EXPERIMENT IN
AUTOBIOGRAPHY

DISCOVERIES AND CONCLUSIONS OF
A VERY ORDINARY BRAIN
(SINCE 1866)

by

H. G. WELLS

British Library Cataloguing-in-Publication Data
A catalogue record for this book is available from
the British Library

CONTENTS

4

5

H. G. Wells

Herbert George Wells was born in Bromley, England in 1866. He apprenticed as a draper before becoming a pupil-teacher at Midhurst Grammar School in West Sussex. Some years later, Wells won a scholarship to the School of Science in London, where he developed a strong interest in biology and evolution, founding and editing the *Science Schools Journal*. However, he left before graduating to return to teaching, and began to focus increasingly on writing. His first major essay on science, 'The Rediscovery of the Unique', appeared in 1891. However, it was in 1895 that Wells seriously established himself as a writer, with the publication of the now iconic novel, *The Time Machine*.

Wells followed *The Time Machine* with the equally well-received *War of the Worlds* (1898), which proved highly popular in the USA, and was serialized in the magazine *Cosmopolitan*. Around the turn of the century, he also began to write extensively on politics, technology and the future, producing works *The Discovery of the Future* (1902) and *Mankind in the Making* (1903). An active socialist, in 1904 Wells joined the Fabian Society, and his 1905 book *A Modern Utopia* presented a vision of a socialist society founded on reason and compassion. Wells also penned a range of successful comic novels, such as *Kipps* (1905) and *The History of Mr Polly* (1910).

Wells' 1920 work, *The Outline of History*, was penned in response to the Russian Revolution, and declared that world would be improved by education, rather than revolution. It made Wells one of the most important political thinkers of the twenties and thirties, and he began to write for a number of journals and newspapers, even travelling to Russia to lecture Lenin and Trotsky on social reform. Appalled by the carnage of World War II, Wells began to work on a project dealing with the perils of nuclear war, but died before completing it. He is now regarded as one of the greatest science-fiction writers of all time, and an important political thinker.

Herbert George Wells

I. — INTRODUCTORY

§ 1. PRELUDE (1932)

I need freedom of mind. I want peace for work. I am distressed by immediate circumstances. My thoughts and work are encumbered by claims and vexations and I cannot see any hope of release from them; any hope of a period of serene and beneficent activity, before I am overtaken altogether by infirmity and death. I am in a phase of fatigue and of that discouragement which is a concomitant of fatigue, the petty things of to-morrow skirmish in my wakeful brain, and I find it difficult to assemble my forces to confront this problem which paralyses the proper use of myself.

I am putting even the pretence of other work aside in an attempt to deal with this situation. I am writing a report about it—to myself. I want to get these discontents clear because I have a feeling that as they become clear they will either cease from troubling me or become manageable and controllable.

There is nothing I think very exceptional in my situation as a mental worker. Entanglement is our common lot. I believe this craving for a release from—bothers, from daily demands and urgencies, from responsibilities and tempting distractions, is shared by an increasing number of people who, with specialized and distinctive work to do, find themselves eaten up by first-hand affairs. This is the outcome of a specialization and a sublimation of interests that has become frequent only in the last century or so. Spaciousness and leisure, and even the desire for spaciousness and leisure, have so far been exceptional. Most individual creatures since life began, have been "up against it" all the time, have been driven continually by fear and cravings, have had to respond to the unresting antagonisms of their surroundings, and they have found a sufficient and sustaining interest in the drama of immediate events provided for them by these demands. Essentially, their living was continuous adjustment to happenings. Good hap and ill hap filled it entirely. They hungered and ate and they desired and loved; they were amused and attracted, they pursued or escaped, they were overtaken and they died.

But with the dawn of human foresight and with the appearance of a great surplus of energy in life such as the last century or so has revealed, there has been a progressive emancipation of the attention from everyday urgencies. What was once the whole of life, has become to an increasing extent, merely the background of life. People can ask now what would have been an extraordinary question five hundred years ago. They can say, "Yes, you earn a living, you support a family, you love and hate, but—*what do you do?*"

Conceptions of living, divorced more and more from immediacy, distinguish the modern civilized man from all former life. In art, in pure science, in literature, for instance, many people find sustaining series of interests and incentives which have come at last to have a greater value for them than any primary needs and satisfactions. These primary needs are taken for granted. The everyday things of life become subordinate to these wider interests which have taken hold of them, and they continue to value everyday things, personal affections and material profit and loss, only in so far as they are ancillary to the newer ruling system of effort, and to evade or disregard them in so far as they are antagonistic or obstructive to that. And the desire to live as fully as possible within the ruling system of effort becomes increasingly conscious and defined.

The originative intellectual worker is not a normal human being and does not lead nor desire to lead a normal human life.

He wants to lead a supernormal life.

Mankind is realizing more and more surely that to escape from individual immediacies into the less personal activities now increasing in human society is not, like games, reverie, intoxication or suicide, a suspension or abandonment of the primary life; on the contrary it is the way to power over that primary life which, though subordinated, remains intact. Essentially it is an imposition upon the primary life of a participation in the greater life of the race as a whole. In studies and studios and laboratories, administrative bureaus and exploring expeditions, a new world is germinated and develops. It is not a repudiation of the old but a vast extension of it, in a racial synthesis into which individual aims will ultimately be absorbed. We originative intellectual workers are reconditioning human life.

Now in this desire, becoming increasingly lucid and continuous for me as my life has gone on, in this desire to get the primaries of life under control and to concentrate the largest possible proportion of my energy upon the particular system of effort that has established itself for me as my distinctive business in the world, I find the clue to the general conduct not only of my own life and the key not only to my present perplexities, but a clue to the difficulties of most scientific, philosophical, artistic, creative, preoccupied men and women. We are like early amphibians, so to speak, struggling out of the waters that have hitherto covered our kind, into the air, seeking to breathe in a new fashion and emancipate ourselves from long accepted and long unquestioned necessities. At last it becomes for us a case of air or nothing. But the new land has not yet definitively emerged from the waters and we swim distressfully in an element we wish to abandon.

I do not now in the least desire to live longer unless I can go on with what I consider to be my proper business. That is not to say that the stuff of everyday life has not been endlessly interesting, exciting and delightful for me in my time: clash of personalities, music and beauty, eating and drinking, travel and meetings, new lands and strange spectacles, the work for successes, much aimless play, much laughter, the getting well again after illness, the pleasures, the very real pleasures, of vanity. Let me not be ungrateful to life for its fundamental substances. But I have had a full share of all these things and I do not want to remain alive simply for more of them. I want the whole stream of this daily life stuff to flow on for me—for a long time yet—if, what I call my work can still be, can be more than ever the emergent meaning of the stream. But only on that condition. And that is where I am troubled now. I find myself less able to get on with my work than ever before. Perhaps the years have something to do with that, and it may be that a progressive broadening and deepening of my conception of what my work should be, makes it less easy than it was; but the main cause is certainly the invasion of my time and thought by matters that are either quite secondary to my real business or have no justifiable connection with it. Subordinate and everyday things, it seems to me in this present mood, surround me in an ever-growing jungle. My hours are choked with them; my thoughts are tattered by them. All my life I have been pushing aside intrusive tendrils, shirking discursive consequences, bilking unhelpful obligations, but I am more aware of them now and less hopeful about them than I have ever been. I have a sense of crisis; that the time has come to reorganize my peace, if the ten or fifteen years ahead, which at the utmost I may hope to work in now, are to be saved from being altogether overgrown.

I will explain later what I think my particular business to be. But for it, if it is to be properly done, I require a pleasant well-lit writing room in good air and a comfortable bedroom to sleep in—and, if the mood takes me, to write in—both free from distracting noises and indeed all unexpected disturbances. There should be a secretary or at least a typist within call and out of earshot, and, within reach, an abundant library and the rest of the world all hung accessibly on to that secretary's telephone. (But it would have to be a one-way telephone, so that when we wanted news we could ask for it, and when we were not in a state to receive and digest news, we should not have it forced upon us.) That would be the central cell of my life. That would give the immediate material conditions for the best work possible. I think I would like that the beautiful scenery outside the big windows should be changed ever and again, but I recognize the difficulties in the way of that. In the background there would have to be, at need, food, exercise and stimulating, agreeable and various conversation, and, pervading all my consciousness, there should be a sense of security and attention, an assurance that what was produced, when I had done my best upon it, would be properly significant and effective. In such circumstances I feel I could still do much in these years before me, without hurry and without waste. I can see a correlated scheme of work I could do that would, I feel, be enormously worth while, and the essence of my trouble is that the clock ticks on, the moments drip out and trickle, flow away as hours, as days, and I cannot adjust my life to secure any such fruitful peace.

It scarcely needs criticism to bring home to me that much of my work has been slovenly, haggard and irritated, most of it hurried and inadequately revised, and some of it as white and pasty in its texture as a starch-fed nun. I am tormented by a desire for achievement that overruns my capacity and by a practical incapacity to bring about for myself the conditions under which fine achievement is possible. I pay out what I feel to be a disproportionate amount of my time and attention in clumsy attempts to save the rest of it for the work in hand. I seem now in this present mood, to be saving only tattered bits of time, and even in these scraps of salvage my mind is often jaded and preoccupied.

It is not that I am poor and unable to buy the things I want, but that I am quite unable to get the things I want. I can neither control my surroundings myself nor can I find helpers and allies who will protect me from the urgencies—from within and from without—of primary things. I do not see how there can be such helpers. For to protect me completely they would have, I suppose, to span my intelligence and possibilities, and if they could do that they would be better employed in doing my work directly and eliminating me altogether.

This feeling of being intolerably hampered by irrelevant necessities, this powerful desire for disentanglement is, I have already said, the common experience of the men and women who write, paint, conduct research and assist in a score of other ways, in preparing that new world, that greater human life, which all art, science and literature have foreshadowed. My old elaborate-minded friend, Henry James the novelist, for example, felt exactly this thing. Some elements in his character obliged him to lead an abundant social life, and as a result he was so involved in engagements, acknowledgments, considerations, compliments, reciprocities, small kindnesses, generosities, graceful gestures and significant acts, all of which he felt compelled to do with great care and amplitude, that at times he found existence more troubled and pressing than many a sweated toiler. His craving for escape found expression in a dream of a home of rest, *The Great Good Place*, where everything that is done was done for good, and the fagged mind was once more active and free. The same craving for flight in a less Grandisonian and altogether more tragic key, drove out the dying Tolstoy in that headlong flight from home which ended his life.

This fugitive impulse is an inevitable factor in the lives of us all, great or small, who have been drawn into these activities, these super- activities which create and which are neither simply gainful, nor a response to material or moral imperatives, nor simply and directly the procuring of primary satisfactions. Our lives are threaded with this same, often quite desperate effort to disentangle ourselves, to get into a Great Good Place of our own, and work freely.

None of us really get there, perhaps there is no *there* anywhere to get to, but we get some way towards it. We never do the work that we imagine to be in us, we never realize the secret splendour of our intentions, yet nevertheless some of us get something done that seems almost worth the effort. Some of us, and it may be as good a way as any, let everything else slide, live in garrets and hovels, borrow money unscrupulously, live on women (or, if they are women, live on men), exploit patronage, accept pensions. But even the careless life will not stay careless. It has its own frustrations and chagrins.

Others make the sort of effort I have made, and give a part of their available energy to save the rest. They fight for their conditions and have a care for the things about them. That is the shape of my story. I have built two houses and practically rebuilt a third to make that Great Good Place to work in, I have shifted from town to country and from country to town, from England to abroad and from friend to friend, I have preyed upon people more generous than myself who loved me and gave life to me. In return, because of my essential preoccupation, I have never given any person nor place a simple disinterested love. It was not in me. I have loved acutely, but that is another matter. I have attended spasmodically to business and money-making. And here I am at sixty-five (Spring 1932), still asking for peace that I may work some more, that I may do that major task that will atone for all the shortcomings of what I have done in the past.

Imperfection and incompleteness are the certain lot of all creative workers. We all compromise. We all fall short. The life story to be told of any creative worker is therefore by its very nature, by its diversions of purpose and its qualified success, by its grotesque transitions from sublimation to base necessity and its pervasive stress towards flight, a comedy. The story can never be altogether pitiful because of the dignity of the work;

it can never be altogether dignified because of its inevitable concessions. It must be serious, but not solemn, and since there is no controversy in view and no judgment of any significance to be passed upon it, there is no occasion for apologetics. In this spirit I shall try to set down the story of my own life and work, up to and including its present perplexities.

I write down my story and state my present problem, I repeat, to clear and relieve my mind. The story has no plot and the problem will never be solved. I do not think that in the present phase of human affairs there is any possible Great Good Place, any sure and abiding home for any creative worker. In diverse forms and spirits we are making over the world, so that the primary desires and emotions, the drama of the immediate individual life will be subordinate more and more, generation by generation, to beauty and truth, to universal interests and mightier aims.

That is our common rôle. We are therefore, now and for the next few hundred years at least, strangers and invaders of the life of every day. We are all essentially lonely. In our nerves, in our bones. We are too preoccupied and too experimental to give ourselves freely and honestly to other people, and in the end other people fail to give themselves fully to us. We are too different among ourselves to get together in any enduring fashion. It is good for others as for myself to find, however belatedly, that there is no fixed home to be found, and no permanent relationships. I see now, what I merely suspected when I began to write this section, that my perplexities belong to the mood of a wayside pause, to the fatigue of a belated tramp on a road where there is no rest-house before the goal.

That dignified peace, that phase of work perfected in serenity, of close companionship in thought, of tactfully changing scenery and stabilized instability ahead, is just a helpful dream that kept me going along some of the more exacting stretches of the course, a useful but essentially an impossible dream. So I sit down now by the reader, so to speak, and yarn a bit about my difficulties and blunders, about preposterous hopes and unexpected lessons, about my luck and the fun of the road, and then, a little refreshed and set-up, a little more sprightly for the talk, I will presently shoulder the old bundle again, go on, along the noisy jostling road, with its irritations and quarrels and distractions, with no delusion that there is any such dreamland work palace ahead, or any perfection of accomplishment possible for me, before I have to dump the whole load, for whatever it is worth, myself and my load together, on the scales of the receiver at journey's end. Perhaps it is as well that I shall never know what the scales tell, or indeed whether they have anything to tell, or whether there will be any scales by which to tell, of the load that has been my life.

§ 2. PERSONA AND PERSONALITY

The preceding section was drafted one wakeful night, somewhen between two and five in the early morning a year or more ago; it was written in perfect good faith, and a criticism and continuation of it may very well serve as the opening movement in this autobiographical effort. For that section reveals, artlessly and plainly what Jung would call my *persona*.

A *persona*, as Jung uses the word, is the private conception a man has of himself, his idea of what he wants to be and of how he wants other people to take him. It provides therefore, the standard by which he judges what he may do, what he ought to do and what is imperative upon him. Everyone has a *persona*. Self conduct and self explanation is impossible without one.

A *persona* may be very stable or it may fluctuate extremely. It may be resolutely honest or it may draw some or all of its elements from the realms of reverie. It may exist with variations in the same mind. We may have single or multiple *personas* and in the latter case we are charged with inconsistencies and puzzle ourselves and our friends. Our *personas* grow and change and age as we do. And rarely if ever are they the whole even of our conscious mental being. All sorts of complexes are imperfectly incorporated or not incorporated at all, and may run away with us in the most unexpected manner.

So that this presentation of a preoccupied mind devoted to an exalted and spacious task and seeking a maximum of detachment from the cares of this world and from baser needs and urgencies that distract it from that task, is not even the beginning of a statement of what I am, but only of what I most like to think I am. It is the plan to which I work, by which I prefer to work, and by which ultimately I want to judge my performance. But quite a lot of other things have happened to me, quite a lot of other stuff goes with me and it is not for the reader to accept this purely personal criterion.

A *persona* may be fundamentally false, as is that of many a maniac. It may be a structure of mere compensatory delusions, as is the case with many vain people. But it does not follow that if it is selected by a man out of his moods and motives, it is necessarily a work of self deception. A man who tries to behave as he conceives he should behave, may be satisfactorily honest in restraining, ignoring and disavowing many of his innate motives and dispositions. The mask, the *persona*, of the Happy Hypocrite became at last his true faces.

It is just as true that all men are imperfect saints and heroes as it is that all men are liars. There is, I maintain, a sufficient justification among my thoughts and acts from quite early years, for that pose of the disinterested thinker and worker, working for a racial rather than a personal achievement. But the distractions, attacks and frustrations that set him scribbling distressfully in the night, come as much from within as without; the antagonisms and temptations could do nothing to him, were it not for that within him upon which they can take hold. Directly I turn from the easier task of posing in an Apology for my life, to the more difficult work of frank autobiography, I have to bring in all the tangled motives out of which my *persona* has emerged; the elaborate sexual complexities, the complexes of ambition and rivalry, the hesitation and fear in my nature, for example; and in the interests of an impartial diagnosis I have to set aside the appeal for a favourable verdict.

A biography should be a dissection and demonstration of how a particular human being was made and worked; the directive *persona* system is of leading importance only when it is sufficiently consistent and developed to be the ruling theme of the story. But this is the case with my life. From quite an early age I have been predisposed towards one particular sort of work and one particular system of interests. I have found the attempt to disentangle the possible drift of life in general and of human life in particular from the confused stream of events, and the means of controlling that drift, if such are to be found, more important and interesting by far than anything else. I have had, I believe, an aptitude for it. The study and expression of *tendency*, has been for me what music is for the musician, or the advancement of his special knowledge is to the scientific investigator. My *persona* may be an exaggeration of one aspect of my being, but I believe that it is a ruling aspect. It may be a magnification but it is not a fantasy. A voluminous mass of work accomplished attests its reality.

The value of that work is another question. A bad musician may be none the less passionately a musician. Because I have spent a large part of my life's energy in a drive to make a practically applicable science out of history and sociology, it does not follow that contemporary historians, economists and politicians are not entirely just in their disregard of my effort. They will not adopt my results; they will only respond to fragments of them. But the fact remains that I have made that effort, that it has given me a considerable ill-defined prestige, and that it is the only thing that makes me conspicuous beyond the average lot and gives my life with such complications and entanglements as have occurred in it, an interest that has already provoked biography and may possibly provoke more, and so renders unavoidable the thought of a defensive publication, at some future date, of this essay in autobiographical self-examination. The conception of a worker concentrated on the perfection and completion of a work is its primary idea. Either the toad which is struggling to express itself here, *has* engendered a jewel in its head or it is nothing worth troubling about in the way of toads.

This work, this jewel in my head for which I take myself seriously enough to be self-scrutinizing and autobiographical, is, it seems to me, a crystallization of ideas. A variety of biological and historical suggestions and generalizations, which, when lying confusedly in the human mind, were cloudy and opaque, have been brought into closer and more exact relations; the once amorphous mixture has fallen into a lucid arrangement and through this new crystalline clearness, a plainer vision of human possibilities and the conditions of their attainment, appears. I have made the broad lines and conditions of the human outlook distinct and unmistakable for myself and for others. I have shown that human life as we know it, is only the dispersed raw material for human life as it might be. There is a hitherto undreamt-of fullness, freedom and happiness within reach of our species. Mankind can pull itself together and take that now. But if mankind fails to apprehend its opportunity, then division, cruelties, delusions and ultimate frustration lie before our kind. The decision to perish or escape has to be made within a very limited time. For escape, vast changes in the educational, economic and directive structure of human society are necessary. They are definable. They are practicable. But they demand courage and integrity. They demand a force and concentration of will and a power of adaptation in habits and usages which may or may not be within the compass of mankind. This is the exciting and moving prospect displayed by the crystal I have brought out of solution.

I do not set up to be the only toad in the world that has this crystallization. I do not find so much difference between my mind and others, that I can suppose that I alone have got this vision clear. What I think, numbers must be thinking. They have similar minds with similar material, and it is by mere chance and opportunity that I have been among the first to give expression to this realization of a guiding framework for life. But I have been among the first. Essentially, then, a main thread in weaving my autobiography must be the story of how I came upon, and amidst what accidents I doubted, questioned and rebelled against, accepted interpretations of life; and so went on to find the pattern of the key to master our world and release its imprisoned promise. I believe I am among those who have found what key is needed. We, I and those similar others, have set down now all the specifications for a working key to the greater human life. By an incessant toil of study, propaganda, education and creative suggestion, by sacrifice where it is necessary and much fearless conflict, by a bold handling of stupidity, obstruction and perversity, we may yet cut out and file and polish and insert and turn that key to the creative world community before it is too late. That kingdom of heaven is materially within our reach.

My story therefore will be at once a very personal one and it will be a history of my sort and my time. An autobiography is the story of the contacts of a mind and a world. The story will begin in perplexity and go on to a troubled and unsystematic awakening. It will culminate in the attainment of a clear sense of purpose, conviction that the coming great world of order, is real and sure; but, so far as my individual life goes, with time running out and a thousand entanglements delaying realization. For me maybe—but surely not for us. For us, the undying us of our thought and experience, that great to-morrow is certain.

So this autobiography plans itself as the crystallization of a system of creative realizations in one particular mind—with various incidental, good, interesting or curious personal things that happened by the way.

§ 3. QUALITY OF THE BRAIN AND BODY CONCERNED

The brain upon which my experiences have been written is not a particularly good one. If there were brain-shows, as there are cat and dog shows, I doubt if it would get even a third class prize. Upon quite a number of points it would be marked below the average. In a little private school in a small town on the outskirts of London it seemed good enough, and that gave me a helpful conceit about it in early struggles where confidence was half the battle. It was a precocious brain, so that I was classified with boys older than myself right up to the end of a brief school career which closed before I was fourteen. But compared with the run of the brains I meet nowadays, it seems a poorish instrument. I won't even compare it with such cerebra as the full and subtly simple brain of Einstein, the wary, quick and flexible one of Lloyd George, the abundant and rich grey matter of G. B. Shaw, Julian Huxley's store of knowledge or my own eldest son's fine and precise instrument. But in relation to everyday people with no claim to mental distinction I still find it at a disadvantage. The names of places and people, numbers, quantities and dates for instance, are easily lost or get a little distorted. It snatches at them and often lets them slip again. I cannot do any but the simplest sums in my head and when I used to play bridge, I found my memory of the consecutive tricks and my reasoning about the playing of the cards, inferior to nine out of ten of the people I played with. I lose at chess to almost anyone and though I have played a spread-out patience called Miss Milligan for the past fifteen years, I have never acquired a sufficient sense of the patterns of 104 cards to make it anything more than a game of chance and feeling. Although I have learnt and relearnt French since my school days and have lived a large part of each year for the past eight years in France, I have never acquired a flexible diction or a good accent and I cannot follow French people when they are talking briskly—and they always talk briskly. Such other languages as Spanish, Italian and German I have picked up from a grammar or a conversation book sufficiently to serve the purposes of travel; only to lose even that much as soon as I ceased to use them. London is my own particular city; all my life I have been going about in it and yet the certitude of the taxicab driver is a perpetual amazement to me. If I wanted to walk from Hoxton to Chelsea without asking my way, I should have to sit down to puzzle over a map for some time. All this indicates a loose rather inferior mental texture, inexact reception, bad storage and uncertain accessibility.

I do not think my brain has begun to age particularly yet. It can pick up new tricks, though it drops them very readily again, more readily perhaps than it used to do. I learnt sufficient Spanish in the odd moments of three months to get along in Spain two years ago without much trouble. I think my brain has always been very much as it is now, except perhaps for a certain slowing down.

And I believe that its defects are mainly innate. It was not a good brain to begin with, although certain physical defects of mine and bad early training, may have increased faults that might have been corrected by an observant teacher. The atmosphere of my home and early upbringing was not a highly educative atmosphere; words were used inexactly, and mispronounced, and so a certain timidity of utterance and a disposition to mumble and avoid doubtful or difficult words and phrases, may have worked back into my mental texture. My eyes have different focal lengths and nobody discovered this until I was over thirty. Columns of figures and lines of print are as a result apt to get a little dislocated and this made me bad at arithmetic and blurred my impression of the form of words. It was only about the age of thirteen, when I got away with algebra, Euclid's elements and, a little later, the elements of trigonometry, that I realized I was not a hopeless duffer at mathematics. But here comes an item on the credit side; I found Euclid easy reading and solved the simple "riders" in my text book with a facility my schoolmaster found exemplary. I also became conceited about my capacity for "problems" in algebra. And by eleven or twelve, in some way I cannot trace, I had taken to drawing rather vigorously and freshly. My elder brother could not draw at all but my other brother draws exactly and delicately, if not quite so spontaneously and expressively as I do. I know practically nothing of brain structure and physiology, but it seems probable to me that this relative readiness to grasp form and relation, indicates that the general shape and arrangement of my brain is better than the quality of its cells, fibres and blood-vessels. I have a quick sense of form and proportion; I have a brain good for outlines. Most of my story will carry out that suggestion.

A thing that has I think more to do with my general build than with my brain structure is that my brain works best in short spells and is easily fatigued. My head is small—I can cheer up nearly every one of my friends by just changing hats; the borrowed brim comes down upon my ears and spreads them wide—my heart has an irregular beat and I suspect that my carotid arteries do not branch so freely and generously into my grey matter as they might do. I do not know whether it would be of any service after I am dead to prepare sections of my brain to ascertain that. I have made an autopsy possible by my will, but my son Gip tells me that all that tissue will have decayed long before a post mortem is possible. "Unless," he added helpfully, "you could commit suicide in a good hardening solution." But that would be difficult to arrange. There may perhaps be considerable differences in mental character due to a larger or smaller lumen of the arteries, to a rapid or sluggish venous drainage, to variations in interstitial tissue, which affect the response and interaction of the nerve

---

cells. At any rate there is and always has been far too ready a disposition in my brain to fag and fade for my taste.

It can fade out generally or locally in a very disconcerting manner. Aphasia is frequent with me. At an examination for a teaching diploma which involved answering twenty or thirty little papers in the course of four days I found myself on the last day face to face with a paper, happily not of vital importance, of which the questions were entirely familiar and entirely unmeaning. There was nothing to be done but go out. On another occasion I undertook to give an afternoon lecture to the Royal Institution. I knew my subject fairly well, so well that I had not written it down. I was not particularly afraid of my audience. I talked for a third of my allotted time—and came to a blank. After an awkward silence I had to say; "I am sorry. That is all I have prepared to-day."

Psycho-analysts have a disposition to explain the forgetting of names and the dissociation of faces, voices and so forth from their proper context as a sub-conscious suppression due to some obscure dislike. If so I must dislike a vast multitude of people. But why should psycho-analysts assume a perfect brain mechanism and recognize only psychic causes? I believe a physical explanation will cover a number of these cases and that a drop in the conductivity of the associated links due to diminished oxygenation or some slight variation in the blood plasma is much more generally the temporarily effacing agent.

I was interested the other night, in a supper-room in Vienna, by a little intimation of the poor quality of my memory. There came in a party of people who sat at another table. One of them was a German young lady who reminded me very strikingly of the daughter of an acquaintance I had made in Spain. He had introduced himself and his family to me because he was the surviving brother of an old friend and editor of mine, Harry Cust, and he had heard all sorts of things about me. "That girl," I said, "is the very image of——" The name would not come. "She is the daughter of Lord B——." I got as far as the "B" and stuck. I tried again; "Her name is—— Cust," I protested, "But I have known her by her Christian name, talked to her, talked about her, liked and admired her, visited her father's home at——." Again an absolute blank. I became bad company. I could talk of nothing else. I retired inside my brain and routed about in it, trying to recover those once quite familiar names. I could recall all sorts of incidents while I was in the same hotel with these people at Ronda and Granada and while I stayed at that house, a very beautiful English house in the midlands, I could produce a rough sketch of the garden and I remembered addressing a party of girl scouts from the front door and even what I said to them. I had met and talked with Lady B and on another occasion met her son within the past year. But that evening the verbal labels seemed lost beyond recovery. I tried over all the peers I had ever heard of whose names began with "B." I tried over every conceivable feminine Christian name. I took a gloomy view of my mental state.

Next morning, while I was still in bed, the missing labels all came back, except one. The name of the house had gone; it is still missing. Presently if it refuses to come home of its own accord I shall look it up in some book of reference. And yet I am sure that somewhere in the thickets of my brain it is hiding from me now. I tell this anecdote for the sake of its complete pointlessness. The psychological explanation of such forgetfulness is a disinclination to remember. But what conflict of hostilities, frustrations, restrained desires and so forth, is here? None at all. It is merely that the links are feeble and the printing of the impressions bad. It is a case of second-rate brain fabric. And rather overgrown and pressed upon at that. If my mental paths are not frequently traversed and refreshed they are obstructed.

Now defects in the brain texture must affect its moral quite as much as its intellectual character. It is essentially the same apparatus at work in either case. If the links of association that reassemble a memory can be temporarily effaced, so can the links that bring a sense of obligation to bear upon a motive. Adding a column of figures wrongly and judging incorrectly a situation in which one has to act are quite comparable brain processes. So in my own behaviour just as in my apprehension of things the outline is better than the detail. The more closely I scrutinize my reactions, the more I find detailed inconsistencies, changes of front and goings to and fro. The more I stand off from the immediate thing and regard my behaviour as a whole the more it holds together. As I have gathered experience of life, I have become increasingly impressed by the injustice we do ourselves and others by not allowing for these local and temporary faintings and fadings of our brains in our judgment of conduct.

Our relations with other human beings are more full and intricate the nearer they are to us and the more important they are in our lives. So, however we may be able to pigeonhole and note this or that casual acquaintance for treatment of a particular sort, when we come to our intimates we find ourselves behaving according to immensely various and complex systems of association, which in the case of such brains as mine anyhow, are never uniformly active, which are subject to just the same partial and irrational dissociations and variations as are my memories of names and numbers. I can have a great tenderness or resentment for someone and it may become as absent from my present thought as that title or the name of that country house I could not remember in Vienna. I may have a sense of obligation and it will vanish as completely. Facts will appear in my mind quite clear in their form and sequence and yet completely shorn of some moving emotional quality I know they once possessed. And then a day or so after it will all come back to me.

Everyone, of course, is more or less like this, but I am of the kind, I think, which is more so.

On the other hand, though my brain organization is so poor that connexions are thus intermittently weakened and effaced and groups of living associations removed out of reach, I do not find in this cerebrum of mine any trace of another type of weakness which I should imagine must be closely akin to such local failure to function, namely those actual replacements of one system of associations by another, which cause what is called double personalities. In the classical instances of double personality psychologists tell of whole distinct networks of memory and impulse, co-existing side by side in the same brain yet functioning independently, which are alternative and often quite contradictory one to the other. When one system is in action; the other is more or less inaccessible and vice versa. I have met and lived in close contact with one or two individuals of this alternating type; it is, I think, more common among women than among men; I have had occasion to watch these changes of phase, and I do not find that in my own brain stuff there are any such regional or textural substitutions. There are effacements but not replacements. My brain may be very much alive or it may be flat and faded out or simply stupefied by sleepiness or apathy; it may be exalted by some fever in the blood, warmed and confused by alcohol, energized, angered or sexually excited by the subtle messages and stimuli my blood brings it; but my belief is that I remain always very much the same personality through it all. I do not think I delude myself about this. My brain I believe is consistent. Such as it is, it holds together. It is like a centralized country with all its government in one capital, even though that government is sometimes negligent, feeble or inert.

One other thing I have to note about this brain of mine and that is—how can I phrase it?—an exceptional want of excitable "Go." I suspect that is due not, as my forgetfulnesses and inconsistencies may be, to local insufficiencies and failures in the circulation, but to some general under-stimulation. My perceptions do not seem to be so thorough, vivid and compelling as those of many people I meet and it is rare that my impressions of things glow. There is a faint element of inattention in all I do; it is as if white was mixed into all the pigments of my life. I am rarely *vivid* to myself. I am just a little slack, not wholly and continuously interested, prone to be indolent and cold-hearted. I am readily bored. When I try to make up for this I am inevitably a little "forced" when dealing with things, and a little "false" and "charming" with people. You will find this coming out when I tell of my failure as a draper's assistant and of my relations to my intimate friends. You will discover a great deal of evasion and refusal in my story.

Nature has a way of turning even biological defects into advantages and I am not sure how far what may be called my success in life has not been due to this undertow of indifference. I have not been easily carried away by immediate things and made to forget the general in the particular. There is a sort of journalistic legend that I am a person of boundless enthusiasm and energy. Nothing could be further from the reality. For all my desire to be interested I have to confess that for most things and people I don't care a damn. Writing numbers of books and articles is evidence not of energy but of sedentary habits. People with a real quantitative excess of energy and enthusiasm become Mussolinis, Hitlers, Stalins, Gladstones, Beaverbrooks, Northcliffes, Napoleons. It takes generations to clean up after them. But what I shall leave behind me will not need cleaning up. Just because of that constitutional apathy it will be characteristically free from individual Woosh and it will be available and it will go on for as long as it is needed.

And now, having conveyed to you some idea of the quality and defects of the grey matter of that organized mass of phosphorized fat and connective tissue which is, so to speak, the hero of the piece, and having displayed the *persona* or, if you will, the vanity which now dominates its imaginations, I will try to tell how in this particular receiving apparatus the picture of its universe was built up, what it did and failed to do with the body it controlled and what the thronging impressions and reactions that constituted its life amount to.

II. — ORIGINS

§ 1. 47 HIGH STREET, BROMLEY, KENT

This brain of mine came into existence and began to acquire reflexes and register impressions in a needy shabby home in a little town called Bromley in Kent, which has since become a suburb of London. My consciousness of myself grew by such imperceptible degrees, and for a time each successive impression incorporated what had preceded it so completely, that I have no recollection of any beginning at all. I have a miscellany of early memories, but they are not arranged in any time order. I will do my best however, to recall the conditions amidst which my childish head got its elementary lessons in living. They seem to me now quite dreadful conditions, but at the time it was the only conceivable world.

It was then the flaxen head of a podgy little boy with a snub nose and a long infantile upper lip, and along the top his flaxen hair was curled in a longitudinal curl which was finally abolished at his own urgent request. Early photographs record short white socks, bare arms and legs, a petticoat, ribbon bows on the shoulders, and a scowl. That must have been gala costume. I do not remember exactly what everyday clothes I wore until I was getting to be a fairly big boy. I seem to recall a sort of holland pinafore for everyday use very like what small boys still wear in France, except that it was brown instead of black holland.

The house in which this little boy ran about, clattering up and down the uncarpeted stairs, bawling—family tradition insists on the bawling—and investigating existence, deserves description, not only from the biographical, but from the sociological point of view. It was one of a row of badly built houses upon a narrow section of the High Street. In front upon the ground floor was the shop, filled with crockery, china and glassware and, a special line of goods, cricket bats, balls, stumps, nets and other cricket material. Behind the shop was an extremely small room, the "parlour," with a fireplace, a borrowed light and glass-door upon the shop and a larger window upon the yard behind. A murderously narrow staircase with a twist in it led downstairs to a completely subterranean kitchen, lit by a window which derived its light from a grating on the street level, and a bricked scullery, which, since the house was poised on a bank, opened into the yard at the ground level below. In the scullery was a small fireplace, a copper boiler for washing, a provision cupboard, a bread pan, a beer cask, a pump delivering water from a well into a stone sink, and space for coal, our only space for coal, beneath the wooden stairs. This "coal cellar" held about a ton of coal, and when the supply was renewed it had to be carried in sacks through the shop and "parlour" and down the staircase by men who were apt to be uncivil about the inconveniences of the task and still more apt to drop small particles of coal along the route.

The yard was perhaps thirty by forty feet square. In it was a brick erection, the "closet," an earth jakes over a cesspool, within perhaps twenty feet of the well and the pump; and above this closet was a rain-water tank. Behind it was the brick dustbin (cleared at rare intervals via the shop), a fairly open and spacious receptacle. In this a small boy could find among the ashes such objects of interest as egg-shells, useful tins and boxes. The ashes could be rearranged to suggest mountain scenery. There was a boundary wall, separating us from the much larger yard and sheds of Mr. Covell the butcher, in which pigs, sheep and horned cattle were harboured violently, and protested plaintively through the night before they were slaughtered. Some were recalcitrant and had to be treated accordingly; there was an element of Rodeo about Covell's yard. Beyond it was Bromley Church and its old graveyard, full then of healthy trees, ruinous tombs and headstones askew—in which I had an elder sister buried.

Our yard was half bricked and half bare earth, and an open cement gutter brought the waste waters of the sink to a soak-away in the middle of the space. Thence, no doubt, soap-suds and cabbage water, seeped away to mingle with the graver accumulations of the "closet" and the waters of the well from which the pump drew our supply. Between the scullery and the neighbour's wall was a narrow passage covered over, and in this my father piled the red earthenware jars and pans, the jam-pots and so forth, which bulk so large in the stock of a crockery dealer.

I "played" a lot in this yard and learnt its every detail, because there was no other open air space within easy reach of a very small boy to play in. Its effect of smallness was enhanced by the erections in the neighbours' yards on either side. On one hand was the yard of Mr. Munday, the haberdasher, who had put up a greenhouse and cultivated mushrooms, to nourish which his boys collected horse-droppings from the High Street in a small wooden truck; and on the other, Mr. Cooper, the tailor, had built out a workroom in which two or three tailors sat and sewed. It was always a matter of uneasiness to my mother whether these men could or could not squint round and see the necessary comings and goings of pots and pans and persons to the closet. The unbricked part of our yard had a small flower-bed in which my father had planted a bush of Wigelia. It flowered reluctantly, and most things grew reluctantly in that bed. A fact, still vividly clear in my mind across an interval of sixty years, is that it was the only patch of turned up earth accessible to the cats of Mr. Munday, Mr. Cooper and our own ménage. But my father was a gardener of some resolution and, against the back of the house rooting in a hole in the brickwork, he had persuaded a grape vine not only to grow but to flourish. When I was ten, he fell from a combination of short ladder, table and kitchen steps on which he had mounted to prune the less accessible shoots of this vine, and sustained a compound fracture of the leg. But of that very important event I will tell a little later.

I dwell rather upon the particulars about this yard, because it was a large part of my little world in those days. I lived mostly in it and in the scullery and underground kitchen. We were much too poor to have a servant, and it was more than my mother could do to keep fires going upstairs (let alone the price of coal). Above the ground floor and reached by an equally tortuous staircase—I have seen my father reduced to a blind ecstasy of rage in an attempt to get a small sofa up it—were a back bedroom occupied by my mother and a front room occupied by my father (this separation was, I think, their form of birth control), and above this again was a room, the boys' bedroom (there were three of us) and a back attic filled with dusty crockery stock. But there was stock everywhere; pots and pans invaded the kitchen, under the dresser and under the ironing board; bats and stumps crept into the "parlour." The furniture of this home had all been acquired second-hand at sales; furniture shops that catered for democracy had still to appear in the middle nineteenth century; an aristocratic but battered bookcase despised a sofa from some housekeeper's room; there was a perky little chiffonier in the parlour; the chairs were massive but moody; the wooden bedsteads had exhausted feather mattresses and grey sheets—for there had to be economy over the washing bills—and there was not a scrap of faded carpet or worn oil-cloth in the house that had not lived a full life of usefulness before it came into our household. Everything was frayed, discoloured and patched. But we had no end of oil lamps because they came out of (and went back into) stock. (My father also dealt in lamp-wicks, oil and paraffin.)

We lived, as I have said, mostly downstairs and underground, more particularly in the winter. We went upstairs to bed. About upstairs I have to add a further particular. The house was infested with bugs. They harboured in the wooden bedsteads and lurked between the layers of wallpaper that peeled from the walls. Slain they avenge themselves by a peculiar penetrating disagreeable smell. That mingles in my early recollections with the more pervasive odour of paraffin, with which my father carried on an inconclusive war against them. Almost every part of my home had its own distinctive smell.

This was the material setting in which my life began. Let me tell now something of my father and mother, what manner of people they were, and how they got themselves into this queer home from which my two brothers and I were launched into what Sir James Jeans has very properly called, this Mysterious Universe, to make what we could of it.

§ 2. SARAH NEAL (1822-1905)

My mother was a little blue-eyed, pink-cheeked woman with a large serious innocent face. She was born on October 10th, 1822, in the days when King George IV was King, and three years before the opening of the first steam railway. It was still an age of horse and foot transit, sailing ships and undiscovered lands. She was the daughter of a Midhurst innkeeper and his frequently invalid wife. His name was George Neal (born 1797) and he was probably of remote Irish origin; his wife's maiden name was Sarah Benham, which sounds good English. She was born in 1796. Midhurst was a little old sunny rag-stone built town on the road from London to Chichester, and my grandfather stabled the relay of horses for the stage coach as his father had done before him. An uncle of his drove a coach, and one winter's night in a snowstorm, being alone without passengers and having sustained himself excessively against the cold and solitude of the drive, he took the wrong turning at the entrance to the town, went straight over the wharf into the pool at the head of the old canal, and was handsomely drowned together with his horses.

It was a characteristic of my mother's family to be easily lit and confused by alcohol, but never subdued to inaction by it. And when my grandfather died he had mortgaged his small property and was very much in debt, so that there was practically nothing for my mother and her younger brother John, who survived him.

The facts still traceable about my grandfather's circumstances are now very fragmentary. I have a few notes my elder brother made from my mother's recollections, and I have various wills and marriage and birth certificates and a diary kept by my mother. George Neal kept the Fountains Inn at Chichester I think, before he kept the New Inn at Chichester; the New Inn he had from 1840 to his death in 1853. He married Sarah Benham on October 30th, 1817. Two infant boys died, and then my mother was born in 1822. After a long interval my uncle John was born in 1836, and a girl Elizabeth in 1838. It is evident my grandmother had very indifferent health, but she was still pretty and winning, says my mother's diary, at the age of fifty-three, and her hands were small and fine. Except for that one entry, there is nothing much now to be learnt about her. I suppose that when she was well she did her best, after the fashion of the time, to teach her daughter the elements of religion, knowledge and the domestic arts. I possess quite a brave sampler worked by my mother when she was in her eighth year. It says, amidst some decorative stitching:

"Opportunity lost can never be recalled; therefore it is the highest wisdom in youth to make all the sensible improvements they can in their early days; for a young overgrown dunce seldom makes a figure in any branch of learning in his old days. Sarah Neal her work. May 26, 1830. 1 2 3 4 5 6 7 8 9 10 11 12 13 14 15 16 17 18."

After which it breaks off and resumes along the bottom with a row of letters upside down.

When my grandmother was too ill to be in control, my mother ran about the inn premises, laid the table for my grandfather's meals, and, as a special treat, drew and served tankards of beer in the bar. There was no compulsory schooling in those days. Some serious neighbours seem to have talked to my grandfather and pointed out the value of accomplishments and scholastic finish to a young female in a progressive age. In 1833 he came into some property through the death of my great-grandfather and thereupon my mother was sent off to a finishing school for young ladies kept by a Miss Riley in Chichester. There in a year or so she showed such remarkable aptitude for polite learning, that she learnt to write in the clear angular handwriting reserved for women in those days, to read, to do sums up to, but not quite including, long division, the names of the countries and capitals of Europe and the counties and county towns of England (with particular attention to the rivers they were "on") and from Mrs. Markham's History all that it was seemly to know about the Kings and Queens of England. Moreover she learnt from Magnell's Questions the names of the four elements (which in due course she taught me), the seven wonders of the world (or was it nine?), the three diseases of wheat, and many such facts which Miss Riley deemed helpful to her in her passage through life. (But she never really mastered the names of the nine Muses and over what they presided, and though she begged and prayed her father that she might learn French, it was an Extra and she was refused it.) A natural tendency to Protestant piety already established by her ailing mother, was greatly enhanced. She was given various edifying books to read, but she was warned against worldly novels, the errors and wiles of Rome, French cooking and the insidious treachery of men, she was also prepared for confirmation and confirmed, she took the sacrament of Holy Communion, and so fortified and finished she returned to her home (1836).

An interesting thing about this school of Miss Riley's, which was in so many respects a very antiquated eighteenth century school, was the strong flavour of early feminism it left in her mind. I do not think it is on record anywhere, but it is plain to me from what I have heard my mother say, that among school mistresses and such like women at any rate, there was a stir of emancipation associated with the claim, ultimately successful, of the Princess Victoria, daughter of the Duke and Duchess of Kent, to succeed King William IV. There was a movement against that young lady based on her sex and this had provoked in reaction a wave of feminine partisanship throughout the country. It picked up reinforcement from an earlier trouble between George the Fourth and Queen Caroline. A favourite book of my mother's was Mrs. Strickland's *Queens of England*, and she followed the life of Victoria, her acts and utterances, her goings forth and her lyings in, her great sorrow and her other bereavements, with a passionate loyalty. The Queen, also a small woman, was in fact my mother's compensatory personality, her imaginative consolation for all the restrictions and hardships that her sex, her diminutive size, her motherhood and all the endless difficulties of life, imposed upon her. The dear Queen could command her husband as a subject and wilt the tremendous Mr. Gladstone with awe. How would it feel to be in that position? One would say this. One would do that. I have no doubt about my mother's reveries. In her latter years in a black bonnet and a black silk dress she became curiously suggestive of the supreme widow....

For my own part, such is the obduracy of the young male, I heard too much of the dear Queen altogether; I conceived a jealous hatred for the abundant clothing, the magnificent housing and all the freedoms of her children and still more intensely of my contemporaries, her grandchildren. Why was my mother so concerned about them? Was not my handicap heavy enough without my having to worship them at my own mother's behest? This was a fixation that has lasted all through my life. Various, desperate and fatiguing expeditions to crowded street corners and points of vantage at Windsor, at Chislehurst near Bromley (where the Empress Eugénie was living in exile) from which we might see the dear Queen pass;—"She's coming. Oh, she's coming. If only I could see! Take off your hat Bertie dear,"—deepened my hostility and wove a stout, ineradicable thread of republicanism into my resentful nature.

But that is anticipating. For the present I am trying to restore my mother's mental picture of the world, as she saw it awaiting her, thirty years and more before I was born or thought of. It was a world much more like Jane Austen's than Fanny Burney's, but at a lower social level. Its chintz was second-hand, and its flowered muslin cheap and easily tired. Still more was it like the English countryside of Dickens' *Bleak House*. It was a countryside, for as yet my mother knew nothing of London. Over it all ruled God our Father, in whose natural kindliness my mother had great confidence. He was entirely confused in her mind, because of the mystery of the Holy Trinity, with "Our Saviour" or "Our Lord"—who was rarely mentioned by any other names. The Holy Ghost she ignored almost entirely; I cannot recall any reference to him; he was certainly never "*our*" Holy Ghost, and the Virgin Mary, in spite of what I should have considered her appeal to feminist proclivities, my mother disregarded even more completely. It may have been simply that there was a papistical flavour about the Virgin; I don't know. Or a remote suspicion of artistic irregularity about the recorded activities of the Holy Spirit. In the lower sky and the real link between my mother and the god-head, was the Dear Queen, ruling by right divine, and beneath this again, the nobility and gentry, who employed, patronised, directed and commanded the rest of mankind. On every Sunday in the year, one went to church and refreshed one's sense of this hierarchy between the communion table and the Free Seats. And behind everyone, behind the Free Seats, but alas! by no means confining his wicked activities to them, was Satan, Old Nick, the Devil, who accounted for so much in the world that was otherwise inexplicable.

My mother was Low Church, and I was disposed to find, even

in my tender years, Low Church theology a little too stiff for me, but she tempered it to her own essential goodness, gentleness and faith in God's Fatherhood, in ways that were quite her own. I remember demanding of her in my crude schoolboy revolt if she really believed in a hell of eternal torment. "We *must*, my dear," she said. "But our Saviour died for us—and perhaps after all nobody will be sent there. Except of course the Old Devil."

And even he, being so to speak the official in charge, I think she would have exempted from actual torture. Maybe Our Father would have shown him the tongs now and again, just to remind him.

There was a picture in an old illustrated book of devotions, Sturm's *Reflections*, obliterated with stamp paper, and so provoking investigation. What had mother been hiding from me? By holding up the page to the light I discovered the censored illustration represented hell-fire; devil, pitchfork and damned, all complete and drawn with great gusto. But she had anticipated the general trend of Protestant theology at the present time and hidden hell away.

She believed that God our Father and Saviour, personally and through occasional angels, would *mind* her; she believed that he would not be indifferent to her prayers; she believed she had to be good, carefully and continually, and not give Satan a chance with her. Then everything would be all right. That was what her "simple faith" as she called it really amounted to, and in that faith she went out very trustfully into the world.

It was decided that she should go into service as a lady's maid. But first she had four years' apprenticeship as a dressmaker (1836-1840) and she also had instruction in hair-dressing, to equip herself more thoroughly for that state of life into which it had pleased God to call her.

It was a world of other ladies'-maids and valets, of house stewards, housekeepers, cooks and butlers, upper servants above the level of maids and footmen, a downstairs world, but living in plentiful good air, well fed and fairly well housed in the attics, basements and interstices of great mansions. It was an old-fashioned world; most of its patterns of behaviour and much of its peculiar idiom, were established in the seventeenth century; its way of talking, its style of wit, was in an unbroken tradition from the *Polite Conversation* of Dean Swift, and it had customs and an etiquette all its own. I do not think she had a bad time in service; people poked fun at a certain simplicity in her, but no one seems to have been malignant.

I do not know all the positions she filled during her years as a lady's maid. In 1845, when her diary begins, she was with the wife of a certain Captain Forde, I know, and in her company she travelled and lived in Ireland and in various places in England. The early part of this diary is by far the best written. It abounds in descriptions of scenery and notes of admiration, and is clearly the record of an interested if conventional mind. Ultimately (1850) she became maid to a certain Miss Bullock who lived at Up Park near Petersfield. It was not so gay as the Forde world. At Christmas particularly, in place of merriment, "Up Park just did nothing but eat," but she conceived a great affection for Miss Bullock. She had left the Fordes because her mother was distressed by the death of her sister Elizabeth and wanted Sarah to be in England nearer to her. And at Up Park she met an eligible bachelor gardener who was destined to end her career as a lady's maid, and in the course of time to be my father. He wasn't there to begin with; he came in 1851. "He seems *peculiar*," says the diary, and offers no further comment. Probably she encountered him first in the Servants' Hall, where there was a weekly dance by candlelight to the music of concertina and fiddle.

This was not my mother's first love affair. Two allusions, slightly reminiscent of the romantic fiction of the time, preserve the memory of a previous experience.

"Kingstown railway," the diary remarks, "is very compact and pretty. From Dublin it is short but the sea appears in view, and mountains, which to one fond of romantic scenery, how dear does the country appear when the views are so diversified by the changes of scene, to the reflective mind how sweet they are *to one alas a voluntary exile* from her dear, her native land, to wander alone to brood over the unkindness, the ingratitude, of a faithless, an absent, but not a forgotten lover. Ah, I left a kind and happy home to hide from all dear friends *the keen, bitter anguish* of my heart. Time and the smiles of dear Erin's hospitable people had made a once miserable girl comparatively happy, but can man be happy who gains an innocent love and then trifles with the girlish innocent heart. May he be forgiven as I forgive him!!!"

And again, some pages later: "I meet kindness everywhere, but there are moments when I feel lonely, which makes me sigh for home, dear England, happy shore, still I do not wish to meet again that *false wicked man*, who gained my young heart and then trifled with a pure love. I hope this early trial will work good in me. I feel it ordered for the best and time will, I trust, prove it to me how mercifully has Providence watched over me, and for a wise purpose taught me not to trust implicitly to erring creatures. Oh, can I ever believe man again? *Burnt all his letters.* I shall now forget quicker I hope, and may he be forgiven his falsehoods."

So, but for that man's treachery, everything might have been different and somebody else might have come into the world in my place, and this biography have never seen the light, replaced by some other biography or by no biography at all.

I know nothing of the earliest encounter of my father and mother. It may have been in the convolutions of Hands Across and Down the Middle, Sir Roger de Coverley, Pop Goes the Weasel, or some such country dance. I like to think of my mother then as innocently animated, pretty and not yet overstrained by dingy toil, and my father as a bright and promising young gardener, son of a head gardener of repute, the head gardener of Lord de Lisle at Penshurst. He was five years younger than she was, and they were both still in their twenties. Presently she was calling him "Joe" and he had modified her name Sarah to "Saddie."

He probably came to the house every day to discuss flowers and vegetables, and so forth, with the cook and the housekeeper and steward and perhaps there was a chance for a word or two then, and on Sundays, when everybody walked downhill a mile and more through the Warren to morning service in Harting Church, they may have had opportunities for conversation. He was not a bad-looking young man, I gather, and I once met an old lady in Harting who recalled that he wore the "most gentlemanly grey trousers."

My parents' relationship had its serious side in those days. It was not all country dances and smiling meetings. I still possess a letter from him to her in which he explains that she has misunderstood an allusion he had made to the Holy Sacrament. He would be the last, he says, to be irreverent on such a topic. It is quite a well written letter.

§ 3. UP PARK AND JOSEPH WELLS (1827-1910)

This Up Park is a handsome great house looking southward, with beechwoods and bracken thickets to shelter the dappled fallow deer of its wide undulating downland park. To the north the estate over-hangs the village of South Harting in the triangle between Midhurst, Petersfield and Chichester. The walled gardens, containing the gardener's cottage which my father occupied, were situated three or four hundred yards or more away from the main buildings. There was an outlying laundry, dairy, butcher's shop and stables in the early eighteenth century style, and a turfed-over ice-house. Up Park was built by a Fetherstonhaugh, and it has always been in the hands of that family.

In the beginning of the nineteenth century the reigning

Fetherstonhaugh was a certain Sir Harry, an intimate of the Prince Regent who was afterwards George IV. Sir Harry was a great seducer of pretty poorish girls, milliners, tenants, singers and servant maids, after the fashion of the time. An early mistress was that lovely young adventuress Emma, who passed into the protection of Greville of the Memoirs, married Sir William Hamilton, and became Romney's and Nelson's Lady Hamilton. In his declining years Sir Harry was smitten with desire for an attractive housemaid, Frances Bullock, and after a strenuous pursuit and a virtuous resistance, valiant struggles on the back stairs and much heated argument, married her. No offspring ensued. She brought her younger sister with her to the house and engaged a governess, Miss Sutherland, to chaperon her and it was after Sir Harry's death that my mother became maid to this younger Miss Bullock.

Queen Victoria and Society never took very eagerly to this belated Lady Fetherstonhaugh, nobody married Miss Bullock, and Sir Harry being duly interred, the three ladies led a spacious dully comfortable life between Up Park and Claridge's. They entertained house parties; people came to them for their shooting and hunting. They changed so little of the old arrangements that I find in a list of guests made by the housekeeper forty years after his death, that "Sir H's bedroom" is still called by his name and assigned to the principal guest. A Mr. Weaver, a bastard, I believe, of Sir Harry's, occupied an ambiguous position in the household as steward and was said—as was probably inevitable—to be Lady Fetherstonhaugh's lover. It could not have been much in the way of love-making anyhow, with everyone watching and disapproving.

In a novel of mine, perhaps my most ambitious novel, *Tono Bungay*, I have made a little picture of Up Park as "Bladesover," and given a glimpse of its life below stairs. (But the housekeeper there is not in the least like my mother.) That is how I saw it in the 'eighties when the two surviving ladies, Miss Bullock (who took the name of Fetherstonhaugh after her sister's death) and Miss Sutherland, were very old ladies indeed. But in the late 'forties when my mother came down from her costumes and mending and hair-dressing to her lunch or tea or supper in the housekeeper's room, or peeped, as I am sure she did at times from some upstairs window towards the gardens, or beamed and curtseyed and set to partners in the country dance, everyone was younger and the life seemed perhaps more eventful. If it was not so gay and various as that now vanished life below stairs in Ireland, it was bright enough.

My father, Joseph Wells, was the son of Joseph Wells, who was head gardener to Lord de Lisle at Penshurst Place in Kent. My father was one of several brothers and sisters, Charles Edward, Henry, Edward, William, Lucy, Elizabeth and Hannah, and although he bore his father's name, he was the youngest of the sons. There were uncles and cousins in the district, so that I suppose the family had been in Kent for at least some generations. My great-grandfather's name was Edward; he had six children and forty grandchildren, and the family is lost at last in a mangrove swamp of Johns, Georges, Edwards, Toms, Williams, Harrys, Sarahs and Lucys. The lack of originality at the Christenings is appalling. The aunts and uncles were all as far as I can ascertain, of the upper-servants, tenant-farmer class, except that one set of my father's first cousins at Penshurst, bearing the surname of Duke, had developed an industry for the making of cricket bats and balls, and were rather more prosperous than the others.

My father grew up to gardening and cricket, and remained an out-of-doors, open-air man to the day of his death. He became gardener at Redleaf, nearby, to a Mr. Joseph Wells, who, in spite of the identical name, was no sort of relation, and in the summer, directly the day's work was over, my father would run, he told me once, a mile and more at top speed to the pitch at Penshurst to snatch half an hour of cricket before the twilight made the ball invisible. He learnt to swim and to handle a muzzle-loading gun and so forth as country boys do, and his schooling gave him reading and writing and "summing," so that he read whatever he could and kept his accounts in a clear well-shaped handwriting; but what sort of school imparted these rudiments I do not know.

Joseph Wells, of Redleaf, was an old gentleman with liberal and æsthetic tastes, and he took rather a fancy to young Joseph. He talked to him, encouraged him to read, and lent and gave him books on botany and gardening. When the old man was ill he liked my father to take his arm when he walked in the garden. My father made definite efforts to improve himself. In our parlour when I was a small boy in search of reading matter there was still the *Young Man's Companion* in two volumes and various numbers of Orr's *Circles of the Science* which he had acquired during this phase. He had an aptitude for drawing. He drew and coloured pictures of various breeds of apple and pear and suchlike fruits, and he sought out and flattened and dried between sheets of blotting paper, a great number of specimen plants.

Old Wells was interested in art, and one of his friends and a frequent visitor at Redleaf was Sir Edwin Landseer, the "animal painter," who could put human souls into almost every sort of animal and who did those grave impassive lions at the base of the Nelson monument in Trafalgar Square. My father served as artist's model on several occasions, and for many years he was to be seen in the National Gallery, peeping at a milkmaid in a picture called *The Maid and the Magpie*. Behind him in the sunshine was Penshurst Church. But afterwards the Landseers were all sent to the Tate Gallery at Millbank and there a sudden flood damaged or destroyed most of them and washed away that record of my father altogether.

I do not know what employment my father found after he left Redleaf, which he did when his employer died, before he came to Up Park and met my mother. I think there was some sort of job as gardener or under-gardener at Crewe. In these days he was evidently restless and uneasy about his outlook upon life. Unrest was in the air. He talked of emigrating to America or Australia. I think the friendliness of Joseph Wells of Redleaf had stirred up vague hopes and ambitions in him, and that he had been disappointed of a "start in life" by the old man's death.

I wish I knew more than I do of my father's dreams and wishes during those early years before he married. In his working everyday world he, like my mother, was still very much in the tradition of the eighteenth century when the nobility and gentry ruled everything under God and the King, when common men knew nothing of the possibility of new wealth, and when either Patronage or a Legacy was the only conceivable way for them out of humdrum and rigid limitation from the cradle to the grave. That system was crumbling away; strange new things were undermining it, but to my mother certainly it seemed an eternal system only to be ended at the Last Trump, and I think it was solely in rare moments of illumination and transparency that my father glimpsed its instability. He and his Saddie walking soberly through the Up Park bracken on a free Sunday afternoon, discussing their prospects, had little more suspicion that their world of gentlemen's estates and carriage-folk and villages and country houses and wayside inns and nice little shops and horse ploughs and windmills and touching one's hat to one's betters, would not endure for ever, than they had that their God in his Heaven was under notice to quit.

But if such was the limitation of his serious talk in the daylight, there could be other moods when he was alone. I had one hint of that which was as good I think as a hundred explicit facts. Once when I was somewhen in my twenties and he was over sixty; as I was walking with him on the open downs out beyond Up Park, he said casually: "When I was a young man of your age I used to come out here and lie oh! half the night, just looking at the stars."

I hadn't thought of him before as a star-gazer. His words opened a great gulf of unsuspected states of mind to me. I wanted him to tell me more, but I did not want to bother him with a cross-examination. I hesitated among a number of clumsy leading questions that would tell me something more of the feelings of that vanished young man of forty years ago who had suddenly reappeared between us.

"What for?" I ventured to ask rather lamely.

"Wondering."

I left it at that. One may be curious about one's father, but prying is prohibited.

But if he could look out of this planet and wonder about the stars, it may be he could also look out of his immediate circumstances and apprehend their triviality by stellar standards. I do not think my mother ever wondered about the stars. God our Father had put them there "for his glory," and that sufficed for her. My father was never at any time in his life, clear and set in that fashion.

My mother's diary is silent about the circumstances of her marriage. There is no mention of any engagement. I cannot imagine how it came about. She left Up Park to be with her mother who was very seriously ill in the spring of 1853. My father visited the inn at Midhurst, I should think as her fiancé, in the summer. He had left Up Park and was on his way to stay with his brother, Charles Edward, in Gloucestershire until he could find another place. Then suddenly she was in a distressful storm. Her father was taken ill unexpectedly and died in August, and her mother, already very ill, died, after a phase of dementia due to grief and dismay, in November. That happened on the 5th, and on the 22nd my mother was married to my father (who was still out of a situation) in the City of London at St. Stephen's Church, Coleman Street. He seems to have been employed a little later as an under gardener at Trentham in Staffordshire, and for a time they could live together only intermittently. She visited him at Trentham, she does not say precisely how; and they spent a Sunday she did not like in "the gardener's cottage" at Crewe. "No church, nothing." She paid visits to relations in between and felt "very unsettled."

I guess they were married on his initiative, but that is only guessing. He may have thought it a fine thing to do. There is nothing like extravagance when one is down. He may have had a flash of imperious passion. But then one should go on in the same key, and that he did not do. My mother may have felt the need of a man to combat the lawyers whom she suspected of making away with her father's estate. If so, my father was very little good to her. Presently he got a job and a cottage at Shuckburgh Park in the midlands. On April 5th, 1854, she is "very happy and busy preparing for my new home." It was to be the happiest and most successful home she ever had, poor little woman! In the diary my father becomes "dearest Joe" and "my dear husband." Previously he had been "Joe" or "J. W." "The Saturday laborious work I do not like, but still I am very happy in my little home." And he did a little water-colour sketch which still exists, of his small square cottage, and I suppose one does not sketch a house unless one is reasonably happy in it. He kept this place at Shuckburgh Park until a daughter had been born to him (in 1855) and then he was at loose ends again.

There seems to have been no intimation of coming trouble until it came. My mother's diary records: "July 17th 1855. Sir Francis gave Joe warning to *leave* (trebly underlined). Oh what a sorrow! It struck to my poor heart to look at my sweet babe and obliged to leave my pretty *home*. May it please God to bless us with another happy quiet home in His own Good Time."

But it did not please God to do anything of the sort at any time any more.

I do not know why my father was unsuccessful as a gardener, but I suspect a certain intractability of temper rather than incapacity. He did not like to be told things and made to do things. He was impatient. Before he married, I gather from an old letter from a friend that has chanced to be preserved, he was talking of going to the gold diggings in Australia, and again after he left the cottage at Shuckburgh he was looking round for some way out of the galling subordinations and uncertainties of "service." He thought again of emigrating; this time to America, there were even two stout boxes made for his belongings, and then his schemes for flight abroad, which perhaps after all were rather half-hearted schemes, were frustrated by the advent of my eldest brother, his second child.

Perhaps it was as well that he did not attempt pioneering in new lands with my mother. She had been trained as a lady's maid and not as a housewife and I do not think she had the mental flexibility to rise to new occasions. She was that sort of woman who is an incorrigibly bad cook. By nature and upbringing alike she belonged to that middle-class of dependents who occupied situations, performed strictly defined duties, gave or failed to give satisfaction and had no ideas at all outside that dependence. People of that quality "saved up for a rainy day" but they were without the slightest trace of primary productive or acquisitive ability. She was that in all innocence, but I perceive that my father might well have had a more efficient help-mate in the struggle for life as it went on in the individualistic nineteenth century.

He was at any rate a producer, if only as a recalcitrant gardener, but he shared her incapacity for getting and holding things. They were both economic innocents made by and for a social order, a scheme of things, that was falling to pieces all about them. And looking for stability in a world that was already breaking away towards adventure, they presently dropped into that dismal insanitary hole I have already described, in which I was born, and from which they were unable to escape for twenty-four dreary years.

Since it was difficult to find a situation as a gardener and still more tiresome to keep it, since there was no shelter or help in the world while one was out of work but the scanty hospitality of one's family, the idea of becoming one's own master and getting a home of one's own even on an uncertain income became a very alluring one. An obliging cousin, George Wells, with a little unsuccessful china and crockery shop in the High Street of Bromley, Kent, offered it to my father on extremely reasonable terms. It was called *Atlas House* because of a figure of Atlas bearing a lamp instead of the world in the shop window. My father anticipated his inheritance of a hundred pounds or so, bought this business and set up for himself. He spent all his available savings and reserves, and my mother with one infant in arms moved into 47 High Street, in time to bring my eldest brother into the world there. And so they were caught. From the outset this business did not "pay," and it "paid" less and less. But they had now no means of getting out of it and going anywhere else.

"Took possession," says the diary on October 23rd 1855. On the 27th, "very unsettled. No furniture sufficient and no capital to do as we ought. I fear we have done wrong." On November 7th she says, "This seems a horrid business, no trade. How I wish I had taken that situation with Lady Carrick!" "November 8th. No customers all day. How sad to be deceived by one's relations. They have got their money and we their old stock."

They both knew they were caught.

And being caught like this was to try these poor things out to the utmost. It grew very plain that my father had neither imagination nor sympathy for the woman's side of life. (Later on I was to betray a similar deficiency.) He had been brought up in a country home with mother and sisters, and the women folk saw to all the indoor business. A man just didn't bother about it. He lived from the shop outward and had by far the best of things; she became the entire household staff, with two little children on her hands and, as the diary shows quite plainly, in perpetual dread of further motherhood. "Anxiety relieved," became her formula. There is a pathetic deterioration in the diary, as infested, impossible, exhausting Atlas House takes possession of her. There were no more descriptions of scenery and fewer and fewer pious and sentimental reflections after the best models. It becomes a record of dates and comings and goings, of feeling ill, of the ill health of her children, growing up, she realized, in unwholesome circumstances, of being left alone, of triter and triter attempts to thank God for his many mercies. "J. W."—he is "J. W." again now and henceforth—"playing cricket at Chislehurst." "J. W. out all day." "J. W. in London." ...

"August 23rd, 1857. Church, morning, had a happy day. J. W. went to church with me!!!"

"August 30th, 1857. Went to church. Mr. J. W. did not go all day, did not feel quite so happy, how often I wish he was more serious."

"Dec. 1st, 1857. Joe resolved on going to New Zealand. Advertisement of business to let or sold. 3rd. Please God to guide us whichever way is for the best."

"Dec. 31st, '57. This year ends with extreme anxiety about the business. How I wish we had never taken it. How unsuited for us. Not half a living and dear parents have all gone. Oh Heavenly Father guide and direct me."

"Jan. 4th. J. W. put a second advertisement in."

"Jan. 6th. Had an answer to advertisement."

These advertisements came to nothing. A "letting notice in the window" came to nothing. "Several enquiries but nothing." More strenuous methods were needed and never adopted. Day follows day in that diary and mostly they are unhappy days. And so it went on. For twenty-four years of her life, and the first thirteen years of mine, dingy old Atlas House kept her going up and down its wearisome staircases in her indefatigable hopeless attempt to recover something of the brightness of that little cottage at Shuckburgh.

My mother used to accuse my father of neglecting the shop for cricket. But it was through that excellent sport as it was then, that the little ménage contrived to hold out, with an occasional bankruptcy, for so long before it was finally sold up. He was never really interested in the crockery trade and sold little, I think, but jampots and preserving jars to the gentlemen's houses round about, and occasional bedroom sets and tea-sets, table glass and replacements. But he developed his youthful ability to play cricket which he had kept alive at Up Park, he revived the local club and was always getting jobs of variable duration as a professional bowler and cricket instructor in the neighbourhood. He played for the West Kent Club from 1857 to 1869 and bowled for the County of Kent in 1862 and 1863. On June 26th, 1862, he clean bowled four Sussex batsmen in four successive balls, a feat not hitherto recorded in county cricket. Moreover his cousin John Duke at Penshurst, whom he had once got out of danger when they were swimming together, let him have long and considerate credit for a supply of cricket goods that ousted the plates and dishes from half the shop window. Among the familiar names of my childhood were the Hoares and the Normans, both banking families with places near Bromley, for whom he bowled; and for some years he went every summer term to Norwich Grammar School as "pro."

§ 4. SARAH WELLS AT ATLAS HOUSE (1855-1880)

My Mother drudged endlessly in that gaunt and impossible home and the years slipped by. Year after year she changed and the prim little lady's-maid, with her simple faith and her definite views about the Holy Sacrament, gave place to a tired woman more and more perplexed by life. Twice more her habitual "anxiety" was not to be relieved, and God was to incur her jaded and formal gratitude for two more "dear ones." She feared us terribly before we came and afterwards she loved and slaved for us intensely, beyond reason. She was not clever at her job and I have to tell it; she sometimes did badly by her children through lack of knowledge and flexibility, but nothing could exceed the grit and devotion of her mothering. She wore her fingers to the bone working at our clothes, and she had acquired a fanatical belief in cod liver oil and insisted that we two younger ones should have it at any cost; so that we escaped the vitamin insufficiency that gave my elder brother a pigeon breast and a retarded growth. No one knew about vitamin D in those days, but cod liver oil had been prescribed for my sister Fanny and it had worked magic with her.

My mother brought my brother Freddy into the world in 1862, and had her great tragedy in 1864, when my sister died of appendicitis. The nature of appendicitis was unknown in those days; it was called "inflammation of the bowels"; my sister had been to a children's tea party a day or so before her seizure, and my mother in her distress at this sudden blow, leaped to the conclusion that Fanny had been given something unsuitable to eat, and was never quite reconciled to those neighbours, would not speak to them, forbade us to mention them.

Fanny had evidently been a very bright, precocious and fragile little girl, an indoor little girl, with a facility for prim piety that had delighted my mother's heart. Such early goodness, says Dr. W. R. Ackroyd (in *Vitamins and other Dietary Essentials*) is generally a sign of some diet deficiency, and that, I fear is how things were with her. Quite healthy children are boisterous. She had learnt her "collect" every Sunday, repeated many hymns by rote, said her prayers beautifully, found her "place" in the prayer book at church, and made many apt remarks for my mother to treasure in her heart. I was born two years and more after her death, in 1866, and my mother decided that I had been sent to replace Fanny and to achieve a similar edification. But again Fate was mocking her. Little boys are different in constitution from little girls, and even from the outset I showed myself exceptionally deficient in the religious sense. I was born blasphemous and protesting. Even at my christening, she told me, I squalled with a vehemence unprecedented in the history of the family.

And later she was to undermine her own teaching with cod liver oil.

My own beginnings were shaped so much as a system of reactions to my mother's ideas and suggestions and feelings that I find some attempt to realize her states of mind, during those twenty-five years of enslavement behind the crockery shop, a necessary prelude to my account of my own education. We had no servants; no nurse-maids and governesses intervened between us; she carried me about until I could be put down to trot after her and so I arose mentally, quite as much as physically, out of her. It was a process of severance and estrangement, for I was my father's as well as my mother's son.

I have tried to give an impression of the simple and confident faith with which my mother sailed out into life. Vast unsuspected forces beyond her ken were steadily destroying the social order, the horse and sailing ship transport, the handicrafts and the tenant-farming social order, to which all her beliefs were attuned and on which all her confidence was based. To her these mighty changes in human life presented themselves as a series of perplexing frustrations and undeserved misfortunes, for which nothing or nobody was clearly to blame—unless it was my father and the disingenuous behaviour of people about her from whom she might have expected better things.

Bromley was being steadily suburbanized. An improved passenger and goods service, and the opening of a second railway station, made it more and more easy for people to go to London for their shopping and for London retailers to come into competition with the local traders. Presently the delivery vans of the early multiple shops, the Army and Navy Co-operative Stores and the like, appeared in the neighbourhood to suck away the ebbing vitality of the local retailer. The trade in pickling jars and jam-pots died away. Fresh housekeepers came to the gentlemen's houses, who knew not Joseph and bought their stuff from the stores.

Why didn't Joe do something about it?

Poor little woman! How continually vexed she was, how constantly tired and worried to the limits of endurance, during that dismal half-lifetime of disillusionment that slipped away at Bromley! She clung most desperately to the values she had learnt at Miss Riley's finishing school; she learnt nothing and forgot nothing through those dark years spent for the most part in the underground kitchen. Every night and morning and sometimes during the day she prayed to Our Father and Our Saviour for a little money, for a little leisure, for a little kindness, to make Joe better and less negligent—for now he was getting very neglectful of her. It was like writing to an absconding debtor for all the answer she got.

Unless taking away her darling, her wonder, her one sweet and tractable child, her Fanny, her little "Possy," without pity or warning was an answer. A lesson. Fanny was well and happy and then she was flushed and contorted with agony and then in three days she was dead. My mother had to talk to her diary about it. Little boys do not like lamenting mothers; Joe was apt to say, "There, there, Saddie," and go off to his cricket; except for Our Lord and Saviour, whose dumbness, I am afraid, wore the make-believe very thin at times, my mother had to do her weeping alone.

It is my conviction that deep down in my mother's heart something was broken when my sister died two years and more before I was born. Her simple faith was cracked then and its reality spilled away. I got only the forms and phrases of it. I do not think she ever admitted to herself, ever realized consciously, that there was no consolation under heaven for the outrage Fate had done her. Our Lord was dumb, even in dreams he came not, and her subconsciousness apprehended all the dreadful implications of that silence. But she fought down that devastating discovery. She went on repeating the old phrases of belief—all the more urgently perhaps. She wanted me to believe in order to stanch that dark undertow of doubt. In the early days with my sister she had been able so to saturate her teaching with confidence in the Divine Protection, that she had created a prodigy of Early Piety. My heart she never touched because the virtue had gone out of her.

I was indeed a prodigy of Early Impiety. I was scared by Hell, I did not at first question the existence of Our Father, but no fear nor terror could prevent my feeling that his All Seeing Eye was that of an Old Sneak and that the Atonement for which I had to be so grateful was either an imposture, a trick of sham self-immolation, or a crazy nightmare. I felt the unsoundness of these things before I dared to think it. There was a time when I believed in the story and scheme of salvation, so far as I could understand it, just as there was a time when I believed there was a Devil, but there was never a time when I did not heartily detest the whole business.

I feared Hell dreadfully for some time. Hell was indeed good enough to scare me and prevent me calling either of my brothers fools, until I was eleven or twelve. But one night I had a dream of Hell so preposterous that it blasted that undesirable resort out of my mind for ever. In an old number of *Chambers Journal* I had read of the punishment of breaking a man on the wheel. The horror of it got into my dreams and there was Our Father in a particularly malignant phase, busy basting a poor broken sinner rotating slowly over a fire built under the wheel. I saw no Devil in the vision; my mind in its simplicity went straight to the responsible fountain head. That dream pursued me into the day time. Never had I hated God so intensely.

And then suddenly the light broke through to me and I knew this God was a lie.

I have a sort of love for most living things, but I cannot recall any time in my life when I had the faintest shadow of an intimation of love for any one of the Persons in the Holy

Trinity. I could as soon love a field scarecrow as those patched up "persons." I am still as unable to account for the ecstasies of the faithful as I was to feel as my mother wished me to feel. I sensed it was a silly story long before I dared to admit even to myself that it was a silly story.

For indeed it is a silly story and each generation nowadays swallows it with greater difficulty. It is a jumble up of a miscellany of the old sacrificial and consolatory religions of the confused and unhappy townspeople of the early Empire; its constituent practices were probably more soothing to troubled hearts before there was any attempt to weld them into one mystical creed, and all the disingenuous intelligence of generation after generation of time-serving or well-meaning divines has served only to accentuate the fundamental silliness of these synthesised Egyptian and Syrian myths. I doubt if one person in a million of all the hosts of Christendom has ever produced a spark of genuine gratitude for the Atonement. I think "love" for the Triune God is as rare as it is unnatural and irrational.

Why do people go on pretending about this Christianity? At the test of war, disease, social injustice and every real human distress, it fails—and leaves a cheated victim, as it abandoned my mother. Jesus was some fine sort of man perhaps, the Jewish Messiah was a promise of leadership, but Our Saviour of the Trinity is a dressed-up inconsistent effigy of amiability, a monstrous hybrid of man and infinity, making vague promises of helpful miracles for the cheating of simple souls, an ever absent help in times of trouble.

And their Sacrament, their wonderful Sacrament, in which the struggling Believers urge themselves to discover the profoundest satisfaction; what is it? What does it amount to? Was there ever a more unintelligible mix up of bad metaphysics and grossly materialistic superstition than this God-eating? Was there anything more corrupting to take into a human mind and be given cardinal importance there?

I once said a dreadful thing to my mother about the Sacrament. In her attempts to evoke Early Piety in me, she worked very hard indeed to teach me the answers in the English Church Catechism. I learnt them dutifully but I found them dull. In one answer (framed very carefully to guard me against the errors of the Church of Rome) I had to say what were the elements in the sacred feast. "Bread and Wine," it ran, "which our Lord hath ordained," *etc., etc.*

Bread and Wine seemed a strange foolish form of refreshment to me, the only wines I knew were ginger wine at Christmas and orange wine, which I took with cod liver oil, and port and sherry which were offered with a cracknel biscuit to housekeepers who came to pay bills, and so it occurred to me it would introduce an amusing element of realism into the solemnity of the recital if I answered "Bread and Butter" and chuckled helpfully....

My mother knew she had to be profoundly shocked. She was shocked to the best of her ability. But she was much more puzzled than shocked. The book was closed, the audition suspended.

She said I did not understand the dreadfulness of what I had said, and that was perfectly true. And poor dear she could not convey it to me. No doubt she interceded with God for me and asked him to take over the task of enlightenment. "Forgive dear Bertie," she must have said.

And anyhow it was made evident to me that a decorative revision of the English Church Catechism was an undesirable enterprise. I turned my attention to the more acceptable effort to say it faster and faster.

My mother in my earliest memories of her was a distressed overworked little woman, already in her late forties. All the hope and confidence of her youth she had left behind her. As I knew her in my childhood, she was engaged in a desperate single-handed battle with our gaunt and dismal home, to keep it clean, to keep her children clean, to get them clothed and fed and taught, to keep up appearances. The only domestic help I ever knew her to have was a garrulous old woman of the quality of Sairey Gamp, a certain Betsy Finch.

In opulent times Betsy would come in to char, and there would even be a washing day, when the copper in the scullery was lit and all the nether regions were filled with white steam and the smell of soapsuds. My mother appears in these early memories, in old cloth slippers, a grey stuff dress or a print dress according to the season, an apron of sacking and a big pink sunbonnet— such as country-women wore in Old and New England alike before the separation. There was little sun in her life, but she wore that headdress, she explained, to keep the dust out of her hair. She is struggling up or down stairs with a dust-pan, a slop-pail, a scrubbing brush or a greasy dishclout. Long before I came into the world her poor dear hands had become enlarged and distorted by scrubbing and damp, and I never knew them otherwise.

Her toil was unending. My father would get up and rake out and lay and light the fire, because she was never clever at getting a fire to burn, and then she would get breakfast while he took down the clumsy shop shutters and swept out the shop. Then came the business of hunting the boys out of bed, seeing that they did something in the way of washing, giving them breakfast and sending them off in time for school. Then airing and making the beds, emptying the slops, washing up the breakfast things. Then perhaps a dusty battle to clean out a room; there were no vacuum cleaners in those days; or a turn at scrubbing—scrubbing the splintery rotten wood of a jerry-built house. There was no O-Cedar mop, no polished floor; down you went to it on all fours with your pail beside you. If Joe was out delivering goods there might at any moment be a jangle of the shop bell and a customer.

Customers bothered my mother, especially when she was in her costume for housework; she would discard her apron in a hurry, wipe her wet hands, pat her hair into order, come into the shop breathless and defensive, and often my father had neglected to mark the prices on the things the customer wanted. If it was cricket goods she was quite at sea.

My father usually bought the meat for dinner himself, and that had to be cooked and the table laid in the downstairs kitchen. Then came a clatter of returning boys through the shop and down the staircase, and the midday meal. The room was dark and intermittently darker because of the skirts and feet going by over the grating. It wasn't always a successful meal. Sometimes there was not much to eat; but there were always potatoes and there was too much cabbage for my taste; and sometimes the cooking had been unfortunate and my father Pished and Tushed or said disagreeable things outright. My mother in those days was just the unpaid servant of everybody. I in particular was often peevish with my food, and frequently I would have headaches and bad bilious attacks in the afternoon. We drank beer that was drawn from a small cask in the scullery, and if it went a little flat before the cask was finished it had to be drunk just the same. Presently father lit his pipe and filled the kitchen air with the fragrance of Red Virginia, the boys dispersed quarrelling or skylarking or rejoicing, and there was nothing left to do of the first half, the heavier half, of my mother's daily routine but wash up the plates at the sink.

Then she could attend to appearances. Instead of the charlady ensemble of the morning, she changed herself into a trim little lady with a cap and lace apron. Generally she sat indoors. Perforce if my father was at cricket, but mainly because there was nothing to do abroad and much to do at home. She had a large confused work-basket—when I was small and exceptionally good it was sometimes my privilege to turn it out—and she had all our clothes to mend. She darned my heels and knees with immense stitches. In addition she made all our clothes until such age as, under the pressure of our schoolfellows' derision, we rebelled against something rather naïve in the cut. Also she made loose covers for the chairs and sofa out of cheap chintz or cretonne. She made them as she cooked and as she made our clothes, with courage rather than skill. They fitted very badly but at least they hid the terrible worn shabbiness of the fundamental stuff. She got tea, she got supper, she put her offspring to bed after they had said their prayers, and then she could sit a little while, think, read the daily-paper, write a line or so in her diary, attend to her correspondence, before she lit her candle and went up the inconvenient staircase for the last time to bed. My father was generally out after supper, talking of men's affairs with men or playing a friendly game of Nap, by which I believe, generally speaking, he profited, in the bar parlour of the Bell.

I know very little about the realities of my father's life at this time. Essentially he was a baffled unsuccessful "stuck" man, but he had a light and cheerful disposition, and a large part of his waking energy was spent in evading disagreeable realizations. He had a kind of attractiveness for women, I think he was aware of it, but I do not know whether he ever went further along the line of unfaithfulness than a light flirtation—in Bromley at any rate. I should certainly have learnt from my schoolfellows of any scandal or scandalous suspicion. He chatted a great deal at the shop door to fellow tradesmen in a similar state of leisure. The voices and occasional laughter came through the shop to my mother alone within.

He read diversely, bought books at sales, brought them home from the Library Institute. I think his original religious and political beliefs were undergoing a slow gentle fading out in those days. Evidently he found my mother, with her rigid standards and her curiously stereotyped mind, less and less interesting to talk to. She was never able to master the mysteries of cards or chess or draughts, so that alleviation of their evenings was out of the question. He felt her voluminous unspoken criticism of his ineptitude, he realized the justice of her complaints, and yet for the life of him he could not see what was to be done. I will confess I do not know what he could have done.

My mother's instinct for appearances was very strong. Whatever the realities of our situation, she was resolved that to the very last moment we should keep up the appearance of being comfortable members of that upper- servant tenant class to which her imagination had been moulded. She believed that it was a secret to all the world that she had no servant and did all the household drudgery herself. I was enjoined never to answer questions about that or let it out when I went abroad. Nor was I to take my coat off carelessly, because my underclothing was never quite up to the promise of my exterior garments. It was never ragged but it abounded in compromises. This hindered my playing games.

I was never to mix with common children, who might teach me naughty words. The Hoptons, the greengrocer's family over the way, were "rough" she thought; they were really turbulently jolly; the Mundays next door were methodists who sang hymns out of church which is almost as bad as singing songs in it, and the Mowatts at the corner she firmly believed had killed poor Possy and were not to be thought of. People who were not beneath us were apt to be stuck-up and unapproachable in the other direction. So my universe of discourse was limited. She preferred to have me indoors rather than out.

She taught me the rudiments of learning. I learnt my alphabet from a big sheet of capital letters pasted up in the kitchen, I learnt the nine figures from the same sheet, and from her, orally, how to count up to a hundred, and the first word I wrote was "butter," which I traced over her handwriting against a pane of the window. Also I began to read under her instructions. But then she felt my education was straining for higher things and I went off with my brother Freddy (who was on no account to let go of my hand) to a school in a room in a row of cottages near the Drill Hall, kept by an unqualified old lady, Mrs. Knott, and her equally unqualified daughter Miss Salmon, where I learnt to say my tables of weights and measures, read words of two or more syllables and pretend to do summing—it was incomprehensible fudging that was never explained to me—on a slate.

Such was my mother in the days when I was a small boy. She already had wrinkles round her eyes, and her mouth was drawn in because she had lost some teeth, and having them replaced by others would have seemed a wicked extravagance to her. I wonder what went on in her brain when she sat alone in the evening by the lamp and the dying fire, doing some last bit of sewing before she went to bed? I began to wonder what went on in her brain when I was in my early teens and I have wondered ever since.

I believe she was profoundly aware of her uncomfortable poverty-stricken circumstances, but I do not think she was acutely unhappy. I believe that she took refuge from reality in a world of innocent reverie. As she sewed, a string of petty agreeable fictions were distracting her mind from unpleasant fears and anxieties. She was meeting someone whom it was agreeable to meet; she was being congratulated on this or that fancied achievement, dear Bertie was coming home with prizes from school, dear Frankie or dear Freddie was setting up in business and doing ever so well, or the postman was coming with a letter, a registered letter. It was a letter to say she had been left money, twenty-five pounds, fifty pounds—why not a hundred pounds? All her own. The Married Woman's Property Act ensured that Joe couldn't touch it. It was a triumph over Joe, but all the same, she would buy him something out of it. Poor Possy should have that gravestone at last. Mr. Morley's bill would be paid.

Should she have a servant? Did she really want a servant—except for what the neighbours thought? More trouble than they are worth most of the time. A silly girl she would have to train—and with boys about! And Joe?... The boys were good as gold, she knew, but who could tell what might not happen if the girl chanced to be a bad, silly girl? Better have in a serious woman, Betsy Finch for example, more regularly. It would be nice not to have to scrub so much. And to have new curtains in the parlour.... Doctor Beeby coming in—just to look at Freddie's finger, nothing serious. "Dear me, Mrs. Wells, dear me! How *pretty* you have made the room!" ...

Some such flow of fancy as that, it must have been.

Without reverie life would surely be unendurable to the greater multitude of human beings. After all opium is merely a stimulant for reverie. And reverie, I am sure, made the substance of her rare leisure. Religion and love, except for her instinctive pride in her boys, had receded imperceptibly from her life and left her dreaming. Once she had dreamt of reciprocated love and a sedulously attentive God, but there was indeed no more reassurance for her except in dreamland. My father was away at cricket, and I think she realized more and more acutely as the years dragged on without material alleviation, that Our Father and Our Lord, on whom, to begin with, she had perhaps counted unduly, were also away—playing perhaps at their own sort of cricket in some remote quarter of the starry universe.

My mother was still a good Churchwoman, but I doubt if her reveries in the lonely evenings at Atlas House ever went into the hereafter and anticipated immortality. I doubt if she ever distracted herself by dreaming of the scenery of the Life to Come, or of anything that could happen there. Unless it was to have a vision of meeting her lost little "Possy" again in some celestial garden, an unchanged and eternal child, and hear her surprised bright cry of "Mummy Mummy!" and hold her in her arms once more.

§ 5. A BROKEN LEG AND SOME BOOKS AND PICTURES (1874)

My leg was broken for me when I was between seven and eight. Probably I am alive to-day and writing this autobiography instead of being a worn-out, dismissed and already dead shop assistant, because my leg was broken. The agent of good fortune was "young Sutton," the grown-up son of the landlord of the *Bell*. I was playing outside the scoring tent in the cricket field and in all friendliness he picked me up and tossed me in the air. "Whose little kid are you?" he said, and I wriggled, he missed his hold on me and I snapped my tibia across a tent peg. A great fuss of being carried home; a painful setting—for they just set and strapped a broken leg tightly between splints in those days, and the knee and ankle swelled dreadfully—and then for some weeks I found myself enthroned on the sofa in the parlour as the most important thing in the house, consuming unheard-of jellies, fruits, brawn and chicken sent with endless apologies on behalf of her son by Mrs. Sutton, and I could demand and have a fair chance of getting anything that came into my head, books, paper, pencils, and toys—and particularly books.

I had just taken to reading. I had just discovered the art of leaving my body to sit impassive in a crumpled up attitude in a chair or sofa, while I wandered over the hills and far away in novel company and new scenes. And now my father went round nearly every day to the Literary Institute in Market Square and got one or two books for me, and Mrs. Sutton sent some books, and there was always a fresh book to read. My world began to expand very rapidly, and when presently I could put my foot to the ground, the reading habit had got me securely. Both my parents were doubtful of the healthiness of reading, and did their best to discourage this poring over books as soon as my leg was better.

I cannot recall now many of the titles of the books I read, I devoured them so fast, and the title and the author's name in those days seemed a mere inscription on the door to delay me in getting down to business. There was a work, in two volumes, upon the countries of the world, which I think must have been made of bound up fortnightly parts. It was illustrated with woodcuts, the photogravure had still to come in those days, and it took me to Tibet, China, the Rocky Mountains, the forests of Brazil, Siam and a score of other lands. I mingled with Indians and naked negroes; I learnt about whaling and crossed the drift ice with Esquimaux. There was Wood's *Natural History*, also copiously illustrated and full of exciting and terrifying facts. I conceived a profound fear of the gorilla, of which there was a fearsome picture, which came out of the book at times after dark and followed me noiselessly about the house. The half landing was a favourite lurking place for this terror. I passed it whistling, but wary and then ran for my life up the next flight. And I was glad to think that between the continental land masses of the world, which would have afforded an unbroken land passage for wolves from Russia and tigers from India, and this safe island on which I took my daily walks, stretched the impassable moat of the English Channel. I read too in another book about the distances of the stars, and that seemed to push the All Seeing Eye very agreeably away from me. Turning over the pages of the Natural History, I perceived a curious relationship between cats and tigers and lions and so forth, and to a lesser degree between them and hyenas and dogs and bears, and between them again and other quadrupeds, and curious premonitions of evolution crept into my thoughts. Also I read the life of the Duke of Wellington and about the American Civil War, and began to fight campaigns and battles in my reveries. At home were the works of Washington Irving and I became strangely familiar with Granada and Columbus and the Companions of Columbus. I do not remember that any story books figured during this first phase of reading. Either I have forgotten them or they did not come my way. Later on, however, Captain Mayne Reid, Fenimore Cooper and the Wild West generally, seized upon my imagination.

One important element in that first bout of reading was the bound volumes of *Punch* and its rival in those days, *Fun*, which my father renewed continually during my convalescence. The bound periodicals with their political cartoons and their quaint details played a curious part in developing my imaginative framework. My ideas of political and international relations were moulded very greatly by the big figures of John Bull and Uncle Sam, the French, the Austrian, and the German and Russian emperors, the Russian bear, the British lion and the Bengal tiger, Mr. Gladstone the noble, and the insidious, smiling Dizzy. They confronted one another; they said heroic, if occasionally quite incomprehensible things to one another. And across the political scene also marched tall and lovely feminine figures, Britannia, Erin, Columbia, La France, bare armed, bare necked, showing beautiful bare bosoms, revealing shining thighs, wearing garments that were a revelation in an age of flounces and crinolines. My first consciousness of women, my first stirrings of desire were roused by these heroic divinities. I became woman-conscious from those days onward.

I do not wish to call in question the accounts the masters of psycho- analysis give us of the awakening of sexual consciousness in the children they have studied. But I believe that the children who furnished material for the first psycho-analysts were the children of people racially different, and different in their conceptions of permissible caresses and endearments from my family. What they say may be true of Austrian Jews and Levantines and yet not true of English or Irish. I cannot remember and I cannot trace any continuity between my infantile physical reactions and my personal sexual life. I believe that all the infantile sensuality of suckling and so forth on which so much stress is laid, was never carried on into the permanent mental fabric, was completely washed out in forgetfulness; never coagulated into sub-conscious memories; it was as though it had never been. I cannot detect any mother fixation, any Oedipus complex or any of that stuff in my make up. My mother's kisses were significant acts, expressions not caresses. As a small boy

I found no more sexual significance about my always decent and seemly mother than I did about the chairs and sofa in our parlour.

It is quite possible that while there is a direct continuity of the sexual subconsciousness from parent to child in the southern and eastern Europeans, due to a sustained habit of caresses and intimacy, the psycho-sexual processes of the northern and western Europeans and Americans arise *de novo* in each generation after a complete break with and forgetfulness of the mother-babe reaction, and so are fundamentally different in their form and sequence. At any rate I am convinced that my own sexual life began in a naïve direct admiration for the lovely bodies, as they seemed, of those political divinities of Tenniel's in *Punch*, and that my first inklings of desire were roused by them and by the plaster casts of Greek statuary that adorned the Crystal Palace. I do not think there was any sub- conscious contribution from preceding events to that response; my mind was inherently ready for it. My mother had instilled in me the impropriety of not wearing clothes, so that my first attraction towards Venus was shamefaced and furtive, but the dear woman never suspected the stimulating influence of Britannia, Erin, Columbia and the rest of them upon my awakening susceptibilities.

It is true that I worshipped them at first in a quasi infantile fashion, but that does not imply continuity of experience. When I went to bed I used to pillow my head on their great arms and breasts. Gradually they ceased to be gigantic. They took me in their arms and I embraced them, but nevertheless I remained fundamentally ignorant and innocent until I went to school after my accident. I found women lovely and worshipful before I was seven years old, and well before I came down to what we call nowadays the "facts of sex." But now that my interest was aroused I became acutely observant of a print or a statuette in a shop window. I do not think my interest at that time was purely hetero-sexual. My world was so clothed and covered up, and the

70

rules of decency were so established in me, that any revelation of the body was an exciting thing.

Now that I had arrived at knickerbockers and the reading of books, I was sent to a little private school in the High Street, Bromley, for boys between seven and fifteen, and from my schoolmates I speedily learnt in the grossest way, imparted with guffaws and gestures, "the facts of sex," and all those rude words that express them, from which my mother had hitherto shielded me.

None of these boys came from bookish homes so that I had from the outset a queer relative wideness of outlook. I knew all sorts of things about lands and beasts and times of which they had never heard. And I had developed a facility for drawing, which in them was altogether dormant. So that I passed for an exceptionally bright and clever little boy and the schoolmaster would invoke "Young Seven Years Old," to shame the obtuseness of my elders. They were decent enough not to visit it upon me. Among boys from more literate homes I should have had none of these outstanding advantages, but I took them naturally enough as an intrinsic superiority, and they made me rather exceptionally self-conceited and confident.

The clash of these gross revelations about the apparatus of sex with my secret admiration for the bodily beauty of women, and with this personal conceit of mine, determined to a large extent my mental and perhaps my physical development. It imposed a reserve upon me that checked a native outspokenness. That a certain amount of masturbation is a normal element in the emergence of sexual consciousness was in those days almost passionately concealed by the English-speaking world. Yet probably no normal individual altogether escapes that response to the stir of approaching adolescence. To my generation it was allowed to come as a horrifying, astounding, perplexing individual discovery. Without guidance and recognition, and black with shame, it ran inevitably into a variety of unwholesome channels. Upon many boys and girls it became localized in the parts more immediately affected and exercised an overwhelming fascination. The school had its exhibitionist and ran with a dirty whispered and giggling undertow. Among the boarders, many of whom slept two in a bed, there was certainly much simple substitutional homosexuality. Personally I recoiled, even more than I cared to show, from mere phallicism. I did not so much begin masturbation as have it happen to me as a natural outcome of my drowsy clasping of my goddesses. I had so to speak a one-sided love affair with the bedding.

I never told a soul about it because I was ashamed and feared ridicule or indignant reproof. Very early I got hold of the idea, I do not know how, that Venus could drain away my energy, and this kept my lapses from ideal "purity" within very definite bounds indeed. There was also a certain amount of superstitious terror to restrain me. Maybe this was that sin against the Holy Ghost that could never be forgiven, that damned inevitably. That worried a brother of mine more than it did me, but I think it worried me also. I was eleven or twelve years old before religion began to fall to pieces in my consciousness.

So at the age of seven (and, to be exact, three quarters), when I went up the High Street to Morley's school for the first time, a rather white- faced little boy in a holland pinafore and carrying a small green baize satchel for my books, I had already between me and my bleak Protestant God, a wide wide world of snowy mountains, Arctic regions, tropical forests, prairies and deserts and high seas, cities and armies, Indians, negroes and island savages, gorillas, great carnivores, elephants, rhinoceroses and whales, about which I was prepared to talk freely, and cool and strange below it all a cavernous world of nameless goddess mistresses of which I never breathed a word to any human being.

III. — SCHOOLBOY

§ 1. MR. MORLEY'S COMMERCIAL ACADEMY
(1874- 1880)

This march up the High Street to Mr. Thomas Morley's Academy begins a new phase in the story of the brain that J. W. and his Saddie had launched into the world. Bromley Academy was a school in the ancient tradition, but the culmination of my schooling was to occur in the most modern and advanced of colleges then in existence, the science schools at South Kensington. It was a queer discontinuous series of educational processes through which my brain was passed, very characteristic of the continual dislocations of that time.

The germinating forces of that Modern World-State which is now struggling into ordered being, were already thrusting destructively amidst the comparative stabilities of the old eighteenth century order before I was born. There was already a railway station on the Dover line and this was supplemented, when I was about twelve years old, by a second line branching off from the Chislehurst line at Grove Park. The place which had been hardly more than a few big houses, a little old market place and a straggling High Street upon the high road, with two coaching inns and a superabundance of small "pull-up" beerhouses, was stimulated to a vigorous growth in population. Steadily London drew it closer and suburbanized it. No one foresaw its growth except a few speculative jerry-builders; no one in the world prepared for even the most obvious consequences of that growth. Shops and dwellings of the type of my home were "run up" anyhow. Slum conditions appeared almost at once in courts and muddy by-ways. Yet all around were open fields and common land, Bromley Common, Chislehurst Common, great parks like Sundridge Park and Camden, and to the south the wide heathery spaces about Keston Fish Ponds and Down.

The new order of things that was appearing in the world when I was born, was already arousing a consciousness of the need for universal elementary education. It was being realized by the ruling classes that a nation with a lower stratum of illiterates would compete at a disadvantage against the foreigner. A condition of things in which everyone would read and write and do sums, dawned on the startled imagination of mankind. The British and the National Schools, which had existed for half a century in order to make little Nonconformists and little Churchmen, were organized into a state system under the Elementary Education Act of 1871 and supplemented by Board Schools (designed to make little Unsectarian Christians). Bromley was served by a National School. That was all that the district possessed in the way of public education. It was the mere foundation of an education. It saw to the children up to the age of thirteen or even fourteen, and no further. Beyond that the locality had no public provision for technical education or the development of artistic or scientific ability whatever. Even that much of general education had been achieved against considerable resistance. There was a strong objection in those days to the use of public funds for the education of "other people's children," and school pennies were exacted weekly from the offspring of everyone not legally indigent.

But side by side with that nineteenth-century National School under the Education Act, the old eighteenth-century order was still carrying on in Bromley, just as it was still carrying on in my mother's mind. In the eighteenth century the lower classes did not pretend to read or write, but the members of the tenant-farmer, shopkeeper, innkeeper, upper servant stratum, which was then, relatively to the labourers, a larger part of the community, either availed themselves of the smaller endowed schools which came down from the mental stir of the Reformation, or, in the absence of any such school in their neighbourhood, supported little private schools of their own. These private schools were struggling along amidst the general dissolution, shuffling and reconstruction of society that was already manifest in the middle nineteenth century, and the Academy of Mr. Thomas Morley was a fairly well preserved specimen, only slightly modernized, of the departing order of things.

He had opened school for himself in 1849, having previously filled the post of usher at an old-established school that closed down in that year. He was Scotch and not of eminent academic attainments; his first prospectus laid stress on "writing in both plain and ornamental style, Arithmetic logically, and History with special reference to Ancient Egypt." Ancient Egypt and indeed most of the History except lists of dates, pedigrees and enactments, had dropped from the school outlook long before I joined it, for even Bromley Academy moved a little with the times, but there was still great stress on copperplate flourishes, long addition sums and book-keeping. Morley was a bald portly spectacled man with a strawberry nose and ginger-grey whiskers, who considered it due to himself and us to wear a top hat, an ample frock-coat, and a white tie, and to carry himself with invariable dignity and make a frequent use of "Sir." Except for a certain assistance with the little ones from Mrs. Morley, a stout ringleted lady in black silk and a gold chain, he ran the school alone. It was a single room built out over a scullery; there were desks round the walls and two, of six places each, in the centre, with a stove between which warmed the place in winter. His bedroom window opened upon the schoolroom, and beneath it, in the corner of the room, was his desk, the great ink bottle from which the ink-wells were replenished, the pile of slates and the incessant cane, with which he administered justice, either in spasmodic descents upon our backs and hindquarters, or after formal accusations, by smacks across the palm of the hand. He also hit us with his hands anywhere, and with books, rulers and anything else that came handy, and his invective and derision were terrific. Also we were made to stand on the rickety forms and hold out books and slates until our arms ached. And in this way he urged us—I suppose our numbers varied from twenty-five to thirty-five—along the path of learning that led in the more successful instances to the examinations, conducted by an association of private schoolmasters, for their mutual reassurance, known as the College of Preceptors, (with special certificates for book-keeping) and then to jobs as clerks.

About half the boys were boarders drawn from London public houses or other homes unsuitable for growing youth. There were a few day-boarders from outlying farms, who took their dinner in the house. The rest were sons of poorish middle-class people in the town. We assembled at nine and went on to twelve and again from two to five, and between these hours, except when the windows were open in warm weather, the atmosphere grew steadily more foetid and our mental operations more sluggish and confused.

It is very difficult to give any facts about this dominie and his Academy which do not carry with them a quality of Dickens-like caricature. He ranted at us from his desk in the quaintest fashion; he took violent dislikes and betrayed irrational preferences; the educational tradition from which he arose and which is so manifest in that first prospectus already quoted, was in the same world with Miss Riley's school at Chichester which did so much to shape my mother; it was antiquated, pretentious, superficial and meagre; and yet there was something good about old Morley and something good for me. I have an impression that with a certain honesty he was struggling out of that tradition and trying to make something of us. That "College of Preceptors" was not only a confederation of private schools to keep up appearances; it was a mutual improvement society, it was a voluntary modernizing movement. It ran lectures on educational method and devised examinations for teaching diplomas. Morley had learnt a lot between his start in 1849 and the days when I was his pupil. He had become an Associate, and then a Licentiate of this self-constituted college, by examination, and each examination had involved a paper or so on teaching method. I believe his teaching, such as it was, was better than that of the crudely trained mechanical grant earners of the contemporary National School which was the only local alternative, and that my mother's instinct was a sound one in sending us all to this antiquated middle-class establishment.

Yet if I describe a day's work in that dusty, dingy, ill-ventilated schoolroom, there will not be a qualified teacher in the world beneath the age of fifty who will not consider it frightful. A lifetime ago it would have seemed perfectly normal schooling.

Few people realize the immense changes that the organization and mechanism of popular teaching have undergone in the past century. They have changed more than housing or transport. Before that dawn of a new way of life, began that slow reluctant dawn in which we are still living, the vast majority of people throughout the world had no schooling at all, and of the educated minority, literate rather than educated, by far the larger proportion—in India and China and Arabia quite as much as in Europe—did their learning in some such makeshift place as this outbuilding of Morley's, in the purlieus of a mosque, for example, under a tree in India or beneath an Irish hedge, as members of a bunch of twenty or so ill-assorted pupils of all ages and sizes and often of both sexes, between six and sixteen. Schools large enough to classify were the exception, and there were rarely more than one or two teachers. Specially built school houses were almost unknown. A room designed and equipped for teaching and containing a manageable class of youngsters in the same phase of development, is comparatively a new thing in human experience, even for the young of the privileged orders.

And necessarily under these old conditions teaching had to be intermittent because the teacher's mind could not confront all that diversity of reaction between childishness and adolescence at the same time; necessarily he had to contrive exercises and activities to keep this group and that quiet while he expounded to another. He was like some very ordinary chess player who had undertaken to play thirty games of chess simultaneously. He was an unqualified mental obstetrician doing his work wholesale. Necessarily the phases and quality of his teaching depended on his moods. At times Morley was really trying to get something over to us; at others he was digesting, or failing to digest, his midday meal; he was in a phase of accidie; he was suffering from worry or grievance; he was amazed at life and revolted by his dependence upon us; he felt the world was rushing past him; he had got up late and omitted to shave and was struggling with an overwhelming desire to leave us all and repair the omission.

So the primary impressions left upon my brain by that Academy are not impressions of competent elucidation and guidance, of a universe being made plain to me or of skills being acquired and elaborated, but of the moods of Mr. Thomas Morley and their consequences. At times his attention was altogether distracted; he was remote upon his throne in the corner, as aloof almost as my mother's God, and then we would relax from the tasks or exercises he had set us and indulge in furtive but strenuous activities of our own. We would talk and tell each other stories—I had a mind suitably equipped by my reading for boyish saga telling and would go on interminably—draw on our slates, play marbles, noughts and crosses and suchlike games, turn out our pockets, swap things, indulge in pinching and punching matches, eat sweets, read penny dreadfuls, do anything, indeed, but the work in hand. Sometimes it would be whispered in the drowsy digestive first hour of the afternoon, "Old Tommy's asleep," and we would watch him sink slowly and beautifully down and down into slumber, terminated by a snore and a start. If at last he got off completely, spectacles askew over his folded arms, a kind of silent wildness would come upon us. We would stand up to make fantastic, insulting and obscene gestures, leave our places to creep noiselessly as far as we dared. He would awaken abruptly, conscience awake also, inflict sudden punishment on some belated adventurer; and then would come a strenuous hour of driving work.

Sometimes he would leave us altogether upon his private occasions. Then it was our bounden duty to kick up all the row we could, to get out of our places and wrestle, to "go for" enemies, to produce the secreted catapult or pea-shooter, to pelt with chewed paper and books. I can taste the dust and recall the din as I write of it. In the midst of the uproar the blind of the bedroom window would be raised, silently, swiftly. Morley, razor in hand and his face covered with soapsuds, would be discovered glaring at us through the glass, marking down sinners for punishment, a terrifying visage. Up would go the window. "You HOUNDS! You Miserable Hounds!" Judgments followed.

The spells of intensive teaching came irregularly, except for Friday afternoon, which was consecrated invariably to the breathless pursuit of arithmetic. There were also whole afternoons of "book-keeping by double entry" upon sheets of paper, when we pursued imaginary goods and cash payments with pen and ruler and even red ink, to a final Profit and Loss Account and a Balance Sheet. We wrote in copybooks and he came, peering and directing, over our shoulders. There was only one way in which a pen might be held; it was a matter of supreme importance; there was only one angle at which writing might slope. I was disposed to be unorthodox in this respect, and my knuckles suffered.

The production of good clerks (with special certificates for book-keeping) was certainly one of the objectives of Mr. Thomas Morley's life. The safety, comfort and dignity of Mr. and Mrs. Thomas Morley and Miss Morley were no doubt a constant preoccupation. But also there was interest in wider and more fundamental things. There was a sense in him that some things were righter than others, a disposition to assert as much, and a real desire for things to be done well. His studies for the diplomas of A.C.P. and L.C.P. (Associate and Licentiate of the College of Preceptors), low though the requirements were, absurdly low by our present standards, had awakened him to the pleasures of certain mental exercises; a mathematical problem, a logical demonstration. When he found that I could be interested by the grammatical analysis of a complicated sentence or the solution of some elementary mathematical problem, he took a liking to me and showed me much more attention than he gave to the more obdurate material he had to deal with, minds stirred to a high level of evasion and resistance by his clumsy, medieval, impatient and aggressive methods of approach. He never gave me a nickname and never singled me out for an abusive tirade.

When I left his school at the age of thirteen (bracketed with a fellow pupil first in all England for book-keeping, so far, that is to say, as England was covered by the College of Preceptors), whatever else I had missed, I had certainly acquired the ability to use English with some precision and delicacy, even if the accent was a Cockney one, and I had quite as good a mathematical apparatus as most boys of the same age get at a public school nowadays. I had read about as much of Euclid as it was customary to read, made a fair start with trigonometry and was on the verge of the calculus. But most of the other stuff I got was bad. Old Tommy taught French out of a crammer's textbook, and, in spite of the fact that he had on several occasions visited Boulogne, he was quite unable to talk in that elusive tongue; so I learnt hardly anything about it except its conjugations and long lists of "exceptions," so useful in written examinations and so unimportant in ordinary life. He crippled my French for life. He made me vowel-shy in every language.

I do not think he read much. He was not generally curious. My reading habit I developed at home and do not recall that

Morley ever directed my attention to any book, unless it was some cheap school textbook used in my work. But at times he would get excited by his morning paper and then we would have a discourse on the geography of the North West Frontier with an appeal to a decaying yellow map of Asia that hung on the wall, or we would follow the search for Livingstone by Stanley in Darkest Africa. He had traces of early Radicalism and a Republican turn of mind; he would discourse upon the extravagant Parliamentary grants made in those days to the various members of the Royal Family when they married, and about the unnecessary costliness of the army and navy. He believed that Mr. Gladstone really stood for "Peace, Retrenchment and Reform." All sorts of Radical principles may have filtered into my receptive mind from these *obiter dicta*.

Geoffrey West, in the exact and careful biography he wrote of me some years ago, is unjust to this old-world pedagogue because he measures him by his own twentieth-century standards with only the later nineteenth century as a background. Against the eighteenth-century background from which he derived, Thomas Morley was by no means so contemptible. West says he favoured a few willing boys with his instructions and let the rest drift. But that happened in all the schools; it was an inevitable aspect of those small miscellaneous schools with single untrained teachers. To-day every teacher still "favours" the willing boy. That sort of favouritism will go on to the end of time. That old gentleman (A.C.P., L.C.P.) walking with a portly gravity that was all his own, hands clasped behind his back, at the tail of the crocodile of ill-assorted undrilled boys, steering them to the best of his ability into the future, taking them to church or for a walk or to the cricket field, is by no means such a dismal memory of inefficiency as West suggests. Bromley Academy had very little of the baseness which pervaded Dotheboys Hall.

But Geoffrey West, in that same book, called my attention to an interesting resemblance between Morley's school and the school of Charles Dickens, a third of a century earlier, of which I should otherwise be ignorant. There was a continual bickering between us and the boys of the National School, bickering which rose occasionally to the level of a pitched battle with staves and sticks upon Martin's Hill, at that time a waste and now a trim recreation ground. For some unknown reason we were called "Morley's Bull Dogs" and the elementary school boys were called, by us at any rate, "Bromley Water Rats" and "Cads." Now the Dickens parallel was "Baker's Bull Dogs" and "Troy Town Rats." Evidently this hostility between the boys of the old type of private schools and those of the new denominational schools, was of long standing, and widespread and almost stereotyped in its expression.

Geoffrey West thinks the antagonism was "snobbish," but that is a loose word to use for a very interesting conflict of divergent ideas and social tendencies. He probably considers the National Schools were "democratic" schools, like the common schools of the United States, "all class" schools, but that is a mistaken view. In spirit, form and intention they were inferior schools, and to send one's children to them in those days, as my mother understood perfectly well, was a definite and final acceptance of social inferiority. The Education Act of 1871 was not an Act for a common universal education, it was an Act to educate the lower classes for employment on lower-class lines, and with specially trained, inferior teachers who had no university quality. If Tommy Morley could not sport a university gown and hood, he could at least claim to wear a gown and hood as an L.C.P. (by royal charter), that was indistinguishable to the common eye from the real thing. He had all the dignity, if little of the substance, of scholarship. The more ancient middle-class schools, whatever their faults, were saturated with the spirit of individual self-reliance and individual dignity, with an idea, however pretentious, of standards "a little above the common," with a feeling (however vulgarized, debased and under-nourished) of *Noblesse oblige*. Certain things we could not do and certain things were expected of us because of our class. Most of the bickering of Morley's Bull Dogs was done against odds, and on the whole we held our own. I think it was a very lucky thing for me personally that I acquired this much class feeling.

I have never believed in the superiority of the inferior. My want of enthusiasm for the Proletarian ideal goes back to the Battle of Martin's Hill. If I was in almost unconcealed revolt against my mother's deferential attitude to royalty and our social superiors, it was because my resentful heart claimed at least an initial equality with every human being; but it was equality of position and opportunity I was after, and not equality of respect or reward; I certainly had no disposition to sacrifice my conceit of being made of better stuff, intrinsically and inherently, than most other human beings, by any self-identification with people who frankly took the defeated attitude. I thought the top of the form better than the bottom of the form, and the boy who qualified better than the boy who failed to qualify. I am not going to argue at this point whether such a state of mind is desirable or creditable to anyone; my biographical duty is to record that so it was with me. So far as the masses went I was entirely of my mother's way of thinking; I was middle-class,—"petty bourgeois" as the Marxists have it.

Just as my mother was obliged to believe in Hell, but hoped that no one would go there, so did I believe there was and had to be a lower stratum, though I was disgusted to find that anyone belonged to it. I did not think this lower stratum merited any respect. It might arouse sympathy for its bad luck or indignation for an unfair handicap. That was a different matter. My thought, as I shall trace its development in this history, has run very close to communist lines, but my conception of a scientifically organized class-less society is essentially of an expanded middle-class which has incorporated both the aristocrat and plutocrat above and the peasant, proletarian and pauper below.

Trotsky has recorded that Lenin, after his one conversation with me, said that I was incurably middle-class. So far Lenin was a sound observer. He, and Trotsky also, were of the same vital social stratum; they had indeed both started life from a far more advantageous level than I had; but the discolouration of their stream of thought by Marxist pretences and sentimentalities, had blinded them to their own essential quality. My conversation with Lenin turned entirely on the "liquidation" of the peasant and the urban toiler—by large-scale agriculture and power machinery. Lenin was just as much for that as I was, we were talking about the same thing in the same spirit; but we said the same thing as though it was a different thing because our minds were tuned in different keys.

§ 2. PUERILE VIEW OF THE WORLD (1878-79)

(August 4th, 1933). I have been trying, for a day or so, to reconstruct my vision of the world as I had it in those days, to restore the state of my brain as it was about 1878 or 9 when I was in mid schoolboy stage. I find it an almost impossible task. I find it impossible to disentangle the things I saw and read before I was thirteen, from the things that came afterwards. The old ideas and impressions were made over in accordance with new material, they were used up to make the new equipment. This reconstruction went on from day to day, and so, in order and detail, they are lost beyond recovery. Yet impossible as it is to get any focussed clearness and exactitude here, it is equally impossible to ignore this phase of completed puerility. My formal education came to a break at that date, was held up for two years and more before it resumed, at a stage at which the brains of great multitudes of English people halted for good, and at which (or at parallel levels) I believe multitudes still halt all over the world. This mass of human beings halting in puerility, is the determining factor in most of the alarming political and social processes of to-day.

In the universe in which my brain was living in 1879 there was no nonsense about time being space or anything of that sort. There were three dimensions, up and down, fore and aft and right and left, and I never heard of a fourth dimension until 1884 or there-about. Then I thought it was a witticism. Space went on for ever in every direction, good Newtonian space. I felt it must be rather empty and cheerless beyond the stars, but I did not let my mind dwell on that. My God, who by this time had become entirely disembodied, had been diffused through this space since the beginning of things. He was already quite abstracted from the furious old hell-and-heaven Thunder God of my childish years. His personality had faded. My mind had been unobtrusively taking the sense of reality out of the Trinity and the Atonement and the other dogmas of official christianity. I felt there must be some mistake about all that, but I had not yet sat down to make any philosophy of my own by which these strange beliefs could be arraigned. I had simply withdrawn my attention. If I had had a catholic upbringing with intercessory individualized saints and local and special Virgins, that tacit withdrawal might have been less easy. Yes or no might have been forced upon me. I might have come earlier to positive disbelief.

Occasionally I would find myself praying—always to God simply. He remained a God spread all over space and time, yet nevertheless he was capable of special response and magic changes in the order of events. I would pray when I was losing a race, or in trouble in an examination room, or frightened. I expected prompt attention. In my first book-keeping examination by the College of Preceptors I could not get my accounts to balance. I prayed furiously. The bell rang, the invigilator hovered over my last frantic efforts. I desisted reluctantly, "All right, God," I said, "catch me praying again." I was then about twelve.

Through this universe with its diffused Space-God spun the

earth, moving amidst the stars along paths that were difficult to understand and still more difficult to remember. I was constantly reading that the earth was a mere pin point in space; that if the sun was as big as St. Paul's dome, the earth would be a strawberry pip somewhere in the suburbs, and many similar illustrative facts, but directly I took my mind off these explicit statements, the pip grew bigger and bigger and I grew even faster. St. Paul's dome stuck where it was and the very Nebulæ came within range again. My mind insisted on that. Just as it insisted that God was always within range. Otherwise it had no use for them.

The earth, directly one let go of one's cosmic facts, expanded again like a vehemently inflated soap bubble, until it filled the entire picture. One did not see all round it in those days. It had mystery at its North and South Poles and Darkest Africa on its equator. Poe's *Narrative of A. Gordon Pym* tells what a very intelligent mind could imagine about the south polar regions a century ago. The poor old earth in those days had a hard crust and a molten interior and naturally suffered from chronic indigestion, earthquakes, rumblings, and eruptions. It has since solidified considerably.

Moreover it already had a past which was rapidly opening out to men's minds in those days. I first became aware of that past in the gardens of the Crystal Palace at Sydenham; it came upon me as a complete surprise, embodied in vast plaster reconstructions of the megatherium and various dinosaurs and a toadlike labyrinthodon (for at first labyrinthodons were supposed to have had toadlike bodies). I was having one of those acute bilious attacks that always happened in the afternoons when I was taken to the Crystal Palace, and that made the impression none the less formidable. My mother explained that these were Antediluvian Animals. They had been left out of the ark, I guessed, on account of their size, but even then there seemed something a little wrong in the suggestion that the ichthyosaurus had been drowned in a flood.

Somewhen later I pored over Humboldt's *Cosmos* and began to learn something of geological time. But by means of accepting the gloss that the Days of Creation meant geological ages, nothing really essential was changed in the past of my universe. There was merely an extension. The Creation, though further off, remained still as the hard and fast beginning of time, before which there was nothing, just as a very pyrotechnic Day of Judgment "when time shall be no more" closed the vista at the other end. Ultimate emptiness bounded my universe in space and time alike. "Someday we shall know all," said my mother in response to my questions about what lay beyond, and with that for a time I had to be content.

Whatever else I doubted, I was incapable at that age of doubting my immortality. I had never known the universe without my consciousness and I could not imagine the universe without my consciousness. I doubt if any young things can really do so. The belief in immortality is tacit and formless in young animals, but it is there. The fear of death is not fear of extinction but a fear of something unknown and utterly disagreeable. I thought I was going on and on—when I thought of continuance at all. I had passed the College of Preceptors' examination very well, so why shouldn't I get through the Day of Judgment? But the world was just then so immediately full of interesting things, that I did not put in much time at the fundamental and eternal questions beyond.

It was made a matter of general congratulation about me that I was English. The flavour of J. R. Green's recently published (1874) History of the English People had drifted to me either directly or at second-hand, and my mind had leapt all too readily to the idea that I was a blond and blue-eyed Nordic, quite the best make of human being known. England was consciously Teutonic in those days, the monarchy and Thomas Carlyle were strong influences in that direction; we talked of our "Keltic fringe" and ignored our Keltic infiltration; and the defeat of France in 1870-71 seemed to be the final defeat of the decadent Latin peoples. This blended very well with the anti-Roman Catholic influence of the eighteenth-century Protestant training, a distrust and hostility that remained quite vivid when much else of that teaching had faded. We English, by sheer native superiority, practically without trying, had possessed ourselves of an Empire on which the sun never set, and through the errors and infirmities of other races were being forced slowly but steadily—and quite modestly—towards world dominion.

All that was quite settled in my head, as I carried my green-baize satchel to and fro between Morley's school and my dismal bankrupt home, and if you had suddenly confronted me with a Russian prince or a rajah in all his glory and suggested he was my equal, I should either have laughed you to scorn or been very exasperated with you about it.

I was taught no history but English History, which after some centuries of royal criminality, civil wars and wars in France, achieved the Reformation and blossomed out into the Empire; and I learnt hardly any geography but British geography. It was only from casual reading that I gathered that quite a number of things had happened and quite a number of interesting things existed outside the world of English affairs. But I looked at pictures of the Taj Mahal, the Colosseum and the Pyramids in very much the same spirit as I listened to stories about the Wonders of Animal Intelligence (beavers, bees, birds' nests, breeding habits of the salmon, *etc.*). They did not shake my profound satisfaction with the self, the township, the county, the nation, the Empire and the outlook that was mine.

In those days I had ideas about Aryans extraordinarily like Mr. Hitler's. The more I hear of him the more I am convinced that his mind is almost the twin of my thirteen year old mind in 1879; but heard through a megaphone and—implemented. I do not know from what books I caught my first glimpse of the Great Aryan People going to and fro in the middle plains of Europe, spreading east, west, north and south, varying their consonants according to Grimm's Law as they did so, and driving the inferior breeds into the mountains. But they formed a picturesque background to the duller facts of ancient history. Their ultimate triumphs everywhere squared accounts with the Jews, against which people I had a subconscious dissatisfaction because of their disproportionate share of Holy Writ. I thought Abraham, Isaac, Moses and David loathsome creatures and fit associates for Our Father, but unlike Hitler I had no feelings about the contemporary Jew. Quite a number of the boarders in the Bromley Academy were Jewish and I was not aware of it. My particular pal, Sidney Bowkett, was I think unconsciously Jewish; the point never arose.

I had reveries—I indulged a great deal in reverie until I was fifteen or sixteen, because my active imagination was not sufficiently employed—and I liked especially to dream that I was a great military dictator like Cromwell, a great republican like George Washington or like Napoleon in his earlier phases. I used to fight battles whenever I went for a walk alone. I used to walk about Bromley, a small rather undernourished boy, meanly clad and whistling detestably between his teeth, and no one suspected that a phantom staff pranced about me and phantom orderlies galloped at my commands, to shift the guns and concentrate fire on those houses below, to launch the final attack upon yonder distant ridge. The citizens of Bromley town go out to take the air on Martin's Hill and look towards Shortland across the fields where once meandered the now dried-up and vanished Ravensbourne, with never a suspicion of the orgies of bloodshed I once conducted there. Martin's Hill indeed is one of the great battlegrounds of history. Scores of times the enemy skirmishers have come across those levels, followed by the successive waves of the infantry attack, while I, outnumbered five to one, manoeuvred my guns round, the guns I had refrained so grimly from using too soon in spite of the threat to my centre, to enfilade them suddenly from the curving slopes towards Beckenham. "Crash," came the first shell, and then crash and crash. They were mown down by the thousand. They straggled up the steep slopes wavering. And then came the shattering counter attack, and I and my cavalry swept the broken masses away towards Croydon, pressed them ruthlessly through a night of slaughter on to the pitiful surrender of the remnant at dawn by Keston Fish Ponds.

And I entered conquered, or rescued, towns riding at the head of my troops, with my cousins and my schoolfellows recognizing me with surprise from the windows. And kings and presidents, and the great of the earth, came to salute my saving wisdom. I was simple even in victory. I made wise and firm decisions, about morals and customs and particularly about those Civil Service Stores which had done so much to bankrupt my father. With inveterate enemies, monarchists, Roman Catholics, non-Aryans and the like I was grimly just. Stern work—but my duty....

In fact Adolf Hitler is nothing more than one of my thirteen year old reveries come real. A whole generation of Germans has failed to grow up.

My head teemed with such stuff in those days. But it is interesting to remark that while my mind was full of international conflicts, alliances, battleships and guns, I was blankly ignorant about money or any of the machinery of economic life. I never dreamed of making dams, opening ship canals, irrigating deserts or flying. I had no inkling of the problem of ways and means; I knew nothing and, therefore, I cared nothing of how houses were built, commodities got and the like. I think that was because nothing existed to catch and turn my imagination in that direction. There was no literature to enhance all that. I think there is no natural bias towards bloodshed in imaginative youngsters, but the only vivid and inspiring things that history fed me with were campaigns and conquests. In Soviet Russia they tell me they have altered all that.

For many years my adult life was haunted by the fading memories of those early war fantasies. Up to 1914, I found a lively interest in playing a war game, with toy soldiers and guns, that recalled the peculiar quality and pleasure of those early reveries. It was quite an amusing model warfare and I have given its primary rules in a small book "for boys and girls of all ages" *Little Wars*. I have met men in responsible positions, L. S. Amery for example, Winston Churchill, George Trevelyan, C. F. G. Masterman, whose imaginations were manifestly built upon a similar framework and who remained puerile in their political outlook because of its persistence. I like to think I grew up out of that stage somewhen between 1916 and 1920 and began to think about war as a responsible adult should.

I recall no marked sexual or personal elements in my early reveries. Until my adolescence, sex fancies came to me only in that dim phase between waking and sleeping. I gave myself gladly and willingly to my warfare, but I was shy of sex; I resisted any urge I may have had towards personal romancing and sensuous fantasies.

My sexual trend was, I think, less marked or more under control when I was twelve and thirteen, than it was when I was nine or ten. My primary curiosities had been satisfied and strong physical urgencies were still unawakened.

My two brothers played only a very small part in this early mental development, my Hitler phase. One was nine years older than I and already bound apprentice to a draper; the other was four years my senior and presently suffered the same fate. They were too far away from me. My elder brother Frank was one of those mischievous boys who mix much natural ingenuity with an aggressive sense of humour. He was, said my mother, a "dreadful tease." He took a lively interest in machinery and fireworks and making people sit up. He fiddled with clocks and steam engines until some accident ensued and with gunpowder until it exploded. He connected all the bell wires in my Uncle

91

Tom's hotel so that with no great extra expenditure of labour, a visitor rang not only his own bell, but every bell in the place. But Frank gained nothing but unpopularity by this device. He haunted the railway station, worshipping the engines and hoping for something to happen. One day at Windsor he got on to a shunting engine standing in a siding and pulled at a lever and found great difficulty in pulling it back. By that time he was half a mile down the line—and no longer a *persona grata* upon the South Western Railway Company's premises. The pursuing driver had to think first of his engine and so my brother got clean away and survived the adventure. This disposition to fiddle with levers made Frank a leader in his generation. A gang followed him to see what would happen next. He was always in trouble. But he found trouble was less complicated if he kept me out of it. I did not share these escapades. Freddy was a more orderly youngster, but he was sent to a different private school for most of my time at Morley's.

Later on I grew up to my brothers, so to speak, and had great talks with them. With Frank, the eldest, indeed, I developed a considerable companionship in my teens and we had some great holiday walks together. But at the time of which I am writing all that had still to come.

Our home was not one of those where general ideas are discussed at table. My mother's ready orthodox formulæ were very effective in suppressing any such talk. So my mind developed almost as if I were an only child.

My childish relations with my brothers varied between vindictive resentment and clamorous aggression. I made a terrific fuss if my toys or games were touched and I displayed great vigour in acquiring their more attractive possessions. I bit and scratched my brothers and I kicked their shins, because I was a sturdy little boy who had to defend himself; but they had to go very easily with me because I was a delicate little fellow who might easily be injured and was certain to yell. On one occasion,

I quite forget now what the occasion was, I threw a fork across the dinner table at Frank, and I can still remember very vividly the missile sticking in his forehead where it left three little scars for a year or so and did no other harm; and I have an equally clear memory of a smashed window behind the head of my brother Freddy, the inrush of cold air and dismay, after I had flung a wooden horse at him. Finally they hit upon an effectual method of at once silencing me and punishing me. They would capture me in our attic and suffocate me with pillows. I couldn't cry out and I had to give in. I can still feel the stress of that suffocation. Why they did not suffocate me for good and all, I do not know. They had no way of checking what was going on under the pillow until they took it off and looked.

I got more mental stimulus from some of my schoolfellows who were of an age with me. I felt the need of some companionship, some relief from reading and lonely reverie. I used to stay on at school after lesson time and go for walks or into the cricket field with the boarders, on holiday afternoons. My cricket was always poor because of my unsuspected astigmatism, but my participation was valued on account of my ready access to stumps and bats and used balls. I had a curious sort of alliance with the son of a London publican, Sidney Bowkett. We started with a great fight at the age of eight, in which we whacked at each other for the better part of an hour, and after that we conceived such a respect for each other that we decided not to fall out again. We became chums. We developed the tactics of combined attack upon bigger boys and so established a sort of joint dominance long before we were the legitimate seniors of the school.

We two talked a lot in and out of school, but what we talked about is not very clear in my mind now. There was probably a lot of bragging about what we meant to do with life. We were both very confident, because we both outclassed all the other boys we knew of our age, and that gave us an unjustified sense of distinctive ability. He was much better looking, more attractive, quicker witted and more aggressive and adventurous than I; his verbal memory was better and his arithmetic quicker and more accurate, but he was quite out of the running with me when it came to drawing, elementary mathematics or that mass of partially digested reading which one may call general knowledge. Sometimes we acted being explorers or great leaders in a sort of dramatized reverie, wherein I supplied most of the facts. Sometimes we helped each other out with long sagas about Puss the Cat, a sort of puss-in-boots, invented by my brother Fred and me, or Ally Sloper, the great comic character of cockneydom at that time, or the adventures of Bert Wells and the Boker Boy. They went to Central Africa, to the Polar regions, down the Maelstrom and up the Himalayas; they made much use of balloons and diving suits, though aeroplanes were outside their imaginations. A great deal of that romancing embodied our bright receptiveness to things about us.

Bowkett's interest was more quickly aroused and livelier than mine, but he had very little invention. He was one of those who see quickly and vividly and say "Look," a sort of people to whom I owe much. Later on I was to have a great friendship with Rebecca West who had that quality of saying "Look" for me, in an even greater degree. I never knew anyone else who could so light up and colour and intensify an impression. Without such stimulus I note things, they register themselves in my mind, but I do not actively notice them of my own accord. Together Bowkett and I could get no end of fun out of a casually encountered rat or an odd butterfly, a stray beetle or an easily climbed tree, which I alone would have ticked off at a glance and passed. We would go through private gardens and trespass together "for to see and to know."

I do not remember talking very much about sexual matters with Bowkett and what we said was highly romanticized and unimportant. We were decent and shy about all that. Yet we knew all the indecent words in the language, we could be astonishingly foul-mouthed in moments of exaltation and showing off; and we were in no way ignorant. But we were not at that time acutely interested. It is only, I think, where small boys in the early teens are in close contact with older youths, youths of sixteen or seventeen whose minds are festering with desire, as they are in English Public Schools, that they can be obsessed by gross sexuality. And then they are not pleasantly obsessed. Naturally boys in the earlier phase are instinctively afraid of intimate detail and avoid it. At any rate, whether we were typical or exceptional, we two avoided it. I have no doubt that Bowkett had his own secret incidental twilight Venus- berg—I will not speculate about that—but sex did not loom large in our ordinary conversation.

At one time we organized a secret society. Unhappily we could never find a secret to put in it. But we had a tremendous initiation ceremony. Among other things the candidate had to hold his fore-finger in a gas jet for thirty seconds. Only two members ever qualified, Bert Wells and the Boker Boy. I still remember the smell of singed flesh and the hard painfulness of the scorched finger. We had a secret language of the "Iway aysay olday anmay owhay areway ouyay" type. We warned a persistent sniffer in the school, by a cabalistic communication, to sniff no more or "incur the Vengeance of the Order" and we chalked up "beware" in the lavatory, in the interests of public morality. How gladly we would have adopted the swastika if we had known of it.

So much for the Hitlerite stage of my development, when I was a sentimentalist, a moralist, a patriot, a racist, a great general in dreamland, a member of a secret society, an immortal figure in history, an impulsive fork thrower and a bawling self-righteous kicker of domestic shins. I will now go on to tell as well as I can how this pasty-faced little English Nazi escaped his manifest destiny of mean and hopeless employment, and got to that broader view of life and those opportunities that have at last made this autobiography possible.

§ 3. MRS. WELLS, HOUSEKEEPER AT UP PARK
(1880-1893)

I have said that a cardinal stroke of good fortune was the breaking of my leg when I was seven years old. Another almost as important was the breaking of my father's leg in 1877, which made the dissolution of our home inevitable. He set himself to prune the grape-vine one Sunday morning in October, and, resolved to make a job of it and get at the highest shoots, he poised a ladder on a bench and came a cropper. We returned from church to find him lying in the yard groaning, and our neighbours, Mr. Cooper and Mr. Munday helped to carry him upstairs. He had a compound fracture of the thigh bone.

Before the year was out it was plain that my father was going to be heavily lame for the rest of his life. This was the end of any serious cricket, any bowling to gentlemen, any school jobs as "pro," or the like for him. All the supplementary income was cut off by this accident which also involved much expense in doctoring. The chronic insolvency of Atlas House became acute.

Things were more tight and distressful than ever, for two years. An increasing skimpiness distinguished our catering. Bread and cheese for supper and half a herring each with our bread and butter at breakfast and a growing tendency for potatoes to dominate the hash or stew at midday in place of meat, intimated retrenchment. Mr. Morley's bill had gone unpaid for a year. Frank who was earning £26 a year (and live in) came home for a holiday and gave my mother half a sovereign to buy me a pair of boots (at which she wept). I was growing fast and growing very thin.

And then suddenly the heavens opened and a great light shone on Mrs. Sarah Wells. Lady Fetherstonhaugh had been dead some years and Miss Bullock, to whom my mother had been maid, either inherited or was given a life tenure of Up Park, with not very plentiful means to maintain it. She took the name of Fetherstonhaugh. Presently arose trouble with the servants and about the household expenses, and Miss Fetherstonhaugh's thoughts turned affectionately towards her faithful maid, between whom and herself there had always been a correspondence of good wishes and little gifts. My mother went to Up Park on a visit. There were earnest conversations. It was still possible for her to find employment. But was it right to leave Joe alone in Atlas House? What would become of the boys? Frank's apprenticeship as a draper was already over and he was in a situation. Freddy's time as a draper's apprentice was up also. He could go out too. My five years of schooling were culminating in special certificates in bookkeeping and hope. The young birds were leaving the nest. Father could rub along by himself for a bit. My mother became housekeeper at Up Park in 1880.

Now if this had not happened, I have no doubt I should have followed in the footsteps of Frank and Freddy and gone on living at home under my mother's care, while I went daily to some shop, some draper's shop, to which I was bound apprentice. This would have seemed so natural and necessary that I should not have resisted. I should have served my time and never had an idea of getting away from the shop until it was too late. But the dislocation that now occurred closed this easy path to frustration. I was awakened to the significance of a start in life from the outset, as my brothers had never been.

But before I tell of the series of starts in life that now began, I must say a little about my mother's achievements in housekeeping. Except that she was thoroughly honest, my mother was perhaps the worst housekeeper that was ever thought of. She had never had the slightest experience in housekeeping. She did not know how to plan work, control servants, buy stores or economize in any way. She did not know clearly what was wanted upstairs. She could not even add up her accounts with assurance and kept them for me to do for her. All this came to light. It dawned slowly upon Miss Fetherstonhaugh; it became clearly apparent to her agent, who came up periodically from Portsmouth, Sir William King; it was manifest from the first to the very competent, if totally illiterate, head housemaid Old Ann, who gave herself her own orders more and more. The kitchen, the laundry, the pantry, with varying kindliness, apprehended this inefficiency in the housekeeper's room. At length I think it dawned even upon my mother.

Not at first. She was frightened, perhaps, but resolute and she believed that with prayer and effort anything can be achieved. She knew at least how a housekeeper should look, and assumed a lace cap, lace apron, black silk dress and all the rest of it, and she knew how a housekeeper should drive down to the tradespeople in Petersfield and take a glass of sherry when the account was settled. She marched down to church every Sunday morning; the whole downstairs household streamed down the Warren and Harting Hill to church; and once a month she took the sacrament. The distressful Atlas House look vanished from her face; she became rounder and pinker, she assumed a tranquil dignity. She contrived that we should have situations round about Up Park, and in our holidays and during phases of being out of a situation, we infested the house. My father came on a visit once or twice and at last in 1887 abandoned Atlas House altogether and settled down on an allowance she paid him, in a cottage at Nyewoods near Rogate Station about four miles away. So the servitude of Atlas House was avenged and J. W. found his level.

She held on to her position until 1893 and I think Miss Fetherstonhaugh was very forbearing that my mother held on so long. Because among other things she grew deaf. She grew deafer and deafer and she would not admit her deafness, but guessed at what was said to her and made wild shots in reply. She was deteriorating mentally. Her religious consolations were becoming more and more trite and mechanical. Miss Fetherstonhaugh was a still older woman and evidently found dealing with her more and more tiresome. They were two deaf old women at cross purposes. The rather sentimental affection between them evaporated in mutual irritation and left not a rack behind.

On several occasions Sir William was "very unpleasant" to my mother. Economy and still more economy was urged upon her and she felt that saving and pinching was beneath the dignity of a country house. The original elation of being housekeeper at Up Park had long since passed away. She began to gossip rather unwisely about some imaginary incidents in the early life of Miss Fetherstonhaugh and her sister, and it came to Miss Fetherstonhaugh's ears. I think that sealed her fate. My mother's downfall came, a month's notice and "much unkindness," in January 1893. The fallen housekeeper, with all her boxes and possessions, was driven to Petersfield station on February 16th, 1893, and the hospitable refuge of Up Park was closed to her and her needy family for ever.

A poor little stunned woman she must have been then, on Petersfield platform, a little black figure in a large black bonnet curiously suggestive now of Her Majesty Queen Victoria. I can imagine her as she wound mournfully down the Petersfield road looking back towards Harting Hill with tears in her blue eyes, not quite clear about why it had all occurred in this fashion, though no doubt God had arranged it "for some good purpose."

Why had Miss Fetherstonhaugh been so unkind?

But luckily, during my mother's thirteen years' sway at Up Park and thanks largely to the reliefs and opportunity that came to me through that brief interval of good fortune in her life, I had been able to do all sorts of things. I was now twenty-six and a married man with a household and I was in a position to arrange a home for her and prevent the family bark from foundering altogether. I had become a Bachelor of Science in the University of London and a successful university crammer and I had published a textbook—a cram book to be exact—on biology as it was understood by the University examiners. I had begun to write for the papers. I had acquired a certain gravity of bearing, a considerable cascade of fair moustache and incipient side whiskers. How these changes had come about and what had happened to my brain and outlook in the process, I will now go on to tell.

§ 4. FIRST START IN LIFE—WINDSOR (SUMMER 1880)

My first start in life was rather hastily improvised. My mother had a second cousin, Thomas Pennicott, "Uncle Tom" we called him, who had always been very much in the margin of her world. I think he had admired her and been perhaps helped by her when they were young folk at Midhurst. He was one of the witnesses to her marriage. He was a fat, round-faced, clean-shaven, black-haired man, illiterate, good humoured and shrewd. He had followed the ruling tendency in my mother's family to keep inns, and he had kept the Royal Oak opposite the South Western Railway Station at Windsor to such good effect, that he was able to buy and rebuild a riverside inn, called Surly Hall, much affected by the Eton wet-bobs, during the summer term. He built it as a gabled house and the gables were decorated with blue designs and mottoes glorifying Eton in the Latin tongue, very elegant and correct. The wet-bobs rowed up in the afternoons and choked the bar and swarmed over the lawn, vociferously consuming squashed flies and other strangely named refreshments. There was a ferry, a number of tethered punts and boats, green tables under the trees, a decaying collection of stuffed birds, ostrich eggs, wampum and sundries, in an outhouse of white plaster and tarred weather boarding, called the Museum, an eyot and a willow-bordered paddock for campers. Surly Hall has long since disappeared from the banks of the Thames, though I believe that Monkey Island, half a mile further up, still carries on.

It was Uncle Tom's excellent custom to invite Sarah's boys for the holidays; it was not an invariable custom but it happened most years, and we had a thoroughly healthy and expansive three weeks or a month, hanging about his licensed premises in an atmosphere faintly flavoured by sawdust and beer. My brothers' times fell into the Royal Oak days, but my lot was to visit Surly Hall for the last three of my school years. There I learnt to punt, paddle and row, but the current was considered too swift for me to attempt swimming without anyone to teach me. I did not learn to swim until I was past thirty.

My uncle was a widower, but he had two grown-up daughters in their early twenties, Kate and Clara; they shared the duties of the one or two barmaids he also employed. They all found me a very amusing temporary younger brother. Kate was the serious sister, a blonde with intellectual aspirations, and she did very much to stimulate me to draw and read. There was a complete illustrated set of Dickens which I read in abundantly, and a lot of bound up *Family Heralds*, in which I best remember a translation of Eugene Sue's *Mysteries of Paris*, which seemed to me at the time, the greatest romance in the world. All these young women encouraged me to talk, because I said such unexpected things. They pretended to flirt with me, they used me as a convenient chaperon when enterprising men customers wanted to gossip on the lawn in the twilight, and Miss King, the chief barmaid, and Clara became competitive for my sentimental devotion. It all helped to educate me.

One day there appeared on the lawn a delightful vision in fluttering muslin, like one of the ladies in Botticelli's*Primavera*. It was that great actress, Ellen Terry, then in her full loveliness, who had come to Surly Hall to study a part and presently be visited there by Mr. Henry Irving. I ceased to consider myself engaged to Miss King forthwith; I had pledged myself heedlessly; and later on I was permitted to punt the goddess about, show her where white lilies were to be found and get her a great bunch of wet forget-me-nots. There was an abundance of forget-me-nots among the sedges, and in a bend above us were smooth brown water surfaces under great trees and a spread of yellow (and some white) water-lilies in which dragon-flies hovered. It was far finer, I thought, than the Keston Fish Ponds, which had hitherto been the most beautiful place in my world, and at Keston there was no boat with oars, paddle and boat-hook complete, in which I could muck about for hours together.

Often when I was going for walks along the rather trite and very pebbly footpaths about Bromley, thirty miles away, I would let my imagination play with the idea that round the next corner and a little further on and then a bit more, I should find myself with a cry of delighted recognition on the road that led immediately to Surly Hall in summer and all its pleasantness. And how was I to suspect that Uncle Tom was losing money and his temper over the place, having borrowed to rebuild it rather too pretentiously, and that he was quarrelling with both his daughters about their lovers and that dark-eyed Clara, dreadfully bored and distressed temperamentally, was taking to drink? I knew nothing of all that, nor how greyly and dismally the Thames sluices by these riverside inns in the winter months.

But this is a mere glimpse of summer paradise on the way to my first start in life. My mother, I think I have made it clear, was within her limits a very determined little woman. Almost as unquestioning as her belief in Our Father and Our Saviour, was her belief in drapers. I know not whether that heartless trifler of her early years was a draper, but she certainly thought that to wear a black coat and tie behind a counter was the best of all possible lots attainable by man—at any rate by man at our social level. She had bound my brother Frank, resisting weakly, to Mr. Crowhurst in the Market Square, Bromley, for five years and she had bound my brother Freddy to Mr. Sparrowhawk of the Pavement for four, to obey those gentlemen as if they were parents and learn the whole art and mystery of drapery from them, and she was now making a very resolute attempt to incarcerate me and determine my future in the same fashion. It did not dawn upon her that my queer gifts of drawing and expression were of any value at all. But as poor father was to be all alone in Atlas House now—the use he made of his eight years of solitude does not concern this story—a Bromley shop was no longer a suitable soil in which to pop me in order to grow up the perfect draper. She did not like to send me away where there was no one to look after me, for she knew there are dangers that waylay the young who are not supervised. So she found a hasty solution to her problem by sending me on trial, with a view to apprenticeship, to Messrs. Rodgers and Denyer of Windsor, opposite the Castle. There my morals would be under the observation of Surly Hall. And from Messrs. Rodgers and Denyer I got my first impressions of the intensely undesirable life for which she designed me. I had no idea of what I was in for. I went to my fate as I was told, unquestioningly, as my brothers had done before me.

I am told that for lots of poor boys, leaving school and going into employment about thirteen or fourteen is a very exhilarating experience. But that is because they get pay, freedom in the evening and on Sundays, and an enhanced dietary. And they are released from the irksomeness of lessons and school tasks. But I had rather liked lessons and school tasks and drapers' apprentices did not get pay. An immense fuss, entirely unjustifiable, was made about the valuable trade apprentices were going to learn, and in the past the parents of the victim, if he "lived in," usually paid a premium of forty or fifty pounds or so for his immolation. I knew that the new start meant a farewell to many childish things. I had seen both my brothers pass into servitude, and I can still remember my brother Freddy having a last game of "marble runs" with toy bricks on the tilted kitchen table, a game of which he was particularly fond, before he submitted to the yoke of Mr. Sparrowhawk and began that ritual of stock-keeping, putting things away, tidying things up, bending over the counter, being attentive and measuring off, that lasted thereafter for forty-odd years of his life. He knew what he was going to, did my brother Fred; and that game was played with sacrificial solemnity. "I enjoyed that game," said Freddy, who has always displayed a certain gentle stoicism. "It's supper time Bert. ...Let's put the things away."

Now it was my turn to put the things away, put the books away, give up drawing and painting and every sort of free delight, stop writing stories and imitations of *Punch*, give up all vain hopes and dreams, and serve an employer.

I hated this place into which I had been put from the outset, but I was far too childish, as yet, to make any real resistance to the closing in of the prison about me. But I would not, I could not, give myself satisfactorily to this strange restricted life. It was just by the luck of that incapacity that the prison rejected me.

I was set down from Uncle Pennicott's dog-cart, with a small portmanteau containing all my earthly goods, at the side door of the establishment of Messrs. Rodgers and Denyer, I was taken up a narrow staircase to the men's dormitory, in which were eight or ten beds and four miserable wash-hand stands, and I was shown a dismal little sitting room with a ground glass window opening on a blank wall, in which the apprentices and assistants might "sit" of an evening, and then I was conducted downstairs to an underground dining-room, lit by naked gas-jets and furnished with two long tables covered with American cloth, where the eating was to be done. Then I was introduced to the shop and particularly to the cash desk, where it had been arranged for the first year of my apprenticeship that I was to sit on a tall stool and receive money, give change, enter the amount on a sheet and stamp receipts. I was further instructed in a ritual of dusting and window cleaning. I was to come down at half past seven in the morning, I learnt, without fail, dust, clean windows, eat a bread-and-butter breakfast at half past eight, prepare my cash sheet and so to the routine of the day. I had to add up my cash at the end of the day, count the money in the till, make sheet and cash agree, help to wrapper-up and sweep out the shop, and so escape at half-past seven or eight to drink the delights of freedom until ten, when I had to be in. Lights out at half past ten. And this was to go on day after day—for ever it seemed to me—with an early closing day once a week at five, and Sunday free.

I did not rise to these demands upon me. My mind withdrew itself from my duties. I did my utmost to go on living within myself and leave my duties to do themselves. My disposition to reverie increased. I dusted abominably; whenever I could manage it I did not dust at all. I smuggled books into my desk or did algebraic problems from my battered Todhunter's Larger Algebra; I gave change absent-mindedly and usually I gave inaccurate change, and I entered wrong figures on the cash sheet out of sheer slovenliness.

The one bright moment during the day was when the Guards fifes and drums went past the shop and up to the Castle. These fifes and drums swirled me away campaigning again. Dispatch riders came headlong from dreamland, brooking no denial from the shop-walker. "Is General Bert Wells here? The Prussians have landed!"

I obeyed, I realize, all the impulses of a developing claustrophobia during that first phase of servitude. I would abandon my desk to sneak down into the warehouse, where I spent an unconscionable time seated in a convenient place of reflection, reading. Or I just stood about down there behind stacks of unpacked bales.

As the afternoon dragged on, the hour of reckoning when the cash sheet was added up drew near. It never by any chance corresponded with the money in the till. There had to be a checking of bills, a scrutiny of figures. Wrong sums had been set down. The adding had been wild work. At first the total error would be anything—more or less. After some weeks it became constantly a shortage. The booking clerk, and one of the partners who did the business correspondence and supervised things, would stay late to wrestle with the problem. They were impatient and reproachful. I had to stay too, profoundly apathetic. Either I was giving change in excess, or in some way the money was seeping away. I did not care a rap.

Rodgers & Denyers 25 High Street
Sunday July 4ᵗʰ 1880

My dear Mother

Here I am sitting in my bed
room after the fatigues of the day
etc.   cough slightly better & so
am tolerably comfortable
I give you an account of one days
work to give you an idea what.
I have to do.
—   morning
We sleep 4 together very 3 apprentices
& 1 of the hands in one room (of
course in separate beds)
We lay in bed until 730 when a
bell rings & we jump up & put
trousers slippers socks & jacket on over
nightgown & hurry down & dust
the shop etc.
about 8 15ᵐ we hurry upstairs & dress
& wash for breakfast.
At 8 30 we go into a sort of vault
underground (lit by gas) & have

Letter dated July 4th, 1880, page 1.

107

breakfast
after breakfast I am in the shop
& desk till dinner at 1
(we have dinner underground
as well as breakfast) & then
work till tea (which we
have in the same place) &
then go on to supper at 8 30
at which time work is done
& we may then go out
until 10·30 . at which time
the apprentices are obliged
to be in the house
I don't like the place much
food it is not at all
like home
Give love to all & give the
Cats my best respects
I am rather tired of being indoors but that's nothing

Letter dated July 4th, 1880, page 2.

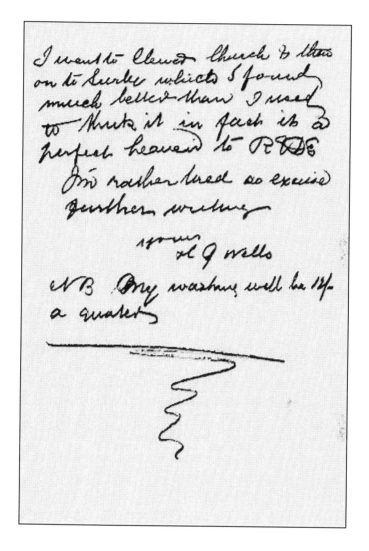

Letter dated July 4th, 1880, page 3.

Rodgers & Deuyers 25 High Street Sunday July 4th 1880

My dear Mother

Here I am sitting in my bed room after the fatigues
of the day etc Cough slightly better & I am tolerably
comfortable

I give you an account of one days work to give you an
idea what I have to do.

Morning

We sleep 4 together very 3 apprentices & 1 of the hands
in one room (of course in separate beds)

We lay in bed until 7.30 when a bell rings & we jump up
& put trousers slippers socks & jacket on over nightgown
& hurry down & dust the shop etc

about 8.15 we hurry upstairs & dress & wash for
breakfast.
At 8.30 we go into a sort of vault underground (lit by
gas) & have breakfast

After breakfast I am in the shop & desk till dinner at 1
(we have dinner underground as well as breakfast) &
then work till tea (which we have in the same place) &
then go on to supper at 8.30 at which time work is done
& we may then go out until 10.30 at which hour the
apprentices are obliged to be in the house

I don't like the place much, for it is not at all like home

Give love to Dad & give the Cat my best respects
I'm rather bored of being indoors but this morning]

I went to Clewet Church & then on to Surly which I
found much better than I used to think it in fact it's a
perfect heaven to R&DE

I'm rather bored so excuse further writing

Yours

H G Wells

NB Any washing will be 12/-a quarter]

    I had always hated money sums and long additions and now
I detested them. I just wanted to get out of that shop before it
was ten o'clock and time to return to the house. I did not realize
the dreadful suspicions that were gathering above my head, nor
the temptation my inaccuracies were offering to anyone who
had access to my desk while I was at meals or otherwise absent.
Nobody thought of that, unless perhaps it was the booking clerk.
    Every early closing night, every Sunday, at every opportunity
I had, I cut off to Surly Hall and took refuge with my cousins.
I went with joy and returned with heavy feet. I did not want to
talk about business there and when they asked me how I was
getting on I said "Oh all right," and turned the talk to more
agreeable topics. I did the long two miles from Windsor to and
fro after dark for the one or two bright hours I spent there. My
cousin Kate or Miss King would play the piano and sing. They
would talk to me as though I was not the lowest thing on earth.
There, I was still esteemed clever, and the queer things I said
were applauded. My cousins, delighted at my appreciation, sang
"Sweet Dreamland Faces," and "Juanita," to me and I sat on a

little stool close to the piano in a state of rapt appreciation—of the music, the shaded lamp, the comfort and the ease of it.

In this world of gramophones, pianolas and the radio, it is worth noting that at the age of thirteen I had heard no music at all except an occasional brass band, the not very good music of hymn singing and organ voluntaries in Bromley Church and these piano songs at Surly Hall.

Then came a terrible inquisition at the shop. I was almost charged with pilfering. But my uncle Tom defended me stoutly. "You better not go saying *that*" said my uncle Tom, and indeed, except that there was now a continual shortage in the cash desk, there was no evidence against me. I had no expensive vices; I had no criminal associates, I was extremely shabby and untidy; no marked money—if they used marked money—or indeed any money except the weekly sixpence allowed me for pocket money, had ever been found upon me and my bearing was one of unconscious but convincing rectitude. Indeed I never realized fully what all the fuss was about until afterwards. Yet the fact remains that as a cash desk clerk I had leaked abominably and somebody—I suppose—had got away with the leakage.

It was plain also that I shirked all my other tasks. And while my start in life was thus already faltering, I had some sort of difference with the junior porter, which resulted in a conspicuous black eye for me. It was a gross breach of social conventions for an apprentice to fight a porter. I had great difficulty in explaining that black eye to my own satisfaction at Surly Hall. Moreover the clothes I had come to Windsor in were anything but stylish, and Mr. Denyer, the most animated of the partners, liked the look of me less and less. I wore a black velvet cap with a peak and that was all wrong. It became plain that my mother's first attempt to give me a start in life had failed. I was not starting. I was not fitted, said Messrs. Rodgers and Denyer, with perfect truth, to be a draper. I was not refined enough.

I do not recall that at Windsor from first to last I made more than the slightest effort to do what was expected of me. It was not so much a resistance as an aversion. And it is a queer thing about that place that though I stayed there a couple of months, I do not remember the name of a single individual except one assistant named Nash, who happened to be the son of a Bromley draper and wore a long moustache. But all the other figures who sat with him at the downstairs dinner table are now blank nameless figures. Did I look at them? Did I listen to them? Nor can I remember the positions of the counters or the arrangement of the goods in the shop. I made no friends. Mr. Denyer, young Mr. Rodgers and old Mr. Rodgers left impressions, because they were like great pantomime heads always looking for me and saying disagreeable things to me, and I was always engaged in getting away from them. They disliked me; I think everybody in that place came to dislike me as a tiresome boring little misfit who made trouble and didn't do his share and was either missing when he was wanted or in the way when he wasn't. My self-conceit, I suppose, has blotted out all the other humiliating details from my memory. I do not even remember whether I felt any chagrin at my failure. All that seems effaced beyond recall. And yet that nocturnal tramp along the Maidenhead Road, which I took whenever I could, is real and living to me still. I could draw a map of the whole way down the hill and through Clewer. I could show where the road was wider and where it narrowed down.

Like most undernourished growing boys I was cowardly and I found the last stretch from Clewer to the inn terrifyingly dark and lonely. It was black on the moonless nights and eerie by moonlight and often it was misty from the river. My imagination peopled the dark fields on either hand with crouching and pursuing foes. Chunks of badly trimmed hedge took on formidable shapes. Sometimes I took to my heels and ran. For a week or so that road was haunted by a rumour of an escaped panther—from Lady Florence Dixie's riverside home, the Fisheries. That phantom panther waited for me patiently; it followed me like a noiseless dog, biding its time. And one night on the other side of the hedge a sleeping horse sighed deeply, a gigantic sigh, and almost frightened me out of my wits.

But nothing of that sort kept me from going at every opportunity to Surly Hall, where there was something to touch my imagination and sustain my self- respect. I was hanging on subconsciously long before I held on consciously, to that life of books and expression and creative living from which the close exactions and economies of employment for private profit were sucking me down. And nothing that my mother and cousins could say to move and encourage me, could induce me to fix my attention on the little flimsy bits of paper with carbon duplicates, that were being slapped down at the guichet of the cash desk.

"One eleven half—two and six. Quick please."

§ 5. SECOND START IN LIFE—WOOKEY (WINTER 1880)

The poor little family commander-in-chief—for that she had become—in lace cap and apron in the housekeeper's room at Up Park had to deal with the situation as her lights and limitations permitted. Joe at Bromley, tied by the leg in insolvent Atlas House, had little to suggest. He had had an idea, in view of my remarkable special certificates for book-keeping that Messrs. Hoare's or Norman's, for whom he had bowled so often, ought to have welcomed me as a bank clerk, but when it became clear that Hoare's and Norman's were unresponsive, he made no further effort to assist my mother in her perplexities. Shelter and nourishment and justifying employment had to be found for the youngster somehow. And at this point Uncle Williams came in with what seemed a hopeful suggestion. He was going to be head of a little national school. I might become a pupil teacher under him.

In those days a great deal of the teaching, such as it was, in elementary schools was done by children scarcely older than the pupils. Instead of leaving school for work they became "P.T.'s" and, after four years, competent to enter a training college for a year or two, before they went on grant earning for the rest of their lives. If an elementary teacher in those days became anything more than a "trained" drudge, it was due to his or her own exertions. My Uncle Williams, hearing of my mother's difficulties, held out hopes that my College of Preceptors achievements might be used to shorten my pupil teacher stage and get me accepted as something which he called an "improver."

So I was packed off from Windsor to Wookey in Somerset, where my Uncle Williams was installed in the school house— but precariously. For he was never really qualified to teach in an English school. He had taught as a young man in Jamaica with qualifications that did not satisfy the Board of Education requirements. There had been a certain lack of explicitness in his application for the post and when that came to light, he had to get out of Wookey again. And the same lack of explicitness extinguished the scholastic career he proposed for me in the course of two or three months.

But it gave me the idea that there was something to be done in teaching and that it was pleasanter to stand in front of a class and distribute knowledge and punishments, than sit at a desk or hover behind a counter, at the beck and call of a hierarchy of seniors.

My Uncle Williams was not my uncle at all; he had married the sister of that "Uncle Tom Pennicott," my mother's cousin who had rebuilt Surly Hall; he had been a teacher in the West Indies, and he was a bright and adventurous rather than a truthful and trustworthy man. He had invented and patented an improved desk for schools, with sunken inkpots that could not upset and could be protected by rotating covers, and he had left teaching to become the active partner of a firm of manufacturers of school appliances, including his desks, at Clewer near Windsor. A sanguine streak in his nature kept his expenses well above his income, and he presently sank to the position of clerk and manager in his own factory, and finally lost even that. Hence his attempt to establish himself in the school house at Wookey by means of inaccuracies.

As I knew him, he was an active centrally bald yellow-faced man with iron grey whiskers, a sharp nose, a chin like the toe of a hygienic slipper, and glasses. Extraordinary quantities of hair grew out of his ears. He had lost one arm, and instead he had a stump in which a hook was screwed, for which a dinner fork could be substituted. He held his food down vindictively and cut it up with a knife, and then put the knife down and ate snappily with another fork in the free hand. He instructed me in the arts and practices of his scholastic process and together, sometimes with a curtain to divide the children between us and sometimes in plenary session, we constituted the school staff. I found teaching heavy going but far more interesting than work in a cash desk. Discipline was difficult to maintain; some of the boys were as big as myself and sturdier, and my cockney accent jarred on Somerset ears. But it had the prestige of being English. Except for occasional hints from Uncle Williams, I had to find out how and what to teach. I taught them dates and geographical lists and sums and tables of weights and measures and reading, as well as I could. I fought my class, hit them about viciously and had altogether a lot of trouble with them. I exacted a full performance of the penalties I imposed and on one occasion pursued a defaulter headlong to his home, only to be routed ignominiously by his indignant mother and chased by her and a gathering rabble of variously sized boys back to the school house.

My Uncle Williams said I was wanting in tact.

My Uncle Williams was a man of derisive conversation with a great contempt for religion and the clergy. His table talk was unrestrained. He talked to me frankly and as if I were an adult; I had never in all my life before had that sort of talk with any grown-up person. It braced me up. He could talk very entertainingly about the church and its faith and about the West Indies and the world as he had seen it. He gave me a new angle from which to regard the universe; I had not hitherto considered that it might be an essentially absurd affair, good only to laugh at. That seemed in many ways a releasing method of approach. It was a fresh, bright way of counter-attacking the dull imperatives of life about me, and taking the implacable quality out of them.

A daughter kept home for him. His wife had remained in Clewer, where two elder daughters had jobs as teachers. My cousin was only three or four years older than I and she was in a phase of great enterprise and curiosity about the business of sex. She pressed her investigations upon me. The urge to experiment was upon her. We went for walks together over the hills in our margin of time; we went one Saturday into Wells and I saw my first cathedral; and generally speaking our talk was instructive rather than what was then considered edifying. This phase in my education was interrupted before it was completed. I took my first lessons in sexual practice with a certain aversion. My mind was prepared with a different formula. The real thing as it was thus presented to me, seemed hot, uncomfortable, shamefaced stuff. But perhaps these conversations at Wookey did something to bring me back from an impracticable isolating dreamland.

I was growing up now. I was past fourteen; I was getting sturdier in my body and less disposed to escape from reality to reverie. The youngster who was returned rather apologetically by Uncle Williams to my mother, may have looked very much like the youngster who went in by the side door of Rodgers and Denyer to try and be a draper, but in fact he was something far more alert and solid. He had heard one or two things which, hitherto, he had avoided facing, spoken of very plainly and directly. And he had been interested by a job. He had really tried to do something instead of merely submitting to a boring routine in a business machine he did not understand. He had come up against material fact with a new nearness and vividness, and he had learnt that laughter was perhaps a better way of dealing with reality than were the evasions of reverie. He certainly owes a great deal more to this second start in life than to the first. A facetious scepticism which later on became his favourite pose may owe a great deal to Uncle Williams.

The collapse of the Wookey situation was so swift and unexpected that it took me and my mother by surprise. There was hasty letter-writing again. I do not know the particulars. I was to go from Wookey to Surly Hall, either to wait there until she could speak to Miss Fetherstonhaugh about me, or because the entire journey from Wookey to Harting was considered too much for me. Even the journey to Windsor was a complicated one. My Uncle Williams packed me off with instructions to catch a certain train, the last possible train, at Maidenhead. There was a kink in the journey between two railway systems. If I missed the connexion I was to stay the night in a Temperance Hotel and then go on the next morning. But the first train available on the next day departed towards midday. (I may have got up late and missed an earlier train;—I cannot remember.) I went for a walk in Maidenhead and came upon a marvellous shop where one could be photographed and get a dozen tintypes for a shilling or a shilling and sixpence. I had never heard of such a thing and the temptation was irresistible. Money had been given me to cover my bill at the Temperance Hotel and my fare on to Windsor, and I felt rich beyond limit. But after the tintypes and a Bath bun and the Temperance Hotel bill, I found myself at the booking-office at half-past eleven with a dozen engaging portraits of myself in my pocket but short of the fare demanded. I had to go round by Slough and change trains; it was a longer journey than I had imagined. I emerged from the station, holding my little portmanteau which had suddenly become very heavy in my hand. "Please can you tell me the way to Windsor?" I asked.

I suppose the distance I covered was a little over four miles, because Surly Hall was on the road between Windsor and Maidenhead. But I still remember that walk as one of the longest in the world. When I had gone fifty yards from Maidenhead station I changed my portmanteau from one hand to the other. Before I had gone a quarter of a mile I put it down and reflected. My reflections were unfruitful. It is muscle and not mind that must carry portmanteaus. Before I had done a mile I was trying to carry that leaden valise on my head for a change. It had to be carried somehow to Surly Hall. I arrived after twilight with arms that felt like limp strings of pain, extremely exhausted and sorry for myself.

And when I got to Surly Hall, I found Surly Hall had changed. It had become cheerless and almost sinister.

The shadow of approaching tragedy hung over it. Dreadful things had happened already. In the interval since my departure from Windsor, my uncle had had a violent quarrel with his daughter Clara about her lover, there had been bitter recriminations and she had gone off to London. How she lived in London nobody knew. Miss King, the barmaid, had gone. Cousin Kate was in a state of dismay and disapproval and threatening to marry a man she had been engaged to for some time and "get away from it all." The river was a swift flood of leaden silver; there were no passing boats to pull up, the hotel was empty, the bar and taproom desolate and the lawn with its green tables sodden and littered with dead leaves. My uncle was greatly embittered at the swift darkening of life about him. I think too he was intensely worried financially. He had mortgaged himself deeply in his rebuilding of the place. He was distressed by the undutifulness of his daughters. He would sit in the taproom talking to a serious potman who had found religion....

Music and song, moonlight on the lawn, forget-me-nots in the sedges and white water-lilies above the brown smooth water; all had become incredible. My education was going on apace....

I did not see Surly Hall again for many years after that visit. But cousin Kate married and went away and cousin Clara followed her destinies in London and came back at last after four years, a broken young woman. Her lover had abandoned her long ago. Uncle Tom, I fear, received her unkindly. All light and hope had gone out of life for her and late one night she flitted in her nightgown down the lawn from a sleepless bed to the river and drowned herself in a deep hole under a pollard willow. The old man died soon after. My cousin Kate died. The place was annexed to an adjacent property and ultimately its license was extinguished. The obliteration of Surly Hall was complete. I do not know of anything that survives of it now except my memories, a passing mention in some Old Etonian's Reminiscences and a fading photograph or so.

§ 6. INTERLUDE AT UP PARK (1880-81)

I am trying to recover the quality of those years between twelve and sixteen or seventeen with as many particulars as I can recall, because I think that the forces and influences in operation then were of primary importance in determining all my subsequent reactions. I am impressed as I look over such documents and records as I can find to revive these days, by the extraordinarily rapid growth of my character and resolution during my fourteenth and fifteenth years. I suppose this hardening and toughening and clearing up of the will was the natural concomitant of puberty. I was perhaps intellectually forward but morally I think I followed an average curve.

But if I did, then I am convinced that this system of terminating the education of an ordinary citizen before the age of fourteen is a wrong one. I do not think that for the new civilization ahead of us education will ever terminate, but certainly thirteen or fourteen is premature for economic citizenship. That age is not a natural turning point in the development of either male or female—at any rate so far as north European races are concerned. The transfer from protected tutelage to quasi responsible employment is premature. At earliest it should not occur until a year or so later when the youngster has become able and willing to take a directive interest in his or her own future. I was relatively precocious, yet clearly thirteen-fourteen was too soon for me. And even if whole-time education is to be prolonged for some years more—as may presently be the case all over the world for everyone—there should still be a break, not according to the present practice in England about twelve or thirteen when a boy goes from a preparatory to a public school, but about fifteen or sixteen. Then is the best time for a change over from instruction and guidance to an intelligent co-operation between teacher and disciple.

Both my brothers and myself, like nearly every boy in the British lower and lower middle classes of that time, were "put to a trade" and bound, before we could exercise any choice in the matter. In relation to any such issue we were children still. If this had been the case only with my brothers and myself, then this aspect of my story would hardly have been worth discussing. It would have been an individual misfortune. It would have been merely the story of three tadpoles who had chanced to be taken out of the water before their legs and lungs would act properly. But this transfer at the wrong age was and still is the common experience. It has therefore had far reaching social consequences. Because of this premature termination of the primary educational phase in the closing years of the last century, a great proportion, perhaps a majority, of British men and women were (and are) employed upon their tasks against their will or at least without their willing assent. The nation almost as a whole is taken out of its tadpole stage too soon. Just as the civilizations of the ancients was based upon the labour of serfs and slaves, so this industrial civilization in which we are still living is based on the toil of masses of people mentally and morally arrested before fourteen. The bulk of the population is neither uneducated and quasi-animal as its servile predecessor was, nor educated as the whole mass should be in a soundly conceived mechanized civilization. It is incompletely metamorphosed; neither one thing nor the other.

One miserable result, though not by any means the only one, is this: that industrial life goes on in a spirit of boredom, with a demand therefore for shorter hours and higher wages as the main expression of the Labour mentality evoked under these conditions. An extraordinary indifference to the amount and quality of the product or service rendered is also manifest. Half Europe still watches the clock just as I watched the clock in Rodgers and Denyer's establishment, and by an inner necessity it tries in every possible way to scamp whatever tiresome task has to be done. Its labour is spiritless labour because it is essentially uninterested labour.

But our already highly mechanized and organized world community, if it is to develop further and sustain an efficient common life requires before everything else interested and participating workers. In this respect as in so many others it has got off from the mark too soon and started at too low a level.

It has taken three quarters of a century for this fact to dawn upon us. Responsible people have still to realize as a class that a happy, stably progressive human community can be made possible only if—among several other necessary primary conditions—the new generation is held back under education until it is at least sixteen years old, before its life rôles are determined and conscious specialized economic citizenship begins. Although, as I have said, relatively precocious I was not fit to have a decisive voice in my own destiny until I was sixteen. For want of a breathing time at this crucial phase, my eldest brother became a complete failure in life—for he did not stick to the shop—and my brother Fred wasted upon haberdashery a fine conscientiousness and an exceptional gift for sensitive meticulous artistic work. And I escaped from becoming a wretched employee in an entirely uncongenial trade not by any merit of my own but by sheer luck.

Against a background of such generalizations my little mother, you see, becomes a symbol of the blind and groping parental solicitude of that age, a solicitude which enslaved and hampered where it sought to aid and establish; and my individual story merges into the story of the handicapped intelligence of our species, blundering heavily towards the realization and handling of vast changes and still vaster dangers and opportunities. My mother becomes a million mothers and my brothers a countless brotherhood. My life is a sample life and not an exceptional one; its distinctive merit has been its expressiveness; its living interest lies in that.

For some weeks after the retreat from Wookey, my mother did not know what to do with me. She asked all sorts of people for information and no doubt she took her troubles to her Heavenly Father, who remained, as ever, speechlessly enigmatical. She spoke to Miss Fetherstonhaugh about me and I was allowed to take refuge, from the gathering gloom of Surly Hall, at Up Park. And there a great snowstorm snowed me up for nearly a fortnight and I produced a daily newspaper of a facetious character, *The Up Park Alarmist*—on what was properly kitchen paper—and gave a shadow play to the maids and others, in a miniature theatre I made in the housekeeper's room.

Now it is one of my firmest convictions that modern civilization was begotten and nursed in the households of the prosperous, relatively independent people, the minor nobility, the gentry, and the larger bourgeoisie, which became visibly important in the landscape of the sixteenth century, introducing a new architectural element in the towns, and spreading as country houses and chateaux and villas over the continually more orderly countryside. Within these households, behind their screen of deer park and park wall and sheltered service, men could talk, think and write at their leisure. They were free from inspection and immediate imperatives. They, at least, could go on after thirteen thinking and doing as they pleased. They created the public schools, revived the waning universities, went on the Grand Tour to see and learn. They could be interested in public affairs without being consumed by them. The management of their estates kept them in touch with reality without making exhaustive demands on their time. Many, no doubt, degenerated into a life of easy dignity or gentlemanly vice, but quite a sufficient number remained curious and interested to make, foster and protect the accumulating science and literature of the seventeenth and eighteenth centuries. Their large rooms, their libraries, their collections of pictures and "curios" retained into the nineteenth century an atmosphere of unhurried liberal enquiry, of serene and determined insubordination and personal dignity, of established æsthetic and intellectual standards. Out of such houses came the Royal Society, the *Century of Inventions*, the first museums and laboratories and picture galleries, gentle manners, good writing, and nearly all that is worth while in our civilization to-day. Their culture, like the culture of the ancient world, rested on a toiling class. Nobody bothered very much about that, but it has been far more through the curiosity and enterprise and free deliberate thinking of these independent gentlemen than through any other influences, that modern machinery and economic organization have developed so as to abolish at last the harsh necessity for any toiling class whatever. It is the country house that has opened the way to human equality, not in the form of a democracy of insurgent proletarians, but as a world of universal gentlefolk no longer in need of a servile substratum. It was the experimental cellule of the coming Modern State.

The new creative forces have long since overflowed, these first nests in which they were hatched and for the most part the European country houses and chateaux that were so alive and germinal, mentally, in the seventeenth and eighteenth centuries, stand now mere empty shells, resorts for week-end gatherings and shooting parties, but no longer real dwelling places, gracefully and hospitably in decay. Yet there still lingers something of that former importance and largeness in outlook, on their walls and hangings and furnishings, if not in their attenuated social life. For me at any rate the house at Up Park was alive and potent. The place had a great effect upon me; it retained a vitality that altogether overshadowed the insignificant ebbing trickle of upstairs life, the two elderly ladies in the parlour following their shrunken routines, by no means content with the bothered little housekeeper in the white panelled room below.

During this visit and subsequent visits, when the weather did not permit of my wandering in the park, I rummaged about in an attic next to my bedroom which was full of odd discarded things. I found several great volumes of engravings of the Vatican paintings of Raphael and Michelangelo. I pondered immensely over the mighty loveliness of these saints and sibyls and gods and goddesses. And there was a box, at first quite mysterious, full of brass objects that clearly might be screwed together. I screwed them together, by the method of trial and error, and presently found a Gregorian telescope on a tripod in my hands. I carried off the wonder to my bedroom. By daylight it showed everything upside down, I found, but that did not matter—except for the difficulty of locating objects—when I turned it to the sky. I was discovered by my mother in the small hours, my bedroom window wide open, inspecting the craters of the moon. She had heard me open the window. She said I should catch my death of cold. But at the time that seemed a minor consideration.

Sir Harry Fetherstonhaugh, like many of his class and time, had been a free-thinker, and the rooms downstairs abounded in bold and enlightening books. I was allowed to borrow volumes and carry them off to my room. Then or later, I cannot now recall when, I improved my halting French with Voltaire's lucid prose, I read such books as *Vathek*and *Rasselas*, I nibbled at Tom Paine, I devoured an unexpurgated *Gulliver's Travels* and I found Plato's *Republic*. That last was a very releasing book indeed for my mind, I had learnt the trick of mocking at law and custom from Uncle Williams and, if anything, I had improved upon it and added caricature to quaint words, but here was something to carry me beyond mockery. Here was the amazing and heartening suggestion that the whole fabric of law, custom and worship, which seemed so invincibly established, might be cast into the melting pot and made anew.

§ 7. THIRD START IN LIFE—MIDHURST (1881)

I do not know how my mother hit upon the idea of making me a pharmaceutical chemist. But that was the next career towards which I (and my small portmanteau) were now directed. I spent only about a month amidst the neat gilt-inscribed drawers and bottles of Mr. Cowap at Midhurst, rolled a few score antibilious and rhubarb pills, broke a dozen soda-water siphons during a friendly broom fight with the errand boy, learnt to sell patent medicines, dusted the coloured water bottles, the bust of Hahnemann (indicating homoeopathic remedies) and the white horse (veterinary preparations), and I do not think I need here devote very much space to him and his amusing cheerful wife, seeing that I have already drawn largely upon this shop, and my experiences in it, in describing aunt and uncle Ponderevo in *Tono Bungay*. Cowap, like uncle Ponderevo, really did produce a heartening Cough Linctus, though he never soared to my hero's feat of commercial expansion. But this time I gave satisfaction, and it was upon my initiative and not upon that of my prospective employer that pharmaceutical chemistry was abandoned as my calling in life. I enquired into the cost of qualification as an assistant and dispenser; the details have long since escaped me;

but I came to the conclusion that the fees and amount of study required, would be quite beyond my mother's limited resources. I pointed this out to her and she saw reason in the figures I gave her.

I was reluctant to abandon this start because I really liked the bright little shop with its drawers full of squills and senna pods, flowers of sulphur, charcoal and such like curious things, and I had taken to Midhurst from the outset. It had been the home of my grandparents, and that gave me a sense of belonging there. It was a real place in my mind and not a morbid sprawl of population like Bromley. Its shops and school and post office and church were grouped in rational comprehensible relations; it had a beginning, a middle and an end. I know no country to compare with West Sussex except the Cotswolds. It had its own colour, a pleasant colour of sunlit sandstone and ironstone and a warm flavour of open country because of the parks and commons and pine woods about it. Midhurst was within three hours' sturdy walking from Up Park. And I had recovered my self respect there very rapidly.

One manifest deficiency in my schooling came to light at the mere suggestion that I should be a chemist. I knew no Latin and much of the dignity of the qualified druggist at that time depended upon a smattering of that tongue. He had to read and to copy and understand prescriptions. Accordingly it was arranged that I should go to the Headmaster of the local Grammar School and have lessons in Latin. I had, I suppose, four or five hours of it before the project of my apprenticeship was abandoned, but in that time I astonished my instructor, accustomed to working against the resistances of Sussex tradesmen's and farmer's sons and the like, by rushing through the greater part of Smith's*Principia* Part I and covering more ground than he had been accustomed to get over with his boys in a year or more. I found this fine structural language congenial just as I had found Euclid's *Elements* congenial. It was a new way of saying things. It was like something I had been waiting for. It braced up my use of English immediately.

The Midhurst Grammar School was an old foundation which had fallen into decay and had been closed in 1859—after a fire which had destroyed the school house. It had been revived by the Endowed Schools Commissioners and the school had been re-opened in 1880, less than a year before my essay in pharmacy. Mr. Horace Byatt, M.A., the new headmaster, was a not very brilliant graduate of Dublin University, an animated and energetic teacher resolved to make a success of his first headmastership. He was a dark, semi-clerical man, plumply active, with bushy hair, side whiskers, a cleft chin, and a valiant rotund voice, and he was quartered with his wife and three small children in a comfortable old house near the South Pond, until the commissioners could rebuild the school house, which was still at that time a weedy heap of ruins.

I know nothing of Byatt's previous history and training, but I doubt if his Latin went very far and I stumped him completely when, some years later, I took some Greek quotation from Paley's *Evidences* to him for elucidation. He had evidently had a considerable experience in teaching elementary science, geometrical drawing and the like, and his rôle at Midhurst was to build up a secondary school on comparatively modern lines. At that time the British Education Department was spreading a system of evening class instruction from which the organized science schools of the next decade were developed. The classes ran through the winter and were examined in May and the teacher received pay according to his results, a pound or two pounds or four pounds for every pass, according to its class and grade. Byatt, who was a university M.A., was considered qualified to conduct classes and earn grants in any of the thirty odd subjects scheduled by the Department, and in addition to his day-time teaching, he was already running evening classes in freehand, perspective and geometrical drawing and in electricity and magnetism, to supplement his fundamental stipend. His interest in the classics was therefore relatively less keen. Latin in such schools as his had ceased to be a language; there was no real thought of either reading it or writing it, much less of speaking it; it was an exercise directed to the passing of various qualifying examinations.

Now Cowap had counted on my premium as an apprentice, and when he realized that I did not intend to go on with that, he betrayed considerable vexation and became urgent to clear me out to make way for a more profitable aspirant. My mother had nowhere for me to go and she arranged to put me as a boarder with the Grammar School headmaster until she could organize a fourth start in life for me. I became the first boarder of the renascent school. I spent about two months there, returning by special request to sit for the May examinations in all the subjects of Byatt's evening classes and so earn grants for him.

Now here again was a new phase in my very jumbled education, and one that I still look back upon with pleasure. I liked Byatt, and he formed an encouragingly high opinion of my grit and capacity. The amount of mental benefit I derived from those few weeks as his pupil, cannot be measured by the work actually done; the stimulus I got was far more important. I went on with Latin but now at a reduced speed, for Byatt preferred to direct me rather towards grant-earning subjects and put text books in such subjects as physiology and physiography into my hands, realizing that I was capable of learning very rapidly by reading alone without any nursing in class. I could understand a book of my own accord and write, and if necessary illustrate, a good answer to a question, and that was something beyond the general capacity of his Midhurst material. I think it was extraordinary good fortune for me, that I had this drilling in writing things down at this time. It gave my reading precision and accustomed me to marshal my knowledge in an orderly fashion. There are many valid objections to a system of education controlled by written examinations; it may tend very easily towards a ready superficiality; but I am convinced that it has at any rate the great merit of imposing method and order in learning. It prevents the formation of those great cavities of vagueness, those preferential obsessions, those disproportions between detail and generalization which are characteristic of gifted people who have never been "examinees."

This broadening out, bucking up and confirmation of my mind by the flood of new experiences at Up Park and Midhurst, were immensely important in my development. I dwell upon this phase because when I look back upon 1880 and early 1881 it seems to me as though these above all others were the years in which the immediate realities about me began to join on in a rational way to that varied world with which books had acquainted me. That larger world came slowly within the reach of my practical imagination. Hitherto it had been rather a dreamland and legend than anything conceivably tangible and attainable. It had been no more credible to me than my mother's imaginative escape to Our Father, Our Saviour, celestial music and the blessedness of heaven. One let one's mind stray away to such things when the rigid uncomfortable imperatives of employment, the inescapable insufficiency and shabbiness of the daily round became insupportable. But one had no belief in any possible escape in fact, and sooner or later the mind had to return to its needy habitation and its fated limitations. Temporary escape and alleviation by reverie were the easier substitutes for positive effort to get out of the imprisoning conditions. But now I was abandoning reverie and working up towards a conscious fight for the positive enlargement of my life.

I wish I could set down with certainty all the main facts in this phase of my adolescence. Then I should be able to separate the accidental elements, the element of individual luck that is to say, from the normal developmental phases. I realize that I was almost beyond comparison a more solid, pugnacious, wary and alert individual in 1881 than I was in 1879, and as I have already suggested that a large factor in this may have been the nervous and chemical changes that are associated with puberty. So far my experience was the general experience. Puberty is certainly a change in much more than the sexual life. The challenge to authority, the release of initiative, the access of courage are at least equally important. But added to this normal invigoration was the escape from the meagre feeding and depressingly shabby and unlit conditions of Atlas House. There I had a great advantage over my two brothers and I think a quite unusual push forward. I was living in those crucial years under healthier conditions; I was undergoing stimulating changes of environment, and, what is no small matter, eating a more varied and better dietary. Yet even when these more fortunate physical circumstances have been allowed for, there remains over and above them, the influence upon my perplexed and resentful mind for the first time, at its most receptive age, of a sudden irruption of new ideas, ideas of scientific precision and confirmation and ideas of leisure, culture and social margin. If I had been the son of an instructive-minded astronomer and had been bothered with early lessons about the stars when I wanted to play with mud pies, I might not have made my first contact with the starry heavens in a state of exaltation, nor pursued Jupiter with the help of *Whitaker's Almanack* until with my own eyes, I saw him and his moons quivering in the field of my telescope, as though I were Galileo come back to earth. Nor should I have realized with anything like the same excitement, had geology been made easy for me in my childhood, that when I stood on the brow of Telegraph Hill and looked across the weald to the North Downs I was standing on the escarpment of a denuded anticlinal, and that this stuff of the pale hills under my feet had once been slime at the bottom of a vanished Cretaceous sea. And again this definite estate of Up Park and the sharply marked out farms, villages and towns of the countryside below, caught me just in the proper phase to awaken a sense of social relationship and history that might never have been roused if I had remained in the catastrophic multitudinousness of suburban development.

The stuff accumulated by the discursive reading of my earlier years, fell rapidly into place in the wider clearer vision of my universe that was coming into being before my eyes. Science in those days insisted, if anything, overmuch upon the reign of law. The march of progress was still being made with absolute assurance, and my emancipation was unqualified. It must be hard for intelligent people nowadays to realize all that a shabby boy of fifteen could feel as the last rack of a peevish son-crucifying Deity dissolved away into blue sky, and as the implacable social barriers, as they had seemed, set to keep him in that path unto which it had pleased that God to call him, weakened down to temporary fences he could see over and presently perhaps hope to climb over or push aside.

But before one breaks or climbs fences one must look over them or through them for a time, and just then I was merely in the stage of peeping with a wild surmise and daring nothing more. I was still a good ten years from the reality of personal freedom.

IV. — EARLY ADOLESCENCE

§ 1. FOURTH START IN LIFE—SOUTHSEA (1881- 1883)

While I was making my first systematic acquaintance with modern science at the Midhurst Grammar School, my mother was busy finding yet another start in life for me. She had consulted Sir William King, who was Miss Fetherstonhaugh's Agent and an important man in Portsmouth affairs, and he had recommended her to Mr. Edwin Hyde, the proprietor of the Southsea Drapery Emporium in Kings Road, Southsea. I learnt at Easter that I was destined once again to try the difficult rôle of a draper, this time under the tutelage of this Mr. Hyde. I was still unprepared with any alternative scheme. I expressed dissent, but my mother wept and entreated. I promised to be a good boy and try.

But this time I went recalcitrant, not indeed against my mother, whose simplicity and difficulties I was beginning to understand, but against a scheme of things which marched me off before I was fifteen to what was plainly a dreary and hopeless life, while other boys, no better in quality than myself, were enjoying all the advantages—I thought they were stupendous advantages in those days—of the public school and university. I conveyed my small portmanteau to Southsea with a sinking heart. I was left upstairs in the dormitory for a time until someone could come to show me round, and I leant upon the window-sill and looked out upon the narrow side street upon which the window gave, with no illusion about what had happened to me. I can still feel the unhappiness and dismay of that moment.

Retail trade, I thought, had captured me for good. I had now to learn to work and to work faithfully for the profit and satisfaction of my prospective employers to the end of my days. I had been at large for a year and found no other way of living. The last chance had gone. At that moment I could not discover in my mind or in my world, as represented by the narrow side street into which I was looking, the little corner pub or the blind alley below me or the strip of sky overhead, the faintest intimation of any further escape.

I turned round from this restricted outer world to survey my dormitory in much the same mood as a condemned prisoner surveying the fittings of the cell he is to occupy for his allotted term....

It is an open question in my mind whether this dismay at the outset, is the common experience of modern youth of the less fortunate classes, or whether because of the enlightenment of my previous starts I happened to see further and more clearly than most of my fellows. A considerable number, I think, get that caught feeling rather later. My brother Frank, after fifteen years of being good, said he could endure the life no longer and broke away as I shall tell in due course. My brother Fred held to the religion of submission longer; he was the good boy of the three of us, and he did subdue himself to the necessary routines for the best part of his life.

What percentage of those who are bound apprentices to drapers, go on to comparative success I do not know, nor what their vital statistics are, but it is beyond all question a meagre distressful life they lead and exceptionally devoid of hope. Caradoc Evans, like myself, has been a draper, and the scene he draws of a draper's existence in the meaner shops of London in *Nothing to Pay* is, I know, true in all substantial particulars. He tells of the perpetual nagging and mutual irritation, the petty "spiffs" and fines, the intrigues and toadyism, the long tedious hours, the wretched dormitories, the insufficient "economized" food, the sudden dismissals, the dreadful interludes of unemployment with clothing growing shabby and money leaking away. There was no dole behind the "swapped" shop assistant in those days. You swam for as long as you could and then, if you could not scramble into some sort of shop, down you went to absolute destitution, the streets and beggary. Hyde was an exceptionally good employer; the place, from an assistant's point of view, was infinitely superior to my previous "crib" at Rodgers and Denyer's, yet still I recall those two years of incarceration as the most unhappy hopeless period of my life. I was indentured for four years, but after nearly two years of it I took matters into my own hands. I rebelled and declared that come what might I would not go on being a draper.

Yet I never got to the worst experiences of an assistant's life. I never knew how it felt to be out of a crib or tasted the full sordidness of the Caradoc Evans type of shop. I learnt about such matters chiefly from my brothers and the assistants at Hyde's. What overwhelmed me immediately was the incessancy of this employment and its lack of compelling interest. I do not know how the modern state as it develops will solve the problem of service in the distributing trades, but I am convinced it will have to be made an employment for short periods, short hours or alternative weeks and months with relays of workers, and that such special education as may be provided for it will link up the mind of the employee with the methods and novelties of manufacture on the one hand and the ultimate use of the goods sold on the other. Then the assistant would go behind the counter or into the stockroom with a sense of function instead of a sense of routine, there would be a minimum of shirking, resentment and lassitude, and he would do his job as a brisk terminable job worth doing and would find it the more interesting the better it was done. Nothing of that sort happened in my case.

It is remarkable how alien and incomprehensible the stuff I had to handle was to me. I was put first into the Manchester department, and there I found fixtures of wrappered blocks labelled incomprehensibly Hard Book or Turkey Twill or the like, rolls of grey and black silesia, flannels with a variety of names, a perplexing range of longcloths and calicoes, endless packages of diaper table-cloths, serviettes, and so forth, and rolls of crash, house cloth, ticking and the like. All that stuff had no origin and no purpose for me, except that it seemed to have been created to make my life burthensome. There were also in this Manchester department cotton dress materials, prints, ginghams and sateens, cretonne and kindred fabrics for covering furniture; stuffs that were rather more understandable but equally irksome to handle. I had to straighten all this stock and pack it up after it had been shown and put it back into the proper fixtures; I had to measure and refold it when the manufacturers delivered it, to block it or to roll it in rolls. This blocking, rolling and folding was skilled work that needed a watchful effort I gave grudgingly, and I never learnt to do it swiftly and neatly. You cannot imagine how maliciously a folded piece of sateen can get askew, how difficult it is to roll huckaback, how unruly a fat blanket is to pack up and how heavy and unwieldy pieces of cretonne can be when you have to carry a score or so of them up narrow folding steps and adjust them neatly on a rising pile. My department also included lace curtains. These had to be unfolded and held up by the junior apprentice while the salesman discoursed to the customer. As the heap of tumbled curtains grew and the customer still wanted to see something a little different, storms of hatred and revolutionary fervour went on behind the apathetic mask of the junior apprentice, doomed before closing time to refold them all and put them away.

Stock keeping, showing goods and clearing up, were the middle duties of the day. We apprentices were roused from our beds at seven, peremptorily, by one of the assistants; he swept hortative through the dormitory and on his return journey pulled the bed-clothes off anyone still in bed. We flung on old suits, tucking our nightgowns into our trousers, and were down in the shop in a quarter of an hour, to clean windows, unwrapper goods and fixtures, dust generally, before eight. At eight we raced upstairs to get first go at the wash basins, dressed for the day and at half-past eight partook of a bread and butter breakfast before descending again. Then came window dressing and dressing out the shop. I had to fetch goods for the window dresser and arrange patterns or pieces of fabric on the brass line above the counter. Every day or so the costume window had to be rearranged and I had to go in the costume room and fetch those headless effigies on which costumes are displayed and carry them the length of the shop, to the window dresser, avoiding gas brackets, chairs and my fellow creatures *en route*. Then I had to see to the replenishing of the pin bowls and the smoothing out and stringing up of paper for small parcels. The tediums of the day were broken for an hour or so while I went out to various other shops in Southsea, Portsmouth and Landport "matching" for the workroom, getting lengths of ribbon and material that were needed and could not be supplied out of stock, taking money from the cash desk to the bank or gettings bags of small change. I loitered as much as I dared on these blessed errands, but by half past eleven or twelve at latest, the shop swallowed me up again and there was no more relief until after closing time, which came at seven or eight according to the season. I had to stand by ready for any helpful job. There were a hundred small fussy things to do, straightening up, putting away, fetching and carrying. It was not excessively laborious but it was indescribably tedious. If there was nothing else to do I had to stand to attention at the counter, as though ready for a customer, though at first I was not competent to serve. The length of those days at Southsea were enormous until closing time; then the last hour fell swiftly past me to "lights out" at half past ten.

Half an hour before closing time we began to put away for the last time and "wrapper up," provided no customer lingered in the department. And as soon as the doors were shut and the last customer gone, the assistants departed and we junior apprentices rushed from behind the counters, scattered wet sawdust out of pails over the floor and swept it up again with great zest and speed, the last rite of the day. By half-past eight we were upstairs and free, supping on bread and butter, cheese and small beer. That was the ritual for every day in the week, thirteen hours of it, except that on Wednesday, Early Closing Day, the shop closed at five.

There was an interval of five minutes at eleven o'clock in the morning when we went upstairs in relays for bread and butter and—my memory is not quite clear here but I think we had a glass of beer. Or it may have been milk or tea. We had a mid-day meal about one for which we had half an hour and we had ten minutes for tea. The dining room was airy, well lit and upstairs, far more agreeable than the underground cellar at Rodgers and Denyer's, and instead of the squalid rooms which characterised the Windsor place, with truckle beds and no accommodation for personal belongings, so that everyone had to keep his possessions in a trunk or valise, high partitions between the beds divided the dormitory into cubicles and everyone had a private chest of drawers, looking glass, pegs, a chair and so forth. For his time and trade, Mr. Edwin Hyde was a fairly civilized employer. He had even provided a reading room, with a library of several hundred books, of which I shall have a word to say in the next section.

Though I began this life of a draper's shopman at the best end, so to speak, I found it insupportable. The unendurable thing about it was that I was never master of my own attention. I had to be thinking continually about pins and paper and packages. If there was nothing for me to do then I had to find something to do and look sharp about it. But the excitement of successful learning, which had come to me at Midhurst, would not die down. For a time Latin was for me, as for Hardy's *Jude the Obscure*, the symbol of mental emancipation. I tried to go on with Latin; I wanted to prepare for more examinations. My mind no longer escaped in reverie, but I was rarely without a book of some sort in my pocket which I would try to read when I should have been combing and grooming Witney blankets for the window, or when I was out of sight of the shop-walker, as I imagined, behind a pile of cotton goods.

It became evident to those who were set in authority over me that I was an inattentive and unwilling worker. This mattered most immediately to Casebow the head of the Manchester department, and the "improver" and senior apprentice who were between him and myself. Casebow was a good sort, but he had to keep up a rain of "Come up!" "Oh, look *sharp!*" "What in heaven are you doing now?" "What on earth are you doing here?" Over him and me ruled the shop walker, Mr. John Key, a stately and quasi-military figure with a good profile and a cherished moustache, very gentlemanly and dreadfully brisk, who marshalled all the forces of the shop together and did not for a moment intend that I or anyone under his sway should sink into sloth and insignificance. When I reflect upon him, I marvel at his all-seeing energy. He lurked watchfully in a little desk in the middle of the main shop, from which he sallied to accost customers, lead them to the appropriate department, summon the proper assistant, "Merton forward!" "Ascough forward!" "Miss Quilter forward!" hover to intervene if the sale did not go well, answer to the cry of "Sign!" and check each transaction, introduce novelties to the departing client,—"We are showing some very pretty sunshades just now Moddum. This for example" (startlingly opened)—and see that no part of our organization (and particularly, it seemed to me, myself) fell out of action. He found me a responsibility, and after a time I got a little on his nerves. He would remember me suddenly and inconveniently. "Wells?" he would ask. "What is Wells doing? Where on earth is that boy now?"

"Jay-Kay's after you," Platt or Rodgers would say.

Wells would become virtuously active at a counter where he had been invisible five minutes before. "Here Sir. I've just been straightening up the longcloths."

"Eugh!"

My life went to the refrain of Mr. Key's disgusted "Eugh."

The proprietor, the "G. V.", I saw less of; he was snappy in his manner and very terrifying. But he came into the department at irregular intervals; he blew over. J. K. who was always about, always keeping me up to the mark, observant of every untidiness in my dress or any slackness in my bearing, an ever present "Eugh" of disapproval, was the living sting of my servitude. At the time I hated him beyond measure. And yet now, when I can pass judgment upon him across an interval of half a century, I see that he was really an excellent man, most anxious to guide my feet into the path of successful drapering and without a grain of malice in his persecution. If he never let me alone for five minutes, then he did me the immense service of bringing home to me in time, just how slack, unsatisfactory and hopeless I was by nature for the calling that had been chosen for me. I could do nothing right for him from the moment when I came into the shop, with an unnecessarily careless slam of the door three minutes late after breakfast, to the time when, broom and pail in hand, I stared malevolently round the corner of a fixture at the lingering customer. The parcels in my department became more and more askew; until they might have been packed, he said, by "old women."

He wasn't "finding fault." The faults obtruded. I wasn't doing things right. Although I tried hard and tried to school myself, the humiliating fact has to be faced by an honest autobiographer, I wasn't equal to the job.

Now it is all claptrap to say that this was so because I was meant for better things. But I was "meant," if I may use that expression, for different things. I don't think I ever had any snobbishness in me about the relative values of Latin and longcloth, but it was an immense consolation to me in those days of drab humiliations, that after all I had been able to race through Euclid's *Elements*, Smith's *Principia* and various scientific text books at a quite unusual speed. That consolation became brighter as my prospect of winning any of the prizes in the trade or even holding my own as a satisfactory assistant, darkened. Manifestly I had not the ghost of a chance of becoming a buyer, a shop walker, a manager, a traveller or a partner. I listened to the tales my seniors would unfold, of the long-drawn despair and hardships of "crib hunting" and rotten shops and what it meant to lose one's "refs," with a growing certitude that that was my part of it, that was the way I should go. And, meditating on my outlook, it was inevitable I should recall the nice authoritative feeling of dictating knowledge to a class and wonder whether even for me with such an appetite for learning as I possessed there might not be prizes and scholarships in the world and some niche of erudition for me to fill.

Possibly my mind would have run naturally towards such ideas, but Mr. Key's expostulating "I never saw such a boy! What do you think will become of you?" was undoubtedly thought-provoking. What *would* become of me?

Might there not be some Wookey where the headmaster's certificates were in order?

This question became more urgent in my mind as I got into my second year. A fresh apprentice came and I was no longer junior; he took over those pleasant errands of matching and so forth that had hitherto fallen to me and I was kept more closely in the shop. (He had by the bye an amusing simplicity of mind, a carelessness of manner, a way of saying "Oo'er," and a feather at the back of his head that stuck in my memory, and formed the nucleus which grew into *Kipps* in my novel of that name.) Junior apprentices wear short black coats, but afterwards they go into black morning coats with tails, and now, at sixteen, I bore these evidences of my increasing maturity. I began to serve small and easy customers. I served them badly. Rodgers and Platt my immediate seniors were far sharper at the job. And the parcels I packed were damnable.

"Get on with it Wells." "Wells Forward." "Has anyone seen Wells?" "Sign!" "But you haven't shown the lady the gingham at six-three! The young man has made a mistake Moddum; we have exactly what you require." "A parcel like that will fall to pieces, man, before it gets home." And at the back of my mind, growing larger and more vivid, until it was like the word of the Lord coming to one of his prophets, was the injunction; "Get out of this trade before it is too late. At any cost get out of it."

141

For some time I did not tell anyone of this amazing urgency to disentangle myself. Then I tried the idea on my brother Frank, who had settled into a reasonably pleasant job at Godalming and was "living out" in lodgings. I used to go to him at Easter and Whitsuntide to spend hilarious friendly Bank Holidays. "But what else can you do?" he asked. The second clerk in the booking desk, named West, was a man of some education who had had dreams of entering the church and who took a sympathetic interest in my spurts with the Latin grammar of an evening. I talked to him. I may have got suggestions from him. Finally I had the brilliant idea of writing to Mr. Horace Byatt at Midhurst. "Weren't there such things as ushers? Might I not be useful in the school?"

He answered that he thought I might be quite useful.

But I was indentured for four years and I had not yet served two. My mother had undertaken to pay a premium of fifty pounds and had already paid forty. She was dismayed beyond measure to find that once again, apparently, I was to come unstuck. She wept and prayed me to "try again"; Freddy was "trying." If only I would "pray for help" in the right quarter. I explained I didn't want help of that sort from any quarter. I had discovered that the drapery business was a dismal trap and I meant to get out of it. My father was invoked and first he supported and then opposed my liberation.

Byatt made an offer. It was the salvation of my situation. It made my revolt reasonable. I might go as a student assistant in the Grammar School; at first he suggested without pay and then decided that he would pay me twenty pounds a year and raise this to forty after a twelve-month. He had a faith in my grant-earning capacity that I was to justify beyond expectation and this inspired him.

I had reached a vital crisis of my life, I felt extraordinarily desperate and, faced with binding indentures and maternal remonstrances, I behaved very much like a hunted rabbit that turns at last and bites. A hunted rabbit that turned and bit would astonish and defeat most ordinary pursuers. I had discovered what were to be for me for some years the two guiding principles of my life. "If you want something sufficiently, take it and damn the consequences," was the first and the second was: "If life is not good enough for you, change it; never endure a way of life that is dull and dreary, because after all the worst thing that can happen to you, if you fight and go on fighting to get out, is defeat, and that is never certain to the end which is death and the end of everything."

Among other things, during that dismal two years, I had thought out some very fundamental problems of conduct. I had really weighed the possibilities of the life before me, and when I used suicide as a threat to shake my mother's opposition to my liberation, it was after a considerable amount of meditation along the Southsea sea front and Portsmouth Hard. I did not think suicide an honourable resort, but it seemed to me a lesser evil than acquiescence. The cool embrace of swift-running, black deep water on a warm summer night couldn't be as bad as crib hunting or wandering about the streets with the last of one's courage gone. There it was in reserve anyhow. Why should I torture myself to earn a living, any old living? If the living isn't good enough, why live?

Not perhaps with that much virility did I think at the time, but in that fashion, I was beginning to think.

I do not remember now the exact order of events in my liberation nor when it was I wrote to Byatt. But I know things were precipitated by some row of which I have forgotten every particular. On some issue I had been insubordinate, deliberately disobeyed orders. There had to be trouble. The matter was something beyond J. K., and I should have to see the G. V. At any rate I got up early one Sunday morning and started off without breakfast to walk the seventeen miles to Up Park and proclaim to my mother that things had become intolerable and this drapery experiment had to end. I think that was the first intimation the poor little lady had of my crisis.

I have told just how that happened in *Tono Bungay* and how I waylaid the procession of servants as they were coming up Harting Hill from Harting Church. I appeared among the beeches and bracken on the high bank. "Cooee Mummy," said I, white-faced and tired, but carrying it off gaily.

The bad shilling back again!

I remember too an act of singular ungraciousness on my part. When at length it had been arranged that my indentures should be cancelled, Mr. Hyde bethought himself of the summer sale that was imminent, when every hand, however incompetent, was welcome. "Would I at least stay on for that?" It meant another month of shop, just four weeks more. I refused obstinately, would not hear of it. There was no real need for me to go to Midhurst for a month yet; the school would not reassemble until September, but I had already anticipated a month of perfervid reading. I felt I was already nearly two years behind those fellows who went to public schools. I had to be after them without any further delay.

Still more vivid is my memory of being alone in a railway compartment between Portsmouth and Petersfield junction,*en route* for Midhurst. My small but faithful portmanteau was on the seat before me. I could not keep still, and after flitting restlessly from one window to another and back again and trying to read, I found it necessary to express my feelings by a staggering dance and a song, a song consisting, I seem to remember, of disrespectful improvisations about the Southsea Drapery Emporium, and more particularly about "old J. K." (Which Emporium was, I insist, after all far above the average of drapers' shops and very decently run, and J. K. an excellent man.) But this chant and breakdown about my exodus from drapery, set to a railway rhythm, is now lost beyond recovery.

"Puff and rumble old J.K. old J.K. old J.K.
"Damn-the-boy has got away, *got* away, *got* away
"Damn-the-boy has got away, got away for ever."

Something in that fashion at any rate.

§ 2. THE Y.M.C A., THE FREETHINKER;
A PREACHER AND THE READING ROOM

This chapter in the history of the adventures of a sample human brain in the latter phase of the Private Capitalist System, must go a little deeper than the story of a misfit, a discontent and an escape, if it is to do justice to the phases through which a clear and firm vision of a world renewed, and a plain satisfying and sustaining objective in life, were built up in it. The educational influence of Up Park was going on during these two years and during the subsequent student period at Midhurst and in London. And, in addition, this now hungry and excited cortex was seizing upon and annexing whatever was relevant to the matters that were becoming of primary importance in the scheme of things it was making for itself. There was a clerk in the office at Southsea, named Field, who had found religion and showed a certain interest in me. He introduced me to the Young Men's Christian Association in Landport, where there was a reading room and a circulating library. And another clerk I have already mentioned, named West, prided himself upon his theology and talked interestingly about religious services. I would spend my Sunday evenings, especially in winter, in attending the various religious services; there was a fashionable high Anglican in Southsea, popular preachers to be heard in the Catholic cathedral, duller but still tolerable entertainment in other chapels and churches. There was also a secularist society in an upstairs room where a number of quiet men rejoiced discreetly when a church was struck by lightning. My still vague and instinctive disbelief in Christianity had now to be put through a closer scrutiny.

Except for a deep resentment of social inequality and particularly of the unfairness of letting those other fellows go to college, I had still hardly the rudiments of social, economic or political ideas. I don't remember any Socialism at this time. There was a "Parliament" which met in the reading room of the Y.M.C.A. and I attended its sessions regularly. It was one of those parodies of the House of Commons, similar to the one in Camden Town wherein figured the parental Harmsworth, the father of Northcliffe and Rothermere. Ambitious barristers, local politicians and embryo journalists, familiarized themselves with the current phrases of politics and the methods of debate, but I found the pedantries of procedure confusing and I could not make head or tail of most of the issues of the time: "Leasehold Enfranchisement" or Our Foreign Policy or Egypt, an Extra Penny on the Income Tax, Licensing Laws and so forth. It bothered me a lot to witness all this mental excitement and not to have a clue to it. Where did it join on—to theology for example?

My mind was still exploring fundamentals in a profoundly dissatisfied mood, and it was working at a level that was too far down to establish any contact between these fundamentals and the political issues of the day. It still seemed to me to be of primary importance to find out if there was, after all, a God, and if so whether he was the Christian God and which sort of Christian God he was. In the absence of a God what *was* this universe and how was it run? Had it ever begun and had it any trend? I knew now something of geology and astronomy and I had a crude conception of Evolution. But the proposition that "somebody must have made it all," had been stuck into my mind early in life and it was only much later that I realized that there was a flaw in this assumption. Such questions seemed to me already of far more importance than satisfying J. K. or securing a satisfactory "ref" when my apprenticeship was up, and they drove that mock Parliament stuff completely off the stage.

I was still much exercised by what might happen when my earthly apprenticeship as a whole, was over. It seemed to me much more important to know whether or no I was immortal than whether or no I was to make a satisfactory shop assistant. It might be a terrible thing to be out of a crib on the Thames Embankment but it would be a far more terrible thing to be out of a crib for ever in the windy spaces of nothingness. Jeering at the Trinity did not dismiss the God idea, nor disbelief in hell the idea of immortality. I realized that unless my memory was very bad indeed I had had a comparatively recent beginning, but I found it difficult to suppose I should ever have an end. I tried to imagine how it would feel not to exist and my imagination failed me. I did all the queer things that everyone, I suppose, does at this stage. I would sit on my bed in my cubicle trying to withdraw my mind from all external things and think through the universe to the Inner Reality. I would lie quite still in my bed invoking the Unknown to "Speak now. Give me a sign."

On my matching expeditions, when I had to go from Southsea to the Landport Drapery Bazaar, I passed through some side streets in which an obscure but spirited newspaper shop displayed a copy of a weekly called the *Freethinker*. Each week had a cheerful blasphemous caricature, which fell in very agreeably with my derisive disposition. I looked for this very eagerly and when I could afford it I bought a copy. In regard to the religions it confirmed my worst suspicions but it left me altogether at a loss for some general statement of my relation to the stars.

Field tried to save my soul. He was strongly evangelical. He took me home to cold supper with his family on several Sunday nights and I participated in some lusty hymn singing. He induced me as a personal favour to pray for faith, but I doubt if I put much power into my prayers. He induced me to read various theological books, but for the most part these deepened my scepticism, by "answering" unconvincingly various objections of which I had been previously unaware. The answer faded and the objection remained. One of those apologetic works stands out in my memory still; I read it with peculiar delight and shared my glee with West. It was Drummond's *Natural Law in the Spiritual World*. Drummond tried to make various leading Christian dogmas more acceptable by instances drawn from natural history. The Virgin Birth for instance was sustained by a dissertation on parthenogenesis and the prolific summer generation of the green fly was invoked to justify the ways of the Holy Ghost to man.

Somewhen during my stay at Portsmouth my mother wrote to me about my confirmation as a Member of the Church of England. I did not take up the suggestion. Then I was summoned to the inner office by Mr. Hyde, who told me my mother had written to him about it, and that I was to go to the Vicar of Portsmouth to be prepared. I remember one interview. Perhaps it was towards the end of my truncated apprenticeship, because I recall only one. I told the vicar that I believed in Evolution and that I could not understand upon that hypothesis, when it was the Fall had occurred. The vicar did not meet my objections but warned me against the sin of presumption. But it seemed to me to be equally presumptuous to affirm a scheme of salvation as to deny it. And if it was presumptuous to set up my private judgment against all the divines of Christendom, it is surely even more presumptuous to set up one's judgment against all the philosophers of China, India, Islam and the Ancient World.

All of which points were subsequently argued with very great heat after "lights out" in the dormitory, until Rodgers the apprentice next above me, set up a great outcry and said he would listen to blasphemy no longer. "Smut," said Rodgers, "I can stand. There's no harm as I can see in a good smutty story. But this here Blasphemy!..."

One picture of this last phase of critical suspense about the quality and significance of Christianity still stands out in my mind. It is a memory of a popular preacher preaching one Sunday evening in the Portsmouth Roman Catholic cathedral. It was in the course of a revivalist mission and I had been persuaded to go with one of the costume room assistants who played elder sister to me. The theme was the extraordinary merit of Our Saviour's sacrifice and the horror and torment of hell from which he had saved the elect. The preacher had a fluting voice and a faintly foreign accent, a fine impassioned white face, burning eyes and self conscious hands. He was enjoying himself thoroughly. He spared us nothing of hell's dreadfulness. All the pain and anguish of life as we knew it, every suffering we had ever experienced or imagined, or read about, was as nothing to one moment in the unending black despair of hell. And so on. For a little while his accomplished volubility carried me with him and then my mind broke into amazement and contempt. This was my old childish nightmare of God and the flaming wheel; this was the sort of thing to scare ten year olds.

I looked at the intent faces about me, at the quiet gravity of my friend and again at this gesticulating voluble figure in the pulpit, earnest, intensely earnest—for his effect. Did this actor believe a word of the preposterous monstrosities he was pouring out? Could anyone believe it? And if not, why did he do it? What was the clue to the manifest deep satisfaction, the fearful satisfaction of the believers about me? What had got hold of them?

And from that my eyes and thoughts went, with all the amazement of new discovery, about the crowded building in which I was sitting, its multitudinous gas and candle flames, its aspiring columns, its glowing altar, the dim arched roof, which had been made to house this spouting fount of horrible nonsense. A real fear of Christianity assailed me. It was not a joke; it was nothing funny as the *Freethinker* pretended. It was something immensely formidable. It was a tremendous human fact. We, the still congregation, were spread over the floor, not one of us daring to cry out against this fellow's threats. Most of us in some grotesque way seemed to like the dreadful stuff.

So far the revolt of my mind had been against the God of Hell in his most Protestant form, it had been as it were a duel; but now I perceived myself in the presence of a different, if parallel attack upon my integrity, the Catholic Church, a mass attack, the attack of an organization, of a great following. I realized as if for the first time, the menace of these queer shaven men in lace and petticoats who had been intoning, responding and going through ritual gestures at me. I realized something dreadful about them. They were thrusting an incredible and ugly lie upon the world and the world was making no such resistance as I was disposed to make to this enthronement of cruelty. Either I had to come into this immense luminous coop and submit, or, I had to declare the Catholic Church, the core and substance of Christendom with all its divines, sages, saints and martyrs, with successive thousands of millions of believers, age after age, wrong.

In the mouth of the Vicar of Portsmouth "presumption" had seemed a light word, but now I saw it as a grave, immense defiance. To deny was to assert that error had ruled the world so far and wisdom was only beginning—with scared little chaps like me. How could I dare?

That was the terrific alternative my friend presently put to me and which West of the booking desk, sitting eloquent on my bed in the dormitory after "lights out," enforced. I had not the wit to say then or the clearness of mind to see, that wisdom begins again with every birth and that there is no arrogance at all in perpetually putting the past on trial.

It was, I think, the illuminated figure of that mellifluous preacher which decided me in my recalcitrance. Cathedrals maintain their argument best when they are beautifully silent or when they echo to music and chanting in strange mysterious phrases. Catholicism should imply everything and assert nothing, and generally it does, but this missioner brought the issue down for me to concrete and personal terms. The beautiful hands haunted me with an immense unconvincingness. Face and voice appealed in vain. My perception was invincible; the man was an actor; he was making the most of a part. At best he had had the will to believe and not the will for truth.

Through him the Church and its authority, were laid bare to me. He had feared and acquiesced where I had not feared and acquiesced, he found a pleasure and excitement in imparting his fear and acquiescence, he had fitted himself into the incredible and I despised him. I had to despise him. I could no other. The thing he believed was so impossible to me that I could not imagine it being believed in good faith. Could anyone who had even tried for truth believe it? And if I despised him then it was natural to proceed to despise all these like-minded individuals and all who succumbed to him.

I found my doubt of his essential integrity, and the shadow of contempt it cast, spreading out from him to the whole Church and religion of which he with his wild spoutings about the agonies of hell, had become the symbol. I felt ashamed to be sitting there in such a bath of credulity.

It marks a new phase in mental development when one faces ideas not simply as ideas but as ideas embodied in architecture and usage and every-day material fact, and still resists. Hitherto I had taken churches and cathedrals as being as much a part of indisputable reality as my hands and feet. They had imposed themselves upon me as a necessary part of urban scenery just as I had taken Windsor Castle and Eton College as natural growths of the Thames valley. But somehow this Portsmouth Cathedral, perhaps because it had been newly built and so seemed more active than a time-worn building, took on the quality of an engine rather than an edifice. It was a big disseminator; it was like one of that preacher's gestures tempered and made into a permanent implement; it was there to put hell and fear and submission into people's minds. And from this starting apprehension, my realization that all religious buildings are in reality kinetic, spread out more and more widely to all the other visible things of human life. They were all, I began to see dimly, ideas,—ideas clothed and armed with substance. It was as impossible just to say that there was no hell and no divine Trinity and no atonement, and then leave these things alone, as to declare myself republican or claim a right to an equal education with everyone else, without moving towards a clash with Windsor and Eton. These things existed and there was no denying it. If I denied the ideas they substantiated then I proposed to push them off my earth; no less.

The ideas I had on my side to pit against these great realized systems seemed terribly bare and feeble from this point of view. But they possessed me. I felt small and scared but obdurate.

I was still half a lifetime away from the full realization that if one does not accept the general ideas upon which the existing world of men is based, one is bound to set about replanning and reconstructing the world on the ideas one finds acceptable. Ultimately I was to come to a vision of a possible state of human affairs in which scarcely one familiar landmark would remain. But revolution on that scale was beyond the courage of my youthful imagination. I was definitely in opposition to the structural concepts of this world into which I had come, and that is as far as I went. I was almost cowed into conformity by the realization of the magnitude of the structures involved. I was in rebellion, but it was still quite impotent rebellion.

I have already mentioned that the Emporium boasted a library for its assistants. This consisted mainly of popular novels. I had made a rule for myself which I kept for several years, never to read a work of fiction or play a game. This was not so priggish as it seems. I was greedy to learn, I had the merest scraps of time to learn in, and I knew the seduction of a good story and the disturbance of a game of skill. So the novels in the bookcase I left alone. But there were also one or two other books to which I owe a good deal. There was one of those compilations for the mentally hungry that have played so important a part in supplementing the deficiencies of formal education in the British communities in the nineteenth century. I cannot trace it now. It may have been Cassell's *Popular Educator*—I seem to have named that to Geoffrey West and he has jumped to the conclusion that I bought that in parts as it was issued. That was due to his natural desire for animating detail. I never did. I hadn't the pocket money to buy anything in parts. On the whole I think that the book I have in mind was more probably some compact encyclopædic production of that sound hardheaded Edinburgh firm, Chambers. It had long summaries of the views of various philosophical schools and of the physical and biological sciences, made I should imagine by competent and conscientious Scots.

I read these cautious and explicit summaries greedily. They cleared up and put my ideas in order. I acquired a number of mental tools at that time; I exercised my mind upon words and phrases and forms of thought. I found myself balancing such oppositions as "subjective" and "objective" and "pessimism" and "optimism." I meditated (with magnificently insufficient data) upon the corpuscular and vibratory conception of a light ray. I asked, what is health? It seems improbable that I did not then encounter the opposition of socialism and individualism, but oddly enough I cannot recall having thought at all about socialism until I read Henry George at Midhurst. I waived my temperamental scepticism before the Conservation of Energy and the sufficiency of Natural Selection. I drew fine distinctions of no practical value between pantheism and atheism.

I tried these new ideas upon West and Platt and others. West was always good for discussion but Platt was uncertain.

"God may be everywhere," said Platt, "or God may be nowhere. That's *His* look out. It doesn't alter the fact we've got to stack these bloody cretonnes before eleven."

Undated Letter c. 1883, page 1.

Undated Letter c. 1883, page 2.

[Number illegible] Kings Road, Southsea

My dear Mother,

By borrowing some money I was enabled to go to

Medhurst on Saturday. Mr Byatt received me very kindly & gave me a dinner & took me over his new house.

He informs me that I am too old to enter the teaching profession in the ordinary way as a pupil teacher in an elementary school and that my only method would be to obtain a position as an assistant teacher in a middle class school. In any case, for about nine or ten months I should have to maintain myself.

He offers to take me in his own school after the next holidays in September. I should have more instruction to receive than work to do for a little while, and he could therefore give me no wages and I should have to keep myself.
There is an assistant master there and he informs me that he pays an old lady 3/- a week for a bed room share in her sitting room and to do his cooking, and he estimates his total expenses (including this 3/-) washing and food to be under 10/- a week.

(Of course the cost of clothes for a schoolmaster is [not?] half that of a draper)

Now I had a talk with this assistant master and he informs me that if I choose to come I can share his room & old ladyfor 2/6 a week.

This means that for a little while you would have to pay 10/- a week for me or, estimating clothes to cost about £10 a year, you would have to pay for me about £35 in the year for one year more.

But then, when the start is made, there is every prospect

of rising to a good position in the world while in my present trade I am a drapers assistant throughout life.

But I must begin at once, if I start at all I must start next September.
Which would you prefer?

I leave the matter in your hands & remain

Your aff son.

H G Wells

PS Have you written to [illegible] about the holidays.

§ 3. FIFTH START IN LIFE—MIDHURST (1883- 84)

Midhurst has always been a happy place for me. I suppose it rained there at times but all my memories of Midhurst are in sunshine. The Grammar School was growing, the school-house had been built and was now occupied by Byatt and his family and filled up with a score or more of boarders; there was already an usher named Harris and presently came a third man Wilderspin who taught French and Latin. I lodged, and shared a bedroom with Harris, over a little sweetstuff shop next to the *Angel* Hotel. For a time, until the school reassembled I had this room alone.

In a novel of mine called *Love and Mr. Lewisham* which is about just such a Grammar School teacher as I was, I have described how he had pinned up on his wall a "Schema," planned to make the utmost use of his time and opportunities. I made that *Schema*, even to the pedantry of calling it that and not calling it plainly a scheme. Every moment in the day had its task. I was never to rest while I was awake. Such things—like my refusal to read novels or play games—are not evidence of an intense and concentrated mind; they are evidence of an acute sense of the need for concentration in a discursive and inattentive brain. I was not attacking the world by all this effort and self-control; I was making my desperate get-away from the shop and the street. I was bracing myself up tremendously. Harris and I would go for one-hour walks and I insisted on a pace of four miles an hour. During this pedestrianism we talked in gasping shouts.

Mrs. Walton my landlady who kept the sweetstuff shop, was a dear little energetic woman with a round friendly face, brown eyes and spectacles. I owe her incalculable things. I paid her twelve shillings a week and she fed me well. She liked cooking and she liked her food to be eaten. My meals at Midhurst are the first in my life that I remember with pleasure. Her stews were marvellously honest and she was great at junket, custard and whortleberry and blackberry jam. Bless her memory.

I taught in the main classroom with Byatt and he kept an eye on what I was doing and gave me some useful advice. He knew how to be lucid, persuasive and helpful. A system of neatly written out homework held his instruction together. I rather suspect he was a trained elementary teacher before he took his Dublin degree and anyhow I learned a lot from him in handling my class of small boys. I was disposed to be over strenuous with them as I was over strenuous with myself, and my discipline was hard at times; I pushed and shoved them about because both I and they preferred that immediate treatment to impositions and detention, but I helped them whenever I grasped their difficulties and I got them along at a good pace.

The brightest and best of the bunch was "Master Horry," Byatt's eldest; he was quick and plastic and my approval gave him just that confidence in his personal quality that sent him right up the school ahead of his age and won him an open scholarship at, I think, *Merchant Taylors*. Half a century later he came to see me at Easton, a dried-up ex- colonial official, Sir Horace Byatt, retired from Uganda and house-hunting in Essex. He had become terribly my senior and terribly an Imperialist, and though I knew Sir Harry Johnston and Sir James Currie well and had some general ideas about African colonial conditions, I could not penetrate his official reticence. It was all too evident that he thought the less that radical fellows of my stamp, knew, said or did about high Imperial matters the better. Mrs. Christabel McLaren had come down from London for lunch that day and she pulled his leg by expressing an extravagant admiration for Trotsky. Sir Horace seemed incapable of regarding a Bolshevik as anything more human than a cuttle fish and his deepening suspicion of her was very amusing. "And *that's* the sort of boy you made," said Mrs. McLaren when he had departed. We met once afterwards, before his death in 1933, at a city dinner to the Colonial Premiers. He still seemed puzzled about me. So far as I know, none of my other Midhurst boys made any notable success in life.

But half the work I did for Byatt was done not as a teacher but as a student. His university degree qualified him to organize evening classes in any of the thirty-odd subjects in the science scheme of the Education Department, and to earn grants on his examination results. Accordingly, in addition to the three or four normal classes of a dozen or so evening students which he had hitherto conducted, he now organized a number of others for my especial benefit. They were, to put it plainly, bogus classes; they included some subjects of which he knew little or nothing, and in none did he do any actual teaching. The procedure was to get me a good textbook, written for the examination in the subject in question, and to set me to read it in the schoolroom, while he at his desk attended to his correspondence. In this way I read up such subjects as physiography (Huxley's revival of the subject-matter of my old friend Humboldt's *Cosmos*), human physiology, vegetable physiology, geology, elementary "inorganic" chemistry, mathematics and so forth. In May came the examinations and, after that, if I got an "advanced" first class he earnt four pounds, two pounds for a second "advanced" and so in diminishing amounts for a first or second "elementary."

The immediate result, so far as my mind was concerned, was to make me read practically the whole outline of physical and biological science, with as much care and precision as the check of a written examination imposes. I learnt a great deal very easily, but I also did a large amount of strenuous "mugging up." I remember for example toiling laboriously through the account of brain anatomy, illustrated by puzzling woodcuts of sections, in an old edition of Kirk's*Anatomy*. To understand the relations of ventricles, ganglion masses and commissures is not by any means difficult if the knowledge is built up in successive phases according to the embryonic development, but attacked at first from the point of view of adult structure, without the help of models and with no one to question upon the meaning of a difficult phrase, that was pretty hard going. And I also remember struggling with diagrams and paper models to grip the elusive demonstration of the earth's rotation by Foucault's pendulum experiment. And after a pretty slick introduction to electricity I got into heavy country, in Deschanel's textbook, where the tubes of force were gathered together. My realization that I knew a great deal more about things in general than most of the people about me, was balanced by another, that there were people in the world whose minds must be able to run and leap easily among these difficulties where mine wriggled and crawled most painfully.

But anyhow my reading was good enough to produce a cluster of A I's when the examination results came to hand.

Unfortunately for my headmaster, who had hoped to repeat this exploit on a still larger scale next year, I passed these May examinations with such a bang, that I was blown out of Midhurst altogether.

The Education Department of that period was not completely

satisfied with the quality of the science teaching it was disseminating about the country, and it was trying to develop its scattered classes into organized science schools and to produce a better type of teacher than the classical graduates, clergymen and so forth, on whom it had at first to rely. Accordingly it was circularizing its successful examinees, with the offer of a certain number of free studentships, at the Normal School of Science, South Kensington, carrying with them a maintenance grant of a guinea a week during the session and second class railway fare to the capital. I read the blue form with incredulity, filled it up secretly and with trepidation, and presently found myself accepted as a "teacher in training" for a year in the biological course under Professor Huxley—the great Professor Huxley, whose name was in the newspapers, who was known all over the world!

Byatt shared my surprise if not my elation.

I had come to Midhurst a happy but desperate fugitive from servitude; I left it in glory. I spent my summer vacation partly at Up Park with my mother and partly with my father at Bromley, and I was hardly the same human being as the desperate, footsore, youngster who had tramped from Portsmouth to Up Park, breathing threats of suicide. My mother did not like to cast a shadow on my happiness, but yet she could not conceal from me that she had heard that this Professor Huxley was a notoriously irreligious man. But when I explained that he was Dean of the Normal School, her fears abated, for she had no idea that there could be such a thing as a lay Dean.

Later on my mother thought and learnt more about the Dean. I have described the quaint simple faith in Providence, Our Father and Our Saviour, by which to the best of her ability she guided her life and the lives of her family. I have guessed at a failure of belief in her after the trials of Atlas House and the loss of her "poor Possy." Whatever reality her religion had had for her ebbed away after that. She wept with dismay when I came blustering from Southsea to say I would not be confirmed, but I think it was social rather than religious dismay. I said I was an "Atheist," a frightful word for her to hear, as bad as swearing. "My dear!" she cried. "Don't say such *dreadful* things!" And then, good little Protestant that she was, she found consolation. "Better than being caught by those Old Priests," she said, "anyhow."

She could never talk about her religion except in set phrases, but slowly the last vestiges of faith faded out. Towards the end of her life her mind flattened and faded very much. She still went to church but I doubt if she prayed with her will and thought any more. Her phases of reverie flowed past with less and less circumstance and definition, ceasing to ripple at last, smoothing down towards a silvery stream of nothingness.

The idea of immortality lost its necessity for her and I think the prospect of a Resurrection began to seem rather an unnecessary and tiresome fuss ahead of her. And that is where Huxley came in. After her death I found this in her little brass-footed work-box, copied out in her old slow angular Italian handwriting on a browning piece of notepaper:

"These lines, once written by Mrs. Huxley, have been placed over the tomb of the late Professor Huxley at his own request:

> "*And if there be no meeting past the grave,*
> "*If all is darkness, silence, yet 'tis rest;*
> "*Be not afraid ye waiting hearts that weep,*
> "*For God still giveth his beloved sleep*
> "*And if an endless sleep He wills, so best.*"

§ 4. FIRST GLIMPSES OF PLATO —AND HENRY GEORGE

Cramming myself with knowledge for examinations as my immediate objective, was by no means the sole occupation of my mind at Midhurst. Now that my theological turmoil was subsiding to a sort of Cause and Effect Deism, I was waking up to the importance of the strands of relationship that held me, though not inflexibly, in my place in the social web. Just as it had dawned upon me with an effect of profound discovery that the Roman Catholic cathedral at Portsmouth *need not be there*, so now it was to become apparent that Up Park need not be there, that the shops in the Midhurst street need not be there, nor the farmers and labourers on the countryside. The world would still turn on its axis, if all these things were replaced by different structures and arrangements.

I have already said that I cannot clearly remember when it was that I read Plato's *Republic*. But it was somewhen before I went to London and it was in summer time, because I remember lying on the grass slope before a little artificial ruined tower that, in the true spirit of the eighteenth century, adorned the brow of the Up Park Down overlooking Harting. The translation of the Dialogues, was all by itself in a single green bound volume, happily free from Introduction or Analysis. I must have puzzled over it and skipped and gone to and fro in it, before its tremendous significance came through. A certain intellectual snobbishness in me may have helped me to persevere. And associated with it, because of its fermenting influence upon my mind, is a book of a very different calibre, a six-penny paper-covered edition of Henry George's *Progress and Poverty* which I bought in a newspaper shop in Midhurst. This last was, I suppose, published by some propagandist Single Tax organization. These two books caught up and gave substance to a drift of dispositions and desires in my mind, that might otherwise have dispersed and left no trace.

Plato in particular, as I got to the mighty intention behind his (to me) sometimes very tedious and occasionally incomprehensible characters, was like the hand of a strong brother taking hold of me and raising me up, to lead me out of a prison of social acceptance and submission. I do not know why Christianity and the old social order permitted the name of Plato to carry an intellectual prestige to my mind far above that of Saint Paul or Moses. Why has there been no detraction? I suppose because the Faithful have never yet been able to escape from a certain lurking self-criticism, and because in every age there have been minds more responsive to the transparent honesty and greatness of Plato and Aristotle than to the tangled dogmatism of the Fathers. But here was a man wearing the likeness of an Olympian God, to whom every scholarly mind and every clerical back bowed down in real or imposed respect, who had written things of a revolutionary destructiveness beyond my darkest mutterings. Hitherto there had always been something insurgent, inferior, doubtful and furtive in my objections to the religious, moral and social systems to which my life had, it seemed, to be adapted. All my thoughts leapt up now in open affirmation to the novel ideas he opened out to me.

Chief of these was the conception of a society in which economic individualism was overruled entirely in the common interest. This was my first encounter with the Communist idea. I had accepted property as in the very nature of things, just as my mother had accepted the Monarchy and the Church. I had been so occupied with my mental rebellion against the ideas of God and King, that hitherto I had not resented the way in which the Owner barred my way here, forbade me to use this or enjoy that. Now with Plato's picture of an entirely different social administration before me, to make a comparison possible, I could ask "*By what right*—is this for you and not for me?" Why are things monopolized? Why was everything appropriated and every advantage secured against me before I came into the world?

Henry George's book came in like a laboratory demonstration to revivify a general theory, with his extremely simplified and plausible story of the progressive appropriation of land, his attack upon the unearned increment of private rents and his remedy of a single tax to make, in effect, rents a collective benefit. His was an easy argument to understand, as he put it, and I was able to modify it and complicate it for myself by bringing in this or that consideration which he had excluded. It was like working kindred mathematical problems of progressive complexity under a common Rule. It was quite easy to pass from the insistence of Henry George upon the inalienable claim of the whole community to share in the benefit of land, to the simpler aspects of interest and monetary appreciation. I became what I may call a Socialist in the Resentful Phase, and what was happening to me was happening to millions of the new generation in Europe and America. Something—none of us knew how to define it but we called it generally the Capitalist System—a complex of traditional usage, uncontrolled acquisitive energy and perverted opportunities, was wasting life for us and we were beginning to realize as much. But at that time in the whole world there was really no explicit realization that this was due not to a system but to an absence of system.

Now it happened to me that the chances, by which one meets or escapes books, so worked at Midhurst that I scarcely heard the name of Karl Marx until I came to London. My socialism was pre-Marxian. I had read something about Robert Owen, I think, in that encyclopædic book in the Southsea Emporium reading-room, and I must have met with some summary of More's *Utopia*, though I do not remember reading it until much later, and essentially my ideas were built on the "primitives" of socialism. I was all for planning a new society. But it seemed plainly unnecessary to clear the old confusion out of the way before the new order came. As a planned order comes, the confusion disappears of itself. It was only after a year and more of biological work at the Normal School of Science, that I came full face upon Marxism and by that time I was equipped to estimate at its proper value its plausible, mystical and dangerous idea of reconstituting the world on a basis of mere resentment and destruction: the Class War. Overthrow the "Capitalist System" (which never was a system) was the simple panacea of that stuffy, ego-centred and malicious theorist. His snobbish hatred of the bourgeoisie amounted to a mania. Blame somebody else and be violent when things go wrong, is the natural disposition of the common man in difficulties all the world over. Marx offered to the cheapest and basest of human impulses the poses of a pretentious philosophy, and the active minds amidst the distressed masses fell to him very readily. Marxism is in no sense creative or curative. Its relation to the inevitable reconstruction of human society which is now in progress, is parasitic. It is an enfeebling mental epidemic of spite which mankind has encountered in its difficult and intricate struggle out of out-worn social conditions towards a new world order. It is the malaria of the Russian effort to this day. There would have been creative revolution, and possibly creative revolution of a far finer type if Karl Marx had never lived.

Still happily unaware of the immense frustrations that awaited the urge towards a new social order, I walked about the russet lanes and green shaded paths of Midhurst, talking over the stuff that was in my mind with Harris, or dreaming of the new rational state that I supposed to be at hand when what was plain to me had become plain to everybody. We were a shabby-looking couple in ready-made clothes, going swiftly and talking volubly. Harris had a grave Red Indian profile and his share in the conversation was mostly nodding judiciously. Or he would say "That's all right; that is," or "I don't see that." I was "shooting up" and growing a little out of my garments, but our generally unkempt appearance was redeemed by the fact that we wore "mortar boards" college caps like those worn by Oxford or

Cambridge undergraduates, to maintain about the Grammar School a suggestion of erudition.

So, by way of Plato, I got my vision of the Age of Reason that was just about to begin. Never did anyone believe more firmly in the promptitude of progress than I. I had to learn even the elements of human behaviour in those days and I had no sense of the immense variety of mind-build and working conviction that was possible. I do not seem to have had a suspicion that there was such a force as social inertia to be reckoned with. I lived no longer in reverie, I looked at the world, but I saw it as yet with a divine simplicity; all that was not simple about it was speedily going to be; all its declensions and verbs were going to be made regular almost immediately and everything conjugated in the indicative mood. Socialism was plainly ahead of us all, when everyone would be active and happy.

It was not only with regard to Economics that my mind had become liberated and moved now with a sanguine simplicity. I was also filled with strange and stimulating ideas about sexual life. Sexual urgencies were becoming more insistent in me with enhanced health and courage. There had been a great amount of smutty and indecent conversation behind the counters at Southsea, but like the foul talk of my schoolfellows at Bromley, it was curious and derisive rather than amorous. It dissipated rather than stimulated desire. Almost completely disconnected in my mind from that stream of not very harmful uncleanness there had been a certain amount of superficial flirtatiousness with the girl apprentices and women assistants, rather after the fashion of the posturing politenesses and pretended devotions I had learnt from my cousins at Surly Hall. The costume hands were by profession young ladies with figures; they attracted the apprentices and professed a sisterly affection for them in order to have them available as escorts and the like, but this relationship never came to kisses or caresses. So far as I was concerned the "good figure" of that period, with its tight long stays, its padded bustle behind, its single consolidated bosom thrust forward and its "Grecian bend" thrust back, had scarcely anything to recall the deep breasted Venuses and Britannias who had first awakened my sexual consciousness. The stark and easy generation of to-day can scarcely realize how completely, from the whalebone-assisted collar round its neck to the flounces round its feet, the body of woman was withheld from masculine observation, and how greatly this contributed to the practical effective resistance to "the nude" in art. Men went to the music halls simply for the rare joy of seeing feminine arms, legs and contours, but I had no money to go to a music hall.

Once, I suppose, that one had penetrated these complicated defences and got to the live body inside, one could think of individualized physical love, but at that I never arrived at Southsea or Midhurst. Mother Nature did what she could to egg me on, and stripped a girl apprentice I thought rather pretty and the costume lady who was my official Sister, in my dreams, but the old harridan accompanied this display with so many odd and unnecessary exaggerations and accessory circumstances, that it made me rather more shy and unreal and decorous than ever when I encountered her victims in my waking life. And moreover, at Southsea, the women were in one wing of the premises and we youths and men in another, inaccessible, dragons intervening. Short of a sort of rape of the Sabines and general social dissolution, little was possible. Once or twice at Southsea or Portsmouth a prostitute would make an alluring gesture to me, but a shilling a week of pocket-money gives no scope for mercenary love. At Midhurst I had no feminine associates at all. Mrs. Walton had two grown-up daughters, but she was always alert about her lodgers, and a playful scuffle with the eldest about a penny, sternly suppressed and reprimanded by mother, was as far as passion went in that direction. In vain did Nature intervene and amplify the scuffle in dreamland.

On one occasion, however, I reached a stage nearer the desired reality. It was at Christmas at Up Park and there was a dance in the Servants Hall and the upper and lower servants mingled together. There was a kitchen maid whom I suddenly discovered was pretty beyond words and I danced and danced again with her, until my mother was moved to find other partners for me. She was a warm-coloured girl with liquid brown eyes and a quick pretty flush of excitement. Her name was Mary and that is all the name I ever had for her. And afterwards in one of the underground passages towards the kitchen, where perhaps I was looking for her, she darted out of a recess and kissed and embraced me. No lovelier thing had ever happened to me. Somebody became audible down the passage and she made a last dash at me, pressed her lips to mine and fled. And that is all. Next morning I trundled off in the dog-cart on the frosty road to Rowlands Castle station for Portsmouth, before sunrise, and when next I went to Up Park for a holiday, Mary had gone. I never saw her again and I could not find her name nor where she had gone. My mother who knew would not tell me. But I can feel her heart beat against mine now, I can recall the lithe body in her flimsy yellow dress, and for all I know I have driven my automobile past Mary—an alert old lady I am certain—on some Hampshire road within the last few weeks.

But after that I knew that love was neither filth nor flirtation and I began to want more of it.

As my mind filled up and broadened out at Midhurst I began to resent the state of sexual deprivation in which I was living, more and more explicitly. All over Europe and America youths and maidens fretted under the same deprivation. Not only were their minds being afflicted by that nightmare story of the Ogre-God and his Hell, not only were they being caught helplessly young and jammed for life into laborious, tedious, uninteresting and hopeless employments, but they were being denied the most healthy and delightful freedoms of mutual entertainment. They were being driven down to concealed and debilitating practices and shameful suppressions. Every year the age of marriage was rising and the percentage of marriages was falling, and the gap of stress and vexation between desire and reasonable fulfilment was widening. In that newspaper shop on the way to Landport where I saw and sometimes bought the *Freethinker*, I also found the *Malthusian* displayed, and one or two numbers had been the subject of a lively discussion with Platt and Ross. The Bradlaugh Besant trial had occurred in 1876 and the light of sanity was gradually breaking into the dark places of English sexual life. There was perhaps a stronger belief current then that births were completely controllable than the actual facts warranted. Now under the stimulus of Plato's Utopianism and my quickening desires I began to ask my imagination what it was I desired in women.

I desired and needed their embraces and so far as I could understand it they needed and desired the embraces of men. It came to me as the discovery of a fresh preposterousness in life as it was being lived about me, that there were endless millions of young people in the world in the same state of sexual suspense and unrest as myself, quite unable to free themselves sweetly and honestly from these entangling preoccupations. Quite enough, there was, of either sex to go round. But I did not want an epidemic of marriages. I had not the slightest wish for household or offspring at that time; my ambition was all for unencumbered study and free movement in pursuit of my own ends, and my mind had not the slightest fixation upon any particular individual or type of individual. I was entirely out of accord with the sentimental patterns and focussed devotions adopted by most people about me. In the free lives and free loves of the guardians of the *Republic* I found the encouragement I needed to give my wishes a systematic form. Presently I discovered a fresh support for these tentative projects in Shelley. Regardless of every visible reality about me, of law, custom, social usage, economic necessities and the unexplored psychology of womanhood, I developed my adolescent fantasy of free, ambitious, self-reliant women who would mate with me and go their way, as I desired to go my way. I had never in fact seen or heard of any such women; I had evolved them from my inner consciousness.

This was my preliminary fantasy of love, before I began love-making. It exerted a ruling influence on my conduct for many years. It is remarkable how much we frame our expectations upon such secret fantasies and how completely we ignore the probability that the lovers we encounter may have quite other systems of imagination. The women of the "Samurai" in my *Modern Utopia* (1905), the most Platonic of my books, are the embodiment of these Midhurst imaginings.

So, before I was eighteen, the broad lines of my adult ideas about human life had appeared—however crudely. I was following a road along which at variable paces a large section of the intelligentsia of my generation was moving in England, towards religious scepticism, socialism and sexual rationalism. I had no idea of that general drift about me. I seemed to be thinking for myself independently, but now I realize that multitudes of minds were moving in precisely the same direction. Like forces acting upon like organizations give like results. I suppose when a flight of starlings circles in the air, each single bird feels it is moving on its own initiative.

One glaring omission from my outlook, as I have sketched it here, will be evident at once to the post-war reader. I had scarcely thought at all and I have nothing to tell of my thoughts concerning the problem of war and international relationship. My untravelled political mind was confined within the limits of the Empire. Flags and soldiers, battleships and big guns were already much in evidence in the European landscape and seascape but, until the Boer War at the end of the century, they had not challenged critical attention. I had no idea that the guns went off—except when pointing right away from civilization, in Afghanistan or Zululand or against remote inadequate batteries at Alexandria. They had an air of being in the order of things, much as mountains, earthquakes and sunsets were in the order of things. They made a background. In England they did not invade the common personal life until after 1914.

This was the most conspicuous blind patch in the English liberal outlook at the close of the nineteenth century, but it was not the only one. I was also blankly unaware of the way in which the monetary organization of the world reflected its general economic injustices and ineptitudes. But then I had never yet seen ten sovereigns together of my own in my life, never touched any paper money except a five pound note, nor encountered a cheque. (Bank of England notes were dealt with very solemnly in those days; the water-mark was scrutinized carefully and the payer, after a suspicious penetrating look or so was generally asked to write his name and address on the instrument.) The bags of money and slips of paper I carried to the Portsmouth bank had not aroused me to any sense of significance. I did not suspect that there was anything more treacherous about money than there was about weights and measures. Either I did not know or it did not seem to matter to me that while a yard was always so much of a metre, the pound and the franc and the lira and the dollar were capable of slipping about in their relations to each other, and that prices could execute the most remarkable and disconcerting changes of level. They were not doing so at the time. In those days they were just sinking very gently, and everything was getting cheaper and cheaper.

There were, as I shall point out in due course, still other primary gaps and disproportions in the radical outlook at the close of the nineteenth century, but these were the chief among them. You will find them equally evident in the autobiography of any labour leader of my generation.

§ 5. QUESTION OF CONSCIENCE

At Midhurst I had a queer little struggle between pride and practical wisdom. I did something that wounded my private honour very deeply. I knelt at the altar rail in the parish church and bowed my head to the bishop's hand and was confirmed, meekly and submissively, a member of the Church of England. You may regard that as a mere formality, but I did not see it in that light. I felt as an early Christian may have felt who for sound domestic and worldly reasons, had consented to burn a pinch of incense to Divus Cæsar.

But I had found myself in an extremely tight corner. Byatt realized that I had not yet been confirmed and that by the statutes of the Grammar School, every member of the teaching staff had to be a communicant. If I was to go on to our mutual benefit devouring and regurgitating scientific fact, the matter had to be put right forthwith. I suggested that I might have "doubts." "My dear Fel-low!" boomed Byatt. "My dear Fel-low! You mustn't talk like that. Let me lend you Paley's *Evidences.* That will put you all right about that.... And positively you know you *must.*" ...

Positively I knew I must. There was no visible job for me in the world if I did not stick now to the Midhurst adventure. To abandon it now would have been like jumping from a liner in mid-Atlantic. I ought to have thought of this confirmation business before. If I refused, the whole burthen of the situation would fall on my mother. The more I grew, the smaller and weaker she seemed and the less I cared to hurt her. I consented, to her great joy. For a time I am sure Our Father got some heartfelt thanks and praises again. Byatt arranged for me to be prepared specially and swiftly by the curate, for the approaching Confirmation Service.

Under happier circumstances I might have had a certain amount of fun out of that curate, but I was too mortified and bitter at my own acquiescence. We sat by lamplight opposite one another at a table in his lodgings. He was a fair aquiline sensitive young man, with a fine resonant service voice, who did his best to keep our conversation away from the business in hand as much as possible. But I was sullenly resolved to make him say—all of it. I asked a string of questions about the bearing of Darwinism and geology on biblical history, about the exact date of the Fall, about the nature of Hell, about Transubstantiation and the precise benefit of the communion service and so forth. After each answer I would say "So that is what I have to believe.... I see." I did not attempt to argue. He was one of those people whose faces flush, whose eyes wander off from you and whose voices get higher in pitch at the slightest need for elucidation.

"It's all a little *subtle* you know——," he would begin.

"Still, people might make difficulties afterwards. I want to know what to say to them."

"Oh—precisely." ...

"I suppose it's all right if I just believe this in—er—a spiritual sense."

"It's much *better* that way. It's ever so much better that way. I'm so *glad* you see that."

The organ played, the service proceeded. Side by side with a real young gentleman of my own age I walked up the aisle and knelt. And afterwards I communicated and consumed a small cube presenting my Redeemer's flesh and had a lick of sweetish wine from the chalice which I was assured contained his blood. I was reminded of a crumb of Trifle. Later to please my mother I repeated this performance at Harting and after that I made an end to Theophagy. I derived neither good or ill, so far as I could trace, from these homoeopathic doses of divinity.

But the wound to my private honour smarted for a long time and it was many years before I could forgive the Church for setting these barriers of conformity in my way to social usefulness. I do not think that I have forgiven her altogether even now.

I record that shame and resentment about my confirmation

because it seems to me that this queer little mood of obduracy was something very important in my development. I do not understand it at all clearly myself and still less can I explain it. What made me attach all that importance to that public lie? I wasn't particularly a George Washington for veracity. If I was never a fluent liar I could at any rate lie quite effectively on occasion. And indeed there was a great deal of material about in my conduct for an officious conscience to play upon, without so entire a concentration on this particular lapse. There was no alternative affirmation in mind. There was no sense of an onlooking divinity in protest. I had no other God. I can only explain my feelings by supposing that there was in my make-up a disinterested element, which attached more importance to the denial of Christianity than to my merely personal advantage. There was something in my brain, an impersonal self, that contested my prior right to welfare at the price of lowering my standard of veracity.

I did what I could to ease this conflict in my being by blasphemous facetiousness, until old Harris became a little scared of me. He did not "believe much" in God but he thought it well not to go too far with him.

Harris had no self-conceit; he had a prominent nose and a wary mouth and he went discreetly and ironically through a world which he had found by experience was apt to prove unexpectedly irascible. Something might be fired at me, some thunderbolt he felt, and it would be like his luck if it hit him. "Don't you *say* such things," he said. "Don't you say it." And presently came the distraction of the May examinations and the end of the school term and after a short stay at Up Park I went off to Atlas House to stay with my father until South Kensington was ready to receive me.

My raw mind was so busy at Midhurst with the scramble to get a comprehensive and consistent conception of the principal parts of the universe, in the place of the orthodox interpretations

I was rejecting, that I paid very little attention to another mind-and-purpose drama that was going on beside me. While I was making my thorny way out of Protestantism in one direction, my senior colleague Wilderspin, who lived in the school house, so that I saw very little of him, was *en route* for Rome. Midhurst is one of those places in England which has retained a Catholic congregation from pre-reformation times and a little proselytizing priest flitted about it, very ready to be friendly with any casual young men he might encounter. He had a slightly lewd streak in his conversation that I found repulsive; he pushed his joke at you slily and laughed fatly first, he belonged to that "jolly" school of propagandist which seeks to make it clear that there is none of your damned Kill-Joy Puritanism about the dear old, merry old church; and after a walk and a talk or so with him I avoided him. Among other things, believing me to be a newly confirmed Anglican and having no idea of my real state of mind, he wanted to dispute with me about the validity of Protestant orders. But I did not care a curse about either the Catholic or the Protestant brand of sacerdotalism, except to dislike them both. I was a universe away from that. I was hampered in my talks with him because I did not know what disconcerting use he might make of any sweeping disavowal of Christianity on my part.

But he got Wilderspin and Wilderspin also vanished from Midhurst at the same time as myself.

Years after, when I had a home at Woking, Wilderspin flickered back into my life for a few days as a full fledged itinerant priest. He called to see me and he seemed to be needy, hungry and uncomfortable. Evidently he was working in a sweated industry. He told me he had to go into the oddest of quarters among the faithful, and that recently he had found the nest of a mouse in a bed he had been given. He gave me the impression of being still slightly astonished at the life he was leading and the mental and material disciplines to which he was subjected. We fixed for him to come to dinner and he showed the keenest interest in planning the menu. We chose a day unrestricted by any fasts or disciplines. He came; we feasted, talked over Midhurst and the school and the boys, laughed together more abundantly than we had ever done before, drank, smoked and parted cordially. It was evidently a spree for him. After which I never saw nor heard of him again. Perhaps my cheerful house upset him, and possibly I was hardly the sort of friend a not very austere and devout priest would be encouraged to frequent.

§ 6. WALKS WITH MY FATHER

I had not seen very much of my father for three years and it was interesting to go back to him and stay with him alone, practically on terms of equality. He had been a large person far above me as a schoolboy, but now I was growing up to him at a great pace. We became excellent friends and companions. Atlas House was extensively unscrubbed and shabbier and more threadbare than ever, but my father camped, so to speak, amidst its disorder very comfortably. He cooked very well, far better than my mother had ever done, in the underground kitchen, and made me wash up and look after my own bedroom, and we did not fuss about the other aspects of housekeeping. He was very lame now and he was getting heavy; he stumped about with the help of a thick cabbage stick but he stumped about actively. He was bald and blue-eyed, with a rosy cheerful face and a square beard like King David. He admired my certificates and ambitions frankly and took a lively interest in the elementary science and philosophy I unfolded to him at second-hand.

The shop was in a sort of coma and gave us very little trouble; the only trade left was the sale of cricket goods. He did more business by locking up the front door after teatime and going round to the cricket field. If people were taken with a craving to buy crockery in the evening they knocked and rattled at the door until the craving left them. On Sundays we were free for a long walk and a bread and cheese lunch—or even a cold meat lunch—miles away from home.

He had always been something of a reader and now he was reading widely and freely. He read the *Daily News*—the *Daily News* of Richard Jeffries and Andrew Lang—and *Longman's Magazine*—in the R. L. Stevenson and Grant Allen days; he got books from the Library Institute and picked them up at sales. We gradually broke down the inhibitions about religion and politics natural between father and son, and had a fine various amount of talk and discussion.

In after years I grew away from my father mentally, though we always remained good friends, but during these last years of his at Bromley, we were very much on a level; if I had a lot of knowledge of one sort, he had a lot of another sort and our conversation was a fair exchange. His was a mind of inappeasable freshness, in the strangest contrast to my mother's. I do not think my mother ever had a new idea after she left Miss Riley's school; her ideas faded out, that was all. But my father kept going to the last. He was playing chess, by correspondence, with my mother-in-law when he was in the late seventies, and about that time he unearthed some old school books of mine and started in upon Algebra and the Elements of Euclid, an unknown world to him, acquiring considerable facility in the solution of quadratic equations and the working of "riders" before he desisted. He began now at Atlas House under the stimulus of my studentship and the writings of W. H. Hudson and Grant Allen, to brush up his gardener's botany anew and his countryman's natural history.

Upon all sorts of counts my father was a better man than myself. He had all the delicate nervous and muscular skill and the rapid hardly conscious mental subtleties of a cricketer, he was an instinctive good shot, and at every sort of game he was ripe good wary stuff. We began chess together in these days but while he went on to a sound game I found it too exacting and irritating and gave it up. At draughts I battled with him incessantly, held my own at last but never established a thorough ascendency. About fields and green things and birds and beasts he had a real intimate knowledge that made my accumulation seem bookish and thin. The country round Bromley was being fast invaded by the spreading out of London; eruptions of new roads and bricks and mortar covered lush meadows and, when I was about fifteen or sixteen, that brown and babbling Ravensbourne between its overhanging trees was suddenly swallowed up by a new drainage system, but my father managed to see and make me see a hundred aspects of the old order of things, a wagtail, a tit's nest, a kingfisher, an indisputable trout under a bridge, sun-dew in a swampy place near Keston, the pollen of pine trees drifting like a mist, the eagle in the bracken root (which I could tell him in return was *Pteris aquilina*). "We'll be after them mushrooms at Camden," he'd say. "They'll be just about right now. We'll take a screw of salt for them, my boy, and eat them raw. Then we won't have any bother about saying where we found them." And when we got to Camden there were the mushrooms as though he had evoked them, white buttons straining up out of the turf for us.

He had the knack of reviving the countryside amidst the deluge of suburbanism, just as he had had the knack of growing a grape vine and making a Wigelia bush flourish in that smutty backyard of ours.

One bank holiday, Whit-Monday no doubt, he took advantage of a cheap fare to go back with me to his boyhood at Penshurst. We walked across the park from Tonbridge. He wanted me to see and feel the open life he had led before the shop and failure had caught him. He wanted to see and feel it again himself. "We used to play cricket here—well, it was just about here anyhow—until we lost sight of the ball in the twilight.... There's more bracken and less turf about here now." He talked of a vanished generation of our cousins, the Dukes, and of a half-sister I had never heard of before. She and he had gone fishing together through the dew-wet grass between sunrise and the beginning of the day's work. She was a tall strong girl who could run almost as fast as he could. He repeated that. So I guess his first dreams of women were not so very unlike mine. He showed me where she sat in Penshurst Church. Also he discoursed very learnedly on the growing of willows to make cricket bats and how long it took for a man to learn to make a first-class cricket ball. That was a great day for my father and me.

All his days my father was a happy and appreciative man with a singular distaste for contention or holding his own in the world. He liked to do clever things with his brain and hands and body, but he was bored beyond endurance by the idea of a continual struggle for existence. So was my elder brother Frank. My brother Fred and I may have the same strain in us, but the world made such ugly, threatening and humiliating gestures at us at the outset that we pulled ourselves together and screwed ourselves up for self-repression and a fight, and we fought and subdued ourselves until we were free. Was that a good thing for us or a bad?

I am inclined to think bad. The disposition to acquire and keep hold and accumulate, to work for a position, to secure precedences and advantages was alien to all four of us. It isn't in our tradition; it isn't in our blood; it isn't in our race. We can do good work and we are responsive to team play, we can "play cricket" as the phrase goes, but we cannot sell, bargain, wait, forestall and keep. In a world devoted to private ownership we secure nothing. We get shoved away from opportunity. It was distortion for us to keep our attention on that side of life. I was lucky, as I shall tell, because quite accidentally I suddenly developed extraordinary earning power, which I am still able to exercise, and for thirty years I had my business looked after for me by an extremely competent wife. But I think some very fine possibilities in my brother Fred were diverted to mere saving and shop-keeping.

In a social order where all the good things go to those who constitutionally and necessarily, watch, grab and clutch all the time, the quality of my father, the rich humour and imagination of my brother Frank, were shoved out of play and wasted altogether. In a world of competitive acquisitiveness the natural lot of my sort of people is to be hustled out of existence by the smarties and pushers. A very strong factor in my developing socialism is and always has been the more or less conscious impulses, an increasingly conscious impulse, to anticipate and disarm the smarty and the pusher and make the world safe for the responsive and candid mind and the authentic, artistic and creative worker. In the *Work, Wealth and Happiness of Mankind* I have written about "Clever Alec." He's "rats" to me and at the smell of him I bristle. I set the highest value on people of my own temperament, which is I suppose, a natural and necessary thing to do, and I believe in the long run our sort will do better than their sort, as men do better than rats. We shall build and what we build will stand at last.

But for thousands of generations yet, the bright-eyed, quick incessant rats will infest our buildings, eat our food, get the better of us in all sorts of ways and gnaw and scuttle and scamper. They will muck about with our money, misrepresent our purpose and disposition, falsify ownership and waste and frustrate millions of genial lives.

My father ended his days in a little house at Liss which I was able to rent and afterwards to buy for him, and my mother and my elder brother joined him there. As I began to prosper I was able to increase the income of that ménage until they were quite comfortable by their not very exacting standards; my brother Fred too, away in South Africa, insisted upon paying his share. When I rebelled against the servitude of the draper's shop, my yawps of liberation had been too much for my elder brother and he had thrown up the yardstick also. He had conceived an ideal of country existence from reading Washington Irving's *Bracebridge*

Hall, and he quartered himself with my father first at Rogate and then at Liss, and wandered about the country repairing clocks, peddling watches, appreciating character and talking nonsense. If it was not particularly profitable, it was amusing—and free. There is a touch of my brother about Mr. Polly,—the character I mean, not the story. My father played nap at times and billiards often in the Liss Club Room. My mother sat in reverie, peeped out of the window of the upstairs parlour at passers-by, wrote prim little letters to Freddie and me, dressed more and more like Queen Victoria and went to Church and Holy Communion. (But she did not go to evening service at Liss because she thought it rather "high," surplices, candles, intonation—"too much of it".) My brother peddled his watches and went off on his bicycle, sometimes for days together.

In 1905 my mother slipped and fell downstairs one evening and was hurt internally and died a few weeks later. In her last illness her mind wandered back to Midhurst and she would fuss about laying the table for her father or counting the stitches as she learnt to crochet. She died a little child again. In 1910 my father woke up very briskly one morning, delivered a careful instruction on the proper way to make suet pudding to his housekeeper Mrs. Smith, insisted that it should be chopped small, protested against "lumps the size of my thumb," glanced over the *Daily Chronicle* she had brought him and prepared to get up. He put his legs out of bed and slid down by the side of the bed a dead man. There is an irregularity in our family pulse, it misses a beat ever and again and sooner or later it misses more than one and that is the end of us. My grandfather had leant over a gate to admire the sunset and then ceased to live in the same fashion. This last spring as I write (1933) heart stoppage came also to my elder brother and as he got up from his breakfast, he reeled and fell down dead. But this was a little premature; he was only seventy-seven and my father and grandfather were both eighty-two. I shall hate to leave the spectacle of life but go I must at last, and I hope when my time is fulfilled that I too may depart in this apparently hereditary manner. It seems to me that whatever other defects we have, we have an admirable way of dying.

V. — SCIENCE STUDENT IN LONDON

§ 1. PROFESSOR HUXLEY AND THE SCIENCE OF BIOLOGY (1884-85)

The day when I walked from my lodging in Westbourne Park across Kensington Gardens to the Normal School of Science, signed on at the entrance to that burly red-brick and terra-cotta building and went up by the lift to the biological laboratory was one of the great days of my life. All my science hitherto had been second-hand—or third or fourth hand; I had read about it, crammed text-books, passed written examinations with a sense of being a long way off from the concrete facts and still further off from the living observations, thoughts, qualifications and first-hand theorizing that constitute the scientific reality. Hitherto I had had only the insufficient printed statements, often very badly and carelessly written, of the text-books, eked out by a few perplexing diagrams and woodcuts. Now by a conspiracy of happy accidents I had got right through to contact with all that I had been just hearing about. Here were microscopes, dissections, models, diagrams close to the objects they elucidated, specimens, museums, ready answers to questions, explanations, discussions. Here I was under the shadow of Huxley, the acutest observer, the ablest generalizer, the great teacher, the most lucid and valiant of controversialists. I had been assigned to his course in Elementary Biology and afterwards I was to go on with Zoology under him.

In a very carefully done short story, *A Slip under the Microscope* (*Yellow Book* 1893) and in an equally careful novel, *Love and Mr. Lewisham* (1900) I have rendered something of the physical and social atmosphere of that early biological laboratory. These descriptions were written so much nearer to the actual experience than I am now, that I will not even attempt to parody them here, and it seems hardly fair to quote them. But I must try, however unsuccessfully, to convey something of my realization of an extraordinary mental enlargement as my mind passed from the printed sciences within book covers to these intimate real things and then radiated outward to a realization that the synthesis of the sciences composed a vital interpretation of the world.

In those days both sides of descriptive biology, botany and zoology, were in a parallel phase; they were passing on from mere classification to morphology and phylogeny. Comparative physiology and genetics had still to come within the scope of the ordinary biological student. It was perhaps inevitable that they should wait upon the establishment and confirmation of the phylogenetic tree, the family tree of life, before they in their turn could take the centre of the stage. The phylogeny of the invertebrata was still in a state of wild generalization, vegetable morphology concerned itself with an elaborate demonstration of the progressive subordination of the oophore to the sporophore, and even the fact of evolution as such was still not universally conceded. The mechanism of evolution remained therefore a field for almost irresponsible speculation. Weismann and his denial of the inheritance of acquired characteristics was in the ascendant. Our chief discipline was a rigorous analysis of vertebrate structure, vertebrate embryology and the succession of vertebrate forms in time. We felt our particular task was the determination of the relationship of groups by the acutest possible criticism of structure. The available fossil evidence was not a tithe of what has been unearthed to-day; the embryological material also fell far short of contemporary resources; but we had the same excitement of continual discoveries, confirming or correcting our conclusions, widening our outlook and filling up new patches of the great jig-saw puzzle, that the biological student still experiences. The study of zoology in this phase was an acute, delicate, rigorous and sweepingly magnificent series of exercises. It was a grammar of form and a criticism of fact. That year I spent in Huxley's class, was beyond all question, the most educational year of my life. It left me under that urgency for coherence and consistency, that repugnance from haphazard assumptions and arbitrary statements, which is the essential distinction of the educated from the uneducated mind.

I worked very hard indeed throughout that first year. The scene of my labours was the upper floor of the Normal School, the Royal College of Science as it is called to-day, a floor long since applied to other uses. There was a long laboratory with windows giving upon the art schools, equipped with deal tables, sinks and taps and, facing the windows, shelves of preparations surmounted by diagrams and drawings of dissections. On the tables were our microscopes, reagents, dissecting dishes or dissected animals as the case might be. In our notebooks we fixed our knowledge. On the doors were blackboards where the demonstrator, G. B. Howes afterwards Professor Howes, a marvellously swift draughtsman, would draw in coloured chalks for our instruction. He was a white-faced, black bearded, nervous man, a sort of Svengali in glasses; swift and vivid, never still, in the completest contrast with the powerful deliberation of the master. Huxley himself lectured in the little lecture theatre adjacent to the laboratory, a square room, surrounded by black shelves bearing mammalian skeletons and skulls displayed to show their homologies, a series of wax models of a developing chick, and similar material. As I knew Huxley he was a yellow-faced, square-faced old man, with bright little brown eyes, lurking as it were in caves under his heavy grey eyebrows, and a mane of grey hair brushed back from his wall of forehead. He lectured in a clear firm voice without hurry and without delay, turning to the blackboard behind him to sketch some diagram, and always dusting the chalk from his fingers rather fastidiously before he resumed. He fell ill presently, and after some delay, Howes, uneasy, irritable, brilliant, took his place, lecturing and drawing breathlessly and leaving the blackboard a smother of graceful coloured lines. At the back of the auditorium were curtains, giving upon a museum devoted to the invertebrata. I was told that while Huxley lectured Charles Darwin had been wont at times to come through those very curtains from the gallery behind and sit and listen until his friend and ally had done. In my time Darwin had been dead for only a year or so (he died in 1882).

These two were very great men. They thought boldly, carefully and simply, they spoke and wrote fearlessly and plainly, they lived modestly and decently; they were mighty intellectual liberators. It is a pity that so many of the younger scientific workers of to-day, ignorant of the conditions of mental life in the early nineteenth century and standing for the most part on the ground won, cleared and prepared for them by these giants, find a perverse pleasure in belittling them. In a thousand respects their work was incomplete and tentative and any little Mr. Whippersnapper who chooses to use the vastly greater resources of to-day against them can find statements made by them that were insufficient or slightly erroneous, and theoretical suggestions that have been abandoned and disproved, and he can catch a bit of personal publicity from the pulpit or the reactionary press by saying that Darwin has been discredited or Huxley superseded. Great joy for Mr. (and Mrs.) Whippersnapper it is, naturally enough, to realize that he knows clearly things that Darwin never heard of, and is able to tatter some hypothesis of Huxley's. Little men will stand on the shoulders of giants to the end of time and small birds foul the nests in which they were hatched. Darwin and

Huxley knew about one per cent of the facts about variation and mutation that are accessible to Mr. Whippersnapper. That does not alter the fundamental magnificence of Darwin's and Huxley's achievement. They put the fact of organic evolution upon an impregnable base of proof and demonstration so that even the Roman Catholic controversialists at last ceased to vociferate, after the fashion of Bishop Wilberforce of the Anglican church on a memorable occasion, "Yah! Sons of apes! You *look* it," and discovered instead that the Church had always known all about Evolution and the place of man in Nature, just as it had always known all about the place of the solar system in space. Only it had said nothing about these things, because it was wiser so. Darwin and Huxley, in their place and measure, belong to the same aristocracy as Plato and Aristotle and Galileo, and they will ultimately dominate the priestly and orthodox mind as surely, because there is a response, however reluctant, masked and stifled, in every human soul to rightness and a firmly stated truth.

This biological course of Huxley's was purely and strictly scientific in its character. It kept no other end in view but the increase and the scrutiny and perfection of the knowledge within its scope. I never heard or thought of practical applications or business uses for what we were unfolding in that year's work, and yet the economic and hygienic benefits that have flowed from biological work in the past forty years have been immense. But these aspects were negligible by the standards of our study. For a year I went shabby and grew shabbier, I was under-fed and not very well housed, and it did not matter to me in the least because of the vision of life that was growing in my mind. I worked exhaustively and spent an even happier year than the one I had had at Midhurst. I was rather handicapped by the irregularity and unsoundness of my general education, but nevertheless I was one of the three who made up the first class in the examinations in zoology which tested our work.

A first-class in the Normal School meant over 80 per cent of the possible marks and the two others who took first-classes were Martin Woodward, a scion of a well-known family of biologists, who was afterwards drowned while dredging for marine zoological material on the west coast of Scotland, and A. V. Jennings, the son of a London private schoolmaster, for whom I formed a considerable friendship. All the rest of the class tailed down through a second class to failure.

Jennings was the only close associate I made in that first year. He was a year or so older than I, a slender grey-clad, red-faced young man with close curly black hair; he had had a sound classical education, and if he had not read as discursively as I he had read much more thoroughly. He was a well- trained student. He liked the strain of blasphemy and irreverence I had evolved for familiar conversational use, it startled him into appreciative chuckles, and once we had surmounted the obstacle of my shyness of sincere discussion, we got through an immense amount of talking about religious, political and scientific ideas. I learnt a great deal from him and polished much crudity and prejudice off my mind against his. For the first time in my life I was coming into touch at South Kensington with minds as lively as or livelier than my own and much better equipped, minds interested as much as I was interested in the significance of life. They saved me to a large extent from developing a shell of defensive reserve about my self conceit.

Once or twice Jennings showed a personal concern for me that still glows bright in my memory. The "Teachers in Training" at the Normal School were paid a maintenance allowance of a guinea weekly, which even in those days was rather insufficient. After I had paid for my lodgings, breakfasts and so forth, I was left with only a shilling or two for a week of midday meals. Pay day was Wednesday and not infrequently my money had run out before Monday or Tuesday and then I ate nothing in the nine-hour interval between the breakfast and the high-tea I had at my lodgings. Jennings noted this and noted that I was getting perceptibly thinner and flimsier, and almost by force he carried me off to a chop house and stood me an exemplary square meal, meat, two vegetables, a glass of beer, jam-roll pudding and a bit of cheese; a memorable fraternal feast. He wanted to repeat this hospitality but I resisted. I had a stupid sort of pride about unrequited benefits or I know he would have done this frequently. "This makes competition fairer," Jennings insisted.

At the end of this invigorating year I had had a vague hope that I should be able to go right on with zoological work but there were no facilities for research available. I cared so much for the subject then that I think I could have sailed away to very sound and useful work in it. I could have built up the full equipment of a professor of zoology upon the basis I had secured, if I had been free to take my own where I could find it. I should have filled up my gaps. I am convinced that for college and university education, keenly interested students—and after all they are the only students worth a rap; the others ought not to be there—should have much more freedom to move about and choose their own courses and teachers than is generally conceded them. However, my first year's performance had impressed the board of selection sufficiently to secure my reappointment as a Teacher in Training for a second and afterwards for a third year in other departments of the school where there were vacancies to be filled.

§ 2. PROFESSOR GUTHRIE AND THE SCIENCE OF PHYSICS (1885- 86)

Unhappily for me there was only one Huxley in the Normal School of Science and the course into which I was now thrown had none of the stimulation and enlargement of that opening year. The process of interest and curiosity was broken, and my mind was unable to turn itself with any energy to the new work that was put before it. It suffered from disruption and shock. I found myself almost at once at cross purposes with my new professors and instructors.

I can see now much more clearly than I did at the time what it was that turned me abruptly from the extravagantly greedy and industrious learner I was in my first year, to the facetious, discontented, restless and tiresome rebel I now became. It is a phase of my life I am only now getting into perspective and seeing as a logical part of a whole.

There were extraordinary faults and inconsistencies in the teaching machinery that had got hold of me. I had no idea of these faults and inconsistencies when I blundered against them, I understood scarcely anything either of the clumsiness of the educational forces to which I was reacting or of the nature of my own reactions; and it was altogether too much for my intelligence and will to get anything but perplexity and a series of partial frustrations and humiliations from the encounters that now lay before me. I am not complaining. Perplexity, frustration, humiliation and waste of energy are the common lot of human beings in a phase of blindly changing conditions, and what is exceptional in my story is not the clumsy struggling that now began but the previous luck of release and encouragement at Midhurst and under Huxley, that bright run of luck between 1883 and 1885, which had invigorated and given me self-confidence and a mulish persistence in the direction in which my feet were set.

The Normal School of Science and Royal School of Mines, to give it the full title it bore in these days, stood with an air of immense purposefulness four-square upon Exhibition Road. When I first took my fragile, unkempt self and my small black bag through its portals, I had a feeling of having come at last under definite guidance and protection. I felt as I think a civilized young citizen ought to feel towards his state education. If I worked hard, did what I was told and followed the regulations, then I thought

I should be given the fullest opportunity to develop whatever fine possibilities were in me and also that I should be used to the best advantage for the world and myself. I thought that the Normal School of Science knew what it meant to do with me. It was only after my first year that it dawned upon me that the Normal School of Science, like most other things in the sliding, slipping civilization of the time, was quite unaware even of what it meant to do with itself. It was an educational miscellany. It had been hastily compiled. Only that big red-brick and terra-cotta building, in which it was then assembled, held it together.

It was a product of the irregular and convulsive thrusts made by the embryonic modern world-state in its unconscious efforts to free itself from the aristocratic national system of eighteenth century Europe. Throughout the nineteenth century, one far-reaching dislocation after another had emphasized the growing need for a general education of the population and for a new type of education based upon the enlightenment due to scientific discovery and a widening range of experience. Already in the eighteen fifties Huxley was hammering away at the importance of biology in education. The drive of this need was resisted by the established religions, the ruling aristocracies and whatever remained over of the "scholarly" mediaeval universities. The new educational organizations essential to the proper working of the new order, had to grow against these resistances and were greatly delayed, dwarfed, distorted and crippled in the process.

The powers in possession conceded the practical necessity for technical and scientific instruction long before they would admit the might and value of the new scientific knowledge. Just as these conservative forces permitted elementary education to appear only on the understanding that it was to be a useful training of inferiors and no more, so they sanctioned the growth of science colleges only on condition that their technical usefulness was recognized as their sole justification.

The great group of schools at South Kensington which is now

known as the Imperial College of Science and Technology, grew therefore out of an entirely technical school, born of the base panic evoked in England by the revelation of continental industrial revival at the Great Exhibition of 1851. The initial institution was situated in the Museum of Practical Geology (note the minatory implication of that "Practical") in Jermyn Street, and its original title was "The Government School of Mines and Science applied to the Arts." To this a chemical school, a lecturer on mineralogy and, later on, physical laboratories were added; it was transferred to South Kensington bit by bit, and upon it a Normal School, to train teachers for the science classes that were being spread belatedly over the country, was rather incongruously imposed (1873 and 1881). It has continued to expand and absorb ever since. It is to-day, a huge fungoid assemblage of buildings and schools without visible centre, guiding purpose or directive brain. It has become a constituent of that still vaster, still more conspicuously acephalic monster, the University of London.

The thumby wisdom of the practical man, with a conception of life based on immediate needs, unanalysed motives and headlong assumptions, and with an innate fear of free and searching thought, is still manifest at a hundred points in the structure and working of this great aggregation. The struggle to blend technical equipment with a carefully cherished illiteracy, an intact oafishness about fundamental things, has been well sustained. South Kensington will still tell you proudly "we are not literary" and explain almost anxiously that the last thing it wants to impart is a liberal education. The ideal output of the Imperial College remains a swarm of mechanical, electrical and chemical business smarties, guaranteed to have no capacity for social leadership, constructive combination or original thought. There is an ineradicable tendency in sound technology to go on to purely scientific interest and breadth of social thought, the higher centres will keep on breaking through, and South Kensington, in spite of itself, does a great deal of real University work and makes men of many of its technicians. But so far the recognition of this tendency in any organized form has been successfully resisted.

Happily for me it happened that the vigorous, persistent far-reaching and philosophical mind of Huxley had become very influential with the Department of Science and Art in the sixties and seventies and particularly at South Kensington, and he had been able not only to establish that general scientific survey, physiography, as a "subject" in the evening class curriculum throughout the country, but he had had also a practically free hand to teach the science of life in his own fashion in the Normal School. This freedom involved, however, a similar freedom for the other professors with whom he was associated and they too without any consultation with their fellows, developed their courses according to their own capacities and their ideas of what was required of them.

Now Professor Guthrie, the Professor of Physics, into whose course I toppled from the top-floor to the ground floor of the Normal School building, was a man of very different texture from the Dean. He appeared as a dull, slow, distraught, heavily bearded man with a general effect of never having fully awakened to the universe about him. He seemed very old to me but as a matter of fact he was fifty-two. It was only after some years that I learnt what it was that made him then so slow and heavy. He was ill, within a year of his death, a still unsuspected cancer in his throat was dragging at his vitality, unknown to anyone. This greatly enhanced the leaden atmosphere of his teaching.

But quite apart from that he was not an inspiring teacher. The biological course from which I came had been a vivid, sustained attempt to see life clearly and to see it whole, to see into it, to see its inter-connexions, to find out, so far as terms were available, what it was, where it came from, what it was doing and where it was going. And, I take it, the task of a properly conceived elementary course in Physics, would be to do the same thing with non-living matter, to establish a fruitful description of phenomena, to clear up our common terminology, dating mostly from mediaeval times, about space, time, force, resistance, to explore the material universe with theory and experiment and so to bring us at last to the real living edge of the subject, the line of open questions on the verge of the unknown. But Guthrie's mind, quite apart from its present sickness, was devoid of the incessant interrogative liveliness necessary to a great man of science. He is best remembered as the initiator of the Physical Society. His original work was not of primary importance. The professorial scientist is by no means inevitably a man of science, any more than your common curate is inevitably a man of faith.

Guthrie, to put it plainly, maundered amidst ill-marshalled facts. He never said a thing that wasn't to be found in a text book and his course of lectures had to be supplemented by his assistant professor C. V. Boys, then an extremely blond and largely inaudible young man, already famous for his manipulative skill and ingenuity with soap bubbles, quartz fibres and measuring mechanisms. Boys lectured on thermo-dynamics. In those days I thought him one of the worst teachers who has ever turned his back upon a restive audience, messed about with the blackboard, galloped through an hour of talk and bolted back to the apparatus in his private room.

His turn came late in the course when I had already developed to a very high degree the habit of inattention to these physics lectures. I lost him from the word Go. If Guthrie was too slow for me, Boys was too fast. If Guthrie gave me an impression that I knew already most of what constituted the science of physics and that, though pretty in places, on the whole it was hardly worth knowing, Boys shot across my mind and vanished from my ken with a disconcerting suggestion that there was a whole dazzling universe of ideas, for which I did not possess the key. I was still in a state of exasperation at this belated discovery when the course came to an end, and in spite of a considerable loss of marks for certain defects, to be described, in the apparatus I had made, I was put in the examination list at the top of the second class. That did not shake my newborn conviction that I had learnt practically nothing about physics.

I do not know how the science of matter is taught to-day, but there is no gainsaying the colossal ineptitude of that particular course of instruction. We had half a school year to devote to our subject day after day and that was none too much for the observations, the demonstrations and the graphic and other mathematical analyses, which would have built up a sound system of conceptions about physical processes in our minds. But I doubt if there was any such system in Professor Guthrie's mind, and if there was in the mind of Boys he was either unable or too indolent to take it out, have a good look at it and explain it to anyone else. And so, instead of being used in real work on the science of physics, the time of the class was frittered away in the most irrelevant and stupid "practical work" a dull imagination has ever contrived for the vexation of eager spirits. Let me try and convey something of my horror of that physics laboratory to the reader.

It would seem that Professor Guthrie, while he was incubating this course, had been impressed with the idea that most of his students were destined to be teachers or experimental workers and that they would find themselves in need of apparatus. Unaware of the economic forces that evoke supply in response to demand, he decided that it was a matter of primary necessity that we should learn to make that apparatus for ourselves. Then even upon desert islands or in savage jungles we should not be at a loss if suddenly an evening class surrounded us. Accordingly he concentrated our energies upon apparatus making. He swept aside the idea that physics is an experimental science and substituted a confused workshop training. When I had gone into the zoological laboratory upstairs, I had been confronted by a newly killed rabbit; I had begun forthwith upon its dissection and in a week or so I had acquired a precise and ample knowledge of mammalian anatomy up to and including the structure of the brain, based upon my dissections and drawings and a careful comparison with prepared dissections of other types. Now when I came into the physics laboratory I was given a blowpipe, a piece of glass tubing, a slab of wood which required planing and some bits of paper and brass, and I was told I had to make a barometer. So instead of a student I became an amateur glass worker and carpenter.

After breaking a fair amount of glass and burning my fingers severely several times, I succeeded in sealing a yard's length tube, bending it, opening out the other end, tacking it on to the plank, filling it with mercury, attaching a scale to it and producing the most inelegant and untruthful barometer the world has ever seen. In the course of some days of heated and uncongenial effort, I had learnt nothing about the barometer, atmospheric pressure, or the science of physics that I had not known thoroughly before I left Midhurst, unless it was the blistering truth that glass can still be intensely hot after it has ceased to glow red.

I was then given a slip of glass on which to etch a millimetre scale with fluorine. Never had millimetre intervals greater individuality than I gave to mine. Again I added nothing to my knowledge—and I stained my only pair of trousers badly with acid.

Then, if I remember rightly, I was required to make a specific gravity bottle, stopper and all, out of more glass tubing. It took days. But by that time I was convinced that Professor Guthrie was playing the fool with me and that he had no intention whatever of imparting whatever he might know and think—if indeed he did know and think anything—about the science of physics to me.

A wiser and more determined character than I, might have held firmly to my initial desire to learn and know about this moving framework of matter in which life is set, might have sought out books and original literature, acquired whatever mathematical equipment was necessary, and come round behind the slow obstructive Guthrie and the swift elusive Boys, outflanking them so to speak, and getting to the citadel, if any, at the centre of the thickets and wildernesses of knowledge they were failing to guide me through. I did not realize it then, but at that time the science of physics was in a state of confusion and reconstruction, and lucid expositions of the new ideas for the student and the general reader did not exist. Quite apart from its unsubstantial equipment and the lack of time, my mind had not the strength and calibre to do so much original exploration as was needed to get near to what was going on. I made a kind of effort to formulate and approach these primary questions, but my effort was not sustained.

In the students' Debating Society, of which I will tell more later, I heard about and laid hold of the idea of a four dimensional frame for a fresh apprehension of physical phenomena, which afterwards led me to send a paper, "The Universe Rigid," to the *Fortnightly Review* (a paper which was rejected by Frank Harris as incomprehensible), and gave me a frame for my first scientific fantasia, the *Time Machine*, and there was moreover a rather elaborate joke going on with Jennings and the others, about a certain "Universal Diagram" I proposed to make, from which all phenomena would be derived by a process of deduction. (One began with a uniformly distributed ether in the infinite space of those days and then displaced a particle. If there was a Universe rigid, and hitherto uniform, the character of the consequent world would depend entirely, I argued along strictly materialist lines, upon the velocity of this initial displacement. The disturbance would spread outward with ever increasing complication.) But I discovered no way, and there was no one to show me a way to get on from such elementary struggles with primary concepts, to a sound understanding of contemporary experimental physics.

Failing that, my mind relapsed into that natural protest of the frustrated—malicious derision of the physics presented to us. I set myself to guy and contemn Guthrie's instructions in every possible way, I took to absenting myself from the laboratory and when I was recalled to my attendances by the registrar of the schools, I brought in Latin and German textbooks and studied them ostentatiously. In those days the matriculation examination of the London University was open to all comers; it was a discursive examination involving among other things a superficial knowledge of French, Latin and either German or Greek and I found German the easier alternative. I mugged it up for myself to the not very exacting standard required. I matriculated in January 1886 as a sort of demonstration of the insufficiency of the physics course to occupy my mind.

My campaign to burlesque Guthrie's practical work was not a very successful one, it was a feeble rebellion with the odds all against me, but it amused some of my fellow students and made me some friends. Even had I been trying to satisfy the requirements of the course, the inattentive clumsiness that had already made me a failure as a shop assistant, would have introduced an element of absurdity into the barometers, thermometers, galvanometers, demonstration apparatus and so forth that I manufactured, but I added to this by demanding a sound scientific reason for every detail in the instructions given me and contriving some other, and usually grotesque, way of achieving the required result if such an imperative reason was not forthcoming. The laboratory instructor Mitchell was not a very quick-minded or intelligent man, bad at an argument and rather disposed to make a meticulous adhesion to instructions a matter of discipline. That gave me a great advantage over him because his powers of enforcement were strictly limited. After a time he began to avoid my end of the laboratory and when he found my bench littered with bits of stuff, a scamped induction coil or such-like object in a state of scandalous incompleteness and myself away, he thanked his private gods and no longer reported my absence.

The decisive struggle which persuaded him to despair of me, turned upon the measurement of the vibrations of a tuning fork giving the middle C of an ordinary piano. We had to erect a wooden cross on a stand with pins at the ends of the arms, and a glass plate, carefully blackened with candle smoke, was hung by a piece of silk passing over these arms in such a way as just to touch a bristle attached to a tuning fork. This tuning fork was thrown into sympathetic vibration by another, the silk thread was burnt in the middle, the plate as it fell rubbed against the bristle and a trace of the vibrations was obtained. A careful measurement of this trace and a fairly simple calculation (neglecting the buoyant effect of the atmosphere) gave the rate of vibration per second. I objected firstly to the neglect of the atmospheric resistance and I tried to worry Mitchell into some definite statement of the extent to which it vitiated the precision of the experiment. Poor dear! all that he could say was that it "didn't amount to much." But we joined issue more seriously upon the cross-piece. I alleged that as a non-Christian I objected to making a cross if that was avoidable. I declared that as a Deist I would prefer to hang my falling plate from one single pin. Also I insisted that it was the duty of a scientific worker always to take the simplest course to his objective. This cross-piece with its two pins was, I argued, a needless elaboration probably tainted by the theological prepossessions of Professor Guthrie. In fact I refused to make it. I could get just as good results with a Monotheistic upright. Mitchell fell into the trap by insisting that that was "how it had to be done." Whereupon I asked whether I was a student of physical science or a convict under discipline. Was I there to learn or was I there to obey?

Obviously Mitchell had no case and as obviously I was making a confounded nuisance of myself for no visible reason. He was acting under direction. My retrospective sympathies are entirely with him.

One example is as good as a score of the silly bickering resistances I put up to annoy my teachers during that futile course of instruction. In the end when my apparatus was assembled for inspection and marking, it was of such a distinguished badness that it drew an admiring group of fellow students and some of it was preserved in a cupboard for several years. As a comment on Professor Guthrie's conception of education it was worth preserving. But I pretended to be prouder of that collection than in my heart I was. Guthrie was taking life at an angle different from mine and I had been betrayed into some very ungracious and insulting reactions. Poor discipline goes with poor teaching. A lecture theatre full of impatient undergraduate students is the least likely of any audience to detect the presence of failing health. His husky voice strained against our insurgent hum. He was irritable and easily "drawn." There was a considerable amount of ironical applause and petty rowdiness during his lectures and in these disturbances I had made myself conspicuous.

I was bad and I was not able to explain why I was bad even to myself. I was not sufficiently mature about the purport of my resistance to make my case clear to anyone. I was not clear about it myself. It was plain I hated and despised the superficialities of that so-called physics course, but it was not at all plain that I was honestly fumbling about to get hold of some clue to a real science of physics. I was. Confusedly my mind was making an effort. I didn't realize that in that effort I was rather in the position of a dwarf who seeks a drinking horn in order to drink the ocean. The drinking horn was certainly not in the laboratory task. The general effect upon the authorities and my contemporaries was that after quite a brilliant start I lacked staying power. Nobody noted anything relevant about the Universal Diagram. My performance in the geological course to which I was now transferred did nothing to qualify that reputation for instability.

* * * * *

I return after fifty years to that old perplexing quarrel with my subject and my teachers. I plead guilty at once to bad manners and a lack of worldly wisdom. I admit I had neither understanding nor humanity for any of my instructors. On the other hand I maintain that my judgment on the kindergarten childishness of that practical course was fundamentally sound. But these are really very superficial and personal issues. There is more to be got out of that baffled phase in my mental development. If, to coin a phrase, we can "de-individualize" what happened, we are left with a fairly bright sample intelligence completely thrown out, in its attempts to grasp what physics was up to. To a certain point it had all been plain sailing, a pretty science, with pretty sub-divisions, optics, acoustics, electricity and magnetism and so on. Up to that point, the time-honoured terms which have crystallized out in language about space, speed, force and so forth sufficed to carry what I was learning. All went well in the customary space-time framework. Then things became difficult.

I realize now that it wasn't simply that neither Guthrie nor Boys was a good teacher. No man can be a good teacher when his subject becomes inexplicable. The truth, of which I had no inkling then, was that beyond what were (and are) the empirical practical truths of the conservation of energy, the indestructibility of matter and force, and so forth, hung an enigmatical fog. A material and experimental *metaphysics* was reached.

The science of physics was peering into this fog, aware that there was some very fundamental misapprehension, getting glimpses of elusive somethings and nothings, making trial guesses and gestures and not getting much further. So far it had travelled upon the common presumptions and now the common presumptions were failing it. Curiously paradoxical facts were coming to light and making those common presumptions seem unsubstantial. Why for instance should there be an absolute zero of temperature? What happened to matter when it got there? Our common presumption was that "more or less" went on for ever in either direction. Why again should there be an invariable relative velocity of light? The common presumption was that if one ran with the light it should go relatively slower. Why was there a limited material universe in apparently limitless space? In an infinitude of stars the whole sky should glow with nebulous light.

There are more of these paradoxical riddles to-day. They have indeed multiplied greatly. The science of physics is even more tantalizing than it was half a century ago, and, above the level of an elementary introduction, optics, acoustics and the rest, even less teachable. The more brilliant investigators rocket off into mathematical pyrotechnics and return to common speech with statements that are, according to the legitimate meaning of words, nonsensical. The fog seems to light up for a moment and becomes denser for these professorial fireworks. Space is finite, they say! That is not space as I and my cat know it. It is something else into which they are trying to frame the vague imperfect concepts they labour to realize. The stars existed before the universe! The universe is expanding into God knows what; and will presently contract! Being is a discontinuous stipple of quanta! In normal everyday language this is sheer nonsense. Ordinary language ought not to be misused in this way. Clearly these mathematical physicists have not made the real words yet, the necessary words that they can hold by, transmit a meaning with and make the base of fresh advance.

How was I, only a year up from the country grammar school and elementary text-books, to guess at that embarrassing fog on the other side of the professor and his assistant?

Biological science can still get along because practically all its questions and phenomena lie within the scope of normal experience. Its subject matter is apparently confined to the earth and to a measurable sphere of time. It frames human history and human life and is itself in its turn completely framed. It can work on indefinitely within the common presumptions. It is only when biology comes into contact with physics and the question What is life? demands an answer in terms of physics, that real mystery is broached. But physical science is far more comprehensive, and in every direction it recedes beyond the scope of experiential thinking and of language based on common experience. It has to misuse and overstrain one familiar term after another. Its progress becomes more and more departure until a degree of remoteness is attained whereat definite consistent statement gives place altogether to philosophical speculation.

Not only was Guthrie no Huxley, but in the whole world of physics at that time there was nobody with the grasp and power of exposition capable of translating the difficulties of material science into language understandable by the eager student or the un-specialized intelligent educated man. My subsequent occupations, interests and limitations, have all stood in the way of my studying physical science and my experience of it has remained that of an outsider trying to adjust his general ideas to what he can overhear. I have never been able to make that adjustment. I am still unable to realize what modern Physics is up to. I do not find myself interrogative *with* those who are conducting research and speculation, but I find myself interrogative about them. My impression is that the Darwin and Huxley of Physics have still to come. There is a gap which has still to be bridged between the ideology and phraseology of normal intelligent people and those specialists who go out from the normal world into this great region of experimental and mathematical exploration.

It is curious to find that to-day the professors of physics are, as a body, still failing to be unanimously lucid upon even such old-world questions as predestination and free-will. A number of them lunge back ambiguously as if towards theological and spiritualistic suggestions. Some have succumbed to the lure of journalism and, writing for the general reader, have become not so much explanatory as popular and sensational.

I have here lying on my writing desk a most interesting and a most significant book. It is called *Where Is Science Going?* It is translated from the German of that indisputably great physicist and innovator Max Planck; it is reinforced by Einstein and very ably edited by a capable scientific journalist Mr. James Murphy. Its interest centres upon the fact that these two cardinal figures in the world of physical science are clearly so perturbed by the misrepresentation and romantic treatment of the trends of physical science by some of the less intellectually scrupulous of their contemporaries and colleagues, that they feel the necessity for a clear statement of the bearing of that work upon ordinary thought. Planck reiterates very clearly the inseparability of the idea of causation from scientific work. He restates the old distinction between the objective conception of events as *caused*, on which all science rests, and our subjective conception of our own personal actions (but not those of the people we observe about us) as wilful and free. So far as our own conduct goes we have free-will; that does not alter the fact that to an external observer our acts are determinate.

But Planck is not as absolute in his insistence upon causation as a universal external fact, as a Victorian man of science would have been. He admits certain difficulties arising out of experimental experiences. A completely comprehended system of causation, which is what I was discussing in that paper the *Universe Rigid* and caricaturing in that Universal Diagram to which I have already alluded, should admit of exact prophecy. In certain cases exact prophecy does not work and consequences, until they occur, appear to be indeterminate. Here, says Planck, we must fall back on our Faith that ultimately finer measurements and a closer analysis will eliminate that quality of indeterminateness.

But *will* they?

I will not add my small yes or no to Planck's decisive Yes, but since I am writing a mental autobiography there is no reason why I should not supplement his repudiation of indeterminateness by a word or so about a collateral line of thought of my own, which may help a little to explain why this scepticism about the adequacy of causation has reappeared in physical theory. I fell into this line of thought as the outcome of the question "What is a species?" which is necessarily raised by the study of organic evolution and much emphasised by classification work in petrology and mineralogy. I happened to have to read a certain small amount of logic and mental science to secure two teaching diplomas (the L.C.P. 1889 and the F.C.P. 1891) and almost simultaneously I had to read some inorganic chemistry for my intermediate examination for the degree of B.Sc. (1889). The chemical, biological and logical conceptions of what constitutes a species were thus thrown into a fruitful juxtaposition. They fermented together.

The first result of this fermentation, was a very ill-written but ingenious paper, *The Rediscovery of the Unique*, which was published in the *Fortnightly Review* in July 1891. It insisted upon the idea that every phenomenon amenable to scrutiny was found to be unique; that therefore there might be no such thing as an identical similarity among outer realities but only approximate similarities, and that though the mind found it necessary to classify in order to operate at all, there was nevertheless a marginal fallacy lurking even in the statement that two and two made four. One set of four would never be quite the same as another set of four; no pair matched completely. Classification was a convenient simplification of realities that would otherwise be incomprehensible. We overlooked this in ordinary practice, though it was plain before our noses if we chose to see it, and we allowed a convenient habit of acquiescence in the identification of merely similar things to harden into a fixed assumption that they were identical repetitions of the same thing. This led us to make such unjustifiable assumptions as that atoms of the same element were identical and to confuse an average result with an unanimous result.

In 1891 this was an anticipation of what physicists now call "statistical causation." The identical similarity of atoms and most other physical units was then an almost universal persuasion. To concede individuality to atoms seemed unnecessary and unprofitable.

Nobody took much notice of this article of mine at the time, but the idea kept alive in my mind; I gave it another form in a *Saturday Review* article, *The Cyclic Delusion*, in 1893; and I revived it in a paper I read before the Oxford Philosophical Society (Nov. 8th, 1903) called *Scepticism of the Instrument*. This was reprinted in *Mind*, vol. XIII N.S., No. 51, and, after revision, in the first edition of my *Modern Utopia* 1905. It insisted not only upon this loose play of the logical process upon which I had already laid stress; "the forceps of our minds are clumsy forceps and crush the truth a little in taking hold of it"; but dwelt also upon the dangerous facility with which such purely negative terms as "the absolute" and infinity could be used with an air of positive significance.

I dug up this old bone of mine and gnawed it again, without getting anything very fresh off it, in *First and Last Things*(1908).

Through this insistence upon the unique individuality of every event, it seems to me, you can arrive by another route at an understanding of that appearance of inexactitude and spontaneity in minute observations which has set some modern physicists talking about objective free-will—to the distress not only of Max Planck and Einstein but of a great number of other scientific workers. All phenomena escape a little from exact statement and logical treatment. Classification is always a little imprecise and every logical process slightly loose in its handle.

"The fact," says Sir James Jeans in a popular work, *The Mysterious Universe* quoted by James Murphy (*op. cit.*), "that 'loose jointedness' of any type whatever pervades the whole universe, destroys the case for absolutely strict causation, the latter being the characteristic of perfectly fitted machinery." But if one starts out with a perception of the universality of uniqueness one never expects perfectly fitted machinery and one demands no more than a consistency in similarity. The fascinating thing about this material world outside our minds is that it is always harmonious with itself, never crazy and anyhow, and yet at the same time never pedantically exact. Like living individuals it has "character"; it is at once true to itself and subtly unexpected. Every time it startles us by breaking away from the assumptions we have made about it, we discover in the long run that our assumptions have been premature and that harmony is still there. Hence every scientific generalization is tentative and every process of scientific reasoning demands checking and adjustment by experiment. The further you go from experimental verification the more sensible becomes the margin of error. The most beautifully reasoned deductions in the world, the most elaborate mathematical demonstrations collapse and must be made over again before the absolute veto of a single contradictory fact, however small this fact may be.

This pragmatical view of nature leaves a working belief in causation intact. We can still believe that exactly the same cause would produce exactly the same effect. We are sustained in that belief almost invincibly by the invariable experience that the more similar the cause the more similar the effect. Our minds seem to have been built up from the beginning of time upon such experiences. Nevertheless we can recognize that there is a quiver of idiosyncrasy in every sequence and that nature never repeats herself. There never has been, it seems, exactly the same cause and exactly the same effect.

Because the universe continues to be unique and original down to the minutest particle of the smallest atom, that is no reason for supposing it is not nevertheless after the pattern of the rational process it has built up in the human mind. But was it not to be expected that the whole of Being would be infinitely more subtle and intricate than any web of terms and symbols our little incidental brains could devise to express it?

We are compelled to simplify because of the finite amount of grey matter we possess. The direct adequate dynamic causation of every event, however minute, remains the only possible working hypothesis for the scientific worker. There is no more need to abandon it than to abandon counting and weighing because no two things are exactly alike. And we may so far agree with Max Planck as to believe that we shall continually approximate to it with increased precision of observation and analysis. But also we may add a conviction that we shall never get to it. We shall never get to it for the excellent reason that there is not the slightest justification, outside the presumptions of our own brain, to believe that it is really there.

This section on the elements of physics grows, I perceive, to an inconvenient length. You see at any rate in what fashion I paddled on the edge of the illimitable ocean of physical speculation and possible knowledge, leaving the glass and stuff on my laboratory bench to take care of itself. After a little paddling I came out of those waters again and dried my feet and ran about on the shore.

In my book, the *Work, Wealth and Happiness of Mankind* (1932) there are twenty pages (Chapter II., §§ 1-4 inclusive) which summarize all that I know about the relations of the human mind to physical reality. Those pages I wrote and rewrote with very great care, I got friends to scrutinize them and make difficulties about them, and I can add nothing to them as a general statement of what I believe. In brief I realize that Being is surrounded east, south, north and west, above and below, by wonder. Within that frame, like a little house in strange, cold, vast and beautiful scenery, is life upon this planet, of which life I am a temporary speck and impression. There is interest beyond measure within that house; use for my utmost. Nevertheless at times one finds an urgency to go out and gaze at those enigmatical immensities. But for such a thing as I am, there is nothing conceivable to be done out there. Ultimately those remote metaphysical appearances may mean everything, but so far as my present will and activities go they mean nothing. The science of physics shrinks to the infinitesimal in a little sparkling flicker in a glass bulb or whirls away vastly with the extra-galactic nebulæ into the deeps of space, and after a time I stop both speck-gazing and star-gazing and return indoors.

§ 3. PROFESSOR JUDD AND THE SCIENCE OF EOLOGY (1886- 87)

Perhaps I had been spoilt by the soundness and beauty of the biological course, but in geology again, I failed to find the inspiration that had come to me under Huxley. Judd was a better teacher than Guthrie, but he was a slow, conscientious lecturer with a large white face, small pale blue eyes, a habit of washing his hands with invisible water as he talked, and a flat assuaging voice; and he had the same lack of militant curiosity as Guthrie in his make-up. His eye watched you and seemed to take no interest in what his deliberate voice was saying. These were superficial characteristics and I am told that not only was Judd's work in stratigraphy sound and patient and excellent but that he was a very good and pleasant man to know. But I never knew him and my antipathy was immediate.

Geology is a badly assembled subject, anyhow. It is rather a lore than a science. In the hands of no teacher who had to cover the whole ground, could it be made as consecutive and exciting as biology and physics, those two fundamental sciences, can be made.

Assuming that my mind is a fairly ordinary one it is worth while, from the point of view of educational theory, trying to state just why it was that while biology as it was taught to me interested and concentrated me and physics interested me and tormented me as something fascinatingly attractive (though withheld, inaccessible and unattainable), geology as a whole failed to interest me at all. The work attracted me acutely in bits but in such a way as to entangle and distract my attention from most of the stuff put before me.

The explanation, I think, is that geology after the passing of that great generation which included Lyell, Murchison and their peers, had been allowed to accumulate great masses of new material without any persistent intelligible application of this new material to its general idea, which was to scrutinize the earth as a whole, say what it is and what it was, ransack it for evidence of how it originated and what it has gone through, focus the superficial evidence available upon the condition of its inaccessible interior and so at last arrive at such a power of ordered knowledge, that the geologist would know of any sediment, rock, mountain or mineral, whence it came, where it was going and what could be done with it and about it.

There is really no point at which good teaching ends and original research begins. From first to last in a science the lash and spur of interrogation must keep the mind alive. But—if I may vary the image—that flame of interrogation which kept Huxley's biological course molten and moving, burnt not at all in the geological course, and, except for bright moments when our own individual curiosity lit up a corner—and went out again, we were confronted by a great array of dark cold assorted facts, lifelessly arranged and presented.

We had a course of stratigraphy; we studied the succession of igneous rocks and of strata, more particularly as they occurred in the British Isles. Now this is a subject that bristles with interrogative possibilities. What is there in the composition of the rock to show the conditions under which it was consolidated? What was the geography of the world when it was made? What has happened to it since? What tale do the organic remains in it tell of climate and change? What is happening to it now? Under such questions there is not a feature about a deposit which does not become significant and interesting.

But such questions were never followed up.

They were barely hinted at. We were confronted with a list of formations and series of beds, with some indications of their local exposures and with drawers of "characteristic" fossils which we had to sketch, handle and learn to recognize. It was about as interesting as learning the names of the streets, houses and residents, with their characteristic articles of furniture, in due order as they were found in a provincial town. That might be useful for certain business purposes, for delivery-van work for example, and no doubt it was useful to a prospector to know just where he was, geologically, and "spot" the formation he was dealing with. But all that could have been learnt *connectedly* with far more ease.

We did neatly tinted cross-sections of country showing faults that were never accounted for and thrusts of unknown origin. Then came mineralogy and petrology and day after day we lifted and looked at lumps of mineral and lumps of rock and put them down again. It was all rote learning; the science that made the examination of a fragment of bone in the comparative anatomy course a beautiful exercise in inference, was entirely wanting. So far as we were taught, a lump of slate or a lump of pitchblende was like it was *because it was*, and that was that. What made the course so peculiarly exasperating was that we were pressed along this training in recognition—at a pace that made it disastrous to follow any incidental hares our own curiosity might start for us. Again I reiterate my profound persuasion that for successful science teaching the rule should be stimulation and a maximum of available information, with a minimum of prescription.

Among other frustrated and crumpled enquiries I remember the flash of excitement I found in crystallography. I learnt that in various series of minerals, the felspar group for example, there were subtle changes in the crystalline axis with changes of chemical composition. There were fluctuations in colour and crystalline form through most of the main mineral groups. What laws lurked in these fluctuations and why?

For petrography the school was at that date exceptionally well equipped. Every student had the use of a petrographical microscope, with polarizing prisms, and we examined a long series of representative rock sections. It would be difficult to exaggerate the beauty and fascination of some of these. They let one into the very heart of those specimen chunks of rock one found so boring in a drawer, they lit them up with a blaze of glorious colour. One saw the jumbled crystals thrust against each other, distorted by unknown pressures, clouded and stained by obscure infiltrations. In many there were odd inclusions of other crystalline substances, and still more entrancingly enigmatical there were often hollows in these crystals (although they had been formed under enormous pressures) and in these hollows there were drops of fluid and bubbles of gas. It was not simply an astounding loveliness, it was, one felt, a profoundly significant loveliness that these sections revealed. They were telling in this bright clear and glowing fashion, of tensions, solutions, releases, the steady creeping of molecule past molecule, age after age. And in their interpretation lay the history and understanding of the Earth as a whole. But the geological course was not out to pursue significance. It would tolerate no loitering for such discursive purposes. Each day brought its drawer of specimens, its tale of slides. That was and is my indictment of all that teaching.

I may perhaps be evolving all this adverse criticism of the courses of science at South Kensington in an unconscious attempt to solace myself for my manifest want of success there as a serious student, after my first year. The reader is better able than I am to judge of that. There can be no doubt of my failure—which led to some painful subsequent years. But when all possible allowance has been made for such a bias on my part, the facts remain that Professor Judd bored me cruelly and that in his course just as in the physics course, my discontent preceded and did not arise out of my failures.

Since those days I have given a reasonable amount of attention to pedagogics and social organization generally. I find it more and more remarkable that the old Normal School and Royal School of Mines, the present Imperial College of Science and Technology, although an important part of its work still consists in preparing teachers of science, has never had, has not now and never seems likely to have, any chair, lecturer or course in educational science and method. Much less is there any study of social, economic and political science, any enquiry as to objectives, or any attempt to point, control and co-ordinate the teaching in the various departments. To the ruling intelligences of South Kensington a course in geology is just a course in geology. When you have gone through a course, any course, then you *know* geology. Isn't that useful for mining and metallurgy? Both Guthrie and Judd were amateurs in science teaching, and neither of them had sound ideas of how to inveigle students into their subjects. And there was in the organization no supervising pedagogic philosopher with the knowledge and authority to tell them as much.

The Imperial College, I realize in the retrospect, was and still is in fact not a college but a sprawl of laboratories and class rooms. Whatever ideas of purpose wrestled together in its beginnings are now forgotten. It has no firm idea of what it is and what it is supposed to do. That is to say it has no philosophy. It has no philosophical organization, no social idea, no rationalized goal, to hold it together.... I do not see how we can hope to arrest and control the disastrous sprawling of the world's affairs, until we have first pulled the philosophical and educational sprawl together.

I had come up to South Kensington persuaded that I should learn everything. I found myself at South Kensington lost and dismayed at the multitudinous inconsecutiveness of everything.

Judd had a disposition very common in conscientious teachers, to over- control his students. He wanted to mess about with their minds. Huxley gave us his science, but he did not watch us digesting it. He was watching his science. Judd insisted not merely on our learning but learning precisely in his fashion. We had to make note-books, after his heart. We had to draw and paint and write down our facts just as a Judd would have done. We had to go at his pace and in his footsteps. We had to send in satisfactory note-books at the end. If not we lost marks in the final examination. To be lopped and sketched to the mental proportion of Judd in this fashion was almost as agonizing as being a victim to Og, King of Bashan.

I made an effort to do what was required of me but an irresistible boredom wrapped me about and bore me down. The habit I had acquired during the physics course of vanishing from my place in the laboratory and resorting to the Education Library or the Dyce and Foster Reading Room presently returned with enhanced strength.

The still favourable opinion of the board of selection kept me at the geological course, elementary and advanced, for an academic year and a half. By that time my career as a science student was in ruins, and that favourable opinion had evaporated. The path to research was closed to me for ever. Academically I had gone to the bad. I had become notoriously unruly. I got a second class at the end of 1886, but I failed the final examination in geology in 1887.

But I carried something out of that geological course nevertheless, for when, after various vicissitudes I presented myself to the London University examiners in 1890 for my B.Sc. degree, I had still enough geology to supplement my first class honours in zoology by taking the first place in second class honours in geology. I doubt if I had read very much in the interim. I think Professor Judd must have mingled considerations of discipline with his estimate of any progress in that final test which killed my scientific career.

§ 4. DIVAGATIONS OF A DISCONTENTED STUDENT
(1884- 1887)

This criticism of the large indeterminateness of the educational bulks and thrusts through which my brain dodged its way, is the outcome of a life's experience. Such, I now realize, were the conditions about me. But at the time I had no grasp of the huge movements and changes that were going on in the world. I had no idea of how the Normal School or the Educational Office or the teaching of science in any form had come about; I did not understand the conflicting forces that had made that teaching as good and as bad as it was, nor what it was had whipped me up out of servitude to be a learner, and was now rather alarmingly losing interest in me. I had been exalted at first and then I was puzzled and dismayed. I acquit myself of blame now much more completely than I acquitted myself at the time. Deep down in me a profound humiliation at my want of outstanding success in physics and geology struggled against the immense self-conceit I had brought up with me from Midhurst. My mind had to find compensating reassurance to save me from the conviction of entire inferiority. It found that reassurance in petty achievements and triumphs in other directions. Blasphemy and the bold and successful discussion of general ideas had already proved very sustaining to my self respect in the drapery emporium. I now found the pose of a philosophical desperado a very present help against my depression under the teaching of Guthrie and Judd.

The startled guffaws of Jennings had already persuaded me that I was something of a wit, and my rather unconventional contributions to the discussions in the Debating Society were also fairly successful and attracted one or two appreciative friends. There were three men, Taylor and Porter and E. H. Smith in that early group, of whom I have lost sight; there were also my life-long friends, A. T. Simmons and William Burton, Elizabeth Healey and A. M. Davies. We loitered in the corridors, made groups in the tea-shop at lunch-time, lent each other books and papers and developed each other's conversational powers.

Curiously enough, though I remember the Debating Society very vividly, I do not remember anything of the speeches I made. I did make speeches because my friends remember them and say they were amusing. The meetings were held in an underground lecture theatre used by the mining school. It was lit by a gas jet or so. The lecturers' platform and the students' benches were surrounded by big models of strata, ore crushers and the like which receded into a profound obscurity, and austere diagrams of unknown significance hung behind the chairman. The usual formula was a paper, for half an hour or so, a reply and then promiscuous discussion. Those who lacked the courage to speak, interjected observations, made sudden outcries or hammered the desks. The desks indeed were hammered until the ink jumped out of the pots. We were supposed to avoid religion and politics; the rest of the universe was at our mercy.

I objected to this taboo of religion and politics. I maintained that these were primary matters, best beaten out in the primary stage of life. I did all I could to weaken and infringe those taboos, sailing as close to the wind as possible, and one or two serious-minded fellow students began to look out for me with an ever ready cry of "Or-der." One evening somebody read an essay on *Superstitions* and cited among others the thirteen superstitions. I took up the origin of that. "A certain itinerant preacher whom I am not permitted to name in this gathering," I began, "had twelve disciples...."

The opposition was up in arms forthwith and we had a lovely dispute that lasted for the better part of an hour. I maintained that the phrase "itinerant preacher," was an exact and proper description of the founder of Christianity, as indeed it was. But the vocabulary of the ordinary Englishman is sticky with stereotyped phrasing and half dried secondary associations. It seemed that "itinerant preacher" connoted a very low type of minister in some dissenting bodies. So much the worse, I said, for the dissenting bodies. The sense of the meeting was against me. Even my close friends looked grave and reproachful. I was asked to "withdraw" the expression. I protested that it was based on information derived from the New Testament, "a most respectable compilation." This did not mend matters. Apparently they could not have it that the New Testament was "respectable" or "compiled." I was warned by the chair and persisted in my insistence upon the proper meaning of words.

I was carried out struggling. To be carried out of an assembly in full fight had recently been made splendid by Charles Bradlaugh. Irish members of parliament were also wont to leave that assembly by the same laborious yet exhilarating method of transport. Except that my hair was pulled rather painfully by someone, a quite momentary discomfort, that experience was altogether bright and glorious.

But I will not expand into this sort of anecdotage. That sample must serve. The Debating Society was a constant source of small opportunities for provocation and irreverence. And about the schools, in lecture theatres, I became almost an expert in making strange unsuitable noises, the wailing of a rubber blowpipe tube with its lips stretched, for example, and in provoking bursts of untimely applause. We, subsidized students, were paid every Wednesday by a clerk with a cash-box and a portfolio, at whose tone when calling out our names we saw fit to take offence. Mockery and ironical applause having failed to mend his manners, a tumult ensued and developed to such riotous behaviour that he fled to the registrar, professed to fear a raid on his tin box of sovereigns, and refused to proceed without police protection.

It seems to me that I must have been a thoroughly detestable hobbledehoy at this stage, a gaunt shabby candidate for expulsion, and it is not anything that I can remember to my credit, but only the constant friendship and loyalty of Jennings and these life-long friends I have named and of R. A. Gregory (now Sir Richard, the Editor of *Nature*) that makes me admit there may have been some qualification of my detestableness which now escapes me. These faithful associates bolstered up my self-respect and kept me from becoming a failure absolutely. They stimulated me to make good in some compensatory way that would atone for my apathy in the school work.

The Education Department had paid all of us scholars, exhibitionists, teachers in training, to come to London, but it had no organization to look after us when we were there. There were no provisions to lodge us or see that we were properly lodged;—it was only in my second year that provision was made in the form of a students' refreshment room to give us midday food at reasonable prices—and except for the registrar, an ex-army man, who noted when we "signed on" late repeatedly, and sent us red underlined copies of the rules when we were observed to be smoking, shouting or loitering in forbidden places, there was no effort to find out what we were doing or how things were with us. No one bothered to find out why I had got loose in my setting, much less did anyone attempt to readjust me in any way. I was not the only straggler from the steady pursuit of the ordained courses. I fainted only mentally, but twice in my time undernourished men fainted altogether in the laboratories. I paid in health for South Kensington all my life, as I shall tell. The schools, I repeat, ignored pedagogics and had no shadow of a general directive control even of our physical lives.

The natural pose to which I resorted to recover my self-esteem, was one of critical hostility to mechanical science and an affectation of literary ambition. I do not think I have ever had very much real literary ambition. And I found in the advancing socialist movement, just the congenial field for the mental energy that was repelled by those courses in physics and geology. After I had matriculated as an ex-collegiate student in London University, I did not go on at once to work for my Intermediate Examination in Science, but I became an active follower of the new propaganda.

I did not at first link the idea of science with the socialist idea, the idea, that is, of a planned inter-co-ordinated society. The socialist movement in England was under the aesthetic influence of Ruskin; it was being run by poets and decorators like William Morris, Walter Crane, Emery Walker and Cobden Sanderson, brilliant intellectual adventurers like Bernard Shaw and Mrs. Annie Besant, teachers with a training in classical philosophy like Graham Wallas, advanced high churchmen like Stuart Headlam and a small group of civil servants like Sidney Webb and Sydney Olivier. These leaders were generally ignorant of scientific philosophy and they had been misled by Herbert Spencer's Individualism into a belief that biological science was anti-socialist. I do not recall any contributions on my part, in those early years, to correct that misunderstanding. Probably there was a certain amount of subconscious antagonism towards science, or at least towards men of science, on my own part during those two latter years at South Kensington.

William Burton, E. H. Smith and I declared ourselves to be out-and-out socialists and signified the same with red ties. The rest of our set came most of the way with us, but with a more temperate enthusiasm. We trailed off to open meetings of the Fabian Society, which reminded me not a little of that Parliament in Landport, and we went on Sunday evenings to Kelmscott House on the Mall, Hammersmith, where William Morris held meetings in a sort of conservatory beside his house. He used to stand up with his back to the wall, with his hands behind him when he spoke, leaning forward as he unfolded each sentence and punctuating with a bump back to position. Graham Wallas, a very good looking young man then with an academic humour, was much in evidence, and Shaw, a raw, aggressive Dubliner, was a frequent speaker. There was a sprinkling of foreigners, who discoursed with passion, and a tendency to length, in what they evidently considered was the English tongue. None of our little group had the confidence to speak at these gatherings, but our applause was abundant, and on our way back to the Underground Railway at Hammersmith, our repressed comments broke through.

My return to South Kensington, after the mediocre examination results of my second year, was rather uncertain. There is a letter from myself to Simmons in which I discuss the possibilities of getting a master's job in a school. This letter recalls something which otherwise I might have forgotten, how very definite my literary ambitions had already become. (In that letter I made a rule sketch of myself with my prospective "works" about me, including "All about God" and a "Design for a New Framework of Society.") My apprehensions though justifiable were not justified; I was given another chance and I did not after all, at that time, write to the scholastic agents. My father arranged for me to stay for a month with my uncle Charles, a small farmer at Minsterworth near Gloucester. There, so soon as my anxiety about my return was dispelled, I set myself to write a paper on Socialism with which to open the autumn session of the Debating Society.

I made not the slightest attempt to get on with my geological reading. I remember I took enormous pains with that paper. I wrote in and altered until it became illegible and then I recopied it and started upon it all over again. I went for a day over to Cheltenham, where E. H. Smith was staying in the parental home, a greengrocer's shop, to plan a scheme for "capturing" the committee of the society "in the socialist interest" and to discuss the possibility of starting a college journal. We resolved that we were going to develop the literary and political consciousness of the Normal School whether the authorities liked it or not.

I do not know how far I may be considered to have cheated the Education Department by drawing my weekly guinea throughout that third year. I was at South Kensington to learn and I certainly learnt a lot, but I gave the very minimum of time and attention possible to the substance of Professor Judd's instructions. I had no sense of cheating at the time. I was certainly working most strenuously in the Education Library, the Art Library and the Dyce and Foster Reading Room, if not in the Advanced Geological Laboratory and the Mineral and Rock collections of the Natural History Museum. If I had relaxed in my efforts to learn about the past, present and implicit future of the planet earth, I was making the most strenuous efforts to get hold of all that was implicit in the idea of Socialism. I was reading not only a voluminous literature of propaganda but discursively in history, sociology and economics. I was doing my best to find out what such exalted names as Goethe and Carlyle, Shelley and Tennyson, Shakespeare, Dryden, Milton, Pope—or again Buddha, Mahomet and Confucius—had had to say about the world and what they mattered to me. I was learning the use of English prose and sharpening my mind against anyone's with whom I could start a discussion.

We got the *Science Schools Journal* going, finding an unexpected ally in A. E. Tutton, a tremendous swatter of chemistry, who hoped for a scientific publication and worked hard for us until he realized that our intentions were amateurish and literary and socialistic. I was the first editor, but in April 1887, the registrar, roused to concern by Professor Judd about the state of my work, made me resign control in favour of Burton. That did not win me back to systematic petrography. I made an effort to conform before it was too late and save my examination, but I could not fix my interest on that stuff, even for a final cram in the last fortnight.

I had just discovered the heady brew of Carlyle's *French*

Revolution and the prophetic works of William Blake. Every day I went off with my note-books and textbooks to either the Dyce and Foster Reading Room or the Art Library. I would work hard, I decided, for two hours, abstracting notes, getting the stuff in order—and then as a treat it should be (let us say) half an hour of Carlyle (whose work I kept at my disposal in the Dyce and Foster) or Blake (in the Art Reading Room). Then, perhaps an observant stroll among the Chantry pictures—they were at Kensington for as yet there was no Tate Gallery to shelter those Victorian masterpieces—the Majolica, the metal work and so forth for ten minutes and then a renewed attack on those minerals. But long before the two hours were up a frightful lassitude, a sort of petrographic nausea, a surfeit of minerals, would supervene. Granite and gabbro and gneiss became all one to me. There seemed no sense in their being different. The extent to which I did not care what bases replaced what in the acid felspars and how an increasing dose of potassium affected their twinning, became boundless and uncontrollable. There, ready to hand on the table, was a folder of Blake's strange tinted designs; his hank-haired rugose gods, his upward whirling spirits, his strained, contorted powers of light and darkness. What exactly was Blake getting at in this stuff about "Albion?" He seemed to have everything to say and Judd seemed to have nothing to say. Almost subconsciously, the note-books and textbooks drew themselves apart into a shocked little heap and the riddles of Blake opened of their own accord before me.

So I spent the last days that were left to me before the June examination made an end for ever to my career as a serious student of science.

§ 5. SOCIALISM (WITHOUT A COMPETENT RECEIVER) AND WORLD CHANGE

In my opening chapters I have tried to put my personal origins into the frame of human history and show how the phases and forces of the education that shaped me, Tommy Morley's Academy, old-fashioned apprenticeship, the newly revived Grammar School at Midhurst, the multiplying colleges at South Kensington, were related to the great change in human conditions that gathered force throughout the seventeenth, eighteenth and nineteenth centuries. World forces were at work tending to disperse the aristocratic estate system in Europe, to abolish small traders, to make work in the retail trades less independent and satisfactory, to promote industrial co-ordination, increase productivity, necessitate new and better informed classes, evoke a new type of education and make it universal, break down political boundaries everywhere and bring all men into one planetary community. The story of my father and mother and all my family is just the story of so many individual particles in the great mass of humanity that was driving before the sweep of these as yet imperfectly apprehended powers of synthesis. Our mental reactions were as remarkable as our physical and in the end, they were more important. What did my sort of people make of what was happening to them?

Nowadays most intelligent people are getting a grasp upon the broad character of the changes and imperatives amidst which we live. An outburst of discovery and invention in material things and of innovation in business and financial method, has, we realize, released so much human energy that, firstly, the need for sustained toil from anyone has been abolished, secondly, practically all parts of the world have been brought into closer interaction than were York and London three centuries ago and, thirdly, the destructive impulses of man have been so equipped, that it is no longer possible to contemplate a planet in which unconditioned war is even a remote possibility. We are waking up to the fact that a planned world-state governing the complex of human activities for the common good, however difficult to attain, has become imperative, and that until it is achieved, the history of the race must be now inevitably a record of catastrophic convulsions shot with mere glimpses and phases of temporary good luck. We are, as a species, caught in an irreversible process. No real going back to the old, comparatively stable condition of things is possible; set-backs will only prolong the tale of our racial disaster. We are therefore impelled to reconstruct the social and economic organization until the new conditions are satisfied. The sooner all men realize that impulsion, the briefer our stresses and the better for the race. That is how an increasing number of minds are coming to see that things are shaping. It is, we perceive, as much a part of the frame in which our lives are set as the roundness and rotation of the earth, as the pressure of the atmosphere or the force of gravitation at the sea level.

But what is matter-of-fact to-day was matter of opinion yesterday and matter for guess and suggestion the day before. What is so manifest to-day was certainly not manifest to anyone in 1887 with the same clearness and completeness. I do not mean simply that it was not manifest to ordinary people, to people like me and my brothers and school-fellows and my fellow students and teachers; it was equally beyond the perceptions of all these clever people who made it their rôle to discuss politico-social questions in and about the Socialist movement.

Perhaps these latter had a more vivid sense of the promise and possibilities of change, some sort of change in our circumstances than the generality, but they were—it is plain to- day—extraordinarily blind to the shapes of whatever change they perceived. How blind they were to the true proportions of things and particularly to the pace of change in things, how blind we all were, I shall try to suggest in this section, although in doing so my comments will carry me in some particulars far beyond my mental states as a student.

I shall give the effect of Socialism as it impressed me at that time and then, as I point out its limitations, I shall tell in what order they dawned upon my own mind and how phase by phase they took the sense of completeness out of the original project.

It is curious to go back now with all that one has since learnt and thought in one's head, and sit in that little out-house at Hammersmith, a raw student again, listening to a lean young Shaw with a thin flame-coloured beard beneath his white illuminated face, or to Graham Wallas, drooping, scholarly, and fastidiously lucid. It is impossible alas! to recover my original naïve participation. I can recall what I saw but not how I felt. I have in that memory a sense of watching people unawares. There they talked, unconscious of their destinies, and we younger outsiders listened and interjected a very occasional word. We were lively and critical disciples but we were disciples surely enough, intensely excited. We listened as they planned their policies. They seemed bold to us in spirit but they seemed extremely sage in method. Morris had his wild moments—of sympathy with the martyred Chicago anarchists for example—but then he was a poet. A vast revolution was going on swiftly and irresistibly all about us, but with perfect sincerity this Fabian group posed as a valiant little minority projecting a revolution reduced to its minimum terms. It was to permeate the existing order rather than change it. There was no real hope in their revolutionary project. It was a protest rather than a plan.

There I think is the profoundest factor in my present sense of remoteness, that vanished persuasion that we were up against essentially immutable institutions. The prevalent sub-consciousness of the time was not a perception of change but an illusory feeling of the stability of established things. That Hammersmith gathering shared it to the full. It needed such a jolt as the Great War to make English people realize that nothing was standing still. There they all felt and spoke as if they were in an absolutely fixed world, even if they thought that it was a world in which stable social injustices called aloud for remonstrance, resistance and remedies.

The Socialist movement was, one may say, a group of mental reaction systems (with very great variations within the group) to the disconcerting consequences of the new change of scale, and it had appeared *pari passu* with that new change. It did not fully understand itself. Nobody troubled to ask why it had appeared when it did and not before. A new movement does not begin by scrutinizing its origins. Its various forms were all responsive adaptations disguised even in the projectors' minds, as heroically revolutionary innovations. It proceeded from men who did not realize they were being pushed towards adaptive effort. It looked to its projectors like a purely constructive proposal, a new thing altogether. Men asked fiercely why should things always be thus and thus when as a matter of fact they had only just become thus and thus and were bound to alter in any case. "Let us have a new world," they said and they called it Socialism. But they did not realize that *some* new world was bound to come and that a new world, new in scale and power, was coming all about them.

Socialism developed at first in England and then in France because both the industrial and the mechanical revolution had hit first England and then France before it struck the rest of the world. From the time of Robert Owen onward, scattered people under the general banner of Socialism had been trying to make new plans for social and economic relationships in the place of those that were being distorted out of recognition or swept altogether away by blind new forces. But they had no real apprehension of the truth that those old social and economic relations would go anyhow without any pushing from them.

There was nothing essentially new in such pseudo-constructive efforts and social stress. England had been the theatre of very profound economic and social mutations from the Wars of the Roses onward, and the influence of these changes upon her social history and literature is very traceable. Long before Owen and the use of the word Socialism, there had been individual socialistic schemers responding to the stresses of the times. Sir Thomas More, for example, was such an early socialistic schemer, deriving from the city-communism of Plato, and the Elizabethan Poor Law was an important early essay in practical social reorganization. Defoe and Fielding were fully conscious of the need to set up new resistances and guiding embankments to the forces of social disintegration. All history is adaptation and the only essential difference between our time and past times is the immense difference in the scale and pace of adaptive urgency.

Socialism, from its christening stage onward, betrayed its incompleteness as a response to the social situation by a profound diversity in its proposals and by that readiness to acquire qualifying labels which is due to dissatisfaction with an original proposition. Here and there it was discovered to be "practical Christianity," and various outbreaks of Christian Socialism occurred, relapsing very readily into mere medieval charitableness towards the poor. Ruskin and Morris arrived at an anti-mechanical aesthetic socialism in recoil from the early degradation of popular art by crude machine processes. The early French socialisms were as partial and fragmentary as the early English, if somewhat more logical. The flight tendency in the new movement was strong: the tendency to get together a little band of the elect and start a new humanity somewhere well out of this apparently inflexible and incurable social system in which their discontents had been engendered. Strong as is my disposition to deflate the reputation of Marx I have to admit that he was the first to conceive of the contemporary social process not as a permanent system of injustice and hardship but as a changing and self-destroying order.

The organization for an effective interplay and criticism of social ideas has still to be invented, and what happened (and what does still to a considerable extent happen) was that each group of thinkers and often each individual thinker, started in on the general problem of readjustment in more or less complete unconsciousness or in contempt and disregard of whatever other nuclei existed. All of them began at some partial experience of the great change-complex in progress. None of them saw their problem whole.

The history of pre-Fabian beginnings is outside my story; by the time I came to London Fabianism was Socialism, so far as the exposition of views and policy went. There was no other Socialist propaganda in England worth considering. But the Fabian Society had gathered together some very angular and incompatible fragments to secure its predominant position, and at every meeting it stirred with mutterings beneath its compromises. Some members denounced machinery as the source of all our social discomfort, while others built their hopes on mechanization as the emancipator of labour, some were nationalist and others cosmopolitan, some were anti-Malthusian and others—with Annie Besant—neo-Malthusian, some Christian and some Atheist (denouncing religion as the opium of the people), some proposing to build up a society out of happy families as units and some wanting to break up the family as completely as did Plato. Many were believers in the capacity of Everyman to control his affairs by universal suffrage, while others had an acuter sense of the difficulties of the task and talked of oligarchies, toryisms and benevolent autocrats.

It was open to the movement either to think out and fight out these differences or to let them cancel each other out and take whatever was left. And since Fabianism was from the first, politic rather than scientific, it adopted the latter alternative. I will quote later on a paragraph in which this deliberate renunciation of exhaustive thoroughness is stated—aggressively. Foreign Socialism had little of our British spirit of compromise. It did go on to think and fight out differences. It rent itself with factions. But foreign Socialism also, if it was less persuaded of the stability of the current order, was under the sway of certain other obsessions which I will presently discuss. It polished and elaborated doctrine much more than the Fabian school, but unhappily not in a practically constructive direction.

Our little group of eager youth from the Kensington schools, going to the new Fabian Society for instruction in this great movement of hope and effort that was to put the world right again, discovered by degrees that this Socialism of theirs was indeed as a whole, almost as planless as the world outside. Anti-Socialists in those far off days used to accuse the Socialists, just as pagans used to accuse the early Christians, of having their wives in common. As a matter of fact the Fabian Socialists did not even have their ideas in common. With a solitary exception. There was one idea which united them all and did indeed constitute them Socialists. This was the idea that the motive of profit, which then dominated economic life, was wrong.

That condemnation of the profit motive was the G.C.M., the greatest common measure of Socialists. There Owen, Ruskin, William Morris, Marx, Webb, Shaw, Hyndmann, Maurice and Kingsley were unanimous. They were at open war with the contemporary theory that the search for gain, the desire to possess and to possess still more and the consequent competition to possess, constituted the main driving force of human association. Proudhon's *La propriété c'est le Vol* was typical. The main contribution made by Marx was a fairly convincing demonstration, that a system of competitive production for profit could not be a permanent system. Competition, he showed, argues the final victory of a dominating competitor (or group of competitors) which will own practically everything and attempt to hold all mankind in unendurable subjection. Unendurable— and hence, he argued, the revolution. All Socialists wished to eliminate profit from economic life and consequently all of them wished to abolish private property in any but the most immediately personal things. Following upon this arose the question, "And then how will the economic life of the community be run?" Thereupon they diverged (and continue to diverge) to all points of the compass.

That paper I prepared so elaborately at Minsterworth, and read to the Debating Society in 1886, was fairly representative of the common man's socialism at that period. It was a statement of the waste arising out of competition and the disproportionate development of what I called "distribution." I was too innocent still about the things of this world to develop any attack upon investment, stock-exchange gambling, speculation and the money-credit system, as the major interceptors and absorbers of "production" in the distributive system. I was thinking rather of the overlapping rounds of competitive milk carts and the needless multiplication of retail shops. I hailed the "stores," which had done so much to overwhelm Atlas House, as the precursors of a state distributing system. I had no use for the rôle of small retailer for my father or anyone else. I wanted distribution and production to be added to the existing functions of the state which I lumped together with a primitive simplicity under the word, "defence." "Production, Distribution and Defence," that was my artless trio of social functions. The state should control them all, I said, not simply confine itself to "defence." I made no definition of the State; apparently I had not become critical of the contemporary state as such.

This primitive Socialism of mine, in spite of my hard narrowness of approach, was well received. In the subsequent debate Burton came in with some quotations from the angle of Ruskin, A. M. Davies raised some individualist objections and cited Herbert Spencer, while E. H. Smith sounded the democratic note (which I had left silent) with considerable emphasis. His sentimental belief in the masses was as near as anyone at South Kensington in these early days came to mystical democratic Marxism. This much I recall of that meeting; E. H. Smith with his foot on a chair, rather harshly rhetorical, Davies slight and Iberian, recalling an early portrait of J. S. Mill, precise and hesitant already with that little cough of his, old Burton, Ruskinian, biblical, as became a man from John Bright's Manchester, and very eloquent and copious. Others spoke but I do not remember them so clearly.

We denounced individualism; we denounced *laissez-faire*. The ownership of land and industrial capital was to be "vested in the community." We did not say what we meant by the "community" because none of us knew—or had even thought it might require knowing. But what we saw as in a vision was a world without a scramble for possession and without the motive of proprietary advantage crippling and vitiating every intellectual and creative effort. A great light had shone upon us and we could see no more.

Socialism was indeed a blinding thing then. It was so dazzled by the profound discovery of itself, in that age of scramble and go-as-you-please, that it seemed unable to get on with its job. It feared to dispel the lovely vision it had conjured up. It remained in a state of exalted paralysis refusing to think further—because that might split the movement—and waiting for the world to come up to it. A similar phase of exalted paralysis has occurred at times in various sciences. After the demonstration of Evolution, biology marked time for a generation, reiterating and elaborating that immense realization. Physics for a period poised at the indivisible atom and the conservation of energy. But Western Socialism has gone on poising, poising itself unprogressively for longer than any science has done. It has been marking time for the past half century.

There were special reasons for this exceptional unprogressiveness of Socialist ideology. In the Fabian Society the desire for politic compromise damped discussion, but there was more in it than that. It was not any dread of dissension that kept continental Socialism impracticable. It was the absence of an experimental and analytical spirit. There had been a conspicuous absence from about the cradle-side of Socialism, of men with the scientific habit of mind. Socialism was essentially a pre-scientific product and it had just that bad disposition to finality of statement which it is the task of experimental science to dispel. Nobody sighed and said "And *now* what?" Nobody said, "Here is a great and inspiring principle which does in general terms meet the stresses of our time, let us go on at once to test it soundly and work out its necessary particulars and methods." Instead Socialism was proclaimed as a completed panacea. It was announced in strange, mystical and dogmatic phrases. The "Proletariat" was to rise against the "Bourgeoisie" and "expropriate" them, *etc., etc.*

The old Calvinistic theologians, equally absolute and unprogressive, announced Salvation by the Blood, and they would never explain what exactly the Blood was, nor how Emmanuel's vein was to be identified, nor anything more about it. Don't argue, don't make difficulties, they said, believe in the Blood and repent. To take difficulties into consideration was to go half way back to apostasy. In exactly the same spirit the Bourgeoisie, industrial and financial leaders, contemporary statesmen, were now exhorted by the Socialists not to ask questions, make difficulties and so damn themselves further, but just repent and consent to "socialization."

No! they were not to ask How.

Now the first difficulty in the way of expropriating the contemporary landowner and capitalist for the common good is the absence of what I have called (in a recent examination of the collectivist idea in the *Work, Wealth and Happiness of Mankind* 1931) a "competent receiver." The Fabian Socialists in their impatience for practical application, did their utmost to ignore this blank in their outlook. They strove to think that any contemporary administrative and governing body, a board of guardians, a bench of magistrates, Parliament, Congress, was capable of playing the rôle of "the community" and "taking over" the most intricate economic tasks. The Webbs (Beatrice and Sidney) whose unparalleled industry and insistence did so much to keep British Socialism in the narrow way, held apparently that almost any sort of administration could be stiffened up and controlled by an "expert" or so, to the required degree of specialized efficiency. They were quite prepared to accept and Fabianize the Tzardom or the tribal chieftainships of the Gold Coast.

The Webb mentality was a peculiar one and it imposed itself with paralysing effect upon the Socialist movement in Britain. Mrs. Webb had been brought up a brilliant girl among politicians, and it took her many years to realize that there could be any other sort of governing class than the class she had seen so closely and intimately. Webb, a clever civil servant by competitive examination, was all too disposed to accept that same governing class, provided it left matters of detail to trusted trained officials. But really the members of that governing class, with its social traditions, its commercial liberalism and its highly developed parliamentary technique of humbugging the new voting democracy, were the last people to submit to their own socialization by indefatigable little civil service officials. There was no autocratic indolence about them when it came to business. They had their own use for parliament. Still less were the existing public bodies elected by the haphazard methods then in use, practicable instruments for the Socialist. And as yet there was nothing else. But since no alternative directorate was at once forthcoming, the discussion of these difficulties seemed to many of the impatient and still exalted faithful, not so much a practical step forward, as a mischievous move to sabotage any progress towards an emancipated world.

There, it seemed to them, stood the aeroplane ready to soar and it was a terrible pity not to get off at once, simply because no one had as yet made even drawings of a possible controlling apparatus. It was hard to wait for that controlling apparatus. "At this rate we shall never get there" and so on. To complete the image, they tried therefore to use the reins from the old gig.

Now I happened to be detached by my circumstances from political and administrative associations and so perhaps I was able to see this hiatus in the Fabian programme with more detachment than its more active members. This problem of direction in a socialist state, this *search for a competent receiver*, troubled my mind more and more throughout the nineties. I cannot now recall what first turned my attention to it. But as I shall tell in my concluding chapter it became at last a dominant idea in my social philosophy.

The failure to develop a conception of organized directive types, a development which is a necessary consequence of the primary socialist assumption, is I believe, due to the association, at once unreasonable and very natural, of Socialism with the opposition and insurrectionary politics of mere temporary social conditions. In 1886, in common with almost all Socialists at that time, I took that association for granted, and it was only as my experience enlarged and as I came to think out the theory of Socialism more thoroughly, that I realized how accidental and in some respects how unfortunate this alliance was.

There was extremely little "democracy" in the original patriarchal socialism of Robert Owen, and it was Marx who finally fettered the two ideas of Socialism and Democracy together. His imagination intensified the insurrectionary impulse in modern democracy and sought in the resentment and discomfort of the disinherited, a sufficient driving force for a revolutionary reconstruction of society. There was a certain plausibility in the suggestion that the mass-losers in the struggle for gain, would necessarily be in favour of the abolition of private property. But it did not follow at all that they would be able to grasp the idea of collectivized property and take an intelligent controlling interest in its collective administration. Over that thin ice the Marxists skated very swiftly and nimbly. Steadily and surely the idea of the class-war was imposed upon the Socialist idea, until for many Socialism ceased to be a movement for a more comprehensive organization of economic life and took on the quality of a violent restitution of stolen goods—to everybody in general and nobody in particular.

Even Socialists who did not adhere textually to the propositions of Marx were carried unconsciously in the direction of his teaching. His misconceptions of the character and possibilities of English Trade Unions had been profound—and infectious. So in Britain and Russia and Germany and everywhere Socialism was taken to the working masses as if it were not simply their chance and hope but their vindication, which is an altogether different matter; and it seemed the most reasonable thing in the world for the Fabians to turn to the Trade Union officials, exhorting them to enter Parliament as our natural leaders in the mighty task of reconstruction before mankind. Though if you only looked at and listened to a few of them——!

I fell in with this prevalent error as readily as most people. I am only being wise after the event. My theoretical dissent from modern democratic theory was contradicted very flatly by some of my actions. In practice at any rate I was not in advance of my time. There was an interesting duplicity in this matter between my persuasions which ran far ahead, and my policy which lagged with the movement. It is only in the retrospect that I perceive that in this matter I was like a later-stage tadpole which has gills and lungs and legs and a tail all at the same time. In 1906 I was responsible for a Fabian report advocating, not indeed identification of the Fabian Society with the new Labour Party, but "cordial co-operation," and in the general elections of 1922 and 1923 I contested London University as an official Labour candidate. Later on in my story I will return to these lapses towards the class-war conception of Socialism. But for the present I am concerned only with my own inconsistencies in so far as they are representative of this curious entanglement of two fundamentally divergent tendencies, which was everywhere apparent between 1880 and 1920. I am discussing the defects and mis-directions of late nineteenth-century Socialism as a working project for world reconstruction.

In another closely associated direction also, the leaders and makers of Socialism misconceived the great problem before them. They did not realize that a change in the size and nature of communities was going on. They did not grasp that modern Socialism demands great administrative areas. To this day many professed Socialists have still to assimilate the significance of this change of scale. The local Socialist parish or town councillor who is the typical unit politician of the Labour Party, is the last person likely to understand and welcome enlargements that will abolish all those parochial intimacies to which he owes his position. Just as Mr. Ramsay Macdonald opposed proportional representation with large constituencies, because the practical impossibility of a poor adventurer working a constituency under such an electoral method would banish Ramsay Macdonalds from political life, so these Labour wardsmen, in close touch with the local builders and contractors, found insuperable subconscious difficulties to the substitution of any large scale administration for their local jobbery. Necessarily theirs was the Socialism of the parish pump and not the Socialism of a comprehensible control of water supply between watershed and watershed. How could it have been otherwise?

I should probably have remained as blind as most other Socialists to this second aspect of the directive difficulty if I had not chanced to build myself a house in Sandgate in 1899 and 1900. I happened to choose a site upon the boundary line between the borough of Folkestone and the urban district of Sandgate, and the experiences I had in securing electricity for my house across that boundary worked upon certain notions I had picked up from Grant Allen about the sizes and distances between villages and towns upon a countryside (which are determined originally by the length of an hour's journey by horse or foot) and started me off thinking in an extremely fruitful direction. I hit upon the principle to which I had already given expression, that not only must a genuine Socialist government be in the hands of a much more closely knit body than were the party governments of our time, but that having regard to the fact that we were no longer in a horse-and-foot world, the proper administrative areas in a modern socialized community must be altogether different in extent and contour from existing divisions. I began to work out the now universally recognized truth that one of the primary aspects of this period of change, is a change in facility and speed of communications, and that among other things this had made almost every existing boundary too small and tight. This truth was not recognized thirty years ago. But it is of quite primary importance. The applications of this principle of change of scale, once it was stated, were, I discovered, unlimited. I was already making them in my *Anticipations* in 1900. Before I had done with this idea it had led me to the realization of the inevitability of a comprehensive world-state, overriding the sovereign governments of the present time.

In 1903, after I had joined the Fabian Society, I launched this disturbing suggestion of the incompatibility of our extensive projects for socialization with the existing local and municipal organizations, in a paper entitled *The Question of Scientific Administrative Areas in Relation to Municipal Undertakings*. (It was reprinted in an appendix to *Mankind in the Making* published in the same year.) I stated my case in the subdued and enquiring manner of a young learner bringing a thesis to his master for correction. I really thought I should tap a fount of understanding. But there I flattered my Fabian audience. The Fabian audience of that phase was not easily excited by ideas, it assembled for edification, and the paper was received as though it did not matter in the least. Graham Wallas made the most understanding comments. He thought that the Fabian disregard of political reform might have been carried too far.

Afterwards, at the Webbs' house in Grosvenor Road, I

succeeded in emphasizing my point in relation to the elaborate studies they were making of local government in the eighteenth century. Finding them disposed to take up the attitude of specialists towards a vexatious pupil I was as rude as I could be about this work of theirs and insisted that so far as contemporary problems of local government were concerned, a study of the methods of Dogberry and Shallow was as likely to be as valuable a contribution to contemporary problems as a monograph on human sacrifice in Etruria. With the coming of electric trams and electric lighting and universal elementary education, every problem of local administration had been changed fundamentally.

And these changes were still going on. I became very emphatic for a time in these and other talks and writings, on the difference between "localized" and "delocalized" types of mind. I was quite sure I had come upon something important that had been previously overlooked. I had. Existing divisions, I argued, left everything in the hands of the "localized" types, and so long as we divided up our administrative areas on eighteenth century lines, the delocalized man with wider interests and a wider range of movements, found himself virtually disenfranchised by his inability to attend intensively to the petty politics about his front door and garden. He might represent a strong body of opinion in the world, but he was in a minority in any particular constituency. We were in fact trying to modernize a world in which the modernized types were deprived of any influence.

Later on the Fabian Society in belated response to these more vivid personal representations of mine, produced the*New Heptarchy Series* (No. 1 at least of it), in which my idea was Fabianized in a tract, *Municipalisation by Provinces*by W. Stephen Sanders. The association of the rank and file of the Socialist movement with contemporary political hopes and ambitions was however too close to admit of any really bold and thorough pursuit of this idea, and after this sixteen page effort by Mr. Sanders and an attempt, by a sort of afterthought, to incorporate two earlier tracts, this *New Heptarchy Series* damped off and expired. It sank back to such obscurity that it is ignored in Pease's official history of the society's achievements, and the Socialist movement produced no further systematic enquiries either in administrative psychology or in political geography. Such enquiries were not "practical politics," the Webbs had administrative and not scientific minds, and the necessary interrogative spirit was lacking.

I was baffled for a time by this tepid reception of my bright idea by my Fabian teachers and perhaps rather too ready to be persuaded that there were sound practical reasons, outside the range of my experience, why my line of suggestion was not followed up with greater zest. I had many other things to occupy me and I did not press my criticism in the society beyond a certain point. When later I contrived a rebellion against the Old Gang (as I shall tell in the proper place), it was upon an entirely different score. Nevertheless the idea of a change in scale as a matter of quite vital importance in human experience had gained a footing in my brain and was stirring about there, and since it could find no adequate outlet in any modification of Fabian policy, it expressed itself in a fantastic story, *The Food of the Gods*(1903-4) which begins in cheerful burlesque and ends in poetic symbolism. And in my *Modern Utopia* (1905), I took the inevitability of a world-state for granted.

Now I think a sedulous examination of the optimum areas for government functions of various types leading up to a critical study of sovereignty, was a line of investigation which Socialism, if it had really shared with modern science the spirit of incessant research and innovation, would have welcomed and followed up with vigour. If this system of relationships had been worked out, it would now be of incalculable benefit. But it never was worked out. The craving for immediate political and practical application shortened the vision of our Socialist leaders. In the discussion of*Fabianism and the Empire* as early as 1900, lip service was paid to Tennyson's "Federation of the World," but it was the contemptuous lip service of men convinced of their own superior common-sense, and the tract itself, drafted by Shaw and evidently revised and patched a great deal by warier minds, assumed that the division of the whole planet amongst a small number of imperialisms, each under the leadership of a Great Power, was destined to be rapidly completed, that further synthesis was hopelessly remote, and that making "our Empire" efficient was a fit and proper limit to the outlook of British Socialism. Those were the days when "efficiency" was a ruling catchword. It implied both the business and military efficiency of the Empire regarded as a competing organization. Just as the Fabians of thirty-odd years ago could not or would not or did not dare see beyond parish councillors, parliaments, trade unions, constituencies of people hardly able to read, and all the obdurate antiquated forms of contemporary law, so they would not and probably could not see beyond the Competing Great Empires of 1900-1914. The *New Statesman*, which was started by the Webbs and their friends in 1913, as a Socialist weekly, remained sedulously disdainful of the "World-State" up to the outbreak of the Great War.... Then came rapid changes of opinion about the permanence and desirability of those "Great Powers" and their imperial systems, and the *New Statesman* of to-day is as much for the World-State as I am.

Let me turn now to another major item in my account-rendered of the essentials that made the Socialism of the eighties and nineties so deficient and ineffective as a key to human frustration.

Socialism was primarily a criticism of private possessiveness in the common weal, and yet in no part of the Socialist movement in Britain or abroad, was there any evidence of an awareness, much less an examination of the connection between proprietary claims and monetary inflation and deflation. The

Socialist movement floated along in a happy unconsciousness of the possible effect of inflation in releasing the debtor and worker from the claims and advantage of ownership. Nowhere was monetary control linked with the process of expropriating the landowner and private capitalist. Yet many of our minds were playing about quite close to that topic. In my *Modern Utopia* (1905) I even threw out the idea of a currency based on energy units. I could do that and still be unaware that I was touching on another vital deficiency in the Socialist project. The normal Fabian gathering had a real horror of the "currency Crank," as it termed anyone who ventured to say that money has ways and tricks of its own which no serious student of social welfare can ignore. Platform and audience rose in revolt together at the mere whisper of such disturbing ideas.

It was not merely that the Fabians refused to think about money; they pushed the thought away from them. A paragraph from *Tract 70* published in 1896, dealing with the "Mission of the Fabians" is probably unequalled in all literature for self-complacent stupidity. "The Fabian Society ... has no distinctive opinions on the Marriage Question, Religion, Art, abstract Economics, historic Evolution, Currency, or any other subject than its own special business of practical Democracy and Socialism." As one reads one can almost hear a flat voice, with a very very sarcastic stress on the capitals, reciting this fatuous declaration.

The same intellectual conservatism, the same refusal to expand its interests beyond the elementary simplicity of its original assumptions, is to be seen in the attitude of the Fabian Society towards education and the instruction of people generally in the aims of the Socialist reconstruction. In 1906 indeed I was already protesting to the Fabian Society that in order to bring about Socialism we must "make Socialists," but the still more searching and difficult proposition that in order to carry on a Socialist state you must make a Socialist population, was beyond even my imaginative courage. In *Mankind in the Making* (1902), I showed myself alive to the interdependence of general education and social structure but my projected curriculum was extremely sketchy and the political and educational propositions do not interlock clinchingly. I attacked the monarchy as a centre of formalism and insincerity. It was a mask and disguised the actual facts of government. It is however only in quite recent works of mine such as the *Work, Wealth and Happiness of Mankind* (1932) and *The Shape of Things to Come*, (1933) that I recognize that public education and social construction are welded by the very nature of things into one indivisible process.

Finally, as a fifth great imperfection of our nineteenth century Socialism, and one that seems now the most incredible, was the repudiation of planning. Socialism sought to make a new world and yet resisted any attempt to scheme or even sketch what the world was to be. In the retrospect this seems the most extraordinary of all the defects of the movement and yet perhaps it was inevitable at the time. Providentialism was in the spirit of the age. Belief in the necessity of progress anyhow, was almost universal. Even Atheists believed in a sort of Providence. The self-complacency of the Wonderful Century has already become incredible to our unsafe, uneasy and critical generation. But the nineteenth century Individualist said in effect, "give everybody the maximum of personal initiative short of permitting actual murder and robbery, and then free competition will give you the best possible results for mankind." And the nineteenth century Socialist answered him, "Destroy the capitalist system, take property out of the hands of individuals and vest it in any old governing body you find about, and all will be well." This belief in the final indulgence of fate was universal.

But the influence of Marx had greatly intensified that general disposition to a fundamental belief in immanent good luck. Marx was an uninventive man with, I think, a subconscious knowledge of his own uninventiveness. He collected facts, scrutinized them, analysed them and drew large generalizations from them. But he lacked the imaginative power necessary to synthesize a project. His exceptionally intense egotism insisted therefore on a pose of scientific necessitarianism and a depreciation of any social inventiveness. He fostered among his associates a real jealousy of the creative imagination, imaginative dullness masqueraded among them as sound common-sense, and making plans, "Utopianism" that is, became at last one of the blackest bugbears in the long lists dictated by Marxist intolerance. Any attempt to work out the details of the world contemplated under Socialism was received by the old Marxists with contemptuous hostility. At the very best it was wasting time, they declared, on the way to that destructive revolution which would release the mechanical benevolence latent in things. Then we should see. They were all (before the Russian revolution knocked practical sense into them) embittered anti-planners. The Faithful may try to deny this nowadays, but their vast dull abusive literature, stored away in the British Museum and elsewhere, bears it heavy witness. Salvation could come only by the Class War and in the Class War, itself inevitable, was all that sufficed for salvation. And their vehemence, their immense pretensions to scientific method, overawed many a Socialist who stood far outside their organization. They sterilized Socialism for half a century. Indeed from first to last the influence of Marx has been an unqualified drag upon the progressive reorganization of human society. We should be far nearer a sanely organized world system to-day if Karl Marx had never been born.

Contact with reality has since insisted upon the most remarkable adjustments of his theories and the completest repudiations of his essential intellectual conservatism and finality. It has obliged Communist Socialism to become progressive and scientific in method, in complete defiance of its founder and of its early evangelical spirit. Lenin conjured government by mass-democracy out of sight, "vanished" it as conjurors say, by his reorganization of the Communist Party so as to make it a directive élite, and by his organization of the soviets in successive tiers. The ultimate adoption of the Five Year Plan and its successor has been the completest change over from the providentialism of Marx to the once hated and despised method of the Utopists. Russia, as we are all beginning to realize nowadays, is now no longer a Communism nor a democratic Socialism, it has come out of these things as a chick comes out of its egg and egg membranes. It is a novel experimental state capitalism, growing more scientific in its methods every year. It is the supposititious child of necessity in the household of theory. Steadily now throughout the world the Socialist idea and its communist intensification sink into subordination to the ampler proposition of planning upon a planetary scale thrust upon mankind by the urgent pressure of reality. World planning takes Socialism in its stride, and is Socialism plus half a dozen other equally important constructive intentions.

If anyone wants a real measure of the essential unfruitfulness of the Socialist movement, if he wants to realize how like it was to the bag of a hopeful but easily diverted collector into which nothing worth-while was ever put, let him turn his mind for a moment to the adventure of flying. Let him compare the amount of hard work and detailed invention, the patient gathering and development of knowledge and experience, the generous mutual help and mental exchange, that have brought flying in a third of a century, from a dream infinitely less hopeful than the original Socialist project, to the world animating reality it is to-day. Side by side with that vigorous contemporary thrust of the human mind, the literature of Socialism is a pitiful repetition of passing remarks and ineffective promises. Is it any wonder that its name ceases to kindle and its phrases are passing out of use?

But in the late eighties and for us students it was different. Socialism was then a splendid new-born hope. How were we to tell it would decline to grow up, become self-centred and self-satisfied and end as a pervasive, under-developed, unconvincing doctrine? Wearing our red ties to give zest to our frayed and shabby costumes we went great distances through the gas-lit winter streets of London and by the sulphurous Underground Railway, to hear and criticize and cheer and believe in William Morris, the Webbs, Bernard Shaw, Hubert Bland, Graham Wallas and all the rest of them, who were to lead us to that millennial world.

The students of to-day know that the way is harder and the road longer than we supposed. But for one of us in those old days, there are now dozens of keen youngsters in the world, more adventurous, better inured to the habit of incessant enquiry, more obstinately industrious and more persistent. The constructive movement to-day has no such picturesque, brilliant and perplexing leaders as we had. It has no Shaw, no William Morris, no galaxy of decorators and poets and speakers, it cannot evoke such exciting meetings, but that is because it has far greater breadth and self-reliance. Nineteenth century revolutionism was intellectual ragging and boys'-play in comparison with the revolutionary effort now required of us. The great changes continue and will yield to the control only of adequately organized directive forces. It is only as I look back to what we thought and knew at South Kensington half a century ago that I realize the greatness of the world's imaginative expansion.

§ 6. BACKGROUND OF THE STUDENT'S LIFE
(1884- 1887)

So far I have been telling of my life in London entirely from the student's end, for that, during these crucial years, was the vitally important end. A vision was being established, in the grey matter of my brain, of the world in which I was to live for all the remainder of my years. Every week-day we students converged from our diversified homes and lodgings upon the schools in Exhibition Road to learn what the gigantic dim beginnings of the new scientific world-order, which had evoked those schools, had, gropingly and confusedly enough, to tell us. That new world-order was saying immensely important things to us, however indistinctly it was saying them as yet, fundamental things about life and its framework of matter and about our planet; and among ourselves we were awakening to our first perceptions of the drama of human politics and economic affairs. The beds we slept in, the meals we ate, the companionships we formed outside the college limits were necessarily individual and secondary things.

They were not so secondary that they did not exercise a profound influence on our personal destinies. In those days the organization of the South Kensington student's life hardly extended beyond the class rooms and laboratories; there were no students' hostels and our times before ten and after five were entirely in our own hands. We dispersed in the evening to the most various lodgings and the oddest of marginal experiences.

My account of the systematic foundation I was given in biological and physical science, of how that foundation was revised, strengthened and extended in subsequent years, and of how I developed a system of social and political concepts upon the framework of the socialism of the period, has carried my story forward in these last respects far beyond my student days. And indeed far away from myself. I must now bring the reader back to the raw youngster of seventeen up from the country, because there are still several things I want to tell of his particular adolescence and of adolescence in general.

Neither my father, my mother nor I, had had the slightest idea of how I could be put up in London, and we knew of no competent adviser. I had to live on my weekly guinea, that was a primary condition. My mother had perhaps an exaggerated idea of the moral dangers of the great city and too little confidence in my innate chastity and good sense. She had had an ancient friendship, dating from the Midhurst days, with the wife of a milkman in the Edgware Road. They had carried on an intermittent and pious correspondence until her friend died. The friend had had a daughter who was married to an employee of a wholesale grocery firm and to her my mother wrote, seeking a lodging for me, a dry pure spot, so to speak, above the flooding corruption of London. She was happy to entrust me to someone she knew—and she did not reflect how little she knew of this daughter of the elect. As a matter of fact my landlady had relapsed with great thoroughness from the austere standards of her Evangelical upbringing. Piety was conspicuously absent from the crowded little house in Westbourne Park to which I was consigned. The establishment was, indeed, another of those endless petty jokes, always, I think in the worst possible taste, which my mother's particular Providence seemed to delight in playing upon her.

The house, though small, was extensively sublet. On the ground floor was a lower-division civil service clerk and his wife, whose recent marriage was turning out badly. On the first floor and upward one were my landlady and her husband, two boys on the top floor, and I and another man lodger each of us in a room of his own. I think my fellow lodger was some sort of clerk, but I cannot now remember very much about him. We got all our food out except breakfast and, in my own case, a meat tea on week-days, and we shared a common Sunday repast. There was no servant. I do not remember that there was any bathroom—a statement which is perhaps best left in that simplicity.

From this lodging I set off with my little bag of books and instruments by way of Westbourne Grove and Kensington Gardens to the vast mental expansions of the schools and in the evening, before the gardens closed at dusk, I hurried back, often having to run hard through the rustling dead leaves, as the keepers whistled and shouted "All out." South of the green spaces and heavy boughs of the Gardens were laboratories, libraries, museums and astronomical observatories; north were the shops of Queens Road and Westbourne Grove, the gas-lit windows of Whiteley's stores and the intensely personal life of this congested houseful of human beings to which my mother had consigned me. Never was there so complete a transition from the general to the particular. There was a small living-room on a half-landing which I shared with the two boys, and where I wrote up my notes or read my textbooks, on an American-cloth-covered table by the light of a gas jet, while they did their school homework or scuffled with each other.

Both the wives in this double ménage were slatternly women entirely preoccupied with food, drink, dress and sex. They were left alone in the house during the day and during that middle period they "cleaned things up" or gave way to lassitude or, when they were in the mood, dressed themselves up in their smartest to go off to some other part of London, to wander in the shops and streets and seek vague adventures. It was a great triumph to be picked up by a man, perhaps treated to refreshment, to play the great and mysterious lady with him, make a rendezvous with him, which might or might not be observed, and talk about it all afterwards excitedly—with anyone but one's husband. The sayings and doings of the gallant were recalled minutely and searched for evidence as to whether he was a gentleman or what manner of man he was. The prize in this imaginative game was an ideal being, the clubman, the man about town; but it always seemed uncertain whether he had been found. He might have been just a chap up from the country on holiday, or some salesman out of work.

Things livened up for these wives in the evening and at the week-end. There were no "pictures" then but there were music-halls where drinks were served in the auditorium and there they went with their husbands. On Saturdays there was shopping for the Sunday dinner and most of the two households went in a sort of band to the shops and stores and stalls in the Edgware Road.

I was invited to join in these rounds on several occasions. We mingled in the human jam between the bawling shopkeepers and the bawling barrow vendors. We stopped and stared, crowding up, at any amusing incident. We bought shrewdly. We saluted acquaintances. We refreshed ourselves in some saloon bar. I stood treat in my turn, condemning myself to go lunchless on the following Monday and Tuesday.

Sunday had a ritual of its own. The men were given clean linen in the morning and driven out to walk along the Harrow Road until by doing three miles they could qualify as "travellers" for refreshment at an inn. This they did with a doggish air. "Whaddleye-*ave* Guv'ner?" Thence home. Meanwhile the wives prepared a robust joint Sunday dinner. This was consumed with cheerfulness and badinage. Then the boys were packed off to Sunday school, and dalliance became the business of the afternoon. The married couples retired to their apartments; the lodger went off to a lady. I was left to entertain a young woman, who was I think, a sister of my landlady's husband. I do not know how she came in, but she was there. I have forgotten almost everything about her except that she was difficult to entertain. I sat on a sofa with her and caressed and was caressed by her, attempting small invasions of her costume and suchlike gallantries which she resisted playfully but firmly. Her favourite expressions were "Ow! *starp* it" and "Nart that." I remember I disliked her and her resistances extremely and I cannot remember any definite desire for her. I am quite at a loss now to explain why it was I continued to make these advances. I suppose because it was Sunday afternoon, and I was too congested with unusual nourishment to attempt any work, and there was nothing else to be done with her. Or if there were I did not know how to set about doing it.

This manner of life was presently grossly animated by a violent quarrel between the two wives. The Sunday dinners were divided; all co-operations ceased. The precise offence I never knew, whether it centred round the lodger, one or both of the husbands or some person or persons unknown. But it involved unending recriminations in the common passage and upon the staircase, and attempts to involve the husbands. The husbands showed themselves lacking in the true manly spirit and came home late with a hang-dog look. My landlady was very insistent upon some defect in the health of her sub-tenant. "She's in a state when no man ought to go near her," is an enigmatical sentence delivered from the half landing, that has survived across the years.

One day my landlady came into my room to change the pillow case while I was there and provoked me into a quasi-amorous struggle. She was wearing a print dress carelessly or carefully unhooked at the neck. Then she became reproachful at my impudence and remarked that I might be a man already, the way I behaved. And afterwards the lodger who seems to have been hovering in the passage, observed at supper in the tone of a warning friend, that if she thought I was too young to bring trouble upon her she might find herself mistaken.

Suchlike small things on the far side, the individual life side, of Kensington Gardens, excited me considerably, bothered me with contradictory impulses, disgusted me faintly and interfered rather vexatiously with the proper copying out of my notes of Professor Huxley's lectures.

It was certainly not the sort of pure safe life away from home that my mother had desired for me, but it did not occur to me to tell her anything about it and I should probably have begun my actual sexual life very speedily, clumsily and grossly and slipped into inglorious trouble if it had not been for the sensible action of a cousin on my father's side, whom he had asked to keep an eye on me.

My father was the sort of man to like, admire and cultivate a friendly niece and his opinion of Janie Gall was a particularly high one. She was an assistant in the costume department at an establishment in Kensington High Street which I see still flourishes, Messrs. Derry & Toms, and she made me call upon her and take her out on several occasions. It was like old times at Southsea to be the escort of an elegant lady from the costumes; I knew the rôle and we got on very well together. In response to her frank enquiries I described to her the more seemly and impersonal defects of my lodgings, considered as quarters for a studious spirit, and she grasped the situation and acted with great promptitude.

A sister-in-law of my father's was letting lodgings in the Euston Road; the situation at Westbourne Park was explained by my father to my mother, who had perhaps allowed the natural jealousy of relations-in-law to blind her to the merits of my Aunt Mary, and I and my small portmanteau were promptly transferred—probably in a four-wheeled "growler"—to my new quarters. A mile was added each way to my daily journey to the schools, but now it was no longer necessary to run at twilight because the new route lay diagonally across Hyde Park—and Hyde Park stands open to our bolder citizens night and day.

It is queer that I do not remember the particulars of that move, nor can I recall the address of that house in which I lodged in Westbourne Park, nor the names of either my landlady, her sub-tenant or her lodger. The few facts I have given and one or two other slightly salacious details remain in my memory, but all the rest of that interlude is forgotten beyond all recalling. It links to nothing else. I disliked it and put it out of my mind. I cannot remember how long it was, whether it was a matter of weeks or months that I lodged there before I went to Euston Road. I looked, so to speak, through a hole in my life of some weeks more or less, into a sort of humanity, coarser, beastlier and baser than anything I had ever known before. None of the other people in my experience before or since were quite so like simmering hot mud as that Westbourne Park household. I cannot recall really pleasant things about anybody in it, whereas there is scarcely any other group of people in my past which had not its redeeming qualifications. I think the peculiar unpleasantness of that episode lies in the fact that we were all too close together. We were as congested as the Zoo monkeys used to be before the benign reign of Sir Chalmers Mitchell. Crowded in that big cage they seemed in those days the nastiest of created things. Now, distributed spaciously under happier and less provocative conditions even the baboons have become—practically—respectable.

I can recall very little about Janie Gall beyond this timely intervention. She was a tall, blonde, sedate young woman whose life had been divided hitherto between England and her father's ship in the far east. She told me once that she was the first white woman ever to visit the Pelew Islands, but she had nothing very much to tell me about those distant scenes. She passed out of my world and afterwards I learnt she had gone to Sweden and had married a Swede named Alsing. I have a perfectly clear picture of myself walking along Knightsbridge and talking with her, and nearly everything else about her is obliterated. Did she go first, or afterwards, to a well-known mourning warehouse in Regent Street? I cannot remember any of these details. They are after all very trifling details.

But 181 Euston Road stands out very bleak and distinct in my memories. In the eighties Euston Road was one of those long corridors of tall gaunt houses which made up a large part of London. It was on the northern boundary of Bloomsbury. Its houses were narrow and without the plaster porticos of their hinterland and of Bayswater, Notting Hill, Pimlico, Kilburn and suchlike regions. They had however, narrow strips of blackened garden between them and the street, gardens in which at the utmost grew a dying lilac or a wilted privet. One went up half a dozen steps to the front door and the eyebrows of the basement windows were on a level with the bottom step.

So far as I can puzzle out the real history of a hundred years ago, there was a very considerable economic expansion after the Napoleonic war, years before the onset of the railways. The steam railway was a great stimulus to still further expansion, its political consequences were tremendous, but it was itself a product of a general release of energy and enterprise already in progress. Under a régime of unrestricted private enterprise, this burst of vigour produced the most remarkable and lamentable results. A system of ninety-nine year building leases was devised, which made vast fortunes for the ground landlords and rendered any subsequent reconstruction of the houses put up almost impossible until the ground lease fell in. Under these conditions private enterprise spewed a vast quantity of extremely unsuitable building all over the London area, and for four or five generations made an uncomfortable incurable stress of the daily lives of hundreds of thousands of people.

It is only now, after a century, that the weathered and decaying lava of this mercenary eruption is being slowly replaced—by new feats of private enterprise almost as greedy and unforeseeing. Once they were erected there was no getting rid of these ugly dingy pretentious substitutes for civilized housing. They occupied the ground. There was no choice; people just had to do with them and pay the high rents demanded. From the individualistic point of view it was an admirable state of affairs. To most Londoners of my generation these rows of jerry-built unalterable homes seemed to be as much in the nature of things as rain in September and it is only with the wisdom of retrospect, that I realize the complete irrational scrambling planlessness of which all of us who had to live in London were the victims.

The recklessly unimaginative entrepreneurs who built these great areas of nineteenth century London and no doubt made off to more agreeable surroundings with the income and profits accruing, seem to have thought, if they thought at all, that there was an infinite supply of prosperous middle-class people to take the houses provided. Each had an ill-lit basement with kitchen, coal cellars and so forth, below the ground level. Above this was the dining-room floor capable of division by folding doors into a small dining-room and a bureau; above this again was a drawing-room and above this a floor or so of bedrooms in diminishing scale. No bathroom was provided and at first the plumbing was of a very primitive kind. Servants were expected to be cheap and servile and grateful, and most things, coals, slops, and so forth had to be carried by hand up and down the one staircase. This was the London house, that bed of Procrustes to which the main masses of the accumulating population of the most swiftly growing city in the world, including thousands and thousands of industrial and technical workers and clerks, students, foreigners upon business missions, musicians, teachers, the professional and artistic rank and file, agents, minor officials, shop employees living out and everyone indeed who ranked between the prosperous householder and the slum denizen, had to fit their lives. The multiplying multitude poured into these moulds with no chance of protest or escape. From the first these houses were cut-up by sub-letting and underwent all sorts of cheap and clumsy adaptations to the real needs of the time. It is only because the thing was spread over a hundred years and not concentrated into a few weeks that history fails to realize what sustained disaster, how much massacre, degeneration and disablement of lives, was due to the housing of London in the nineteenth century.

(But the autobiography of any denizen of any of the swelling great cities of the nineteenth century who wished to place his story in regard to the historical past and the future would have, I suppose, a similar story to tell of housing conditions; the same tale of growth without form—like a cancer. New York was almost as bad and St. Petersburg far worse. There is a dreadful flavour of mortality about these city growths of the past hundred years, so that one wonders at times whether the world will ever completely recover from them. Nowhere was there, nowhere is there yet, an intelligent preparation of accommodation for the specialized civilians in the endless variety rendered inevitable by the enlarging social body. Nowhere was there protection from those Smart Alecs, the primary poison of the whole process, who piled up the rents. Even when the tenants were people who did work of vital importance to the community, the ground had been so sold under their feet that they came back from work to needlessly restricted and devitalizing quarters for their sleep and leisure.)

My uncle William had been no better business man than my father and he had had no skill in cricket or any other earning power to fall back upon. He had been a draper and, my mother said, extravagant. I had seen him on one occasion, a dark shabby unhappy man clad in black, who came to Atlas House one wintry afternoon, ate with us, talked apart with my father, borrowed a half sovereign from our insufficiency and departed—to die not long afterwards in a workhouse infirmary. He had married one of two sisters named Candy, daughters of a small Hampshire farmer; the other had remained unmarried and, after their father's death, with a van load of furniture and a few pounds, she and my widowed aunt had come to London to live by letting lodgings. They planned to occupy the basement, cooking in the back kitchen and living in the front and doing all the work up and down the house; the dining-room floor to be let to one tenant and the drawing-room floor to another and all the rest of the bedrooms to nice young men or respectable young ladies; and thus they would get a living. They made no provision in their estimates for the wear and tear of their furniture nor the wear and tear of themselves, and so, year by year, their rooms and their services became less and less attractive and desirable. That was what happened to countless widows, old servants with a scrap of "savings," wives of employees who wanted to help their husbands a bit and all that vast miscellany of dim and dingy women, the London landladies, who were guyed so mercilessly in the popular fiction of the time. The larger, more successful, lodging houses had a "slavey," a poor drudge to do the heavier carrying and scrubbing, but people like my aunt and her sister, had to be their own slaveys.

When my cousin Janie Gall took me to tea at Euston Road the Saturday afternoon before my removal, my aunt and her sister were in company costume with caps and small aprons, like my mother at Up Park. But even then I thought them grimy, and, poor dears! they *were* grimy. They were far grimier than my mother had ever been in the worst days at Atlas House. How could they have been anything else, seeing that the house was warmed throughout by coal-fires and that they were perpetually carrying up scuttles of coal (at sixpence a scuttle) to their various lodgers, and dusting and scrubbing and turning out rooms and dealing with slops and ashes? My aunt Mary was a little bright-eyed woman and very affectionate and lovable from the beginning; her sister was larger, with a small eye and profile faintly suggestive of a parrot, judicious in her manner and given to moods of gloom and disapproval. As we sat talking politely, a dark-eyed girl of my own age, in the simple and pretty "art" dress that then prevailed came shyly into the room and stood looking at us. She had a grave and lovely face, very firmly modelled, broad brows and a particularly beautiful mouth and chin and neck. This was my cousin Isabel whom later I was to marry.

It was arranged that I should have a room upstairs and work at my notes in the evening by the gas light in the underground front room. This was a rather crowded room with hanging shelves for books, a what-not and a piano upon which at times my cousin played not very skilfully the few pieces of music she had learnt. My aunt would darn stockings and her sister fret over accounts, or sometimes we would play whist, at which Miss Candy, aunt Arabella, was as precise as Lamb's Mrs. Battle. She found the way her sister Mary played particularly trying. "I'm silly," said my aunt Mary anticipating her reproof. "You *shouldn't* be silly, Mary," said auntie Bella. They had been saying that over and over again since they were girls—far back in the eighteen fifties.

On occasion, when the upstairs lodgers were away or the rooms unlet, we transferred our evenings to the drawing-room or dining-room. If I wanted to concentrate I went to my own bedroom and there I would work by candle-light, often in an overcoat, with my feet wrapped about with my clean underlinen and stuck into the lowest drawer of my chest of drawers to keep them out of the draught along the floor.

I forget most of the lodgers. There was a woman student at University College who had the drawing-room floor for some years, and a German woman in the dining-room whose visitors roused Auntie Bella's censorious curiosity. Some of them were men, and foreigners at that. "We mustn't come to that sort of thing," said Aunt Arabella darkly, but went no further in the matter.

On the top floor was a poor old clergyman and his wife, who presently died one after the other, the wife first. He had either never had a vicarage or he had lost one, and he earned a precarious income by going off to churches for a week-end or a week or so on "supply," to relieve the regular incumbent. Until, one wintry week-end, some careless person sent an open dog- cart to meet him at the railway station and gave him pneumonia. Apparently he had no surviving friends or if he had they did not come forward; he died intestate and practically penniless, and I escorted my aunt one wet and windy morning to Highgate cemetery where we were the only mourners at his funeral. Another old clerical derelict, with a dewdrop at his nose-tip, hurried through the service. It was my first funeral. I had never dreamt that a clergyman could end so shabbily, or that the Establishment could discard its poor priests so heartlessly. It was quite a new light on the church. My little aunt was his sole creditor and executor and I doubt if, when the doctor was satisfied, there was much left to set against the arrears of the poor old fellow's bill.

I lodged at 181 Euston Road for all the rest of my student life. Every day in the session, unless I got up too late, I walked to South Kensington. I would go through the back streets as far as the top of Regent Street with Isabel; she worked in Regent Street as a retoucher of photographs; there we said good-bye for the day and I went on for all the length of Oxford Street to the Marble Arch and thence across the Park to Exhibition Road. If I was late however I left my cousin unescorted and went by train from Gower Street Station (Euston Square they call it now) to Praed Street at a cost of three half-pence, and then ran across the Gardens. And as I went down Exhibition Road, Euston Road passed out of my mind and my student life resumed again as if it were a distinct and separate stream of experience. I thought again upon the scale of astronomical distances and geological time and how, when presently Socialism came, life would be valiant and spacious and there would be no more shabbiness or darkness in the world.

§ 7. HEART'S DESIRE

I want to make my physical presence at the time I left South Kensington, as real as possible to the reader. I have given five sections to tell how my picture of life in the universe was built up in my brain; I now want to show what sort of body it was that carried this brain about and supplied it with blood and obedient protection. By 1887, it had become a scandalously skinny body. I was five foot five and always I weighed less than eight stone. My proper weight should have been 9 st. 11 lbs., but I was generally nearer to seven, and that in my clothes. And they were exceedingly shabby clothes. It did not add to the charm of my costume that frequently I wore a waterproof collar, an invention now happily forgotten again. It was a glossy white rubber-covered thing that cost nothing for laundry. That was the point of it. You washed it overnight with soap and a sponge, and then it was ready in the morning. But after a time it accumulated something rather like the tartar that discolours teeth. It marks one difference that is worth noting between the eighties and the present time, that never a Kensington student, however needy, would have dreamed of appearing in the classroom or laboratory without what could at least be considered a white collar. Now, I suppose, a good half of the Kensington crowd wear open-necked shirts. A certain proportion of us in those days, and all the staff, wore top hats.

I was as light and thin as I have said, because I was undernourished. I ate a hastily poached egg and toast in the morning before going off for my three mile tramp to the schools and I had a meat-tea about five when I got back—and a bread and cheese supper. Most of my time I was so preoccupied with my studies and my intellectual interests that I did not observe what was happening to me, but occasionally and more especially in my third year, I would become acutely aware of my bad condition. I would survey my naked body, so far as my bedroom looking-glass permitted, with extreme distaste, and compare it with the Apollos and Mercuries in the Art Museum. There were hollows under the clavicles, the ribs showed and the muscles of the arms and legs were contemptible. I did not realize that this was merely a matter of insufficient food and exercise. I thought it was an inferior body—perhaps past hope of mending.

To me, in my hidden thoughts, the realization that my own body was thin and ugly was almost insupportable—as I suppose it would be to most young men or women. In the secret places of my heart I wanted a beautiful body and I wanted it because I wanted to make love with it, and all the derision and humour with which I treated my personal appearance in my talking and writing to my friends, my caricatures of my leanness and my unkempt shabbiness, did not affect the profundity of that unconfessed mortification. Each year I was becoming much more positively and urgently sexual and the desire to be physically strong and attractive was intense. I do not know how far my psychology in these matters is exceptional, but I have never been able to consider any sort of love as tolerable except a complete encounter of two mutually desirous bodies—and they have to be reasonably lovely bodies. The circumstances must be beautiful or adventurous or both. I believe this is how things are with nine people out of ten; as natural as hunger and thirst.

The fact that I was slovenly to look upon and with hollows under my collar-bones and with shoulder-blades that stuck out, could not alter these insistent demands of the life in me. No doubt these realizations reinforced those balancing inhibitions and that wariness and fastidiousness which are as natural as the primary cravings, and made me more than normally secretive; but to hold down an urgency is not to diminish it. I had quite another set of motives, ambition, a desire for good intellectual performance and that vague passion for service which expressed itself in my socialism, and I tried, not always successfully, to take refuge in these from my more vital and intimate imperatives.

Beautiful girls and women do not come the way of poor students in London. One was nearer to such beings among the costume hands and counter assistants of the draper's shop. There were a few friendly women fellow-students in the laboratories, but they deliberately disavowed sex in their dress and behaviour. Sex consciousness broke out to visibility only among the Art students, and these we saw but rarely during brief promenades in the Art Museum, which made a kind of neutral territory between the Art Schools and ourselves. On my long march back to Euston Road I would see women walking in the streets, especially along Oxford Street and Regent Street, and sometimes in the light of the shops, one would shine out with an effect of loveliness and set my imagination afire. I would be reminded of Ellen Terry walking in the sunshine upon the lawn at Surly Hall. Or I would see some handsome girl riding in the Row or taking a dog for a run in the park. They were all as inaccessible as the naked women in the Chantry pictures.

It was practically inevitable that all this suppressed and accumulating imaginative and physical craving in me should concentrate upon the one human being who was conceivable as an actual lover; my cousin Isabel. She and I had from the outset a subtle sense of kindred that kept us in spite of differences, marriage and divorce, friendly and confident of one another to the end of her days, but I think that from the beginning we should have been brother and sister to each other, if need, proximity and isolation had not forced upon us the rôle of lovers, very innocent lovers. She was very pleasant to look upon, gentle mannered, kind and firm, and about her I released all the pent up imaginations of my heart. I was devoted to her, I insisted, and she was devoted to me. We were passionate allies who would conquer the world together. In spite of all appearances, there was something magnificent about us. She did her best to follow me, though something uncontrollable in her whispered that this was all nonsense. And whenever we could avoid the jealous eye of Auntie Bella, we kissed and embraced. Aunt Mary did not embarrass us because she had taken to me from the beginning.

Across a gulf of half a century I look with an extreme detachment and yet with an intense sympathy upon these two young Londoners, walking out together, whispering in a darkened staircase, hugging in furtive silence on a landing. Isabel wore simple dresses after the Pre-Raphaelite fashion. We should think them graceful to-day except that the sleeves would seem big and puffy to us and the pretty neck unaccountably hidden. Abroad she wore a cloak in winter and her hats were usually those velvet caps that also came out of the Cinquecento.

Having stripped my youthful self for your edification I will now cover up my worst physical deficiencies with my clothes again. They were rather shabby but very respectable, a grey "mixture" suit and a grey overcoat in winter. The collar was white even if it was waterproof and the hat was a hard bowler. There were no soft felt hats until much later and a cap, in London, would have been disgraceful behaviour. And we lived in an age when everyone had best clothes. On Sunday we two walked out together with a certain added seriousness; we walked in Regents Park or we went to a church or a picture gallery, when there was a picture gallery open, or to some public meeting, and then I wore a morning coat and a top hat.

In my desire for correct particulars in this autobiography, I have spent some time trying to trace the beginnings, the rise and fall of my successive top hats. They mark periods in human history as surely as do the ramshackle houses in which I spent the first half of my life and the incoherent phases of my upbringing and education. In the mind of a febrile psycho-analyst, these top hats might be made to show the most curious and significant phases in the upward struggle of the human intelligence. They were more voluntary and so more subtle in their fluctuating intimations than were turbans, fezzes, pigtails and the like which outlasted whole generations. But that history of the rise and fall of the top hat has yet to be written. When I was born it had already passed its zenith; cricketers no longer played the game in top hats—though my father had begun in that fashion; but it still seemed the most natural thing in the world for me to take out my cousin on Sundays in this guise. Half the young men I met on that day sported similar glossy cylinders. In the city and west-end, on a week day, you rarely saw a man wearing anything else. The streets below repeated the rhythms of the clustering chimney pots on the roofs above. I must have acquired my first specimen, when I acquired my morning coat and its tails, during the second year of my apprenticeship at Southsea. But was that the one I wore in London? I think it was and if so it went right on with me to 1891, when it died a natural death—as I shall tell in its place—in the presence of Mr. Frank Harris, the editor of the *Fortnightly Review*. After that I think I bought another to attend a funeral and a third seems to have marked a phase of social acquiescence before the War. I went to Bond Street picture shows, and the Academy, in the latter. It ended as a charade property for my sons at Easton Glebe. Since then I have had no more top hats.

But it is just that indication of social acquiescence which justifies this digression and makes the top hat of my student days so significant. It was the symbol of complete practical submission to a whole world of social conventions. It was not, in my case at any rate, just a careless following of the current fashion, for peace and quietness. That early top hat in particular had been economized for, it expressed an effort, it had *had* to be worn.

Now as my cousin and I walked along the broad path between the flower beds of Regents Park—bright and gay they were then but not nearly so beautiful as they are now—I would be talking very earnestly of atheism and agnosticism, of republicanism, of the social revolution, of the releasing power of art, of Malthusianism, of free-love and such-like liberating topics. In a tail coat and top hat. My mind was twenty years ahead of my visible presence. It was indeed making already for the gardens of Utopia.

But my cousin who was as direct and simple as she was sane, honest and sweet, was just walking in her Sunday best in Regents Park.

In my eagerness to find in her the mate of my imaginings, I quite overlooked the fact that while I had been reading and learning voraciously since the age of seven, she had never broken a leg and so had never been inoculated with the germ of reading. While I had gone to school precociously equipped, she had begun just the other way about as a backward girl, and she had never recovered from that disadvantage. It was a purely accidental difference to begin with, I am sure her brain was inherently as good as or better than mine, but an inalterable difference in range and content was now established. Her world was like an interior by a Dutch master and mine was a loose headlong panorama of all history, science and literature. She tried valiantly to hang on to what I was saying, but the gap was too wide. She thought I must be dreadfully "clever" to talk such nonsense and she comforted her mind with the reflection that it had not the slightest relation to things about us. She liked me by nature and she did not like to irritate me, but sometimes something I said was too much for her, and she "stood up for" the old Queen, or the landlords, or business men, or Church; whatever it was I happened to be abolishing. It was a fixed principle in her broad and kindly mind that they were all "doing their best" and that in their places we should do no better. Then, since what she said spoilt the picture I wanted to make of her in my imagination, I would become rude and over-bearing.

I tried to get her to read books and particularly the books of Mr. John Ruskin, but like so many people who have had the benefit of a simple English education she was book-shy. The language she met in books was not the language of her speech and thoughts. I doubt if she read a hundred books in all her life.

I was far too much in a ferment myself to reduce my ideas to terms that would have persuaded her. I hadn't that much grasp of my own views. "Everybody doesn't think alike," said my cousin. "But that's no earthly reason why you shouldn't think at all," I bit, and after that the young couple would go on their way in a moody silence, dimly aware that there was something unjust and wrong about it all, but quite unable to find out what was wrong or in any way set it right. Why was I always talking of these queer and out-of-the-way things? Because otherwise and particularly in my silk hat and so forth, I was quite a nice boy. And again why was I sometimes so pressing about love-making—in a way that one ought not to think about until one was in a position to marry? And that might not be for years. A little love-making there might be, no doubt, but one must not go too far.

My mind in those days refused absolutely to recognize the

incompatibility that is so plain as I state it here. I had laid hands on Isabel, so to speak, to love her and I would not be denied. She was to be my woman whether she liked it or not. I tethered my sexual and romantic imagination to her so long as I was in London—and that, quite as much as my poverty, saved me from the squalor of the street-walker. With a devotion that was more than half jealousy, whenever work did not hold me at South Kensington I used to devour my meat tea and then set off out again down to Regent Street to meet her and bring her home, and always when she was working in the evening at some art classes at the Birkbeck Institute, I made my way through the dark Bloomsbury Squares to meet her. These evening assiduities kept me exercised physically but they made grave inroads upon the time I should have given to my proper work. And I loved her smile, I loved her voice, I loved her feminity, I loved to feel that—provided I did not go too far—she was mine. And someday, somewhen, I should do something fine and successful and the world would be at my feet; her tacit reservations would vanish and she would realize that everything I said, did and wanted, was right.

I was always wanting to board and storm and subjugate her imagination so that it would come out at last of its own accord to meet mine. It never came out to meet me.

Through some mysterious instinct my little Aunt Mary understood and believed in my heart's desire, but Auntie Bella was sterner stuff, with a more sceptical disposition and an acuter sense of reality. She thought it a pity that Isabel and I were so much together.

That was the naïve intensely personal other side of my life, to which I walked back daily across Hyde Park from that interplay of lectures room, laboratory, debating society and student talk described in the earlier sections of this chapter.

One of the queer things about us human beings is the way the obvious consequences of our actions take us by surprise. I will not now apply this to the large scale instances of the great wars of 1914 and, shall we say?—1940. But I do remember very vividly how unprepared I was to walk the plank as a condemned science student in the summer of 1887. I had done practically everything necessary to ensure failure and dismissal, but when these came they found me planless and amazed. I suppose that is the way of youth—and all animals. Foresight is among the latest and incompletest of the acquisitions of mankind.

Abruptly the self confidence which had never really failed me since my escape from the Southsea Drapery Emporium, collapsed like a pricked bladder. I had no outlook, no qualifications, no resources, no self-discipline and no physique.

"And what is to become of me *now*?" I asked, in a real panic for the first time since my triumphant exodus from the draper's shop.

VI. — STRUGGLE FOR A LIVING

§ 1. SIXTH START IN LIFE OR THEREABOUTS (1887)

I have to thank my lucky stars—and a faithful friend or so—that I did not sink as a result of my insubordinations, inattentions, digressions and waste of energy at South Kensington into absolute failure. Most of the orderly students in my generation made good as professors and fellows of the Royal Society, as industrial leaders, public officials, heads of important science schools; knighthoods and the like are frequent among them; I am probably the only completely unsatisfactory student turned out by the Normal School, who did not go the pace there and who yet came up again and made a comparative success in life. I was now nearly of age and able to realize the dangers of my position in the world, and I put up a fight according to my lights. But it was a wild and ill-planned fight, and the real commander of my destinies was a singularly facetious Destiny, which seemed to delight in bowling me over in order to roll me through, kicking and struggling, to some new and quite unsuspected opportunity. I have already explained how I became one of the intelligentsia and was saved from a limited life behind a draper's counter by two broken legs, my own first, and then my father's. I have now to tell how I was guided to mental emancipation and real prosperity by a smashed kidney, a ruptured pulmonary blood vessel, an unsuccessful marriage and an uncontrollable love affair.

My very obstinate self-conceit was also an important factor in my survival. I shall die, as I have lived, the responsible centre of my world. Occasionally I make inelegant gestures of self-effacement but they deceive nobody, and they do not suit me. I am a typical Cockney without either reverence or a sincere conviction of inferiority to any fellow creature. In building up in my mind a system of self-protection against the invincible fact that I was a failure as a student and manifestly without either the character or the capacity for a proper scientific career, I had convinced myself that I was a remarkable wit and potential writer. There must be compensation somewhere. I went on writing, indeed, as a toy-dog goes on barking I yapped manuscript, threateningly, at an inattentive world.

With every desire to be indulgent to myself I am bound to say that every scrap of writing surviving from that period witnesses that the output was copious rubbish, imitative of the worst stuff in the contemporary cheap magazine. There was not a spark of imagination or original observation about it. I made not the slightest use of the very considerable reservoir of scientific and general knowledge already accumulated in my brain. I don't know why. Perhaps I was then so vain that I believed I could write *down* to the public. Or so modest that I thought the better I imitated the better I should succeed. The fact remains that I scribbled vacuous trash. The only writing of any quality at all is to be found in the extremely self-conscious letters I wrote to my friends. Here I really did try to amuse and express myself in my own fashion. These letters are adorned with queer little drawings and A. T. Simmons and Elizabeth Healey among others, seem to have found them worth keeping so that a number of them have been preserved to this day. There is fun in them. I doubt if I could possibly have carried on and become a writer without the support of those two people. They were my sole "public" for years. No letters I wrote to my cousin Isabel survive. I cannot remember writing to her though certainly I must have done so. I doubt if I wrote to her with the same zest and certainty of appreciation.

My plans for a rally against my richly deserved disaster as student, had a certain reasonableness. I was now in a shocking state of bodily unfitness, very thin, under-exercised and with no muscular dexterity, loose in gesture, slow on the turn and feeble in the punch; and it seemed to me that if I got a job as an assistant in a school deep in the country, with good air, good food and good games, (I had my previous invigoration at health-giving Midhurst in my mind) I might pick up the neglected beginnings of my bodily manhood and at the same time get a little leisure to learn, by the method of trial and error, what was the elusive vital thing I didn't yet know about this writing business. I had had, by the bye, one small success and earned a guinea. I had sent a short story, now happily untraceable, to the most popular fiction weekly of those days, the *Family Herald*. It was a very misleading success. It was a sloppy, sentimental, dishonest, short story and its acceptance strengthened me in my delusion that I had found the way to do it.

Meanwhile I had to live by teaching. In spite of my rather wilted qualifications, there were plenty of residential school jobs at forty or fifty pounds a year to be got; I had matriculated as an ex-collegiate in London University, I was qualified to earn grants in a number of subjects, and I had had teaching experience. The Holt Academy, Wrexham, seemed, on paper, the most desirable of all the places offered me by the agencies. It was a complex organization. A boys' school plus a girls' school plus a college for the preparation of young men for the Calvinistic Methodist ministry, promised variety of teaching and possibilities of talk and exercise with students of my own age. I expected a library, playing fields, a room of my own. I expected fresh air and good plain living. I thought all Wales was lake and mountain and wild loveliness. And the Holt Academy had the added advantage of re-opening at the end of July and so shortening the gap of impecuniosity after the College of Science dispersed.

But when I got to Holt I found only the decaying remains of a once prosperous institution set in a dismal street of houses in a flat ungainly landscape. Holt was a small old town shrunk to the dimensions of a village, and its most prominent feature was a gasometer. The school house was an untidy dwelling with what seemed to be a small whitewashed ex-chapel, with broken and dirty windows and a brick floor, by way of schoolroom. The girls' school was perhaps a score of children and growing girls in a cramped little villa down the street. The candidates for the ministry were three lumpish young men apparently just off the fields, and the boys' school was a handful of farmers' and shopkeepers' sons. My new employer presented himself as a barrel of a man with bright eyes in a round, ill-shaven face, a glib tongue and a staccato Welsh accent, dressed in the black coat, white tie and top hat dear to Tommy Morley, the traditional garb of the dominie. He was dirty,—I still remember his blackened teeth—and his wife was dirty, with a certain life-soiled prettiness. He conducted me to a bedroom which I was to share, I learnt, with two of the embryo Calvinistic ministers.

My dismay deepened as I went over the premises and discovered the routines of the place. The few boarders were crowded into a room or so, sleeping two and three in a bed with no supervision. My only colleague was a Frenchman, Raut, of whom I heard years afterwards, because he claimed to have possessed himself of the manuscript of a story by me which he was offering for sale. (I found myself unable to authenticate that manuscript.) Meals were served in a room upon a long table covered with American cloth and the food was poor and the cooking bad. There was neither time-table nor scheme of work. We started lessons just anyhow. Spasmodic unexpected half-holidays alternated with storms of educational energy, when we worked far into the evening. Jones had a certain gift for eloquence which vented itself in long prayers and exhortations at meals or on any odd occasion. He would open school with prayer. On occasions of crisis he would pray. His confidence in God was remarkable. He never hesitated to bring himself and us to the attention of an Avenging Providence. He did little teaching himself, but hovered about and interfered. At times, the tedium of life became too much for him and his wife. He would appear unexpectedly in the schoolroom, flushed and staggering, to make a long wandering discourse about nothing in particular or to assail some casual victim with vague disconcerting reproaches. Then for a day or so he would be missing and in his private quarters, and Raut and I and the theological students would keep such order as we found practicable and convenient.

These theological students aimed at some easy, qualifying examination for their spiritual functions. The chief requirement for their high calling was a capacity for intermittent religious feeling and its expression in Welsh, and that they had by birth and routine. They were instructed in "divinity" (poor God!) and the elements of polite learning when it seemed good to Jones that this should happen. They were not without ambitions. Their hopes, I learnt, were not bounded by their own sect. A qualified minister of the Calvinistic Methodists might sometimes be accepted as a recruit and further polished by—I think it was—the Wesleyans. A Welsh-speaking Wesleyan again might have scruples of conscience and get into the Anglican priesthood. The Anglican priesthood had always openings for Welsh speakers and so, far up the vistas of life, a living in the established church beckoned to my room-mates. I know not how far this process of ratting might be carried. An unmarried Anglican can, I believe, become a Roman Catholic priest. In Christendom all roads lead to Rome, and so my room-mates were potential, if highly improbable, popes.

I improvised lessons in the boys' school and in the girls' school, I taught scripture on Sunday afternoons, played cricket and Association football to the best of my ability, and made my first attendances at a Calvinistic Methodist service. It was more vivid and personal than the Anglican ritual and Rouse, the minister, was more copiously eloquent even than Jones. I found some of the hymns very effective. I was particularly fond of that frequent favourite which begins:

> *Not all the blood of goats*
> *Shall for my sins atone.*

I liked the lusty voices singing together all out, and there was a satisfying picturesqueness about the spiritual geography of Beulah Land and Jordan's Stream, Hermon and Carmel, that let one out, in imagination at least, from Holt.

> *Christian dost thou hear them On the Holy ground;*
> *How the Hosts of Midian Prowl and prowl around?*
> *Christian, up and SMITE them....*

But it was very plain to me, as a surviving letter to Miss Healey testifies, that I realized my career had got into a very awkward cul-de-sac. There was no getting away from this place that I could see, however much I disliked it. I had no money to get away with. There was nothing for me now but to stick it for at least a year, get some better clothes, save a few pounds, hammer away at my writing, and hope for some chance of escape. For a few weeks the weather was very good and I developed a tendency to let things drift. I seem to have forgotten my romantic devotion to my cousin very easily; I suppose her inability to carry on a correspondence had something to do with that. For a time she just went out of the scheme of happenings. I met the daughter of the minister of an adjacent parish, Annie Meredith, a mistress in a high school on holiday, we liked each other at sight and we carried on a brisk and spirited flirtation. I find I boast about this in my letters—not to Miss Healey but to A. M. Davies—say she is well read and talk of spending "whole hours by shady river banks where I talk grotesquely to her and she very intelligently to me." Had that summer weather and my returning health and vigour lasted for ever, I suppose I should have slackened slowly from my futile literary efforts and reconciled myself altogether to the rôle of a second rate secondary teacher. I should have awakened one day to find myself thirty and still in a school dormitory.

But this is where the peculiar humour of my Guardian Angel came in. Annie Meredith went off to her school work leaving Holt remarkably dull again, and the football season began. I played badly but with a desperate resolve to improve. The lean shock-headed intellectual doing his desperate tactless best in open-air games is never an attractive spectacle. I had a rough time on the field because that was where the bigger louts got back upon me for my English accent and my irritating assumption of superior erudition. One bony youngster fouled me. He stooped, put his shoulders under my ribs, lifted me, and sent me sprawling.

I got up with muddy hands and knees to go on playing. But a strange sickness seized upon me. There was a vast pain in my side. My courage failed me. I couldn't run. I couldn't kick. "I'm going in," I said, and returned sulkily to the house regardless of the game, amidst sounds of incredulous derision.

In the house I was violently sick. I went to lie down. Then I was moved to urinate and found myself staring at a chamber-pot half full of scarlet blood. That was the most dismaying moment in my life. I did not know what to do. I lay down again and waited for someone to come.

Nothing very much was done about me that evening, but in the night I was crawling along the bedroom on all fours, delirious, seeking water to drink. The next day a doctor was brought from Wrexham. He discovered that my left kidney had been crushed.

He was a good doctor but he made one mistake which did very much to restore my prestige at Holt. I had been shocked and sickened but I had had no acute pain at all. He declared however that I must have suffered and still be suffering the greatest agony. I did not care to dispute his ruling. After all he was a specialist and I was an amateur. As it impressed Jones and Mrs. Jones and seemed likely to raise the low standard of nursing and sympathy in the place, I adopted the bearing of a stoical Red Indian under torture, very successfully. I gave the whole school a most edifying and inexpensive lesson in patient lip-biting heroism.

I lay in bed in that bleakly furnished bedroom for as long as I could, meditating on my future. I spent my coming of age in bed. I had, I decided, to carry on at Holt. I had no money and practically nowhere to go. My father at Bromley was being sold up. Up Park was wearying of Mrs. Wells's family.

At intervals Mr. Jones came and looked at me and I regarded him with that serenity which comes to men who know no alternatives. At first, being afraid that I might die and under the spell of my heroic self control, he was effusive for my comfort. "Would I like some books?" He was going in to Wrexham. I said I had never read *Vanity Fair*. I had always wanted to read *Vanity Fair* and this might be my last chance. "But in your state," protested Jones, sincerely shocked. "The vera name of the book! It must be a vera vera baaad book."

I didn't get it.

In a few days his attentions faded away. I began to be hungry. The doctor said I ought to lie some days longer and be kept warm and well fed. Jones came to suggest I should go home to my friends—unpaid. I explained that I proposed to get up and resume my duties. The weather was turning cold and Jones would have no fires until the first of October, but with a stiffness and ache in my side I got up and went on with my classes in the brick-floored schoolroom. Presently I had a bad cough which grew rapidly worse. Then I discovered that my lungs were imitating my kidney and that the handkerchief into which I coughed was streaked with blood. The Wrexham doctor, calling to see how I was getting on, pronounced me consumptive. But consumptive or not, I meant to see the half year out at least and pocket Jones's twenty pounds. I had a faint malicious satisfaction in keeping Jones to that.

§ 2. BLOOD IN THE SPUTUM (1887)

In those days we knew very little about tuberculosis. People talked of consumption. It was not understood to be infectious and since it produced no symptoms of importance below the diaphragm, it was found particularly suitable for the purposes of sentimental fiction. The fragile sympathetic consumptive with his (or her) bright eyes, high colour and superficially hopeful spirits, doomed to an untimely end—for it was also supposed to be incurable—had unlimited encouragement to brave self-pity and the most unscrupulous demands, for toleration and sacrifice, upon the normal world. So even the intimations, as everyone supposed them to be, of an early death, were not without their compensations.

To a certain extent I fell in with the pattern of behaviour expected of me. I played the interesting consumptive to the best of my ability. But there were forces in both my body and mind that resented this graceful cutting down of my sprawling expectations of life. I don't know how a modern specialist would define my case but it certainly traversed all the accepted medical science of the eighties. No tuberculous germs were ever detected, but there was certainly some degenerative process at work in my lung, breaking down tissue and breaching the walls of blood vessels. This process went on for about five years, rising to a maximum and then being arrested and ceasing, leaving a scarred lung. There was an attack and there were resistances that finally won. But in my case, as in so many cases, there was (and is) no medical science adequate to define the evidently very complex tangle of stimulations and pro and anti-functional forces at work. A degenerative adjustment of my damaged kidney began in 1898 to complicate the hidden business still further. Consequently, beginning with my condemnation by the Wrexham doctor as a consumptive, there were a series of misleading diagnoses, each one creating expectations and holding out prospects to which I tried to adjust my plans of life, and each diagnosis failing in its turn to come true. As late as 1900, I was building a house at Sandgate specially facing towards the sun, with bedrooms, living rooms, loggia and study all on one floor, because I believed I should presently have to live in a bath-chair and be wheeled from room to room. And all the while an essential healthiness was doing its successful utmost to bring me back to physical normality.

Not only were my blood and tissues resisting the suggestion that I was one of those transitory gifted beings too fine and fragile for ordinary life, but my mind also was in active revolt against that idea. I had, I will admit, some beautiful moments of exquisite self-pity, tender even to tears, but they were rare. In my bones I disliked the idea of dying, I disliked it hotly and aggressively. I was exasperated not to have become famous; not to have seen the world. Still more deeply exasperated was I at the nets of restraint about me that threatened that I should die a virgin. I had an angry insurgence of sexual desire. I began to accumulate a curious resentment against my cousin Isabel because she had had no passion for me. I wanted to go out and pursue strange women. I reproached myself with my discretion about the street walkers of London during my student days. I make no apology for these moods; that is how the thought of enfeeblement and death stirred my imagination. This resentment at being cheated out of a tremendous crowning experience was to survive into my later sexual life, long after the obsession with death, from which it had arisen, had lifted. My imagination exaggerated the joy of embracing a woman until it became maddeningly desirable.

There was also a considerable amount of pure fear in my mind, a sort of claustrophobia, for though I disbelieved intellectually in immortality I found it impossible to imagine myself non-existent. I felt I was going to be stifled, frozen and shut up, but still I felt I should know of it. I had a nightmare sense of the approach of this conscious nothingness.

In no respect I think does the mature mind differ so widely from the youthful mind as in its fear of death. I doubt if a young mind is really capable of grasping the idea of a cessation of experience, although it may be acutely alive to defeat and deprivation. But as life unfolds into realization, death loses that sting. For the past quarter of a century at any rate my death, as death, has had no terror or distress for me. It does not, I realize, concern me. I want to complete certain things, but if death sees fit to come before I have done them, I shall never know of it. Maybe I do not speak for all oldish men here. When I talked with Sigmund Freud in Vienna this spring, he did not seem to feel as I do about death. He is older than I and he was in bad health, but he seemed to be clinging to life and to his reputation and teaching much more youthfully than I do to mine. But then perhaps he was just drawing me out.

Quite apart from the general fear of death, disappointment

and frustration which weighed so heavily upon my imagination at times during my consumptive phase, there were unpleasant minor fears and anxieties that I can still recall acutely. Every time I coughed and particularly if I had a bout of coughing, there was the dread of tasting the peculiar tang of blood. And I can remember as though it happened only last night, the little tickle and trickle of blood in the lungs that preceded a real hæmorrhage. Don't cough too soon? Don't cough too much? There was always the question how big the flow was to be, how long it would go on, what was to be the end of it this time. And as one lay exhausted, dreading even to breathe, there was still the doubt whether it was really over.

I can tell of these disagreeable and dismaying things now that they lie so far behind me, but at the time I did not confess my states of dread and dismay to any human being. Here again I can thank my Fate for my sustaining vanity. I posed consistently as the gay consumptive. Indeed I carried it off with Holt to the end that I was the invincible Spartan. My letters to those loyal correspondents of mine, were cheerfully fatalist and more blasphemous than ever.

My fellow student William Burton, who had followed me as editor of the *Science Schools Journal,* had got a good job as chemist with Wedgwoods the potters. The firm had lost many of its old recipes and his work was to analyse old potsherds and rediscover how the original Wedgwoods used to mix their more famous wares. He had just married, and he came out of his honeymoon way with his brightly new little wife to see me. I had a meal with them in the Holt Inn. It was a good and sustaining thing for me to have them thus concerned about me. They excited me and cheered me up, but they were secretly distressed to find me more fragile and emaciated than ever. They departed, bless their friendly hearts! scheming helpfully about me.

The magic word consumptive softened the heart of Up Park towards me. The defences erected against any further invasions by Mrs. Wells's family were lowered. I came to what I considered a fair arrangement with Jones and set out upon my journey to Harting. I think I must have stopped the night at 181 Euston Road but I cannot remember. I was installed in a room next to my mother's at Up Park and celebrated my arrival by a more serious hæmorrhage than any I had had hitherto.

It chanced that a certain young Dr. Collins was staying in the house and he was summoned to my assistance. I was put upon my back, ice-bags were clapped on my chest and the flow was stopped. I was satisfying all the conventional expectations of a consumptive very completely. I lay still for a day or so and then began to live again in a gentle fashion in a pleasant chintz-furnished, fire-warmed, sunlit room. My previous few weeks at Holt assumed the quality of a bad dream, a quality it has never quite lost. A few days later came a box of books from Burton, an unforgettable kindness.

I must have stayed at Up Park for nearly four months. It was an interlude not only of physical recovery but mental opportunity. I read, wrote and thought abundantly. I got better and had relapses, but none were so grave as the breakdown on arriving. Collins was a brilliant young heretic in the medical world of those days, altogether more modern than my Wrexham practitioner, and he rather dashed my pose as a consumptive and encouraged my secret hope of life by refusing to recognize me as a tuberculous case. He held—and events have justified him—that with a year or so of gentle going I might make a complete recovery. But he was rather distrustful of the stability of my damaged kidney and there again he was right. And he spoke of the possibility of diabetes and now I am diabetic. We had one or two interesting talks about things in general. He was a leading Comtist and an Individualist, as his father was before him, and a valiant man in the affairs of London University. He is now Sir William Job Collins, as obstinately Positivist as ever and only a few weeks ago I reminded him of his excellent diagnosis in our Reform Club.

Geoffrey West, my indefatigable biographer, knows more about these months I spent at Up Park in 1887-88 than I do, for he has exhumed quite a remarkable number of letters written by me during that time. I seem to have had alternations of recovery and hope with relapse and stoicism. I seem to have hoped very readily and taken risks forthwith. At one time I am confined to my room, at another I boast of a sunlit seven mile walk in thawing snow. But that was followed by a "rustling lung." Up Park below stairs was gay at Christmas and I was gay with it. My father had been sold up and had come with the vestiges of that old furniture in Atlas House to a small cottage at Nyewoods by Rogate station, three miles from Up Park. He had relinquished the idea of earning anything, modestly but firmly. My elder brother, who had fretted as a draper's assistant from the glorious days of my revolt, had joined him there. He proposed to make a new start in life as a watch and clock peddler and repairer. Freddie came to this Rogate cottage for his Christmas holiday and the whole family was shockingly in evidence for the Christmas feast in the Servants Hall, in excellent appetite and the most shameless and unjustifiable high spirits. A letter to Davies, quoted by West, makes it apparent that I danced abundantly and larked about and amused the company by some sort of performance with my brother Frank; but what it was about I cannot now remember. I am sure my mother chuckled with happiness to see her four menfolk so happy. I seem to have been concealing from my mother the fact that there was still blood in my sputum either to spare her feelings or else to escape excessive coddling, but Heaven knows how much posing and exaggeration there is in these letters to my friends.

What is however very plain in them is the gradual transition from the forced courage of a genuine invalid to the restlessness and irritability of a convalescent. I began to find my very comfortable quarters irksome and unstimulating. I had no one to talk to except the Harting curate, and that probably accounts for the voluminousness of these letters West unearthed. Other frustrations were becoming more and more vexatious. I fretted for some lovely encounter that never occurred. Yet, though I did not realize it, I was getting through something of very great importance in my education during these months of outward inaction. I was reading and reading poetry and imaginative work with an attention to language and style that I had never given these aspects of literature before. I was becoming conscious of the glib vacuity of the trash I had been writing hitherto. When I look back upon my life, there is nothing in it that seems quite so preposterous as the fact that I set about writing fiction for sale, after years of deliberate abstinence from novels or poetry. Now, belatedly, I began to observe and imitate. I read everything accessible. I ground out some sonnets. I struggled with Spenser; I read Shelley, Keats, Heine, Whitman, Lamb, Holmes, Stevenson, Hawthorne, and a number of popular novels. I began to realize the cheapness and flatness of my own phrasing. I went on indeed with the "novel" I had worked upon at Wrexham, but with a growing distaste. I hadn't the vigour to scrap it forthwith and begin all over again. And I dislike leaving things unfinished. But I began to write other stuff, I aired the most extraordinary critical opinions in my letters to Miss Healey and apparently I sent her some verse. Because I find West quoting me to her: "You say my lines are lacking in metre—metres are used for gas, not the outpourings of the human heart. You say my poem has no feet! The humming bird has no feet, the cherubim round the Mater Dolorosa have no feet. The ancients figured the poetic afflatus as a horse *winged* to signify the poet was sparing of his feet."

Later on in the year, with a quickened sense of what writing could be and do, I read over with shame and contrition all that I had written and I burnt almost all of it. That seemed the only proper way of finishing it. I realized that I had still to learn the elements of this writing business. I had to go back to the beginning, learn to handle short essays, short stories and possibly a little formal verse, until I had acquired the constructive strength and knowledge of things in general demanded for any more ambitious effort. I had not, I saw, been *writing* so far. I had just been playing at writing. I had been scribbling and assuring myself and my friends that it signified something. I had been covering my failure at South Kensington with these unfounded literary pretensions. But it is very illuminating to note that I never showed these copious scribblings to anyone. No human being, not even myself, knows now what *Lady Frankland's Companion* was supposed to be about. I remember only sheets and sheets of boyish scrawl. I saw myself at last with a rare and dreadful plainness. Should I always be too conceited to learn? I knew I had a gift, a quality, but apparently I was too vain and confident about that quality ever to make use of it. I chewed the bitter cud of these reflections as I prowled through the beech-woods and bracken-dells of Up Park or over the yew-dotted downs by Telegraph House.

Every bit of strength I recovered, every ounce of weight I added, deepened my dissatisfaction with the indolent life I was leading, and the feebleness of my invalid efforts. I wanted to resume my attack upon the world, but on a broader basis now and with more soundness and deliberation. My idea of getting a job to keep me while writing had been a sound one, even if it had chanced upon disaster at Holt. I realized that I must insert in the place of "while writing" a preliminary stage "while learning to write" but otherwise the plan of campaign was sound. Better luck next time—if I was to have a next time.

And presently the Burtons, installed in a newly furnished new little house conveniently close to the Wedgwood pot-bank at Etruria, wrote to say that they had a visitor's room quite at my disposal. It was a most enticing invitation and I accepted very eagerly. I found the Burtons and their books and their talk, and the strange landscape of the Five Towns with its blazing iron foundries, its steaming canals, its clay whitened pot-banks and the marvellous effects of its dust and smoke-laden atmosphere, very stimulating. As I went about the place I may have jostled in the streets of Burslem against another ambitious young man of just my age who was then clerk to a solicitor, that friendly rival of my middle years, Arnold Bennett.

There is a letter I wrote in February 1888, to Dr. Collins, which shows very clearly my conception of my position at that time. I lift it in its entirety from West's book. It is interesting as a sample of my early prose. There is something more than a little suggestive of Babu English in the phrasing. I had not yet fused my colloquial with the literary language which was still slightly foreign to me.

"You pointed out when you last did me the favour of examining my chest, how difficult it would be to get any employment compatible with my precarious health, without special concessions and personal influence. Miss Fetherstonhaugh holds out very small hope of assisting me in this way, and Sir William King, her agent, to whom she mentioned the matter, spoke in an exceedingly depreciating way of the prospects of obtaining anything of the kind required. I am very ignorant of social conditions above my own level, but it appears to me that you, moving, as you are, among people who as a class are engaged in more vigorous intellectual employments and who are more intricately involved in the business of life than those with whom Miss Fetherstonhaugh comes chiefly into contact, would be far more influential in this present matter than she is. A very large portion of the visitors here is of the three orders of military gentry, clerical dignitaries, or that fortunate independent class whose only business is to live happily, and it seems to me that the only employment that such a connection could offer above the rank of an unmitigated menial, is a private tutorship, for which I should, even after a very unwholesome meal of my principles, be vastly less suitable than the most rejected young gentleman that ever behaved himself at Oxford. You, on the other hand, are acquainted with men like Harrison, Bernard Shaw, the Huxleys, who must from the active and extensive nature of their engagements of necessity employ numerous fags to assist in the more onerous and less responsible portions of their duties. It was this that I had especially in view when I mentioned my desire for employment to you, but I am afraid that I failed to express myself with sufficient definiteness on that occasion, and that I led you to understand that I appreciated wine and oil above a consistent position and the prospects of self-advancement. My constitutional tendencies all incline me to prefer staking the preservation of my life on my utility, to imperilling, as everyone counsels, my utility to preserve my life; I would rather do what I wanted and felt was right to be done, and retire soon with some faint irradiation of human dignity and self-applause, than survive for a long period to my own discontent and the general impoverishment. (This is applied Socialism.) This is my second and more powerful reason for coming upon you in this way to help me to some work, because I consider you are not only more able to assist me, but that you are the only person who is willing and in a position to bring me into contact with that world of liberal thought in which alone the peculiar circumstances of my education render me capable of attaining to any degree of success."

Collins replied kindly but nothing further ensued and I stayed at Etruria for nearly three months waiting for opportunity to come and find me. I think I must have been a handful as a guest though neither my host or hostess betrayed any impatience. I was always on hand. I was very untidy. I had a teasing habit of luring Burton after his day's work into exasperating discussions. But, they say—for they are still alive and good friends of mine—that I used to amuse them greatly by wild caricatures of life at Holt and Up Park, and by sudden flights of fantasy. And at Etruria my real writing began. I produced something as good at least as my letters, something I could read aloud to people I respected without immediate shame. It was good enough to alter and correct and write over again.

I projected a vast melodrama in the setting of the Five Towns, a sort of Staffordshire *Mysteries of Paris* conceived partly in burlesque, it was to be a grotesque with lovely and terrible passages. Of this a solitary fragment survives in my collected short stories as *The Cone*. Moreover I began a romance, very much under the influence of Hawthorne, which was printed in the *Science Schools Journal*, the *Chronic Argonauts*. I broke this off after three instalments because I could not go on with it. That I realized I could not go on with it marks a stage in my education in the art of fiction. It was the original draft of what later became the *Time Machine*, which first won me recognition as an imaginative writer. But the prose was over-elaborate and with that same flavour of the Babu, to which I have called attention in my letter to Dr. Collins. And the story is clumsily invented, and loaded with irrelevant sham significance. The time traveller, for example, is called Nebo-gipfel, though manifestly Mount Nebo had no business whatever in that history. There was no Promised Land ahead. And there is a lot of fuss about the hostility of a superstitious Welsh village to this Dr. Nebogipfel which was obviously just lifted into the tale from Hawthorne's *Scarlet Letter*. And think of "Chronic" and "Argonauts" in the title! The ineptitude of this rococo title for a hard mathematical invention! I was over twenty-one and I still had my business to learn. I still jumbled both my prose and my story in an entirely incompetent fashion. If a young man of twenty-one were to bring me a story like the *Chronic Argonauts* for my advice to-day I do not think I should encourage him to go on writing.

But it was a sign of growing intelligence that I was realizing my exceptional ignorance of the contemporary world and exploring the possibilities of fantasy. That is the proper game for the young man, particularly for young men without a natural social setting of their own.

Spring passed into summer and I grew stronger every day. It became manifest that I could not go on living upon the Burtons indefinitely. One bright afternoon I went out by myself to a little patch of surviving woodland amidst the industrialized country, called "Trury Woods." There had been a great outbreak of wild hyacinths that year and I lay down among them to think. It was one of those sun-drenched afternoons that are turgid with vitality. Those hyacinths in their upright multitude were braver than an army with banners and more inspiring than trumpets.

"I have been dying for nearly two-thirds of a year," I said, "and I have died enough."

I stopped dying then and there, and in spite of moments of some provocation I have never died since.

I went back to Burton. I had got the two halves of a five-pound note from my mother against such an eventuality. (People sent divided five-pound notes in separate letters in those days, for safety.) I told Burton I was going to London the day after to-morrow.

"What for?" said Burton.

"To find a job."

"My dear chap!" cried Burton, but I think it must have been an immense relief to him.

I posted letters to various scholastic and employment agencies that night, and said I would call upon them in two or three days' time. I was astonished that I had not done so a couple of months before.

§ 3. SECOND ATTACK ON LONDON (1888)

I have given up counting my starts in life. This return to London was, I suppose, about the seventh or eighth in order.

When I read over my biography by Geoffrey West, I realize the peculiar advantages of an autobiographer. For a year between

June 1887 and June 1888 I had been an active volcano of letters—and letters that chanced to be kept. Geoffrey West set about collecting these letters with great ability and industry. He got more matter than he bargained for and it is only the mercy of Heaven and my timely holocaust, that saved him from the manuscript of *Lady Frankland's Companion* (35,000 words) and other unpublished outpourings. But in 1888 the eruption died down. Except for a sketch I sent Simmons of myself very lean and unkempt standing at a street corner considering an advertisement for sandwichmen, with the pithy announcement, "I am in London seeking work but at present finding none," there is very little documentation of the next six months, at the end of which I turn up suddenly, with my epistolary vigour much restored, as an assistant master in Henley House School, Kilburn. I even find myself at a loss now to fix the dates and circumstances of that intervening period. I have nothing to go upon but patchy memories with the connecting events forgotten.

I did not want to bother my friends or be bothered by them until I got that job. I knew that in the last resort I could get money from my mother, but she had now to support my father at Nyewoods with very little assistance from brother Frank, and I was ashamed to press on her too heavily. It is doubtful if she had anything much in hand just at that time. It was possible I might not find a job because among other things I was extremely shabby. I arrived, with that old small portmanteau of mine, at St. Pancras and found a lodging that night in Judd Street, which I considered to be just within my means; a rather disconcerting lodging. The room had three beds and one of my fellow occupants, the lodging-house keeper told me, was "a most respectable young man who worked at a butcher's." I forget him and I forget if the third bed was occupied that night. I went to bed early because the journey up had tired me. The next morning I breakfasted in a coffee house—one could get a big cup of coffee, a thick slice of bread and butter and a boiled or fried egg for fourpence or fivepence—and then set out to find a room of my own in the streets between Grays Inn Road and the British Museum.

I got one for four shillings a week, in Theobalds Road. It was not really a whole room but a partitioned-off part of an attic; it had no fireplace, and it was furnished simply with a truckle bed, a wash-hand-stand, a chair and a small chest of drawers carrying a looking glass. The partition was so thin, that audibly I was, so to speak, in the next room. My neighbours were a young couple on whom I never set eyes, but their voices became very familiar to me and I learnt much about their intimate lives. When the intimacy seemed to be rising to a regrettable level, I would cough vigorously, make my bed creak or move my chair about, and the young couple would instantly sink out of existence into a profound silence like a frightened fish in a deep pool.

In this lair I tried to do some writing and my correspondence, and from it I sallied out to find that job that was to carry me and all my fortunes until I had really mastered this writing business. I went the round of the scholastic agents, I put myself on the lists of any employment agency that did not attempt to exact a fee for registration, and I answered many impossible and some possible advertisements. I ate at irregular intervals and economically. There were good little individual shops where sausages or fish sizzled attractively over gas jets in the windows; the chops in chop houses were not bad, tea shops were multiplying; a "cut from the joint and two vegs" in a public house cost eightpence or ninepence. In Fleet Street I tried a very cheap vegetarian restaurant once or twice, but it left me hungry in the night. The scholastic agents said I was late in the field for a permanent job that year, but they put me down for possible visiting teaching in science. I did get a little special coaching in geology and mineralogy, with an army crammer, but that was all. My first substantial employer was my old fellow-student Jennings.

Jennings was trying to build up a position as a biological coach. He found his pay as a junior demonstrator in geology at the

Science Schools insufficient, and he was using some of his capital to assemble teaching equipment. He was also lecturing in biology at the Birkbeck Institute in Chancery Lane. For these purposes he needed a collection of wall diagrams and, knowing me to be a sufficient draughtsman for the purpose, he commissioned me, so soon as he learnt I was in want of work, to make him a set. His idea was to have these copied from textbooks and high priced series of diagrams, mostly German, which I could sketch in the British Museum Reading Room. He bought a piece of calico and paints for me, I procured one of those now superseded, green, reader's tickets of very soft card, which lasted a life-time, or until they fell to pieces, and I made my sketches under the Bloomsbury dome and enlarged them as diagrams in a small laboratory Jennings shared with a microscopist named Martin Cole in 27, Chancery Lane. Cole, at the window, prepared, stained and mounted the microscope slides he sold, while I sprawled over a table behind him and worked at my diagram painting. Cole's slides were sold chiefly to medical students and, neatly arranged upon his shelves were innumerable bottles containing scraps of human lung, liver, kidney and so forth, diseased or healthy, obtained more or less surreptitiously from post-mortems and similar occasions.

My job with Jennings came none too soon, for my original five pounds had ebbed away to nothing. Before I could draw upon him, I came to the bottom of my resources. I had a sporting wish to carry the thing through if I possibly could, without a further appeal to my mother. I did some very fine computations outside small fried-fish shops and the like during these last days before Jennings and I struck our bargain. At last I came to an evening when I turned out my pocket and found a small piece of indiarubber, a pocket knife and a halfpenny. Even in that cheaper time there was nothing in the way of supper to be done on a halfpenny. And since even a postcard cost three farthings I had cut myself off from writing to anyone. I had cut it altogether too fine. I went to bed to reflect upon the problem.

Since I had no watch nor rings or anything of that sort I had not yet discovered the routines of the pawnshop, and it was difficult to fix upon anything in my possession that I felt would appeal to a pawnbroker's appetite. I imagined in my innocence he would only consider "valuables." I had a bone-handled cane that had originally cost two and sixpence, some fine vestiges of surplus underclothing, socks all worn into holes at the heel, two waterproof collars, discoloured, and half a dozen normal linen ones, frayed, and so forth.

As I got up next morning I looked by chance at that halfpenny and something unusual in the design and colour caught my eye. It was a shilling, blackened by contact with the lump of ink eraser! You cannot imagine the difference that sudden windfall of eleven pence ha'penny, made to my world. And first I broke my fast.

My week-days during that period of stress were fully occupied by small activities. The British Museum Reading Room and the Education Library at South Kensington were good places for light, shelter and comfort. You could sit in them indefinitely so long as they were open. And the streets and shops were endlessly interesting. I loitered and watched the crowds. It was encouraging to see how many people seemed able to get food and clothing. But I found the Sundays terrible. They were vast, lonely days. The shuttered streets were endless and they led nowhither but to chapels and churches which took you in and turned you out at inconvenient hours. Except in St. Paul's Cathedral there was nowhere to sit and think. In the smaller places of worship one had to be sitting down or standing up or kneeling and pretending to participate. Loneliness weighed upon me more and more. I began to wonder what my cousin Isabel was doing and whether I might not chance to meet her in the street. At last she seemed round every corner.

When I got an advance from Jennings I gave way to a growing desire for companionship and wrote to ask if I might come to tea with her on Sunday afternoon. My cousin was now earning good money by retouching photographs. The gaunt house in Euston Road had been abandoned, Auntie Bella had found a situation as housekeeper to a Wiltshire farmer, and my cousin and her mother were installed on the drawing-room floor of a little house in Fitzroy Road near Regents Park. Thither I went and over the tea-cups and hot buttered toast my aunt Mary, who loved me like a son, rated me soundly in her earnest thin little voice for coming to London without telling her, and pointed out the economies and advantages of joining forces with them. There was a little bedroom on the landing to let. She was longing to look after me.

Within a week I had left Theobalds Road and transferred most of my paints and rolls of calico to Fitzroy Road, and something like the old pattern of my life with Isabel was restored. Directly I was in her presence again I forgot whatever I had forgotten about her. We were less children than we had been and she was more self-reliant than in Euston Road under the distrustful sway of Auntie Bella, but she had the same restrained sweetness and gentleness, the same sound and limited wisdom, the same withheld feminity to which my emotional life had been adjusted during my student days. We resumed our old familiarity as though there had been no interval. We went about again side by side with our thoughts and reveries worlds apart.

The restored sense of home and care at the back of me gave fresh vigour to my hunt for work and money. I went on with Jennings and his diagrams, did a bit of coaching, arranged to share Cole's room and steer Simmons, who had become an assistant schoolmaster, during his Christmas vacation through the dissections for the biology of his Intermediate Science examination, and also I picked up small but useful sums of money, if not by journalism at least in the margin of journalism. At that time a number of new penny weeklies were coming into existence to challenge the ascendancy of the old *Family Herald* with the new boardschool public. There were *Tit Bits, Answers* and a little later*Pearson's Weekly*. I think it was *Tit Bits* which first devised a page called "Questions worth Answering" open to outside contributors. A dozen or so questions appeared one week and the best answer to each question was published the next. It was a popularization of *Notes and Queries*. For a question accepted, one got half-a-crown; for an answer one was paid according to length. If one were lucky, one might send in an acceptable answer to one's own question. My copious reading and my special biological lore came in very usefully here. Every week I contrived in this way to add anything between two and sixpence and fourteen or fifteen shillings to the Fitzroy Road budget.

My lungs stood the onset of winter fairly well. My aunt Mary kept her bird-like eye upon me and knew I had a cough before I did, and did something about it. By the end of the year I had arranged to begin a job in Kilburn after Christmas, that was more like firm ground under my feet than anything I had been upon for a year and a half.

§ 4. HENLEY HOUSE SCHOOL (1889-90)

From my departure from Southsea in 1883 to my return to London in 1888, the history of this brain of mine was mainly a story of growth and learning things. It acquired as much, decided as much and was exercised as much as if it had been inside the skull of a university scholar. It developed a coherent picture of the world and learnt the use of the English language and the beginnings of literary form. But from my emergence from St. Pancras Station to find lodgings and a job, this brain, for the better part of a year, was so occupied with the immediate struggle for life, so near to hunger and exposure and so driven by material needs, that I do not think it added anything very much to either its content or power. It was only after a term or so at Henley House School, that it began to take notice of external things again and resume its criticism of, and its disinterested attack upon, existence in general.

This Henley House School was, financially, a not very successful private school in Kilburn. It was housed in a brace of semi-detached villas, very roughly adapted to its educational needs. It drew its boys from the region of Maida Vale and St. John's Wood; the parents were theatrical, artistic, professional and business people who from motives of economy or affection preferred to have their sons living at home. There were only a few boarders. It was a privately owned school and J. V. Milne, the proprietor, was responsible to no earthly authority for what he did or did not teach. In one of the houses he lived with his family and in the other were the various class-rooms and the assistants' room of the school. The playground was a walled gravelly enclosure that had once been two back gardens. It was too small for anything but the most scuffling of games. Equipment was little better than it had been in Morley's school; the desks were not so age-worn and there were more blackboards and maps. But it remained—skimpy. When I entered upon my duties, J. V. came to me and pressed a golden sovereign into my hand. "Get whatever apparatus you require for your science teaching," he said.

"And if there is any change?" I asked with this fund, this endowment, in my hand.

"You can give me an account later."

I had to administer this grant very carefully. The existing apparatus was huddled into what had once been a small bedroom cupboard on the second floor, and was in an extremely ruinous condition. My predecessor had been a Frenchman and very evidently a man of great persistence of character. His chemical teaching had apparently reached a climax in the production of oxygen by heating potassium permanganate in a glass flask. Young Roberts, the son of Arthur Roberts, the comedian, said it had been a very great lesson indeed. Those were primitive times in glass manufacture and the ordinary test-tube or Florentine flask was not of a special refractory glass as it is now, and it cracked and flew at the slightest irregularity in its heating. My predecessor had put his permanganate in a flask, put the flask on a tripod, set a Bunsen burner beneath it and made all the necessary arrangements for collecting his oxygen. But before there was any oxygen worth mentioning to collect, the flask flew with a loud crack and its bottom descended upon the flame. My predecessor rallied his forces and put a second Florentine flask into action, with exactly the same result. A certain joyousness invaded the class as, with the spirit of the French at Waterloo, a third flask was thrown into the struggle. And so on, *da capo*; joy increased and open demonstrations had to be repressed. At the end there were no more Florentine flasks and the applause broke out unhindered. The cupboard was chiefly occupied by these shattered flasks neatly arranged, each over its own proper detached bottom.

I meditated upon these vestiges of experimental science and upon what seemed to me to be the evidence of an attempt to make carbon-dioxide out of blackboard chalk—an attempt fore-ordained to failure because blackboard chalk is not chalk and contains no carbon dioxide. And I considered my still intact sovereign.

I discussed the matter with J. V. "Mr. Milne," I said, "I think experimental demonstrations before a class are a great mistake."

"They certainly have a very bad effect on discipline," he remarked.

"I propose," I said, "with your permission, to draw all my experiments upon the blackboard—in coloured chalks which I shall buy out of this pound—to explain clearly and fully exactly what happens and to make the class copy out these experiments in a note-book. I have never known an experiment on a blackboard go wrong. On the other hand, these attempts at an excessive realism——"

"I am quite of your mind," he said.

"Later on, however, I may dissect a rabbit bit by bit and make them draw that. I may dissect it under water because that is cleaner and prettier than a heap of viscera on a board, and I shall have to buy a large baking-dish and cork and lead and pins."

"It will not be—indelicate?"

"It need not be. I will show them what to see on the blackboard."

"One never knows what parents will find to object to. However—if you want to do it...."

In this way I contrived, without extravagance, to train my classes to draw, write and understand about a great many things that would have been much more puzzling for them if they had encountered them in all the rich confusion of actuality. I never attempted to use the chemical balance for example; chemical balances, especially if they have been left to brood in the darkness of bedroom cupboards, will seize upon the slightest pretext to confute the hasty experimentalist; and moreover my predecessor had lost most of the weights. My boys therefore missed the usual stinks and bangs of scientific instruction and acquired instead a real grasp of scientific principles and scientific quantities, together with a facility in illustrating examination answers that stood them in good stead in the years immediately before them.

I found Milne a really able teacher, keen to do his best for his boys and with a curious obstinate originality, and I learnt very much from him about discipline and management. Finance, I knew, was worrying him a good deal, but he watched his boys closely and would slacken, intensify or change their work, with a skilled apprehension of their idiosyncrasies. He would think of them at night. The boys had confidence in him and in us and I never knew a better mannered school. He was friendly and sympathetic with me from the outset. He was a little grey-clad extremely dolichocephalic man with glasses, a pointed nose and a small beard, rather shy in his manner; he had a phantom lisp and there was a sort of confidential relationship between his head and his shoulders. His original proposal was that I should be resident English, science and drawing master at £60 a year. But I wanted to go on living with my aunt and cousin at Fitzroy Road, I detested Sunday duty and I wanted to write or to work at my preparation for the Intermediate Examination in the London University, in all the spare time I could get. So I offered to forego my residence and all my meals except the midday one, if I could come at nine and vanish at or before five. And I stipulated that I should do no scripture teaching, as I felt I could not do it in good faith. The arrangement worked very well for us both. He liked my putting in that conscience clause at the risk of not getting a job I evidently wanted.

The midday meal was an excellent one, attended by a number of the day- boys. With memories of Holt in my mind, I wrote to Simmons effusively, praising the cleanliness, the table napkins and particularly the flowers on the table. In my world hitherto there had been no flowers on the meal table anywhere. And at the end of the table, facing me, sat Mrs. Milne, rather concerned if I did not eat enough, because I was still, she thought, scandalously thin.

I suppose the day is not so very remote when the last of these private schools will have vanished from the earth. Fifty years ago they were still responsible for the education, or want of education, of a considerable fraction of the British middle-class. They were under no public control at all. Anyone might own one, anyone might teach in one, no standard of attainment was required of them; the parents dipped their sons into them as they thought proper and took them out when they thought they were done. Certain university and quasi-public bodies conducted examinations to which a number of the brighter pupils were submitted in order to enhance the prestige of the establishment, and these examining bodies exerted a distinct influence upon the choice of subjects. For the most part these private schools passed the middle-class youth of England on to business or professional life incapable of any foreign language, incapable indeed of writing or speaking their own except in the clumsiest manner, unable to use their eyes and hands to draw or handle apparatus, grossly ignorant of physical science, history or economics, contemptuous of the board school boy and with just enough consciousness of their deficiencies to make them suspicious of, and hostile to, intellectual ability and equipment.

It is only when the nature of the English private school education is grasped that it becomes possible to understand why the enormous possibilities of world predominance and world control, manifest in the British political expansion during the nineteenth century, wilted away so rapidly under the stresses of the subsequent years. Its direction was dull, ignorant, pretentious and blundering. I have given a glimpse of the British private school at its worst in my brief account of Holt Academy; J. V. Milne and Jones were almost at opposite poles of conscience and intelligence; Milne was a man who won my unstinted admiration and remained my friend throughout life; nevertheless it is useless to pretend that Henley House was more than a sketch of good intentions or that we stirred up a tithe of the finer possibilities of the boys who passed under our hands. We taught them a few tricks, we got them a few "certificates," we did something for their manners and personal bearing, we dropped some fruitful hints into them, but we gave them no coherent and sustaining vision of life. One or two of the Henley House boys were destined to play a fairly conspicuous rôle in English affairs. Our prize boy, our whale so to speak, was Lord Northcliffe, who did so much to create the modern newspaper and died controlling owner of *The Times*. He can very well be studied as a sample of the limitations of the English private school education—and indeed of English education generally.

In making these criticisms I am not blaming J. V. Milne. In view of his conditions and resources he did wonderfully. He could hardly pay his way; the two rather battered villas and that one golden sovereign for all the apparatus required for science teaching, give the measure of his means. When later on an opportunity offered, he got out of Kilburn and ran a more spaciously equipped school, Streete Court at Westgate-on-Sea. But for Henley House, he could not pick and choose his assistants; economies and compromises cramped his style, and in endless respects the school made itself in spite of all his efforts to mould and direct it.

Nevertheless he had in operation an honour system of discipline that was far in advance of the times. It is a little too complex to explain here, but it was decidedly better than the discipline under Sanderson of Oundle, which I was to study later. A cane hung in Milne's study, a symbol of force as the ultimate sanction, but it was never used in my time and I do not think it had been used for some years before. He was understandingly interested by my abandonment of the worst pretences of "practical" demonstration in my science teaching, he watched and discussed my use of the note-book system of binding work together that I had picked up from Byatt and seen misapplied by Judd, and when later I innovated in the mathematical work, threw out all the muddling-about with money sums, weights and measures, business "practice" and so forth that cumbered the teaching (and examining) of arithmetic, and took a class of small boys between six and eight straight away from the first four rules to easy algebra, he was delighted. In those days that was a new and bold thing to do. We got to fractions, quadratics and problems involving quadratics in a twelvemonth and laid the foundations of two or three university careers by way of mathematics. A. A. Milne, the novelist and playwright, was one of that band of young hopefuls, and his brother Ken and Batsford the publisher.

The sense of Milne's observation and interest quickened my teaching greatly. I would prepare little stunts for him and the boys. It was amusing to stroll up to the blackboard in an off-hand way and draw the outline of England or Scotland or North America from memory. (One had to be particularly wary about the relative latitude of the east and west coasts and the rest followed.) One could stand with one's back to a whole class and yet have every boy still and interested. The wickedest would be following the chalk line and comparing it with his Atlas if only in the hope of saying, "Please Sir," and making a correction.

Where Henley House was most defective from a modern point of view was in its failure to establish any social and political outlook. But there J. V. suffered not only from the limitations of a poorly financed private adventurer who had to make his school "pay," but also from the lax and aimless mentality of the period in which he was living. The old European order, as I have pointed out already in the chapter on my origins, was far gone in decay, and had lost sight of any conception of an object in life. The new order had still to discover itself and its objectives. In the eighteenth century, a school in Protestant England pointed every life in it, either towards hell-fire or eternal bliss; its intellectual and moral training was all more or less relevant to and tested by the requirements of that pilgrimage; for that in the long run you were being prepared. That double glow of gold and red had faded out almost completely from the school perspectives of 1890, but nothing had taken its place. The idea of the modern world-state must ultimately determine the curriculum and disciplines of every school on earth, but even to-day only a few teachers apprehend that, and in my Henley House days the idea of that social and political necessity had hardly dawned. The schools and universities just went on teaching things in what was called the "general education"—because they had always been taught. "Why do we learn Latin, Sir?" asked our bright boys. "What is the good of this chemistry, Sir, if I am to go into a bank?" Or, "Does it really matter, Sir, now, *how* Henry VII was related to Henry IV?"

We were teaching some "subjects," as the times went, fairly well, we were getting more than average results in outside examinations. But collectively, comprehensively we were teaching nothing at all. We were completely ignoring the primary function of the school in human society, which is to correlate the intelligence, will and conscience of the individual to the social process. We were unaware of a social process. Not only were Henley House, and the private schools generally, imparting this nothingness of outlook, but except for a certain gangster esprit-de-corps in various of the other public schools and military seminaries, "governing class" sentiment and the like, the same blankness pervaded the whole educational organization of the community. We taught no history of human origins, nothing about the structure of civilization, nothing of social or political life. We did not make, we did not even attempt to make participating citizens. We launched our boys, with, or more commonly without, a university "local" or matriculation certificate, as mere irresponsible adventurers into an uncharted scramble for life.

And this is where our big specimen of output, our whale, Northcliffe, comes in. His story is a very illuminating demonstration of the effects of private school insufficiencies upon social development.

He was eldest of the numerous family of an adventurous barrister, Harmsworth, from Dublin, who came to London with a capable and energetic wife, to make a great career, and did not do so. He won only a moderate measure of success; he was "Counsel to the Great Northern Railway" and so forth; and his political activities never advanced beyond one of those mock parliaments, the Camden Town equivalent of the Parliament of the Landport Y. M. C. A., mentioned earlier in this book, in which politically minded men displayed their quality and tempered themselves for real political activities. Camden Town, like Landport, never got down to any social or economic principles. It was a training in saying "Mr, Speaker, Sir, the right honourable member for Little Ditcham," in moving "the previous question" and suchlike necessary superficialities of the political game. He died in 1889 when his eldest son was twenty-four years old, but the mother, a woman oddly reminiscent in her vitality and character of Laetitia Bonaparte, survived to 1925, three years after the death of Northcliffe.

Alfred was born in 1865, a little more than a year before me, and he seems to have entered Henley House School when he was nine or ten years old. He made a very poor impression on his teachers and became one of those unsatisfactory, rather heavy, good-tempered boys who in the usual course of things drift ineffectively through school to some second-rate employment. It was J. V.'s ability that saved him from that. Somewhen about the age of twelve, Master Harmsworth became possessed of a jelly-graph for the reproduction of MS. in violet ink, and with this he set himself to produce a mock newspaper. J. V. with the soundest pedagogic instinct, seized upon the educational possibilities of this display of interest and encouraged young Harmsworth, violet with copying ink and not quite sure whether he had done well or ill, to persist with the *Henley House Magazine* even at the cost of his school work. The first number appeared in 1878; the first printed number in 1881 "edited by Alfred C. Harmsworth," and I possess all the subsequent issues up to the end of 1893, when Milne transferred his school to Streete Court. During my stay at Henley House, I contributed largely, and among others who had a hand in the magazine was A. J. Montefiore, who was later to edit the *Educational Review* and A. A. Milne ("aged six"—at his first appearance in print) the novelist, essayist and playwright.

Now neither Milne nor anyone in the Harmsworth family, as they scanned the early issues of this little publication, had the faintest suspicion of the preposterous thrust of opportunity that it was destined to give its youthful editor. But in the eighties the first school generation educated under the Education Act of 1871 was demanding cheap reading matter and wanting something a little easier than *Chambers Journal* and a little less simply feminine than the *Family Herald*. A shrewd pharmaceutical chemist named Newnes tried to make a modest profit out of a periodical, originally of cuttings and quotations, *Tit Bits*, and made a great fortune. Almost simultaneously our Harmsworth, pursuing print as if by instinct, tried to turn a modest hundred or so, by creating *Answers to Correspondents* (1888) which, among other things, provided me as I have told, with a few useful shillings a week during its first year of issue. He had been ill for a brief period after leaving school in 1882 and he had worked not so very successfully at outside journalism. *Answers* hung fire for a time until it dropped its initial idea and set out to imitate and beat *Tit Bits* at its own game, with the aid of prize competitions.

Neither Newnes nor Harmsworth, when they launched these ventures, had the slightest idea of the scale of the new forces they were tapping. They thought they were going to sell to a public of at most a few score thousands and they found they were publishing for the million. They did not so much climb to success; they were rather caught by success and blown sky high. I will not even summarize the headlong uprush of Alfred C. Harmsworth and his brother Harold; how presently they had acquired the *Evening News*, started the *Daily Mail* and gone from strength to strength until at last Alfred sat on the highest throne in British journalism, *The Times*, and Harold was one of the richest men in the world.

Only one item in this rocket flight is really significant here. The second success of the Harmsworth brothers was a publication called *Comic Cuts*. Some rare spasm of decency seems to have prevented them calling this enormously profitable, nasty, taste-destroying appeal for the ha'pence of small boys, *Komic Kuts*. They sailed into this business of producing saleable letterpress for the coppers of the new public, with an entire disregard of good taste, good value, educational influence, social consequences or political responsibility. They were as blind as young kittens to all those aspects of life. That is the most remarkable fact about them from my present point of view and I think posterity will find it even more astonishing. In pristine innocence, naked of any sense of responsibility, with immense native energy, they set about pouring millions of printed sheets of any sort of trash that sold, into the awakening mind of the British masses. The "instantaneous success" of *Comic Cuts* was hailed by J. V. in *Henley House Magazine* (May 1890) without a word of criticism or a sign of disapproval. He tells the "Short History of A Henley House Boy" and writes that *Answers* returns to its proprietors close upon £10,000 per annum.

> "Mr. Alfred Harmsworth is now only twenty-four years of age," he writes. "He has written two successful books, *A Thousand Ways of Earning a Living*, of which 25,000 were sold, and *All About our Railways*. He attributes most of his success to—what do you think?—*downright hard work*. 'I usually spend twelve hours a day on the paper,' he writes me. I wanted him to give me some facts showing the magnitude of the work—the staff, the management, *etc.*, of his paper—and some facts about himself, but he writes, 'I really do not like biography. You can say this (what I have said to many other people), that the generous and thoughtful way in which I was educated at Henley House must have had a very great influence on my career. Though I was never much of a student, I did manage in those three years to pick up a vast amount of reasoning and fact, which often, even now, are useful. But there! I am ashamed to say any more. You can say what you like about my opinion of Henley House, and you cannot put it too strongly. Yours affectionately, Alfred C. Harmsworth.'

"Now that you have just been reading of an old Henley House School boy, may I get in a word. If there is an idle boy in the school, let him take this lesson to heart—that sheer hard work is the magician's wand. Should there be any of you drifting along, and hoping, like Mr. Micawber, that something may turn up, let me tell you that the things that generally 'turn up' are disappointments, failure, poverty and remorse. May the last never be yours."

J. V. Milne could write like that and teach like that—in a vein of pure competitive individualism. His own conscience and practice were happily better than his theories.

In twenty years these two young ruffians (ruffians so far as any sense of social obligations goes), these creators of *Comic Cuts*, had been flung up to the working ownership of *The Times*, and peerages; they had become immense factors in the chaos of English affairs, and with them and under the controlling counsels of their magnificent mother, they had carried their bunch of brothers to positions of importance and opulence in our social disorder. My friend Geoffrey Harmsworth, the son of Northcliffe's brother Lester, has planned to tell the story under the title of the *Harmsworth Adventure*. It is absurdly like the Bonaparte adventure. During my time at Henley House School, one last Harmsworth of the original vintage remained, a sturdy and by no means brilliant youngster, St-John. A year or so ago before he died I met him at Cannes, a princely invalid, the proprietor of *Perrier*, preposterously wealthy, surrounded by obsequious valets, male nurses, maîtres d'hôtel and so forth.

With Northcliffe I maintained an intermittent friendship; I co-operated with him for a time at Crewe House during the war and afterwards he came over to Easton to lunch and talk with me when I returned from Russia in 1920. But my articles were already ear-marked for the *Daily Express*. He was then in the grip of an obscure malady that distressed his mind, arrested its development and prevented sustained work. The doctors advised him to go for long wandering excursions by automobile or afoot, watching the world go by him. He must learn to be idle. I met him for a last encounter, walking alone in Westminster, "just looking at the shop windows." That must have been in 1920 or 1921. Finally these doctors sent him wandering round the world and he wandered right out of sanity. I saw enough of him to see the extraordinary mental and moral conflict created by the real vastness of the opportunities and challenges that crowded upon him on the one hand and, on the other, the blank inadequacy of his education at Henley House School for anything better than a career of push and acquisition.

In an autobiography it is permissible to compare his mind with my own. Mine—peace to its defects!—was a system of digested and assimilated ideas; it was an assembled mind; his was a vast jumble into which fresh experiences were for ever tumbling. I was educated—self- educated. He was uneducated. He was blown up so rapidly that he was never free to think out his rôle in the world. He never had the chances for weeks and months of reflection and readjustment given me by my various disablements and set-backs. When he was ill—and ever and again he was ill and took refuge with his mother at Totteridge—he was mentally disordered and lost grip altogether. And he was prone to the easy flattery of women. Nevertheless a certain admirable greatness of mind appeared eventually and he travelled far from the mere headlong vulgarity of his first drive into prosperity. He realized with a mixture of astonishment, exaltation and dismay, that a big newspaper proprietor, whether he liked it or not and whether or no the fact met with any formal recognition, was an immensely responsible figure in the world. He had vivid intimations that amidst the catastrophic shifts and changes of Western life, a new social order was finding its way into existence.

He never had the time nor the mental coolness to get this clear.

But long before the Great War jolted the intelligence of Europe into a new system of aims and understandings, he was trying to fill up the gap that Henley House School—and all that went with it in tone and period—had left in his equipment. He had an almost pathetic belief that somewhere, just outside his world, were a lot of clever fellows who had better knowledge and ideas than his. He did not understand the breadth and slowness of the process by which the modern world-state has been and is still coming to self- realization. It had not dawned upon him what a heaving pretentious mess economic, social and educational science still was, because he had never come to grips with the stuff as I had done. But he felt the looseness and insecurity of things about him and he tried in his impatient way to get something constructive and stabilizing. He "ran" Norman Angell for a time and the question of world peace and, after my *Anticipations* and *Modern Utopia*, he wanted very much to organize a following for me. He found me at once stimulating and disappointing. I did not want to be organized; I did not even want to be hurried. His experience had been that you only had to advertise a thing well or offer a prize about it, to get all you wanted. And when you had got it you rushed on to something else. If you wanted world peace, or a cure for cancer or tuberculosis, or a machine to fly round the world, you offered a prize for it, you made an enormous fuss about it and then, he thought, some of those clever fellows at the back of things would set to work upon it, as he had set to work upon the *Daily Mirror*, and win it. He wanted to attack the economic riddles of the world long before any diagnosis had been made, in precisely the same energetic fashion. I shall mention later the articles upon "The Labour Unrest" that I wrote for him in this phase.

The World War and the world peace was a tremendous strain upon him. It was a forcible education for all of us and for him it brought both growth and disorganization. A really intimate record of Northcliffe's brain processes, his ambitions, his likes and dislikes, his general motivation, is impossible; but in regard to his period it would be the most illuminating historical document in the world. It would be as typical a story as anyone could find of the stresses of transition from that blind confidence in Providence, that implicit confidence in the good intentions of the natural order of things, no matter what were our mistakes and misdeeds, characterizing the human mind in the nineteenth century, to that startled realization of the need for men to combine against the cold indifference, the pitiless justice, if you will, of nature, which is our modern attitude. The effort to achieve an adult behaviour under the stresses of ulcerative endocarditis and after forty odd years of triumphant puerility, shattered and killed him. Confounded by the catastrophe of the Great War and its still more terrifying sequels, spun giddily into the vortex of leadership and responsibility without the restraints of a tradition or the preparation of a philosophy, embittered into a clumsy personal feud by the way in which he was jostled by Lloyd George out of any honourable participation in the War Settlement—and so abruptly stranded, Northcliffe's mind was shattered very much, indeed, as was Woodrow Wilson's. It was burst by opportunity.

I shall have more to say of him when I tell at the proper time how my sample mind, and the English mind of which it was a part, were put through the mill of the Great War. But after this brief excursion forward into consequences, let me return for the present to that little ill-equipped private school in Kilburn from which it started, that little school in which, with the best intentions in the world, Milne and his staff taught neither human history, economics nor social duty, and from which they launched boys into the gathering disaster of civilization as though they were sending them into a keen but merciful prize competition, in which "sheer hard work" was the "magician's wand," and so forth and so on.

Only now are we beginning to suspect there should be more

in education than that.

§ 5. THE UNIVERSITY CORRESPONDENCE COLLEGE (1890- 1893)

During 1889 my efforts to "write," so far as I can remember or trace them now, died down to hardly anything at all. My hope of an income from that source had faded, and it seemed to me that such prospects in life as remained open to me, lay in school teaching. They were not brilliant prospects anyhow, because I was quite obstinately resolved not to profess Christianity, but my self-conceit was in a phase of unwholesome deflation and a mediocre rôle seemed a good enough objective for my abilities. Milne had interested me in teaching method, and I decided that if I secured a teaching diploma and took up my degree in the London University, I might, in spite of my religious handicap, get a sufficiently good position to marry upon. I wanted to marry; I had indeed a gnawing desire to marry, and my life in close proximity to my cousin was distressing and humiliating me in a manner she could not possibly comprehend. I was keen and eager and she was tepid and rational. Plain risks dismayed her. It seemed the most obvious thing in the world to her that I should first win my way to a fairly safe place and the status of a householder before my devotion was rewarded. In pursuance of this intensely personal objective, I took my Intermediate Science Examination in July '89 with only second-class honours in zoology, and I got the diploma of licentiate of the College of Preceptors at the end of the year.

I have already said a word or two about this College of Preceptors in my account of Morley's Academy. Its requirements were not very exacting, and its diplomas were sought chiefly by teachers without university degrees. It offered papers in a number of subjects, and it allowed candidates to pass in one subject at one time and another later on, so that the grade of competing examinee was a lowly one. I took the whole range of subjects at a swoop, got what was called honours—80 per cent of the maximum marks—in most of the subjects and secured the three prizes for the theory and practice of education (£10), mathematics (£5) and natural science (£5). That itself was a useful accession of money, but the greater benefit of this raid upon the college was that I was obliged to read something of the history and practice of education, some elementary psychology, (a mere rudiment of a science at that date) and logic. I was greatly interested in these subjects and, superficial though the standard was, they cleared up my mind upon various issues and started some valuable trains of thought. I planned to go on with mental and moral science and to take that, with zoology and geology, for my degree examination in London University in 1890, but I did not do so because I found that botany would be a more immediately marketable commodity and so I went back to botany.

Armed with this L.C.P. diploma and my second class intermediate honours, I became exacting with J. V. Milne. He raised my salary £10 a year and agreed to cut down the hours I had to spend at Henley House. I looked about for supplementary employment and presently found myself in correspondence with a certain William Briggs, M.A., the organizer of a University Correspondence College at Cambridge, an institution which I still think one of the queerest outgrowths of the disorderly educational fermentations of that time. It flourishes still. Briggs was able not only to offer me just the additional work I wanted to keep me going until I took my degree of B.Sc., but his peculiar requirements enabled him to set a premium upon my taking honours in that examination. I went down to Cambridge to see him; we fixed up an immediate arrangement for me to earn at least £2 a week by doing his correspondence tuition in biology which was in urgent need of attention, and we further agreed that if I took my degree in October, I should leave Henley House School and have a permanent appointment with him in a Tutorial College he was developing in London, at a rate of pay to be determined by my class in honours. He was to give me at least thirty hours' work a week all over the year at 2s. 2d., 2s. 4d. or 2s. 6d. an hour, according to whether I obtained third-, second- or first-class honours. Honours were very important to him from the prospectus point of view. His list of tutors displayed an almost unbroken front of Cambridge, Oxford and London "firsts." High honours men in biology were rare in those days, and it was characteristic of Briggs that he should decide to make one out of me for himself.

I left Henley House at the end of the summer term, I took my degree with first-class honours in zoology and second-class honours in geology. I had already been working for some months in my surplus time with Briggs, and I carried on first with classes in a small room above a bookshop in that now vanished thoroughfare Booksellers Row, and afterwards in a spacious well-lit establishment in Red Lion Square. There I had a reasonably well furnished teaching laboratory, with one side all blackboards and big billiard-room lamps for night teaching. Briggs gave me enough work to make an average of nearly fifty hours a week, on a system of piecework that enabled me at times to compress a number of nominal half-crown hours into a normal one and so, by the middle of 1891, I found myself in a position to satisfy my cousin's requirements, take a small house, 28 Haldon Road in East Putney, and release her from her daily journey to that Regent Street workroom. She intended, however, to retouch at home and to take pupils.

A word about our budget will be interesting to-day. We paid £30 a year rent for our house, an eight-roomed house, (the eight included a kitchen, a bathroom and a box-room); we estimated 10s. a head as a maximum expenditure for food, and in January 1893 I opened a banking account in Wandsworth, which endures to this day, with a cheque from Briggs for £52 10s. 5d. Until then we had carried only a small reserve of twenty pounds or less in the Post Office Savings Bank. This Post Office Savings Bank account had been opened in the Fitzroy Road days with my first instalment of salary from Milne. Before then our only reserve for emergency money had been a few pawnable articles of silver and an old watch belonging to my Aunt Mary....

We were married very soberly in Wandsworth Parish Church on October 3st, 1891. My cousin was grave and content but rather anxious about the possibility of children, my aunt was very happy and my elder brother Frank, who had come up for the ceremony, was moved by a confusion of his affections and wept suddenly in the vestry.

But I will tell what matters about my domestic life later. What is of much more general interest, is the peculiar organization of that University Correspondence College of which I had now become a tutor. Briggs in his way was as accidental and marvellous as Northcliffe, and as illustrative of the planless casualness of our contemporary world.

To write an autobiography as the history and adventures of a brain, involves the unfolding of an educational panorama in the background. In what has gone before I have tried to display the strain upon and the disorganization of the petty educational organizations of the small-scale horse-foot, hand-industry civilizations that culminated in the seventeenth and eighteenth centuries, by the change of pace and scale due to mechanical invention. In two swift centuries the material structures of a single modern world-state came into being. Without any correlated mental structure. Social and political adaptation dragged further and further behind that headlong advance. Our world to-day is at the climax of that discord. And not only were the illiterate traditionalism of the general mass and the private schools and tutoring of the better sort, exhibited as wildly inadequate to the demands of the new occasions, but all the organization of professional training and the colleges, universities, academies and so forth, which had served the old order, were also tossed about, dwarfed and pressed upon by the huge dumb necessities of a world metamorphosis.

Nowhere yet was there a really comprehensive apprehension of what was happening. The gist of my individual story is the growth of that apprehension, belatedly, in one fairly quick-witted but not very powerful brain. But a partial and reluctant disposition to adaptation became more and more operative in the nineteenth century and produced a structure of universal elementary education throughout Europe, a great multiplication of technical and secondary schools, a growth in the numbers upon existing university rolls and the foundation of a great number of new universities. This adaptation was more quantitative than qualitative. The need for more and more widely extended education was realized long before the need for a new sort of education. Schools and universities were multiplied but not modernized. The spirit of the old educational order was instructive and not constructive; it was a system of conservation, and to this day it remains rather a resistance than a help to the growing creative will in man.

So to the multitudinous demand of the advancing new generations for light upon what they were, upon what was happening to them and whither they were going, the pedagogues and professors replied in just as antiquated and unhelpful forms as possible. They remained not only out of touch themselves with new knowledge and new ideas, but they actually intercepted the approach to new knowledge and new ideas, by purveying the stalest of knowledge and the tritest, most exhausted ideas to these hungry swarms of a new age groping blindly for imperfectly conceived mental food. It is illuminatingly symbolical that everywhere the new universities dressed themselves up in caps and gowns and Gothic buildings and applied the degrees of the mediaeval curricula, bachelor, master, doctor, to the students of a new time. I have already pointed out the oddity—seeing that I had little Latin and no Greek—of my calling my early plan of study at Midhurst a "Schema" and my first draft of the *Time Machine*, the "Chronic Argonauts." But this snobbish deference to the pomps, dignities and dialects of a vanishing age, ran through the whole world of education. There was no possibility of teaching (profitably and successfully), or indeed of practising any profession, without a university degree embodying great chunks of that privileged old learning. And when by means of clamour from without, such subjects as physical science and biology were thrust into the curricula, they underwent a curious standardization and sterilization in the process.

Now the urge to spread new knowledge of the modern type widely through the community, was so imperative, and the resistance of the established respectable educational organization, the old universities and the schools with prestige and influence, to any change and any adequate growth, was so tough, that a vast amount of educational jerry-building went on, precisely analogous to that jerry-built housing of London in the nineteenth century on which I have already expatiated. London was jerry-built because the ground landlords were in possession: English national education was jerry-built because Oxford and Cambridge were in possession. The British elementary teacher was an extremely hasty improvisation and I have already given a glimpse of Horace Byatt, Esq., M.A. (Dublin) earning grants for teaching me "advanced" sciences of which he knew practically nothing. Equally jerry-built and provisional were the first efforts to create an urgently needed supply of teachers and university graduates beyond the expensive limits of Oxford and Cambridge. New degree-giving universities were brought into existence with only the most sketchy and loosely connected colleges and laboratories, or with evening classes or with no definite teaching arrangements at all. Most typical of these was our London University. This at first was essentially an examining board. It aimed primarily at graduating the students in the great miscellany of schools and classes that was growing up in London, but its examinations and degrees were open to all comers from every part of the world. I for instance was examined by my own professors in the South Kensington Science Schools, but the examinations I passed to take my degree in London University, were entirely independent of these college tests.

And this is where the great work of Mr. (afterwards Dr.) William Briggs comes in. It was at once preposterous and necessary. The practice of general examination boards is almost bound to be narrow and rigidly stereotyped. They must never do the unexpected because that might be unfair. The outside student working without direction or working under teachers who had no regard for the requirements of an examining board, was all too apt to wander into fields of interest that were not covered by the syllabus or to fail to get up prescribed topics because his attention had not been drawn to them. His tendency was to be as variable as the examining board was invariable. All the more to the credit of the intelligent student, you will say, but that is beside the present explanation. The ambitious new outsider had to be standardized—because for a time there was no other way of dealing with him. At that early stage in the popularization of education and the enlargement of the educational field, it is hard to see how the stimulus and rough direction of these far flung Education Department, school certificate and London University examinations could have been dispensed with. It was the only way of getting any rapid diffusion of learning at all. Quality had to come later. It was a phase of great improvisations in the face of much prejudice and resistance.

Waste and absurdity stalk mankind relentlessly, and it is impossible to ignore the triumphs of waste and absurdity occurring in that early struggle to produce an entirely educated community. It was the most natural thing for the human mind to transfer importance from the actual learning of things, a deep, dark, intricate process, to the passing of examinations, and to believe that a man who had a certificate in his hand had a subject in his head. With only the facilities for teaching at the utmost a few thousand men to experience chemical fact and know chemical science, there were produced hundreds of thousands with certificates in chemistry. When I matriculated in London University my certificate witnessed that I had passed in Latin, German and French and nevertheless I was quite unable to read, write or speak any of these tongues. About a small and quite insufficient band of men who knew and wanted to teach, seethed everywhere an earnest multitude of examinees. Briggs began life as an examinee. He was a man of great simplicity and honesty. To the end of his days I do not think he realized that there was any possible knowledge but certified knowledge. He became almost a king among examinees. All his life he was adding letters to the honourable cluster at the end of his name; LL.D., D.C.L., M.A., B.Sc., and so forth and so on. He was a thick-set, shortish, dark, round-faced earnest-mannered man with a tendency to plumpness. I never knew him laugh. He was exactly five years older than myself, to a day. Having passed some sort of teachers' examinations—I believe in Yorkshire—he coached a few other candidates for the same distinction. But unlike most coaches he was modest about his abilities and honest in delivering the goods, and for some of the subjects he called in help. He employed assistant tutors. He had organizing power. Presently he turned from little teachers' qualifying examinations, to the widely sought after London University Matriculation. His pupils multiplied and he engaged more tutors. No doubt, like Northcliffe, he began with the ambition of making a few hundred pounds and like Northcliffe he was blown up to real opulence and influence. When I went down to Cambridge to interview him about his biological work, he already had a tutorial staff with over forty first-class honours men upon it, and he was dealing with hundreds of students and thousands of pounds.

The Briggs tutorial method was broadly simple. It rested upon the real absence of any philosophy or psychology in the educational methods of the time. The ordinary professor knew hardly anything of teaching except by rule of thumb and nothing whatever of the persistent wickedness of the human heart and, when this poor specialized innocent became an examiner in the university, almost his first impulse was to look over the papers of questions set in preceding years. These questions he parodied or if they had not turned up for some years he revived them. Rarely did he ever look at the syllabus of his subject before setting a paper, and still more rarely did he attempt any novelties in his exploration of the way in which that syllabus had been followed. Accordingly in almost every subject the paper set repeated various combinations and permutations of a very finite number of questions. Meditating upon these phenomena, Briggs was struck by the idea that if his pupils were made to write out a hundred or so model answers and look over these exercises freshly before entering the examination room, they would certainly be fully prepared and trained to answer the six or seven that would be put to them.

Accordingly he procured honours-men already acquainted with the examination to be attacked, and induced them to divide the proper textbook into thirty equal pieces of reading and further to divide up a sample collection of questions previously set, so as to control the reading done. The pupil after reading each of his thirty lessons sat down and answered the questions assigned to that lesson in a special copy-book supplied for the purpose and sent it in to the tutor, who read, marked, criticized and advised in red ink. "You must read £35 again" he wrote or "You have missed the v.i. (vitally important) footnote on p. 11." Or "the matter you have introduced here is not required for a pass." This was a systemization of the note-book style of teaching I have already described as a success at the Midhurst Grammar School, and as, under circumstances of wider opportunity, a mental torture in Professor Judd's geological work. A few University Correspondence students, I believe, became insane, but none who pursued the thirty lessons to the end, failed to pass the examination for which they had been prepared. It was merely their thirty-first paper and differed from its predecessors merely by containing no novel questions.

Now "elementary biology" had long been regarded as a difficult subject. It was required for the Intermediate examination of all Bachelors of Science and for the Preliminary Scientific examination for the medical degrees, and it stood like a barrier in the way of a multitude of aspirants to the London B.Sc., M.B. and M.D. There were no textbooks that precisely covered the peculiar mental habits of the university examiners, and the careless student ran very grave risks of learning things outside the established requirements and becoming an intellectual nomad. Moreover there was a practical examination which proved an effectual "stumper" to men who had merely crammed from books. I set to work under Briggs to devise the necessary disciplines and economies of effort for making both the written and the practical examinations in biology safe for candidates.

That was an absolutely different thing from teaching biological science. I took over and revised a course of thirty correspondence instruction papers and later on expanded them into a small *Textbook of Biology* (my first published book for which I arranged to charge Briggs four or five hundred hours, I forget which), and I developed an efficient drilling in the practical work to cover about forty hours or so of intensive laboratory work. These forty odd hours could be spread over a session of twenty or more evening classes of two hours each, or compressed, for the convenience of students coming to London for the vacation or a last revision, into a furious grind of five or six hours a day for a fortnight. We met the demand for biological tutoring as it had never been met before and if it was a strange sort of biology we taught, that was the fault of the university examinations.

My classes varied in numbers from half a dozen to our maximum capacity of about thirty-two. For the bigger classes I had an assistant, who was my understudy in case of a breakdown. My students sat with their rabbits, frogs, dogfish, crayfish or other material before them and I stood at the black-board, showed swiftly and clearly what had to be done and then went round to see that it was done. I had to organize the supply and preparation of material and meet all sorts of practical difficulties. For instance it was impossible in those days to buy a student's microscope in London for less than five pounds; this was a prohibitive price for many of our people until we discovered and imported a quite practicable German model at half the price, and arranged for its resale at second-hand after it had done its work for its first owner. I carried the books of answers of my correspondence students in buses and trains to and from the Red Lion Square laboratories and marked them in any odd time, with a red-filled fountain pen. Each book was a nominal twenty minutes' work for me, but I became very swift and expert with them, swifter indeed than expert. My notes and comments were sometimes more blottesque than edifying, but on the whole they did their work.

I must confess that for a time I found this rapid development of an examiner defeating mechanism very exciting and amusing, and it was only later on that I began to consider its larger aspects. Briggs had a bookshop in Booksellers Row, which also dealt with those microscopes, his Tutorial College in Red Lion Square and a little colony of small villas for his resident tutors and students, and postal distribution in Cambridge. Later, I think, in the order of things was his printing plant at Foxton and the workers' cottages and gardens. I liked the persistent vigour with which he expanded his organization. My exploit with the L.C.P. diploma and my success in honours for the B.Sc. had made me an amateur examinee of some distinction and won his sympathetic respect. At the end of 1891 I raided the College of Preceptors again, took its highest diploma of Fellow and carried off a Doreck scholarship of £20.

Briggs hailed my marriage with warm approval. He liked his tutors to marry young and settle down to his work. I cannot estimate how much the early marriage of university honours men made his constellation of first-classes possible, but it was indisputably a factor of some importance. These prize boys, these climbers of the scholarship ladder, trained to lives of decorum, found themselves in the course of nature, as I found myself, the prey to a secret but uncontrollable urge towards early marriage. Emerging at last as the certified triumphs of the university process, missing immediate promotion to orthodox academic posts and finding no other employment open to them except teaching at schools, in which they were at a great disadvantage because of their feebly developed skill at games, the offer from Briggs of a secure three or four hundred pounds a year and probably more, seemed like the opening of the gates of Paradise with Eve just inside. Hastily selecting wives and suitable furniture for a villa, they entered the University Correspondence organization, and found it extremely difficult thereafter to return to legitimate academic courses. For there can be no denying that at the outset both the University Correspondence College and the Tutorial College had an extremely piratical air and awakened the perplexed suspicion and hostility of more respectably constituted educational organizations to a very grave extent. I was never under any illusion that my classes would open up a way of return for me to genuine scientific work and my spirit resounded richly to this piratical note.

The success of these classes of ours in satisfying the biological requirements of the examiners in London University without incurring any serious knowledge of biology, was great and rapid. We drew away a swarm of medical students from the rather otiose hospital teaching in biology, we got a number of ambitious teachers, engineering and technical students who wanted the B.Sc. degree, and so forth, and in the school holidays we packed our long black-boarded room with the cream of the elementary teachers up from the country, already B.A.'s, and taking an intensive course in order to add B.Sc. to their caudal adornments and their qualifications for a headmastership. We passed them neatly and surely. In one year, the entire first class in Preliminary Scientific consisted of my men; we had so raised the examinee standard, that all the papers from other competing institutions were pushed into the second class. Harley Street is still dotted with men who found us useful in helping them over an unreasonable obstacle, and I am continually meeting with the victim-beneficiaries of my smudgy uncomplimentary corrections and my sleight of hand demonstrations. Lord Horder was one, the late Rt. Hon. E. S. Montagu, the Secretary of State for India (1917-22) another. We put all sorts of competing coaches out of business. One of those for whom we made life harder was Dr. Aveling, the son-in-law of old Karl Marx, at Highgate, and I suppose I contributed, unaware of what I was doing, to the difficulties my old friend A. V. Jennings encountered in his efforts to establish a private laboratory of his own.

At various times I have thought of making a large rambling novel out of William Briggs and his creations; *Mr. Miggs and the Mind of the World*, or some such title. There were many technical difficulties in the way, but the more serious one lay in the uniqueness of his effort. It would have needed to be recognizably him and his staff because there was nothing else in the world like them. And, quite apart from the probability of blundering into libel, there was the impossibility of varying the personalities and relationships sufficiently to alleviate a touch of personal cruelty to the tutors and so forth in the foreground. These of course could be invented, but whatever one invented, that type of reader who insists upon reading between the lines would say "that is old X" or "that is Mrs. Y. Now we know about her." Which is enormously regrettable, because the whole Briggs adventure from start to finish, done on a big canvas and with an ample background of education ministries and immensely dignified university personages and authorities, is fraught with comedy of the finest sort. Apart from the endless quaintness of the detail there is the absurdity of the whole thing. That general absurdity, at least, we can glance at here.

At one pole of the business, you have the remote persons and wills and forces which are presumably seeking or tending to produce a soundly educated community. That, if you will, is the spirit in things which makes for the modern world-state, that is the something not ourselves that makes for righteousness, or—the dawning commonsense of mankind. At that pole it is realized that in the new activities of biological science there is illumination and inspiration of a very high order. Thence comes a real drive and effort to bring this powerful new knowledge into effective relation to as much of the general mind as can be reached by formal teaching.

But this drive towards biological education has to work not only against passive resistances, but also against a great multitude of common desires, impulses and activities, that are not so much plainly antagonistic as running counter to the creative power. First the new subject has to establish its claim to a leading place in education. It is claiming space in a curriculum already occupied. Everyone in authority who as yet knows nothing about it, and everyone teaching a subject already established and already suffering from the progressive overloading of curricula, will resist its claims. When they cannot exclude it altogether they will try compromises, they will try to cut down the share of time and equipment conceded to it, to a minimum.

They will accuse the new subject of being "revolutionary" and they will do so with perfect justice. Every new subject involves a change in the general attitude. Biology was and is a particularly aggressive and revolutionary subject, and that is why so many of us are urgent to make it a basal and primary subject in a new education. But in order to attain their ends many of the advocates of the innovation, minimize its revolutionary quality. To minimize that is to minimize its value. So they are led to consent to an emasculated syllabus from which all "controversial matters" are excluded by agreement. In our biological syllabus for instance there was not a word about evolution or the ecological interplay of species and varieties. Biology had indeed been introduced to the London University examination, rather like a ram brought into a flock of sheep to improve the breed, but under protest and only on the strictest understanding and with the most drastic precautions that there should be no breach of chastity.

The fact that biology as we examination-ruled teachers knew it, was a severely *blinkered* subject, might not in itself have prevented our introducing scientific habits of interrogation and verification to our students, if we had had any sort of linkage with, or intelligent backing from, the men who were directly carrying on the living science and who were also the university examiners. But we were thrust out of touch with them. We never got to them, though we certainly got at them.

It is not always the professors, experts and researchers in a field of human interest who are the best and most trustworthy teachers of that subject to the common man. This is a point excessively ignored by men of science. They do not realize their specialized limitations. They think that writing and teaching come by nature. They do not understand that science is something far greater than the community of scientific men. It is a culture and not a club. The Royal Society resists the admission that there is any science of public education or social psychology whatever, and contemporary economists assembled at the British Association are still reluctant to admit the possibility of a scientific planning of public affairs.

Of all that I may write later. But here it has to be recorded that biology, having got its foot into the door of the university education, was wedged at that. It was represented only by a syllabus which presented a sort of sterilized abbreviation of the first half year of the exemplary biological course of Professor Huxley at Kensington. It began and ended with the comparative anatomy of a few chosen animal and vegetable types. It was linked with no other subject. Such reflection as it threw upon the problems of life was by implication. The illuminating structural identities and contrasts between the vertebrated types, were the most suggestive points to seek, and such real teaching of biological generalizations as was possible in my classes, was done in casual conversation while I and my assistant went round the dissections. In spite of such moments, the fact remains that when we had done with the majority of our students and sent them up for their inevitable passes, they knew indeed how to dissect out the ovary of an earthworm, the pedal ganglion of a mussel or the recurrent laryngeal nerve of a rabbit, and how to draw a passable diagram of the alimentary canal of a frog or the bones of its pelvic girdle or the homologies of the angiosperm oophore, but beyond these simple tricks they knew nothing whatever of biology.

My realization of what I was doing during my three years with Briggs was gradual. The requirements for the diplomas of L.C.P. and F.C.P. were not very exacting, but they involved a certain amount of reading in educational theory and history; I had to prepare a short thesis on Froebel for the former and on Comenius for the latter; and I presently added to my income by writing, in conjunction with a colleague on Briggs' staff, Walter Low, who was, until his untimely death in 1895, my very close friend, most of a monthly publication called the *Educational Times*. For the *Educational Times* I reviewed practically every work upon education that was being published at that time. Educational theory was forced upon me. This naturally set me asking over again, what I had already asked myself rather ineffectively during my time at Henley House School: "What on earth am

I really up to here? Why am I giving these particular lessons in this particular way? If human society is anything more than a fit of collective insanity in the animal kingdom, what *is* teaching for?"

At intervals, but persistently, I have been working out the answer to that all my life, and it will play an increasing rôle in the story to follow.

Later on, having perhaps that early *Textbook of Biology*, already alluded to, on my conscience, I exerted myself to create a real textbook of biology for the reading and use of intelligent people. I got Julian Huxley and my eldest son Gip, both very sound and aggressive teachers of biology, to combine with me in setting down as plainly and clearly as we could everything that an educated man—to be an educated man—ought to know about biological science. This is the *Science of Life* (1929). It really does cover the ground of the subject, and I believe that to have it read properly, to control its reading by test writing and examination, and to substantiate it by a certain amount of museum work and demonstrations, would come much nearer to the effective teaching in general biology which is necessary for any intelligent approach to the world, than anything of the sort that is so far being done by any university. Other interests would arrange themselves in relation to it....

But I am moving ahead of my story. The main moral I would draw from this brief account of these two remarkable growths upon the London University, the University Correspondence College and the Tutorial College, is this: that the progressive spirit must not only ask for education but see that he gets it. And seeing that you get it is the real job. We did not so much exploit London University as expose it. The unsoundness was already there. We were its *reductio ad absurdum*. The new expanded educational system was not yet giving a real education at all, and Briggs' widely advertised and ever growing lists of graduated examinees merely stripped the state of affairs down to its fundamental bareness.

Could the organization of this correspondence and extra-collegiate teaching have been made, could it even yet be made, of real educational use to the community? I believe it could. It was the dream of Briggs' later years to be formally incorporated in the English university system. I believe the defects of our tuition were and are not so much in the tuition itself as in the indolence and slovenly incompetence of the University examiners and in the lack of full and able direction in the university syllabuses. There is nothing inherently undesirable in the direction and testing of reading by correspondence, and nothing harmful in intelligent examining. But, as it was, we were, with the greatest energy and gravity, just missing the goal. We went beside the mark. The only results we produced were examination results which merely looked like the real thing. In the true spirit of an age of individualistic competition, we were selling wooden nutmegs or umbrellas that wouldn't open, or brass sovereigns or a patent food without any nourishment in it, or whatever other image you like for an unsound delivery of goods. And our circumstances almost insisted upon that unsound delivery. We could not have existed except as teachers who did not teach, but pass.

§ 6. COLLAPSE INTO LITERARY JOURNALISM
(1893-94)

The first phase of all my resistances to the world about me has been derision. I suppose I gathered my courage in that way for more definite revolt. And now I began to be ironical and sarcastic about this job by which I earned my living and sustained my household. The loss of genuine keenness about my teaching, and a corresponding release of facetiousness brightened my style in the *Educational Times*, and presently Briggs asked me to edit (at so many hours per number) a little advertising and intercommunicating periodical of his own, *The University Correspondent.*

Both Walter Low and I were very sarcastic young men and we had excellent reason so to be. The *Educational Times* was the property of the College of Preceptors. It paid Low £50 a year as editor and another £50 a year for contributors. He and I found it convenient that I should be the contributors—all of them. It saved him a great deal of correspondence. He was older and more experienced in newspaper matters than I, and I learnt a good deal of journalistic *savoir faire* from him. I acquired dexterity in swinging into a subject and a variety of useful phrases and methods of reviewing. We went about together, prowling about London, two passably respectable but not at all glossy young men, with hungry side glances at its abounding prosperity, sharpening our wits with talk. I was not so flimsy as I had been; I was beginning to look more compact and substantial. Low was tall and dark, not the Jew of convention and caricature, the ambitious and not the acquisitive sort, mystical and deliberate. He had an extensive knowledge of foreign languages and contemporary literature. He knew vastly more about current political issues than I did. We argued endlessly about the Jewish question, upon which he sought continually to enlighten me. But I have always refused to be enlightened and sympathetic about the Jewish question. From my cosmopolitan standpoint it is a question that ought not to exist. So, though we never quarrelled, we had some lively passages and if we convinced each other of nothing we considerably instructed each other.

Walter Low was one of a numerous and interesting family which came to England, I think from Hungary, after the political disturbances of '48. His father prospered at first and then lost his business flair without losing his enterprise; and so the family fortunes were dissipated. Consequently the elder children had greater advantages than the younger. Sidney and Maurice both went to Oxford, became eminent journalists and ended with knighthoods. One of the sisters married well, and an elder one, Frances, became a prominent journalist. She wrote particularly in a ladies' paper called the *Queen* and scolded the girl of the period—with the usual absence of result. The younger members of the family had to fight for education by winning scholarships. The youngest sister, Barbara, is a psycho-analyst and has written an excellent little book on her subject. Walter's education fell into the trough of the family depression and instead of going to Oxford or Cambridge he worked in London and took a London M.A. degree, with exceptional distinction in foreign languages. The difficulties he had experienced gave him much the same discontented and disadvantaged feeling about life that pervaded my thoughts. We were in our twenties now and still getting nowhere. It wasn't that we were failing to climb the ladder of success. We had an exasperating realization that we could not even get our feet on the ladder of success. It had been put out of our reach.

We had both toiled hard for outside university distinctions and we found they had led us into nothing but this fundamentally unsatisfactory coaching. We had both worked strenuously at writing and discovered that the more we learnt of that elusive art the less satisfaction we derived from the writing we did, because of the haste with which we had to do it and sell it. Both of us, following some shy dream of sensuous loveliness and tender intimacy, had married and become householders, and neither for our wives nor for ourselves, was married life, upon restricted means, fulfilling the imaginations that romance and music had aroused in us. At the back of our minds was a vague feeling that we would like to begin life all over again and begin it differently; but although this feeling may have coloured our subconsciousness and certainly deflected our behaviour, it found no more definite expression. We did not own up to it. We scoffed and assumed a confident air.

My guiding destiny was presently to wrench me round into

a new beginning again, but Walter Low never got away to good fortune. He caught a cold, neglected it and died of pneumonia in 1895. He left a widow who presently married again, and three bright little daughters. One of them, Ivy, wrote two quite good short novels in her teens, *Growing Pains*, and *The Questing Beast*, and then married a young Russian exile and conspirator named Litvinoff, who is now the very able Foreign Minister of the Russian government. We met at my home at Grasse and afterwards in London, in the spring of 1933, and Ivy talked with great affection and understanding about her father.

I did what I could to stifle my fundamental dissatisfaction with life during this period as a correspondence tutor. There was no one about me whom by any stretch of injustice I could blame for the insufficiencies of my experience, and I tried not to grumble about them even to myself. My correspondence fell away; I had quite enough correspondence without writing personal letters. The zest may have gone out of my interest in myself and there is little or no record of the moods of this time. But between myself and Low there was a considerable mute understanding. Under the influence of his efforts I was beginning to write again in any scraps of time I could snatch from direct money-earning. I was resuming my general criticism of life. I had already had one curious little gleam of success. In the winter of 1890-91 after taking my degree, I had broken down and had a hæmorrhage, and Dr. Collins—who believed steadfastly in my ultimate recovery—had got me nearly a month's holiday at Up Park. This had given me a period of intellectual leisureliness in which my mind could play with an idea for days on end, and I wrote a paper *The Rediscovery of the Unique* which was printed by Frank Harris in the *Fortnightly Review* (July 1891). I have already mentioned this paper in § 2 of Chapter V, in my account of the development of my conception of the physical universe. This success whetted my appetite for print and I sent Harris a further article, the *Universe Rigid*, which he packed off to the printers at once and only read when he got it in proof. He found it incomprehensible and his immediate staff found it incomprehensible. This is not surprising, since it was a laboured and ill-written description of a four dimensional space-time universe, and that sort of thing was still far away from the monthly reviews in 1891. "Great *Gahd!*" cried Harris, "What's the fellow up to?" and summoned me to the office.

I found his summons disconcerting. My below-stairs training reinforced the spirit of the times on me, and insisted that I should visit him in proper formal costume. I imagined I must wear a morning coat and a silk hat and carry an umbrella. It was impossible I should enter the presence of a Great Editor in any other guise. My aunt Mary and I inspected these vitally important articles. The umbrella, tightly rolled and with a new elastic band, was not so bad, provided it had not to be opened; but the silk hat was extremely discouraging. It was very fluffy and defaced and, as I now perceived for the first time, a little brownish in places. The summons was urgent and there was no time to get it ironed. We brushed it with a hard brush and then with a soft one and wiped it round again and again with a silk handkerchief. The nap remained unsubdued. Then, against the remonstrances of my aunt Mary, I wetted it with a sponge and then brushed. That seemed to do the trick. My aunt's attempt to restrain me had ruffled and delayed me a little, but I hurried out, damply glossy, to the great encounter, my début in the world of letters.

Harris kept me waiting in the packing office downstairs for nearly half an hour before he would see me. This ruffled me still more. At last I was shown up to a room that seemed to me enormous, in the midst of which was a long table at which the great man was sitting. At the ends were a young man, whom I was afterwards to know as Blanchamp, and a very refined looking old gentleman named Silk who was Harris's private secretary. Harris silently motioned me to a chair opposite himself.

He was a square-headed individual with very black hair parted in the middle and brushed fiercely back. His eyes as they met my shabby and shrinking form became intimidatory. He had a blunt nose over a vast black upturned moustache, from beneath which came a deep voice of exceptional power. He seemed to me to be of extraordinary size, though that was a mere illusion; but he was certainly formidable. "And it was *you* sent me this Universe R-R-Rigid!" he roared.

I got across to the table somehow, sat down and disposed myself for a conversation. I was depleted and breathless. I placed my umbrella and hat on the table before me and realized then for the first time that my aunt Mary had been right about that wetting. It had become a disgraceful hat, an insult. The damp gloss had gone. The nap was drying irregularly and standing up in little tufts all over. It was not simply a shabby top hat; it was an improper top hat. I stared at it. Harris stared at it. Blanchamp and Silk had evidently never seen such a hat. With an effort we came to the business in hand.

"You sent me this Universe Gur-R-R-Rigid," said Harris, picking up his cue after the pause.

He caught up a proof beside him and tossed it across the table. "Dear Gahd! I can't understand six words of it. What do you *mean* by it? For Gahd's sake tell me what it is all *about*? What's the sense of it? What are you trying to *say*?"

I couldn't stand up to him—and my hat. I couldn't for a moment adopt the tone and style of a bright young man of science. There was my hat tacitly revealing the sort of chap I was. I couldn't find words. Blanchamp and Silk with their chins resting on their hands, turned back from the hat to me, in gloomy silent accusation.

"Tell me what you *think* it's about?" roared Harris, growing more merciless with my embarrassment, and rapping the proof with the back of his considerable hand. He was enjoying himself.

"Well, you see——" I said.

"I don't see," said Harris. "That's just what I don't do."

"The idea," I said, "the idea——"

Harris became menacingly silent, patiently attentive.

"If you consider time is space like, then—— I mean if you treat it like a fourth dimension like, well then you see...."

"*Gahd* the way I've been let in!" injected Harris in an aside to Gahd.

"I can't use it," said Harris at the culmination of the interview. "We'll have to disperse the type again,"—and the vision I had had of a series of profound but brilliant articles about fundamental ideas, that would make a reputation for me, vanished. My departure from that room has been mercifully obliterated from my memory. But as soon as I got alone with it in my bedroom in Fitzroy Road, I smashed up that hat finally. To the great distress of my aunt Mary. And the effect of that encounter was to prevent my writing anything ambitious again, for a year or more. If I did, I might get into the presence of another editor, and clearly that was far worse than having one's MS. returned. It needed all the encouragement and rivalry of Walter Low to bring me back to articles once more and even then I confined myself mainly to the ill-paid and consequently reasonably accessible educational papers. They paid so badly that their editors had no desire whatever to look their contributors in the face.

Harris broke up the type of that second article and it is lost, but one or two people, Oscar Wilde was one, so praised to him the *Rediscovery of the Unique*, that he may have had afterthoughts about the merits of the rejected stuff. At any rate, when in 1894 he became proprietor editor of the *Saturday Review* and reorganized its staff, he remembered and wrote to me and I became one of his regular contributors.

But before then there had been some violent convulsions in my affairs. That humorous, that almost facetious Destiny that rules my life, seems to have resented the possibility that I might settle down in the position of one of Briggs' married, prize tutors, with occasional lapses into journalism and aspiration, and proceeded to knock my solidifying world to pieces again with characteristic emphasis.

Its course of action was threefold. It made its attack in three phases. First it concentrated the diffused discontent and self-criticism in my life into an acute emotional situation. I think I have already made plain how incompatible was my outlook of things from that of my wife. I want to make certain aspects of that relationship very clear. There is a traditional disposition to import blame or sympathy into every breach between a man and a woman. The people who tell the story about them say that he was false to her or that she was unworthy of him or that he or she made no effort and so forth and so on. But in most breaches between men and women, the want of harmony was there from the beginning and the atmosphere of a conflict and moral compulsions is imposed upon them by laws and customs that exact an impossibly stereotyped universality of behaviour from a world of unique personalities. My cousin and I had been thrown closely together by the accidents of life, we had been honest allies and we liked and admired innumerable things in each other. That we should marry had seemed the logical outcome of our situation. We both wanted now to be honest mates and adapt ourselves to each other completely. We were both perplexed and distressed by our failure to do that. We were in love with each other, quite honestly and simply desirous of being "everything" to each other. But there was an unalterable difference not only in our mental equipment and habits, but in our nervous reactions. I felt and acted swiftly and variously and at times very loosely and superficially, in the acutest contrast to her gentler and steadier flow. There was no contact nor comparison between our imaginative worlds, but within her range her quality was simpler and nobler than mine. If we had not been under the obligation of our marriage and our sentimental bias to agree in a hundred judgments and act together upon some common interpretation of life, all would have been well with us. But that need for a community of objective was the impossible condition which separated us.

The ideas which made me more and more discontented with the cramming of examinees by which we lived, were outside her world. She could not understand why I mocked and fretted perpetually at Briggs' grave and industrious organization of tutoring, because she had no inkling of the ultimate futility of the whole process. Examinations to her were like alarming but edible wild animals, they were in the order of nature, and it was my business as the man to go out and overcome them and bring back the proceeds. I on the other hand thought they were distortions of an educational process for which I felt dimly responsible. Mentally she lived inside a system, and I was not only in the system but also consciously and responsibly a part of that system in which I lived. She said, with perfect justice, that Briggs had always treated me very fairly and that I ought not to make fun of him. In her gentle but obstinate way she "stood up for him" when I talked about him. But indeed we brought in such different data that with regard to everyone in our world, her friends and my friends, we had hardly a judgment in common. She was equally unable to see why some issues of the *University Correspondent* satisfied me and others overwhelmed me with strain and fury because they wouldn't come right by certain impossible standards of my own. Why did I sit at my desk getting more and more put out by my work, while my dinner was getting cold? She thought I "fussed about little things" too much. She was perplexed, seeing how much I had to do, that I should want to do quite other writing besides. And again it seemed to her on the verge of unreason that I could fly off from something in the newspaper to scorn, bitterness and denunciation. I can still see her dear brown eyes dismayed at some uncontrollable outburst. Throughout our married life, with no sense of personal antagonism, unconsciously, she became the gently firm champion of all that I felt was suppressing me. Conversation between us died away as topic after topic ceased to be a neutral topic. It shrank to occasional jests and endearments or to small immediate things; to the sweet-peas in the garden or the gift of a kitten. My unaccountable irritability was a perpetual threat to our peace.

Meanwhile I talked outside my home and began to find an increasing interest in the suggestions of personality in the girls and women who flitted across the background of my restless, toilsome little world. Then it was that my Destiny saw fit to bring a grave little figure into my life who was to be its ruling influence and support throughout all my most active years. When I came into my laboratory to meet the new students who were assembling for the afternoon class of 1892-93 I found two exceptionally charming young women making friends at the end table. One of them was a certain Adeline Roberts, so dazzlingly pretty and so essentially serious, that she never in all her life had time to fall in love with a man before he was in a state of urgent and undignified protestation at her feet. So that she is still Adeline Roberts, M.D., L.C.C., and a soundly conservative influence in the affairs of the county of London. The other, Amy Catherine Robbins, was a more fragile figure, with very delicate features, very fair hair and very brown eyes. She was dressed in mourning, for her father had been quite recently killed in a railway accident, and she wanted to get the London B.Sc. degree before she took up high school teaching.

If either of these young ladies had joined my class alone I should probably never have become very intimate with either. It would not have been within my range of possibility to single out any particular student for more than a due meed of instruction. It would have been "conspicuous." But with two students capable of asking intelligent questions, it was the most natural thing in the world to put a stool between them, sit down instructively, and let these questions expand. They were both in a phase of mental formation and student curiosity, they were both reading widely, and it was the most natural thing in the world that comparative anatomy should lead to evolutionary theory and that again point the way to theological questions and social themes. They revived the discursive interests of my Kensington days. The disposition of Adeline Roberts was towards orthodoxy; her mind had been built upon an unshaken and wholly accepted Christian faith; Catherine Robbins had read more widely and had a bolder curiosity. She was breaking away from the tepid, shallow, sentimental Church of England Christianity in which she had been brought up. The snatches of talk for four or five minutes at a stretch that were possible during the class session were presently not enough for us, and we developed a habit of meeting early and going on talking after the two hours of rigorous biology were over. Little Miss Robbins was the more acutely interested and she was generally more punctually in advance of her time than her friend, so that we two became a duologue masked as a three-cornered friendship.

This was a new outlet for my imagination. I was under no necessity here of assuming the cynical tone I adopted with Walter Low, and I could talk of my ideas and ambitions more freely than I had ever done before. I could release old mental accumulations that had been out of action since my student phase had ended. I posed as a man of promise and effort and, as I posed, I began to believe in my pose. I cannot now retrace the easy steps through interest to intimate affection. We lent each other books; we exchanged notes; we contrived to walk together once or twice and to have tea together. It was a friendship that assured itself with the most perfect insincerity that it meant to go no further, and it kept on going further.

It came to me quite suddenly one night that I wanted the sort of life that Amy Catherine Robbins symbolized for me and that my present life was unendurable. That was the realization of a state of affairs that had been accumulating below the level of consciousness for some time. It did not in the least prevent that present life continuing. And the sexual element in this shift of desire was very small.

I became profoundly preoccupied with this realization of a better companionship. I did not know how to state my situation, even to myself. I did not clearly understand the fundamentals of my trouble. I tried over all sorts of explanations for this sudden sense of insufficiency in my cousin, whom nevertheless I still loved with pride, proprietorship and jealousy, and this distressing and overpowering desire to be together with a new companion. My habitual disposition to respect an obligation, to accept my immediate world and respond to its urgencies and imperatives was very strong. But almost equally strong was another system of dispositions not so immediate, but begotten of reading and thought and discussion, which denied the final claim of these immediate imperatives to control and shape my life, a system of dispositions which conformed to a code of right and wrong and duties—and excuses, that could at times run absolutely counter to the primary set. Seen in the perspective of forty-five years it is all clear enough. Indeed the primary theme of this autobiography is this conflict between the primary and the secondary values of life, and here it approached an acute phase. But I had still to realize that. I found myself divided against myself, contradicting myself, saying something that seemed on one day to be a revelation of the profoundest truth and the next day a feat of humbug. I had become inexplicable even on my own terms, and my humour and expressiveness had deserted me.

Every convention required that I should regard the business as a simple choice between two personalities, and I had not the acuteness to see through that at the time. The formula imposed upon my mind was that I had been "mistaken" in regarding myself as loving Isabel, which was not in the least true, and that now I had found my "true affinity" and fallen in love with her, which again was a misstatement. My sub-conscious intelligence was protesting against this simplification but it never struggled up to explicitness.

But I think it will be more convenient to postpone the dissection of these emotional perplexities for another chapter and to go on here with the odd tangle of associated accidents which now in little more than a year transformed me from an industrious tutor into an ambitious writer. My sentimental education is a story by itself and it shall have a chapter to itself.

Having brought me to this phase of fluctuation between two conflicting streams of motive, my peculiar Destiny set itself by a series of decisive blows to change all the circumstances about me. The precarious hold of my family upon a living had already been loosened in the case both of my father, who was in that cottage at Nyewoods earning nothing, and of my brother, who was with him repairing and trading watches on a small scale. Now it was that Miss Fetherstonhaugh rebelled against my mother's increasing deafness and inefficiency and dismissed her, and almost simultaneously, my brother Freddy, who had seemed safely established in the confidence of his firm at Wokingham, discovered that he was presently to be replaced in his job by a son of his employer.

His heart burned within him. He had been happy at Wokingham and satisfied with himself for some years; he had saved perhaps a hundred pounds, and his head spun with schemes of getting in a little more capital and credit and setting up for himself in the town and—just showing them. He consulted me. I found myself forced into the position of head of the family. My mother took refuge with me in February and I learn from an undated letter preserved by my brother Frank, that I actually went down to Wokingham, a trip I have completely forgotten, probably in the early spring, to consider the prospects of Wells Bros. Drapers (and Watchmakers) there. I did not find those prospects very bright.

I had none of the Bonaparte-Northcliffe disposition to control and use my family. My impression is that I was hasty, harsh and stupid about all this tangle and almost uncouthly regardless of the humiliations and distressed desires involved therein, I seem to have experimented with my father and mother, possibly at my mother's suggestion, in giving them sheets of lessons to copy out. Poor dears, they were about as qualified to do that properly, as they were to make translations from Sanscrit. I also discover, in letters my brother Freddy has kept, that I wanted him to turn from drapery and try his luck for an art scholarship at South Kensington. There were various unstable plans for partnerships and business enterprises that vanished as they came, like summer snow. In addition to all the other little jobs I had in hand I seem at that time to have undertaken, to organize on the appearance of one or two possible examinees, a special course in geology for the London degree examination. This in itself was a complicated task needing close attention, reading and a balanced judgment. I never carried it out. Freddy was dislodged from Wokingham sometime in April or May. By that time my mother had gone to join my father and my brother Frank at Nyewoods and Freddy occupied the spare bedroom at Haldon Road, went into London daily, dividing his time there between the dismal pursuit of crib-hunting and, with a diminishing hopefulness, enquiries about the possibility of setting up in business for himself with practically no capital at all. Upon reflection he decided he could not work in partnership with brother Frank and it became clearer and clearer to us both that with so small a capital as we possessed, it would be impossible to get goods at proper wholesale prices. We should fall into the hands of intermediaries who specialize in eating up the hopeful beginnings of would-be small retailers. We were both very innocent about finance but not so innocent as all that.

I still have my old bank books. At the beginning of 1893 I opened the account already noted at the Wandsworth Branch of what is now the Westminster Bank, and from the first of these little volumes which presently grow larger and fatter, I learn that in that year I earned £380 13s. 7d. My quarterly balance was usually round about £50. At the end of the year however it fell to £25 15s. 1d. A pound meant more then than it does now, but manifestly the fortunes of the Wells family were still being carried within a very narrow margin of safety. I seem to have paid out cheques to various Wellses, identities now untraceable, to the amount of £109. Most, if not all of this, probably went to my parents at Nyewoods.

One evening I gave a couple of hours to my new geological aspirant. I have quite forgotten him now, but apparently I introduced him to a few typical fossils. Where I procured these fossils, I do not know, but possibly they were hired. At any rate I found myself about nine or ten at night hurrying down the slope of Villiers Street to Charing Cross Underground Station, with a heavy bag of specimens. I was seized by a fit of coughing. Once more I tasted blood and felt the dismay that had become associated with it and when I had got into the train I pulled out my handkerchief and found it stained brightly scarlet. I coughed alone in the dingy compartment and tried not to cough, sitting very still and telling myself it was nothing very much, until at last I got to Putney Bridge. Then it had stopped. I was hungry when I got home and as I did not want to be sent to bed forthwith, I hid my tell-tale handkerchief and would not even look at it myself because I wanted to believe that I had coughed up nothing but a little discoloured phlegm, and I made a hearty supper. It was unendurable to think that I was to have yet another relapse, that I should have to stop work again. I got to bed all right. At three o'clock in the morning I was trying for dear life not to cough. But this time the blood came and came and seemed resolved to choke me for good and all. This was no skirmish; this was a grand attack.

I remember the candle-lit room, the dawn breaking through presently, my wife and my aunt in nightgowns and dressing-gowns, the doctor hastily summoned and attention focussed about a basin in which there was blood and blood and more blood. Sponge-bags of ice were presently adjusted to my chest but I kept on disarranging them to sit up for a further bout of coughing. I suppose I was extremely near death that night, but I remember only my irritation at the thought that this would prevent my giving a lecture I had engaged myself to give on the morrow. The blood stopped before I did. I was presently spread out under my ice-bags, still and hardly breathing, but alive.

When I woke up after an indefinite interval it was as if all bothers and urgencies had been washed out of my brain. I was pleasantly weary and tranquil, the centre of a small attentive world. I had to starve for a week except for a spoonful or so of that excellent stimulant, Valentine's Extract. Much the same beautiful irresponsibility descended upon me, as came to many of the men who were sent out of the Great War to hospitals or England. There was nothing more for me to do, nothing I could possibly attend to and I didn't care a rap. I had got out of my struggle with honour and no one could ask me to carry on with those classes any more. I was quit of them. I might write or I might die. It didn't matter. The crowning event of this phase of my life came after seven days, when I was given a thin slice of bread and butter.

Within a day or so of this disaster I was writing heroically indistinct pencil notes to my friends and having a fine time of it. "I almost sent in p.p.c. cards on Thursday morning, but it occurred to me in time that they were out of fashion"—that was the style of it. "No more teaching for me for ever," I write to Miss Healey. Sympathetic responses came to hand. Adeline Roberts, honestly appalled at my situation, felt it her duty to write me a letter, a most kind and affectionate letter of religious exhortation. I do not remember how I answered her, but it was something in the manner of a Cockney Voltaire. I'm sorry for that to this day. Dr. Collins heard of my plight and wrote also. I detected a helpful motive and wrote among other things to assure him that I had "reserves" for a year or so.

As I grew stronger I found myself exceptionally clear-headed and steady- minded. I amused myself in my convalescence by playing draughts and chess with brother Fred. Hitherto he had always been the better player and I had been hasty and inaccurate. Now for a time I found I saw all round him and he hadn't a chance with me. And suddenly I grasped the essentials of his problem. There came a demand from South Africa for an assistant, the rate of pay sounded very good in comparison with English salaries, and he was half alarmed and half attracted by the proposal. This was the very thing for him. He was honest, sober, decent and pleasant, he was trustworthy to the superlative degree and he lacked the sort of push, smartness and self assertion needed to make any sort of business success in England. In the colonies shop assistants do not run as straight or as steadily as they are compelled to do at home, they feel the breath of opportunity and the lure of personal freedom, so that out there his assets of steadiness and trustworthiness would be a precious commodity, and therefore I determined he must go. I had to overbear a strong sentimental resistance on the part of my mother, but Freddy was greatly sustained by my agreement with him, and in a week or so the engagement was made and the adventurer was buying his outfit and packing for the Cape,—to prosper, to acquire property and at last to return to England on the verge of sixty "comfortably off," to marry a first cousin on our maternal side, and present me with my one and only niece. With Freddy thus provided for and having undertaken to carry a share of the expenses of Nyewoods so soon as his first money came in, my mind was liberated to go into the details of my own problem.

I was not without a solution. There had already been a set-back to my earning power in the middle of 1891, when after a lesser hæmorrhage I had proposed to throw up my class teaching with Briggs. At that time he had found no properly qualified substitute and I had taken on the class work again after a rest. My classes had grown and multiplied steadily since then and we had already added a permanent assistant, J. M. Lowson, a very much better botanist than I, and a loyal and pleasant colleague. We arranged for my friend and former fellow student A. M. Davies, now a distinguished geologist, to relieve me of the rest of the class teaching, while my name remained on Briggs' glittering list of first-class honours men as the biological tutor, and I carried on with the correspondence work and undertook a text book of geography that was never completed. Fate was pushing me to the writing desk in spite of myself. I decided that henceforth I must reckon class teaching in London as outside the range of my possibilities and so we were free to move out of town to some more open and healthy situation. But before doing that we resolved, as my little aunt was now also in rather shaky health, to take a fortnight's holiday, all three of us, and pick up our strength at Eastbourne.

I see I drew a cheque for £30, payable to "self" in May, and I have no doubt this gigantic withdrawal represents that Eastbourne expedition.

As I look over these yellowing old bank-books I see close to that another item: May 19th Gregory £10. It recalls one of the brightest incidents in my life and I cannot omit it here. My old fellow student R. A. Gregory was in a tighter corner just then even than I was; he had no ready money at all and I lent him that! (What courage and confidence we had in those days!) In a week or so he had paid it back to me. Never in all my days since has anyone returned me a borrowed fiver or tenner, except Gregory. And after that he and I put our heads together and arranged to collaborate in a small but useful cram-book to be called *Honours Physiography*, which we sold outright to a publisher for £20— which we shared, fifty-fifty.

When I had been at Eastbourne for two or three days, I hit quite by accident upon the true path to successful free-lance journalism. I found the hidden secret in a book by J. M. Barrie, called *When a Man's Single*. Let me quote the precious words through which I found salvation. "You beginners," said the sage Rorrison, "seem able to write nothing but your views on politics, and your reflections on art, and your theories of life, which you sometimes even think original. Editors won't have that, because their readers don't want it.... You see this pipe here? Simms saw me mending it with sealing-wax one day, and two days afterwards there was an article about it in the *Scalping Knife*. When I went off for my holidays last summer I asked him to look in here occasionally and turn a new cheese which had been sent me from the country. Of course he forgot to do it, and I denounced him on my return for not keeping his solemn promise, so he revenged himself by publishing an article entitled 'Rorrison's Oil-Painting.' In this it was explained that just before Rorrison went off for a holiday he got a present of an oil-painting. Remembering when he had got to Paris that the painting, which had come to him wet from the easel, had been left lying on his table, he telegraphed to the writer to have it put away out of reach of dust and the cat. The writer promised to do so, but when Rorrison returned he found the picture lying just where he left it. He rushed off to his friend's room to upbraid him, and did it so effectually that the friend says in his article, 'I will never do a good turn for Rorrison again!'"

"But why," asked Rob, "did he turn the cheese into an oil-painting?"

"Ah, there you have the journalistic instinct again. You see a cheese is too plebeian a thing to form the subject of an article in the *Scalping Knife*, so Simms made a painting of it. He has had my Chinese umbrella from several points of view in three different papers. When I play on his piano I put scraps of paper on the notes to guide me, and he made his three guineas out of that. Once I challenged him to write an article on a straw that was sticking to the sill of my window, and it was one of the most interesting things he ever did. Then there was the box of old clothes and other odds and ends that he promised to store for me when I changed my rooms. He sold the lot to a hawker for a pair of flower-pots, and wrote an article on the transaction. Subsequently he had another article on the flower-pots; and when I appeared to claim my belongings he got a third article out of that."

Why had I never thought in that way before? For years I had been seeking rare and precious topics. *Rediscovery of the Unique! Universe Rigid!* The more I was rejected the higher my shots had flown. All the time I had been shooting over the target. All I had to do was to lower my aim—and hit.

I did lower my aim and by extraordinary good fortune I hit at once. My friendly Destiny had everything ready for me. It had arranged that an American millionaire, Mr. W. W. Astor, not very well informed about the journalistic traditions of Fleet Street, should establish himself in London and buy the *Pall Mall Gazette*. As soon as the transaction was completed he called the Editor to him, and instructed him to change his politics. The Editor and most of the staff resigned, to the extreme surprise of Mr. Astor who, casting about for an immediate successor and meeting at dinner, a handsome and agreeable young man, Harry Cust, heir to the Earl of Brownlow, whose knowledge of literature and the world were as manifest as his manners were charming, offered him the vacant editorship, then and there. Cust was a friend of W. E. Henley, the editor of the small, bright and combative *National Observer*, and to him he went for advice and help. A staff was assembled on which experienced journalists mingled with writers of an acuter literary sensibility, and in the highest of spirits and with a fine regardlessness of expenditure— for was not Astor notoriously a multi-millionaire—Cust set out to make the *Pall Mall Gazette* the most brilliant of recorded papers. Large and extravagant offices were secured in the West End near Leicester Square. Everyone available in Cust's social circle and Henley's literary world, was invoked to help, advise, criticize. Among other strange rules in the office was one that no contribution offered should go unread. The rate of pay was exceptionally good for the time, and there was less space devoted to news and politics and more to literary matter than in any other evening paper.

Quite unaware of this burgeoning of generous intentions within the cold resistances of the London press, I lay in the kindly sunshine beneath the white headland of Beachy Head and read my Barrie. Reading him in the nick of time. How easy he made it seem! I fell into a pleasant meditation. I reflected that directly one forgot how confoundedly serious life could be, it did become confoundedly amusing. For instance those other people on the beach....

I returned to my lodgings with the substance of an article *On Staying at the Seaside* scribbled on the back of a letter and on its envelope. My cousin Bertha Williams at Windsor was a typist and I sent the stuff for her to typewrite. Then I posted this to the *Pall Mall Gazette* and received a proof almost by return. I was already busy on a second article which was also accepted. Next I dug up a facetious paper I had written for the *Science Schools Journal* long ago, and rewrote it as *The Man of the Year Million*. This appeared later in the *Pall Mall Budget*. It was illustrated there and someone in*Punch* was amused by it and quoted it and gave another illustration. I had been learning the business of writing lightly and brightly for years without understanding that I was serving an apprenticeship. *The Science Schools Journal*, the*University Correspondent*, the *Educational Times*, the *Journal of Education*, had been, so to speak, my exercise books, and my endless letters to such appreciative friends as Elizabeth Healey and even my talks to quick-witted associates like Walter Low, had been releasing me from the restricted vocabulary of my boyhood, sharpening my phrasing and developing skill in expression. At last I found myself with the knack of it.

I do not now recall the order of the various sketches, dialogues and essays I produced in that opening year of journalism. They came pouring out. Some of the best of them are to be found collected in two books, still to be bought,*Certain Personal Matters* and *Select Conversations with an Uncle*. Much of that stuff was good enough to print but not worth reprinting. Barrie was entertained by one of these articles and asked Cust who had written it. When Cust expressed his approval of my work to me and demanded more, I asked him to let me have some reviewing and routine work to eke out my income when I was not in the mood to invent, and he agreed. Books for review came to hand....

In a couple of months I was earning more money than I had ever done in my class-teaching days. It was absurd. I forgot all the tragedy of my invalidism and in August in a mood of returning confidence, we moved to a house my wife had found in Sutton, 4 Cumnor Place. Nyewoods read the articles, heard of the monthly cheques, participated, rejoiced and was glad. Editors of other papers began to write to me. I still went on with correspondence tuition, my textbook of geography and my collaboration with Gregory.

I lived at Sutton until after Christmas, when as I will tell more fully in the next chapter, I left my cousin. We parted and Catherine Robbins joined me in London, in lodgings at 7 Mornington Place (January, 1894). She was reading and making notes for her B.Sc. degree and we scribbled side by side in our front room on the ground floor, prowled about London in search of stuff for articles and had a very happy time together.

I continued to write with excitement and industry, I found ideas came to hand more and more readily, and now the return of a manuscript was becoming rare. Editors were beginning to look out for me and I was learning what would suit them. But the particulars of these journeyman years I will deal with later. Here I will give only the testimony of my little bank books to show how the financial pressure upon me was relieved and overcome. In 1893 I had made £380 13*s*. 7*d*. and it had been extremely difficult to keep things going. I seem to have carried off Catherine Robbins on a gross capital of less than £100. In 1894 I earned £583 17s. 7d.; in 1895 £792 2s. 5d. and in 1896 £1,056 7s. 9d. Every year for a number of years my income went on expanding in this fashion. I was able to put Nyewoods on a satisfactory basis with regular payments, pay off all the costs of my divorce, pay a punctual alimony to Isabel, indulge comfortably in such diminishing bouts of ill health as still lay ahead of me, accumulate a growing surplus and presently build a home and beget children. I was able to move my father and mother and brother from Nyewoods to a better house at Liss, Roseneath, in 1896 and afterwards buy it for them. My wilder flounderings with material fortune were over; my Destiny seemed satisfied with my further progress and there were no more disastrous but salutary kickings into fresh positions and wider opportunities. The last cardinal turning point on the road to fortune had been marked by that mouthful of blood in Villiers Street on the way down to Charing Cross.

§ 7. EXHIBITS IN EVIDENCE

This I think is the place for various documents, mostly letters written between 1890 and 1900, which give the tone and quality of my relations to my family and to one or two other people who were playing an important part in my life at that period. I have had to pick them out from a very considerable heap of material. One of the most difficult things in my task of relating the development of an ordinary brain during what I believe to be a very crucial phase in human history, has been to select. I doubt if anybody reads collections of So and So's letters right through and I doubt if many readers will go through this section closely. Yet these scribbles set down for some particular recipient without the remotest idea of publication and subsequent judgment, do, I think, catch some subtle phases in mental transition. A few sheets I have had reproduced in reduced facsimile, to get the still puerile flavour of the handwriting and the still puerile habit of facetious sketching. The rest have been transcribed and are given in small print. As we used to say in our correspondence tuition: it is not absolutely essential that this material should be read. They are for expansion and confirmation of what has been related already. I wish I could have had all of them done in facsimile. The browning old sheets have a reality and veracity impossible to convey in any other fashion. They add very few new facts; they are living substance rather than record; there they are.

These letters are full of the little jokes and allusions of a reluctantly dispersing household. None of us realized how we were drifting apart, each one of us to new associations that the other would never share. There is a sort of "listen to my wonders" in these letters which I find now just a little pathetic, the desire to make the most of any little success; behind the apparent egotism and vanity is a living desire to keep up the old closeness of interest and the old intimacy of humour. That impulse fades out steadily, and in still later correspondence it has gone almost completely. The funny little inept sketches become rare and die out at last— cropping up finally only when Christmas or a birthday revives the fading family spirit. In the end the last umbilical threads are severed and hardly anything remains but a friendly memory of those vanished ties.

I suppose every biography, if fully told, would reveal this early predominance of home affections and the successive weakening out and subordination of one strand of sympathy after another, as new ones replaced them. It is clear that up to my thirtieth year there was still a very powerful web of feeling between me and the scattered remains of my home group. I was at least half way through life before my emotional release from that original matrix was completed. That, I think, must be the normal way of the individual life. It is a pilgrimage from familiarity to loneliness. I doubt whether any subsequent association systems, the dependences upon those persons and groups to whom we turn to replace that confirmation and reassurance our families gave us in the beginning, have ever the same influence over us that our primary audience exercised. It is not that we break away but that we are broken away. We cling to friendships, social circles, cliques, clubs, movements, societies, parties, descendants: but for all our clinging we are forced towards the open. We lose the trick of easy clinging. In the long run, if we live long enough, we find ourselves standing alone, grown up at last altogether, in the face of the universe and life—and what remains to us of death.

The strongest secondary system of reference I ever developed was to my second wife, the moral background of half my life. For long years it seemed as though many things had not completely happened until I had told her of them. And even now, although she has been dead for seven years I find myself thinking "This would amuse Jane." I write a bit of a letter in my head or I think of a "picshua," before I remember.

Many of these letters were undated. These I have given an approximate date in italics in square brackets. I have corrected some of the dating by Ephgrave's useful calendar.

* * * * *

College of Preceptors,
Bloomsbury Square, W.C.
July 5th, 1890.

DEAR OLD FRED,

Just a line to mention the fact that you *have* a brother in London to whom your memory is a precious possession and *wild flowers very acceptable.*[*] Dog daisies, dandelions, violets, in fact anything in that way, the meanest flower that blows—a LARGE box.

I hope you keep healthy and happy. I am overworked of course, but my appetite is still unimpaired and while that lasts, I will keep happy.

"Our jokes are little but our hearts are great." Tennison

Believe me,

Very respectfully yours,

BERTIE.

[*I wanted these flowers for teaching botany in Milne's school.]

What is this? Why do the people in the tram car shrink from his presence? Why, in this hot weather sit there in a heap together? Can it be—Satan? Or the Hangman? Or the Whitechapel Murder(er)? No—it is none of these things. It is simply a young biological demonstrator who has been dissecting with a large class that particular form of life known as the Dog Fish (*scylla canicula*). HE STINKS.

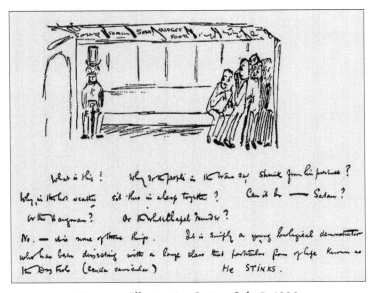

Drawing Illustrating Letter: July 5, 1890.

* * * * *

46, Fitzroy Road, N.W.
Monday 15/6/90 [?91]

DEAR G.V.,

I have sent you your glasses—they were done long ago
but I could not forward them on account of my illness—
they were forgotten in fact.

I had influenza about three weeks ago, and congestion
of the right lung on the top of it. I have had to resign my
class work with Briggs, and so I am—now that I am a

350

little stronger again—hunting round for work to do at home.

I wrote to mother four or five days ago but she has not answered my letter.

It is no good going into the details of the disaster. It is a smash. Still living is not so impossible now as it would be if I had not a degree. My thing is to come on in the next *Fortnightly* and if they send me copies I will send one to you. The editor has written for me to call on him, about a second paper they have taken and perhaps there is something in that.[*]

Faithfully your son,

BERTIE.

I have had to pay a substitute for all my classes.

Marriage postponed—for ever?

[* What there was in that has already been told. See p. 293.]

* * * * *

Wednesday evening.
[Sep. 21st, 1892.]

DEAR MOTHER,

You observe a doubtless familiar figure above, keeping his 26th birthday. In the background are bookshelves recently erected by your eldest, who came up here Thursday and has been doing things like that ever since. He has laid hands upon all the available reading in the house and seems to be going at it six books at a time. Isabel is at work doing some—— (The rest of the letter is not to be found.)

Drawing Illustrating Letter: Sept. 21st, 1892.

* * * * *

[January ? 1893.]

DEAR FRED,

Of course mother can come here and live with us. She
will not be happy, however, if Nyewoods is not kept on. If
I keep her will you contribute 3/-a week or 12/-a month
to that concern. I propose to leave things entirely in
Frank's hands there and to pay all money to him. If you
will do this I will see to all the rest myself. Let me hear.
Very busy—excuse more.

BUSS.

You stick where you are, my boy, and don't let this little
affair upset you.

Write and tell mother to come straight here, bag and
baggage, and assure her it will be all right with the G.V.

* * * * *

May 22 (?) 1893

MY DEAR MISS ROBBINS,

When we made our small jokes on Wednesday afternoon
anent the possible courses a shy man desperate at
the imminence of a party might adopt, we did not
realize that the Great Arch Humorist also meant to
have his joke in the matter. For my own part I was so
disgusted, when I woke in the dismal time before dawn

on Thursday morning, to find myself the butt of *His* witticism, that I almost left this earthly joking ground in a huff. However by midday on Thursday, what with ice and opium pills, and this soothing bitterness and that, my wife and the doctor calmed the internal eruption of the joker outjoked, and since that I have been lying on my back, moody but recovering. I *must* say this for chest diseases; they leave one remarkably cheerful, they do not hurt at all and they clear the mind like strong tea. My poor wife has had all the pain of this affair, bodily and mental, fatigue and fear. For my share I shall take all the sympathy and credit.

It was very kind of you to call this morning but my wife would have liked to have seen you. Next week—if I do not go to pieces again—I expect I shall be coming downstairs, and a visitor who would talk to me and take little in return, would be a charity. Will you thank Miss Roberts for the letter of condolence which—quite contrary, as she must be aware, to all etiquette, following your bad example—she wrote to my wife.

I guess class teaching is over for me for good, and that whether I like it or not, I must write for a living now.

With best wishes,

Yours very faithfully,

H. G. WELLS.

* * * * *

[*May 26th, 1893.*]
Thursday.

OFFICIAL BULLETIN

Mr. Wells tasted meat for the first time since Wednesday the 17th, yesterday, he also turned over on his side and sat up with assistance—cheerful. No recurrence of symptoms of hæmorrhage, no fever. Slept well. To-day stronger. Has eaten an egg, some boiled mutton, and other trifles. Pulse quiet, no fever or inflammation. No blood or clot expectorated now for eighty-five hours. Much stronger, able to sit up and turn about without help. *Getting a trifle troublesome.* Insists on writing letters in ink to everybody he knows—quilt spoilt and two sheets ditto—also in preference to tinkling little bell, upsets table when he wishes to call attendance— also wants books to read and if those procured are not to his taste throws them at nurse—also plays Freddy at draughts and insists upon winning. Hopes are entertained that he may get up by Saturday. No definite plans. Possibly a month at Ventnor, and then if practicable remove from London.
It is particularly requested that in all letters of condolence it shall *not* be remarked that it may be for the best after all.

＊ ＊ ＊ ＊ ＊

28, Haldon Road,
Wandsworth, S.W.
May 26th, 93.

MY DEAR MISS ROBBINS,

Your unworthy teacher of Biology is still—poor fellow—
keeping recumbent, though he knows his ceiling pretty
well by this time, but no doubt he is a-healing and
by Saturday he will be, he hopes, put out in the front
parlour in the afternoon. But he will be an ill thing to
see, lank and unshaven and with the cares of this world
growing up to choke him as he sprouts out of his bed.
However that is your affair, only you must not make it a
matter of mockery.

During my various illnesses I have derived much
innocent amusement from letters of condolence but your
Vice Principal Briggs thing capped it with a brief note
written out by Miss Thomas and signed,
John Briggs,
S. T.

After that I can believe the story of the typewritten love
letter signed by a pardonable slip of the pen, Holroyd,
Barker and Smith.

Remember me kindly to Miss Roberts and Miss Taylor,
especially Miss Roberts. Tell the girl not to trifle with
Bronchitis, whatever other giddiness she may be guilty
of. And believe me

Yours very faithfully,

H. G. WELLS.

P.S. I think he will not be fit to see you before Sunday but

I will write you before then.

Yours faithfully,

I.M.W.

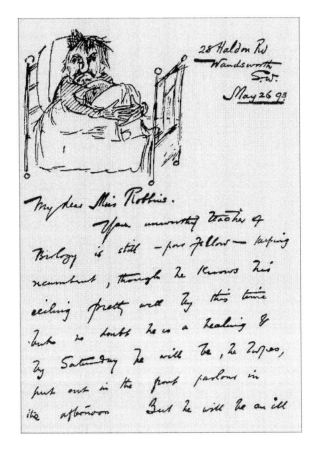

Drawing illustrating Letter: May 26th, 1893.

* * * * *

6, New Cottages,
Meads Road.
Eastbourne.
Tuesday.

MY DEAR MISS ROBBINS,

Your humble servant has been at this gay place now
for eight long days. He has been led out daily to an
extremely stony beach and there spread out in the sun
for three, four or five hours as it might be, and he has
there inhaled sea air into such lung as Providence has
spared him, sea air mingled with the taint of such crabs
as have gone recently from here to that bourne from
which no traveller returns. His evenings have passed in
the marking of examination papers and correspondence
tuiting, and his nights in uneasy meditations on Death
and the Future Life, and Hope and Indeterminate
Equations. Moreover I have sorrowed greatly over Miss
Roberts. When I was near the lowest point of my illness
she sent me a wicked book by some evangelist—a word
I have long used as a curse—about how that Huxley will
not look his (the evangelist's) substitutes for arguments
in the face, how that geology supports the book of
Genesis (which is a lie) how that the gospel of St. Mark
was written before A.D. 38 (which is idiotic) and all
those dismal things. Egged on by this wicked book
I wrote two letters to Miss Roberts blaspheming her
gods, saying I knew God was a gentleman and could not
possibly have any connexion with her evangelist and the
like painful things. I am sorry now because I certainly

was uncivil, but this particular form of Religion arouses all the latent 'Arry in my composition. But I know Miss Roberts will never approve of me any more.

This Providence has seen fit to increase the tale of my wife's troubles by sending her mother very ill. Of the two she is much worse than I am now, and I am still in a hectic unstable condition. A more serious man than myself would be horribly miserable at his inability to play his part of man in all these troubles. Everything is pressing on my wife's shoulders now, and I dare not exert myself to help for fear I shall give her a greater trouble still.

I sincerely hope you are working hard for your examination. I shall take anything but a first class pass very much to heart, so that I hope you will out of consideration for a poor suffering soul who must not be depressed by any means, do your best. I am looking forward to visiting Red Lion Square next week and seeing you again and conversing diversely with you. Very faithfully yours,

H. G. WELLS.

Concerning literature to which you would have directed me, I have done nothing. One dismal article full of jocularities like the rattling of peas in a bladder has seen the light in the *Globe*. Moreover I tried a short story for *Black and White*, which impressed me when I had done it as being unaccountably feminine and acid—much what a masculine old maid would write. What *Black and White* thinks of it I do not know. I think my mind stagnates. It is blocked up with a lot of things. I shall come and talk to you a long time I think and deliver myself.

* * * * *

[*Late June or July 1893.*]

MY DEAR FREDDIE,

I have nothing to tell you except to keep your courage up and work hard and bear in mind that there are plenty of sympathetic friends over here anxious to hear about you whenever you can write. Things are going very evenly with us. We have not found a house yet, but we have hardly hunted for it. I have been and am very busy. I have almost written my share of Gregory and Wells' Honours Physiography which I arranged for a day or two before you sailed and a lot of small coachings jobs have dropped in for me, and next week (which will be about the time of your landing at Cape Town) I shall be sitting in glory above my roomful of candidates.

Izzums sends her love to you, Mummie is writing to you herewith.

With love from us all and best wishes

Your very affte brother

BUSSUMS.

The "roomful of candidates" refers to either some London University or College of Preceptors examination at which I earnt a guinea or so as invigilator. My mother seems to have visited me in London again after my brother's departure. The four figures in the illustration are myself, my mother, my Aunt Mary and my cousin Isabel.

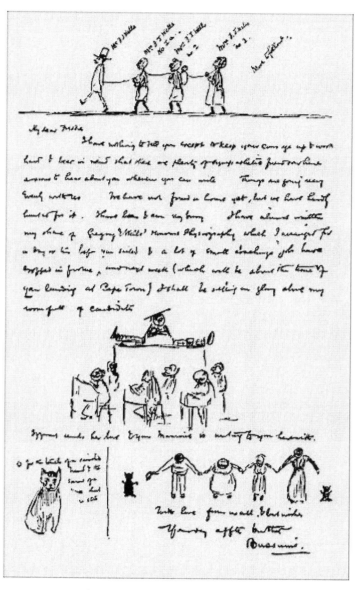

Reproduction of Letter: late June or July, 1893.

* * * * *

[*No date of entry, probably early August 1893.*]
4, Cumnor Place, Sutton.

DEAR MISS ROBBINS,

I am in the tail end of the stream of congratulations,
but I am happy to say I was the first person not in the
confidence of the university to see that you were in the
first division. And our Adeline has passed in Biology,
she and her riotous school of boys, or at least Wells and
Johns. Miss Saunders is in the second class, and one Miss
Knight—you will remember a romantic young thing
with expressive dark eyes, is, I am very sorry to see,
missing.

Everyone will be in superlatives about this success of
yours but as a matter of fact it is a mere beginning and
not at all beyond my expectation. I should have been
secretly disappointed if anything else had happened. You
must not touch degree grinding for two or three years
yet, though it is time for you to select your subjects. You
must take an honours degree—that is a mere debt you
owe your disinterested teachers.

This choice of degree subjects is a very serious one, and
one you ought to make now. For mental greatness—
such as mine—you must attack the biological group.
I sincerely regard mathematics as on a lower level
intellectually than biology. On the other hand you have
done enough in mathematics to show you can get to
brilliant things in that direction, while your biology is a

brief growth of one year. However we must talk over this when you return. It will of course affect your attack upon South Kensington very considerably. I am glad your visit is to last another week. Putney for the last three days has been a melancholy oven. However I hope you will return before we leave here, because I would very much like to deal with this matter of the future at a greater length than is possible in a letter.

My wife sends her sincerest congratulations on your success. How did Painter get on? They have let me sign an article in the *Pall Mall Gazette*, by the bye, and signed articles in dailies is a distinct advance for a poor wretch like me.

Very faithfully yours,

H. G. WELLS.

* * * * *

[*November ? 1893*]
class="cp">4, Cumnor Place,
Sutton.

MY DEAR FREDDIE,

I suppose, if I write to you now, this letter will reach you about Christmas time, and I daresay you will like to have our good wishes in season, even if we have to send them off unseasonably early to reach you. But over here already we are beginning to think of Christmas, there is a hard frost to-day and the roads are all hard, and last Sunday there was the first fall of snow. All the bookstalls are bright with the Christmas numbers of the magazines, and the London shops are getting brilliant with cards and presents. My two books[*] have been published now, and I have been writing articles for all kinds of publications since you left. The stories I wrote do not seem to be a great success but I have found a good market for chatty articles, and I am doing more and more of these. I had a cheque of £14 13s. from the *Pall Mall Gazette*the day before yesterday for *one month's* contributions. Not bad is it? But that may be a lucky month. However I am not drawing upon my small savings, thank goodness, and I am keeping indoors, and I think pulling round steadily. How are things going with you? I hope everything glides along, and that you are striking root in South Africa. Do you ever play draughts or chess? If so I hope you are improving, for your play with me was simply abominable.

[* The Textbooks of Biology.]

Isabel and Mummie and the Cat are well, and we find ourselves very comfortable in our new home. We are only about twenty minutes walk from the downs, and we can go by Banstead and Epsom to Dorking over them all the way. We have had a lot of Sutton people call upon us, so that we already feel much more at home than we did in Putney, where the London custom of ignoring your neighbour is in fashion.

I have not been to see either Father or Mother since you left us
but I daresay I shall run down there some of these days.

I judge
they are all right. Neither have I seen Frank now for
some months.

I think now I am almost at the end of my news. It is not a
very eventful record, but as someone has written, we are
happiest when we have least history. Things have been
going easily with us, and so I hope they may continue.

With very many wishes for a happy Christmas and a
prosperous New Year.

Believe me my dear Freddie

Your very affectionate Brother

THE BUSSWHACKER.

Isabel and Auntie send their love.

* * * * *

4, Cumnor Place,

Sutton.

Dec. 15th, 1893.

MY DEAR MOTHER,

I had hoped to run down to Rogate for a day or so before
Xmas to settle my accounts with father and to wish you

all a pleasant time, but I am afraid it will scarcely be possible now, so I am sending a little cheque (payable to father) to pay for what he has done for me and the balance I hope *you* will dispense in making things festive on the great anniversary. As Frank has possibly told you I am still contriving to make both ends meet by writing articles. There are two more when the previous ones are returned. Did the G.V. notice that *To-day* had a note and sketch about my million year man?

I and Isabel are going off this afternoon to stop with Mrs. Robbins at Putney until Monday—you will remember Miss Robbins who came to tea one Sunday—and we are going to a concert to-night with them. My cold and so on it is needless to say are better, or I should not be doing this.

We are looking forward to Frank's visit directly after Christmas.

With love from all.

Believe me dear Mother

Your affectionate Son

BERTIE.

It is not all jam this book writing. Part II of my Biology has been slashed up most cruelly in this week's *Nature* in a review.

* * * * *

7, Mornington Place,
N.W.
Feb. 8th, 1894.

MY DEAR MOTHER,

Do not be anxious about me. This trouble of ours is
unavoidable, but I really do not care to go into details.
Isabel and I have separated and she is at Hampstead and
I am here. The separation is almost entirely my fault. I
am with very nice people here and very busy. Yesterday I
went over a microscope factory for an article for the *Pall
Mall Gazette* similar to the one I sent a proof of to the
G.V. Did I tell you that they had made me one of their
reviewers? I keep very well, no cough in the morning
or any of those troubles. I hope Frank will run up soon
to see me and reassure you. Let me know when he is
coming as sometimes I am away all day. Love to the G.V.
I will see to that Zoology soon. Ask him to send a letter
card to Ellerington saying that no more B.Sc. Zoology
will be sent for four weeks to give him an opportunity of
getting the work up to date.

Your loving son

BERTIE.

Will Father send me one copy each of the scheme for
Zoology and for Biology and of the last lesson and test he
has of each of those courses, please?

* * * * *

Tusculum Villa,
Sevenoaks, KENT.
August 10th, 94.

MY DEAR FATHER,

I had intended to come along this week but more delays
have arisen and so I suppose I had better fill up the
gap with a letter. I thought Frank who came up to see
me a few weeks ago would have explained affairs to
you. The matter is extremely simple. Last January I ran
away with a young lady student of mine to London. It's
not a bit of good dilating on that matter because the
mischief is done and what remains now is to get affairs
straight again. Isabel left the house at Sutton and went
to Hampstead where she is now living (at my expense)
and she has now got through about half the necessary
divorce proceedings against me. I expect to be divorced
early next year and then I shall marry Miss Robbins.

The house at Sutton the landlord took off my hands upon
my paying the rent up to June. Since then I have been in
apartments with Miss Robbins (passing as my wife) but
now Mrs. Robbins has joined us. She owns a house at
Putney and has let that now on a twenty one years lease
at a rent of £90. We think of taking a house down here—
as we are not very comfortable in apartments—and
settling down. My wife will take her degree of B.Sc. (of
which one examination still remains) and go on with me
with literary work.

About my work. The *P.M.G.* is still my bread and cheese.
I do from six to ten columns a month and get two
guineas a column. I have been doing work for Briggs that

brings in about £60 a year but it takes too much time and I am resigning that. I am also dropping the *Journal of Education* which comes to about £12 a year and takes nearly a day a month. I do *Educational Times* work from 2 to 5 or more cols. a month at half a guinea col. and in addition drop articles at *Black and White* and the *National Observer*, when I get the time free. Then there are short stories which are difficult to plant at present, but I expect this series in *P. M. Budget* will get my name up. They are paid at a slightly higher rate than articles but are much more profitable in the end because they can be republished as a book. Besides this I have been writing a longer thing on spec and have been treating through an agent to get some of my *P.M.G.* articles published as a book.

I think that is a pretty complete statement of my affairs. Naturally things are a little tight with me at present as the divorce business is heavy but after that bill is settled I see no reason why things should not go easily with all of us. I shall have to pay Isabel £100 a year or more, but my income by hook or by crook can always be brought up to £350 and it may be more in future. Mrs. Robbins is going to raise the ready money for our furniture by a small mortgage on her house and the interest on that with the ground rent will come to £30 out of her £90. Still I don't expect to be pinched and I have no doubt that I shall be able to do my filial duty by mother and yourself all right.

My health hasn't given me any trouble, save for one cold and a bit of overwork this year.

Give my love to mother and believe me,

Yours ever,

BERTIE.

Of course I want you to hand this to mother to read as well. Mother will remember Miss Robbins—she came to tea one Sunday afternoon.

The letting of Mrs. Robbins' house was not a success. Her tenant did not pay his rent and "flitted" at night with his furniture. The house was then sold and the money invested.

* * * * *

12, Mornington Road, N.W.
5/12/94.

MY DEAR LITTLE MOTHER,

I'm anticipating Christmas and sending you a little present (I wish it could be larger). I'm keeping very well this Christmas and at about the same level of prosperity. I don't do so much for the *P.M.G.* but I do stuff for the *Saturday*which is rather better pay and I have some hope of the *New Review*....

This day week I'm giving my lecture at the Coll of Preceptors.
There's nothing settled about any of my books yet but I think there
will be two if not three in March.

Let me hear all about you. Have you heard from Fred?

Yours ever affectionately

BERTIE.

* * * * *

Drawing illustrating Letter: Dec. 5th, 1894.

Little Bertie writing away for dear life to get little things for all his little people—sends his love to Little Clock Man and Little Daddy and Little Mother.

* * * * *

12 Mornington Road, N.W.
5/2/95.

MY DEAR FATHER AND MOTHER,

Thanks very much for your letters in the last few days. It's very kind of the Father to say £40 a year will do to go on with. However I think I can manage £60, though just now is a tight time. Take £10 of the £15 to go on with and put £5 by for next quarter, say, as an experiment. You know the method is to put the cheque I send into the Savings bank—which will take cheques now—and draw out whatever you want as you want it. Later on I hope to do better things for you if I can only get hold of a little money. It's a dream of mine to get you into rather a better house, either by buying one or leasing it but that can't happen this year and may never happen. Whatever success I have, you are responsible for the beginnings of it. However hard up you were when I was a youngster you let me have paper and pencils, books from the Institute and so forth and if I haven't my mother to thank for my imagination and my father for skill, where did I get these qualities?

Believe me my dear Parents

Your very affectionate son

BERTIE.

* * * * *

12, Mornington Rd, N.W.
Sunday October 13th. (1895)

MY DEAR MOTHER,

Just a line to tell you that I am back with my old landlady here for three weeks (getting married). We've been up about a week. My last book seems a hit—everyone has heard of it—and all kinds of people seem disposed to make much of me. I've told nobody scarcely that we were coming up and already I'm invited out to-night and every night next week except Monday and Friday. I've had letters too from four publishing firms asking for the offer of my next book but I shall, I think, stick to my first connexion. It's rather pleasant to find oneself something in the world after all the years of trying and disappointment.

What is Fred's address at Johannesburg? I'm rather anxious to know. I sent a copy of the "Wonderful Visit" to him just before I had your letter, addressed to Messrs Garlick. I'd like to know all about him. There's no doubt that country is rising at an immense pace. I know one of the bank managers there and might be able to help Fred through him. He was my colleague at Milne's school. He's a Scotchman and bound to die rich, a long headed friendly man who might—if he chose—put Fred up a lot of good tips. His name is Johnston. I'm getting his address from Milne.

Love to the Dad and Frank.

Your very affectionate son,

BERTIE.

* * * * *

Lynton, Maybury Rd.,
Woking, Surrey.

Friday, Jan. 24th, 1896.

MY DEAR LITTLE BROTHER AT THE SEAT OF WAR,

How goes it with you? For a day or two in the new year, while Jameson was astonishing the world, I was seriously anxious about your safety, and I should have cabled to know if all was well, had not the wires been choked with graver matter. I suppose we shall soon have a lengthy and vivid account of the whole business from you. Here things have been of the liveliest, war rumours, all the Music Halls busy with songs insulting the German Emperor, fleets being manned, and nobody free to attend to the works of a poor struggling author from Lands End to John o' Groats. Consequently a book I was to have published hasn't been published, and won't be until March. You see how far reaching your Uitlander bothers are?

I'm going on very well altogether. I made between five and six hundred last year, and expect to make more rather than less, this year. I've married and ended all those troubles, and I've just taken a pretty little house at Liss with seven decent rooms and a garden and things all comfortable for the old folks. They are moving in next week. Frank is to expand his watchmaking business and altogether I think things are on the move towards comfort. I was down there about Christmas time and all three seemed very well and jolly. Frank's business seems picking up. The new home is one of a dozen or so decent little houses, and within comfortable reach of a church.

I'm riding a bicycle now and went a few weeks ago to a place called Odiham, which may perhaps awaken old memories.

Since I wrote the above I've received your letter. I'm glad to find you're all right. As you say, the Invasion was a Capitalistic enterprise, though Jameson himself is a gallant man enough. But the Transvaal has no business to intrigue with Germany for all that. Do you see any papers now? There's usually something about me in the *Review of Reviews*.

Go and see Johnston if you possibly can. He's a first rate man you'll find. Some of these days I must come and see you out there. I hope your getting on all right with the Dutch language and your business. What are the chances of opening for yourself out there? I should think that if you could pick up Dutch and master the habits and requirements, you'd have a better chance than you had in this crowded country. Don't dream of any speculation in gold mines or that kind of thing. Stick tight to your savings. If you want to invest trust old Johnston. He's a first rate, square headed, thoroughly honest man. What do you think of your move out of England? It wasn't so bad for you altogether—was it?

However time slips by. I've got to write a story before next week for a new monthly magazine, so I mustn't write any more now to you.

With kindest regards

Your very affectionate Brother

THE BUSSWHACKER.

* * * * *

[*July:1896*]
Brosley.
This does not represent a Dutchman but an elderly gentleman of distinguished manners who has recently been staying at Heatherlea, Worcester Park, Surrey. He plays chess with considerable skill, draughts and whist—croquet he learnt rapidly—and he answers to the names of "Gov'ner" "Dad" or the "Old Man" with equal facility. When returning to Liss he took away all the tobacco and a box of Brosley clay pipes. In the place of him a short lady of pleasing demeanour is shortly expected (as per accompanying illustration). She will probably be here on the birthday of her middle and favourite son, whom she speaks of variously as "Freddy"

"Fezzy" "Fizzums" and "Master Freddie." Needless to
say his health will be drunk on that anniversary both
at Liss and Heatherlea with the warmest feelings. This
person (illustration) it is scarcely necessary to explain
is your long lost brother Buss. You will observe that he
has with growing years and prosperity developed—a
projection which he keeps in bounds only by the most
strenuous bicycle riding. He rejoices to say that things
go very well with him, books selling cheerfully and so
forth, in spite of the Jubilee. And speaking of the Jubilee
he saw nothing of it whatever, except that he went to see
the ironclads—hundreds of 'em lying all along Spithead
and the Solent for miles and miles and miles.—He went
round the show twice in a steamboat accompanied by
[symbol of right-pointing hand] that chap! And while he
was going round the King of Siam in his yacht came out
of Portsmouth Harbour and every blessed ironclad let off
a gun (illustration). This is a sort of Birthday card really.
I've heard from mother once or twice that things were
going very well with you and I was very glad to get your
own letter. May your good luck keep on for you deserve
it richly. Many happy returns of the day and a light heart
to you, old boy!

From BUSS.

Drawing illustrating Letter: July, 1896.

* * * * *

Heatherlea, Worcester Park.
New Year's Eve. 1896.

MY DEAR LITTLE BRUZZER FREDDY,

I had your funny card for which, Bruzzer Freddy, there was one and a penny to pay! but I would have cheerfully paid much more than that rather than not have had it. And as it is New Year's Eve and I have been thinking over the past year and all that has happened, I don't think I can do better than write this letter to you before the New Year begins. And to begin with myself, I have been still on the rise of fortune's wave this year, and it seems as though I must certainly go on to still larger successes and gains next for my name still spreads abroad, and people I have never seen, some from Chicago, one from Cape Town, and one from far up the Yung Tse Kiang in China, write and tell me they find my books pleasant. So far it has meant more fame than money to me, but I hope next year that the gilt edge will come to my successes. This year I have made between eight hundred and a thousand and next year it will be more and after that still more, and then I hope to put in operation little plans I have. You know the old people are now pretty comfortable at Liss, and Frank's business really seems on the move. There were two packing cases of clocks and things in the passage of the house when I went down there yesterday. And next year I hope to be able (though I don't want him to know yet for fear of disappointment) to put him firmly on his legs. I think it will be possible to get him into a shop in a good position in Liss, and to let the old folks have a better cottage than they are in at present. But you know the old maxim— hasten slowly. I want everything safe and straight first. Then when Frank is a really efficient citizen again—we shall be seeing you back I expect, brown and strong I hope and with a little something in your pocket. And then we must see whether at Wokingham or Petersfield or some such place, it won't be possible for you to start with fair prospects. Eigh? The little old lady is rosy and active—fit for twenty years I shouldn't wonder, and before that time perhaps she will see all three of us flourishing in our own homes, and as cheerful as can be. The old man too is none so dusty a chap when you get him on the right side—and he seems hale enough for a century. So that this New Year's Eve I feel uncommonly cheerful and hopeful, not only for myself but for the whole blessed family of us.

Good luck Bruzzer Freddy

Yours ever,

H. G. BUSSWHACKER.

I don't know if you see *Pearson's Magazine* out there—in April next a long story of mine will begin and go on until December, and I expect great things of it. *Pearson's Magazine* mind!—not *Pearson's Weekly*.

Remember me kindly to Johnston who's a nice old chap isn't he? When is he coming over? If ever he comes I shall expect him to come and stop here for a time to gossip about old times.

Look out for the *Saturday Review* if you get a chance of seeing it. You will see among the reviews every week now H.G.W. which is me.

And don't forget to write to a chap and tell him all about
yourself.

* * * * *

Beach Cottage,
Granville Road.
December 18th, 98.

MY DEAR FATHER,

I've been meaning to write to you all this past week and
tell you about the work in hand. I don't know anything
about the*Bookman* paragraph of which you speak—
could I see it? Possibly Nicol got hold of something
through Barrie (who came to see us). But the paragraphs
in the *Academy* were written by Hind the editor after a
visit here in which we talked about our work. The serial
about the year 2100 will appear very soon now in the
Graphic with coloured illustrations. I've altered it a good
deal for the book which, will be published in April or
May by Harper Bros., and then this long silence of a year
and more will be over. It's rather in the vein of the *Time
Machine* but ever so much larger in every way. I don't
think people will have forgotten me in the interval. The
old books keep on selling—each at the rate of four to six
copies a week bringing in little cheques for five pounds
or so for the half year. The other book the *Academy*
spoke of, is now being put on the market by Pinker, it's
a sentimental story in rather a new style, and I think he
has offered it to *Harper's Magazine.* It's called *Love and
Mr. Lewisham.* I'm also under a contract to do stories

for the *Strand Magazine* but I don't like the job. It's like talking to fools, you can't let yourself go or they won't understand. If you send them anything a bit novel they are afraid their readers won't understand. Two stories they have had, I consider bosh, but they liked them tremendously. Another I have recently done they don't like although it is an admirable story. So that will go elsewhere. Just now I am writing rather hard—though this is between ourselves—at a comic novel rather on the old fashioned Dickens line, a lot of entertaining characters doing ordinary things.[*] I keep better here than I've been since I was at South Kensington and get good work out of myself every day. There are more ideas in a day here than in a week of Worcester Park.

[* Kipps.]

Amy wants me to say there is a Turkey at Shoolbreds simply gobbling to get at you, and it has some minor luggage under its wing. Our love to you all. Perhaps we may travel your way next Spring. It seems ages since I saw you. Best wishes for a Merry Christmas,

Yours ever,

BERTIE.

Our Fat Cat has fled. Break it gently to Frank.

No colds I hope?

No trouble with that liver?

A little sketch shows a turkey *en route* for Nyewoods.)

* * * * *

Arnold House,
Sandgate,
Kent.
June 7th, 1900.

MY DEAR LITTLE MOTHER,

As it is so near quarter day I am sending you on £15 and
I hope that in another week I shall see you. It was very
jolly was it not? getting that letter from Fred and by this
time I daresay he is reading all the letters you have been
writing him since the war began. What a budget it will
be for him!

But I don't like to hear you have "put by" £5. I don't want
you to go pinching and saving out of the money I send
you. It isn't any too much anyhow and you ought to
spend it all upon things to make life pleasant.

I am sending you a first review of *Love and Mr.
Lewisham.* They have sold 1,600 copies in England and
2,500 in the colonies before publication, and I think the
book is almost certain to beat any previous book I have
written in the matter of sales.

Give my love to Father and Frank. And believe me

Your very affectionate son,

BERTIE.

* * * * *

There survive scores of such letters, but these samples I think give the quality of all of them and my texture at that time. As I look over them I seem to realize for the first time the devitalization of relationship that seems to be an inevitable consequence of an ever widening divergence of experiences, associations and standards. And in turning over the pages of the *Saturday Review* (1894-97) in an attempt to identify all my contributions, I found a queer little intimation that this loss of dearness and nearness was troubling my mind at the time. It has never been reprinted and I think it may very well come in as a rider to these letters. It embalms a mood of over-work and doubt. There is real nostalgia for the close warmth of the Family peeping out in it, and an exaggerated sense of dislocation. Those forebodings of social isolation and inaccessible intimacies have not been justified. I was gradually learning an art, which I will call the Art of Modus Vivendi—not quite the same thing as Arnold Bennett's "Savoir Faire," but a very similarly necessitated accomplishment. I cannot complain of the share of friends and lovers life has given me or pose even to this day as a lonesome man. And though I missed horsemanship and good sound flannelled sport, most of what are called the good things of life, got to me in time.

EXCELSIOR

"To rise in the world, in spite of popular illusions, is by no means an unmixed blessing. The young proletarian, playing happily in his native gutter, scarcely realizes this. So soon as he begins to think at all about himself, his teachers begin the evil lesson of ambition; he lifts his eyes to the distant peaks, and the sun is bright upon them and they seem very fair. The garrulous Smiles comes his way with his stories of men who have "got on"—

without a word of warning against the sorrows of success. No one warns him of the penalties. Every one speaks of climbing as though it were bliss unspeakable. And so the young proletarian, finding his limbs are stout and the strength is in him, starts confidently enough, by the way of book or barter as his tastes incline.

"Let the epic Smiles tell of the career of those who win. Let no one tell of those who fall, who drop by the way with bodies enfeebled by overstudy, underfed, who are lost amidst the mountain fogs of commercial morality. Our concern is with those who win, to whom a day comes when they can see their schoolmates far below them, still paddling happily in the gutter, can look down on venerable heads to which they once looked up, and, turning the other way, behold the Promised Land. One might think it would be all exultation, this Nebo incident, the happiest of all possible positions in the sad life of man. It may be even, that the man from below tells himself as much. And then he looks round for some sympathetic participator.

"With that he discovers, though perhaps not all at once, the peculiar discomfort of worldly success. In his new stratum he finds pleasant people enough, people who were born in that station, educated to keep in it, and who regard it—perhaps correctly—as properly their own. To them he is an intruder, and largely inexplicable. He knows that any allusion to that steep pathway of broken heads over which he has clambered—for all human success is relative, and if one man rises some other must fall—and which he has found such excitement in ascending, any such allusion he knows will be the mental equivalent to putting his thumbs in the armholes of his waistcoat. Usually the man from below has a more than average brain, and is sensitive enough to keep his Most Interesting Topic, his Life, to himself. He knows, too, the legend of the Bounder, knows that these people credit all men who rise from his class with an aggressive ostentation, with hair-oil and at least one massive gold chain if not two, besides a complete inversion of the normal aspirate. He imagines that people expect breaches of their particular laws, and he knows, too, that there is some ground for that expectation. He blunders at times from sheer watchfulness.

"You begin to perceive the hair-shirt. To speak in the tongue of Herbert Spencer, the man from below is not adapted to his environment. That is not all; he is adapted to no environment. Though the language of the people of the new stratum is not his mother tongue, though their manners and customs fit him like a slop suit, he has acquired just enough of these things to be equally out of his element below. He is a kind of social miscellany, a book of short stories, a volume of reminiscences of People I have Met. And that friend, that dear friend, who is the salt of life, with whom he may let his mind run free, whose prejudices are the same, whose habits coincide—the man from below knows him not. There was A in the pound a week stage, 'tis true, and B at the three hundred phase, and C in the early thousands; but in some mysterious way they were all aggrieved. A time came when each remarked in a tone that rang false, 'You're getting such a Swell now, you know,' and he saw a new light in the erstwhile friendly eye, and therewith yawned a gulf. His friends are not life companions but epochs, influences. And he has worse troubles. One of two things happens to the man from below in his marrying. Either he marries early some one down below there, and she cannot keep pace with him, or he marries late up above—some one very charming and young, and he cannot keep pace with her.

"For by the time he has risen to his highest stratum, and donned the stiffest, prickliest hair-shirt of all, the man from below begins to feel old. He has never been a youth at that level, and he does not know how to begin. The perennial youthfulness of your retired general—who is perhaps half his age again—appalls him. You see him watching cricket in a puzzled way—he had no time for cricket—or hanging over the railings of Rotten

Row (in an attitude that he feels instinctively is a little incorrect), and staring at the handsome, healthy, well-dressed people who ride by. Theirs is the earth. *His* means for horse exercise came when his nerve for it had gone. The wine of life does not wait. After all the man he has ousted had drunk the best of the cup. For the conqueror, the dregs.

"That is the disillusionment of the successful proletarian. Better a little grocery, a life of sordid anxiety, love, and a tumult of children, than this Dead Sea fruit of success. It is fun to struggle, but tragedy to win. Happy is the poor man who clutches that prize in the grip of death and never sees it crumble in his hand."

To which betrayal of a mood I add thirty-nine years later only one word: "Nonsense."

But let me get on with my story which this exhibition of documents has delayed. This divorce put me askew to the usages and institutions of my times in a very elementary, provocative and stimulating way. It affected my attempts at fiction and my social and political reactions profoundly and I must do my best now to dissect out the complex of motives and suggestions that was determining my conduct at this crucial phase.

VII. — DISSECTION

§ 1. COMPOUND FUGUE

If you do not want to explore an egoism you should not read autobiography. If I did not take an immense interest in life, through the medium of myself, I should not have embarked upon this analysis of memories and records. It is not merely for the benefit of some possible reader, but to satisfy my own curiosity about life and the world, that I am digging down into these obscurities of forty years ago. The reader's rôle, the prospect of publication, is kept in view chiefly to steady and control these operations, by the pervading sense of a critical observer. The egoism is unavoidable. I am being my own rabbit because I find no other specimen so convenient for dissection. Our own lives are all the practical material we have for the scientific study of living; the rest is hearsay.

The main theme of this book has been exposed in the Introductory Chapter and recalled at intervals. Essentially this autobiography treats of the steady expansion of the interests and activities of a brain, emerging from what I have called a narrow-scope way of living, to a broader and broader outlook and a consequent longer reach of motive. I move from a backyard to Cosmopolis; from Atlas House to the burthen of Atlas. This theme appears and reappears in varying forms and keys; in the story of my early reading, in the story of my escape from retail trade, in the story of my student perplexities and my attempts to make my geology scientific and my physics philosophical, and so on. More and more consciously the individual adventurer, as he disentangles himself from the family associations in which he was engendered, is displayed trying to make himself a citizen of the world. As his *persona* becomes lucid it takes that form. He is an individual becoming the conscious Common Man of his time and culture. He is a specimen drop from the changing ocean of general political opinion.

But the making of that world scheme is not the only driving force present in the actual life as it has to be told. In many passages it has not been even the dominant driving force. Other systems of feeling and motive run across or with or against the main theme. Sometimes they seem to have a definite relation to it; they enhance its colour and interest or they antagonize it, but often there is no possibility of regularizing their intervention. As in all actual fugues the rules are broken and, judged by the strict standard, the composition is irregular.

The second main system of motive in the working out of my personal destiny, has been the sexual system. It is not the only other system of motive by any means. Certain fears and falterings, an undeniable claustrophobia for example, run through the narrative. The phases of disintegration and healing in my right lung, the resentment and slow resignation of my squashed kidney, have interpolated themes of their own, with their own irrelevant developments. Nevertheless the sexual complexes constitute the only other great and continuing system. I suspect the sexual system should be at least the second theme, when it is not the first, in every autobiography, honestly and fully told. It seizes upon the essential egoism for long periods, it insists upon a prominent rôle in the dramatizations of the *persona* and it will not be denied.

I realize how difficult an autobiography that is not an apology for a life but a research into its nature, can become, as I deal with this business of my divorce. I have already emphasised the widening contrast between the mental range of myself and my cousin. I have shown a disposition to simplify out the issue between myself and Catherine Robbins and Isabel to an issue between how shall I put it?—wide-scope lives and narrow-scope lives. That makes a fairly acceptable story of it, with only one fault, that it is untrue. It is all the more untrue because like a bad portrait there is superficial truth in it. The reality was far more complicated. Much more was entangled in the story. I confess that I feel that there are elements in it that I myself apprehend only very imperfectly. Let me take up this fresh chapter, as though I were a portrait painter taking a fresh canvas and beginning over again. Let me alter the pose and the lighting of my experiences so as to bring out in its successive phases the emotional and sensual egoism rather than the intellectual egoism that has hitherto been the focus of attention.

391

And as I turn over old letters, set date against date, and try and determine the true inter-relation of this vivid memory with that, it grows clearer and clearer to me that my personal unity, the consistency of my present *persona* has been achieved only after a long struggle between distinct strands of motivation, which had no necessary rational relation one to another and that, at the period of which I am writing, this unity was still more apparent than real.

For the normal man, as we have him to-day, his personal unity is a delusion. He is always fighting down the exposure of that delusion. His first impulse is to rationalize his inconsistencies by telling himself fanciful stories of why he did this and that. The tougher job, which all men and women will ultimately be educated to undertake, is to recognize the ultimately irreconcilable quality of these inconsistencies and to make a deal between them.

It is because of this almost universal desire to impose a sort of rational relationship upon the alternation of motives that I (and my biographer Geoffrey West, following my promptings) have represented this early divorce of mine, this first revelation of increasingly powerful strands of sexual force at work in me, as if it were almost entirely a part of my progressive detachment from my world of origin. But it merely chanced to help detach me. Later on, this sexual drive was to hamper and confuse my progress very considerably.

The simple attractive story I am half disposed to tell, of myself as an ugly duckling who escaped from the limitations and want of understanding of his cousin and of his family generally, to discover itself a swan in Fleet Street and Paternoster Row, is made impossible by two things: an awkward trick my memory has had of stowing away moments of intense feeling and vivid action quite regardless of the mental embarrassment their preservation may ultimately cause my *persona*, and an analogous disposition already noted, on the part of my friends and family to keep letters I have written. I am astonished at the multitude of my letters that have never been destroyed. I have recovered now some thousand or so of them; as I turn them over past events live again, vanished details are restored, and insist upon a readjustment of the all too plausible values I have long set upon them.

And now let me try to get a little nearer to Isabel's true rôle in my life.

§ 2. PRIMARY FIXATION

I have told what I know of my childish and boyish sexual development. It was uncomplicated and I think very normal. There was only a very slight slant towards homosexuality. Less I think than is usual. As a small boy I had adorations for one or two big fellows and as a boy of twelve or thirteen I had affection for one or two little chaps, who obviously played the rôle of girls in my unoriented imagination. These were nothing more than early explorations of my emotional tentacles. All this, as sexual knowledge and discrimination developed, dissolved away to nothing, and by sixteen I was entirely heterosexual in my fantasies. I had a bright strong vision of beautiful women, the sort of women revealed by classical statuary and paintings, reciprocally worshipped and beautifully embraced, which I connected only very remotely with the living feminine personalities I met clothed and difficult, and with whom I "flirted," at times, weakly and formally. I had one or two warning experiences that the hidden happiness of sex was not easy of attainment. My gleams of intimacy at Westbourne Park were not pretty; plainly my Venus Urania did not live down that frowsty scuffling alley. Later on (I cannot fix the date but it must have been while I was in my twenties and a biological demonstrator) my secret shame at my own virginity became insupportable and I went furtively and discreetly with a prostitute. She was just an unimaginative prostitute. That deepened my wary apprehension that round about the hidden garden of desire was a jungle of very squalid and stupid lairs.

Now my cousin had a real sweetness and loveliness that our closeness did nothing to abolish. All the cloudy drift of desire and romantic imagination in my mind centred more and more upon her. I became so persuaded and satisfied that with her I could get to this fundamental happiness of love which now obsessed me, that for all the years between my student days and our marriage my imagination never wandered very far from her. I played the devoted impatient lover. There was a deep-seated fixation of my mind upon her.

She loved me I knew, but with a more limited and temperate imagination than mine. The jangle of our thoughts and outlooks, that difference in scope, would not have mattered very much if our passions had been in tune. We should have managed then. Our real discord was not mental but temperamental. And she was afraid, and the worldly wisdom of that retouching studio in Regent Street did not help her in the least. My nature protested at having to wait for her so long, protested against having to marry her in church instead of at a registry office. I didn't believe in marriage anyhow, I insisted. The great thing was not marriage but love. I invoked Godwin, Shelley, Socialism.

Streaks of vindictiveness crept into my passion. And I was a very ignorant as well as an impatient lover. I knew nothing of the arts of wooing. I should probably have thought that sort of thing dishonest. My idea was of flame meeting flame.... We are so much wiser about that sort of thing nowadays. It is rarer for avid and innocent young bridegrooms to be flung upon shrinking and innocent brides.

It mattered nothing to me, then, that Isabel was manifestly fond of me, cared greatly for me. It was a profound mortification to me, a vast disappointment, that she did not immediately respond to my ardours. She submitted. I had waited so long for this poor climax. "She does not love me," I said in my heart. I put as brave a face as I could upon the business, I dried her tears, blamed my roughness, but it was a secretly very embittered young husband who went on catching trains, correcting correspondence answer books, eviscerating rabbits and frogs and hurrying through the crowded business of every day.

Here was something more organic than any difference in mental scope. And I want to make it quite clear that for a long time my emotional pride, my secret romanticism was still centred quite firmly in my cousin. It is true that I was presently letting my desires wander away from her and that I was making love to other people. I wanted to compensate myself for the humiliation she had so unwittingly put upon me. I was in a phase of aroused liveliness. That did not alter her unpremeditated and unconscious dominance of my imagination, my deep-lying desire for passionate love with her.

Quite soon after my marriage indeed came an adventure, that did much to restore my baffled self confidence. There was a certain little Miss Kingsmill who came to Haldon Road first as a pupil to learn retouching and then as a helper with the work. She was cheerfully a-moral and already an experienced young woman. She was about the house before and after my marriage; the business stirred her; she may have had confidences from my cousin and a quickening interest became evident in her manner towards me. I found myself alone with her in the house one day; I was working upon a pile of correspondence books, my aunt was out shopping and my wife had gone to London with some retouched negatives. I forget by what excuse Ethel Kingsmill flitted from her retouching desk upstairs, to my study. But she succeeded in dispelling all the gloomy apprehensions I was beginning to entertain, that lovemaking was nothing more than an outrage inflicted upon reluctant womankind and all its loveliness a dream. The sound of my returning aunt's latch-key separated us in a state of flushed and happy accomplishment. I sat down with a quickened vitality to my blottesque red corrections again and Ethel, upstairs, very content with herself, resumed her niggling at her negative. Sentimentally and "morally" this is a quite shocking incident to relate; in truth it was the most natural thing in the world.

After that one adventure I looked the world in the eye again. But it did nothing to change my attachment to Isabel. Our separation did not alter the fact that still for many years she retained the dominant place among my emotional possibilities. I do not know what might have happened if at any time in the course of our estrangement she had awakened and turned upon me with a passionate appeal.

I can see to-day, as I dissect the dead rabbit of my former self, what I never saw before, why it was that after years of complete orientation to my cousin, now that she was my wife, my eye and fancy wandered. Less consciously than instinctively I was trying to undo the knot I had tied and release myself from the strong, unsatisfying bond of habit and affection between us. I still wanted to keep her, if only she would quicken and come alive to me; and quite as strongly I wanted to escape from the pit of disappointment into which I had fallen with her.

As I sit over this specimen of human life, pickled now in correspondence and ineffaceable memories for forty years, I find this replacement, in the course of a few weeks, of a very real simple honesty of sexual purpose by duplicity quite the most interesting fact about my early married life. After six "engagement" years of monogamic sincerity and essential faithfulness, I embarked, as soon as I was married, upon an enterprising promiscuity. The old love wasn't at all dead, but I meant now to get in all the minor and incidental love adventures I could.

I am disposed to think, on the strength I admit, of my one only personal experiences, that for the normally constituted human being there must be two contrasted types of phase, fixation upon an individual as one end of the series and complete promiscuity of attention and interest as the other. Anyone, at any time, may be in one or other phase, or moving from one to the other. We are not monogamic by nature, or promiscuous by nature, but some of us happen to get *fixed* for longer or shorter periods. There is a general desire to concentrate. We tend towards attachment but a shock or a mounting subconscious resistance may suddenly interfere. It is like the accumulation of a sediment, in a test tube which may at any time happen to be heated or shaken. We become dispersed then, perhaps for an indefinite time, until a new trend towards fixation appears. These are matters not within the control of will or foresight, they happen to us before willing begins. That, I think, gives some expression to these alternations of fairly strict loyalty, such as I observed before my marriage, with my subsequent infidelities, which phase again gave place to a second, less powerful, fixation and that to a second discursiveness.

But as I sit and speculate about what really happened to me more than half a life-time ago in 1892 and 1893, I begin to suspect that I am still simplifying too much and that there was another independent strand of motive playing among the others. Is there a strain of evasion in my composition? Does the thought of being bound and settling down, in itself, so soon as it is definitely presented, arouse a recalcitrant stress in me? And how far is that fugitive impulse exceptional, and how far is its presence an ordinary thing in the human make-up? Is this string also tugging at everybody? Is there potential flight as well as attraction in every love affair? I remember clearly how much I desired my cousin to become my mistress before I married her and how much I wished to go on living in lodgings for a time even after we were married, instead of taking a house.

In my case the break between the pull and the drive came to a climax very abruptly. I find I was writing from my home in Sutton in mid-December 1892 as though I intended to live on there indefinitely; and I find myself living in Mornington Place with Catherine Robbins early in the following January! The circumstances of that very abrupt change defeat my memory. Something happened which I cannot recall. I have been inclined to suppose a fit of claustrophobia. Did I perhaps wake up suddenly in the night and say "I must get out of this"? I may have had one of those spasmodic resolutions that do come up sometimes out of the welter of the half-conscious and the subconscious! If so I do not remember it. But I do find indications of precisely the opposite thing, a considerable amount of shilly-shally. Even after I had eloped I was, I know, trying very earnestly to persuade my cousin not to divorce me. Having got away from her I wanted to keep her. It is only now, in this cold and deliberate retrospect, that I admit even to myself how disingenuous, how confused and divided in purpose I was at that time.

Isabel and I paid a visit to the Robbins' household on December 15th and stayed until December 18th. This probably brought on the crisis. Isabel may have given way to a fit of jealousy. My brother Freddy, who was always greatly attached to her and who talked the affair over with her years afterwards, tells me now that she ascribed our separation to her own initiative. She told him she had put it to me that either I must end this continually more intimate and interesting friendship altogether or part from her. She had had a similar phase of possessiveness during my student days at South Kensington. She felt at a disadvantage with these people who could "talk." I do not now recall any such ultimatum, but in the circumstances it was a very natural and probable one and the visit to Putney may have precipitated it. The retort, "Very well, if you can let me go like this, I will go," was equally natural and obvious. There we have exactly the pride and resentment on either side necessary for a sudden separation. She made what is otherwise an unaccountable decision, easy for me.

Brother Freddy comes in very usefully here. Later on, he tells me, she regretted our parting profoundly. I too regretted it. She reproached herself, he says, for failing to "understand" me and for having broken before I was ready to break. She said she had been headstrong and selfish; she had said her say, I had taken her at her word, and she found there was no going back upon it. There was certainly a deep bond of dearness between us still, we realized that as our anger abated, but, once we were launched upon our several courses, there was no return.

Perhaps it was well that there was no return. There was a superficial volatility and a profound impatience in my make-up that would have taxed her ultimately beyond the limit of her adaptability. We might have gone on dragging out the estrangement. A later breach might have been a less generous one.

My little Aunt Mary, who died two years later, was distressed and perplexed beyond measure by our divorce and, as Isabel told me long afterwards, her opinion of the whole affair expressed itself in a "good scolding" for "losing" me. My mother too was so amazed at Isabel "letting me go," and so near to indignation about it, that she quite forgot to be shocked at the immorality of my situation. I cannot make up my mind how far this disposition on the part of women to make their own sex wholly responsible for the infirmity of purpose of their menfolk is due to deep seated and ancient traditions, and how far it is innate. But that was how my aunt and my mother behaved.

When my second wife was dying in 1927, she said to me, "I have never destroyed a single letter of yours, I cannot destroy them now. There they are in my bureau, with all my own letters that you have asked me to keep. You must do as you please with them." So that I am able, after a little trouble with some undated letters, to check back every main phase in our reactions throughout our long married life. The record is even fuller than a mere keeping of letters would imply. Not only did we write to each other daily when we were apart, but for all our time when we were together, I had a queer little custom of drawing what we called "picshuas" to amuse her and myself, little sketches of fancy, comment or caricature. I began this in Mornington Place in 1893. These picshuas carried on the tradition of those scratchy odd little drawings with which I used to decorate my letters to my family and friends. Many were destroyed as they were done, but many were thrust into drawers and survived. The growth and changes of tone in our relations is, I say, traceable by means of this accumulation over thirty-five years. And it is quite evident that these letters are those of two loving friends and allies, who are not and never had been passionate lovers. That is the point of importance here.

The earliest of all my letters, the ones written before matters came to a crisis, were the ordinary letters of a self-conscious young man putting his best foot forward in a friendly correspondence. They were letters that might have to be shown to "mother" and eminently discreet. There is no essential change of tone right up to the breach with Isabel. But then came letters written during our crisis, and I find a curiously false and unconvincing note sounding through them. They are plainly the attempts of an extremely perplexed mind to make a fair story out of a muddle of impulses. They are not straightforward, they pose and flatter, they exaggerate. The ring of simple and honest passion is not there; I would hate to quote a line of them. Fortunately that is not only unnecessary but impossible. They vary so much that no quotations would be really representative.

The resort to heroics in these letters is frequent and facile. I was acting a part. I may have been acting in good faith, to the best of my ability, but I was acting. It is plain that I resolved suddenly at any cost to get my little student to come away and give herself to me, but there is not the slightest indication that I was really possessed by her personality or that at that time I had the smallest apprehension of its sterling quality. Sifting over all my evidence now, not as my apologist but as my scientific historian, I am inclined to think that the most powerful drive at work in me was the longing to relieve my imagination not of the real Isabel but of that Venus Urania, that torment of high and beautiful desire, who had failed to embody herself in Isabel and yet had become so inseparable from her. My mind was seizing upon Amy Catherine Robbins to make her the triumphant rival of that elusive goddess.

On my new mistress, in her turn, I was trying to impose a rôle. Like so many other desperate young love affairs, ours was to be such a love affair as the world had never seen before. Other people were different. We were by mutual agreement two beings of an astonishing genius with an inherent right to turn accepted morality upside down. It was an explosion of moral light....

There was some coming and going between Mornington Place and the Robbins' home in Putney after our first departure. The mother declared herself to be dying of grief, she wept continuously and incredibly, and the daughter went back to her home for some days. Attempts were then made to delay her return to me. Various men friends of the family were invoked to remonstrate and threaten. I stuck to my purpose grimly. Miss Amy Catherine Robbins stuck to my purpose. Vast arguments unfolded about us. She was consumptive; I was consumptive; we were launching on a desperate experiment. We replied magnificently that if we were going to die so soon, the more reason there was that we should spend all that was left of our brief time on earth together. But let her at any rate remain in the shelter of her home until I was divorced, they argued. I answered that I was not sure I wanted to be divorced. We did not believe in the Institution of Marriage and we did not intend to marry. We were both very sure that we did not intend to marry.

The resolve to get the best of an argument may link two people as closely as inherent mutual desire. We hadn't our backs to the wall; there was indeed nothing in the nature of a wall behind us; we had only each other. We saw the thing through in spite of immense secret disillusionments. I found this fragile delicate little being of Dresden china, was altogether innocent and ignorant of the material realities of love, it was impossible to be rough or urgent with her and so the deep desired embraces of Venus Urania were now further off from me than ever. But not a soul in the world about us knew anything of that for some years. We stuck to each other stoutly and forged the links of a chain of mutual aid, tolerance and affection that held us close to each other to the day of her death. We got over the worst of our difficulties; we established a *modus vivendi*. Insensibly the immense pretentiousness of our first beginning evaporated and we began to jest and mock at ourselves very cordially. The "picshuas" began. We worked in close association and sympathy. But there arose no such sexual fixation between us, as still lingered in my mind towards my cousin.

If I am to tell this story at all I must tell here of two illuminating incidents that happen to be known now to no one in the whole world but myself. They seem to me to be profoundly illuminating; but the reader must judge for himself whether I am disposed to exaggerate their significance. They show at any rate how little I had really finished with my cousin when I separated myself from her and how much of that separation was concerned with her and not with her successor. The first of these incidents occurred when I visited her somewhen about 1898 or 99 at a poultry farm she was running, not very profitably, at Twyford between Maidenhead and Reading. I think the pretext of our meeting again was the discussion of some extension of that enterprise. I bicycled to the place and found her amidst green things and swarming creatures depending upon her, in the rustic setting to which by nature she belonged. We spent a day together at Virginia Water, a day without tension, with an easy friendliness we had never known before. We used our old intimate names for each other. Suddenly I found myself overcome by the sense of our separation. I wanted fantastically to recover her. I implored her for the last time in vain. Before dawn the house had become unendurable for me. I got up and dressed and went down to find my bicycle and depart. She heard me moving about, perhaps she too had not slept, and she came down, kindly and invincible as ever, and as amazed as ever at my strangeness.

Because you see it was all so unreasonable.

"But you cannot go out at this hour without something to eat," she said, and set about lighting a fire and boiling a kettle.

Her aunt could be heard moving about upstairs, for they occupied adjacent rooms. "It's all right Auntie," she said, and prevented her from coming down to witness my distress.

All our old mingling of intense attraction and baffling reservation was there unchanged. "But how can things like that be, now?" she asked. I gave way to a wild storm of weeping. I wept in her arms like a disappointed child, and then suddenly pulled myself together and went out into the summer dawn and mounted my bicycle and wandered off southward into a sunlit intensity of perplexity and frustration, unable to understand the peculiar keenness of my unhappiness. I felt like an automaton, I felt as though all purpose had been drained out of me and nothing remained worth while. The world was dead and I was dead and I had only just discovered it.

After that I set myself to forget my imaginations about her, by releasing my imaginations for other people. But in that I was unsuccessful for a long time. Five or six years afterwards she married; I do not know the exact date because for more than a year she kept this from me. And then came a still more illuminating incident. When at last I heard of it, I was overwhelmed by a storm of irrational organic jealousy. It took the form of a deliberate effacement of her. I destroyed all her photographs and letters and every souvenir I possessed of her; I would not have her mentioned to me if I could avoid it; I ceased all communications. The portraits I have reproduced here I have had to borrow. That bitterness again is quite incompatible with the plausible and conventional theory that she was nothing more to me than an illiterate young woman whom I "dropped" because she was unequal to a rôle in the literary world. I burnt her photographs. That was a symbolization. If we had lived ten thousand years ago I suppose I should have taken my axe of stone and set out to find and kill her.

And to complete this history here, the still stranger thing is that in another five years all this fixation had vanished. It had been completely swept out of my mind by other disturbances of which I must tell at some later date. The sting had vanished. I was able to meet her again in 1909 in a mood of limitless friendliness, free from all the glittering black magic of sex; and so things remained with us until the end of her life. Some friend we had in common mentioned her to me, brought us into communication again, and we met and continued to meet at intervals after that. Following her marriage, the order for her alimony had been discharged but now, realizing she had to practice many economies, I arranged an income for her, exactly as one might do for a married sister. In quite the same mood of brotherliness I bought a laundry for her when the fancy took her to possess a business of her own. That enterprise was crippled by an operation for appendicitis; she had no great facilities for being nursed in her own house and she came to mine and stayed through her convalescence with my wife and myself until she was well again. No one about us knew her story; she was my cousin and that sufficed; we were in a world far removed from the primitive jealousies, comparisons and recriminations of our early years. We walked about the garden discussing annuals and perennials and roses and trees. When she was growing stronger I took her for my favourite round through the big gardens of Easton Lodge. She was particularly pleased by the lily tank before the house, and by the golden pheasants Lady Warwick had turned loose in the wood behind the ponds.

That was the last walk we ever had together.

She wrote to me in her simple gentle fashion when my wife died, praising and lamenting her. Afterwards she wanted to build a house of her own and asked me to help her. When I saw that her heart was set upon it I agreed to that, though it did not seem to me to be what Americans call a sound proposition. We inspected the site and she showed me the plans. But the house was barely begun before she died and it was abandoned. She died quite unexpectedly. She had been diabetic and making use of insulin for some years. I had just discovered that I too was diabetic and I was looking forward to her coming to a lunch with me, at which I would surprise her by an admirable menu of all the best permissible things. I thought it was a cousinly touch that we should share the same diathesis. But something went wrong with her insulin injections and one day in France I got a letter from her husband saying that she was dead. She had been well on Saturday and she became comatose on Monday and died without recovering consciousness.

So ends this history of the rise and fall and sequel of that primary fixation that began when my cousin came downstairs to meet me in that basement tea-party in the Euston Road forty-seven years before. I offer no moral lesson. I have tried to tell things as they happened.

§ 3. MODUS VIVENDI

The mixture of high-falutin with sincere determination on the part of this Miss Amy Catherine Robbins and myself in the early stages of our joint adventure, deserves a little more attention. We were both in reality in flight from conditions of intolerably narrow living. But we did not know how to state that properly, we were not altogether clear about it, and we caught at the phrasing of Shelley and the assumption of an imperative passion. She was the only daughter of an extremely timid and conventional mother with no ideas for her future beyond marriage to a safe, uneventful *good* man, and her appearance in my mixed classes was already an expression of her struggle and revolt. My own recalcitrance to the life fate had presented to me

I have already dealt with. My intimations of freedom and social and intellectual enterprise (on the noblest scale) went to her head very readily and it was an overwhelming desire for emancipation from consuming everyday obligations for both of us rather than sexual passion, that led to our wild dash at opportunity.

That alliance for escape and self development held throughout our lives. We never broke it. As our heroics evaporated we found ourselves with an immense liking and respect for each other and a great willingness to turn an awkward corner with a jest and a caricature. We discovered a way of doing that. We became and remained the best companions in the world. But our alliance never became an intense sexual companionship, which indeed is why my primary fixation upon my cousin remained so powerful in my mind for ten years, or more, and why, later on, as we emerged to success and freedom I was in a phase of imaginative dispersal and began to scandalize the whisperers about us.

Here again it would be easy to dress up my story in a highly logical and creditable manner. But I have never quite succeeded in that sort of dressing- up. A few tactful omissions would smooth out the record beautifully. And if the record is not beautifully smoothed out it is not for want of effort. Between the ages of thirty and forty I devoted a considerable amount of mental energy to the general problem of men and women. And never with any real disinterestedness. I wanted to live a consistent life, I wanted a life that would stand examination, I hated having to fake a front to the world, and yet not only were my thoughts and fancies uncontrollable, but my conduct remained perplexingly disingenuous. I did my best to eliminate my sense of that disingenuousness by candid public theorizing. I spoke out for "Free Love." I suppose I was going through phases roughly parallel with those through which Shelley had passed eighty years before. Hundreds of thousands have passed that way. I did my best to maintain that love-making was a thing in itself, a thing to thank the gods for, but not to be taken too seriously and carried into the larger constructive interests of life.

The spreading knowledge of birth-control,—Neo-Malthusianism was our name for it in those days—seemed to justify my contention that love was now to be taken more lightly than it had been in the past. It was to be refreshment and invigoration, as I set out quite plainly in my *Modern Utopia* (1905) and I could preach these doctrines with no thought of how I would react if presently my wife were to carry them into effect, since she was so plainly not disposed to carry them into effect, and what is much more remarkable, with my recent storm of weeping in that little farm kitchen at Twyford, very conveniently—but quite honestly—forgotten. This again I think is after the common fashion. We are not naturally aware of our two-phase quality. We can all think in the liberal fashion in our phases of dispersal; there is always a Free Love contingent in any community at any time; but its membership varies and at any time any of its members may lapse towards a fixation and towards its attendant exclusiveness and jealous passion. People drop out of the contingent or return to it. At one time love is the happy worship of Venus, the goddess of human loveliness, the graceful mutual complement of two free bodies and spirits; at another it is the sacred symbol of an intense and mystical personal association, a merging of identities prepared to live and die for one another. It is this variation of phase that plays havoc with every simple dogmatic ruling upon sexual behaviour.

Advocates of free love, in so far as they aim at the liberation of individual sexual conduct from social reproach and from legal controls and penalties, are, I believe, entirely in the right. Nevertheless, with such a liberation, very little is attained. Circumstances are simplified, but the problem itself remains unchanged. We are still confronted with the essential riddle of our own phases of development as we pass from youth to maturity and, as I have already insisted, with this other, more persistent, alternation of phase between dispersal and intensification. The tangle is further complicated by the absolute right of society to intervene directly the existence of children is involved, and by a third mass of difficulties due to the fact that emotionally and physically, and thence to an increasing degree in its secondary associations and implications, love is a different thing for men and women. In a universe of perfect adaptations these differences would reciprocate; in this world they do nothing of the sort.

But here I approach questions and experiences that will be better deferred until I come to that phase of my middle years during which I produced various hesitating yet enterprising love novels. Then, almost in spite of myself, I was forced by my temperament and circumstances to face the possibility that men and women as such, when it comes to planning a greater world order, may be disposed to desire incompatible things. Feminine creativeness and feminine devotion may differ from their masculine parallels and though women radicals and men radicals are members of the same associations and speak to the same meetings, their ends may lie far apart. There may have to be a new treaty of mutual tolerance between the sexes.

But in the early days of my second marriage I did not even suspect the possibility of these fundamental disagreements in the human project. My wife and I had still to win the freedom to think as we liked about our world. What we were then going to think about it, lay some years ahead of us. While we struggled we liked each other personally more and more, we dropped our heroics and laughed and worked together, we made do with our physical and nervous incompatibilities and kept a brave face towards the world.

We dropped our disavowal of the Institution of Marriage and married, as soon as I was free to do so, in 1895. The behaviour of the servants of that period and the landladies and next-door neighbours, forced that upon us anyhow. Directly the unsoundness of our position appeared, servants became impertinent and neighbours rude and strange. How well we came to know the abrupt transition from a friendly greeting "passing the time of day" to a rigid estrangement. Were they really horrified when they "heard about it," or is there a disposition to hate and persecute awaiting release in every homely body? I believe that there has been a great increase in tolerance in the last forty years but in our period, if we had not married, half our energy would have been frittered away in a conflict of garden-wall insults and slights and domestic exactions. We had no disposition for that kind of warfare.

And having got together and found how evanescent were our heroics, and having discovered that our private dreams of some hidden splendour of loving were evaporating, we were nevertheless under both an inner and an outer obligation to stand by one another and pull our adventure through. We refrained from premature discussion and felt our way over our situation with tentatives and careful understatement. We could each wait for the other to take on an idea. She, even less than I, had that terrible fluidity of speech that can swamp any situation in garrulous justification and headlong ultimatums. And our extraordinary isolation, too, helped us to discover a *modus vivendi*. Neither of us had any confidants to complicate our relations by some potent divergent suggestion, and there was no background of unsympathetic values that either of us respected. Neither of us bothered in the least about what so and so would think. In many matters we were odd and exceptional individuals but in our broad relations to each other and society we may have come much nearer to being absolute and uncomplicated sample man and woman, than do most young couples. The research for a *modus vivendi* is a necessary phase of the normal married life to-day.

Now in this research for a *modus vivendi* certain apparently very trivial things played a really very important part. Although I have published only four lines of verse in my life, I used to be in the habit of making endless doggerel as I got up in the morning, and when we were sitting together in the evening, with my writing things before me I would break off my work to do "picshuas," these silly little sketches about this or that incident which became at last a sort of burlesque diary of our lives and accumulated in boxes until there were hundreds of them. Many—perhaps most—are lost but still there remain hundreds. I invented a queer little device in a couple of strokes to represent her head, and it somehow seemed to us to resemble her; also a kindred convention, with a large nose and a wreath of laurel suggestive of poetic distinction and incipient baldness, for myself. Like so many couples, we found it necessary to use pet names; she became Bits or Miss Bits or Snitch or It, with variations, and I was Bins or Mr. Bins. A burlesque description I gave, after a visit to the Zoological Gardens, of the high intelligence and remarkable social life of the gopher, amused us so much that we incorporated a sort of gopher chorus with the picshuas. Whatever we did, whatever was going on in the world, the gophers set about doing after their fashion. Into this parallel world of burlesque and fancy, we transferred a very considerable amount of our every-day life, and there it lost its weight and irksomeness. We transferred our own selves there also. Miss Bits became an active practical imperious little being and Mr. Bins a rather bad, evasive character who went in great awe of her. He was frequently chastised with an umbrella or "Umbler pop." All this funny-silly stuff is so much of the same quality that I find it hard to pick out specimens, but I do not see how I can tell of it without reproducing samples. Here for instance are various "études," some very early sketches of Miss Robbins in her academic gown, done before our elopement, a very characteristic figure of her engaged in literary effort, from about 1896, four later studies of the conventional head of Miss Bits, It usually, It at the slightest hint of impropriety, It sad and It asleep, a treatment of the advent of reading glasses, and a sort of frieze of every-day; the Same, Yesterday, To-day and for Ever. These may seem at the first glance to be the most idle of scribblings but in fact they are acute statements in personal interpretation. Mostly they were done on sheets of manuscript paper, so that here they suffer considerable reduction and compression. This, says my publisher was unavoidable.

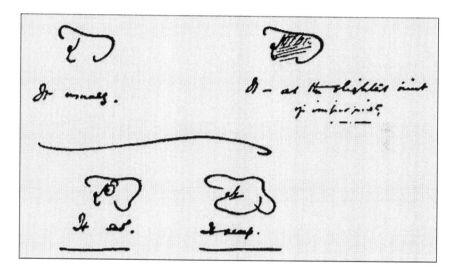

Picshua: Four Studies of "It."

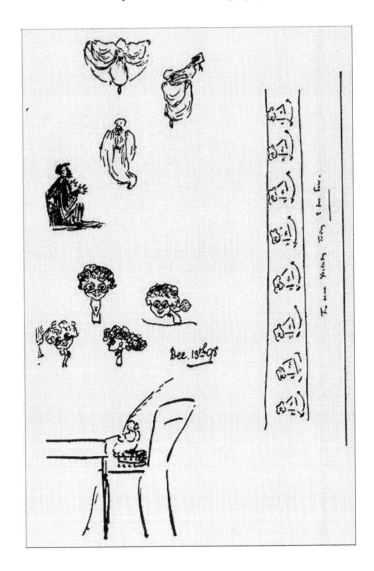

Picshuas: Academic Robes, Reading Glasses,
Literary Composition, Frieze Design.

* * * * *

Here is a Satirical Picshua, on one side of the paper is "Bits as she *finks* she is" and on the other, "the real Bits, really a very dear Bits indeed." She writes, sleeps, eats and rides a bicycle with me.]

Picshua: A Satirical Picshua.

* * * * *

Here again is the text of a sympathetic but relentless poem, undated but probably about 1898, showing still more clearly how she was being, to use Henry James's word "treated," for mental assimilation:

> *CHANSON*
> *It was called names*
> *Miss Furry Boots and Nicketty and Bits,*
> *And P.C.B., and Snitterlings and Snits,*
> *It was called names.*
>
> *Such names as no one but a perfect 'Orror*
> *Could ever fink or find or beg or borror*
> *Names out of books or names made up to fit it*
> *In wild array*
> *It never knew when some new name might hit it*
> *From day to day*
> *Some names it's written down and some it 'as forgotten*
> *Some names was nice and some was simply ROTTEN.*
> *Sometimes they made it smile,*
> *Sometimes they seemed to flatter*
> *Sometimes they made it weep—it really did not matter.*
> *Some made it pine quite fin, but fin or fat or fatter*
> *It was called names.*

* * * * *

Here again is a gardening picture from either Woking or the early Worcester Park days, representing an encounter with a slug. The Wreath on my head "dates" the picture as an early one, probably 1895 or 1896. This wreath was my symbol for literary ambitions; it appears constantly in my earlier student's letters to A.T. Simmons and Miss Healey, and it becomes infrequent after 1898.

Picshua: Salutary Lesson.
Determined Behaviour of a Lady Horticulturist.

* * * * *

Here you have a "Fearful Pome" intended to bring home to
an insolent woman her dependence on her lord. This doggerel
variant of Lear's nonsense rhyme, brings out the queer little fact

415

that even in these early days at Heatherlea, Worcester Park, the money of the alliance was already under her control. We were living indeed exactly like an honest working-class couple and the man handed over his earnings to his "missus" and was given out his pocket money.

Fearful Pome To Scare And Improve A Bits

The Pobble who has no Toes
Had once as many as Ten
(Now here is a Strange and Horrible Thing
All of his Toes were Men)

Some there are who wrongly hold
His toes did number eleven
But none dare count the Hairs of his Head
(Though the Stars in his Hair are Seven)

Such as would count the Hairs of His Head
peedily Painfully Die
(Aunt Jobiska he never had
All that tale is a Lie).

All who meet the Pobble abroad
Come to infinite Harm
May you never meet him (Pray the Lord),
Clothed in his Sinister Charm

(Softly (yet dreadfully fast) He goes
That Terrible Pobble who has no Toes)
(It's no good saying you do not care
This Awful Pobble goes everywhere)

Should you meet him, cover your face
Leave your shoes in that Terrible Place
The Pobble—the Foe of the Human Race—and Flee
Your only shelter from his Clutch
Your only Refuge he dare not Touch
The only Being he cares for Much is Me (H.G.)

Me what you fink is simply Fungy
Me what you keep so short of Mungy
Me what you keep so short of Beer
Is your only chance when the Pobble is near
Nex time you go for your Umbler Pop
Fink of that Terrible Pobble and Stop.

Reproduction of Fearful Pome, Page 1.

Reproduction of Fearful Pome, Page 2.

* * * * *

Here is a gentle protest against an unfair invasion of table space. The lamp dates it as before 1900 and the spectacles as after 1898.

419

Picshua: Invasion of Table Space.

* * * * *

Here is a much later sketch, dated 1911, celebrating the return of the Tangerine season. We had enjoyed tangerines together at Mornington Place, seventeen years before. I thought we might enjoy them again in seventeen years' time—but in 1911 there were only sixteen years left to us; she died in 1927. And note the "some day" at the bottom.... That picshua has become the oddest little epitome of our third of a century together.

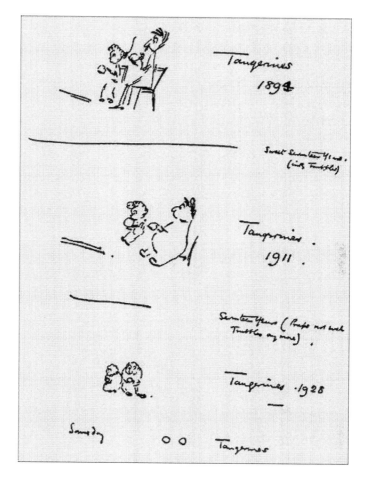

Picshua: Tangerines.

* * * * *

Here is an earlier picshua again (March 31st, 1899). It commemorates a removal from Beach Cottage, Sandgate, to Arnold House. The helplessness of the male on these occasions of

421

domestic upheaval is contrasted with the ruthless energy of the female. The first thing is "Gup! Movals!", *i.e.* "Get up—removal!" Then the embarrassed master of the house misses his trousers. He finds himself being carried from house to house and protests, "But Bits why can't I walk like I usually does?" He is crushed by the stern reply "Cos it's Movals". And so on.

Picshua: Removal to Arnold House.

* * * * *

On the following two pages is a casual specimen for 1898. The reader may do his best to interpret it. A lens may be needed, but that is due to the unavoidable reduction in printing. By this time the reader has either given up looking at these picshuas or he has learnt their peculiar language. The idea of building a house was already under discussion. We had had a visit from J.M. Barrie (of which a word may be said later) and he and Jane are represented measuring heights (Mezzerinites). There had been trouble over a building site, with a Mr. Toomer. The gophers appear in full cry in pursuit of the said Toomer. The Atom reflects upon her diminutive size. Other points may be guessed at.

Picshua: J.M. Barrie, etc., 1st Drawing.

Picshua: J.M. Barrie, etc., 2nd Drawing.

* * * * *

This rather more ambitious attempt commemorates the completion of *Love and Mr. Lewisham*. What the little figures rocketing across the left hand corner of the picture intimate I do not know. They are, I think, just a decorative freak.

424

Picshua: Waiting For The Verdik.
Love and Mr.Lewisham

* * * * *

Finally let me quote a hymn, celebrating our first seven years together. "Mr. Boo" I may explain was a cat that ran away, and the "Bites" were Harvesters, which we had gathered unwittingly on the Downs behind Folkstone.

Lines Written On This Piece Of Paper, Oct. 11th, 1900.

Our God is an Amoosing God. It is His Mercy that
This Bins who formerly was ill is now quite well and Fat
And isn't going Bald no more nor toofaking and such
For all of which This Bins who writes congratulates
Him much.

Our God is an Amoosing God, although he let that site,
What first we chose, be Toomerized, he more than made
things right
By getting us a better site, a more amoozing chunk
And finding us the Voysey man and Honest Mr. Dunk.

Our God is an Amoosing God. Although he stole our Boo.
(A rather shabby sort of fing for any God to do)
Although he persecuted us for several orful nights
With fings which I can only name by calling of em—Bites.
Although he made me orful ill when I came back from
Rome.
Although he keeps the windows back, what's ordered for
our mome,
Although, if I aint precious sharp, he gets my socks on odd
And blacks my flangle trowsers. Still—

He's an Amoosing God.

Yes God is an Amoozing God, and that is why I am
By way of Compliment to Him, so much the Woolly Lamb.
He gives me little woolly Momes and little Furry Bits
He's lately added to my store a Mackintosh that fits.
He gives me Tankards full of Beer and endless pleasant
Fings
And so to show my Gratitude to God I sits and sings.
I sits and sings to Lordy God with all my little wits.

*(But all the same I don't love 'Im not near what I love
Bits.)*

* * * * *

But altogether many hundreds of these sketches and
scribblings have escaped the dustbin and the fireplace; and they
are all at about the same level of skill and humour. There is no
need to reproduce more of them. What matters here is the way
in which they wrapped about the facts of life and created for us
a quaint and softened atmosphere of intercourse. They falsified
our relations to the pitch of making them tolerable and workable.
The flow of this output was a little interrupted when I took to
drawing Good Night Pictures for our children, but it never really
ceased. I was drawing picshuas for her within a few weeks of her
death, and one day during those last months we had together, we
turned the whole collection out and looked them over together,
remembering and reminding.

The reader may think I have wandered away from the subject
of dispersal and fixation with which I began this section. But
indeed it is essential to that subject that I should explain how
it was that we two contrived in the absence of a real passionate
sexual fixation, a binding net of fantasy and affection that proved
in the end as effective as the very closest sexual sympathy could
have been in keeping us together. And we were linked together
also by our unreserved co-operation in work and business
affairs. At first I sent my MSS. to be typed by a cousin, (the
daughter of that cousin Williams who kept school for a time
at Wookey), but later on my wife learnt to typewrite in order
to save the delay of posting and waiting to correct copy, which
latter process often necessitated retyping. She not only typed,
she scrutinized my text, watched after my besetting sin of verbal
repetitions, and criticized and advised. Quite early in our life

together, so soon as I had any money, I began handing over most of it to her, and for the greater part of our married life, we had a joint and several banking account on which either of us could draw without consulting the other, and she had complete control of my investments. She spent exactly what she thought proper, she made up my income tax returns without troubling me, I ceased more and more to look into things, satisfied when she told me that everything was "all right," and, when she died, I found myself half as much again better off than I had ever imagined myself to be. Another thing between us that seems extremely significant to me as I look back upon it, was this, that I disliked both of her names, Amy and Catherine, and avoided using either. The reader may have noticed that there has been a curious awkwardness hitherto in alluding to her. That is because in actual fact I spoke of her only by the current nickname. Then on the heels of a string of nicknames, I was suddenly moved to call her "Jane" and Jane she became and remained. I do not know exactly when I did this, but very rapidly it became her only name, for me and our friends. "Amy" she dropped altogether; she disliked it as much as I did. Her mother used it abundantly, and perhaps too much, for remonstrance and advice.

But Catherine she liked and as I have told in The Book of Catherine Wells she kept it for her literary work. In that volume I have gathered together almost every piece of writing that she completed and in the preface I have given an account of her rather overshadowed but very distinctive literary personality. Her literary initiatives were of a different order and quality from mine, and she insisted upon that and would never avail herself of my name or influence in publishing her own none too abundant writing. We belonged to different schools. Her admiration for Katherine Mansfield, for instance, was unbounded while my appreciation was tempered by a sense of that young woman's limitations; and she had a leaning towards Virginia Woolf, whose lucubrations I have always regarded with a lack-lustre eye. She liked delicate fantasy after the manner of Edith Sitwell, to whom I am as appreciatively indifferent as I am to the quaint patterns of old chintzes, the designs on dinner plates or the charm of nursery rhymes. Again, she found great interest in Proust who for me is far less documentary and entertaining than, let us say, Messrs. Shoolbred's catalogue of twenty years ago, or an old local newspaper, which is truer and leaves the commentary to me.

Catherine Wells was indeed not quite one of us, not quite one with Jane and me, I mean; she was a quiet, fine spirited stranger in our household; she was all that had escaped from the rough nick-naming and caricaturing and compromise that would have completely imposed upon her the rôles of Miss Bits and Jane. Our union had never incorporated her. I had glimpses of her at times; she would look at me out of Jane's brown eyes, and vanish. All I know of her I have let appear in that book. Much later, after the war, when our accumulating means afforded it, Catherine Wells took rooms of her own in Bloomsbury, rooms I never saw; she explained what she wanted and I fell in with her idea, and in this secret flat, quite away from all the life that centred upon me, she thought and dreamt and wrote and sought continually and fruitlessly for something she felt she had lost of herself or missed or never attained. She worked upon a story in that retreat, a fastidious elusive story that she never brought to any shape or ending; some of it she polished and retyped many times. It was a dream of an island of beauty and sensuous perfection in which she lived alone and was sometimes happy in her loneliness and sometimes very lonely. In her dream there was a lover who never appeared. He was a voice heard; he was a trail of footsteps in the dewy grass, or she woke and found a rosebud at her side....

A year or so before her last illness she gave up that flat and ceased to work upon her unfinished book.

It is evident that this marriage of ours had some very distinctive features. Its originality did not end at that perfect business confidence and that queer play of silly humorous fantasy, mental caressing and imposed interpretations already described. At the back of all that, two extremely dissimilar brains were working very intelligently at the peculiar life problem we had created for each other. We came at last to a very explicit understanding about the profound difference in our physical and imaginative responses.

Jane thought I had a right to my own individual disposition and that luck had treated me badly in mating me first to an unresponsive and then to a fragile companion. About that she was extraordinarily dispassionate and logical and much more clearheaded than I was. She faced the matter with the same courage, honesty and self-subordination with which she faced all the practical issues of life. She suppressed any jealous impulse and gave me whatever freedom I desired. She knew as well as I did that for all its elements of artificiality, our alliance was indissoluble; we had intergrown and become parts of each other, and she realized perhaps sooner than I, how little that alliance demanded a monopoly of passionate intimacy. So long as we were in the opening phase of our struggle for a position and worldly freedom, this question was hardly a practical issue between us. There was neither time nor energy to indulge any form of wanderlust. But with the coming of success, increasing leisure and facility of movement, the rapid enlargement of our circle of acquaintance, and contact with unconventional and exciting people, there was no further necessity for the same rigid self-restraint. The craving, in a body that was gathering health and strength, for a complete loveliness of bodily response, was creeping up into my imagination and growing more and more powerful. This craving dominated the work of D. H. Lawrence altogether. For my own part, I could never yield it that importance. I would justify it if I could, but not at the price of that joint attack upon the world to which I was committed with Jane.

My compromise with Jane developed after 1900. The *modus*

vivendi we contrived was sound enough to hold us together to the end, but it was by no means a perfect arrangement. That escape of the personality of Catherine Wells from our unison was only one mark of its imperfection. Over against that are to be set the far more frequent escapades of a Don Juan among the intelligentsia. I record our understanding, as I want to record all the material facts of my life; it was an experiment in adjustment, but there was nothing exemplary about it. All life is imperfect: imperfection becomes a condemnation only when it reaches an intolerable level. Our imperfections we made quite tolerable and I do not believe that in making them tolerable we injured anybody else in the world. Compromises of some sort between ill-fitted yet congenial people must, I suppose, become more frequent in our advancing world as individuality intensifies. The more marked the individuality the more difficult is it to discover a complete reciprocity. The more difficult therefore is it to establish an exclusive fixation.

Yet the normal human being gravitates naturally towards an exclusive and complete fixation, with its keen possessiveness and its irrational infinitude of jealousy. What I have called the discursive phase of a human being is the unstable and transitory phase; there is no such thing as complete promiscuity; there is always preference and there is no limit set to the possible swift intensifications of preference; the casual lover loves always on a slippery slope. The French with their absurd logicality distinguish between the *passade*, a stroke of mutual attraction that may happen to any couple, and a real love affair. In theory, I was now to have *passades*.

But life and Latin logic have always been at variance, and it did not work out like that. There is no such distinction to be drawn. There are not small preferences that do not matter and big ones that do; there are all sizes and grades of preferences. For women even more than for men, the frequent *passade* seems unattractive. A woman understands much more than a man the undesirability of inconsequent discursive bodily love. She gives her Self, there is personality as well as her person in the gift; she may reckon on a greater return than she gets, but indeed it is a poor sort of lovemaking on either side in which, at the time at any rate, there is not the feeling that selves are being given. Otherwise it would be the easiest thing in the world to solve all this riddle of incompatible temperaments by skilled prostitution.

Clearly Jane and I were persuaded of the possibility of some such solution, though presumably in terms rather less brutally simple. I do not think we could have made our treaty if we had not thought so. On either side, we supposed, there were men and women with an excess of sexual energy and imagination. On either side there were restless spirits with a craving for variety. What could be more rational than for such super-animated men and women to find out and assuage one another?

And everything else would remain as it was before.

But as a matter of fact, short of some rare miracle of flatness, nothing does remain as it was before. Two worlds are altered every time a man and woman associate. The alterations may vary widely in extent but an alteration is always there. It would indeed be a very remarkable thing if Nature, for all her general looseness and extravagance, had contrived it otherwise. Jane's humour and charity, and the fundamental human love between us, were to be tried out very severely in the years that lay ahead. Suffice it here to say that they stood the test.

§ 4. WRITINGS ABOUT SEX

And here, I think, and not later, is the place for a compact account of my writings so far as they concern the relations of men and women. These books and papers arose very directly out of my own personal difficulties. They were essentially an eversion, a generalization, an attempt to put my case in the character of

Everyman.

In my earlier writings the topic of sex is conspicuously absent, I felt then that I knew nothing about it that could possibly be communicated. I muddled with my own problems in my own fashion, shamefacedly. Then, because I still felt I knew nothing about it, I began asking questions.

I think that as the waters of oblivion swallow up my writings bulk by bulk, the essays and booklets and stories and novels I wrote about love and sex-reactions will be the first section to go right out of sight and memory. If any survive they will survive as a citation or so, as historical sidelights for the industrious student. They had their function in their time but their time has already gone by. They were essentially negative enquiries, statements of unsolved difficulties, protests against rigid restraints and suppressions; variations of "Why not?" They helped to release a generation from restriction and that is about all they achieved. Aesthetically they have no great value. No one will ever read them for delight.

Love and Mr. Lewisham was published in 1900. The "love" in it is the most naïve response of youth and maiden imaginable, and the story is really the story of the "Schema" of a career and how it was torn up. The conflict and disharmony between the two main strands in what I have called my "Compound Fugue," was troubling my mind. Mr. Lewisham was a teacher and science student as I had been, and his entanglement is quite on all fours with mine. But he has a child. Because he loved his Ethel, Mr. Lewisham had to tear up his Schema and settle down. Domestic claustrophobia, the fear of being caught in a household, which I have suggested may have played a part in my departure from Sutton, is evident in this book. At the time of writing it (1898-99), I did not consciously apply the story of Mr. Lewisham to my own circumstances, but down below the threshold of my consciousness the phobia must have been there. Later on, in 1910, it had come to the surface and I sold Spade House deliberately, because I felt that otherwise it would become the final setting of my life.

The *Sea Lady* (published in 1902 and planned two years earlier) is a parallel story of the same two main strands of motive, but it is told under quite a different scheme of values. Something new comes to light; a sensuous demand. There is an element of confession in the tale but it is a confession in motley. And love, instead of leading to any settling down, breaks things up. But the defeat of the disinterested career is just as complete. Chatteris, the lover, plunges not into domesticity but into the sea, glittering under a full moon. A craving for some lovelier experience than life had yet given me, is the burthen in this second phase. Not only Catherine Wells but I too could long at times for impossible magic islands. Chatteris is a promising young politician, a sort of mixture of Harry Cust and any hero in any novel by Mrs. Humphry Ward, and he is engaged to be married to a heroine, quite deliberately and confessedly lifted, gestures, little speeches and all, from that lady's *Marcella*. All the hopes of this heroine are shattered by a mermaid who comes ashore as the Bunting family, the heroine's hosts, are bathing from the end of their garden at Sandgate. For at Sandgate people's gardens go right down to the beach. The mermaid is—beauty. And the magic of beauty. She drives Chatteris into a madness of desire for "other dreams," for a life beyond reason and possibility. The book ends as lightly as it began—in a "supreme moment"—of moonshine.

The next book of mine in which unsolved sexual perplexities appear is *A Modern Utopia* (1905). Plato ruled over the making of that book, and in it I followed him in disposing of the sexual distraction, by minimizing the differences between men and women and ignoring the fact of personal fixation altogether. That is and always has been the intellectual's way out. My Samurai are of both sexes, a hardy bare-limbed race, free lovers among themselves—and mutually obliging. Like the people of the original Oneida community in New York State they constituted one comprehensive "group marriage." Possibly among such people fixations would not be serious; that is hypothetical psychology. I may have stressed the mutual civility of the order. The book was popular among the young of our universities; it launched many of them into cheerful adventures that speedily brought them up against the facts of fixation, jealousy and resentment. It played a considerable part in the general movement of release from the rigid technical chastity of women during the Victorian period.

So far as there can be any general theory of sexual conduct and law, the *Modern Utopia* remains my last word. Within that comprehensive freedom, individuals, I believe, must work out their problems of fixation and co- operation, monopolization, loyalty and charity, each for himself and herself. For everyone and every couple there is a distinctive discord and perhaps in most cases a solution. The key to the progressive thought of our time is the frank realization of this immense variety in reaction and the repudiation of the rigid universal solutions of the past. We do not solve anything by this realization, but we liberate and individualize the problem. It is an interesting paradox that Socialism should involve extreme sexual individualism and Competitive Individualism clip the individual into the rigid relationships of the family.

A Modern Utopia was leading up to *Ann Veronica* (1909) in which the youthful heroine was allowed a frankness of desire and sexual enterprise, hitherto unknown in English popular fiction. That book created a scandal at the time, though it seems mild enough reading to the young of to- day. It is rather badly constructed, there is an excessive use of soliloquy, but Ann Veronica came as near to being a living character as anyone in my earlier love stories. This was so because in some particulars she was drawn from life. And for that and other reasons she made a great fuss in the world.

The particular offence was that Ann Veronica was a virgin who fell in love and showed it, instead of waiting as all popular heroines had hitherto done, for someone to make love to her. It was held to be an unspeakable offence that an adolescent female should be sex-conscious before the thing was forced upon her attention. But Ann Veronica wanted a particular man who excited her and she pursued him and got him. With gusto. It was only a slight reflection of anything that had actually occurred, but there was something convincing about the behaviour of the young woman in the story, something sufficiently convincing to impose the illusion of reality upon her; and from the outset Ann Veronica was assailed as though she was an actual living person.

It was a strenuous and long sustained fuss. The book was banned by libraries and preached against by earnest clergymen. The spirit of denunciation, latent in every human society, was aroused and let loose against me. I have turned over my memories and records of that fuss and I find it so abundant and formless an accumulation of pettiness that I cannot put it together into a narrative. It is a jumble of slights, injustices and hasty condemnations, plus a considerable amount of exacerbated resentment and ineffective reprisal on my own part. I do not make a good or dignified martyr. There was not only a "bad press" and a great deal of public denunciation of me but there was an attempt, mainly on the part of people who did not know me, to ostracize me socially. The head and front of the public attack was Mr. St. Loe Strachey, the proprietor of the *Spectator*. A reviewer in his columns rallied the last resources of our noble language, made no bones about it, pulled himself together as men must do when the fundamentals of life are at stake, and said in so many words that Ann Veronica was a whore. It was I think an illegitimate extension of the term.

He was a fine fellow, that reviewer. "The muddy world of Mr. Wells's imaginings," said he, was "a community of scuffling stoats and ferrets, unenlightened by a ray of duty and abnegation." That was rough on the Samurai of my*Modern Utopia*. He writhed with "loathing and indignation" and so on and so on, mounting and shouting, up to that last great manly word.

That denotes the quality of the fuss and gives the clue to my resentment. Strachey's hostility, if a little clumsy and heavy, was perfectly honest, and before he died we met—as witnesses in defence of a birth-control pamphlet—and became very good friends. I was indignant and expostulatory at the time, but on the whole I really had very little to complain of. The social attack did me no harm. It made no perceptible difference in my life that we two were sent to Coventry by people we had never met. The people who had met us did not send us to Coventry. Most of my friends stood the proof very delightfully; people as various as G. K. Chesterton, C. F. G. Masterman, Sydney Olivier and his family, Ray Lankester, Shaw, Harry Cust, and Lady Mary Elcho, came out stoutly for me and would have nothing to do with any social boycott. Altogether it was no sort of martyrdom, as martyrdoms go nowadays, and its general ineffectiveness amounted to a victory. My ostracism had its use as a filter to save me from many dull and dreary people. And my ultimate victory was no mere personal one. Mr. Fisher Unwin had bought the book outright and did very well by it. It sold and went on selling in a variety of editions. After *Ann Veronica*, things were never quite the same again in the world of popular English fiction; young heroines with a temperamental zest for illicit love-making and no sense of an inevitable Nemesis, increased and multiplied not only in novels but in real life.

But for a time the uproar about *Ann Veronica* put me quite out of focus with the public and the literary world. The fact that the great bulk of my work displayed an exceptional want of reference to sex or love-making, or the position of woman, was ignored; and if I had been a D. H. Lawrence, with every fig leaf pinned aside, I could not have been considered more improper than I was. This brought me a quite new type of reader, and books like *Kipps*, *The War of the Worlds*, *The First Men in the Moon* and *The Wonderful Visit* were bought by eager seekers after obscenity—

to their extreme disillusionment. They decided after a baffled perusal that I was dreadfully overrated and superficial, and my brief reputation in the cloacal recesses of the bookish world evaporated speedily enough.

In 1911 this conflict was revived upon a broader basis, if with less intensity, over my *New Machiavelli*. I would not drop the subject of the passionate daughter, and there was, I admit, considerable defiance of manner if not of matter, both in the *New Machiavelli* and in *Marriage* which followed it. Quite manifestly I had refused to learn my lesson and, this time, I was to be squashed for good. But this final attack was delivered two years too late. Many people were beginning to be ashamed of the violence of their reactions to *Ann Veronica* and others were plainly bored by the demands of my more persistent antagonists for a fresh effort to erase me, and the result of this second attempt to end Wells was on the whole distinction rather than destruction. Instead of being made an outcast, finally and conclusively, I was made a sort of champion.

The *New Machiavelli* was first printed as a serial in Ford Madox Hueffer's *English Review* and persistent rumours that no publisher would consent to issue it led to a considerable sale of the back numbers of that periodical at enhanced prices—with the usual disappointment for the purchasers. "What is all the fuss about?" the poor dears demanded. "There is nothing in it!" There was indeed furtive work with the publishers on the part of what are called influential people, but I neither know nor care who were these influential people, and I do not know what was said and done. The respectable firm of Macmillan was already under contract to publish the book and could not legally or honourably back out, but it presently appealed to me in a state of great embarrassment, for permission to publish in this particular case under the imprint of John Lane, who was less squeamish about his reputation for decorum. I consented to that, and so the gentility of Macmillan, or whatever else was threatened by those influential people, was preserved.

The *New Machiavelli* is all the world away from overt eroticism. The theme is simply a fresh variant upon the theme of*Love and Mr. Lewisham* and the *Sea Lady*; it stressed the harsh incompatibility of wide public interests with the high, swift rush of imaginative passion—with considerable sympathy for the passion. The Marcella- like heroine of the *Sea Lady* is repeated, but the mermaid has become a much more credible young woman, and it is to exile in Italy and literary effort, and not to moonshine and death, that the lovers go. There is some good characterization in it, one or two well-written passages and an amusing description of a fire at an actual dinner-party, given by Cust, at which I was present. But it is nothing outstanding in the way of a novel.

I was not indulging myself and the world in artistic pornography or making an attack upon anything I considered moral. I found nothing for self reproach in my private conduct, I did not know for some time that the imaginations of the back benches of the Fabian Society and the riff-raff of the literary world were adorning my unwitting and undeserving head with a rakish halo. I did not realize how readily my simple questionings could be interpreted as the half confessions of a sort of Fabian Casanova, an inky Lovelace, the satyr-Cupid of Socialism. I was asking a "Why not?" that had been accumulating in my mind all my life, and the intensity of my questioning had no doubt been greatly enhanced by the peculiar inhibitions of my first wife and the innocent fragility of my second. I was releasing, in these books, a long accumulation of suppression. So far as I can remember my phases, however, the influence of my particular experiences was quite subconscious at the time and I think I should have come to that particular "Why not?" in some fashion—anyhow. I was asking my question in perfect good faith and I went on asking it.

I was working out the collateral problems with an ingenuous

completeness, and I did not mean to relinquish that enquiry. I had come to the conclusion that sex-life began with adolescence, which after all was only discovering what "adolescence" means, and that when it began—it ought to begin. I thought it preposterous that any young people should be distressed by unexplained desires, thwarted by arbitrary prohibitions and blunder into sexual experiences, blindfold. The stories of Isabel and my wife and myself were plainly stories of an excessive, artificial innocence. I contemned that "chastity" which is mere abstinence and concealment more and more plainly. I believed and said that a normal human being was not properly balanced, physically and mentally, without an active sexual life; that this was as necessary and almost as urgently necessary, as fresh air and free movement, and I have never found any reason to change that opinion.

But a propaganda of more and franker and healthier love-making was not, I found,—as Plato found before me—a simple proposition. It carried with it certain qualifying conditions. Some of these, but not all of them, I brought into the discussion. In a world where pressure upon the means of subsistence was a normal condition of life, it was necessary to compensate for the removal of traditional sexual restraints, and so my advocacy of simple and easy love-making had to be supplemented by an adhesion to the propaganda of the Neo-Malthusians. This I made in my *Anticipations* (1900) and I continued to write plainly on that subject in a period when Neo-Malthusianism was by no means the respectable movement it has since become.

In some of these earlier essays on sexual liberation, I seem now, to be skirmishing about on the marginal conventions of the business and failing to come to grips with its more intimate realities. I was condemning a great system of suppressions and prohibitions as unreasonable; but at first I did not face up steadily to the fact that they were as natural as they were unreasonable. I was giving a fair hearing to one set of instincts and not allowing another set to come into court. I had not examined by what necessary processes the net of restraints I was denouncing had been woven to entangle pleasure and happiness. In spite of my own acute experience, I was ignoring that gravitation towards fixation in love, with its intense possessiveness, dominance, jealousy and hatred of irresponsible indulgence, which lies at the heart of the problem. I had been suppressing it in myself and I was ignoring it in my arguments.

Gradually as my disputes and controversies went on, my attention was forced back, almost in spite of myself, towards these profounder elements in the human make-up which stand in the way of a cheerful healthy sexual go-as-you-please for mankind. I was obliged to look jealousy in the face. All this tangle of restriction, restraint, opposition and anger, could be explained as so much expansion, complication and organization of jealousy. Jealousy may not be a reasonable thing, but it lies at least as close to the springs of human action as sexual desire. Jealousy was not merely a trouble between competitive lovers. Parents, onlookers, society could be jealous.

I set myself to examine the credentials of jealousy. At some time I had read Lang and Atkinson's *Human Origins*, probably under the influence of Grant Allen, and the book illuminated me very greatly. I realized the rôle played by the primitive taboos in disciplining and canalizing the dominant jealousy of the more powerful males so as to make possible the development of tribal societies. I saw the history of expanding human associations as essentially a successive subjugation of the patriarchal group to wider collective needs, by jealousy-regulating arrangements. Continually civilization had been developing, by buying off or generalizing, socializing and legalizing jealousy and possessiveness, in sex as in property. We were debarred from sexual ease, just as we were debarred from economic ease, by this excessive fostering in our institutions of the already sufficiently strong instinct of ownership. The Family, I declared, was the inseparable correlative of private proprietorship. It embodied jealousy in sexual life as private ownership embodied jealousy in economic life. And to the very great dismay of the strategists and tacticians of the Fabian Society, and to the immense embarrassment of the Labour Party socialists, I began to blurt out these ideas and attempt to sexualise socialism.

I should naturally like to present my mental process in this matter as completely lucid, consistent and far-seeing from the beginning, and if it were not for that family habit of filing letters and accumulating records to which I have already alluded, I think I should have been able to do that. Nobody now would remember my tergiversation if my files did not. But it is clear that though my association with Labour Socialism had very little effect upon my stories and romances, it did affect various pamphlets, discussions and letters I wrote upon the subject.

Let me deal with the novels first. They do follow a fairly consistent line. The topic of jealousy dominated *In the Days of the Comet* (1906). The swish of a comet's tail cools and cleanses the human atmosphere, and jealousy, and with it war and poverty, vanish from the world. Jealousy is also the dominant trouble in the *Passionate Friends* (1913) and *The Wife of Sir Isaac Harman* (1914), while *Marriage* (1912), once more presents the old conflict between broad intentions and passionate urgencies, that had furnished the motif of three earlier tales, *Love and Mr. Lewisham*, *The New Machiavelli* and the *Sea Lady*. In all these novels the interest centres not upon individual character, but upon the struggles of common and rational motives and frank enquiry against social conditions and stereotyped ideas. The actors in them are types, therefore, rather than acutely individualized persons. They could not be other than types. For reasons that will become plainer as I proceed, my output of this "discussion-fiction" between men and women became relatively much less important after the outbreak of the war. Christina Alberta in *Christina Alberta's Father* (1925) is a much more living figure than Ann Veronica and her morals are far easier; but times had changed and not a voice was raised against her. That *Spectator* reviewer, and much else, had died since 1909. That particular liberation had been achieved.

Apart from these, only three of my stories can be put into the category of sex-discussion,—*The Secret Places of the Heart* (1922) in which I was thinking not so much of the problem of jealousy, as of love-making considered as a source of waste of energy, and, to a lesser degree and interwoven with quite other ideas, *Meanwhile* (1927) which betrays a similar trend. I may be able to return later to the rather different issue of these more recent books. They are raising the question whether after all a woman can be a good citizen and if she can, in what way, a problem also appearing *inter alia* in *The World of William Clissold* (1926). In the last "book" of the latter, there is also a sketch of a feminine personality "Clementina" which stands by itself, an incidental lark, because it is so manifestly objective and interrogative.

Turning from my novels to the various papers, pamphlets and letters I was putting out through this same period, I discover a much less candid display of view and attitude. I began well, but I found I was speedily entangled and bemused by various political and propagandist issues. I find a quite straightforward statement of my ideas in a paper I read to the Fabian Society in October 1906, under the title of *Socialism and the Middle Classes*. Therein I say plainly that I "no more regard the institution of marriage as a permanent thing than I regard a state of competitive industrialism as a permanent thing" and the whole paper sustains this attitude. But subsequently I published this, bound-up with a second article which had appeared in the *Independent Review* (*Socialism and the Family* 1906) and, in this last, the phrasing is, to say the least of it, more discreet. I am advocating in both what is plainly a correlative of the break-up of the family, the public endowment of motherhood. But the question as to whether this endowment is to be confined to women under some sort of marriage contract recognized by the state, or extended to all mothers indiscriminately is not distinctly stated. The issue was vague in my own mind; there were questions of fatherly influence and of eugenics to consider, and I had still to think them out. It is regrettable that those perplexities still clouded my attitude; otherwise I find the record satisfactory up to this point.

But then came an ingenious misstatement by Mr. Joynson-Hicks (as he was then) while campaigning against Labour Socialism in the Altrincham division (Lancashire), and a more or less deliberate misquotation by Mr. J. H. Bottomley, a conservative election agent for the Newton division, which lured me into an excess of repudiation. Joynson-Hicks had declared that Socialists would part husband and wife, and subject every woman to a sort of communal prostitution. Challenged to justify this statement, which greatly shocked the rank and file of the Labour battalions, he defended himself by an appeal to my works. "He was not in the habit of making a statement without some kind of justification, and one had only to read Mr. Wells' book, where it clearly stated that 'Wives no less than goods, were to be held in common'; and 'Every infant would be taken away from the mother and father and placed in a State nursery.' (*Daily Dispatch*. Oct. 12th, 1906.)"

Mr. Bottomley had put it in this way, in a pamphlet for local circulation: "Essentially the Socialist position is a denial of property in human beings; not only must land and the means of production be liberated, but women and children, just as men and things must cease to be owned. *So in future it will be not my wife or your wife, but our wife.*" The words in italics were his own addition but, somehow, they got inside the quotation marks.

Two quotations, one from *The Times Literary Supplement*, in a review of *In the Days of the Comet*, and one from the *Spectator* for October 19th, 1907, in an article on *Socialism and Sex Relations*, also got into the dispute. *The Times Literary Supplement* said: "Socialistic men's wives, we gather, are, no less than their goods, to be held in common. Free love, according to Mr. Wells, is to be of the essence of the new social contract." And the words of the *Spectator* were as follows: "For example we find Mr. Wells in his novel, *In the Days of the Comet*, making Free Love the dominant principle for the regulation of sexual ties in his regenerated State. The romantic difficulty as to which of the two lovers of the heroine is to be the happy man is solved by their both being accepted. Polyandry is 'the way out' in this case, as polygamy might be in another."

Now the proper reply to this sort of attack was to stick to the phrase Free Love, insist that this did not mean indiscriminate love, point out that the words supposed to be quoted had not been used, and explain with patience and lucidity, that personal sexual freedom and collective responsibility for the family, did not mean "having wives in common" or taking children away from their parents or practising polyandry or polygamy or anything of that sort. But instead of explaining, I spluttered into exaggerated indignation at the dishonesty of those misplaced inverted commas of Mr. Bottomley's, I repudiated "Free Love," which was obviously wrong of me, simply because, like the word atheist, the phrase had acquired an unpopular flavour, and unsaid, more or less distinctly, much that I had been saying during the previous half a dozen years. I was entangling myself with politics, and I found my socialistic associates were embarrassed by my speculations. I did not want them to reproach me. In *New Worlds for Old* (1908) first published as a serial in the *Grand Magazine* in 1907, I went still further along the line of self-repudiation, and I read with contrition to-day, this dreadful passage of quite Fabian understatement:

"Socialism has not even worked out what are the reasonable conditions of a State marriage contract, and it would be ridiculous to pretend it had. This is not a defect in Socialism particularly, but a defect in human knowledge. At countless points in the tangle of questions involved, the facts are not clearly known. Socialism offers no theory whatever as to the duration of marriage, as to whether, as among the Roman Catholics, it should be absolutely for life, or, as some hold, for ever; or, as among the various divorce-permitting Protestant bodies, until this or that eventuality; or even, as Mr. George Meredith suggested some years ago, for a term of ten years. In these matters Socialism does not decide, and it is quite reasonable to argue that Socialism need not decide. Socialism maintains an attitude of neutrality."

This is a false attitude. Socialism, if it is anything more than a petty tinkering with economic relationships is a renucleation of society. The family can remain only as a biological fact. Its economic and educational autonomy are inevitably doomed. The modern state is bound to be the ultimate guardian of all children and it must assist, replace, or subordinate the parent as supporter, guardian and educator; it must release all human beings from the obligation of mutual proprietorship, and it must refuse absolutely to recognize or enforce any kind of sexual ownership. It cannot therefore remain neutral when such claims come before it. It must disallow them. But in these incriminatory documents I find myself being as vague, tactful and reassuring about sentimental interpretations—as if I had set out in life to become a Nationalist Prime Minister.

These skirmishes with politicians and pamphleteers occurred in 1906-7 and 8 and I touched my nadir of compromise and understatement in that last year. Later on, when I tell of my relations to accepted religious forms and beliefs I shall have to deal again with this politic, conciliatory strain in me. It can be excused. It can be explained as the deference of modesty and as a civilized inclination to conformity; it has its amiable aspects. But whatever may be possible in larger brains, mine is not clever and subtle enough to be disingenuous to that extent; my proper rôle is to say things plainly and still more plainly, to be aggressive and derisive and let persuasion go hang. It is better to offend rather than mislead. When I am diplomatic I am lost. It was really an extraordinarily good thing for me that circumstances conspired with my innate impulse, when I am at the writing desk, to let statement and story rip, to put me quite openly where I was, with the *Ann Veronica* shindy in 1909 and the subsequent campaign, in 1910 and 1911, against the *New Machiavelli*. After that it was plain where I stood, and that in spite of our pretty, orderly home and the general decorum of our industrious lives, Jane and I were not to be too hastily accepted as a nice, deserving young couple respectfully climbing the pleasant stairway of English life from quite modest beginnings, to social recognition, prosperity, and even perhaps "honours."

It was not only that the Fabian and Labour politician found my persistent development of "Why not?" in regard to the family and marriage, inconvenient, but also that I was at cross purposes upon the same score with the feminist movement in the new century. My realization of how far away I was to the left of the official left movements of my time had something to do, I think, with these lapses towards compromise I am now deploring.

The old feminist movement of the early nineteenth century had undergone a sort of rejuvenation in the eighties and nineties. It had given up its bloomers and become smart, energetic and ambitious. There was a growing demand on the part of women for economic and political independence, and at first it seemed to me that here at last advancing upon me was that great-hearted free companionship of noble women of which I had dreamed from my earliest years.

As the hosts of liberation came nearer and could be inspected more accurately I found reason to qualify these bright expectations. If women wanted to be free, the first thing was surely for them to have complete control of their persons, and how could that happen unless Free Love and Neo-Malthusianism replaced directed and obligatory love and involuntary child-bearing, in the forefront of their programme. Their inferiority was a necessary aspect of the proprietary, patriarchal family, and there was no way of equalizing the economic disadvantage imposed upon them by the bearing and care of children, short of the public endowment of motherhood. These things and not any petty political enfranchisement, I reasoned, must surely constitute the real Magna Charta of Women, and I set myself to explain this with the same tactless simplicity and lucidity that had already caused such inconvenience to the politicians of the Labour Party.

But the leaders of the feminist revival were no more willing than were the socialists to realize where they were going. They were alive to the wrongs that set them moving but not to the ends towards which their movement would take them. Confronted by the plain statement of the Free Citizen Woman as opposed to the Domesticated Woman their hearts failed them. It became increasingly evident that a large part of the woman's suffrage movement was animated less by the desire for freedom and fullness of life, than by a passionate jealousy and hatred of the relative liberties of men. For one woman in the resuscitated movement who wanted to live generously and nobly, a score were desirous merely of making things uncomfortable for the insolent, embarrassing, oblivious male. They did not want more life; their main impulse was vindictive.

They wanted to remain generally where they were and what they were, but to have it conceded that they were infinitely brighter and better and finer than men, that potentially they were finer poets, musicians, artists, social organizers, scientific investigators and philosophers than men could ever be, that a man owed everything to his mother and nothing to his father and so forth and so on; that women therefore ought to be given unlimited control over the goods and actions of their lawful partners, be empowered to impose upon these gross creatures complete chastity, or otherwise, as the fancy might take them, and, instead of establishing a free and liberal equality, entirely reverse the ascendency of the sexes. This was a very wholesome tu quoque for ages of arrogant masculine bad manners, but it was not practical politics and it did not penetrate to the more fundamental realities of the sexual stress.

That feminism had anything to do with sexual health and happiness, was repudiated by these ladies with flushed indignation so soon as the suggestion was made plain to them. Their modesty was as great as their boldness. Sex—what was sex? Get thee behind me Satan! They were not thinking of it. They were good pure women rightly struggling for a Vote, and that was all they wanted. The Vote was to be their instrument of dominance. They concentrated all the energy of their growing movement upon that claim. The new Feminist Movement had no more use for me therefore than the Labour Socialists. To both these organizations I was an *enfant terrible* and not to be talked about.

It is no part of the plan of this book to tell the tale of that nagging, ignoble campaign which ended abruptly with the Declaration of War in 1914, to detail once again the window-smashing, the burning of country houses, churches and the contents of letter boxes, the squawking at meetings, "votes for women" until the discussion of public affairs became impossible, the consequent expulsion of the struggling heroines with all kinds of ignoble and indelicate reprisals, the ensuing discovery by indignant young women of good family, of the unexpected dirtiness and nastiness of police cells and prisons—one good by-product anyhow—and all the rest of it. In *The Wife of Sir Isaac Harman* (1914) I tried to explain to myself and my readers the suppressions and resentments that might lead a gentle woman to smash a plate-glass window. I studied my model carefully and I think the figure lives, but no suffragette saw herself in my mirror. Nor will I relate here how as Europe collapsed into war, the Vote was flung to women simply to keep them quiet, and how the only traceable consequence has been the further enfeeblement of the waning powers of Democracy.

449

In those gentler days before the return towards primitive violence began, it was possible for girls and women to pester mankind and presume upon the large protective tolerance of civilization. Since then, the progressive disintegration of social order, the increasing amount of gangsterism and terrorism in political life, has made the atmosphere too grim and heavy for the definite organization of women as such, for social and political aggression. Their understanding of the disintegrative forces at work seems to be a feeble one, and in the conscious constructive effort of to-day they count as a sex for remarkably little. There has been no perceptible woman's movement to resist the practical obliteration of their freedoms by Fascists or Nazis. The sex war has died away and in England only the gentle sarcasms and grumblings of Lady Rhondda and her group of clever ladies in *Time and Tide* remain to remind us of it. Over most of the world it has died down altogether.

I can look back now with sympathetic amusement upon the encounter of my former self, that rising and decidedly over-confident young writer of half my age with this new and transitory being: the Militant Suffragette. What a surprise and perplexity she was! The young man's disposition to lump all the feminity in the world, in its infinite variety, into a class, to indict it and judge it as a class, after having felt a strong disposition to adore it—as a class, was perfectly natural, superficially reasonable and fundamentally absurd. Still heavily under the sway of organic illusion he prepared to welcome these goddesses, at last in splendid revolt, and to do his utmost for them, and, instead of goddesses escaping, he encountered a fluttering swarm of disillusioned and wildly exasperated human beings, all a little frightened at what they were doing, and with no clearer conception than any other angry crowd of what had set them going and what was to be done about it. Helpfully and with the brightest hopes he produced his carefully reasoned diagnosis of their grievances; he spread his ingenious arrangement of Neo-Malthusianism, Free Love ("ton corps est *à* toi"), economic independence, the endowment of motherhood and the systematic suppression of jealousy as an animal vice, and he found his lucid and complete statement thrust aside, while the riot passed on, after the manner of riots, vehemently loudly and vacuously, to a purely symbolic end—the Vote in this case—and essential frustration and dispersal.

Slowly as the blaze of antagonism created by the open sex-war of 1900-14 has died down, men and women under an inexorable need for each other and an imperative necessity for co-operation, have returned again to the commanding and infinitely varied problems of mutual adjustment, to the million and one perennial problems of man and woman. I do not know how far the main attack and the capture of the actual Vote was of value to humanity but I have no doubt of the service done by that slower and wider campaign of "Why not?" in which I played my little part. A tiresome and obstructive accumulation of obsolete restraints, conventions and pretences, was cleared out of the way for a new generation. That did not put an end to the facile self-deceptions of sex because these are of the very stuff of life, nor could it abolish the see-saw between the chronic mutual need and the chronic resistance to entanglement, but it did clear the way for an individual management of the glamour and its ensuing centrifugal strain. It put the glamour in its place and made the fugitive impulse controllable and tolerable. When goddesses and Sea Ladies vanish and a flash back to the ancestral chimpanzee abolishes the magic caverns of Venus, human beings arrive. Instead of a rigid system of obligations and restrictions which would solve, for everyone, the Woman Problem, in one simple universal fashion, we are left with an almost infinite series of variations of the problem of association between men and women, and an infinitude of opportunities for mutual charity.

§ 5. DIGRESSION ABOUT NOVELS

I find before me a considerable accumulation of material first assembled together in a folder labelled "Whether I am a Novelist." It has been extremely difficult to digest this material into a presentable form. It refuses to be simplified. It is like a mental shunting yard in which several trains of thought have come into collision and I feel now that the utmost I can do with it is not so much to set these trains going again as to salvage some few fragmentary observations from the wreckage.

One of these trains comes in from the previous section. It is an insistence upon the importance of individuality and individual adjustment in life; "Problems of association between men and women and an infinitude of opportunities for mutual charity." That carries on very obviously towards the idea of the novel as an expanding discussion of "How did they treat each other? How might they have treated each other? How should they treat each other?" I set out to write novels, as distinguished from those pseudo-scientific stories in which imaginative experience rather than personal conduct was the matter in hand, on the assumption that problems of adjustment were the essential matter for novel-writing. *Love and Mr. Lewisham* was entirely a story about a dislocation and an adjustment.

But across the track of that train of thought came another in which the novel presented itself not as an ethical enquiry but as the rendering of a system of impressions. In this distended and irregularly interesting folder, which I find so hard to reduce to straightforward explicitness, I find myself worrying round various talks and discussions I had with Henry James a third of a century ago. He was a very important figure in the literary world of that time and a shrewd and penetrating critic of the technique by which he lived. He liked me and he found my work respectable enough to be greatly distressed about it. I bothered him and he bothered me. We were at cross purposes based as I shall show later on very fundamental differences, not only of temperament but training. He had no idea of the possible use of the novel as a help to conduct. His mind had turned away from any such idea. From his point of view there were not so much "novels" as The Novel, and it was a very high and important achievement. He thought of it as an Art Form and of novelists as artists of a very special and exalted type. He was concerned about their greatness and repute. He saw us all as Masters or would-be Masters, little Masters and great Masters, and he was plainly sorry that "Cher Maître" was not an English expression. One could not be in a room with him for ten minutes without realizing the importance he attached to the dignity of this art of his. I was by nature and education unsympathetic with this mental disposition. But I was disposed to regard a novel as about as much an art form as a market place or a boulevard. It had not even necessarily to get anywhere. You went by it on your various occasions.

That was entirely out of key with James's assumptions. I recall a talk I had with him soon after the publication of *Marriage*. With tact and circumlocution, James broke it to me, that he found a remarkable deficiency in that story. It was a deficiency that he had also observed in a vast proportion of contemporary fiction, it had exercised him very fruitfully, and his illuminating comments spread out from that starting point to a far-reaching tentacular discussion of what a novel should do and be.

The point he was stressing was this: *Marriage* is the story of a young man of science, Trafford, who, apparently without much previous experience, pilots a friend's aeroplane (in 1912!) and crashes, he and the friend together, into a croquet party and the Pope family and the life of Marjorie Pope. Thereupon there is bandaging, ambulance work and much coming and going and Marjorie, who is already engaged to a Mr. Magnet, falls deeply in love with Trafford. She drives to the village in a donkey cart to do some shopping and meets the lamed Trafford, also driving a donkey cart and their wheels interlock and they fall talking.

All that—except for the writing of it—was tolerable according to James. But then, in order to avoid the traffic in the high road the two young people take their respective donkey carts into a side lane and remain there talking for three hours. And this is where James's objection came in. Of the three hours of intercourse in the lane the novel tells nothing, except that the young people emerged in open and declared love with each other. This, said James, wasn't playing the game. I had cut out an essential, after a feast of irrelevant particulars. Gently but firmly he insisted that I did not myself know what had happened and what was said in that lane; that there was even a touch of improbability about their staying there so long and that this lack of information and probability at a crucial point was due to the fact that I had not thought out the individualities concerned with sufficient care and thoroughness. I had not cared enough about these individualities. Moreover in the conversations between the two principals, the man in particular supplied information about himself and his position in life in such a way as to talk at the reader instead of to the girl. The talk was in fact more for the benefit of the former. Trafford had to supply this information because I had been too inept or hasty to convey it in any other way. Or because there was too much to convey in any other way. Henry James was quite right in saying that I had not thought out these two people to the pitch of saturation and that they did not behave unconsciously and naturally. But my defence is that that did not matter, or at least that for the purposes of the book it did not matter very much.

Now I do not exactly remember the several other points he made in that elaborate critical excursion, nor did I attempt any reprisals upon his own work, but his gist was plain. If the Novel was properly a presentation of real people as real people, in absolutely natural reaction in a story, then my characters were not simply sketchy, they were eked out by wires and pads of non-living matter and they stood condemned. His discourse, which had evidently been maturing against my visit, covered not only my work but that of several of my contemporaries whom he had also read with interest and distaste. And the only point upon which I might have argued but which I did not then argue, was this, that the Novel was not necessarily, as he assumed, this real through and through and absolutely true treatment of people more living than life. It might be more and less than that and still be a novel.

To illustrate with what lovely complication of veracity and disingenuousness, with what curious intricate suavity of intimation he could develop his point I will quote from a letter of his, also bearing upon the same book *Marriage*. His intricate mind, as persistent and edentate as a pseudopodium, was still worrying round and about the question raised by that story. "I have read you," he says, "as I always read you, and as I read no one else, with a complete abdication of all those 'principles of criticism,' canons of form, preconceptions of felicity, references to the idea of method or the sacred laws of composition, with which I roam, with which I totter, through the pages of others attended in some dim degree by the fond yet feeble theory of, but which I shake off, as I advance under your spell, with the most cynical inconsistency. For under your spell I do advance— save when I pull myself up stock still in order not to break it even with so much as the breath of appreciation; I live with you and in you and (almost cannibal-like) *on* you, on you H. G. W., to the sacrifice of your Marjories and your Traffords, and whoever may be of their company; not your treatment of them, at all, but, much more, their be-fooling of you (pass me the merely scientific expression—I mean your fine high action in view of the red herring of lively interest they trail for you at their heels) becoming thus of the essence of the spectacle for me, and nothing in it all 'happening' so much as these attestations of your character and behaviour, these reactions of yours as you more or less follow them, affect me as vividly happening. I see you 'behave' all along much more than I see them even when they behave, (as I'm not sure they behave *most* in *Marriage*) with whatever charged intensity or accomplished effect; so that the ground of the drama is somehow most of all in the adventure for *you*—not to say *of* you, the moral, temperamental, personal, expressional, of your setting it forth; an adventure in fine more appreciable to me than any of those you are by way of letting *them* in for. I don't say that those you let them in for don't interest me too, and don't 'come off' and people the scene and lead on the attention, about as much as I can do with; but only, and always, that you beat them on their own ground and that your 'story,' through the five hundred pages, says more to me than theirs. You'll find this perhaps a queer rigmarole of a statement; but I ask of you to allow for it just now as the mumble, at best, of an invalid; and wait a little till I can put more of my hand on my sense. Mind you that the restriction I may seem to you to lay on my view of your work, still leaves that work more convulsed with life and more brimming with blood than any it is given me nowadays to meet. The point I have wanted to make is that I find myself absolutely unable, and still more unwilling, to approach you, or to take leave of you, in any projected light of criticism, in any judging or concluding, any comparing, in fact in any aesthetic or 'literary' relation at all...."

Tried by Henry James's standards I doubt if any of my novels can be taken in any other fashion. There are flashes and veins of character duly "treated" and living individuals in many of them, but none that satisfy his requirements fully. A lot of *Kipps* may pass, some of *Tono Bungay, Mr. Britling Sees It Through* and *Joan and Peter* and let me add, I have a weakness for Lady Harman and for Theodore Bulpington and—— But I will not run on. These are pleas in extenuation. The main indictment is sound, that I sketch out scenes and individuals, often quite crudely, and resort even to conventional types and symbols, in order to get on to a discussion of relationships. The important point which I tried to argue with Henry James was that the novel of completely consistent characterization arranged beautifully in a story and painted deep and round and solid, no more exhausts the possibilities of the novel, than the art of Velasquez exhausts the possibilities of the painted picture.

The issue exercised my mind considerably. I had a queer feeling that we were both incompatibly right. I wrote one or two lectures and critical papers on the scope of the novel, and I argued with myself and others, that realism and exhaustive presentation were not its only objectives. I think I might have gone further and maintained that they were not even its proper objectives but at best only graces by the way, but at the time I was not clear enough to say that. I might have made a good case by asserting that fiction was necessarily fictitious through and through, and that the real analogy to Velasquez who painted straight from dwarfs and kings, would be biography, character drawn straight from life and not an invented story. James was very much against the idea that there was a biographical element in any good novel, and he and his brother William were very severe upon Vernon Lee when she produced a character in a short story (*Lady Tal* 1892) markedly like Henry. But it is beyond the power of man to "create" individuals absolutely. If we do not write from models then we compile and fabricate. Every "living" character in a novel is drawn, frankly or furtively, from life—is filched from biography whole or in scraps, a portrait or a patch-up, and its actions are a reflection upon moral conduct. At whatever number of "removes" from facts we may be, we are still imputing motives to somebody. That is the conclusion I am coming to now, but I did not have it ready at that time. I allowed it to be taken for granted that there was such a thing as The Novel, a great and stately addendum to reality, a sort of super-reality with "created" persons in it, and by implication I admitted that my so-called novels were artless self-revelatory stuff, falling far away from a stately ideal by which they had to be judged.

But now I ask when and where has that great ideal been realized—or can it ever be realized?

Competent critics have since examined this supreme importance of individualities, in other words of "character" in the fiction of the nineteenth century and early twentieth century. Throughout that period character-interest did its best to take the place of adjustment-interest in fiction. With a certain justice these authorities ascribe the predominance of individuation to the example of Sir Walter Scott. But more generally it was a consequence of the prevalent sense of social stability, and he was not so much a primary influence as an exponent. He was a man of intensely conservative quality; he accepted, he accepted wilfully, the established social values about him; he had hardly a doubt in him of what was right or wrong, handsome or ungracious, just or mean. He saw events therefore as a play of individualities in a rigid frame of values never more to be questioned or permanently changed. His lawless, romantic past was the picturesque prelude to stability; our current values were already potentially there. Throughout the broad smooth flow of nineteenth century life in Great Britain, the art of fiction floated on this same assumption of social fixity. The Novel in English was produced in an atmosphere of security for the entertainment of secure people who liked to feel established and safe for good. Its standards were established within that apparently permanent frame and the criticism of it began to be irritated and perplexed when, through a new instability, the splintering frame began to get into the picture.

I suppose for a time I was the outstanding instance among writers of fiction in English of the frame getting into the picture.

I did not see this clearly in those opening years of this century, but in 1912 I made a sort of pronouncement against the "character" obsession and the refusal to discuss values, in a paper on *The Contemporary Novel* delivered to The Times Book Club, in which I argued for an enlarging scope for the novel.

My attack upon the creation-of-character idea was oblique and subconscious rather than direct. "We (novelists) are going to deal with political questions and religious questions and social questions. We cannot present people unless we have this free hand, this unrestricted field. What is the good of telling stories about people's lives if one may not deal freely with the religious beliefs and organizations that have controlled or failed to control them? What is the good of pretending to write about love, and the loyalties and treacheries and quarrels of men and women, if one must not glance at those varieties of physical temperament and organic quality, those deeply passionate needs and distresses, from which half the storms of human life are brewed? We mean to deal with all these things, and it will need very much more than the disapproval of provincial librarians, the hostility of a few influential people in London, the scurrility of one paper," (one for St. Loe Strachey and that bold bad word) "and the deep and obstinate silences of another, to stop the incoming tide of aggressive novel-writing. We are going to write about it all. We are going to write about business and finance and politics and precedence and pretentiousness and decorum and indecorum, until a thousand pretences and ten thousand impostures shrivel in the cold, clear draught of our elucidations. We are going to write of wasted opportunities and latent beauties until a thousand new ways of living open to men and women. We are going to appeal to the young and the hopeful and the curious, against the established, the dignified, and defensive. Before we have done, we will have all life within the scope of the novel."

These are brave trumpetings. In effect in my hands the Novel proved like a blanket too small for the bed and when I tried to pull it over to cover my tossing conflict of ideas, I found I had to abandon questions of individuation. I never got "all life within the scope of the novel." (What a phrase! Who could?)

In the criticism of that time there was a certain confusion between this new spreading out of the interest of the novel to issues of custom and political and social change, and the entirely more limited "Novel with a Purpose" of the earlier nineteenth century. This examined no essential ideas; its values were established values, it merely assailed some particular evil, exposed some little-known abuse. It kept well within the frame. The majority of the Dickens novels were novels with a purpose, but they never deal with any inner confusion, any conflicts of opinion within the individual characters, any subjective essential change. A much closer approximation to the spread-out novel I was advocating is the propaganda novel. But I have always resented having my novels called propaganda novels, because it seems to me the word propaganda should be confined to the definite service of some organized party, church or doctrine. It implies direction from outside. If at times I have been inclined to thrust views upon my readers, they were at any rate my own views and put forward without any strategic aim.

To return to this novel *Marriage*, the story tells how masculine intellectual interest met feminine spending and what ensued. Trafford is not so much a solid man as a scientific intelligence caught in the meshes of love, and Marjorie Pope's zest in buying and arrangement is emphasized to the exclusion of any minor tricks and turns. But the argument of the book would not have stood out, if there had been any such tricks and turns. Marjorie's father is an intrusion of character drawing who really had no business in the book at all. Mr. Magnet also is a slightly malicious irrelevance; the humourless speech he makes in London on humour is, for example, transcribed verbatim from a reported speech by a distinguished contemporary.

Indisputably the writing is scamped in places. It could have been just as light and much better done. But that would have taken more time than I could afford. I do not mean by that I could have earned less money and been a more conscientious writer, though that consideration very probably came in, but I mean that I had very many things to say and that if I could say one of them in such a way as to get my point over to the reader I did not worry much about finish. The fastidious critic might object, but the general reader to whom I addressed myself cared no more for finish and fundamental veracity about the secondary things of behaviour than I. I did not want to sweep under the mat for crumbs of characterization, nor did he want me to do so. What we wanted was a ventilation of the point at issue.

It required some years and a number of such experiments and essays in statement as the one I have quoted, before I got it really clear in my own mind that I was feeling my way towards something outside any established formula for the novel altogether. In the established novel, objective through and through, the characteristic exterior reactions of the character were everything and the conflicts and changes of ideas within his brain were ignored. (That according to the jargon of the time would have been to "introduce controversial matter.") But I was becoming more and more interested in the interior conflict, this controversial matter stewing and fermenting in all our brains, and its ventilation in action. There is no satisfactory device I knew for exhibiting a train of reasoning in a character unless a set of ideas similar to those upon which the character thinks exists already in the reader's mind. Galsworthy's Soames Forsyte *thinks* for pages, but he thinks along recognized British lines. He does not grapple with ideas new and difficult both for the reader and himself. I could not see how, if we were to grapple with new ideas, a sort of argument with the reader, an explanation of the theory that is being exhibited, could be avoided. I began therefore to make my characters indulge in impossibly explicit monologues and duologues. As early as 1902, Chatteris in the *Sea Lady* talks a good deal more than is natural. Ann Veronica soliloquises continually. In *Marriage* (1912), Trafford and Marjorie go off to Labrador for a good honest six months' talk about their mutual reactions and argue at the reader all the time. Mr. Brumley in *The Wife of Sir Isaac Harman* (1914) exercises

461

a garrulous pressure upon the flow of the story throughout. *The Research Magnificent* (1915) is largely talk and monologue. I try in that book the device of making the ostensible writer speculate about the chief character in the story he is telling. The ostensible writer becomes a sort of enveloping character, himself in discussion with the reader. Still more expository is the *Soul of a Bishop* (1917).

Incidentally I may complain that *The Research Magnificent* is a book deserving to be remembered and yet seems to be largely forgotten. I liked it when I re-read it and I find it remarkably up to date with my present opinions. It was blotted out by the war. But Amanda is alive and Benham has his moments of vitality.

By 1919, in *The Undying Fire*, I was at last fully aware of what I was doing and I took a new line. I realized I had been trying to revive the Dialogue in a narrative form. I was not so much expanding the novel as getting right out of it. *The Undying Fire* is that great Hebrew imitation of the Platonic Dialogue, the Book of Job, frankly modernized. The arrangement of the ancient book is followed very closely; the speakers even to their names are recognizably the same. The man of Uz is Mr. Job Huss; Eliphaz the Temanite becomes Sir Eliphaz Burrows, manufacturer of a new building material called Temanite; Bildad is Mr. William Dad and Elihu becomes Dr. Elihu Barrack. They parallel their ancient arguments; even their speeches in their order correspond closely with the pattern of the ancient book. In many ways I think *The Undying Fire* one of the best pieces of work I ever did. I set great store by it still.

But after all these protests of the excellence and intelligence of my intentions, I have to admit that the larger part of my fiction was written lightly and with a certain haste. Only one or two of my novels deal primarily with personality, and then rather in the spirit of what David Low calls the caricature-portrait, than for the purpose of such exhaustive rendering as Henry James had in mind. Such caricature-individualities are

Hoopdriver in *The Wheels of Chance*(1896), *Kipps* (1905) and Mr. Polly in *The History of Mr. Polly* (1910). My uncle and aunt in *Tono Bungay* (1909), one or two minor characters in *The Dream* (1924), *Christina Alberta's Father* (1925) and *The Bulpington of Blup* (1932), are also caricature-individualities of which I am not ashamed. Theodore Bulpington is as good as Kipps. Please. But I doubt if any of these persons have that sort of vitality which endures into new social phases. In the course of a few decades they may become incomprehensible; the snobbery of Kipps for example or the bookish illiteracy of Mr. Polly may be altogether inexplicable. *The Dream* is an attempt to show how our lives to-day may look to our happier descendants. It is in the same class as *In the Days of the Comet*.

My experimentation with what I may call the Dialogue Novel, was only one of the directions in which I have wandered away from the uncongenial limitations of the novel proper. The plain fact is that I have never been willing to respect these limitations or to accept the Novel as an art form. *Mr. Britling Sees It Through* is a circumstantial story, but it ends in Dialogue and Monologue. *Joan and Peter* (1918) again starts respectably in large novel form and becomes dialogue only towards the end. It is as shamelessly unfinished as a Gothic cathedral. It was to have been a great novel about Education but it grew so large that Peter's public-school experiences, among other things, had to be left out. He just jumps from the preparatory school to the War and the flying corps. The missing public-school stage is to be found in *The Story of a Great School-master*. Joan I like as a character; A. A. Milne has said nice things about her, but nobody else has had a good word for her—or indeed a bad one. *The Dream* (1924) has some good minor characters, but it is plainly a social criticism from a new angle, rather than a novel proper. A young man of the great world of the future on a holiday walk in the mountains, injures his hand, falls into a fever and dreams "through a whole life" of our present world. *The World of William Clissold* (1926) again is quite unorthodox in shape and approach. It is an attempt to present a thesis upon contemporary life and social development, in the form of a fictitious autobiography. A young chemist, like Trafford in *Marriage*, gives up pure research for industrial organization, grows rich, finds his successful life boring and retires to a house in Provence to think things out and find a better use for himself. He writes the one book that every man has it in him to write. The main strand of the earlier novels reappears in this, the perplexity of the man with general ideas and a strong constructive impulse when he finds that the women he meets do not enter into this stream of motive, but, except for the odd concluding "book," this obsession of so much of my fiction sits lightly here because of the predominance of economic and political questioning. I shall return to *The World of William Clissold* when I deal with my political ideas and later on I may be free to discuss its autobiographical significance. It anticipated a more serious attempt at social analysis, *The Work, Wealth and Happiness of Mankind* (1931), *The Open Conspiracy* (1928) and *The Shape of Things to Come* (1933).

The Autocracy of Mr. Parham (1930) is a rather boisterous caricature not of the personality but of the imaginations of a modern British imperialist of the university type. It might have been dedicated to Mr. L. S. Amery. It amuses me still, but few people share my liking. Reality has outdone fiction since and Mosley fooling it in the Albert Hall with his black shirts (1934) makes Parham's great dream-meeting there seem preposterously sane and sound. *Men Like Gods* frankly caricatures some prominent contemporaries. Another breach of established literary standards with which, in spite of its very tepid reception, I am mainly content, was *Mr. Blettsworthy on Rampole Island* (1928). I laughed when writing both it and *Men Like Gods* and *The Autocracy of Mr. Parham*. The gist of Rampole Island is a caricature-portrait of the whole human world. I wish I could hear at times of people still reading these three stories. They got,

I think, a dull press.

Exhaustive character study is an adult occupation, a philosophical occupation. So much of my life has been a prolonged and enlarged adolescence, an encounter with the world in general, that the observation of character began to play a leading part in it only in my later years. It was necessary for me to reconstruct the frame in which individual lives as a whole had to be lived, before I could concentrate upon any of the individual problems of fitting them into this frame. I am taking more interest now in individuality than ever I did before. As mankind settles down into the security of that modern world-state with which contemporary life is in labour, as men's minds escape more and more from the harsh urgencies and feelings of a primary struggle, as the conception of the modern world-state becomes the common basis of their education and the frame of their conduct, the discussion of primary issues will abate and the analysis of individual difference again become a dominating interest. But then surely people will be less round-about in their approach to expression and the subterfuge of fiction will not be so imperative as it is to-day.

Our restraints upon the written discussion of living people are antiquated. Why should David Low say practically what he likes about actual people with his pencil, while I must declare every character in a novel is fictitious? So I am disposed to question whether the Novel will have any great importance in the intellectual life of the future because I believe we are moving towards a greater freedom of truthful comment upon individuals; if it survives I think it will become more frankly caricature-comment upon personalities and social phases than it is at present, but it seems equally probable to me that it will dwindle and die altogether and be replaced by more searching and outspoken biography and autobiography. Stories, parables, parodies of fact will still be told, but that is a different matter. The race of silly young men who announce that they are going to write The Novel may follow the race of silly young men who used to proclaim their intention of writing The Epic, to limbo. In my time The Novel, as projected, was usually a "Trilogy." Perhaps in 1965 the foolish young men will all be trailing in the wake of Lytton Strachey and Philip Guedalla and announcing colossal biography-sequences. They will produce vast mosaics of pseudo-reality, galleries of portraits, presenting contemporary history in a state of exaltation.

Who would read a novel if we were permitted to write biography—all out? Here in this autobiography I am experimenting—though still very mildly, with biographical and auto-biographical matter. Although it has many restraints, which are from the artistic point of view vexatious, I still find it so much more real and interesting and satisfying that I doubt if I shall ever again turn back towards The Novel. I may write a story or so more—a dialogue, an adventure or an anecdote. But I shall never come as near to a deliberate attempt upon The Novel again as I did in *Tono Bungay* (1909).

Next to *Tono Bungay*, *Mr. Britling Sees It Through* and *Joan and Peter* come as near to being full-dress novels as anything I have written. They are both fairly sound pictures of contemporary conditions. *Mr. Britling Sees It Through* was a huge success more particularly in America, where it earnt about £20,000; *Tono Bungay* did well; but *Joan and Peter* never won the recognition I think it deserved. To me it seems a far finer piece of work than *Mr. Britling Sees It Through*.

Even *Tono Bungay* was not much of a concession to Henry James and his conception of an intensified rendering of feeling and characterization as the proper business of the novelist. It was an indisputable Novel, but it was extensive rather than intensive. That is to say it presented characters only as part of a *scene*. It was planned as a social panorama in the vein of Balzac. That vein has produced some physically and mentally great books, and it continues to this day to produce evidences of the nervous endurance of ambitious writers, vast canvasses, too often crude or conventional in interpretation, superficial in motivation and smeary and wholesale in treatment. I cannot imagine it holding out against a literature of competent historical and contemporary studies. *The Forsyte Saga*, as a broadly conceived picture of prosperous British Philistia by one of its indigenes, is not so good and convincing as a group of untrammelled biographical studies of genteel successful types might be. An industrious treatment of early nineteenth century records again would make Balzac's *Comédie Humaine* seem flighty stuff. Yet in *War and Peace* one may perhaps find a justification for the enhancement and animation of history by fictitious moods and scenes.

I will confess that I find life too short for many things I would like to do. I do not think I am afraid of death but I wish it had not to come so soon. In the natural course of things I shall be lucky, I suppose, if I live a dozen years more, and beyond measure fortunate if I last as a fully living brain for another twenty years. This is barely time to turn round in. Good biography requires more time than that—let alone that I have other things to do. Yet I have known some intensely interesting people whom it would be delightful and rewarding to treat! It is a pity. If I could have forty good years or so more of vigour, I could find a use for every day of it, and then I would write those copious intimate character studies, character in relation to changing values and conditions, that now I fear I shall never be able to do. They would have to be copious. Impermanent realities are not to be rendered without an abundance of matter. In a changing world there cannot be portraits without backgrounds and the source of the shifting reflected light upon the face has to be shown. Here at page 424 of this experiment in autobiography I have to assure the possibly incredulous reader that my attempt to compress it and reduce it to a quintessence, has been strenuous and continual.

XIII. — FAIRLY LAUNCHED AT LAST

§ 1. DUOLOGUE IN LODGINGS (1894-95)

This is an experiment in autobiography and again, I insist, I am writing for myself quite as much as for my reader. In turning over my memories of my early marriage and divorce and the documents that preserve the facts of the case, I learned in the sight of the reader, a great deal about myself and I found it natural to carry on from those early and determining thoughts and experiences to their reflection in my novels and my public discussion of personal relationships. I brought that account of my novels and pseudo-novels down to the present time. These discursive sections have served a useful purpose, they have functioned as a siding, so to speak, into which it has been possible to shunt a number of things that would otherwise have turned up later to complicate the main story of this brain with which I am dealing. That main story, is the development, the steady progressive growth of a modern vision of the world, and the way in which the planned reconstruction of human relationships in the form of a world-state became at last the frame and test of my activities. It is as much the frame and test of my activities as the spread of Islam was the frame and test of an early believing Moslem and the kingdom of God and salvation, of a sincere Christian. My life in the fact that it has evolved a general sustaining idea has become, at least psychologically a religious life; its *persona* is deoriented from the ego. My essential purpose is that world-vision. I shall try to express it, as fully and effectively as I can, in a last culminating chapter, a sort of testamentary chapter, which I shall call *The Idea of a Planned World*.

But before I can get on to this a further amount of anecdotage and incident is needed to make this development clear. My struggle for a footing is still only half told. I come back now to the point from which I launched out into a dissection of my sexual impulses and conduct, when at the beginning of 1894, at the age of twenty-seven and a half, I left my house, 4 Cumnor Place, Sutton and went to live in sin and social rebellion first at Mornington Place and then in Mornington Road.

The last decade of the nineteenth century was an extraordinarily favourable time for new writers and my individual good luck was set in the luck of a whole generation of aspirants. Quite a lot of us from nowhere were "getting on." The predominance of Dickens and Thackeray and the successors and imitators they had inspired was passing. In a way they had exhausted the soil for the type of novel they had brought to a culmination, just as Lord Tennyson (who died as late as 1892), Tennyson of the Arthurian cycle, had extracted every poetical possibility from the contemporary prosperous bourgeoisie. For a generation the prestige of the great Victorians remained like the shadow of vast trees in a forest, but now that it was lifting, every weed and sapling had its chance, provided only that it was of a different species from its predecessors. When woods are burnt, it is a different tree which reconstitutes the forest. The habit of reading was spreading to new classes with distinctive needs and curiosities. They did not understand and enjoy the conventions and phrases of Trollope or Jane Austen, or the genteel satire of Thackeray, they were outside the "governing class" of Mrs. Humphry Ward's imagination, the sombre passions and inhibitions of the Brontë country or of Wessex or Devonshire had never stirred them, and even the humours of Dickens no longer fitted into their everyday experiences.

The Education Act of 1871 had not only enlarged the reading public very greatly but it had stimulated the middle class by a sense of possible competition from below. And quite apart from that, progress was producing a considerable fermentation of ideas. An exceptional wave of intellectual enterprise had affected the British "governing class." Under the influence of such brilliant Tories as Arthur Balfour and George Wyndham, a number of people in society were taking notice of writing and were on the alert for any signs of literary freshness. Such happy minor accidents as the invasion of England by the Astor family with a taste for running periodicals at a handsome loss, contributed also in their measure to the general expansion of opportunity for new writers. New books were being demanded and fresh authors were in request. Below and above alike there was opportunity, more public, more publicity, more publishers and more patronage. Nowadays it is relatively hard for a young writer to get a hearing. He (or she) plunges into a congested scramble. Here as everywhere production has outrun consuming capacity. But in the nineties young writers were looked for. Even publishers were looking for them.

For a time the need to be actually new was not clearly realized. Literary criticism in those days had some odd conventions. It was still either scholarly or with scholarly pretensions. It was dominated by the mediaeval assumption that whatever is worth knowing is already known and whatever is worth doing has already been done. Astonishment is unbecoming in scholarly men and their attitude to newcomers is best expressed by the word "recognition." Anybody fresh who turned up was treated as an aspirant Dalai Lama is treated, and scrutinized for evidence of his predecessor's soul. So it came about that every one of us who started writing in the nineties, was discovered to be "a second"—somebody or other. In the course of two or three years I was welcomed as a second Dickens, a second Bulwer Lytton and a second Jules Verne. But also I was a second Barrie, though J. M. B. was hardly more than my contemporary, and, when I turned to short stories, I became a second Kipling. I certainly, on occasion, imitated both these excellent masters. Later on I figured also as a second Diderot, a second Carlyle and a second Rousseau....

Until recently this was the common lot. Literature "broadened down from precedent to precedent." The influence of the publisher who wanted us to be new but did not want us to be *strange*, worked in the same direction as educated criticism. A sheaf of secondhand tickets to literary distinction was thrust into our hands and hardly anyone could get a straight ticket on his own. These secondhand tickets were very convenient as admission tickets. It was however unwise to sit down in the vacant chairs, because if one did so, one rarely got up again. Pett Ridge for instance pinned himself down as a second Dickens to the end of his days. I was saved from a parallel fate by the perplexing variety of my early attributions.

Of course Jane and I, starting life afresh in our guinea-a-week ground floor apartments in Mornington Place, had no suspicion how wise we had been in getting born exactly when we did. We did not realize we were like two respectable little new ordinary shares in a stock-exchange boom. We believed very gravely in the general sanity of things and we took the tide of easy success which had caught us up, as the due reward of our activity and efforts. We thought this was how things had always been and were always going to be. It was all delightfully simple. We were as bright and witty as we knew how, and acceptance, proofs and a cheque followed as a matter of course. I was doing my best to write as other writers wrote, and it was long before I realized that my exceptional origins and training gave me an almost unavoidable freshness of approach and that I was being original in spite of my sedulous efforts to justify my discursive secondariness.

Our life in 1894 and 95 was an almost continuous duologue. In Mornington Place and in Mornington Road we occupied a bedroom with a double bed and came through folding doors to our living room. All our clothing was in a small chest of drawers and a wardrobe and I did my work at a little table with a shaded paraffin lamp in the corner or, when it was not needed for a meal, at the table in the middle of the living room. All my notes and manuscripts were in a green cardboard box of four drawers. Our first landlady in Mornington Place was a German woman, Madame Reinach, and her cooking was so emphatic, her sympathy with our romantically unmarried state so liberally expressed, her eagerness for intimate mutual confidences so pressing, and her own confidences so extraordinary, that presently Jane went off by herself to Mornington Road and found another lodging for us.

Here our landlady, whose name by some queer turn I have forgotten, mothered us very agreeably. She was a tall, strong-faced, Scotswoman. For a London landlady she was an exceptionally clean, capable, silent and stoical woman. She had been housemaid, if I remember rightly, in the household of the Duke of Fife, and she began to approve of me when she found I worked continuously and never drank. I think that somewhere between the housemaid stage and this lodging house of hers, someone may have figured who lacked my simple virtues. (An old friend with a better memory than mine tells me her name was Mrs. Lewis. But I still do not remember.)

We would wake cheerfully and get up and I would invent rhymes and "pomes" of which I have already given sufficient samples, as we washed and dressed and avoided collisions with each other. We had no bathroom and our limited floor space was further restricted by a "tub," a shallow tin bird-bath in which we sponged and splashed. Perhaps we would peep through the folding doors and if the living room was empty, one of us, I in trousers and nightshirt—those were pre-pyjama days—or Jane in her little blue dressing gown and her two blonde pigtails reaching below her waist, would make a dash for the letters. Usually they were cheering letters. Perhaps there was a cheque; perhaps there was an invitation to contribute an article or maybe there was a book for review. As we read these, a firm tread on the stairs, a clatter and an appetizing smell and at last a rap-rap on the folding doors announced our coffee and eggs and bacon.

How vividly I remember the cheerfulness of that front room; Jane in her wrapper on the hearthrug toasting a slice of bread; the grey London day a little misty perhaps outside and the bright animation of the coal-fire reflected on the fireirons and the fender!

After breakfast I would set to work upon a review or one of the two or three articles I always kept in hand, working them up very carefully from rough notes until I was satisfied with them. Jane would make a fair copy of what I had done, or write on her own account, or go out to supplement our landlady's catering, or read biology for her final B.Sc. degree examination. After the morning's work we might raid out into Regents Park or up among the interesting shops and stalls of the Hampstead Road, for a breath of air and a gleam of amusement before our one o'clock dinner. After dinner we would prowl out to look for articles.

This article hunt was a very important business. We sought unlikely places at unlikely times in order to get queer impressions of them. We went to Highgate Cemetery in the afternoon and protested at the conventionality of the monumental mason, or we were gravely critical, with a lapse into enthusiasm in the best art-critic manner, of the Parkes Museum (sanitary science), or we went on a cold windy day to Epping Forest to write "Bleak March in Epping Forest." We nosed the Bond Street windows and the West End art and picture shows to furbish forth an Uncle I had invented to suit the taste of the *Pall Mall Gazette*—a tremendous man of the world he was, the sort of man who might live in the Albany. (*Select Conversations with an Uncle*, is the pick of what we got for him.) I was still a fellow of the Zoological Society (afterwards my subscription went into abeyance) and we sought articles and apt allusions from cage to cage. Whenever we hit upon an idea for an article that I did not immediately write, it was put into the topmost of my nest of green drawers for future use.

On wet afternoons or after supper when we could work no more we played chess (which yielded an article) and bézique, which defied even my article extracting powers. Bézique was introduced to us by my old fellow student Morley Davies, who had taken on my Correspondence Classes and was working for his B.Sc. He lodged near by and he would come in after supper and gravely take down a triple pack with us.

We went very little to concerts, theatres or music-halls for the very sound reason that we could not afford it. Our only exercise was "going for a walk." And for a time except for occasional after-supper visitors like Davies, or my distant cousin Owen Thomas, who was arranging my divorce upon the most economical lines, or a tea at Walter Low's, we had no social life at all. But then I never had had any social life and Jane's experience had been chiefly of little dances, tea parties, croquet parties and lawn tennis in the villadom of Putney, formal entertainments of which she was now disposed to be very scornful.

It is perhaps not surprising that as the Spring came on, Jane and I, in spite of our encouraging successfulness, displayed signs of being run down. I had something wrong with a lymphatic gland under my jaw and when I called in a Camden Town doctor to clean it up for me, he insisted that Jane was in a worse state than I and that she ought to be much more in the fresh air and better nourished if she was not to become tuberculous. He ordered her Burgundy and we went out and bought an entire bottle at once,—Gilbey's Burgundy, Number—something or other—and Jane consumed it medicinally, one glass per meal. We decided to transfer ourselves to country lodgings for the summer. Except for the facilities of getting books and the advisability of being near one's editors, there seemed to be no particular reason why we should be tied to London. Moreover Jane's mother, Mrs. Robbins, had let her house at Putney; she had been lodging with some friends in North London and she too was ailing and in need of the open air. She had accepted our irregular situation by this time and was quite ready to join us. And while we were hesitating on the verge of this necessity came an accession of work that seemed to make an abandonment of London altogether justifiable.

I was invited one day to go and see my editor, Cust of the *Pall Mall Gazette*—either that or I had asked to see him, I forget which. I went down to the office for my second encounter with an editor but this time I wore no wetted top-hat to shame me by its misbehaviour and no tail coat. I was evidently wearing quite reasonable clothes because I have forgotten them. I was learning my world. The *Pall Mall Gazette* was installed in magnificent offices in the position now occupied by the Garrick Theatre. I was sent up to the editor's room. I remember it as a magnificent drawing-room; Fleet Street hath not its like to-day. There was certainly one grand piano in it, and my memory is inclined to put in another. There was a vast editor's desk, marvellously equipped, like a desk out of Hollywood. There were chairs and sofas. But for the moment I saw nobody amidst these splendours. I advanced slowly across a space of noiseless carpet. Then I became aware of a sound of sobbing and realized that someone almost completely hidden from me lay prostrate on a sofa indulging in paroxysms of grief.

In the circumstances a cough seemed to be the best thing.

Thereupon the sound from the sofa ceased abruptly and a tall blond man sat up, stared and then stood up, put away his pocket handkerchief and became entirely friendly and self-possessed. Whatever emotional crisis was going on had nothing to do with the business between us and was suspended. Yes, he wanted to see me. He liked my stuff and it was perfectly reasonable that I should want to make up my income by doing reviewing. There wasn't any job he could give me on the staff just now. So soon as there was he would think of me. Did I know W. E. Henley? I ought to go and see him.

He asked me where I got my knowledge and how I had learnt to write and what I was and I told him to the best of my ability. He put me at my ease from the beginning. There was none of the Olympian balderdash of Frank Harris about him. He combined the agreeable manners of an elder brother with those of a fellow adventurer. It wasn't at all Fleet Street to which he made me welcome but a Great Lark in journalism. I suppose he knew hardly more of Fleet Street than I did. I must certainly go and see Henley, but just now there was someone else I must meet.

He touched a bell and presently across the large spaces of the room appeared Mr. Lewis Hind. Hind was a contrast to Cust in every way, except that he too was an outsider in the journalistic world. He was tall, dark and sallow, with a reserved manner and an impediment in his speech. He had begun life in the textile trade and at one time he had gone about London with samples of lace. He had been an industrious student, with Clement K. Shorter and W. Pett Ridge at the Birkbeck Institute and he had adventured with them into the expanding field of journalism. He had been taken up and influenced in the direction of catholicism by Mrs. Alice Meynell and he had found a permanent job as sub-editor of the *Magazine of Art* under Henley and, through his introduction and that of Mrs. Meynell he had come aboard Mr. Astor's *Pall Mall* adventure. The *Gazette* had thrown off a weekly satellite, the *Pall Mall Budget*, which was at first merely a bale of the less newsy material in the *Gazette*. My *Man of the Year Million* had appeared in it, with some amusing illustrations, and had made a little eddy of success for me. Hind edited this budget and it was proposed to expand it presently into an independent illustrated weekly with original matter, all its own. He was looking for "features." He carried me off from Cust's room to his own less palatial quarters and there he broached the idea of utilizing my special knowledge of science in the expanded weekly, in a series of short stories to be called "single sitting" stories. I was to have five guineas for each story. It seemed quite good pay, then, and I set my mind to imagining possible stories of the kind he demanded.

We left Cust in his office. Whether he went on with his crisis or forgot about it I cannot say, but from my later acquaintance with him, I think he most probably forgot about it.

The first of the single sitting stories I ground out was the *Stolen Bacillus* and after a time I became quite dexterous in evolving incidents and anecdotes from little possibilities of a scientific or quasi-scientific sort. I presently broadened my market and found higher prices were to be got from the *Strand Magazine* and the *Pall Mall Magazine*. Many of these stories, forty perhaps altogether, have been reprinted again and again in a variety of collections and they still appear and reappear in newspapers and magazines. Hind paid me £5 for them, but the normal fee I get nowadays for republication in a newspaper, is £20, and many have still undeveloped dramatic and film possibilities. I had no idea in those energetic needy days of these little tips I was putting aside for my declining years.

At about the same time that Hind set me writing short stories, I had a request from the mighty William Ernest Henley himself for a contribution to the *National Observer*. I went to see the old giant whose "head was bloody but unbowed" at his house upon the riverside at Putney. He was a magnificent torso set upon shrunken withered legs. When I met President Franklin Roosevelt this spring I found the same big chest and the same infirmity. He talked very richly and agreeably and, as he talked, he emphasized his remarks by clutching an agate paper weight in his big freckled paw and banging it on his writing table. Years afterwards when he died his wife gave me that slab of agate and it is on my desk before me as I write. I resolved to do my very best for him and I dug up my peculiar treasure, my old idea of "time-travelling," from the *Science Schools Journal* and sent him in a couple of papers. He liked them and asked me to carry on the idea so as to give glimpses of the world of the future. This I was only too pleased to do, and altogether I developed the notion into seven papers between March and June. This was the second launching of the story that had begun in the *Science Schools Journal* as the *Chronic Argonauts*, but now nearly all the traces of Hawthorne and English Babu classicism had disappeared. I had realized that the more impossible the story I had to tell, the more ordinary must be the setting, and the circumstances in which I now set the Time Traveller were all that I could imagine of solid upper-middle-class comfort.

With these *Time Traveller* papers running, with quite a number of stories for Hind germinating in my head, with a supply of books to review and what seemed a steady market for my occasional, my frequent occasional, articles in the *Gazette*, it seemed no sort of risk to leave London for a lodging at Sevenoaks, and thither we went, all three of us, as London grew hot and dusty and tiring. For awhile things were very pleasant at Sevenoaks. We went for long walks and Jane recovered rapidly in health and energy. We explored Knole Park and down the long hill to Tunbridge and away to the haunts of my grandfather, Penshurst Park. Jane was still working for her final degree, though she never actually sat for the examination; botany was to be one of her three subjects and we gathered and brought home big and various bunches of flowers so that she might learn the natural orders.

At first Mrs. Robbins was not with us. When she joined us she was in ill health; she had recovered only very partially from her disapproval of our unmarried state, and her presence was a considerable restraint upon our jests and "picshuas" and daily ease. At times the tension of her unspoken feelings would oblige her to take to her room and eat her meals there. This slight and retreating shadow upon our contentment was presently supplemented by graver troubles. There was a sudden fall in my income. Abruptly the *National Observer* changed hands. This was quite a sudden transaction; the paper had never paid its expenses and its chief supporter decided to sell it to a Mr. Vincent who also took over the editorial control from Henley. Mr. Vincent thought my articles queer wild ramblings and wound them up at once. At the same time the *Pall Mall Gazette* stopped using my articles. The literary editor, Marriott Watson, always a firm friend of mine, was away on holiday and his temporary successor did not think very much of my stuff. I did not know of this, and I was quite at a loss to account for this sudden withdrawal of support. I thought it might be a permanent withdrawal. For the first time we found our monthly expenditure exceeding our income. A certain dismay pervaded our hitherto cheerful walks. And then an equally unexpected decision by Mr. Astor announced an approaching end to the brief bright career of the *Pall Mall Budget* and with it my sure and certain market and prompt pay for a single-sitting story.

Just then came an emissary from the divorce court with a writ, couched in stern uncompromising phrases, and instead of locking this securely away, Jane put it in a drawer accessible to the curiosity of our landlady. There had been some little trouble with her already; she wanted to charge an extra sixpence for every meal Mrs. Robbins took in her own room, she said we littered up the place with our wild flowers, and she thought I consumed an unconscionable amount of lamp-oil by writing so late. She was faintly irritated about Jane's disinclination for womanly gossiping with her, she felt we were "stuck-up" in some way, and when she realized that we had no marriage lines, her indignation flared. She could not immediately tax us with our flagrant immorality, for that would have been to admit her own prying, but she became extremely truculent in her bearing and negligent in her services. Dark allusions foreshadowed the coming row. We were not the sort of people everybody would want to take in. There were people who were right and you could tell it, and people who were not. Life assumed a harsh and careworn visage.

It seemed rather useless to go on writing articles. All the periodicals to which I contributed were holding stuff of mine in proof and it might be indiscreet to pour in fresh matter to such a point that the tanks overflowed and returned it. But I had one thing in the back of my mind. Henley had told me that it was just possible he would presently find backing for a monthly. If so, he thought I might rewrite the *Time Traveller* articles as a serial story. Anyhow that was something to do and I set to work on the *Time Machine* and rewrote it from end to end.

I still remember writing that part of the story in which the *Time Traveller* returns to find his machine removed and his retreat cut off. I sat alone at the round table downstairs writing steadily in the luminous circle cast by a shaded paraffin lamp. Jane had gone to bed and her mother had been ill in bed all day. It was a very warm blue August night and the window was wide open. The best part of my mind fled through the story in a state of concentration before the Morlocks but some outlying regions of my brain were recording other things. Moths were fluttering in ever and again and though I was unconscious of them at the time, one must have flopped near me and left some trace in my marginal consciousness that became a short story I presently wrote, *A Moth, Genus Novo*. And outside in the summer night a voice went on and on, a feminine voice that rose and fell. It was Mrs.—— I forget her name—our landlady in open rebellion at last, talking to a sympathetic neighbour in the next garden and talking through the window at me. I was aware of her and heeded her not, and she lacked the courage to beard me in my parlour. "Would I *never* go to bed? How could she lock up with that window staring open? Never had she had such people in her house before,—never. A nice lot if everything was known about them. Often when you didn't actually know about things you could feel them. What she let her rooms to was summer visitors who walked about all day and went to bed at night. And she hated meanness and there were some who could be mean about sixpences. People with lodgings to let in Sevenoaks ought to know the sort of people who might take them...."

It went on and on. I wrote on grimly to that accompaniment. I wrote her out and she made her last comment with the front door well and truly slammed. I finished my chapter before I shut the window and turned down and blew out the lamp. And somehow amidst the gathering disturbance of those days the *Time Machine* got itself finished. Jane kept up a valiant front and fended off from me as much as she could of the trouble that was assailing her on both sides. But a certain gay elasticity disappeared. It was a disagreeable time for her. She went and looked at other apartments and was asked unusual questions.

It was a retreat rather than a return we made to London, with the tart reproaches of the social system echoing in our ears. But before our ultimate flight I had had a letter from Henley telling me it was all right about that monthly of his. He was to start *The New Review* in January and he would pay me £100 for the *Time Machine* as his first serial story. One hundred pounds! And at the same time the mills of the *Pall Mall Gazette* began to go round and consume my work again. Mrs. Robbins went back to stay with friends in North London and Jane and I found our old rooms with our Scotch landlady at 12, Mornington Road, still free for us.

We seem to have stuck it in London for the rest of the year. Somewhere that Autumn Frank Harris, who was no longer editing the *Fortnightly Review*, obtained possession of the weekly *Saturday Review*. He proceeded to a drastic reconstruction of what was then a dull and dignified periodical. He was mindful of those two early articles of mine, the one he had published and the one he had destroyed, and he sent for me at once. He sent also for Walter Low and a number of other comparatively unknown people. The office was in Southampton Street, off the Strand, and it occupied the first and second floors. I found people ascending and descending and the roar of a remembered voice told me that Harris was on the higher level. I found Blanchamp in a large room on the drawing-room floor amidst a great confusion of books and papers and greatly amused. Harris was having a glorious time of it above. He had summoned most of the former staff to his presence in order to read out scraps from their recent contributions to them and to demand, in the presence of his "Dear Gahd" and his faithful henchman Silk, why the hell they wrote like that. It was a Revolution,—the twilight of the Academic. But Professor Saintsbury, chief of that anonymous staff, had been warned in time by Edmund Gosse and so escaped the crowning humiliation.

Clergymen, Oxford dons, respectable but strictly anonymous men of learning and standing, came hustling downstairs in various phases of indignation and protest, while odd newcomers in strange garments as redolent of individuality as their signatures, waited their turn to ascend. I came late on the list and by that time Harris was ready for lunch and took Blanchamp, Low and myself as his guests and audience to the Café Royal, where I made the acquaintance of Camembert of the ripest and a sort of Burgundy quite different from the bottle I had bought for Jane in her extremity. I don't think we talked much about my prospective contributions. But I gathered that our fortunes were made, that Oxford and the Stuffy and the Genteel and Mr. Gladstone were to be destroyed and that under Harris the *Saturday Review* was to become a weekly unprecedented in literary history.

It did in fact become a very lively, readable and remarkable publication. It was never so consciously and consistently "written" as Henley's defunct *National Observer*, but it had a broader liveliness and a far more vigorous circulation. Among other rising writers Harris presently had at work upon it was a lean, red-haired Irishman named Shaw, already known as a music critic and a Socialist speaker, who so far broke through its traditional anonymity as to insist upon his initials appearing after his dramatic criticisms, D. S. McColl (also presently initialled), J. F. Runciman (ditto), Cunninghame Graham (full signature), Max Beerbohm, Chalmers Mitchell, Arthur Symons, J. T. Grein.... I cannot remember half of them. Signed articles increased and multiplied and all sorts of prominent and interesting people made occasional contributions. A "Feature," a series of articles on "The Best Scenery I know" was begun and a "Correspondence" section broke out. No man, it seems, had ever been stirred to write letters to the old "Saturday" or he had been snubbed when he did. Now some were invited and others were stung to contribute the most interesting letters. What Saintsbury thought of it all has never, I think, been recorded. But then Saintsbury very rarely brought his critical acumen to bear upon contemporary writing.

Our City articles also, I gathered, were developing a vigour all their own under the immediate direction of Harris. "I'm a blackmailer," he announced, time and again, and represented himself as a terrible wolf among financiers. Possibly he did something to justify his boasts, in later life he seems to have told Hugh Kingsmill some remarkable stories of cheques extorted and bundles of notes passing from hand to hand but manifestly in the long run it came to very little and he died a year or so ago at Nice in anything but wealthy circumstances.

England in my time has been very liable to adventurous outsiders; Bottomley and Birkenhead, Ramsay Macdonald and Loewenstein, Shaw and Zaharoff, Maundy Gregory and me—a host of others; men with no legitimate and predetermined rôles, men who have behaved at all levels of behaviour but whose common characteristic it has been to fly across the social confusion quite unaccountably, scattering a train of interrogations in their wake. Only the court, the army and navy, banking and the civil service have been secure against this invasion. Such men are inevitable in a period of obsolete educational ideas and decaying social traditions. Whatever else they are they are not dull and formal. They quicken, if it is only quickening to destroy. Harris was certainly a superlative example of the outside adventurer. He was altogether meteoric.

Nobody seemed to know whence Harris had come. He was supposed to be either a Welsh Jew or a Spanish Irishman; he spoke with an accent, but he had done so much to his accent that I doubt whether Shaw could place it precisely. It had a sort of "mega-celtic" flavour—if I may coin a word. His entirely untrustworthy reminiscences give Galway as his birth-place. The meticulous student may find these matters fully discussed in the *Life* by A. I. Tobin and Elmer Gertz and in Hugh Kingsmill's *Frank Harris*. He emerged as a bright pressman in Chicago, made his way to London, pushed into journalism, and when he was sent to write up the bad treatment of the tenants on the Cecil estates, achieved a reputation for vigour and mental integrity by praising instead of cursing. He was taken notice of. He clambered to the editorship of the *Evening News*. From that, before it fell away from him, he leapt still higher. Legend has it that he went to Chapman, the proprietor of the *Fortnightly Review*, and told him his paper was dull because he did not know enough prominent people and then to one or two outstanding people and pointed out the value of publicity in this democratic age, and particularly the value of the publicity to be got through a personal acquaintance with Mr. Chapman; that he invited him to meet them and them to meet him, to the great social gratification of Mr. Chapman, and emerged triumphantly from the resultant party as editor of the *Fortnightly Review*. He infused a certain amount of new life into it and challenged the established ascendency of the *Nineteenth Century*. He married a wealthy widow, a Mrs. Clayton, who had a small but charming house in the then socially exalted region of Park Lane. There he reached his zenith. He saw himself entering parliament; he cultivated the constituency of Hackney, he aspired, he told Hugh Kingsmill, to become the "British Bismarck" (whatever he imagined that to mean. He may have been thinking of his moustache) and all sorts of prominent and interesting people went to the dinner parties at Park Lane. But he could not stay the course. His sexual vanity was overpowering, he not only became a discursive amorist but he talked about it, and there ensued an estrangement and separation from his wife and her income and Park Lane. His dominating way in conversation startled, amused and then irritated people, and he felt his grip slipping. The directors of the *Fortnightly*became restive and interfering. He began to drink heavily and to shout still louder as the penalties of loud shouting closed in on him. When I met him for the second time as the editor with a controlling interest in the *Saturday Review*, he had already left his wife and lost her monetary support, but he was still high in the London sky. He was still a star of the magnitude of Whistler or Henley or Oscar Wilde and we, his younger contributors, were little chaps below him.

I think his blackmailing in the *Saturday Review* period was almost pure romancing, for he achieved neither the wealth nor the jail that are the alternatives facing the serious blackmailer. He was far too loud and vain, far too eager to create an immediate impression to be a proper scoundrel. I have been hearing about him all my life and I have never heard convincing particulars of any actual monetary frauds; the *Saturday Review*, I can witness, paid punctually to the end of his proprietorship. His claims to literary flair, if not to literary distinction, were better founded. He read widely and confusedly but often with vivid appreciation, and he pretended to great learning. He was the sort of man who will prepare a long quotation in Greek for a dinner party. Kingsmill says he sported an Eton tie at times and talked of the "old days" at Rugby. Also he insisted that he had been a cowboy, a foremast hand and a great number of other fine romantic things, as occasion seemed to demand. I never saw him do anything more adventurous than sit and talk exuberantly in imminent danger of unanswerable contradiction.

That was what he lived for, talking, writing that was also loud talk in ink, and editing. He was a brilliant editor for a time and then the impetus gave out and he flagged rapidly. So soon as he ceased to work vehemently he became unable to work. He could not attend to things without excitement. As his confidence went he became clumsily loud.

His talk was most effective at the first hearing; after some experience of it, it began to bore me so excessively that I avoided the office when I knew he was there. There was no variety in his posing and no fancy in his falsehoods. I do not remember that he said a single good thing in all that uproar; his praise, his condemnations, his assertions, his pretensions to an excessive villainy and virility, have all dissolved in my memory into a rich muddy noise. Always he was proclaiming himself the journalistic Robin Hood, bold yet strangely sensitive and tender-hearted— with the full volume of his voice. The reader may get the quality of it best in his book *The Man Shakespeare*.

I went on writing for him until 1898, but with diminishing frequency. Throughout that period he shrank in my mind from his original dimensions of Olympian terror to something in retreating perspective that kept on barking. Sometimes I relented towards him and did my best to restore him to his original position in my esteem as a Great Character, or at least a Great Lark. But really he had not the versatility and detachment for the Great Lark. He could never get sufficiently away from his ugly self. He had nothing of the fresh gaiety of Harry Cust who was everything a Great Lark should be.

After 1898 I saw Harris only intermittently. He left London. Something obscure happened to the *Saturday Review* and he sold his interest in it and went to France.

Thereafter I heard him rumbling about, for the most part below the horizon of my world, a distant thunder. He came up to visibility again for a time as the editor of an old and long respectable monthly called *Hearth and Home*. He desecrated the Hearth and got rid of the Homelike quality very rapidly and thoroughly. Before or after that (I forget which) he was editor of a periodical with menace even in the title, *The Candid Friend*, which was abusive rather than candid, and faded out. Afterwards he worked his mischief upon *Vanity Fair* and then upon a publication called*Modern Society*. But he did nothing extraordinarily or gallantly wicked though he did much that was noisily offensive.

We had a quarrel during the *Vanity Fair* phase. He sent me a book called *The Bomb*. I thought the first part good and the second tawdry and bad and I asked him which part of it was really his. I had touched a tender spot. His idea of a retort was to publish terrific "slatings" of my *Tono Bungay*, which for reasons still obscure to me he called Tono-the-Bungay. That did not alter the fact that *The Bomb* is curiously unequal.

Modern Society got him into prison but only on the score of contempt of court. He commented on the private character of the defendant in a divorce case that was *sub judice*. His "martyrdom," as he called it later, lasted a month. Then for a time I heard no more of him.

One morning in war time, somewhen in 1915, my neighbour Lady Warwick came sailing down from Easton Lodge to Easton Glebe, my house on the edge of her park. It is not her way to beat about the bush. "Why does Frank Harris say I am not to tell you he is here?" she asked.

Was he here? He was at Brook End with his wife—in fear of prosecution. He had found reason for bolting from Paris and he had thrown himself upon her never-failing generosity. Brook End was a furnished house just beyond the far gates of the park which she was in the habit of lending to all and sundry who appealed to her. He had been boasting too much in Paris about his German sympathies and his influence with the Indian princes, and the French who are a logical people and take things said far too seriously, made themselves disagreeable and inquisitive. They are quite capable of shooting a man on his own confession. He gave way to panic. He fled to England with Mrs. Harris and a couple of valises. He still saw denunciation in every tree and the rustle of the summer leaves outside the windows at Brook End seemed the prelude to arrest.

I explained that he and I had been exchanging abusive letters and I supposed that he was expecting me to behave as he would have behaved if our positions had been reversed. Jane came in and we agreed that it was a case for cordial and even effusive hospitality. Mrs. Harris is a very pleasant and loyal lady and there was little need for effort in our welcome to her. Harris—a very subdued Harris it was—brightened up and we did what we could to make his stay in Essex pleasant until he could get a passage to America. He sat at my table and talked of Shakespeare, Dryden, Carlyle, Jesus Christ, Confucius, me and other great figures; of poetry and his own divine sensitiveness and the execrable cooking in Brixton jail.

Presently they got a passage for America and departed.

He had been gone some days when I had another visit from Lady Warwick. This time she did not come to the point so directly. As we walked in my rose garden she asked me what I really thought of Frank Harris. Didn't she know?

You see, she had had a number of letters—quite interesting letters from a certain royal personage.

"And you gave them to him?"

"Oh *no*! But he asked to look through them. He thought he might advise me about them. One doesn't *care* to destroy things like that. They have historical importance."

"And they are now in his valise on their way to America?"

"Yes. How did you know that?"

It seemed to me, I am afraid, an altogether amusing situation. "Even if the ship is torpedoed," I said, "Harris will stick to those letters."

It was a lengthy and costly business to recover and place those carelessly written and very private documents in the hands most likely to hold them discreetly. Meanwhile Harris took over *Pearson's Magazine* in America and ran it as a pro-German organ until America came into the war. He reduced a circulation of 200,000 to 10,000. He published a hostile and quite imaginary interview with me to show how entirely ignorant and foolish was my attitude in the struggle.

But this is my autobiography and not a biography of Harris. I never saw him again. I found myself very near him when I made a winter home for myself near Grasse, but I kept any craving I had to hear his voice once more, well under control. Messages passed between us and I promised to go and see him—when I could manage it. But I never did manage and I am rather sorry now. He died in 1932 and after all, by that time, he was an old man of seventy-seven or seventy-eight, and it would have done me no harm to have gone over and listened to him for an hour or so.

Shaw was far kinder to him. When he was staying at Antibes in the summer of 1928 he went over to Nice on several occasions, and renewed the old acquaintance. It was an odd friendship. Harris never wearied and bored Shaw as he wearied and bored me. Shaw found something attractive in all those boastings of sentimentalized villainy and passionate virility. And moreover he could hold his own with Harris in a way that I could not do. In his earlier years he had been wont to face and sway the uproar of excited public meetings. Talking to Harris must have seemed almost like old times come again. But Harris in talk went over me like a steam roller and flattened me out completely.

Very generously Shaw allowed Harris to write a *Life* of himself. It is the work of an ego-centred, sex-crazy old man. And it reveals more than anything else the profound resentment of Harris at the relative success of his former contributor. Shaw, he says, was a miracle of impotence in art, in affairs and in love. That is the main thesis. The analysis is pseudo- physiological throughout. Shaw took these outpourings with an admirable good humour and helped the book greatly by adding elucidatory contributions of his own. But so far as I and my autobiography are concerned, the latter years of Harris at Nice are no more than "noises heard off." I know nothing of that redoubtable suppressed *Life and Loves* of his, in four volumes, which is sought after by collectors of "curious" books, except that it must certainly be tumultuous and unveracious.

So much for that hot, vehement brain which went roaring past my own less audible hemispheres of grey matter on their way through this world. I am told that *The Life and Loves of Frank Harris* is a warning to all autobiographers, and I can quite believe it. Apparently it is a hotch potch of lies, self-pity, vain pretensions and exhibitionism and the end is unhappiness and despair. Nevertheless I do not feel urged, even for my own good, to go to the pains needed to procure and read a surreptitious copy of it. I do not think I should learn anything more about this awful example of undisciplined egoism than I know and have told already. The core of the matter is this, that this man drank and shouted and had to go on drinking and shouting all through his life because the tireless pursuit of self-discovery upon his heels gave him no peace; he never had the courage to face round at his reality and he was never sufficiently stupefied to forget it. He was already in flight before the horror of The Man Frank Harris, before ever he came to London. And yet, perhaps, if he had turned, he might have made something quite tolerable of his repudiated and falsified self. I cannot tell. It would have been a stiff job anyhow with that dwarfish ill-proportioned body, that ugly dark face and with lust-entangled vanity and greediness of overpowering strength.

* * * * *

I return from this digression to the years 1894-95 and my visits to Southampton Street to get books for review from Frank Harris and Blanchamp and to carry them off, whole armfuls, in a hansom cab to 12 Mornington Road. There I sat down and Jane and I mugged up our reviews of them, whenever the light of invention burnt low and an original article seemed out of the question.

I was now in a very hopeful and enterprising mood. Henley had accepted the *Time Machine*, agreed to pay £100 for it, and had recommended it to Heinemann, the publisher. This would bring in at least another £50. I should have a book out in the spring and I should pass from the status of journalist—"occasional journalist" at that, and anonymous—to authorship under my own name. And there was talk of a book of short stories with Methuen. Furthermore John Lane was proposing to make a book out of some of my articles, though for that I was to get only £10 down. The point was that my chance was plainly coming fast. I should get a press—and I felt I might get a good press—for the *Time Machine*anyhow. If I could get another book out before that amount of publicity died away I should be fairly launched as an author and then I might be able to go on writing books. This incessant hunt for "ideas" for anonymous articles might be relaxed and the grind of book-reviewing abated.

I find in my archives a "picshua" commemorating my Christmas dinner for 1894. Very few picshuas survive from the first year of my life with Jane. I did not draw so very many then, and she did not begin methodically to save what I drew until we had a house and storage. The early pictures were not nearly so neat and dexterous as the later. But this one shows our tall landlady (bless her!) giving a last glance at the table she has laid for myself and Jane and Mrs. Robbins. The fare is recognizably a turkey. Detail however is hasty and inadequate. The interested reader will note the folding doors. He will note too a queer black object on the table to the left of Jane. That represents, however inadequately, a black glass flagon. In this flagon there was a wine—I do not know if it is still sold by grocers—a golden wine, called "Canary Sack." I am not at all sure if it was the same as

Falstaff's sack; it was a sweetish thin sherry-like wine.

That wine on the table, even more than the turkey and the presence of Mrs. Robbins, marks the fact that already in the first year Jane and I felt we were winning our queer little joint fight against the world, for the liberty of our lives and the freedom of our brains. We had had a serious talk about our social outlook. People, often strange people, were beginning to ask us out. All sorts of unfamiliar food and drink might be sprung upon us, for the dietary Jane had been brought up upon was scarcely less restricted than my own. We knew no wines but port and sherry. Accordingly we decided to experiment with food and drink so far as the resources of the Camden Town and Tottenham Court Road luxury trade permitted. We tried a bottle of claret and a bottle of hock and so forth and so on, and that is why we "washed down" our Christmas fare with Canary Sack. So that if anyone asked us to take Canary Sack we should know what we were in for. But nobody ever did ask us to take Canary Sack. My knowledge of Canary Sack is still waste knowledge.

Picshua: Xmas 1894.

And we discussed whether we would go out to a dinner or so in a restaurant in preparation for our social emergence. There was the Holborn Restaurant and there were restaurants in Soho which offered dinners from 1*s*. 6*d*. upwards, where we might acquire the elements of gastronomic *savoir faire*.

I had already been to one formidable dinner party, the "Wake" of Henley's *National Observer*. It was perhaps not in the best possible taste to call it a wake, seeing that the new editor proprietor who had undertaken to carry on the life of the deceased, was present as a guest. George Wyndham, Nathaniel Curzon, Walter Sickert, Edgar Vincent (better known nowadays as Lord D'Abernon), G. S. Street, Arthur Morrison, Bob Stevenson, Charles Baxter (R. L. S.'s business manager), H. B. Marriott Watson and other contributors to the paper were present. I am not sure whether J. M. Barrie and Rudyard Kipling were there, but both had been among Henley's men. I sat at the tail of a table, rather proud and scared, latest adherent to this gallant band. And because I was there at the end I was first to be served with a strange black blobby substance altogether unknown to me. I was there to enjoy myself and I helped myself to a generous portion. My next door neighbour—I rather fancy it was Basil Thomson—eyed the black mound upon my plate.

"I see you *like* caviar," he remarked.

"Love it," I said.

I didn't, but I ate it all. I had my proper pride.

That dinner was at Verrey's in Regent Street and I remember walking very gravely and carefully along the kerb of the pavement at a later hour, to convince myself that the exalted swimming in my head which had ensued upon the festival, was not in the nature of intoxication. If there had been a tight-rope handy leading straight out over the bottomless pit I suppose that in that mood of grave investigation I should have tried it. I decided that I was not drunk, but that I was "under the influence of alcohol." My literary ambitions were bringing me into a quite unanticipated world, full of strange sorts of food and still more various sorts of drink. A certain discretion might, I decided with a wary eye on the kerb, be necessary.

It was a good thing for me that behind the folding doors at 12 Mornington Road slept a fine and valiant little being, so delicate and clean and so credulous of my pretensions, that it would have been intolerable to appear before her unshaven or squalid or drunken or base. I lived through my Bohemian days as sober as Shaw if not nearly so teetotally.

Which reminds me of a bitter complaint I once heard in the *Saturday Review* office from one of Harris's satellites. "When we're here'n the'vning all com'fly tight tha' fella Shaw comes in— dishgrashful shtate shobriety—talks and *talks*... AND TALKS."

§ 2. LYNTON, STATION ROAD, WOKING (1895)

I began the new year with my first and only regular job on a London daily. Cust had promised that I should have the next vacancy, whatever it was, on the *Pall Mall*, and the lot fell upon the dramatic criticism. I was summoned by telegram. "Here," said Cust and thrust two small pieces of coloured paper into my hand.

"What are these?" I asked.

"Theatres. Go and do 'em,"

"Yes," I said and reflected. "I'm willing to have a shot at it, but I ought to warn you that so far, not counting the Crystal Palace pantomime and Gilbert and Sullivan, I've been only twice to a theatre."

"Exactly what I want," said Cust. "You won't be in the gang. You'll make a break."

"One wears evening dress?"

It was not in Gust's code of manners to betray astonishment. "Oh yes. To-morrow night especially. The Haymarket."

We regarded each other thoughtfully for a moment, "Right O," said I and hurried round to a tailor named Millar in Charles Street who knew me to be solvent. "Can you make me evening clothes by to-morrow night?" I asked, "Or must I hire them?"

The clothes were made in time but in the foyer I met Cust and George Steevens ready to supply a criticism if I failed them and nothing came to hand from me. But I did the job in a fashion and posted my copy fairly written out in its bright red envelope before two o'clock in the morning in the Mornington Road pillar box. The play was "*An Ideal Husband*, a new and original play of modern life by Oscar Wilde."

That was on the third of January 1895, and all went well. On the fifth I had to do *Guy Domville*, a play by Henry James at the St. James's Theatre. This was a more memorable experience. It was an extremely weak drama. James was a strange unnatural human being, a sensitive man lost in an immensely abundant brain, which had had neither a scientific nor a philosophical training, but which was by education and natural aptitude alike, formal, formally æsthetic, conscientiously fastidious and delicate. Wrapped about in elaborations of gesture and speech, James regarded his fellow creatures with a face of distress and a remote effort at intercourse, like some victim of enchantment placed in the centre of an immense bladder. His life was unbelievably correct and his home at Rye one of the most perfect pieces of suitably furnished Georgian architecture imaginable. He was an unspotted bachelor. He had always been well off and devoted to artistic ambitions; he had experienced no tragedy and he shunned the hoarse laughter of comedy; and yet he was consumed by a gnawing hunger for dramatic success. In this performance he had his first and last actual encounter with the theatre.

Guy Domville was one of those rare ripe exquisite Catholic Englishmen of ancient family conceivable only by an American mind, who gave up the woman he loved to an altogether coarser cousin, because his religious vocation was stronger than his passion. I forget the details of the action. There was a drinking scene in which Guy and the cousin, for some obscure purpose of discovery, pretended to drink and, instead, poured their wine furtively into a convenient bowl of flowers upon the table between them. Guy was played by George Alexander, at first in a mood of refined solemnity and then as the intimations of gathering disapproval from pit and gallery increased, with stiffening desperation. Alexander at the close had an incredibly awkward exit. He had to stand at a door in the middle of the stage, say slowly "Be keynd to Her.... *Be* keynd to Her" and depart. By nature Alexander had a long face, but at that moment with audible defeat before him, he seemed the longest and dismallest face, all face, that I have ever seen. The slowly closing door reduced him to a strip, to a line, of perpendicular gloom. The uproar burst like a thunder-storm as the door closed and the stalls responded with feeble applause. Then the tumult was mysteriously allayed. There were some minutes of uneasy apprehension. "Au-thor" cried voices. "Au-thor!" The stalls, not understanding, redoubled their clapping.

Disaster was too much for Alexander that night. A spasm of hate for the writer of those fatal lines must surely have seized him. With incredible cruelty he led the doomed James, still not understanding clearly how things were with him, to the middle of the stage, and there the pit and gallery had him. James bowed; he knew it was the proper thing to bow. Perhaps he had selected a few words to say, but if so they went unsaid. I have never heard any sound more devastating than the crescendo of booing that ensued. The gentle applause of the stalls was altogether overwhelmed. For a moment or so James faced the storm, his round face white, his mouth opening and shutting and then Alexander, I hope in a contrite mood, snatched him back into the wings.

That was my first sight of Henry James with whom I was later to have a sincere yet troubled friendship. We were by nature and training profoundly unsympathetic. He was the most consciously and elaborately artistic and refined human being I ever encountered, and I swam in the common thought and feeling of my period, with an irregular abundance of rude knowledge, aggressive judgments and a disposition to get to close quarters with Madame Fact even if it meant a scuffle with her. James never scuffled with Fact; he treated her as a perfect and unchallengeable lady; he never questioned a single stitch or flounce of the conventions and interpretations in which she presented herself. He thought that for every social occasion a correct costume could be prescribed and a correct behaviour defined. On the table (an excellent piece) in his hall at Rye lay a number of caps and hats, each with its appropriate gloves and sticks, a tweed cap and a stout stick for the Marsh, a soft comfortable deer-stalker if he were to turn aside to the Golf Club, a light-brown felt hat and a cane for a morning walk down to the Harbour, a grey felt with a black band and a gold-headed cane of greater importance, if afternoon calling in the town was afoot. He retired at set times to a charming room in his beautiful walled garden and there he worked, dictating with a slow but not unhappy circumspection, the novels that were to establish his position in the world of discriminating readers. They are novels from which all the fiercer experiences are excluded; even their passions are so polite that one feels that they were gratified, even at their utmost intimacy, by a few seemly gestures; and yet the stories are woven with a peculiar humorous, faintly fussy, delicacy, that gives them a flavour like nothing else in the language. When you want to read and find reality too real, and hard story-telling tiresome, you may find Henry James good company. For generations to come a select type of reader will brighten appreciatively to the *Spoils of Poynton*, *The Ambassadors*, *The Tragic Muse*, *The Golden Bowl* and many of the stories.

I once saw James quarrelling with his brother William James, the psychologist. He had lost his calm; he was terribly unnerved. He appealed to me, to me of all people, to adjudicate on what was and what was not permissible behaviour in England. William was arguing about it in an indisputably American accent, with an indecently naked reasonableness. I had come to Rye with a car to fetch William James and his daughter to my home at Sandgate. William had none of Henry's passionate regard for the polish upon the surfaces of life and he was immensely excited by the fact that in the little Rye inn, which had its garden just over the high brick wall of the garden of Lamb House, G. K. Chesterton was staying. William James had corresponded with our vast contemporary and he sorely wanted to see him. So with a scandalous directness he had put the gardener's ladder against that ripe red wall and clambered up and peeped over!

Henry had caught him at it.

It was the sort of thing that isn't done. It was most emphatically the sort of thing that isn't done.... Henry had instructed the gardener to put away that ladder and William was looking thoroughly naughty about it.

To Henry's manifest relief, I carried William off and in the road just outside the town we ran against the Chestertons who had been for a drive in Romney Marsh; Chesterton was heated and I think rather swollen by the sunshine; he seemed to overhang his one-horse fly; he descended slowly but firmly; he was moist and steamy but cordial; we chatted in the road for a time and William got his coveted impression.

But reminiscence is running away with me. I return to the raw young dramatic critic standing amidst the astonished uneasy stallites under the storm that greeted *Guy Domville*. That hissing and booing may have contributed something to the disinclination I have always felt from any adventure into The Theatre.

On that eventful evening I scraped acquaintance with another interesting contemporary, Bernard Shaw. I had known him by sight since the Hammersmith days but I had never spoken to him before. Fires and civil commotions loosen tongues. I accosted him as a *Saturday Review* colleague and we walked back to our respective lodgings northward while he talked very interestingly about the uproar we had left behind us and the place of the fashionable three-act play amidst the eternal verities. He laid particular stress on the fact that nobody in the audience and hardly any of the cast, had realized the grace of Henry James's language.

Shaw was then a slender young man of thirty-five or so very

hard-up, and he broke the ranks of the boiled shirts and black and white ties in the stalls, with a modest brown jacket suit, a very white face and very red whiskers. (Now he has a very red face and very white whiskers, but it is still the same Shaw.) He talked like an elder brother to me in that agreeable Dublin English of his. I liked him with a liking that has lasted a lifetime. In those days he was just a brilliant essayist and critic and an exasperating speaker in Socialist gatherings. He had written some novels that no one thought anything of, and his plays were still a secret between himself and his God.

From that time onward I saw him intermittently, but I did not see very much of him until I went into the Fabian Society, six or seven years later. Then he was a man in the forties and a much more important figure. He was married and he was no longer impecunious. His opinions and attitudes had developed and matured and so had mine. We found ourselves antagonistic on a number of issues and though we were not quite enough in the same field nor near enough in age to be rivals, there was from my side at any rate, a certain emulation between us.

We were both atheists and socialists; we were both attacking an apparently fixed and invincible social system from the outside; but this much resemblance did not prevent our carrying ourselves with a certain sustained defensiveness towards each other that remains to this day. In conversational intercourse a man's conclusions are of less importance than his training and the way he gets to them, and in this respect chasms of difference yawned between Shaw and myself, wider even than those that separated me from Henry James. I have tried to set out my own formal and informal education in a previous chapter. Shaw had had no such sustained and constructive mental training as I had been through, but on the other hand he had been saturated from his youth up in good music, brilliant conversation and the appreciative treatment of life. Extreme physical sensibility had forced him to adopt an austere teetotal and vegetarian way of living, and early circumstances, of which Ireland was not the least, had inclined him to rebellion and social protest; but otherwise he was as distinctly over against me and on the aesthetic side of life as Henry James. To him, I guess, I have always appeared heavily and sometimes formidably facty and close-set; to me his judgments, arrived at by feeling and expression, have always had a flimsiness. I want to get hold of Fact, strip off her inessentials and, if she behaves badly put her in stays and irons; but Shaw dances round her and weaves a wilful veil of confident assurances about her as her true presentment. He thinks one can "put things over" on Fact and I do not. He philanders with her. I have no delusions about the natural goodness and wisdom of human beings and at bottom I am grimly and desperately educational. But Shaw's conception of education is to let dear old Nature rip. He has got no further in that respect than Rousseau. Then I know, fundamentally, the heartless impartiality of natural causation, but Shaw makes Evolution something brighter and softer, by endowing it with an ultimately benevolent Life Force, acquired, quite uncritically I feel, from his friend and adviser Samuel Butler. We have been fighting this battle with each other all our lives. We had a brisk exchange of letters after the publication of the *Science of Life*.

But let me return to those theatrical first nights of mine. None of the criticism I wrote was ever anything but dull. I did not understand the theatre. I was out of my place there. I do not think I am made to understand the theatre but at any rate, I never sat down to ask myself, "What is all this stage stuff about? What is the gist of this complex unreality?" If I had done so, then I should have emerged with a point of view and data for adequate critical writing—even if that writing had turned out to be only a denunciation of all the existing methods and machinery.

Shaw like James and like his still more consciously cultivated disciple, Granville Barker, believed firmly in The Theatre as a finished and definite something demanding devotion; offering great opportunities to the human mind. He perceived indeed there was something very wrong with it, he demanded an endowed theatre, a different criticism, a different audience than the common "Theatre-goer" we knew, but in the end he could imagine this gathering of several hundred people for three hours' entertainment on a stage becoming something very fine and important and even primary in the general life. I had no such belief. I was forming a conception of a new sort of human community with an unprecedented way of life, and it seemed to me to be a minor detail whether this boxed-up performance of plays, would occur at all in that ampler existence I anticipated. "Shows" there will certainly be, in great variety in the modern civilization ahead, very wonderful blendings of thought, music and vision; but except by way of archaeological revival, I can see no footlights, proscenium, prompter's box, playwright and painted players there.

Of course this wasn't clear in my mind in the nineties, but I did fail to find The Theatre sufficiently important adequately to stir my wits and so if for no other reason my work as a dramatic critic was flat and spiritless. Yet I saw some good plays. In Wilde's *Importance of Being Earnest* Alexander did a magnificent piece of work that completely effaced his Guy Domville from my mind, and in Pinero's *Notorious Mrs. Ebbsmith* I saw and heard young Mrs. Pat Campbell, with her flexible body and her delightful voice, for the first time.

After the wear of a month or so for my new dress clothes my rough but essentially benevolent personal Providence appreciated the listlessness of this forced uncongenial work and intervened to stop it. I caught a bad cold, streaks of blood appeared again, and once more the impossibility of my moving about in London in all weather was demonstrated. I resigned The Theatre into better hands, those of G. S. Street, who was later to be a gentle and understanding Censor of Plays, and I set about finding a little house in the country, where I could follow up with another book the success that I felt was coming to the *Time Machine* and my short-story volume.

Our withdrawal to Woking was a fairly cheerful adventure. Woking was the site of the first crematorium but few of our friends made more than five or six jokes about that. We borrowed a hundred pounds by a mortgage on Mrs. Robbins' house in Putney and with that hundred pounds, believe it or not, we furnished a small resolute semi-detached villa with a minute greenhouse in the Maybury Road facing the railway line, where all night long the goods trains shunted and bumped and clattered—without serious effect upon our healthy slumbers. Close at hand in those days was a pretty and rarely used canal amidst pine woods, a weedy canal, beset with loose-strife, spiræa, forget-me-nots and yellow water lilies, upon which one could be happy for hours in a hired canoe, and in all directions stretched open and undeveloped heath land, so that we could walk and presently learn to ride bicycles and restore our broken contact with the open air. There I planned and wrote the *War of the Worlds*, the *Wheels of Chance* and the *Invisible Man*. I learnt to ride my bicycle upon sandy tracks with none but God to help me; he chastened me considerably in the process, and after a fall one day I wrote down a description of the state of my legs which became the opening chapter of the *Wheels of Chance*. I rode wherever Mr. Hoopdrive rode in that story. Later on I wheeled about the district marking down suitable places and people for destruction by my Martians. The bicycle in those days was still very primitive. The diamond frame had appeared but there was no free-wheel. You could only stop and jump off when the treadle was at its lowest point, and the brake was an uncertain plunger upon the front wheel. Consequently you were often carried on beyond your intentions, as when Mr. Polly upset the zinc dust-bins outside the shop of Mr. Rusper. Nevertheless the bicycle was the swiftest thing upon the roads in those days, there were as yet no automobiles and the cyclist had a lordliness, a sense of masterful adventure, that has gone from him altogether now.

Jane was still a very fragile little being and as soon as I had sufficiently mastered the art of wheeling I got a tandem bicycle of a peculiar shape made for us by the Humber people and we began to wander about the south of England, very agreeably. But here I think a photograph and a selection of picshuas may take up the story again. The first picshua shows us starting out upon an expedition that carried us at last across Dartmoor to Cornwall and the second shows Jane engaging her first domestic servant.

Picshua: Cycling.

Picshua: Engaging A Servant.

We lived very happily and industriously in the Woking home for a year and a half and then my mother-in-law fell ill and for a time it was necessary that she should live with us, so that we had to move to a larger house at Worcester Park. We had married as soon as I was free to do so. By the time of our removal, our circle of acquaintances and friends had increased very considerably. I will not catalogue names but one friendly figure stands out amidst much other friendliness, that once much reviled and now rather too much forgotten writer, Grant Allen. I do not think I have ever made a fair acknowledgment of a certain mental indebtedness to him. Better thirty-five years late than never.

He was about twenty years older than I. He had been a science teacher in the West Indies and he was full of the new wine of aggressive Darwinism. He came back to England and, in that fresh illumination, began writing books for the general reader and essays in natural history. He was a successful popularizer and he had a very pronounced streak of speculative originality. But he had the schoolmaster trick of dogmatism and a rash confidence in every new idea that seized upon him. In these days no editor paid very much for scientific contributions and James Payne, the editor of the *Cornhill Magazine*, showed him that the better way to prosperity was to travel abroad and write

505

conventional novels about places of interest to British tourists. The middle-class British and Americans who were beginning to travel very freely in Europe were delighted to read easy stories of sentiment and behaviour introducing just the places they had visited and the sights they had seen. With this work Grant Allen achieved a reasonable popularity and prosperity. But he was uneasy in his prosperity. He had had an earlier infection of that same ferment of biology and socialism that was working in my blood. He wanted not merely to enjoy life but to do something to it. Social injustice and sexual limitation bothered his mind, and he was critical of current ideas and accepted opinions. I myself was destined to go through roughly parallel phases of uneasiness and to fall even more definitely under the advancing intimations of the different life of the coming world-state.

Like myself Grant Allen had never found a footing in the professional scientific world and he had none of the patience, deliberation—and discretion—of the established scientific worker, who must live with a wholesome fear of the Royal Society and its inhibitions before his eyes. Grant Allen's semi-popular original scientific works such as his *Origin of the Idea of God* (1897) and his *Physiological Aesthetics* (1877) were at once bold and sketchy, unsupported by properly verified quotations and collated references, and regardless or manifestly ignorant of much other contemporary work. They were too original to be fair popularization and too unsubstantiated to be taken seriously by serious specialists, and what was good in them has been long since appropriated, generally without acknowledgment, by sounder workers, while the flimsy bulk of them moulders on a few dusty and forgotten shelves. His anthropology became an easy butt for the fuller scholarship and livelier style of Andrew Lang.

His attempt to change himself over from a regularly selling, proper English "purveyor of fiction" to the novelist with ideas and initiative and so contribute materially to vital literature was equally unfortunate. In that also he was, so to speak, an undecided amphibian, an Amblystoma, never quite sure whether he had come out of the water for good or not. He had always to earn a living, and the time left over from that, just as it had not been enough either for the patient and finished research needed to win respect in the scientific world, was now not enough for the thorough and well thought-out novel of aggressive reality.

Later on I was to be in much the same case. In his spare time, so to speak, and unaware that the devices and methods of the ordinary trade novel are exactly what cannot be used for fresh matter, he wrote what was really a sentimental novelette, *The Woman Who Did*. He tried (I am sure with a hurried pen) to present a woman who deliberately broke the rigid social conventions of the period and bore an illegitimate child as "her very own," and, without any intensive effort to conceive her personality, he tried to tell the story so that she should be sympathetic for the common-place reader. That was a most dangerous and difficult thing to attempt, and since, later on, I was to try out something of a kindred sort in *Ann Veronica*, *The New Machiavelli* and *The Wife of Sir Isaac Harman*, I can bear my expert witness to the difficulty of the technical miracle he was so glibly setting about to perform. My mature persuasion is that the distance a novel can carry a reader out of his or her moral and social preconceptions is a very short one. I think a novel can do more than a play in this way; I don't believe an audience in a theatre has ever budged a bit from its established standards of conduct for anything that has been put on the stage; but in either case what principally occurs is recognition and response. The most fatal thing that can be done is to "assume" the Tightness of the new standard you are putting over. This was done excessively in *The Woman Who Did*. Stupid people will never read anything with which they do not agree, so what is the good of trying to write down to them? And even quite intelligent people will read and consider an account of strange defiant behaviour only if it is neither glorified nor extenuated but put before them simply as a vitalized statement. "Look here!" you must say, "What do you think of this?" So long as they are interested, judging freely, and not bristling with resentful resistance, you are doing the job. But everybody bristled at *The Woman Who Did.*

I bristled. I was infuriated. I was the more infuriated because I was so nearly in agreement with Grant Allen's ideas, that this hasty, headlong, incompetent book seemed like a treason to a great cause. It was, I felt, opening a breach to the enemy. So I slated him with care and intensity, in this style:

> "We have endeavoured to piece this character together, and we cannot conceive the living woman. She is, he assures us with a certain pathos, a 'real woman.' But one doubts it from the outset. 'A living proof of the doctrine of heredity' is her own idea, but that is scarcely the right effect of her. Mr. Grant Allen seems nearer the truth when he describes her as 'a solid rock of ethical resolution.'" Her solidity is witnessed to by allusions to her 'opulent form' and the 'lissom grace of her rounded figure.' Fancy a girl with an 'opulent' form! Her 'face was, above all things, the face of a free woman,' a 'statuesque' face, and upon this Mr. Grant Allen has chiselled certain inappropriate 'dimples,' which mar but do not modify that statuesque quality. 'She was too stately of mien ever to grant a favour without granting it of pure grace and with a queenly munificence'— when Alan kissed her. She dresses in a 'sleeveless sack embroidered with arabesques,' and such-like symbolic garments. So much goes to convey her visible presence. The reader must figure her sackful of lissom opulence and her dimpled, statuesque features for himself—the picture eludes us. She had a 'silvery voice.' The physical expression of her emotions was of two kinds, a blush,

and a 'thrill to the finger-tips.' This last phrase is always cropping up, though we must confess we can attach no meaning to it ourselves and cannot imagine Mr. Grant Allen doing so. Her soul is 'spotless.' Never did she do anything wrong. (And this is a 'real woman'!) When Alan called to see her on some trivial business 'she sat a lonely soul, enthroned amid the halo of her own perfect purity'—a curious way of receiving visitors. She is 'pure' and 'pellucid' and 'noble,' and so forth on every page almost. And at the crisis she 'would have flaunted the open expression of her supreme moral faith before the eyes of all London,' had not Alan, the father of the baby in question, with 'virile self-assertion' restrained her.

"Clearly this is not a human being. No more a human being than the women twelve hands tall of the fashion magazines. Had her author respected her less he might have drawn her better. Surely Mr. Grant Allen has lived long enough to know that real women do not have spotless souls and a physical beauty that is invariably overpowering. Real women are things of dietary and secretions, of subtle desires and mental intricacy; even the purest among them have at least beauty spots upon their souls. This monstrous Herminia—where did he get her? Assuredly not of observation and insight. She seems to us to be a kind of plaster-cast of 'Pure Womanhood' in a halo, with a soul of abstractions, a machine to carry out a purely sentimental principle to its logical conclusion. Alan, her lover, is a kind of ideal prig, 'a pure soul in his way, and mixed of the finer paste' from which the heroes of inferior novels are made. The Dean, her father, is the sympathetic but prejudiced cleric of modern comedy. The source of Ethel Waterton is acknowledged: she 'was a most insipid blonde from the cover of a chocolate-box.' Dolores, for whom Mr. Grant Allen feels least, for or against, is far and away the best character in the book. She is so, we think, for that very reason.

"Now the book professes to be something more than an artistic story, true to life. It is, we are led to infer, an ethical discussion. But is it? The problem of marriage concerns terrestrial human beings, and the ingratitude of the offspring of a plaster-cast, though wonderful enough, bears no more on our moral difficulties than the incubation of Semele, or the birth of the Minotaur. In these problem novels at least, truth is absolutely essential. But to handle the relation of the sexes truly needs a Jean Paul Richter, or a George Meredith. It is not to be done by desiring.

"And the gospel Mr. Grant Allen—who surely knows that life is one broad battlefield—is preaching: what is it? It is the emancipation of women. He does not propose to emancipate them from the narrowness, the sexual savagery, the want of charity, that are the sole causes of the miseries of the illegitimate and the unfortunate. Instead he wishes to emancipate them from monogamy, which we have hitherto regarded as being more of a fetter upon virile instincts. His proposal is to abolish cohabitation, to abolish the family—that school of all human gentleness—and to provide support for women who may have children at the expense of the State. We are all to be foundlings together, and it will be an inquisitive child who knows its own father. Now Mr. Grant Allen must know perfectly well that amorous desires and the desire to bear children are anything but overpowering impulses in many of the very noblest women. The women, who would inevitably have numerous children under the conditions he hopes for, would be the hysterically erotic, the sexually incontinent. *Why* he should make proposals to cultivate humanity in this direction is not apparent. We find fine handsome sayings about Truth and Freedom, but any establishment for his proposition a reviewer much in sympathy with him on many of his opinions fails altogether to discover in his book. A fellowship of two based on cohabitation and protected by jealousy, with or without the marriage ceremony, seems as much the natural destiny of the average man as of the eagle or the tiger.

"And we have a quarrel, too, with the style of the book. Had Mr. Grant Allen really cared, as he intimates he cared, for truth and beauty, had he really loved this Herminia of his creation, would he have put her forth in such style as he has done? 'Ordinary,' 'stereotyped,' 'sordid,' 'ignoble,' are among the adjectives he applies to the respectable villadom he identifies with the English people. Yet every one of them fits the workmanship he has considered worthy of his heroine."

And so on. Twenty years later I was, by the bye, to find myself in a position almost parallel to that of Grant Allen with my *Passionate Friends*, which in its turn was slated furiously and in much the same spirit by the younger generation in the person of Rebecca West. But I have never been able to persuade myself that I deserved that trouncing quite as much as Grant Allen merited his.

He behaved charmingly. He wrote me a very pleasant invitation to come and talk to him and I ran down by train one Sunday, walked up from Haslemere station and lunched with him in Hindhead. In these days Hindhead was a lonely place in a great black, purple and golden wilderness of heath; there was an old inn called The Huts and a score of partly hidden houses. Tyndall had built a house there, Conan Doyle was close by, Richard Le Gallienne occupied a cottage as tenant, motor cars and suburbanism were still a dozen years away. Le Gallienne came in after lunch. His sister was staying in the house with her husband, James Welsh, the actor. We sat about in deck chairs through a long sunny summer afternoon under the pines in the garden on the edge of the Devil's Punch Bowl.

Across the interval of years I do not recall that wandering conversation with any precision. Probably we talked a lot about writing and getting on in the world of books. I was a new and aggressive beginner in that world and I was being welcomed very generously. And also I suppose we must have talked of the subject of *The Woman Who Did* and its related issues. Grant Allen and I were in the tradition of Godwin and Shelley. Its trend was to force a high heroic independence on women—even on quite young women. But Grant Allen who had something in him—I will not say like a Faun or a Satyr, but rather like the earnest Uncle of these woodland folk, was all for the girls showing spirit. I was rather enwrapped then in my private situation. Le Gallienne was an Amorist and he trailed a flavour of Swinburne and Renascence Italy—Browning's Renascence Italy, across our talk.

When history is properly written, it will be interesting to trace the Amorist through the ages. There have been phases when the Amorist has dominated manners and costume and decoration and phases when he has been rather shamefaced and occasional in the twilight and the bushes and the staircase to the ballroom. The Amorist just then was in the ascendant phase, and Richard Le Gallienne was the chief of our Amorists. He was busy then with prose fancies in which roses and raptures and restaurants were very attractively combined, and he was inciting the youth of our period to set out upon the Quest of the Golden Girl. He was long and slender with a handsome white half-feminine face, expressive hands and a vast shock of black hair. I found him an entertaining contrast to myself and we got on very well together until suddenly he went out of the literary world of London to America.

I add three other picshuas from the Woking period here. They will amuse some readers. Others will find them detestable, but after all, this is my autobiography. One records a horticultural triumph not uncommon in suburban gardens. The other two are vain-glorious to the ultimate degree. The last of the three reeks with the "shop" of authorship; one observes also the pride of Jane, the author's family in a state of wonder, the envious hostile reviewer with a forked tail, press cutting (from Romeike), much sordid exultation about royalties and cheques. But we were very young still, we had had a hard and risky time and it was exciting to succeed.

Picshua: We Cut Our First Marrow.

[The Author's Syndicate.
14th March 1896

Dear Mr. Wells,

Mr. Pearson is anxious to see the remainder of your story "The War of the Worlds" as soon as possible. As far as he has read he likes it very much, but says that a great deal depends on the finish of the story. I shall be glad If you will let me know when you think you can send me

514

the remainder.

Faithfully yours,...]

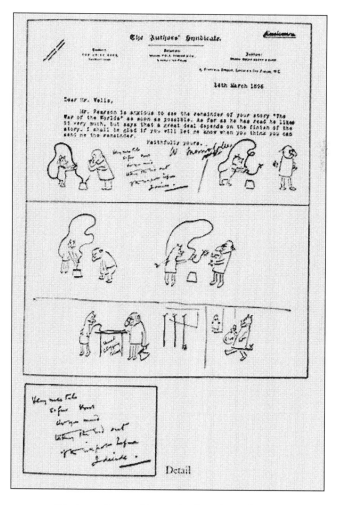

Picshua: Letter From Authors' Syndicate.

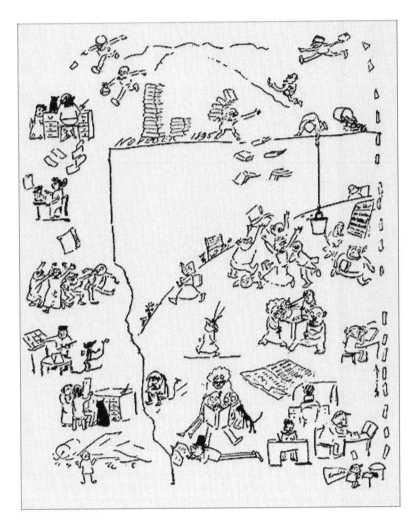

Picshua: November 1895.

§ 3. HEATHERLEA, WORCESTER PARK (1896-97)

I think I have sufficiently conveyed now the flavour of my new way of life and I will not go with any great particularity into the details of my history after we had moved to Worcester Park. I will trust a few picshuas to carry on the tale. This Worcester Park house had two fairly big rooms downstairs, a visitor's room and a reasonably large garden and we started a practice of keeping open house on Saturday afternoons which improved our knowledge of the many new friends we were making. Among others who stayed with us was Dorothy Richardson, a schoolmate of Jane's. Dorothy has a very distinctive literary gift, acute intensity of expression and an astonishingly vivid memory; her *"Pilgrimage"* books are a very curious essay in autobiography; they still lack their due meed of general appreciation; and in one of them, *The Tunnel*, she has described our Worcester Park life with astonishing accuracy. I figure as Hypo in that description and Jane is Alma.

The first picshua here shows our daily routine and our domestic humour in full swing. This is documentary evidence of Jane's participation in my early work and of the punishments and discipline alleged to prevail during the writing of *When the Sleeper Awakes* and *Love and Mr. Lewisham*. The next records my return to the *Fortnightly Review* and what I think must have been a dinner at the *New Vagabonds Club* at which I seem to have been the guest of honour. The third records details of this glorious occasion. The waiter seems to have missed me for ice pudding; the figures who bow before Jane are J. K. Jerome, Sidney Low, Douglas Sladen and Kenneth Grahame (of the immortal *Wind in the Willows*). Vain-glory is again offensively evident.

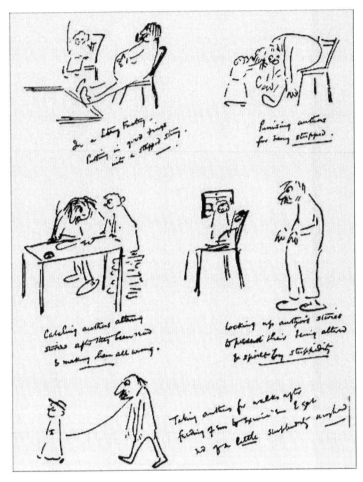

Picshua: November 18th, 1896.

Picshua: Letter from "Fortnightly Review."

Picshua: New Vagabonds Club.

The next picshua records our industry in our Heatherlea garden under the direction of our jobbing gardener (one day a week) Mr. Tilbury. The date of this particular picshua, as the small figure in the corner indicates, was the day of publication of the *Invisible Man*, a tale, that thanks largely to the excellent film recently produced by James Whale, is still read as much as ever it was. To many young people nowadays I am just the author of the *Invisible Man*. The writing on Jane's foot, by the bye, is "gloshers," which is so to speak, idiotic for galosh. But why I wrote that word in that fashion, is—like the mating cry of the pterodactyl and the hunting habits of the labyrinthodon, lost in the mist of the past.

Picshua: Gardening.
Publication of "Invisible Man," September 8th, 1897.

Next comes a picshua full of self-congratulations. "The improvement of a certain person's mind" has been resumed. Jane made a brief attempt to take up her B.Sc. degree work again, but that was presently abandoned. The shelf of our books is filling up. At an Omar Khayyam dinner I had met George Gissing and he was very anxious for us to go with him to Italy in the spring. We study a guide to Italy.

Picshua: October 1897.

The next picshua shows the Italian project maturing. Jane was still far from strong and she had been ordered an iron tonic. We brace ourselves to face the danger of malaria and austerities of a Roman breakfast. Neither of us had ever been across the channel before; Jane had some French and German, but my knowledge of languages was limited to the decaying remains of my swift matriculation cramming of exceptions. All that had been written work and I did not so much pronounce as block out rude masses of misconceived sound. "Abroad" was a slightly terrifying world of adventure for us. And we were not going to just nibble at the continent. We were going straight through, at one bite, to Rome.

Picshua: February 1898.

We did go to Rome in the spring of 1898. We spent a month there with Gissing and then went on by ourselves to Naples, Capri, Pompeii, Amalfi and Paestum. Capri and Paestum cropped up a little later in a short story, *A Vision of Armageddon*. We acquired a traveller's smattering of Italian, a number of photographs, some glowing memories and brighter ideas about diet and wine. We returned by way of Switzerland and Ostend. The uneasy social life of nineteenth century Europe was in a phase of inflammation. In Naples people were rioting for "Pane e Lavoro!" and in the square outside our hotel in Brussels there was a demonstration, and the crowd was singing the Marseillaise and fired a revolver or so.

George Gissing was a strange tragic figure, a figure of internal tragedy, and it is only slowly that I have realized the complex of his misfortunes. There is a novel about him by Morley Roberts *The Private Life of Henry Maitland* (1912) which tells the substance of his tale with considerable inaccuracy, and there is an admirable study of his life and work by Frank Swinnerton, so good that it would be officious and impertinent for me to parallel it, however briefly, here. The portrait by Sir William Rothenstein which figures in Swinnerton's book could hardly be bettered. I had read and admired Gissing's *In the Year of Jubilee* and his *New Grub Street* before I met him and I began our first conversation by remarking upon the coincidence that Reardon, in the latter book, lived like myself as a struggling writer in Mornington Road with a wife named Amy. This was at an Omar Khayyam dinner whither I had gone as the guest of either Grant Allen or Edmund Clodd (I forget which). Gissing was then an extremely good-looking, well-built man, slightly on the lean side, blond, with a good profile and a splendid leonine head; his appearance betraying little then of the poison that had crept into his blood to distress, depress and undermine his vitality and at last to destroy him. He spoke in a rotund Johnsonian manner, but what he had to say was reasonable and friendly. I asked him to come over to us at Worcester Park and his visit was the beginning of a long intimacy.

He talked very much of ill health and I tried to make him a cyclist, for he took no exercise at all except walking, and I thought it might be pleasant to explore Surrey and Sussex with him, but he was far too nervous and excitable to ride. It was curious to see this well-built Viking, blowing and funking as he hopped behind his machine. "Get on to your ironmongery," said I. He mounted, wabbled a few yards, and fell off shrieking with laughter. "Iron-mongery!" he gasped. "Oh! riding on ironmongery!" and lay in the grass at the roadside, helpless with mirth. He loved laughter and that was a great link between us—I liked to explode him with some slight twist of phrase. He could be very easily surprised and shocked to mirth, because he had a scholar's disposition to avoid novel constructions and unusual applications of words. In the summer of 1897, Jane and I spent some weeks or so at Budleigh Salterton near to a lodging he had taken and then it was that our daring adventure "abroad" was conceived.

I knew nothing in those days of his early life, of how in his precocious teens he had wrecked his career as a scholar by a liaison with a young street-walker, a liaison which had led to some difficulties about money and a police court. Friends appeared to rescue him but nobody seems to have troubled about her. He was sent to America for a fresh start and the effect of a fresh start under conditions of sexual deprivation in Boston, had been to send him in flight to Chicago and then bring him back in a recoil to England, to hunt out and marry his mistress. They lived dismally in lodgings while he tried to write great novels. For her it was an intolerable life. She left him and died in hospital.

Clearly there was for him something about this woman, of which no record remains, some charm, some illusion or at any rate some specific attraction, for which he never had words. She was his Primary Fixation. For him she had been Woman. All this was past, but he had created a new situation for himself by picking up a servant girl in Regents Park one Sunday afternoon and marrying her. Told thus baldly the thing is almost incredible, and an analysis of his motives here would take an extravagant amount of space. His home training had made him repressive to the explosive pitch; he felt that to make love to any woman he could regard as a social equal would be too elaborate, restrained and tedious for his urgencies, he could not answer questions he supposed he would be asked about his health and means, and so, for the second time, he flung himself at a social inferior whom he expected to be easy and grateful. This second marriage was also a failure; failure was inevitable; the new wife became a resentful, jealous scold. But we never saw her and I cannot judge between them. To us Gissing was just himself. "I cannot ask you to my home," he said. "Impossible—quite impossible. Oh quite impossible. I have to dismiss any such ideas. I have no home."

He did not always keep such ideas dismissed, but for the most part they were out of the picture. He kept his own family also, the custodians of those strangling early standards, out of our way, just as he kept his wife out of our way. He was terrified at the prospect of incompatibility. His sensitiveness to reactions made every relationship a pose, and he had no natural customary *persona* for miscellaneous use.

The Gissing I knew, therefore, was essentially a specially posed mentality, a personal response, and his effect upon me was an extraordinary blend of a damaged joy-loving human being hampered by inherited gentility and a classical education. He craved to laugh, jest, enjoy, stride along against the wind, shout, "quaff mighty flagons." But his upbringing behind the chemist's shop in Wakefield had been one of repressive gentility, where "what will the neighbours *think* of us?" was more terrible than the thunder of God. The insanity of our educational organization had planted down in that Yorkshire town, a grammar school dominated by the idea of classical scholarship. The head was an enthusiastic pedant who poured into that fresh and vigorous young brain nothing but classics and a "scorn" for non-classical things. Gissing's imagination, therefore escaped from the cramping gentilities and respectability of home to find its compensations in the rhetorical swagger, the rotundities and the pompous grossness of Rome. He walked about Wakefield in love with goddesses and nymphs and excited by ideas of patrician freedoms in a world of untouchable women. Classics men according to their natures are all either "Latins" or "Hellenes."

Gissing was a Latin, oratorical and not scientific, unanalytical, unsubtle and secretly haughty. He accepted and identified himself with all the pretensions of Rome's triumphal arches.

His knowledge of classical Rome was extraordinarily full. We found him, there, an unsparing enthusiastic guide. With a sort of a shamed hostility indeed he recognized the vestiges of mediaevalism and the Renascence that cumbered the spectacle. But that was just a subsequent defilement, like mud on the marble of a submerged palace. At the back of his mind, a splendid Olympus to our Roman excursions, stood noble senators in togas, marvellous matrons like Lucrece, gladiators proud to die, Horatiuses ready to leap into gulfs *pro patria*, the finest fruit of humanity, unjudged, accepted, speaking like epitaphs and epics, and by these standards also he measured the mundane swarm he pictured *In the Year of Jubilee*. For that thin yet penetrating juice of shrewd humour, of kindly stoicisms, of ready trustfulness, of fitful indignations and fantastic and often grotesque generosities, which this dear London life of ours exudes, he had no palate. I have never been able to decide how much that defect of taste was innate or how far it was a consequence partly of the timid pretentiousness of his home circumstances, and partly of that pompous grammatical training to which his brain was subjected just in his formative years. I favour the latter alternative. I favour it because of his ready abundant fits of laughter. You do not get laughter without release, and you must have something suppressed to release. "Preposterous!" was a favourite word with him. He told me once of how he was awakened at three in the morning in a London hotel by a clatter of milk cans under his window. He lay in bed helpless with laughter that civilization should produce this marvel of a chamber designed for sleeping, just over a yard where the rattling of milk cans was an inevitable nightly event.

At the back of my mind I thought him horribly mis-educated and he hardly troubled to hide from me his opinion that I was absolutely illiterate. Each of us had his secret amusement in the other's company. He knew the Greek epics and plays to a level of frequent quotation but I think he took his classical philosophers as read and their finality for granted; he assumed that modern science and thought were merely degenerate recapitulations of their lofty and inaccessible wisdom. The transforming forces of the world about us he ascribed to a certain rather regrettable "mechanical ingenuity" in our people. He thought that a classical scholar need only turn over a few books to master all that scientific work and modern philosophy had made of the world, and it did not disillusion him in the least that he had no mastery of himself or any living fact in existence. He was entirely enclosed in a defensive phraseology and a conscious "scorn" of the "baser" orders and "ignoble" types. When he laughed he called the world "Preposterous," but when he could not break through to reality and laughter then his word was "Sordid." That readiness to call common people "base" "sordid" "mean," "the vulgar sort" and so forth was less evident in the man's nature than in his writings. Some of his books will be read for many generations, but because of this warping of his mind they will find fewer lovers than readers. In Swinnerton's book one can see that kindly writer starting out with a real admiration and sympathy for his subject and gradually being estranged by the injustice, the faint cruelty of this mannered ungraciousness towards disadvantaged people.

Through Gissing I was confirmed in my suspicion that this orthodox classical training which was once so powerful an antiseptic against Egyptian dogma and natural superstitions, is now no longer a city of refuge from barbaric predispositions. It has become a vast collection of monumental masonry, a pale cemetery in a twilight, through which new conceptions hurry apologetically on their way to town, finding neither home nor sustenance there. It is a cemetery, which like that churchyard behind Atlas House, Bromley, can give little to life but a certain sparkle in the water and breed nothing any more but ghosts, *ignes fatui* and infections. It has ceased to be a field of education and become a proper hunting ground for the archæologist and social psychologist.

So, full of friendly antagonisms, Gissing, Jane and I went about Rome together, our brains reacting and exchanging very abundantly. It was Rome before the mischiefs of Mayor Nathan, before the vast vulgarity of the Vittorio Emmanuele monument had ruined the Piazza Venezia, and when the only main thoroughfare was the Corso. The Etruscan tombs still slept undiscovered in the Forum and instead of Boni's flower beds there were weeds and wild flowers. Walking through some fields near Tivoli the *Story of Miss Winchelsea's Heart* came into my head—and I remember telling it to Gissing.

Gissing, like Gibbon, regarded Christianity as a deplorable disaster for the proud gentilities of classicism and left us to "do" the Vatican and St. Peter's by ourselves. In many of the darkened, incense-saturated churches, I felt old Egypt and its mysteries still living and muttering, but the papal city and its swarming pilgrims, its libraries and galleries, its observatory, its Renascence architecture, filled me with perplexing impressions. Much more than pomp, tradition and decay was manifest in these activities. The Scarlet Woman of my youthful prejudices was not in evidence. Protestantism, I perceived, had not done justice to Renascence Rome.

Here, quite plainly, was a great mental system engaged in a vital effort to comprehend its expanding universe and sustain a co-ordinating conception of human activities. That easy word "superstition" did not cover a tithe of it.

It dawned upon me that there had been a Catholic Reformation as drastic as and perhaps profounder than the Protestant Reformation, and that the mentality of clerical Rome, instead of being an unchanged system *in saecula saeculorum* had been stirred to its foundations at that time and was still struggling—

like everything else alive—in the grip of adaptive necessity. In spite of my anti-Christian bias I found something congenial in the far flung cosmopolitanism of the Catholic proposition. Notwithstanding its synthesis of decaying ancient theologies and its strong taint of other-worldishness, the Catholic Church continues to be, in its own half-hearted fashion, an Open Conspiracy to reorganize the whole life of man. If the papal system had achieved the ambitions of its most vigorous period, it would have been much more in the nature of that competent receiver for human affairs, the research for which has occupied my mind so largely throughout my life, than that planless Providentialism which characterized almost all the political and social thought of the nineteenth century. Catholicism is something greater in scope and spirit than any nationalist protestantism and immeasurably above such loutish reversions to hate as Hitlerism or the Ku-Klux-Klan. I should even hesitate to call it "reactionary" without some qualification.

I have lived for many years in open controversy with Catholicism and though, naturally enough, I have sometimes been insulted by indignant zealots, I have found the ordinary Catholic controversialist a fair fighter and a civilized man—worthy of that great cultural system within which such minds as Leonardo and Michelangelo could develop and find expression. He has an antiquated realist philosophy which too often gives him a sort of pert hardness, but that is another matter. It is a question too fine for me to discuss whether I am an outright atheist or an extreme heretic on the furthest verge of Christendom—beyond the Arians, beyond the Manichaeans. But certainly I branch from the Catholic stem.

Let me however return from this Vatican excursion to George Gissing. That disposition to get away from entangling conditions which is manifest in almost every type of imaginative worker, accumulated in his case to quite desperate fugitive drives. In Italy with us he was in flight from his second wife. The dreadful intimacy of that isolated life at Ewell, without a thought in common, an intimacy of perpetual recrimination, had become intolerable. A well-known educationist, a woman who had evidently a very great admiration for Gissing, had proposed to take in Mrs. Gissing and the children and try to establish tolerable relations with her, to "educate" her in fact, while Gissing recovered his mental peace in his beloved Italy. But the experiment was not working well; the helpful lady was meddling with things beyond her experience and the poor wife, perplexed and indignant beyond measure by this strange man who had possessed himself of her life, was progressing through scenes and screams towards a complete mental breakdown; she was behaving very badly indeed, and letters would arrive at the Hotel Aliberti in Rome, that left Gissing white and shaking between anger and dismay for the better part of a day. The best thing then was to go off with him outside Rome to some wayside albergo, to the Milvian bridge, or towards Tivoli or along the Appian Way, drink rough red wine, get him talking Italian to peasants, launch out upon wild social, historical and ethnological discussions, and gradually push the gnawing trouble into the background again.

This poor vexed brain—so competent for learning and aesthetic reception, so incompetent, so impulsive and weakly yielding under the real stresses of life—went on from us into Calabria and produced there *By the Ionian Sea* and, later on, after returning to England, *The Private Papers of Henry Ryecroft*. The interest of these books, with their halting effort to pose as a cultivated leisurely eighteenth century intelligence, is, I think, greatly intensified by the realization that beneath the struggle to sustain that *persona*, the pitiless hunt of consequences, the pursuit of the monstrous penalties exacted for a false start and a foolish and inconsiderate decision or so, was incessant. Perhaps Gissing was made to be hunted by Fate. He never turned and fought. He always hid or fled.

Presently we were back at Worcester Park and he was

established with a "worthy housekeeper," a cook general in fact, in a cottage in Dorking. The wife was still being hushed up by the friend in London and did not know of his whereabouts. He was intensely solitary and miserable at Dorking. One day he came to us with a request. There was a proposal from a Frenchwoman to translate his novels into French. He wished to confer with her. Impossible for a lone man to entertain a strange lady at Dorking; would we arrange a meeting?

They lunched with us and afterwards they walked in our garden confabulating. She was a woman of the intellectual bourgeoisie, with neat black hair and a trim black dress, her voice was carefully musical, she was well read, slightly voluble and over-explicit by our English standards, and consciously refined and intelligent. To Gissing she came as the first breath of Continental recognition, and she seemed to embody all those possibilities of fine intercourse and one-sided understanding for which he was craving. For Gissing carried the normal expectancy of the male, which I have already dealt with in my own dissection, to an extravagant degree. Never did a man need mothering more and never was there a less sacrificial lover.

Presently we learnt from a chance remark that the lady had visited him one day at Dorking. She had become "Thérèse" He made no further confidences. Then he broke up his Dorking establishment and left for Switzerland, where he was joined by Thérèse and her mother. He confided that there was to be a joint ménage and to ease things with the French relations, the mother carried the relationship so far towards a pseudo-marriage as to circulate cards with the surname of Thérèse erased in favour of "Gissing." All this had, of course, to be carried out with absolute secrecy towards his actual wife and most of his English friends. Those of us who knew, thought that if he could be put into such circumstances as would at last give his very fine brain a fair chance to do good work, connivance in so petty a deception was a negligible price to pay.

Presently he published a novel called *The Crown of Life*. It is the very poorest of his novels but it is illuminating as regards himself. The "crown of life" was love—in a frock coat. This was what Gissing thought of love or at any rate it was as much as he dared to think of love. But after all, we argued, something of the sort had to happen and now perhaps he would write that great romance of the days of Cassiodorus.

But things did not work out as we hoped. When, a year or so later, Jane and I, returning from an excursion to Switzerland, visited him in Paris, we found him in a state of profound discontent. The apartment was bleakly elegant in the polished French way. He was doing no effective work, he was thin and ailing, and he complained bitterly that his pseudo mother-in-law, who was in complete control of his domestic affairs, was starving him. The sight of us stirred him to an unwonted Anglo-mania, a stomachic nostalgia, and presently he fled to us in England. An old school friend of his, Henry Hick, a New Romney doctor, of whom I shall have a word or so to say later, came over to look at him, and declared he was indeed starved, and Jane set to work and fed him up—weighing him carefully at regular intervals—with marvellous results.

I was glad to have him in our house, but it carried a penalty. For suddenly Thérèse began to write me long, long, wonderfully phrased letters—on thin paper and crossed—informing me that she could not bring herself to write to him directly and demanding my intervention. I had still to realize the peculiar Latin capacity for making copious infusions of simple situations. Presently when Gissing went off for some days to Hick, he too began to write at Thérèse to me—long letters in his small fine handwriting.

But I was busy upon work of my own and after one or two rather hasty attempts at diplomacy I brutalized the situation. I declared that the best thing for Gissing to do would be to decide never to return to France, since there was an evident incompatibility of appetite between him and the lady, or alternatively if there was any sort of living affection still between them, which I doubted, he must stipulate as a condition of his return that the catering should be taken out of the hands of the mother and put in those of the daughter under his own direction, and finally I announced that in no circumstances would I read through, much less paraphrase, consider or answer any further letters from Thérèse. Whatever she wrote to me, I should send to him for him to deal with directly. And with that I washed my hands of their immediate troubles.

He went back to her on the terms I had suggested, so I suppose there was still some sort of tenderness between them. Then these three poor troubled things full of the spirit of mute recrimination, perplexed and baffled by each other's differences, went down to a furnished house at St. Jean-de-Luz and, afterwards, to St. Jean-Pied-de-Port in the mountains above, and there he set to work writing what was to have been, what might have been under happier circumstances, a great historical picture of Italy under the Gothic kings, *Veranilda*. He had had this book in mind almost all the time I had known him. He had been reading Cassiodorus for it in 1898. Towards Christmas 1903 some of Thérèse's relations came to visit them. On some excursion with them he caught a cold, which settled on his chest. Neither Thérèse nor her mother was the nursing type of woman. A sudden hatred seized him of the comfortless house he was in, of the misty mountain village, of economized French food and everything about him and a sudden fear fell upon him of the crackling trouble in his lungs and the fever that was gathering in his veins. He had been writing with deepening distress to Morley Roberts in November. Just on the eve of Christmas came telegrams to both of us: "George is dying. Entreat you to come. In greatest haste."

I had private bothers of my own and I was supposed to be nursing a cold, but as Roberts did not seem to be available and made no reply to a telegram I sent him, I decided to go. It was Christmas Eve. I had no time to change out of my garden clothes and I threw some things into a handbag and went off in a fly to Folkestone Pier to catch the afternoon boat. I made my Christmas dinner of ham at Bayonne station.

I found the house a cheerless one. I saw nothing, or at least I remember seeing nothing of Thérèse's mother; I think she had retired to her own room. Thérèse was in a state of distress and I thought her extremely incompetent. The visitors were still visiting but I insisted upon their departure. There was however a good little Anglican parson about, with his wife, and they helped me to get in a nurse (or rather a "religieuse," which is by no means the same thing) and made some beef-tea before they departed for their home in St. Jean-de-Luz.

Gissing was dying of double pneumonia and quite delirious all the time I was there. There was no ice available and his chest had to be kept cool by continually dipping handkerchiefs in methylated spirit and putting them on him. Also his mouth was slimy and needed constant wiping. I kept by him, nursing him until far into the small hours while the weary religieuse recuperated, dozing by the fire. Then I found my way back to my inn at the other end of the place through a thick fog. St. Jean-Pied-de-Port is a lonely frontier town and at night its deserted streets abound in howling great dogs to whom the belated wayfarer is an occasion for the fiercest demonstrations. I felt like a flitting soul hurrying past Anubis and hesitating at strange misleading turnings on the lonely Pathway of the Dead. I forget every detail of the inn but I still remember that sick-room acutely.

It is one of the many oddities of my sheltered life that until the death of Gissing I had never watched a brain passing through disorganization into a final stillness. I had never yet seen anyone dying or delirious. I had expected to find him enfeebled and anxious and I had already planned how we could get a civil list pension from Mr. Balfour, to educate his boys and how I would tell him of that and what other reassurances I might give him. But Gissing aflame with fever had dropped all these anxieties out of his mind. Only once did the old Gissing reappear for a moment, when abruptly he entreated me to take him back to England. For the rest of the time this gaunt, dishevelled, unshaven, flushed, bright-eyed being who sat up in bed and gestured weakly with his lean hand, was exalted. He had passed over altogether into that fantastic pseudo-Roman world of which Wakefield Grammar School had laid the foundations.

"What are these magnificent beings!" he would say. "Who are these magnificent beings advancing upon us?" Or again, "What is all this splendour? What does it portend?" He babbled in Latin; he chanted fragments of Gregorian music. All the accumulation of material that he had made for *Veranilda* and more also, was hurrying faster and brighter across the mirrors of his brain before the lights went out for ever.

The Anglican chaplain, whose wife had helped with the beef-tea, heard of that chanting. He allowed his impression to develop in his memory and it was proclaimed later in a newspaper that Gissing had died "in the fear of God's holy name, and with the comfort and strength of the Catholic faith." This led to some bitter recriminations. Edward Clodd and Morley Roberts were particularly enraged at this "body-snatching" as they called it, and among other verbal missiles that hit that kindly little man in the full publicity of print were "crow," "vulture" and "ecclesiastical buzzard." But he did not deserve to be called such names. He did quite honestly think Gissing's "Te Deums" had some sort of spiritual significance.

Another distressful human being in the sick chamber that night was Thérèse. I treated her harshly. She annoyed me because I found a handkerchief was being used to wipe his mouth that had been dipped in methylated spirit, and her thrifty soul resisted me when I demanded every clean handkerchief he possessed. Her sense of proportion was inadequate and her need for sympathy untimely. As I was hurrying across the room to do him some small service, I found her in my way. She clasped her hands and spoke in her beautifully modulated voice. "Figure to yourself Mr. Wells, what it must mean to me, to see my poor Georges like this!"

I restrained myself by an effort. "You are tired out," I said. "You must go to bed. He will be safe now with the nurse and me."

And I put her gently but firmly out of the room....

So ended all that flimsy inordinate stir of grey matter that was George Gissing. He was a pessimistic writer. He spent his big fine brain depreciating life, because he would not and perhaps could not look life squarely in the eyes,—neither his circumstances nor the conventions about him nor the adverse things about him nor the limitations of his personal character. But whether it was nature or education that made this tragedy I cannot tell.

§ 4. NEW ROMNEY AND SANDGATE (1898)

I came back from Italy to Worcester Park in the summer of 1898, on the verge of the last bout of illness in my life before my health cleared up, quite unaware of the collapse that hung over me. I ascribed a general sense of malaise, an inability to stick to my work—I was then writing *Love and Mr. Lewisham*—to want of exercise and so the greater my lassitude the more I forced myself to exertion. What was happening was a sort of break-up of the scars and old clotted accumulations about my crushed kidney, and nothing could have been worse for me than to start, as we did, upon a cycling journey to the south coast. I was ashamed of my bodily discomfort—until I was over forty the sense of physical inferiority was a constant acute distress to me which no philosophy could mitigate—and I plugged along with a head that seemed filled with wool and a skin that felt like a misfit. Somewhere on the road I caught a cold.

We struggled to Lewes and then on to Seaford. We decided I must really be overdoing this exercise and we went into lodgings for a rest. All this is brought back to me by the hieroglyphics of the picshuas. Here under date of July 29th is one of them. Our sitting-room was evidently furnished with unrestrained piety. We were physically unhappy and our discomfort breaks out in hatred of our fellow visitors to Seaford. Jane has complained that she is dull. Some forgotten joke about a hat is traceable; I fancy I may have used her hat as a waste-paper basket; and noises (buniks) upstairs are afflicting me. By way of rest I am struggling to complete *Love and Mr. Lewisham*. Whenever I felt ill I became urgent to finish whatever book I was working on, because while a book unfinished would have been worth nothing, a finished book now meant several hundred pounds. Before going to Rome I had already scamped the finish of *When the Sleeper Wakes* (which afterwards I rechristened in better English *When the Sleeper Awakes*) and I came near to scamping *Love and Mr. Lewisham*. But the suppuration that was going on in my now aching side, was too rapid to allow that. *Love and Mr. Lewisham* was finished with much care and elaboration some months later. My erring kidney began apparently to secrete ink. Jane, after brooding over my condition, was struck by an idea and went out and bought a clinical thermometer. We found my temperature had mounted to 102 F.

Picshua: July 29th, 1898.

We had no established doctor but I had met a friend of Gissing's, Henry Hick, who was medical officer of health for Romney Marsh and who had asked us to stay a night with him in the course of our cycling tour. New Romney seemed close at hand, we exchanged telegrams and I went to him at once by little cross country lines and several changes of train. I was now in considerable pain, the jolting carriages seemed malignantly uncomfortable, I suffered from intense thirst, I could get nothing to drink and the journey was interminable. With an unfaltering gentleness and no sign of dismay, Jane steered this peevish bundle of suffering that had once been her "Mr. Binder" to its destination. Hick was a good man at diagnosis and he did me well. An operation seemed indicated and he put me to bed and starved me down to make the trouble more accessible to the scalpel, but when the surgeon came from London it was decided that the offending kidney had practically taken itself off and that there was nothing left to remove. Thereupon I began to recover and after a few years of interrogative suspense and occasional pain not even a reminiscent twinge remained of my left kidney.

I find the picshuas resume after a couple of months. Before October I did some little drawings as I lay in bed, and amused myself by colouring them and these I think prevented the immediate resumption of the picshua diary. Mrs. Hick had just presented the world with a daughter; I became her godfather and began an elaborate illustrated story dedicated to this young lady called *The Story of Tommy and the Elephant*. This little book was preserved, and years afterwards when my god-daughter needed some money to set up as a medical practitioner she sold it and the copyright with my assent, and it was published in facsimile. It had an artless quaintness that pleased people and it did well and still sells as a Christmas present book.

On October 5th the picshuas testify that I hatched out a new project called *Kipps*, and completed *Love and Mr. Lewisham*. By this time I had left Hick's helpful home and was, in a rather invalidish fashion, taking up my work again. I had been driven in a comfortable carriage to Sandgate and after a week or so in a boarding house we had installed ourselves in a little furnished house called Beach Cottage. Hick did not think it advisable for me to go back to Worcester Park and I never entered that house again.

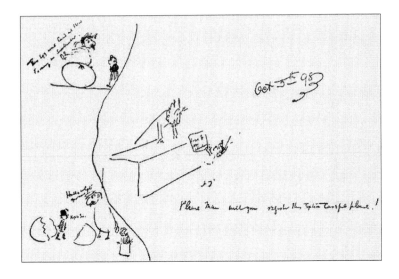

Picshua: October 5th, 1898.

On October 8th there seems to have been a bout of drawing
to put all the momentous events of the previous two months on
record. The picshuas recall a score of particulars that I should
otherwise have forgotten completely. I am reminded of a "horrid
medicine," and that I began to drink Contrexeville water, and
there is a vivid rendering of Jane's dismay at a possible operation,
while Hick and the specialist discuss my case. I think that Jane
looking at the knife and saying "Wow" marks one of the high
points of my peculiar artistic method. I assume my first dressing
gown, I get up, leaning heavily on Jane, I gambol (galumph) to
her great alarm, and she takes me out to the sea front in a bath
chair. Then as my strength returns and I can run alone, Jane
takes to sea bathing (in a costume that "dates") and I buy a new
cotton hat—"not a halo this time after all."

Picshua: October 8th, 1898. Reminiscences Of August 1898.

The next drawing records merely the interruption of a picnic by intrusive cows during the period of recovery. Jane was never afraid of death, I have seen her twice when she thought she would be killed and she was quite steady, but she was town bred and she did not like cows. She distrusted these kind fragrant animals.

*Picshua: October 8th, 1898. Reminiscences
of New Romney in September.*

The next picshua records that we amused ourselves by shooting
with an air gun, and then there began the serious business of
finding a new0 Accordng to the best advice available, a long
period of invalidism was before me. I had to reconcile myself to
complete exile from London, and contrive to live in dry air with
no damp in the subsoil and in as much sunshine as possible.

Picshua: October 8th, 1898. Bits The Cow Girl. House Hunting.

Beach Cottage was a temporary refuge and so close to the sea that in rough weather the waves broke over the roof. Jane planted me there and then went off to pack up the furniture in Heatherlea and bring it down to an unfurnished house, Arnold House, into which we presently moved on a short lease, until we could find something better suited to our needs. That was difficult. Already in the picshuas given we are manifestly thinking of having to build a house and at last we decided to set about that adventure. I have already given a picshua of our removal from Beach Cottage to Arnold House in § 3 of Chapter Seven.

Picshua: October 8th, 1898.
Reminiscences Of September 24th, 1898.

A queer little incident in my illness which it would be ungrateful to omit, was the sudden appearance of Henry James and Edmund Gosse at New Romney, riding upon bicycles from the direction of Rye. They took tea with Dr. Hick and us and were very charming and friendly, and Jane and I were greatly flattered by their visit. It never dawned upon me that they had any but sociable motives in coming over to see me. And later on, when I was in Beach Cottage, J. M. Barrie came in to see me. I gathered he had taken it into his head to spend a day at the seaside and visit me. (There is a picshua in § 3 of Chapter Seven commemorating his visit.) Barrie talked slowly and wisely of this and that, but particularly of his early struggles and the difficulties of young writers. There were times when a little help might do much for a man who was down. It never entered my head that I myself might be considered "down" just then, and I argued the matter with him. Once a man borrowed or was subsidized, I said, the "go" went out of his work. It was a dangerous and perhaps a fatal thing to deprive a man's cheques of the sharp freshness of an unencumbered gain. "Perhaps you're right," meditated Barrie, and went on after a pause to tell of how when he first came to London he did not understand the nature of a cheque. "I just put them in a drawer and waited for the fellow to send me the real money," he said. "I didn't see the sense of them."

He helped himself to a buttered bun. "When first I came to London," he remarked, "I lived almost entirely on boons...."

The experience of later years has made me realize that in this way the Royal Literary Fund was making its enquiries about me, and that I was not so completely outside the range of assistance as I imagined. But I never had any assistance of that kind and at that time I did not want it. I was now some hundreds of pounds on the solvent side and thinking of building a house with my balance. I knew nothing of investment and having a house of my own seemed as good a use for savings as I could imagine.

§ 5. EDIFYING ENCOUNTERS.
SOME TYPES OF PERSONA; AND TEMPERAMENTAL
ATTITUDE (1897-1910)

I had a three years' agreement for Arnold House and I stayed out my full time in it, gradually rebuilding my overstrained body and recovering resisting power to colds and suchlike infections. It was a semi-detached villa and it had a long narrow strip of grass which ended in a hedge of tamarisk along the sea wall. Upon the beach one day the *Sea Lady* appeared, very lovely in a close fitting bathing dress and with the sunlight in her hair, and took possession of my writing desk.

Our next door neighbours were a very pleasant couple named Popham, small rentiers with cultivated tastes who read well and thought of doing something to mend the world. They were the children of that serious Nonconformity which founded so many sound businesses in the mid Victorian epoch, turned them into honest joint-stock companies and left its children just independent enough to travel, trifle with the Arts and supply the backbone of the new British intelligentsia. The Pophams were always handy to play with. They taught me to swim, so far as I have ever learnt to swim, we moored a raft twenty or thirty yards from shore and I struggled out to it, and I found Popham as good a companion as Bowkett for long bicycle rides into Kent. Mrs. Popham was a sister-in-law of Graham Wallas whom I had already heard speaking in the old days in William Morris's greenhouse meetings. Presently he came down to Sandgate with his wife and we found we had a lot to talk about together.

Wallas was a rather slovenly, slightly pedantic, noble-spirited man and I cannot measure justly the influence of the disinterested life he led on my own. It was I think very considerable. The Wallases, the Oliviers and the Webbs were quite the best of the leading Fabians—Shaw I refuse to count as a typical Fabian; they lived lives devoted to the Res Publica right out to the end of their days. They took the idea of getting a living as something by the way; a sort of living was there for them anyhow; and the real business of life began for them only after that had been settled and put on one side.

From what I have told of myself it must be plain that in those days I was full of mercenary *go*; "price per thousand" and "saleable copy" were as present in my mind as they are in the picshuas I have shown. My commercialism is not, I think, innate, but my fight with the world for Jane and myself and my family, had set a premium upon money making. I was beginning to like the sport. I was beginning to enjoy being able to pay for things. I was getting rather keen on my literary reputation as a saleable asset. It was as good for my mind as uninfected mountain air in an early case of tuberculosis to go for walks with Wallas, worlds away from any thought of prices, agents, serializations, "rights." We even went off to Switzerland together for a couple of weeks and walked among the passes of Valais, over the Gemmi, over the Aletsch Glacier to Bel Alp, up to Zermatt, up the Furka, over the St. Gotthard, talking.

Essentially Wallas was a talker and a lecturer. He liked picking a case to pieces with a quiet fastidious deliberation far more than he liked the labour of putting things together. My journalistic experiences since my student days had bitten into me the primary need of sending in copy in time or even a little in advance of time. All my life I have been "delivering the goods" even if the packing has been hasty and the execution scampered at any rate, if not actually*scamped*. The habit is ingrained. I had meant to loiter over this autobiography for years—and perhaps not publish it in the end. I sketched an opening for it two years ago. And here it is being pressed to a finish. But the bad side of Wallas's rentier unworldliness was that he was under no inner compulsion to get things positively done. If he had not had very definite academic ambitions and a real joy in answering questions, he might have sunken altogether into sterile erudite wisdom. As it is, the

London School of Economics will testify how much the personal Graham Wallas outdid the published Graham Wallas. Alfred Zimmern and Walter Lippmann were among his particular pupils and there is scarcely any considerable figure among the younger generation of publicists who does not owe something to his slow, fussy, mannered, penetrating and inspiring counsels. He was a classical scholar, but Hellenic rather than Roman—in contrast to Gissing—a Platonist and not a Homerist. His grasp upon modern scientific philosophy was a firm one.

Our Swiss conversations centred upon our common feeling that there had to be some firmer basis, a better thought-out system of ideas, for social and political activities than was available at that time. He had been greatly impressed by the book of Professor Ostrogorski on *Democracy and the Organization of Political Parties* (1902). It was an early break towards realism in political science. It swept aside legist conceptions of government by a frank treatment of parliamentary actuality. It was plain to Wallas that realistic acid might be made to bite still deeper into political conventionality. He wanted to make a psychological examination of mass- political reactions the new basis for a revision of governmental theory, and he thought of calling this study "A Prolegomenon to Politics." Finally he produced it as *Human Nature in Politics* (1908). Walter Lippmann, under his inspiration, produced *A Preface to Politics*, and the Alpine sunlight of that mental hike of ours is also very evident in my own *Modern Utopia* (1905). We were all branching out in characteristic directions from the Ostrogorski stimulus.

Wallas and I never lost contact completely. Within a few months of his death (1932) he was in my study reading and commenting very illuminatingly and usefully upon the political chapters of my *Work, Wealth and Happiness of Mankind*. He had been reading a good deal of Bentham at that time, digging out long forgotten books, and I remember his glasses gleaming appreciatively as he squatted in my lowest easy chair and dilated on the "old boy's" abundance and breadth of range. Bentham, too, had been a sort of encyclopædist. I do not think Wallas wrote anything about this aspect of Bentham, though I know he dealt with him largely in his lectures on local government; he was just going over him for pleasure, gathering a bright nosegay of characteristic ideas—to be presently dropped by the wayside.

Somewhere between my own tendency to push on to conclusions and Wallas's interminable deliberation, lies I suppose the ideal method of the perfect student working "without haste and without delay."

My opinion of the texture and mental forms of the brain of Graham Wallas was very high, and I formed an almost equal respect for the intelligence of another of those early Fabians, Sydney Olivier who became Lord Olivier. Both the Webbs also I found very good, if antagonistic, stuff. Beatrice had (and has) a delightful way that is all her own, of throwing out bold general propositions about things in the most aggressive manner possible. I should call her style of talk experimental dogmatism. If you disagree, you say "Oh Nonsense!" and restate her proposition in a corrected form. Then she fights with unscrupulous candour and invincible good temper. Sidney is not nearly so exploratory; his convictions are less vivid and plastic; his aim is rather persuasion than truth, he is politic rather than philosophical. Of Shaw's mind I have already given an impression.

In my account of *fin-de-siècle* socialism I have criticized the peculiar limitations of pseudo "practicality" and anti-Utopianism that went with the academic and civil-service associations of the Fabian group. In particular I have shown how they shirked and delayed the problem of the competent receiver. Here I am dealing not so much with these ideological limitations with which I presently fell foul, as with their pervading sense of the importance of social service as the frame of life, and the way in which Jane and I were probably influenced by them. We may have had that in us from the beginning, Jane particularly, but they brought it out in us. They may have done much to deflect me from the drift towards a successful, merely literary career into which I was manifestly falling in those early Sandgate days. I might have become entirely an artist and a literary careerist and possibly a distinguished one, and then my old friend Osborn of the *National Observer*, the *Morning Post* and "Boon" would never have had occasion to call my books "sociological cocktails."

A much more tawdry brain in the Fabian constellation which played its part in teaching me about human reactions was that of Hubert Bland. As my personal acquaintances with the Fabians extended we found the Blands had a house at Dymchurch, within an easy bicycle ride of us, to which they came in summertime. They were the strangest of couples and they played a large part in the Fabian comedy. Doris Langley Moore has recently given a very frank account of them in her excellent life of Mrs. Bland (*E. Nesbit* 1933), to which I make my acknowledgments. E. Nesbit was a tall, whimsical, restless, able woman who had been very beautiful and was still very good-looking; and Bland was a thick-set, broad-faced aggressive man, a sort of Tom-cat man, with a tenoring voice and a black ribboned monocle and a general disposition to dress and live up to that. The two of them dramatized life and I had as yet met few people who did that. They loved scenes and "situations." They really enjoyed strong emotion. There was no such persistent pursuit of truth and constructive ends in them as in their finer associates. It was not in their imaginative scheme.

Much of her activity went into the writing of verse, rather insincere verse, rather sentimental stories for adults and quite admirable tales for children. The Bastable family she created is still a joy to little people between ten and seventeen. She earned the greater part of the joint income. She ran a great easy-going hospitable Bohemian household at Well Hall, Eltham, an old moated house with a walled garden. Those who loved her and those who wished to please her called her royally "Madame" or "Duchess," and she had a touch of aloof authority which justified that. A miscellany of people came and went there and to lodgings handy-by the smaller house at Dymchurch; the Chesterton brothers, Laurence Housman, Enid Bagnold, Horace Horsnell, Arthur Watts, Oswald Barren, Edgar Jepson, Alfred Sutro, Berta Ruck, Jack Squire, Clifford Sharp, Monseigneur Benson, Frederick Rolfe (Baron Corvo), a multitude of young writers, actors and aspirants in an atmosphere of talk, charades, mystifications and disputes. And there also I and Jane visited and learnt to play Badminton and gossip and discuss endlessly.

At first it seemed to be a simple agreeable multitudinousness from which literary buds and flowers sprang abundantly, presided over by this tall, engaging, restless, moody, humorous woman. Then gradually the visitor began to perceive at first unsuspected trends and threads of relationship and scented, as if from the moat, a more disturbing flavour. People came to Well Hall and went, and some of them went for good. There had been "misunderstandings."

I thought at first that Well Hall was a new group for us and now in the retrospect I realize that it was a new sort of world. It was a world of rôles and not of realities. Perhaps that is the more usual type of world, the sort of world in which people do not say "I am thus and thus," but "I will be thus and thus." From what I have told in the earlier part of this autobiography it is plain that my own people, my parents, brothers, aunt, cousin and so forth, and the people with whom I came in contact, were either very simple-minded people indeed or else they were people with the sustained and developed simplicity and coherence of scientific training or people with whom my contacts were simple and unrevealing. But the Blands were almost the first people I met at all intimately, who were fundamentally intricate, who had no primary simple idea. They had brains as active and powerful as most other brains in my world, but—as I began to realize only after some disconcerting experiences—they had never taken them down to any sort of philosophy; they had never focussed them on any single objective, and they started off at all sorts of levels from arbitrarily adopted fantasies and poses.

The incongruity of Bland's costume with his Bohemian setting, the costume of a city swell, top-hat, tail-coat, greys and blacks, white slips, spatterdashes and that black-ribboned monocle, might have told me, had I had the ability then to read such signs, of the general imagination at work in his *persona*, the myth of a great Man of the World, a Business Man (he had no gleam of business ability) invading for his own sage strong purposes this assembly of long-haired intellectuals. This myth had, I think, been developed and sustained in him, by the struggle of his egoism against the manifest fact that his wife had a brighter and fresher mind than himself, and had subtler and livelier friends. For many years, says Miss Moore, she carried on a long correspondence with Laurence Housman and I guess that Bland had had to protect his self-esteem against many such intimations of insufficiency in his own equipment. He could not pervade her. That particular correspondence, the biographer relates, was ended when E. Nesbit, against her character and disposition, followed Bland on the anti-feminist side of the suffrage dispute.

In the end she became rather a long-suffering lady, but her restless needle of a mind, her quick response, kept her always an exacting and elusive lady. It was I am convinced because she, in her general drift, was radical and anarchistic, that the pose of Bland's self-protection hardened into this form of gentlemanly conservatism. He presented himself as a Tory in grain, he became—I know of no confirmation—a man of good old family; he entered the dear old Roman Catholic church. These were all insistencies upon soundness and solidity as against her quickness and whim. He was publicly emphatic for social decorum, punctilio, the natural dependence of women and the purity of the family. None of your modern stuff for *him*.

All this socialism he assured you, so far as it was any good, was a reaction from nineteenth century liberalism to the good old social organization that flourished in England before the days of Adam Smith.

She acquiesced in these posturings. If she had not, I suppose he would have argued with her until she did, and he was a man of unfaltering voice and great determination. But a gay holiday spirit bubbled beneath her verbal orthodoxies and escaped into her work. The Bastables are an anarchistic lot. Her soul was against the government all the time.

This discordance of form and spirit lay on the surface of their lives. Most of us who went to them were from the first on the side of the quicksilver wife against the more commonplace, argumentative, cast-iron husband. Then gradually something else came into the *ensemble*. It came first to the visitor at Well Hall as chance whisperings, as flashes of conflict and fierce resentment, as raised voices in another room, a rush of feet down a passage and the banging of a door.

Miss Langley Moore in her careful and well informed book lays the whole story bare with many particulars I never knew before. There was a more primitive strand in Bland's make-up. He was under an inner compulsion to be a Seducer—on the best eighteenth century lines. That, and not Tory-Socialism, was his essential preoccupation; that was what he talked to himself about when he was in his own company. His imaginations may have been running into this mould before he met her, it is not a very rare mould, but the clash of their personalities confirmed the tendency. That I suppose was where he really got even with her wit and freaks and fantasies and with a certain essential physical coldness in her. And in return he gave her some romantically difficult situations. The astonished visitor came to realize that most of the children of the household were not E. Nesbit's but the results of Bland's conquests, that the friend and companion who ran the household was the mother of one of these young people, that young Miss so and so, who played Badminton with a preoccupied air was the last capture of Hubert's accomplished sex appeal. All this E. Nesbit not only detested and mitigated and tolerated, but presided over and I think found exceedingly interesting.

Everywhere fantastic concealments and conventions had been arranged to adjust these irregularities to Hubert's pose of ripe old gentility. You found after a time that Well Hall was not so much an atmosphere as a web.

In company, in public, Bland talked and wrote of social and political problems and debated with a barrister-like effectiveness, but when I was alone with him, the fundamental interest insisted upon coming to the surface. He felt my unspoken criticisms and I could not check his assertive apologetics. He would talk about it. He would give hints of his exceptional prowess. He would boast. He would discuss the social laxities of Woolwich and Blackheath, breaking into anecdotes, "simply for the purpose of illustration." Or he would produce a pocket-worn letter and read choice bits of it—"purely because of its psychological interest." He did his utmost to give this perpetual pursuit of furtive gratification, the dignity of a purpose. He was, he claimed to me at least, not so much Don Juan as Professor Juan. "I am a student, an experimentalist," he announced, "in illicit love."

"Illicit love"! It had to be "illicit" and that was the very gist of it for him. It had to be the centre of a system of jealousies, concealments, hidings, exposures, confrontations, sacrifices, incredible generosities—in a word, drama. What he seemed most to value was the glory of a passionate triumph over openness, reason and loyalty—and getting the better of the other fellow. The more complex the situation was, the better it was fitted for Bland's atmosphere.

It is curious how opposed this mentality of what I may call, the seventeenth and eighteenth century "Buck," is to the newer, rationalist, go-as-you-please of the Shelley type, to which my own mind was being attracted in those days. I wanted to abolish barriers between the sexes and Bland loved to get under or over or through them. The more barriers the better. In those days I would have made illicit love impossible—by making almost all love-making *licit*. There was no real inconsistency therefore between Bland's private life and his enthusiasm for formal conventionality and it was perfectly logical that though we were both disposed to great freedoms by the accepted standards, we were in diametrically antagonistic schools. He thought it made a love affair more exciting and important if one might be damned for it and I could not believe these pleasant intimacies could ever bring real damnation to anyone. He exalted chastity because so it meant a greater sacrifice, and I suppose he would have thought it a crowning achievement to commit incest or elope with a nun. He was sincerely disgusted at my disposition to take the moral fuss out of his darling sins. My impulses were all to get rid of the repressions of sexual love, minimize its importance and subordinate this stress between men and women as agreeably as possible to the business of mankind.

So now, with the detachment of half a lifetime, I define the forces that first attracted me to Well Hall and then made Well Hall jar upon me; but at that time I did not see so clearly and I found these two people and their atmosphere and their household of children and those who were entangled with them, baffling to an extreme degree. At the first encounter it had seemed so extraordinarily open and jolly. Then suddenly you encountered fierce resentment, you found Mrs. Bland inexplicably malignant; doors became walls so to speak and floors pitfalls. In that atmosphere you surprised yourself. It was like Alice through the Looking Glass; not only were there Mock Turtles and White Queens and Mad Hatters about, but you discovered with amazement that you were changing your own shape and stature.

The web of concealments and intrigue that radiated from the Bland ménage and met many other kindred if less intricate strands among that miscellany of enquiring and experimenting people which constituted the Fabian Society, spread like the mycelium of a fungus throughout that organization. The Blands were among the earliest founders of that "Fellowship of the New Life" from which the Fabian Society sprang. They were original members of the latter, and Bland, because he was neither the chief bread winner of his family nor restrained by any fundamental mental consistency nor preoccupied with any really ordered creative aims, was able to devote all the time and energy that could be spared from fluttering the Blackheath dovecotes, to Fabian manoeuvres. He was always there, just as dry old Quaker-trained Edward Pease, the salaried trustworthy secretary, was always there, and Pease was by nature a very honest desiccating pedant and Bland by nature a politician. Bland was as loose internally as Pease was rigid and they were inspired by a natural antagonism. The little society was setting out upon the most gigantic enterprise that humanity has ever attempted, a New Life (Think of it!) and even if that new life was restricted by subsequent provisos to economic reconstruction only, it still meant a vast long trying game of waiting and preparation; the society was not only poor, small and with everything to learn about its job, but from the very beginning it had these two personalities, like the germs of a congenital disease, vitiating and diverting its energies.

Long before my innocence came into the society, some deep feud between Pease and the Blands had established itself when Pease and not Bland became the salaried secretary; and the mysterious concealments, reservations, alliances, imputations, schemes and tactics of these obscure issues played havoc with the affairs of our middle-class socialist propaganda. The larger purposes of the Wallases, Webbs and Shaw had to defer continually to the dark riddle of "what the Blands will do about it." There was no reckoning without them for they turned up, excited and energetic, with satellites, dependents, confederates and new associates at every meeting. In the dusty confusion of personalities and secondary issues created by them, rumour moved darkly and anonymous letters flittered about like bats at twilight. By the time I came into the society Bland, the able politician, was established in the mind of Shaw, for example, as a necessary evil and Pease as an unavoidable ally. When Shaw faced towards social and political problems, this implacable animosity loomed so large for him that at times it blotted out the stars.

The topic of *Human Nature in Politics* (to borrow a title from Graham Wallas) is a vast one, and here was a hard specimen for my frustration and education. Following Ostrogorski, Wallas dealt with this trouble from the point of view of mass reactions, but now here I am approaching it—or rather blundering into it—from the opposite direction, by way of biography. What are we to do with these energetic vital types who will not subdue themselves to a broad and consistent aim; who choose a pose, stage situations, fly off at a tangent and never table their objectives? Shall we never be able to keep secondary issues and idiosyncrasies in their place? How far is it inevitable that we should live in a world of personal "misunderstandings"? How far is directive simplicity possible? What can be done to keep our public and social objectives untangled and simple and clear?

Before it had existed half a dozen years, the Fabian Society was in urgent need of a searching psycho-analysis, and there has never yet been a government or party, an educational directorate, or a religion that has not presently diverged into morasses of complication and self-contradiction. How far is that to be the case with us for ever?

How far might some more universal and more efficient education, more penetrating, better planned and better administered, have started and sustained our Fabian Society— every one of us well meaning—in a better understanding and a less wasteful co-operation? Were the complexities of Bland

and his wife, the intellectual freakishness of Shaw, the intricate cross-purposes of that bunch of animated folk, unavoidable and incurable?

The Federation of the New Life passed like a dreamer's sigh, but within some fated term of years, unless mankind is to perish, there must be a real Federation of the New Life. I find myself on the verge here of slipping away from my already sufficiently copious autobiographical purpose into what might prove a limitless dissertation on human behaviour, a sort of outline, a digest, of all available biography. It is time to recall my enquiring pen—as one calls a roving dog to heel—and return to my personal story, to return from cosmo-biography to autobiography, and to go on telling how I, at any rate, in spite of all those deflections and entanglements, found at last a satisfactory simplification and orientation of my own existence in the idea of an educational, political and economic world unification.

Of that mental and moral consolidation my last chapter must tell. In the early Sandgate days not only was I being attracted more and more powerfully towards the civil service conception of a life framed in devotion to constructive public ends à la Webb, but I was also being tugged, though with less force, in a quite opposite direction, towards the artistic attitude. I have never been able to find the artistic attitude fundamentally justifiable but I understand and sympathize with the case for it. It was expressed in varying modes and very engagingly by a number of brains through whose orbits my own was travelling. Professor York Powell had come to know me, through the Marriott Watsons and the *Pall Mall Gazette* group, and he was very strong in his assertion that the "artist" lived in a class apart, having a primary and over-riding duty to his "gift." He might be solvent if he liked and political in his off time, but his primary duty was to express the divine juice that was in him.

York Powell, a big bearded man with a deep abundant chuckle, came very frequently to Sandgate, where he had an old gnarled boatman friend, who was something of a character, Jim Payne. I did my best to be initiated by York Powell into the charms of sea-fishing and a sort of tarry wisdom peculiar to Jim Payne, but the inoculation never really took. York Powell was always trying to draw Jim out for my benefit and Jim was harder to draw out than a badger. I never saw him drawn.

To a lodging in Sandgate also came Bob Stevenson, the "Spring- Heeled Jack" of his cousin Robert Louis' *Talk and Talkers*, after a stroke, for the ending of his days. I had known him before his illness and had heard him do some marvellous talks; a dissertation upon how he would behave if he was left nearly two millions, still lingers in my mind. One million was just to keep—one could never bear to break a single million—but all the rest was to be spent and distributed magnificently. He described his dinner before his benefactions began. He was particular about a large deed-box full of cheque books to be brought to him by bank messengers "in scarlet coats with *new* gold bands round their top hats." He chose among his friends those whose presence and advice would be most conducive to wise and generous giving. He planned the most ingenious gifts and the most remarkable endowments. I have tried to give a faint impression of his style of imaginative talking in Ewart's talk about the City of Women in *Tono Bungay*. But Ewart is not even a caricature of Bob; only Bob's style of talk was grafted on to him. Bob Stevenson, like York Powell, was all on the side of aesthetic concentration and letting the rest go hang. He could not imagine what these Fabians were up to. They were not real in his universe.

Henry James, too, had developed expressionism into an elaborate philosophy; it is a great loss to the science of criticism that he should have died before his slowly unfolding autobiography reached a point where he could state his mature attitude. In several talks we hovered on the abundant verge of it but even the evenings at Lamb House were too short for anything but intimations and preliminaries.

Another very important acquaintance of my early Sandgate time, now too little appreciated in the world, was the American Stephen Crane. He was one of the earliest of those stark American writers who broke away from the genteel literary traditions of Victorian England and he wrote an admirable bare prose. One or two of his short stories, *The Open Boat*, for example, seem to me imperishable gems. He made his reputation with a short book about the Civil War,*The Red Badge of Courage*. It was an amazing feat of imaginative understanding. It was written, as Ambrose Bierce said, not with ink but blood. And forthwith the American newspapers pounced upon him to make him a war correspondent. He was commissioned to go to Cuba, to the Spanish-American war and to the Turko-Greek war of 1897. He was a lean, blond, slow-speaking, perceptive, fragile, tuberculous being, too adventurous to be temperate with anything and impracticable to an extreme degree. He liked to sit and talk, sagely and deeply. How he managed ever to get to the seats of war to which he was sent I cannot imagine. I don't think he got very deeply into them. But he got deeply enough into them to shatter his health completely.

In Greece he met and married an energetic lady who had been sent out by some American newspaper as the first woman war correspondent. With, perhaps, excessive vigour she set out to give her ailing young husband a real good time. Morton Frewen (the wealthy father of Clare Sheridan) lent them a very old and beautiful house, Brede House near Rye and there they inaugurated a life of gay extravagance and open hospitality. I forget the exact circumstances of our first meeting but I remember very vividly a marvellous Christmas Party in which Jane and I participated. We were urged to come over and, in a postscript, to bring any bedding and blankets we could spare. We arrived in a heaped-up Sandgate cab, rather in advance of the guests from London. We were given a room over the main gateway in which there was a portcullis and an owl's nest, but at least we got a room. Nobody else did—because although some thirty or forty invitations had been issued, there were not as a matter of fact more than three or four bedrooms available. One of them however was large and its normal furniture had been supplemented by a number of hired truckle-beds and christened the Girls' Dormitory, and in the attic an array of shake-downs was provided for the men. Husbands and wives were torn apart.

Later on we realized that the sanitary equipment of Brede House dated from the seventeenth century, an interesting historical detail, and such as there was indoors, was accessible only through the Girls' Dormitory. Consequently the wintry countryside next morning was dotted with wandering melancholy, preoccupied, men guests.

Anyhow there were good open fires in the great fireplaces and I remember that party as an extraordinary lark—but shot, at the close, with red intimations of a coming tragedy. We danced in a big oak-panelled room downstairs, lit by candles stuck upon iron sconces that Cora Crane had improvised with the help of the Brede blacksmith. Unfortunately she had not improvised grease guards and after a time everybody's back showed a patch of composite candle-wax, like the flash on the coat of a Welsh Fusilier. When we were not dancing or romping we were waxing the floor or rehearsing a play vamped up by A. E. W. Mason, Crane, myself and others. It was a ghost play, and very allusive and fragmentary, and we gave it in the School Room at Brede. It amused its authors and cast vastly. What the Brede people made of it is not on record.

We revelled until two or three every night and came down towards mid-day to breakfasts of eggs and bacon, sweet potatoes from America and beer. Crane had a transient impulse to teach some of the men poker, in the small hours, but we would not take it seriously. Mason I found knew my old schoolfellow Sidney Bowkett and had some anecdotes to tell me about him. "In any decent saloon in America," said Crane, "you'd be shot for talking like that at poker," and abandoned our instruction in a pet.

That was the setting in which I remember Crane. He was profoundly weary and ill, if I had been wise enough to see it, but I thought him sulky and reserved. He was essentially the helpless artist; he wasn't the master of his party, he wasn't the master of his home; his life was altogether out of control; he was being carried along. What he was still clinging to, but with a dwindling zest, was artistry. He had an intense receptiveness to vivid work; he had an inevitably right instinct for the word in his stories; but he had no critical chatter. We compared our impressions of various contemporaries. "That's Great," he'd say or simply "*Gaw!*" Was so and so "any good"? So and so was "no good."

Was he writing anything now?

His response was joyless. Pinker the agent had *fixed* some stories for him. "I got to do them," he said, "I got to do them."

The tragic entanglement of the highly specialized artist had come to him. Sensation and expression—and with him it had been well nigh perfect expression—was the supreme joy of his life and the justification of existence for him. And here he was, in a medley of impulsive disproportionate expenditure, being pursued by the worthy Pinker with enquiries of when he could "deliver copy" and warnings not to overrun his length. The good thing in his life had slipped by him.

In the night after the play Mrs. Crane came to us. He had had a haemorrhage from his lungs and he had tried to conceal it from her. He "didn't want anyone to bother." Would I help get a doctor?

There was a bicycle in the place and my last clear memory of that fantastic Brede House party is riding out of the cold skirts of a wintry night into a drizzling dawn along a wet road to call up a doctor in Rye.

That crisis passed, but he died later in the new year, 1900. He did his utmost to conceal his symptoms and get on with his dying. Only at the end did his wife wake up to what was coming.

She made a great effort to get him to Baden-Baden. She conveyed him silent and sunken and stoical to Folkestone by car, regardless of expense, she had chartered a special train to wait for him at Boulogne and he died almost as soon as he arrived in Germany.

Two other important men of letters were also close at hand to present the ideal of pure artistry to me rather less congenially. These were Ford Madox Hueffer and Joseph Conrad, of whom the former—through certain defects of character and a copious carelessness of reminiscence—is, I think, too much neglected, and the latter still placed too high in the scale of literary achievement. Joseph Conrad was really Teodor Jozef Konrad Korzeniowski. He had very wisely dropped his surname and was content to be Joseph Conrad to English readers. He had been excited by a review I wrote of his *Almayer's Folly* in the *Saturday Review*; it was his first "important" recognition and he became anxious to make my acquaintance.

At first he impressed me, as he impressed Henry James, as the strangest of creatures. He was rather short and round-shouldered with his head as it were sunken into his body. He had a dark retreating face with a very carefully trimmed and pointed beard, a trouble-wrinkled forehead and very troubled dark eyes, and the gestures of his hands and arms were from the shoulders and very Oriental indeed. He reminded people of Du Maurier's Svengali and, in the nautical trimness of his costume, of Cutliffe Hyne's Captain Kettle. He spoke English strangely. Not badly altogether; he would supplement his vocabulary—especially if he were discussing cultural or political matters—with French words; but with certain oddities. He had learnt to read English long before he spoke it and he had formed wrong sound impressions of many familiar words; he had for example acquired an incurable tendency to pronounce the last *e* in these and those. He would say, "*Wat* shall we do with *thesa* things?" And he was always incalculable about the use of "shall" and "will." When he talked of seafaring his terminology was excellent but when he turned to less familiar topics he was often at a loss for phrases.

Yet he wove an extraordinarily rich descriptive English prose, a new sort of English of his own, conspicuously and almost necessarily free from stereotyped expressions and hack phrases, in which foreign turns and phrases interlaced with unusual native words unusually used. And I think it was this fine, fresh, careful, slightly exotic quality about his prose, that "foreign" flavour which the normal Anglo-Saxon mind habitually associates with culture, that blinded criticism to the essentially sentimental and melodramatic character of the stories he told. His deepest theme is the simple terror of strange places, of the jungle, of night, of the incalculable sea; as a mariner his life was surely a perpetual anxiety about miscalculations, about the hidden structural vices of his ship, about shifting cargo and untrustworthy men; he laid bare with an air of discovery what most adventurers, travellers and sailors habitually suppress. Another primary topic with him—best treated in that amazingly good story *Amy Foster,* a sort of caricature autobiography, was the feeling of being incurably "foreign." He pursued a phantom "honour"—in *Lord Jim* for instance; his humour in *The Nigger of the Narcissus,* is dismal, and you may search his work from end to end and find little tenderness and no trace of experienced love or affection. But he had set himself to be a great writer, an artist in words, and to achieve all the recognition and distinction that he imagined should go with that ambition, he had gone literary with a singleness and intensity of purpose that made the kindred concentration of Henry James seem lax and large and pale. *The Mirror of the Sea* was his favourite among his own writings, and I think that in that he showed a sound critical judgment.

He came into my ken in association with Ford Madox Hueffer and they remain together, contrasted and inseparable, in my memory. Ford is a long blond with a drawling manner, the very spit of his brother Oliver, and oddly resembling George Moore the novelist in pose and person. What he is really or if he is really, nobody knows now and he least of all; he has become a great system of assumed *personas* and dramatized selves. His brain is an exceptionally good one and when first he came along, he had cast himself for the rôle of a very gifted scion of the Pre-Raphaelite stem, given over to artistic purposes and a little undecided between music, poetry, criticism, The Novel, Thoreau-istic horticulture and the simple appreciation of life. He has written some admirable verse, some very good historical romances, two or three books in conjunction with Conrad, and a considerable bulk of more or less autobiographical—unreality. As a sort of heir to Pre-Raphaelitism, he owned among other things a farm called the Pent at the foot of the Downs above Hythe; it had been occupied previously by Christina Rossetti and Walter Crane the artist; and he had let it to Conrad; Conrad wrote about *The Heart of Darkness* and *The Secret Agent* on a desk that may have creaked to the creative effort of *Goblin Market*; and thither Hueffer and I walked to our meeting.

One goes downhill to the Pent, the windows of the house are low and my first impression of Conrad, was of a swarthy face peering out and up through the little window panes.

He talked with me mostly of adventure and dangers, Hueffer talked criticism and style and words, and our encounter was the beginning of a long, fairly friendly but always rather strained acquaintance. Conrad with Mrs. Conrad and his small blond haired bright-eyed boy, would come over to Sandgate, cracking a whip along the road, driving a little black pony carriage as though it was a droshky and encouraging a puzzled little Kentish pony with loud cries and endearments in Polish, to the dismay of all beholders. We never really "got on" together. I was perhaps more unsympathetic and incomprehensible to Conrad than he was to me. I think he found me Philistine, stupid and intensely English; he was incredulous that I could take social and political issues seriously; he was always trying to penetrate below my foundations, discover my imaginative obsessions and see what I was really up to. The frequent carelessness of my writing, my scientific qualifications of statement and provisional inconclusiveness, and my indifference to intensity of effect, perplexed and irritated him. Why didn't I *write*? Why had I no care for my reputation?

"My dear Wells, what is this *Love and Mr. Lewisham about*?" he would ask. But then he would ask also, wringing his hands and wrinkling his forehead, "What is all this about Jane Austen? What is there *in* her? What is it all *about*?"

I remember a dispute we had one day as we lay on the Sandgate beach and looked out to sea. How, he demanded, would I describe how that boat out there, sat or rode or danced or quivered on the water? I said that in nineteen cases out of twenty I would just let the boat be there in the commonest phrases possible. Unless I wanted the boat to be important I would not give it an outstanding phrase and if I wanted to make it important then the phrase to use would depend on the angle at which the boat became significant. But it was all against Conrad's over-sensitized receptivity that a boat could ever be just a boat. He wanted to see it with a definite vividness of his own. But I wanted to see it and to see it only in relation to something else—a story, a thesis. And I suppose if I had been pressed about it I would have betrayed a disposition to link that story or thesis to something still more extensive and that to something still more extensive and so ultimately to link it up to my philosophy and my world outlook.

Now here perhaps—if I may deal with Conrad and others and myself as hand specimens—is something rather fundamental for the educationist. I have told in my account of my school days (Ch. 3 §1) how I differed from my schoolmate Sidney Bowkett, in that he felt and heard and saw so much more vividly, so much more emotionally, than I did. That gave him superiorities in many directions, but the very coldness and flatness of my perceptions, gave me a readier apprehension of relationships, put me ahead of him in mathematics and drawing (which after all is a sort of abstraction of form) and made it easier for me later on to grasp general ideas in biology and physics. My education at Kensington was very broad and rapid, I suggest, because I was not dealing with burning and glowing impressions—and when I came to a course where sense impressions were of primary importance, as they were in the course in mineralogy (see Ch. 5 §3), I gave way to irrepressible boredom and fell down. My mind became what I call an educated mind, that is to say a mind systematically unified, because of my relative defect in brightness of response. I was easy to educate.

These vivid writers I was now beginning to encounter were, on the contrary, hard to educate—as I use the word educate. They were at an opposite pole to me as regards strength of reception. Their abundant, luminous impressions were vastly more difficult to subdue to a disciplined and co-ordinating relationship than mine. They remained therefore abundant but uneducated brains. Instead of being based on a central philosophy, they started off at a dozen points; they were impulsive, unco-ordinated, wilful. Conrad, you see, I count uneducated, Stephen Crane, Henry James, the larger part of the world of literary artistry. Shaw's education I have already impugned. The science and art of education was not adequate for the taming and full utilization of these more powerfully receptive types and they lapsed into arbitrary inconsistent and dramatized ways of thinking and living. With a more expert and scientific educational process all that might have been different. They lapsed—though retaining their distinctive scale and quality—towards the inner arbitrariness and unreality of the untrained common man.

Not only was I relatively equipped with a strong bias for rational associations but, also, accident threw me in my receptive years mostly among non-dramatizing systematic-minded people. My mother dramatized herself, indeed, but so artlessly that I rebelled against that. My scientific training and teaching confirmed and equipped all my inherent tendency to get things ruthlessly mapped out and consistent. I suspected any imaginative romancing in conduct. I defended myself against romancing by my continual self-mockery and caricature—what you see in this book therefore as a sort of bloom of little sketches is not really an efflorescence but something very fundamental to this brain-story. I am holding myself down from pretentious impersonations. But they were there, trying to get me. A man is revealed by the nature of his mockeries.

Such mentalities as my wife, Graham Wallas and the Webbs, and the general Socialist proposition, did much to sustain the educational consolidation that was going on in me. So that by the time I encountered such vigorously dramatizing people as the Blands and such vivid impressionists as Conrad I was already built up and set in the most refractory and comprehensive forms of conviction. I had struggled with a considerable measure of success against the common vice of self-protective assumptions. I had, I have, few "complexes." I would almost define education as the prevention of complexes. I was seeing myself as far as possible without pretences, my *persona* was under constant scrutiny, even at the price of private and secret sessions of humiliation, and not only was I trying to avoid posing to myself but I kept up as little pose as possible to the world. I eschewed dignity. I found therefore something as ridiculous in Conrad's *persona* of a romantic adventurous un-mercenary intensely artistic European gentleman carrying an exquisite code of unblemished honour through a universe of baseness as I did in Hubert Bland's man-of-affairs costume and simple Catholic piety.

When Conrad first met Shaw in my house, Shaw talked with his customary freedoms. "You know, my dear fellow, your books won't *do*"—for some Shavian reason I have forgotten—and so forth.

I went out of the room and suddenly found Conrad on my

heels, swift and white-faced. "Does that man want to *insult*me?" he demanded.

The provocation to say "Yes" and assist at the subsequent duel was very great, but I overcame it. "It's humour," I said, and took Conrad out into the garden to cool. One could always baffle Conrad by saying "humour." It was one of our damned English tricks he had never learnt to tackle.

Later on he wanted Ford Madox Hueffer to challenge me. If Conrad had had his way, either Hueffer's blood or mine would have reddened Dymchurch sands. I thought an article Hueffer had written about Hall Caine was undignified and I said that he had written it as if he was a discharged valet—or something equally pungent. Hueffer came over to tell me about it. "I tried to explain to him that duelling isn't done," said Hueffer.

In those days Hueffer was very much on the rational side of life; his extraordinary drift towards self-dramatization—when he even changed his name to Captain Ford—became conspicuous only later, after the stresses of the war. In the light of that his last book, *It Was the Nightingale*, is well worth reading. I think Conrad owed a very great deal to their early association; Hueffer helped greatly to "English" him and his idiom, threw remarkable lights on the English literary world for him, collaborated with him on two occasions, and conversed interminably with him about the precise word and about perfection in writing.

They forced me to consider and define my own position in such matters. Did I really care for these things? I like turning a phrase as well as any man, I try my utmost to achieve precision of statement where precision is important, and some passages of mine, the opening sections (§§1-4) in the chapter on "How Man Has Learnt to Think" in the*Work, Wealth and Happiness of Mankind* for instance, I rewrote a dozen times. But I have a feeling that the happy word is the gift, the momentary capricious gift of the gods a flash of mother-wit. You cannot *train* for it; you cannot write well and forcibly without at times writing flatly, and the real quality of a writer is, like divinity, inalienable. This incessant endeavour to keep prose bristling up and have it "vivid" all the time defeats its end. I find very much of Conrad oppressive, as overwrought as an Indian tracery, and it is only in chosen passages and some of his short stories that I would put his work on a level with the naked vigour of Stephen Crane. I think Tomlinson's more loosely written *By Sea and Jungle* is more finely felt and conveys an intenser vision than most of Conrad's sea and jungle pieces.

All this talk that I had with Conrad and Hueffer and James about the just word, the perfect expression, about this or that being "written" or not written, bothered me, set me interrogating myself, threw me into a heart-searching defensive attitude. I will not pretend that I got it clear all at once, that I was not deflected by their criticisms and that I did not fluctuate and make attempts to come up to their unsystematized, mysterious and elusive standards. But in the end I revolted altogether and refused to play their game. "I am a journalist," I declared, "I refuse to play the 'artist.' If sometimes I am an artist it is a freak of the gods. I am journalist all the time and what I write *goes now*—and will presently die."

I have stuck to that declaration ever since. I write as I walk because I want to get somewhere and I write as straight as I can, just as I walk as straight as I can, because that is the best way to get there. So I came down off the fence between Conrad and Wallas and I remain definitely on the side opposed to the aesthetic valuation of literature. That valuation is at best a personal response, a floating and indefinable judgment. All these receptive critics pose for their work. They dress their souls before the glass, add a few final touches of make-up and sally forth like old bucks for fresh "adventures among masterpieces." I come upon masterpieces by pure chance; they happen to me and I do not worry about what I miss.

Throughout my life, a main strand of interest has been the

endeavour to anchor *personas* to a common conception of reality. That is the structural idea of my *Research Magnificent*. I shall tell more of that endeavour in the next chapter. But this theme of the floating *persona*, the dramatized self, recurs at various levels of complexity and self-deception, in Mr. Hoopdriver in *The Wheels of Chance*, in the dreams of Mr. Parham, in *Christina Alberta's Father*, and most elaborately of all, in *The Bulpington of Blup*. This last is a very direct caricature study of the irresponsible disconnected aesthetic mentality. It is friendship's offering to the world of letters from the scientific side. E. Nesbit, by the bye, did some short stories in which she dealt with this same unreality in the world as she knew it. She saw through herself enough for that. They are collected together under the title of *The Literary Sense*.

So far in this section I have tried to show the pull of two main groups of divergent personalities and two main sets of tendency upon my character, during those still plastic days at Sandgate, and to indicate something of the quality of my response. These brains passed so to speak to the right of me and the left of me; I felt their gravitational attraction. The scientific pull was the earlier and stronger. I moved more and more away from conscious artistry and its exaltations and chagrins; I was strengthened against self-dramatization and confirmed in my disposition to social purposiveness. This definition and confirmation of my mind was the principal thing that was happening to me in those early Sandgate years. But I should be simplifying my story over much if I left that chapter in my life merely as a sort of straightforward tug-of-war in my brain, in which the systematizing, politically directed impulse won. There were other thrusts and drifts, interests and attractions, quite outside this particular conflict as to whether I should keep my mental effort based on an objective or float off into cloudland.

For instance at an entirely different level from these issues of poise and aim in my development, something else was going on,—I was busy "getting on in the world." One does not get on without giving a considerable amount of one's waking time to it. It is plain from the letters home already quoted and the "picshuas" here reproduced, that this was a very constant and lively interest in our early days. Jane and I were concerned in questions of "rights" and royalties and "price per thou" in a manner that was altogether ungenteel. We affected no innocence about "publicity" and we welcomed a large bundle of press-cuttings and felt anxious if the little blue packets were unpunctual and meagre. And somehow it is here and not in relation to whether writing was an end or an implement that the figure of Arnold Bennett with his bright and busy brain seething in a fashion all its own, comes in. We two, he and I, got on in the world abreast—and it was extremely good fun for both of us. Later on we diverged.

He wrote to me first, in September 1897, on the notepaper of a little periodical he edited, called *Woman*, to ask how I came to know about the Potteries, which I had mentioned in the *Time Machine* and in a short story, and after that we corresponded. In a second letter he says he is "glad to find the Potteries made such an impression" on me, so I suppose I had enlarged upon their scenic interest, and adds "only during the last few years have I begun to see its possibilities." In a further letter he thanks me for telling him of Conrad. He had missed *Almayer's Folly* in a batch of other novels for his paper and I had discovered it. That was one up for me. Now under my injunction he is rejoicing over *The Nigger of the Narcissus*. "Where did the man pick up that style and that synthetic way of gathering up a general impression and flinging it at you?... He is so consciously an artist. Now Kipling isn't an artist a bit. Kipling doesn't know what art is—I mean the art of words; il ne se préoccupe que de la chose racontée" Follow praises of George Moore. That unnecessary scrap of French is very Bennett. He was already deliberately heading for France and culture, learning French, learning to play the piano, filling up the gaps of a commonplace middle-class education with these accomplishments—and all with the brightest efficiency. Presently he came to Sandgate to see us and his swimming and diving roused my envy.

Never have I known anyone else so cheerfully objective as Bennett. His world was as bright and hard surfaced as crockery—his *persona* was, as it were, a hard, definite china figurine. What was not precise, factual and contemporary, could not enter into his consciousness. He was friendly and self assured; he knew quite clearly that we were both on our way to social distinction and incomes of several thousands a year. I had not thought of it like that. I was still only getting something between one and two thousand a year, and I did not feel at all secure about getting more. But Bennett knew we couldn't stop there. He had a through ticket and a timetable—and he proved to be right.

Our success was to be attained straightforwardly by writing sound clear stories, lucidly reasonable articles and well constructed plays. His pride was in craftsmanship rather than in artistic expression, mystically intensified and passionately pursued, after the manner of Conrad. Possibly his ancestors had had just the same feel about their work, when they spun the clay of pots and bowls finely and precisely. He was ready to turn his pen to anything, provided it could be done well. He wrote much of the little weekly paper, *Woman*, he was editing—including answers to correspondents—often upon the most delicate subjects—over the signature, if I remember rightly, of "Aunt Ellen." He did it as well as he knew how. He declared he did it as well as it could be done. His ancestors on the potbanks had made vessels for honour or for dishonour. Why should not he turn out whatever was required? Some years ago he and Shaw and I were all invited by an ingenious advertisement manager to write advertisements for Harrods' Stores, for large fees. We all fell into the trap and wrote him letters (which he used for his purposes) for nothing. Shaw and I took the high attitude. We were priests and prophets; we could not be paid for our opinions. Bennett frankly lamented the thing could not be done because it "wasn't *done*." But he could see no reason why a writer should not write an advertisement as an architect builds a shop.

We were both about of an age; to be exact he was six months younger than I; we were both hard workers, both pushing up by way of writing from lower middle-class surroundings, where we had little prospect of anything but a restricted salaried life, and we found we were pushing with quite surprising ease; we were learning much the same business, tackling much the same obstacles, encountering similar prejudices and antagonisms and facing similar social occasions. We both had a natural zest for life and we both came out of a good old English radical tradition. We were liberal, sceptical and republican. But beyond this we were very different animals indeed. While I was becoming more and more set upon changing my world and making it something entirely different and while Conrad was equally set upon wringing an unprecedented intensity of phrasing out of his, Bennett was taking the thing that is, for what it was, with a naïve and eager zest. He saw it brighter than it was; he did not see into it and he did not see beyond it. He was like a child at a fair. His only trouble was how to get everything in in the time at his disposal, music, pictures, books, shows, eating, drinking, display, the remarkable clothes one could wear, the remarkable stunts one could do, the unexpected persons, the incessant fresh oddities of people; the whole adorable, incessant, multitudinous lark of it.

There it was. What more could you want?

Since I have just been writing about educated and uneducated types I perceive I am exposed to the question whether Bennett was an educated type. I would say that in my sense of the word he was absolutely immune to education and that he did not need it. He was impermeable. He learnt with extraordinary rapidity and precision. He was full of skills and information. The bright clear mosaic of impressions was continually being added to and all the pieces stayed in their places. He did not feel the need for a philosophy or for a faith or for anything to hold them together. One of the most characteristic, if not the best of his books, is *Imperial Palace*, a most competent assemblage of facts, but told with an exultation, a slight magnification. His self-explanation— explanation rather than analysis—is the *Card*. In that book he shows that he could see himself as plainly and directly as he saw anything else. It is not a self dramatization; it is pleased recognition, even of his own absurdities. *A Great Man* again is delighted self-caricature—even to his youthful bilious attacks. If there was any element of self-deception in his *persona* it was a belief in the luck that comes to men who are "Cards"—Regular Cards. His investments for example were too hopeful. When he died—and he died a well spent man—he left a holding of Russian securities, which he had bought for a rise that never came.

His work was extraordinarily unequal. Working with cultivated and conscious craftsmanship upon things intimately known to him, he produced indubitable masterpieces. There are few novels in our period to put beside *The Old Wives Tale* and *Riceyman Steps* and few stories to equal *The Matador of the Five Towns*. And yet he could write a book about death and eternity like *The Glimpse*—a glimpse into an empty cavern in his mind. He wrote a vast amount of efficient yet lifeless fiction from which his essential work is slowly being disinterred.

After his first visit to Sandgate, we never lost touch with each other. We never quarrelled, we never let our very lively resolve to "get on" betray our mutual generosity; we were continually interested in one another and continually comparing ourselves with each other. He thought me an odd card; I thought him an odd card. I became more and more involved in the social and political issues I shall describe in the next chapter, I made all sorts of contacts outside literary circles, I broadened and spread myself; and maybe I spread myself thin; while he retracted and concentrated. The boundaries of my personality became less definite and his more and more firmly drawn. I have told already how I put my banking account under the control of my wife, did not know of my own investments, allowed matters of furnishing, house-building, invitations and so forth to go right out of my control. I have never had any household in which my rôle has not been essentially that of the paying guest. But Bennett's control of the particulars of his life remained always (the word was one of his favourite ones) meticulous. He loved the direction of organization; the thing breaks out in his *Imperial Palace*. His home at Thorpe le Soken; his home in Cadogan Square were beautifully managed—by himself. His clothes were carefully studied. At the Reform Club we used to note with all respect the accordance of shirt and tie and sock and handkerchief, and draw him out upon the advisability of sending our laundry to Paris. I would ask him where to buy a watch or a hat. "Do you mind," he would say to me, "if I just arrange that tie of yours?"

The difference between Bennett and myself, particularly in our later developments, is perhaps interesting from a psychological point of view, though I do not know how to put it in psychological language. We contrasted more and more in our contact with the external world as our work unfolded. He developed his relation to the external world and I developed the relation of the external world to myself. He increased in precision and his generalizations weakened; I lost precision and my generalizations grew wider and stronger. This is something superficially parallel but certainly not identical with the comparison I have been making between the systematized mental life of those who are both scientifically disposed and trained and those who are moved to the unco-ordinated vivid expressiveness of the artist.

I will venture here to throw out a wild suggestion to the brain specialist. The artistic type relative to the systematizing type may have a more vigorous innervation of the cortex, rather more volume in the arteries, a richer or more easily oxygenated blood supply. But the difference between the meticulous brain and the loose *sweeping* brain may be due not to any cortical difference at all, but to some more central ganglionic difference. Somewhere sorting and critical operations are in progress, concepts and associations are called up and passed upon, links are made or rejected, and I doubt if these are cortical operations. The discussion of mind working is still in the stage of metaphor, and so I have to put it that this "bureau" of co-ordination and censorship, is roomy, generous and easy going in the Bennett type, and narrow, centralized, economical and exacting in my own. I believe that, corresponding to these mental differences, there was a real difference in our cerebral anatomy.

It was perhaps a part of his competent autonomy that Bennett was so remarkably free from the normal infantilism of the human male. He was not so dependent upon women for his comfort and self-respect as most of us are; he was not very deeply interested in them from that point of view. And he had not that capacity for illusion about them which is proper to our sex. The women in his books are for the most part good hard Staffordshire ware, capable, sisterly persons with a tang to their tongues. He seemed always to regard them as curious, wilful creatures—to be treated with a kind of humorous wariness. There were pleasures in love but they had their place among other pleasures. To have a mistress in France was, he felt, part of the *ensemble* of a literary artist, and afterwards it seemed to him right that the household of a rapidly rising novelist should have a smart, attractive wife, a really well-dressed wife. So that he set about marrying rather as he set about house-hunting. For him it was as objective a business as everything else. Marriage wasn't by any means that organic life association at once accidental and inevitable, that ingrowing intimacy, that it is for less lucidly constituted minds.

Yet he was not cold-hearted; he was a very affectionate man. Indeed he radiated and evoked affection to an unusual degree, but in some way that I find obscure and perplexing his sexual life did not flood into his general life. His personality never, so to speak, fused with a woman's. He never gave the effect of being welded, even temporarily, with the woman he was with. They did not seem really to have got together.

I think there was some obscure hitch in his make-up here, some early scar that robbed him of the easy self-forgetfulness, that "egoism expanded out of sight," of a real lover. I associate that hitch with the stammer that ran through his life. Very far back in his early years something may have happened, something that has escaped any record, which robbed him of normal confidence and set up a lifelong awkwardness.

He experienced certain chagrins in that search for a wife, he was not able to carry it through with complete detachment, and when he came to the English home he had chosen at Thorpe le Soken, he brought with him a French wife who had previously been his close friend, a lady of charm and lucidity but with a very marked personality which failed to accord in every particular with his realization of what the wife of a successful London novelist should be. I will not go into the particulars of their gradual disagreement and legal separation, his abandonment of Thorpe le Soken for Cadogan Square, nor of his subsequent pseudo-marriage, at which "all London" connived, to the mother of his one child. I think these affairs bothered him a lot but they did not trouble him fundamentally. He reflected on this and that, and laughed abruptly. And anyhow this part of his story is outside this present autobiography.

He left a tangle behind him full of possibilities of recrimination and misadjustment. There have been post-testamentary proceedings, and one lady has taken to journalistic reminiscences about him, reminiscences which, it seems to me, show chiefly how little a woman may understand a man in spite of having lived with him. But perhaps I am prejudiced in this matter. The real Arnold Bennett who is cherished in the memories of his friends, was remarkably detached from this matrimonial and quasi-matrimonial byplay.

Having been more than a little frustrated in his ambitions to run a well- managed wife in two brilliantly conducted establishments in London and the country, he fell back upon the deliberate development of his own personality. It was no self-dramatization he attempted; no covering up of defects by compensatory assumptions; it was a cool and systematic exploitation of his own oddities. He was as objective about himself and as amused about himself as about anything else in the world. He improved a certain swing in his movements to a grave deliberate swagger; he enriched his gestures. He brushed up his abundant whitening hair to a delightful cocks-comb. The stammer he had never been able to conquer was utilized for a conversational method of pauses and explosions. He invented a sort of preliminary noise like the neigh of a penny trumpet. He dressed to the conception of an opulent and important presence. He wore a fob. He made his entry into a club or a restaurant an event. It pleased his vanity no doubt, but why should pleasing one's vanity by evoking an effusive reception in a room or restaurant be any different from pleasing one's palate with a wine? It was done with a humour all his own. Deep within him the invincible Card rejoiced. He knew just how far to carry his mannerisms so that they never bored. They delighted most people and offended none.

I wish Frank Swinnerton who was his frequent associate during his last phase would Boswellize a little about him before the memories fade. Only Swinnerton could describe Bennett calling up the chef at the Savoy to announce the invention of a new dish, or describe him dressing a salad. And Swinnerton could tell of his water-colour painting and his yacht. He ran a yacht but he never let me see it. It was a bright and lovely toy for him, and I think he felt I might just look at it and then at him, with the wrong expression. He was a member of the Yacht Club. I have it on my conscience that I said an unkind thing about his water colours. "Arnold," I said, "you paint like Royalty."

* * * * *

Let me return from Arnold Bennett to the tale of how Jane and I "got on" in the years between 1895 and 1900. In the beginning of this Chapter I brought the history of our social education up to my first encounter with caviar and our tentative experiments with Canary Sack and the various vintages of Messrs. Gilbey available in Camden Town. We soon got beyond such elementary investigations. The enlargement of our lives, once it began, was very rapid indeed, but we found the amount of *savoir-faire* needed to meet the new demands upon us, not nearly so great as we had supposed.

I think my glimpses of life below stairs at Up Park helped me to meet fresh social occasions with a certain ease. A servant in a big household becomes either an abject snob or an extreme equalitarian. At Up Park there was a footman who kept a diary of the bad English and the "ignorance" he heard while he was waiting at table; he would read out his choice items with the names and dates exactly given, and he may have helped importantly to dispel any delusion that social superiority is more than an advantage of position. I never shared the belief, which peeps out through the novels of George Meredith, Henry James, Gissing and others, that "up there somewhere" there are Great Ladies, of a knowledge, understanding and refinement, passing the wit of common men. The better type of social climbers seek these Great Ladies as the Spaniards sought El Dorado. And failing to find them, invent them.

Jane and I never started with that preoccupation. We did not so much climb as wander into the region of Society. We found ourselves lunching, dining and week-ending occasionally with a very healthy and easy-minded sort of people, living less urgently and more abundantly than any of the other people we knew; with more sport, exercise, travel and leisure than the run of mankind; the women were never under any compulsion to wear an unbecoming garment, and struck Jane as terribly expensive; and everybody was "looked after" to an enviable degree. They had on the whole easier manners than we had encountered before. But they had very little to show us or tell us. The last thing they wanted to do was to penetrate below the surface of things on which they lived so agreeably.

Among the interesting parties I remember in those early days, were several at Lady Desborough's at Taplow Court, and Lady Mary Elcho's at Stanway. There I used to meet people like Arthur Balfour, various Cecils and Sedgwicks, George Curzon, George Wyndham, Sir Walter Raleigh, Judge Holmes, Lady Crewe, Mrs. Macguire, Maurice Baring.... But never mind all that. Samples must serve for a catalogue. There was sometimes good talk at dinner and after dinner, but mostly the talk was allusive and gossipy. Balfour for the most part played the rôle of the receptive, enquiring intelligence. "Tell me," was a sort of colloquial habit with him. He rarely ventured opinions to be shot at. He had the lazy man's habit of interrogative discussion. Close at hand to us at Sandgate was the house of Sir Edward Sassoon. Lady Sassoon was a tall witty woman, a Rothschild, very much preoccupied with speculations about a Future Life and the writings of Frederic W. H. Myers. Philosophers like McTaggart, who were expected to throw light on her curiosity about the Future Life, mingled with politicians like Winston Churchill, trying over perorations at dinner, and Edwardians like the Marquis de Soveral. Most of these week-end visits and dinner parties were as unbracing mentally, and as pleasant, as going to a flower show and seeing what space and care can do with favoured strains of some familiar species. In these days there were also such persistent lunch givers as Mrs. Colefax (now Lady Colefax) and Sir Henry Lucy (Toby M.P.) of *Punch*, who gathered large confused tables of twenty or thirty people. There one met "celebrities" rather than people in positions; the celebrities anyhow were the salt of the feast; and as Jane and I were much preoccupied with our own game against life, the chief point of our conversation was usually to find out as unobtrusively as possible who we were talking to and why. And by the time we were beginning to place our neighbours, the lunch party would break up and sweep them away.

We would compare notes afterwards. "I met old So and So." "And what did he say?" "Oh, just old nothing."

None of these social experiences had anything like the same formative impressions upon my mind as the encounters with the politico-social workers and with the writers in earnest, and the artists, upon which I have enlarged. The best thing that these friendly glimpses of the prosperous and influential did for us was to remove any lurking feeling of our being "underneath" and to confirm my natural disposition to behave as though I was just as good as anybody and just as responsible for our national behaviour and outlook.

Picshua: Royal Institution Audience.

We were "getting on." At first it was very exciting and then it became less marvellous. We still found ourselves rising. I remember about this time—to be exact in January 24th, 1902—I was asked to read a paper to the Royal Institution and I wrote and read *The Discovery of the Future*, about which I shall have more to say in my concluding chapter. An impression I sketched at the time of a Royal Institution audience may very fitly conclude this chapter. I regard this picshua as a masterpiece only to be compared to the Palæolithic drawings in the Caves of Altamira. It marks our steady invasion of the world of influential and authoritative people. I remember that Sir James Crichton-Browne (who was about as young then as he is now; he was born in 1840) was very kind and polite to us on this occasion and that after the lecture was delivered I met Mrs. Alfred and Mrs. Emile Mond, long before there was any Lord Melchett, when Brunner Mond and Co. was only the embryo of I.C.I. They wanted to collect us socially, and it was suddenly borne in upon us that we had become worth collecting—eight years from our desperate start in Mornington Place.

§ 6. BUILDING A HOUSE (1899-1900)

In the present section there is little need for writing. Two photographs and two picshuas will serve to tell the tale. We found a site for the house we contemplated, we found an architect in C. F. A. Voysey, that pioneer in the escape from the small snobbish villa residence to the bright and comfortable pseudo-cottage. Presently we found ourselves with all the money we needed for the house and a surplus of over £1,000. And my health was getting better and better.

Picshua: June 11th, 1901.

The house was still being built when it dawned upon us as a novel and delightful idea that we were now justified in starting a family. A picture of the pretty little study in which I was to work for ten years finishing *Kipps*, producing *Anticipations, A Modern Utopia, Mankind in the Making, Tono Bungay, Ann Veronica, The New Machiavelli* and various other novels, may very well be included in this picture chapter.

Voysey wanted to put a large heart-shaped letter plate on my front door, but I protested at wearing my heart so conspicuously outside and we compromised on a spade. We called the house Spade House. The men on the lift beside my garden, which used to ascend and descend between Folkestone and Sandgate, confused my name with that of another Wells, "the Man who Broke the Bank at Monte Carlo"—and they told their passengers that it was "on the ace of spades" that the trick was done. I was no longer lean and hungry-looking (as the second picshua shows), I was "putting on weight" and in order to keep it down I pulled a roller about my nascent garden in the sight of the promenaders on the Leas, unconscious at first of my sporting fame. But soon I went about Sandgate and Folkestone like a Wagnerian hero with a motif of my own—whenever there was a whistling errand boy within ear shot.

Spade House faced the south with a loggia that was a suntrap. The living- rooms were on one level with the bedrooms so that if presently I had to live in a wheeled chair I could be moved easily from room to room. But things did not turn out in that fashion. Before the house was finished, Voysey had revised his plans so as to have a night and day nursery upstairs, and presently I was finishing *Kipps* and making notes for what I meant to be a real full-length novel at last, *Tono Bungay*, a novel, as I imagined it, on Dickens-Thackeray lines, and I had got a bicycle again and was beginning the exploration of Kent. I became a Borough magistrate and stability and respectability loomed straight ahead of us. I might have been knighted; I might have known the glories of the O.M.; I might have faced the photographer in the scarlet of an honorary degree.

Picshua: March 28th, 1901.

Such things have nestled in the jungle beside my path. But Ann Veronica (bless her!) and my outspoken republicanism saved me from all that. There is only one honour I covet, and I will say nothing about it because it will never come my way, and there is only one disappointment I have ever had in this field, and that was when Jane was not put upon the Essex county bench— for which she was all too good.

IX. — THE IDEA OF A PLANNED WORLD

§ 1. ANTICIPATIONS (1900)
AND THE "NEW REPUBLIC"

In this newly built Spade House I began a book *Anticipations* which can be considered as the keystone to the main arch of my work. That arch rises naturally from my first creative imaginations, *The Man of the Year Million* (written first in 1887) and *The Chronic Argonauts* (in the *Science Schools Journal* 1888), and it leads on by a logical development to*The Shape of Things to Come* (1933) and to the efforts I am still making to define and arrange for myself and for a few other people who inhabit my world, the actual factors necessary to give a concrete working expression to a world-wide "Open Conspiracy" to rescue human society from the net of tradition in which it is entangled and to reconstruct it upon planetary lines.

Necessarily this main arch, the structural frame of my life, is of supreme importance to me, and naturally it is of supreme importance in this picture of my world. It is unavoidable therefore that at times I should write as if I imagined that—like that figure of Atlas which stood in my father's shop window—I sustained the whole world upon my shoulders.

That is the necessary effect of an autobiographical perspective. Every man who has grown out of his infantile faith in the sanity of things about him and developed a social consciousness, carries his whole world upon his shoulders. In an autobiography he is bound to tell about that. He cannot pretend to be unaware of what his mind is doing. He becomes perforce the judge of all the world. He cannot add, "in my opinion" or, "though it is not for me to judge," to every sentence. If he is afraid to appear self-important and an arrogant prig, he had better leave out the story of his brain altogether. But then, what will remain?

I once met a very eminent American who regaled me with an anecdote. He said, "I once saw Abraham Lincoln."

"Yes?" I said eagerly.

"He was as close to me as you are. Closer."

"Well?"

"I saw him."

"And *what* did you see?"

"Abraham Lincoln of course. Surely you've heard of Abraham Lincoln?"

That was really modest autobiography, a *locus* and, beyond that, nothing. But the alternative would have been to pronounce a judgment on Abraham Lincoln.

I should probably romance about it, fill in gaps and simplify unduly, if I tried to give an orderly account of how preoccupation with the future became dominant in my conscious life. But I think my contact with evolutionary speculation at my most receptive age played a large part in the matter. I cannot judge, I do not know how to judge, whether the accident of writing those two early pieces about the remote future and mankind and time-travelling gave me a bias in this matter, and whether, having once made a little success in forecasting, it seemed natural to give the public more from the same tap, or whether on the other hand there was an innate disposition to approach things in general from that unusual side. The idea of treating time as a fourth dimension was, I think, due to an original impulse; I do not remember picking that up. But I may have picked it up, because it was in the air. If I did not then the bias was innate.

The future depicted in the *Time Machine* (1894) was a mere fantasy based on the idea of the human species developing about divergent lines, but the future in *When the Sleeper Awakes* (1898) was essentially an exaggeration of contemporary tendencies:

higher buildings, bigger towns, wickeder capitalists and labour more down-trodden than ever and more desperate. Everything was bigger, quicker and more crowded; there was more and more flying and the wildest financial speculation. It was our contemporary world in a state of highly inflamed distension. Very much the same picture is given in *A Story of the Days to Come* (1899) and *A Dream of Armageddon* (1903). I suppose that is the natural line for an imaginative writer to take, in an age of material progress and political sterility. Until he thinks better of it. Michael Arlen betrayed the same tendency in his *Man's Mortality* as recently as 1932. But in 1899 I was already beginning to realize there might be better guessing about the trend of things.

Along came the end of the century, just apt to my thoughts, and I arranged with W. L. Courtney, who had succeeded Frank Harris as editor of the *Fortnightly Review*, to publish a series of papers discussing what was likely to happen in the new century.

Now *Anticipations* was not only a new start for me, but, it presently became clear, a new thing in general thought. It may have been a feeble and vulnerable innovation, but it was as new as a new-laid egg. It was the first attempt to forecast the human future as a whole and to estimate the relative power of this and that great system of influence. Partial forecasts and forebodings existed in abundance already; we had estimates for instance, of the length of time it would take to exhaust the world's coal supply, of the prospects of population congestion if the birth-rate remained stable, of the outlook for this planet as the solar system cooled, as it was then supposed to be doing, very rapidly; but most of these conclusions were based on such narrowly conditioned calculations that they could be dismissed quite easily by challenging the validity of the assumptions. A comprehensive attempt to state and weigh and work out a general resultant for the chief forces of social change throughout the world, sober forecasting, that is to say, without propaganda, satire or extravaganza, was so much a novelty that my book, crude though it was and smudgily vague, excited quite a number of people. Macmillan, my English publishers, were caught unawares by the demand and had sold out the first edition before they reprinted. It sold as well as a novel.

Among other people who were excited by *Anticipations* was myself. I became my own first disciple. Perhaps at the outset of this series I was inspired chiefly by the idea of producing some timely interesting articles. But before I was half way through the series I realized that this sort of thing could not remain simply journalistic. If I was not doing something widely and profoundly important I was at least sketching out something widely and profoundly important. I was carrying on the curves instead of the tangents of history. I was indicating, even if I was not to some extent providing, new data of quite primary importance for rationalized social political and economic effort. I was writing the human prospectus.

One of the things I would like to see done in the world is the foundation of a number of chairs for the teaching of an old subject in a new spirit. If I belonged to the now rapidly vanishing class of benevolent multi-millionaires I would create Professorships of Analytical History. Instead of presenting the clotted masses of un-digested or ill-digested fact which still encumber academic history to-day, my Professors would be doing fully, systematically and soundly, just what I did, though in the flimsiest way, in these *Anticipations*. From the biological point of view my Professors would be human ecologists; indeed Human Ecology would be a good alternative name for this new history as I conceive it. Then there need be no challenge to those who are still in endowed possession of "history" as such. My new men and the students under them would be working out strands of biological, intellectual, economic consequences. Periods, nations and races they would consider only in so far as these provided them with material facts. They would be related to the older school of historians much as vegetable physiologists ecologists and morphologists are related to the old plant-flattening, specimen-hunting, stamen-counting botanists. The end of all intelligent analysis is to clear the way for synthesis. The clearer their new history became the nearer they would be to efficient world-planning. All this is very obvious to-day but it was by no means clear in 1900. It took me some years to grasp the magnitude of my own realization.

Sooner or later Human Ecology under some name or other, will win its way to academic recognition and to its proper place in general education—in America sooner than in Europe, I guess—but the old history made up of time-worn gossip and stale and falsified politics, is deeply embedded in literature and usage. The invasion of the field of history by the scientific spirit is belated and slow. The old history, barbarically copious and classically fruitless, is strongly entrenched in the centres of learning throughout the world; it is closely interwoven with the legal profession and the current politico-social organization, and has all the resistant vigour of hierarchic dignity on the defensive. For years yet, I am afraid, the young will still have to learn the more significant facts about Queen Elizabeth's doubtful virginity, memorize such legal documents as the Constitutions of Clarendon and the Bill of Rights and discuss those marvellous world policies invented for examination purposes by dons addicted to self-identification with Julius Cæsar or Napoleon Bonaparte or Charles the Fifth or Disraeli or some other of the many exaggerated and inflammatory figures about which history has festered. But this material has no more educational value than the reading of detective stories, until a sound analytical treatment brings it right into the texture of contemporary affairs and points on through their confusion to the broad lines of probability ahead.

I made a first attempt to formulate this idea in my Royal Institution lecture in January 1902. I called this lecture the*Discovery of the Future* and I drew a hard distinction between what I called the legal (past-regarding) and the creative (future regarding) minds. I insisted that we overrated the darkness of the future, that by adequate analysis of contemporary processes its conditions could be brought within the range of our knowledge and its form controlled, and that mankind was at the dawn of a great change-over from life regarded as a system of consequences to life regarded as a system of constructive effort. I did not say that the future could be foretold but I said that its conditions could be foretold. We should be less and less bound by the engagements of the past and more and more ruled by a realiazation of the creative effect of our acts. We should release ourselves more and more from the stranglehold of past things.

An attack upon the assumption that history is made by "Great Men" is clearly implied in this view. Napoleon and Cæsar were typical "Great Men." I hold they were as much an outcome of systemic processes as are the pustules that break out through the skin of many growing young people. Just now we are living in a world where such boils are breaking out everywhere; everywhere there are dictators and "leaders"; everywhere there are "movements" festering about anything from the highly distended Mussolini to our own little black- head, Mosley. It is a spotty stage in the adolescence of mankind, a spotty stage that will pass. It is the Great Man idea and method in final pathological decay.

My lecture was printed in *Nature* (February 6th, 1902) and afterwards reprinted as a pamphlet. I find it, when I re-read it now and measure it by the present certainties of my mind, vague, inexact and rhetorical, but that is the measure of the progress in definition that has been going on in the intervening third of a century. When it was read, that lecture was well abreast of its time.

In 1902 I returned to the *Fortnightly Review* in which *Anticipations* had appeared and contributed a second series of papers under the general title of *Mankind in the Making*, which was published as a book in 1903. This is less in the vein of Analytical History and more in the nature of a general prospectus for the human enterprise. In 1905, I published *A Modern Utopia*, also after a serialization in the *Fortnightly*, and in this I presented not so much my expectations for mankind as my desires.

Let me however return to *Anticipations* for a while. The full title of the book is *Anticipations of the Reaction of Mechanical and Scientific Progress upon Human Life and Thought*. It begins with a statement of what is now a matter of world-wide recognition, the fundamental change in the scale of human relationships and human enterprises brought about by increased facilities of communication. It goes on to apply this generalization to one after another of the fundamental human interests, to show how it affects the boundaries of political divisions, the scope and nature of collective organisations, working loyalties and educational necessities. I had discovered no new principle here. It was too obvious a thing to be a discovery, and it had already been applied most illuminatingly by Grant Allen in an unpretending essay on the distances between country towns. I never read anything more germinal in my life, unless it was Lang and Atkinson's *Primal Law and Social Origins*, than this particular magazine article. It woke me up to the reciprocal relationship between facilities of locomotion and community-size, and so to a realization of what was happening to the world. I was, I think, the first to apply this relationship comprehensively to historical analysis. If I did not discover this principle I was certainly among the first to call attention to its far-reaching implications.

Anticipations begins with two papers on land-traction and the redistribution of population through the evolution of transport. Then follows an examination of the way in which the change of scale is destroying a long established social order and creating a social confusion in which no new classifications are yet apparent. Here again I was in a region of possible knowledge which was then immensely unexplored. There are two chapters on this social flux, and some guessing at its possible recrystallization, and these lead on naturally to a "Life History of Democracy." Modern Democracy is shown to be not an organic method of social organization but the political expression of a phase of social liquefaction. This chapter on Democracy, the chapter called the "Great Synthesis" and the concluding chapter on "Faith, Morals and Public Policy in the Twentieth Century" are from my present point of view, the most imperfect and the most interesting parts of *Anticipations*. The forecasts of modern war, striking as their partial fulfilment has been, of the interplay of languages, of the probability of defeat for Germany in the war that was then already threatening us, the renascence of Poland and the prospective movements of boundaries and predominances, though they show a considerable amount of shrewdness, have now been so much overtaken by events and proved or disproved, that they need not concern me here. My great miss in these early shots at forecasting was that I never guessed at the possibility of a modernized planning régime arising in Russia—of all countries. I saw the approaching decivilization of Ireland but I wrote that Russia would be only another and vaster Ireland. I was quite out about Russia.

The fact that in 1900 I had already grasped the inevitability of a World State and the complete insufficiency of the current parliamentary methods of democratic government is of more than merely autobiographical interest. Everybody in 1900 was shirking the necessity for great political reconstructions everywhere. Even the raising of the question carried my book outside the sphere of "practical politics" as they were then understood.

At that early date I was somehow already alive to the incompatibility of the great world order fore-shadowed by scientific and industrial progress, with existing political and social structures. I was already searching about in my mind, and in the facts about me, for ideas about the political and social will and mentality that were demanded by these inevitable material developments. The fact that I regarded myself as a complete outsider in public affairs, and that I felt debarred from any such conformity as would have given me a career within the established political and educational machinery, probably helped importantly in the liberation of my mind to these realizations, and supplied the disinterested vigour with which I worked them out. I could attack electoral and parliamentary methods, the prestige of the universities and the ruling class, the monarchy and patriotism, because I had not the slightest hope or intention of ever using any of these established systems for my own advancement or protection. For a scientific treatment of the theory of government my political handicap was a release. I had the liberty of that irresponsible child in the fable of the Emperor's Clothes. I could say exactly what I thought because it was inconceivable that I could ever be a successful courtier.

In *Anticipations*, I take up the contemporary pretensions of democracy and state the widely unspoken thought of the late Victorians: "This will not work." I then consider existing governments and ruling influences and say as plainly, "These do not work." What most active people were saying was, "They will work well enough for a few years more." And so, through circumstances and simplicity rather than through any exceptional intelligence, I arrived ahead of everyone at the naked essential question, which everyone about me was putting off for to-morrow, "What, then, will work?" And the attempt to answer that has been the cardinal reality of my thought and writing ever since.

The first tentative answer, as I made it in *Anticipations*, was something I called "The New Republic." It was an answer in the most general terms and it was given in a thoroughly Nineteenth Century spirit. I have written already, in Chapter the Fifth, § 5 of the peculiar fatuous hopefulness of the Nineteenth Century and here I am—true to my period.

This New Republic was to consist of all those people throughout the world whose minds were adapted to the demands of the big scale conditions of the new time.

> "I have sought to show" I wrote "that in peace and war alike a process has been and is at work, a process with all the inevitableness and all the patience of a natural force, whereby the great swollen, shapeless, hyper-trophied social mass of to-day must give birth at last to a naturally and informally organized, educated class, an unprecedented sort of people, a New Republic dominating the world. It will be none of our ostensible governments that will effect this great clearing up; it will be the mass of power and intelligence altogether outside the official state systems of to-day that will make this great clearance, a new social Hercules that will strangle the serpents of war and national animosity in his cradle.... It will appear first, I believe, as a conscious organization of intelligent and quite possibly in some cases wealthy men, as a movement having distinct social and political aims, confessedly ignoring most of the existing apparatus of political control, or using it only as an incidental implement in the attainment of these aims. It will be very loosely organized in its earlier stages, a mere movement of a number of people in a certain direction, who will presently discover with a sort of surprise the common object towards which they are all moving."

After the fatalistic optimistic fashion of the time, you see, I assumed that this "New Republic" would appear of its own accord, would "emerge." This was Liberalism—after the Tennysonian pattern. But even then some doubt was lurking at the back of my mind whether it might not prove necessary to *assist* the process of emergence. That there was something to be done about it, and that waiting for the great civilization of the future to arrive was not enough, grew clearer and clearer in my mind, year after year. Destiny, like the God of the Jews, gives no unconditional promises.

In § 5 of Chapter Five of this book I have already made a general criticism of the Socialism of the opening century and told, as one of the newer generation at that time, of my reactions to the assumptions and limitations of the Socialist movement. In several of my books my dawning sense that both Marxism and Fabian Socialism were failing to complete their first intentions and beginning to "date," found expression. Here I have to touch again upon the issues of that section, but from a new angle. What concerns me now is the story of my own disentanglement and the curious way in which I was using my prestige and possibilities as an imaginative writer, to do the thinking-out of this problem of human will and government, under fantastic forms. Just as Pope found it easier to discuss natural theology in verse, so at this stage, I found it more convenient to discuss sociology in fable. While in the Fabian Society I was raising *The Question of Scientific Administrative Areas* (1903), I was also writing a story based on exactly the same idea, *The Food of the Gods* (serialized in 1903 and published as a book in 1904), which began with a wild burlesque of the change of scale produced by scientific men and ended in the heroic struggle of the rare new big-scale way of living against the teeming small-scale life of the earth. Nobody saw the significance of it, but it left some of its readers faintly puzzled. They were vastly amused and thrilled by my giant wasps and rats, but young Caddies was beyond them. And later on in the same way the research for some means of changing the collective drive of human motives threw off the fable of *In the Days of the Comet* (1906), when an impalpable gas from a comet's tail sweeps into our atmosphere, does the work of centuries of moral education in the twinkling of an eye, and makes mankind sane, understanding and infinitely tolerant.

The more formal research for the realization of the New Republic was pursued in *Mankind in the Making*. I was realizing that the correlative of a new republic was a new education and this book is a discursive examination, an all too discursive examination of the formative elements in the social magma. The best part is the criticism and the rejection of selective breeding as giving any immediate hope of human improvement. Much of the rest shirks the harder task of scrutinizing the "man-making forces in society," in favour of a series of sketchy suggestions and rhetorical passages. Sometimes the text degenerates into mere scolding. Here is the conclusion of this, the most completely forgotten of my books. This stuff, you will observe, is not really getting on with the business at all; it is revivalism, field preaching. It is the exhortation of a man who has not yet been able to establish, at any point, working contacts for the realization of his ideas. Plainly he is exhorting himself as well as others. Just to keep going.

> "Assuredly youth will come to us, if this is indeed to
> be the dawn of a new time. Without the high resolve of
> youth, without the constant accession of youth, without
> recuperative power, no sustained forward movement
> is possible in the world. It is to youth, therefore, that
> this book is finally addressed, to the adolescents, to the
> students, to those who are yet in the schools and who
> will presently come to read it, to those who, being still
> plastic, can understand the infinite plasticity of the
> world. It is those who are yet unmade who must become
> the makers.... After thirty there are few conversions
> and fewer fine beginnings; men and women go on in
> the path they have marked out for themselves. Their
> imaginations have become firm and rigid, even if they

have not withered, and there is no turning them from the conviction of their brief experience that almost all that is, is inexorably so. Accomplished things obsess us more and more....

"With each year of their lives they come more distinctly into conscious participation with our efforts. Those soft little creatures that we have figured grotesquely as dropping from an inexorable spout into our world; those weak and wailing lumps of pink flesh, more helpless than any animal, for whom we have planned better care, a better chance of life, better conditions of all sorts; those larval souls, who are at first helpless clay in our hands, presently, insensibly, have become helpers beside us in the struggle. In a little while they are beautiful children, they are boys and girls and youths and maidens, full of the zest of new life, full of an abundant, joyful receptivity. In a little while they are walking with us, seeking to know whither we go, and whither we lead them, and why.... In a little while they are young men and women, and then men and women, save for a fresher vigour, like ourselves. For us it comes at last to fellowship and resignation. For them it comes at last to responsibility, to freedom, and to introspection and the searching of hearts.... To know all one can of one's self in relation to the world about one, to think out all one can, to take nothing for granted except by reason of one's unavoidable limitations, to be swift, indeed, but not hasty, to be strong but not violent, to be as watchful of one's self as it is given one to be, is the manifest duty of all who would subserve the New Republic. For the New Republican, as for his forerunner the Puritan, conscience and discipline must saturate life. He must be ruled by duties and a certain ritual in life. Every day and every week he must set aside time to read and think, to commune with others and himself; he must be as jealous of his health and strength as the Levites of old. Can we in this generation make but a few thousands of such men and women, men and women who are not afraid to live, men and women with a common faith and a common understanding, then, indeed, our work will be done. They will in their own time take this world as a sculptor takes his marble, and shape it better than all our dreams."

That I think is my style at its worst and my matter at its thinnest, and quoting it makes me feel very sympathetic with those critics who, to put it mildly, restrain their admiration for me. But it is a proper part of the story to record a phase when I did come to the surface and spout like that, before I took breath and went down into things again.

§ 2. THE SAMURAI—IN UTOPIA AND IN THE FABIAN SOCIETY (1905-1909)

A Modern Utopia goes half way towards the fantastic story for its form, in a fresh attack upon the problem of bringing the New Republic into existence. It is fairly plain to me that I felt I was going ineffectively nowhere, in those discursive utterances in *Mankind in the Making*, where the only tolerable stuff was the plain and simple squashing of "Positive Eugenics." But I had still to discover how to get at a fruitful presentation of New Republican organization. I now tried an attack upon my difficulties, so to speak, from the rear, by dropping the study of existing conditions and asking first, "What is it that has to be done? What sort of world do we want?" I took a leaf; in fact I took a number of pages; from Plato in that. Only after the answer to that question had begun to appear, would it be possible to take up the consideration of how to get there with any hope of success.

Of course, as I have already explained in my criticism of Fabian Socialism and classical Marxism, this was flying in the face of potent and sacred dogmas. Both schools were so ignorant of the use of the imagination in scientific exploration, that they thought Utopianism "unscientific"—and their snobbish terror of that word "unscientific" had no limits. That does not alter the fact that my Utopian attack upon the problem of socialist administration was thoroughly worth the making.

In February 1906, I find that I was defending my method of approach to the problem of administration, at a meeting of the Sociological Society, in a paper entitled "The so-called Science of Sociology." This was afterwards reprinted in *An Englishman Looks at the World* (1914). In this paper I insisted that in sociology there were no units for treatment, but only one single unit which was human society, and that in consequence the normal scientific method of classification and generalization breaks down. "We cannot put Humanity into a museum, or dry it for examination; our one, single, still living specimen is all history, all anthropology, and the fluctuating world of men. There is no satisfactory means of dividing it, and nothing else in the real world with which to compare it. We have only the remotest ideas of its 'life-cycle' and a few relics of its origin and dreams of its destiny.... Sociology must be neither art simply, nor science in the narrow meaning of the word at all, but knowledge rendered imaginatively and with an element of personality, that is to say, in the highest sense of the term, literature."

There were, I argued, two literary forms through which valid sociological work may be carried on; the first, the fitting of "schemes of interpretation" to history and the second, smaller in bulk and "altogether under-rated and neglected," the creation and criticism of Utopias. This I maintained should be the main business of a sociological society. This essay was a little excursion by the way and the subsequent discussion was entirely inconclusive. Mr. Wilfred Trotter thought it was an "Attack on Science" and Mr. Swinny defended Comte from my ingratitude. (Probably I am unjust to Comte and grudge to acknowledge a sort of priority he had in sketching the modern outlook. But for him, as for Marx, I have a real personal dislike, a genuine reluctance to concede him any sort of leadership. It is I think part of an inherent dislike of leadership and a still profounder objection to the subsequent deification of leaders. Leaders I feel should guide as far as they can—and then vanish. Their ashes should not choke the fire they have lit.)

Although it has never had any great popular sale, *A Modern Utopia* remains to this day one of the most vital and successful of my books. It is as alive to-day as *Mankind in the Making* is dead. It was the first approach I made to the dialogue form, and I am almost as satisfied with its literary quality as I am with that of *The Undying Fire*. The trend towards dialogue like the basal notion of the Samurai, marks my debt to Plato. *A Modern Utopia*, quite as much as that of More, derives frankly from the *Republic*.

In this *Modern Utopia* I made a suggestion for a temperamental classification of citizens as citizens. For the purposes of the state I proposed a division into four types of character, the poietic, the kinetic, the dull and the base. A primary problem of government was to vest all the executive and administrative work in the kinetic class, while leaving the poietic an adequate share in suggestion, criticism and legislation, controlling the base and giving the dull an incentive to kinetic effort.

The device of the order of the Samurai, as I worked it out in this book, does I think solve this problem better than any other method that has ever been suggested. Membership of the Samurai was voluntary, but was made difficult by qualifications and severe disciplinary tests and, on the principle that the bow need not always be strung, could be abandoned and resumed, under proper safeguards, according to the way of living desired by the individual at any time. In the Utopian constitution, free-speech and great fields of initiative were jealously guarded from repressive controls. The kinetic were trained to respect them. The "base" were merely those who had given evidence of a strong anti-social disposition and were the only individuals inalterably excluded from the Samurai. Membership of either of these four classes, was regulated by the filtering processes of education and of the tests of social life, and was never hereditary.

The experience of the thirty years that have passed since I launched this scheme, and particularly the appearance of such successful organizations as the Communist party and the Italian fascists has greatly strengthened my belief in the essential soundness of this conception of the governing order of the future. A Samurai Order educated in such an ideology as I have since tried to shape out, is inevitable if the modern world-state is ever to be fully realized. We want the world ruled, not by everybody, but by a politically minded organization open, with proper safeguards, to everybody. The problem of world revolution and world civilization becomes the problem of crystallizing, as soon as possible, as many as possible of the right sort of individuals from the social magma, and getting them into effective, conscious co-operation.

Before working out my sketch *A Modern Utopia*, I was disposed to think that this ruling order, which I had called at first the New Republic, would appear of its own accord. After I had published and seen something of the effect of *A Modern Utopia*, I realized that an Order of the Samurai was not a thing that comes about of itself and that if ever it were to exist, it must be realized as the result of very deliberate effort. After publishing *A Modern Utopia* in 1906, I went to America and wrote a series of impressions, *The Future in America* in which I dwelt upon the casual and chaotic elements in American development, noted the apparent absence of any "sense of the State" and speculated on the possibility of supplying that deficiency. Then I returned to begin a confused, tedious, ill-conceived and ineffectual campaign to turn the little Fabian Society, wizened already though not old, into the beginnings of an order, akin to these Samurai in *A Modern Utopia*, which should embody for mankind a sense of the State.

I envisaged that reconditioned Fabian Society as becoming, by means of vigorous propaganda, mainly carried on by young people, the directive element of a reorganized socialist party. We would attack the coming generation at the high school, technical college and university stage, and our organization would quicken into a constructive social stratum.

The idea was as good as the attempt to realize it was futile. On various occasions in my life it has been borne in on me, in spite of a stout internal defence, that I can be quite remarkably silly and inept; but no part of my career rankles so acutely in my memory with the conviction of bad judgment, gusty impulse and real inexcusable vanity, as that storm in the Fabian tea-cup. From the first my motives were misunderstood, and it should have been my business to make them understandable. I antagonized Shaw and Beatrice Webb for example, by my ill-aimed aggressiveness, yet both these people have since shown by their behaviour towards Fascism and Communism respectively, that their trend of mind is all towards just such a qualification of crude democracy as in 1906 I was so clumsily seeking. I was fundamentally right and I was wrong-headed and I left the Society, at last, if possible more politically parliamentary and ineffective than I found it. If I were to recount the comings and goings of that petty, dusty conflict beginning with my paper *The Faults of the Fabian* (February 1906) and ending with my resignation in September 1908, the reader would be intolerably bored. Fortunately for him it would bore me far more to disinter the documents, fight my battles over again and write it all down. And nobody else will ever do it.

I can but mention in passing the crowded meetings in Cliffords Inn, the gathered "intelligentsia"—then so new in English life— the old radical veterans and the bubbling new young people; the fine speeches of Shaw; Sidney Webb, with his head down talking fast with a slight lisp, terribly like a Civil Servant dispensing information; the magnificent Bland in a frock-coat and a black ribboned monocle, debating, really debating Sir, in a rococo variation of the front bench parliamentary manner; red-haired Haden Guest, being mercurial, and Edward Pease, the secretary, invincibly dry; myself speaking haltingly on the verge of the inaudible, addressing my tie through a cascade moustache that was no sort of help at all, correcting myself as though I were a manuscript under treatment, making ill-judged departures into parenthesis; the motions, the amendments, the disputes with the chairman, the shows of hands, the storms of applause; the excited Socialists disgorging at last, still disputing, into philistine Fleet Street and the Strand, swirling into little eddies in Appenrodt's, talking a mixture of politics and personalities. Our seriousness was intense. We typed and printed and issued Reports and Replies and Committee Election Appeals and Personal Statements, and my original intentions were buried at last beneath a steaming heap of hot secondary issues.

The order of the Fabian Samurai perished unborn. I went, discoursing to undergraduate branches and local branches, to Oxford, Cambridge, Glasgow, Manchester and elsewhere pursuing the lengthening threads of our disputes. The society would neither give itself to me to do what I wished with it, nor cast me out. It liked the entertainment of its lively evenings. And at last I suddenly became aware of the disproportionate waste of my energy in these disputes and abandoned my attack. Now there was the New Republic to be discovered. By me at any rate.

Reflections of that queer conflict are to be found in *The New Machiavelli* (1911). For some time I was a baffled revolutionary. I did not know what to do next. My Theory of Revolution by Samurai hung in the air and I could not discover any way of bringing it down to the level of reality. At the very time when I was failing, Lenin, under the stresses of a more pressing reality, was steadily evolving an extraordinarily similar scheme, the reconstructed Communist Party. Whether there was any genetic connection between his scheme and mine I have never been able to ascertain. But the in-and-out arrangement whereby a man or woman could be a militant member of the organization and then drop out of its obligations and privileges, the imposition of special disciplines and restrictions upon the active members and the recognition that there are types of good citizens who will live best and work best outside the responsible administrative organization, are common alike to my project and the Russian reality. Moreover they resemble each other in insisting upon a training in directive ideas as part of the militant qualification. If Russia has done nothing else for mankind, the experiment of the Communist Party is alone sufficient to justify her revolution and place it upon an altogether higher level than that chaotic emotional release, the first French Revolution.

§ 3. "PLANNING" IN THE DAILY MAIL (1912)

If for a time I could not get on with the project of an organized "New Republic" as such, this did not prevent my making an occasional attack upon the general problem of social reconstruction. In 1912 Northcliffe asked me to write a series of articles for his *Daily Mail* on the Labour Unrest. Here again I displayed a certain prophetic quality. I got a year or so ahead of the general movement. "Planning" is a world-wide idea nowadays, but in 1912 this that follows was strange stuff for the readers of the leading half-penny daily to find upon their breakfast tables:

"No community has ever yet had the will and the imagination to recast and radically alter its social methods as a whole. The idea of such a reconstruction has never been absent from human thought since the days of Plato, and it has been enormously reinforced by the spreading material successes of modern science, successes due always to the substitution of analysis and reasoned planning for trial and the rule of thumb. But it has never yet been so believed in and understood as to render any real endeavour to reconstruct possible. The experiment has always been too gigantic for the available faith behind it, and there have been against it the fear of presumption, the interests of all advantaged people, and the natural sloth of humanity. We do but emerge now from a period of deliberate happy-go-lucky and the influence of Herbert Spencer, who came near raising public shiftlessness to the dignity of a national philosophy. Everything would adjust itself—if only it was left alone.

"Yet some things there are that cannot be done by small adjustments, such as leaping chasms or killing an ox or escaping from the roof of a burning house. You have to decide upon a certain course on such occasions and maintain a continuous movement. If you wait on the burning house until you scorch and then turn round a bit or move away a yard or so, of if on the verge of a chasm you move a little in the way in which you wish to go, disaster will punish your moderation. And it seems to me that the establishment of the world's work upon a new basis—and that and no less is what this Labour Unrest demands for its pacification—is just one of those large alterations which will never be made by the collectively unconscious activities of men, by competitions and survival and the higgling of the market. Humanity is rebelling against the continuing existence of a labour class as such, and I can see no way by which our present method of weekly wages employment can change by imperceptible increments into a method of salary and pension—for it is quite evident that only by reaching that shall we reach the end of these present discontents. The change has to be made on a comprehensive scale or not at all. We need nothing less than a national plan of social development if the thing is to be achieved.

"Now that, I admit, is, as the Americans say, a large proposition. But we are living in a time of more and more comprehensive plans, and the mere fact that no scheme so extensive has ever been tried before is no reason at all why we should not consider one. We think nowadays quite serenely of schemes for the treatment of the nation's health as one whole, while our fathers considered illness as a blend of accident with special providences; we have systematized the community's water supply, education, and all sorts of once 'chaotic services, and Germany and our own infinite higgledy-piggledy discomfort and ugliness have brought home to us at last even the possibility of planning the extension of our towns and cities. It is only another step upward in scale to plan out new, more tolerable conditions of employment for every sort of worker and to organize the transition from our present disorder."

And again:

"I have attempted a diagnosis of this aspect of our national situation. I have pointed out that nearly all the social forces of our time seem to be in conspiracy to bring about the disappearance of a labour class as such and the rearrangement of our work and industry upon a new basis. That rearrangement demands an unprecedented national effort and the production of an adequate National Plan. Failing that, we seem doomed to a period of chronic social conflict and possibly even of frankly revolutionary outbreaks that may destroy us altogether or leave us only a dwarfed and enfeebled nation...."

(But all this was complicated with an advocacy of "proportional representation" and one or two other minor reforms which I now find myself less willing to revive. Not so much because I have lost faith in them as because I realize that they are of such secondary importance that any insistence upon them distorts the proportions of the general proposition. If ever they are mentioned people say: "So *that's* your panacea!" and everything else is ignored.)

§ 4. THE GREAT WAR AND MY RESORT TO "GOD" (1914-1916)

The onset of the Great War hung portentously over us all throughout the three years between the Agadir incident (July 1911) and the invasion of Belgium in August 1914. The inevitability of a crash was more and more manifest, and my reluctant attention was swung round to this continually more immediate threat to the structure of civilization. In 1913, in a short series of articles in the *Daily Mail*, I was writing about the modernization of warfare. (They are reprinted together with the Labour Unrest series and other articles in *An Englishman Looks at the World*, 1914) and early in 1914 I published a futuristic story *The World Set Free*, in which I described the collapse of the social order through the use of "atomic bombs" in a war that began, prophetically and obviously enough, with a German invasion of France by way of Belgium.

After this collapse there was to be a wave of sanity—a disposition to believe in these spontaneous waves of sanity may be one of my besetting weaknesses—and a wonderful council at Brissago (near Locarno!) was to set up the new world order. Yet, after all, the popular reception of President Wilson in 1919 was more like a wave of sanity than anything that had ever occurred in history before. Already in 1908 in *The War in the Air*, written before any practicable flying had occurred, I had reasoned that air warfare, by making warfare three dimensional, would abolish the war front and with that the possibility of distinguishing between civilian and combatant or of bringing a war to a conclusive end. This I argued, must not only intensify but must alter the ordinary man's attitude to warfare. He can no longer regard it as we did the Boer War for example as a vivid spectacle in which his participation is that of a paying spectator at a cricket or base-ball match.

No intelligent brain that passed through the experience of the Great War emerged without being profoundly changed. Our vision of life was revised in outline and detail alike. To me, as to most people, it was a revelation of the profound instability of the social order. It was also a revelation of the possibilities of fundamental reorganization that were now open to mankind—and of certain extraordinary weaknesses in the collective mentality. I was intensely indignant at the militarist drive in Germany and, as a convinced Republican, I saw in its onslaught the culminating expression of the monarchist idea. This, said I, in shrill jets of journalism, is the logical outcome of your parades and uniforms! Now to fight the fighters!

People forget nowadays how the personal imperialism of the Hohenzollerns dominated the opening phase of the war. I shouted various newspaper articles of an extremely belligerent type. But my estimate of the moral and intellectual forces at large in the world, was out. I would not face the frightful truth. I anticipated an explosion of indignant commonsense that would sweep not simply the Hohenzollerns but the whole of the current political system, the militant state and its symbols, out of existence, leaving the whole planet a confederated system of socialist republics. Even in *In the Fourth Year* (1918) I denounced the "Krupp-Kaiser" combination and took it almost as a matter of course that such a thing as a private-profit armament industry could not survive the war. Perhaps in the long run its cessation may be the tardy outcome of the cataclysm, but that outcome, I must admit, is still being most tragically delayed. It is being delayed by the general inability to realize that a "sovereign state" is essentially and incurably a war- making state. My own behaviour in 1914-15 is an excellent example of that inability.

The fount of sanguine exhortation in me swamped my warier disposition towards critical analysis and swept me along. I wrote a pamphlet, that weighed, I think, with some of those who were hesitating between participation and war resistance, "*The War that will end War.*" The title has become proverbial. The broken promise of the phrase is still used as a taunt by the out-and-out pacificist against anyone who does not accept the dogma of non-resistance in its entirety. But in some fashion armed forces that take action have to be disarmed and I remain persuaded that there will have to be a last conflict to inaugurate the peace of mankind. Rather than a war between sovereign governments, however, it is far more likely to be a war to suppress these wherever they are found.

Anatole France in regard to the war was in much the same case as myself. We had met several times before 1914 and formed a very friendly estimate of each other, and when *The Book of France* was compiled and published, for relief funds in the devastated regions, he contributed an article *Debout pour la Dernière Guerre*, which he insisted I should translate. I did so under the title of *Let Us Arise and End War*.

As I reassemble all that I can of my hasty, discursive and copious writings during the early stages of the war, and do my utmost to recover my actual states of mind, it becomes plain to me that for a time—in spite of my intellectual previsions—the world disaster, now that it had come, so overwhelmed my mind that I was obliged to thrust this false interpretation upon it, and assert, in spite of my deep and at first unformulated misgivings, that here and now, the new world order was in conflict with the old. Progress was arrested, its front was shattered under my eyes, so shattered that even to this day (1934) it has not reformed, and I convinced myself that on the contrary it was the old traditional system falling to pieces, and the world state coming into being (as the world alliance) under my eyes. The return to complete sanity took the greater part of two years. My mind did not get an effective consistent grip upon the war until 1916.

I remember distinctly when the first effectual destructive tap came to my delusion. It was a queer and a very little, but, at the same time, very arresting, incident. For some British readers there will be a shock, when they read of it, quite different in its nature from the shock that came to me. But I have given fair warning in this book that I am a Republican, and that the essential disavowals of my soul go deeper than the merely theological beliefs of my fellow country-men. Perhaps they do not get enough of this sort of shock.

I was walking from my flat in St. James's Court to lunch and talk at the Reform Club. Upon the wall at the corner of Marlborough House as it was then, I saw a large bill; it was an unusual place for an advertisement and I stopped to read it. It was a Royal Proclamation. I forget what matter it concerned; what struck me was the individual manner of the wording. King George was addressing "my people." There was no official "we" and "our" about it.

I had been so busy with the idea of civilization fighting against tradition, I had become so habituated to the liberal explanation of the monarchy as a picturesque and harmless vestigial structure, that this abrupt realization that the King was placing himself personally at the head of his people, was like a bomb bursting under my nose. My mind hung over that fact for a moment or so.

"Good God!" I said in the greatest indignation, "what has *he* got to do with our war?"

I went my way digesting it.

"*My* people"—me and my sort were *his* people!

So long as you suffer any man to call himself your shepherd sooner or later you will find a crook round your ankle. We were not making war against Germany; we were being ordered about in the King's war with Germany.

It took me some months of reluctant realization to bring my mind to face the unpalatable truth that this "war for civilization," this "war to end war" of mine was in fact no better than a consoling fantasy, and that the flaming actuality was simply this, that France, Great Britain and their allied Powers were, in pursuance of their established policies, interests, treaties and secret understandings, after the accepted manner of history and under the direction of their duly constituted military authorities, engaged in war with the allied central powers, and that under contemporary conditions no other war was possible. The World-State of my imaginations and desires was presented hardly more by one side in the conflict than by the other. We were fighting for "King and Country" and over there they were fighting for "Kaiser and Fatherland"; it was six of one and half a dozen of the other, so far as the World-State was concerned.

The efforts of my brain to grasp the vast possibilities of human violence, feebleness and docility that I had neglected and ignored so long in my eagerness to push forward to the modern State, and further to adjust my guiding *persona* to these reluctant realizations, were, I suppose, paralleled in hundreds of thousands of brains. We couldn't get out of it for a time and think it out— and, the young men, particularly were given no time to think. They thought it out in the trenches—and in No Man's Land. And I, exempt from service and free to express myself, had offered them nothing better than the "War to end War"!

Naturally, in my autobiography, my mind must occupy the central position of this story of disillusionment, as a rabbit on the table represents its species, but the conscious and subconscious conflicts I tell on my own behalf were general and not particular to me. I documented the process with exceptional abundance; that is my only distinction. Before the end of 1914, I had already set to work upon a record of my mental phases, elaborated in a novel, *Mr. Britling Sees It Through*. It is only in the most general sense autobiographical—and I lost no son. But the story of Mr. Britling's son and Mr. Britling's grey matter could be repeated with ten thousand variations. Mr. Britling is not so much a representation of myself as of my type and class, and I think I have contrived in that book to give not only the astonishment and the sense of tragic disillusionment in a civilized mind as the cruel facts of war rose steadily to dominate everything else in life, but also the passionate desire to find some immediate reassurance amidst that whirlwind of disaster.

Mr. Britling after much tribulation "found God." He has lost his son and he sits in his study late at night trying to write to the parents of his boy's German tutor who is also among the dead.

"*These boys, these hopes, this war has killed.*'

"The words hung for a time in his mind.

"'No!' said Mr. Britling stoutly. 'They live!'

"And suddenly it was borne in upon his mind that he was not alone. There were thousands and tens of thousands of men and women like himself, desiring with all their hearts to say, as he desired to say, the reconciling word. It was not only his hand that thrust against the obstacles.... Frenchmen and Russians sat in the same stillness, facing

the same perplexities; there were Germans seeking a
way through to him. Even as he sat and wrote. And
for the first time clearly he felt a Presence of which he
had thought very many times in the last few weeks, a
Presence so close to him that it was behind his eyes and
in his brain and hands. It was no trick of his vision; it
was a feeling of immediate reality. And it was Hugh,
Hugh that he had thought was dead, it was young
Heinrich living also, it was himself, it was those others
that sought, it was all these and it was more, it was the
Master, the Captain of Mankind, it was God, there
present with him, and he knew that it was God. It was
as if he had been groping all this time in the darkness,
thinking himself alone amidst rocks and pitfalls and
pitiless things, and suddenly a hand, a firm strong hand,
had touched his own. And a voice within him bade him
be of good courage. There was no magic trickery in that
moment; he was still weak and weary, a discouraged
rhetorician, a good intentioned ill-equipped writer;
but he was no longer lonely and wretched, no longer in
the same world with despair. God was beside him and
within him and about him.... It was the crucial moment
of Mr. Britling's life. It was a thing as light as the passing
of a cloud on an April morning; it was a thing as great
as the first day of creation. For some moments he still
sat back with his chin upon his chest and his hands
dropping from the arms of his chair. Then he sat up and
drew a deep breath....

"For weeks his mind had been playing about this idea.
He had talked to Letty of this Finite God, who is the
king of man's adventure in space and time. But hitherto
God had been for him a thing of the intelligence, a
theory, a report, something told about but not realized....

Mr. Britling's thinking about God hitherto had been like
some one who has found an empty house, very beautiful
and pleasant, full of the promise of a fine personality.
And then as the discoverer makes his lonely, curious
explorations, he hears downstairs, dear and friendly, the
voice of the Master coming in....

"There was no need to despair because he himself was
one of the feeble folk. God was with him indeed, and he
was with God. The King was coming to his own. Amidst
the darknesses and confusions, the nightmare cruelties
and the hideous stupidities of the great war, God, the
Captain of the World Republic, fought his way to empire.
So long as one did one's best and utmost in a cause so
mighty, did it matter though the thing one did was little
and poor?

"'I have thought too much of myself,' said Mr. Britling,
'and of what I would do by myself. I have forgotten *that
which was with me....*'"

But the exact truth of the matter is that he had forgotten that
which was *in* him, the impersonal, the man in general, which is
as much our inheritance as our human frame. He was trying to
project his own innate courage so as to feel it external to himself,
independent of himself and eternal. Multitudes were doing the
same thing at this time.

I went to considerable lengths with this attempt to deify
human courage. I shocked many old friends and provoked
William Archer's effective pamphlet *God and Mr. Wells*. In the
long run I came to admit that by all preceding definitions of
God, this God of Mr. Britling was no God at all. But before I
returned to that completeness of sincerity, there had to be some
ingenious theological contortions. I was perhaps too aware of

the numbers of fine-minded people who were still clinging not so much to religion as to the comfort of religious habits and phrases. Some lingering quality of childish dependence in them answered to this lapse towards a "sustaining faith" in myself. What we have here is really a falling back of the mind towards immaturity under the stress of dismay and anxiety. It is a very good thing at times to hear such words as "Let not your Heart be troubled; neither let it be afraid" spoken as if with authority. It is a good thing to imagine the still companionship of an understanding Presence on a sleepless night. Then one can get to sleep again with something of the reassurance of a child in its cot. Everywhere in those first years of disaster men were looking for some lodestar for their loyalty. I thought it was pitiful that they should pin their minds to "King and Country" and suchlike claptrap, when they might live and die for greater ends, and I did my utmost to personify and animate a greater, remoter objective in *God the Invisible King*. So by a sort of *coup d'état* I turned my New Republic for a time into a divine monarchy.

I cannot disentangle now, perhaps at no time could I have disentangled, what was simple and direct in this theocratic phase in my life, from what was—*politic*. I do not know how far I was being perfectly straightforward in this phase, how far I was—as the vulgar have it—"codding myself," and how far I was trying to make my New Republicanism acceptable in a different guise to that multitude which could not, it seemed, dispense with kingship. But what these God-needing people require is the sense of a Father on whom they can have the most perfect reliance. They are straining back to the instinctive faith of "little children," that ultimately everything is all right. They are frightened people who want to be told that they need not brace up to the grimness before them. With all the will in the world I could not bring myself to present my God as that sort of God. I could invent a heartening God but not a palliating God. At his best my deity was far less like the Heavenly Father of a devout Catholic or a devout Moslem or Jew than he was like a personification of, let us say, the Five Year Plan. A Communist might have accepted him as a metaphor. No mystic could have used him because of the complete lack of miraculous aid or distinctive and flattering personal response. As he is presented in*God the Invisible King* he is no better than an inspiring but extremely preoccupied comrade, a thoroughly hard leader.

At no time did my deistic phrasing make any concessions to doctrinal Christianity. If my gestures were pious, my hands were clean. I never sold myself to organized orthodoxy. At its most artificial my religiosity was a flaming heresy and not a time-serving compromise. I never came nearer to Christianity than Manicheism—as Sir John Squire pointed out long ago.

I followed up *God the Invisible King*, with *The Soul of a Bishop* (also 1917)—in which I distinguish very clearly between the God of the Anglican Church and this new personification of human progressiveness—and both *Joan and Peter*(1918) and *The Undying Fire* (1919) are strongly flavoured with deified humanism. Another God indeed, God the Creator, appears for a brief interview with Peter in the hospital—and a very strange untidy God he is. He is evidently the male equivalent, humorous and self exculpatory, of what I have called elsewhere "that old harridan, Dame Nature." And in the last meditation of Joan and Peter's Uncle Oswald, "God," he feels, is "a name battered out of all value and meaning."

The Undying Fire is artistically conceived and rather brilliantly coloured; I have already expressed my satisfaction with it as the best of my Dialogue-Novels; and it crowns and ends my theology. It is the sunset of my divinity. Here is what Mr. Huss got from his God when at last he met him face to face.

"It was as if the dreamer pushed his way through the outskirts of a great forest and approached the open, but it was not through trees that he thrust his way but through bars and nets and interlacing curves of blinding, many-coloured light towards the clear promise beyond. He had grown now to an incredible vastness so that it was no longer earth upon which he set his feet but that crystalline pavement whose translucent depths contain the stars. Yet though he approached the open he never reached the open; the iridescent net that had seemed to grow thin, grew dense again; he was still struggling, and the black doubts that had lifted for a moment swept down upon his soul. And he realized he was in a dream, a dream that was drawing swiftly now to its close.

"'Oh God!' he cried, 'answer me! For Satan has mocked me sorely.
Answer me before I lose sight of you again. Am I right to fight? Am
I right to come out of my little earth, here above the stars?'

"'Right if you dare.'

"'Shall I conquer and prevail? Give me your promise!'

"'Everlastingly you may conquer and find fresh worlds to conquer.'

"'*May*—but *shall* I?'

"It was as if the torrent of molten thoughts stopped suddenly. It was as if everything stopped.

"'Answer me,' he cried.

"Slowly the shining thoughts moved on again.

"'So long as your courage endures you will conquer....

"'If you have courage, although the night be dark, although the present battle be bloody and cruel and end in a strange and evil fashion, nevertheless victory shall be yours—in a way you will understand—when victory comes. Only have courage. On the courage in your heart all things depend. By courage it is that the stars continue in their courses, day by day. It is the courage of life alone that keeps sky and earth apart.... If that courage fail, if that sacred fire go out, then all things fail and all things go out, all things—good and evil, space and time.'

"'Leaving nothing?'

"'*Nothing.*'

"'Nothing,' he echoed, and the word spread like a dark and darkening mask across the face of all things."

But before that, Mr. Huss following in the footsteps of Job had said:

"'I will not pretend to explain what I cannot explain. It may be that God is as yet only foreshadowed in life. You may reason, Doctor Barrack, that this fire in the heart that I call God, is as much the outcome of your Process as all the other things in life. I cannot argue against that. What I am telling you now is not what I believe so much as what I feel. To me it seems that the creative desire that burns in me is a thing different in its nature from the blind Process of matter, is a force running contrariwise to the power of confusion.... But this I do know, that once it is lit in a man, then his mind is alight—thenceforth. It

622

rules his conscience with compelling power. It summons him to live the residue of his days working and fighting for the unity and release and triumph of mankind. He may be mean still, and cowardly and vile still, but he will know himself for what he is.... Some ancient phrases live marvellously. Within my heart *I know that my Redeemer liveth....*'"

Is not that very like prevarication? But I prevaricate in the footsteps of a famous exemplar. Have you ever thought over St. Paul's ambiguities in his Epistle to the Corinthians (I., xv. 35)? Could the resurrection of the body be more ingeniously evaded and "spiritualized" and adapted to all tastes?

After *The Undying Fire*, God as a character disappears from my work, except for a brief undignified appearance, a regrettable appearance, dressed in moonshine and armed with Cupid's bow and arrows in *The Secret Places of the Heart* (1922). My phraseology went back unobtrusively to the sturdy atheism of my youthful days. My spirit had never left it. If I have used the name of God at all in the past ten years it has been by way of a recognized metaphor as in "God forbid," or, "At last God wearied of Napoleon." I have become more and more scrupulous about appropriating the prestige of this name for my own ends.

In *What Are We to Do with Our Lives?* (1932) I make the most explicit renunciation and apology for this phase of terminological disingenuousness. In spite of the fact that it yielded Peter's dream of God Among the Cobwebs and *The Undying Fire* I wish, not so much for my own sake as for the sake of my more faithful readers, that I had never fallen into it; it confused and misled many of them and introduced a barren détour into my research for an effective direction for human affairs.

§ 5. WAR EXPERIENCES OF AN OUTSIDER

That theological excursion of mine was not the only détour I made. I made a still longer détour through the tangle of international politics. I attempted amateurish diplomacies, so to speak, in my writings, and they also need explanation. Everyman almost was imagining diplomacies and treaties in those days, but mine, to a quite exceptional degree, were documented.

Let me return first to the disillusionment about the beneficence of our war-making (1915-16-17) that followed my first attempt in 1914 to find a justifying purpose in "our" war. I did not become "anti- war." I found the simple solution of the conscientious objectors and war resisters generally, too simple for me altogether. My brain was quite prepared for conflict on behalf of the law and order of the world-state. I believe that is necessary to this day. Peace will have to be kept—forcibly. For ages. The distinction people draw between moral and physical force is flimsy and unsound. Life is conflict and the only way to universal peace is through the defeat and obliteration of every minor organization of force. Carrying weapons individually or in crowds, calls for vigorous suppression on the part of the community. The anti-war people made me the more impatient because of the rightness of much of their criticism of the prevailing war motives. I was perhaps afraid, if I yielded to them, of being carried back too far towards the futility of a merely negative attitude. What they said was so true and what they did was so merely sabotage, I lost my temper with them.

And with less stress upon the "perhaps" I was reluctant to admit how gravely I had compromised myself by my much too forward belligerence and my rash and eager confidence in the liberalism, intelligence and good faith of our foreign office and war office in the first month or so of the war. My pro-war zeal was inconsistent with my pre-war utterances and against my profounder convictions. As I recovered consciousness, so to speak, from the first shock of the war explosion and resumed my habitual criticism of government and the social order, I found myself suspect to many of my associates who had become pacificists of the left wing. They regarded me as a traitor who was betraying them to the "war-mongers," while the reactionists in a position of authority, with equal justification and perhaps a nicer sense of my fundamental quality, were extremely suspicious of me as an ally. The hardest line to take is the middle way, especially if one is not sure-footed oneself, and there can be no doubt my staggering course was perplexing to many a friendly observer. Whatever I wrote or said went to an exasperating accompaniment of incredulity from the left, and I felt all the virtuous indignation natural to a man who has really been in the wrong. I was in the wrong and some of the things I wrote about conscientious objectors in *War and the Future* were unforgivable. I turned on the pacificists in*Joan and Peter*, savaged them to the best of my ability, imputed motives, ignored honourable perplexities and left some rankling wounds. Some of those war-time pacificists will never forgive me and I cannot complain of that. I made belated amends in the *Bulpington of Blup*. But that is a minor matter. The thing that occupied most of my mind was the problem of getting whatever was to be got for constructive world revolution out of the confusion of war, and being pro-German and non-combatant, finding endless excuses for the enemy and detracting from the fighting energy of the allies, seemed to me of no use at all towards my end.

I turn over a number of faded and forgotten writings as I try to judge and summarize my behaviour in these crucial years. There is an illuminating sketch of a story "The Wild Asses of the Devil" in *Boon* (1915). In 1915 I find I was already writing about the *Peace of the World* and the *End of the Armament Rings*. In 1916 I produced *What Is Coming?* made up of a number of 1915 newspaper articles. The leaves of my copy of this book are already carbonized, copies of it would be hard to find, if anyone wanted to find them, and if I were to put my reputation before my autobiographical rectitude, I think I should just let this little volume decay and char and disappear and say nothing about it. Most of it is very loose-lipped indeed. In it I am feeling my way about not only among ideas but among what I then thought were insurmountable popular prejudices, in a very blind and haphazard fashion. My propagandist and practical drive was still all too powerful for my scientific and critical disposition. I wanted something done and I did not want to seem to propose extravagant and impossible things.

Most of these 1915 articles were written with a curious flavour of clumsy propitiation or still clumsier menace, with an evident sense that they might be quoted in Germany, and there is a powerful flavour of ignorance, inexperience and self-importance about them. But I felt it was better to blurt out some things badly than not have them put about at all. I insist in this book that Germany will lose the struggle through exhaustion and that in the final settlement Britain must work closely with the United States (not then in the war). I also forecast the repudiation of the Hohenzollerns by Germany and the establishment of a German republic, but I did not anticipate that this would happen as soon as it actually did. There are some flashes of intuition. It was less widely recognized then than it is now that the way to liquidate a bankrupt world is through a rise in prices and a revaluation of gold. In some way I have got at that in this early war-book, and I am also clear that for any conclusive settlement there must be a grouping of states in larger systems. I talk of some hypothetical combination, which I call the "Pledged Allies," which must pursue a policy in common after the war, and I insist that a republican Germany will be altogether more capable of an understanding with such a combination than a monarchy. The Allies—pledged already not to make a separate peace—ought, I argue, to define a policy *now* before the war ends and pledge themselves to insist upon its realization. The idea of an ultimate

Peace Conference becoming a sort of permanent world control is foreshadowed. The boldest paper of all in this amateurish collection of suggestions is a discussion of the possibility of pooling the tropical possessions of the great powers in order to end imperialist rivalries. This particular paper closes with this adumbration of the League of Nations idea, and it shows how far constructive liberal thought had got at that date (1916):

> "And so the discussion of the future of the overseas 'empires' brings us again to the same realization to which the discussion of nearly every great issue arising out of this war has pointed, the realization of the imperative necessity of some great council or conference, some permanent overriding body, call it what you will, that will deal with things more broadly than any 'nationalism' or 'patriotic imperialism' can possibly do. That body must come into human affairs. Upon the courage and imagination of living statesmen it depends whether it will come simply and directly into concrete reality or whether it will materialize slowly through, it may be, centuries of blood and blundering from such phantom anticipations as this, anticipations that now haunt the thoughts of all politically-minded men."

So I was already trying to get the World State recognized as a war objective in 1916.

In the late summer of 1916 I visited the Italian, French and German fronts. There was a fashion in that year of inviting writers and artists to go and see for themselves what the war was like and to report their impressions. I was kept loafing about in Paris for some week or so, I had a talk with Papa Joffre and was presented solemnly with a set of coloured postcards of all the chief French generals, and very good postcards they made. I went through North Italy by Gorizia to the Carso, returned to France to the front near Soissons and then went at my own request to the British front about Arras, to compare the British and French organizations for aerial photography. It was an interesting but rather pointless trip. At Arras I met and went about with O. G. S. Crawford, whose ingenious readings of the air photographs delighted me very much—he is now largely responsible for that interesting periodical*Antiquity*, and he has applied all that he learnt in warfare to the nobler uses of scientific survey. At Amiens I was under the wing of C. E. Montague, the author of *A Hind Let Loose*, *Disenchantment* and *Rough Justice*. Montague was a curious mixture of sixth-form Anglican sentimentality (about dear old horses, dearer old doggies, brave women, real gentlemen, the old school, the old country and sound stock: Galsworthyissimus in fact), with a most adventurous intelligence. He was a radical bound, hide bound, in a conservative hide. He was a year younger than I, he had concealed his age and dyed his silvery hair to enlist at the outbreak of the war, he had accepted a commission with reluctance and I had been warned he was not the safest of guides. We got on very well together. I remember vividly walking with him across the shell-hole-dotted, wire-littered open towards the front line trenches. The sun was shining brightly and there was just the faintest whiff of freshness and danger in the air. I doubt if anything was coming over; what shelling was audible overhead was British. We had agreed that blundering up the wet and narrow communication trench was intolerable in such sunshine and we walked bare-headed and carried our shrapnel helmets, like baskets, on our arms. We had confessed to each other what a bore the war had become to us, how its vast inconsequence weighed us down, and we talked as we trudged along very happily of the technical merits of Laurence Sterne.

In the front line although he insisted on my keeping my head below the parapet, he was exposing himself freely, standing up and craning his neck in the hope of seeing a German "out there."

"At twilight sometimes you can see them hopping about from one shell hole to another."

But there was nothing doing that day, there had been some "strafing" overnight but that was over, everyone in the trenches was sleeping and we returned through the tranquil desolation disputing whether there was any reason for anticipating a great outburst of literary activity as a result of the war. He thought that there ought to be and I thought that outbursts of literary activity were due to such secondary conditions as to have no directly traceable relation to the great events of history....

At the time of this pointless sight-seeing I might have been doing extremely useful war-work at home. I was still convinced that the war had to be won by the Allies and I was only too eager to give my time and risk my life and fortune in any task that used me effectively. But I meant to be used effectively. I refused absolutely to volunteer and drill and acquire the saluting habit for the protection of railway bridges and culverts against imaginary nocturnal Germans in the byways of Essex, or for sentinel-go in prisoners' camps or anything of that sort. But an old notion of mine, the *Land Ironclads* (published in the *Strand Magazine* in 1903) was being worked out at that time in the form of the Tanks, and it is absurd that my imagination was not mobilized in scheming the structure and use of these contrivances. These obvious weapons were forced upon the army by Winston Churchill against all the conservative instincts of the army; Kitchener had turned them down as "mechanical toys," and when at length they were put into action, it was done so timidly and experimentally and with so inadequate an estimate of their possibilities that their immense value as a major surprise that might have ended the war, was altogether wasted. Later some were bogged in Flanders mud, to the great delight of the contemporary military mind. If the tanks could not be prevented, the next best thing from the old army point of view was to spoil them. "Can't use the damned things. Look at *that!*"

Nowadays things have altered in form but not in essence and the British military intelligence, with its unerring instinct for being two decades out of date, is plainly and dangerously tank-mad.

When I heard about the tanks I felt bitter and frustrated, but that did not save me from getting into conflict later with the rigid intelligence of the professional soldiers.

I was lying snug in bed one night and I could not sleep. My window was open and the rain was pouring down outside and suddenly in an imaginative flash I saw the communication trenches swamped and swimming in mud and a miserable procession of overloaded "Tommies" struggling up to the front line along the wet planks. Some stumbled and fell. I knew men were often drowned in this dismal pilgrimage and that everyone who got to the front line arrived nearly worn out and smothered in mud. Moreover the utmost supplies these men could carry were insufficient. Suddenly I saw that this was an entirely avoidable strain. I tumbled out of bed and spent the rest of the night planning a mobile telpherage system. My idea was to run forward a set of T shaped poles with an erector wire, so that they could be all pulled up for use or allowed to lie flat and that two tractor wires could then work on the arms of the T. Power could be supplied by a motor lorry at the base of this line.

Either just before this or just after it I met Winston Churchill at lunch in Clare Sheridan's studio in St. John's Wood. I think it was just before. I had aired my grievance about the tanks and so I was able to get going with him about this telpherage project forthwith. He saw my points and put me in touch with capable men to supplement my mechanical insufficiency. Upon his instructions, E. V. Haigh, who was at the Ministry of Munitions, set the Trench Warfare Department in motion, and a temporary lieutenant Leeming—I think from Lancashire—worked out the apparatus with a group of men and made a reality of my dream.

We invented a really novel war accessory—I contributed nothing except the first idea and a few comments—and it was available as a perfected pattern before the end of the war, though never in sufficient quantity to produce perceptible effects. The "tin hats" did not like it. It would have saved multitudes of casualties and greatly facilitated the opening phases of the Allied offensive in 1918.

This telpherage of ours was no mere static transport system. It could be run forward almost as fast as infantry could advance; any part could be carried by a single man, it could be hauled up for action and lie when not in use; an ordinary lorry, the lorry that had brought up the poles and wire, could work it from a protected emplacement and it could carry an endless string of such loads as a wounded man on a stretcher or an equivalent weight of food or ammunition. We worked a rough trial length on Clapham Common and then installed, in Richmond Park, more than a mile which behaved admirably. If the line were disabled by a shell it was easy to repair and replace, and it was extremely light to bring up. It was practically invisible from the air, since its use wore no track and it could be shifted laterally and dismantled as easily as it was erected. (A description of the "Leeming" Portable and Collapsible Aerial Ropeway is documented with prints and photographs, under date November 26th 1917, in the archives of the Ministry of Munitions.)

This work brought me into closer touch with the military caste than I had ever been before. I had known plenty of men, politicians and so forth, who had been in regular regiments for brief periods, but these men I now encountered were the real army and nothing else. They were the quintessence of Service mentality. They impressed me extraordinarily—excessively. My memories of them I am persuaded must be exaggerated. They remain in my memory as an incredible caricature.

I remember vividly a conference we had in a shed upon the Thames embankment. The soldiers came "well groomed" as the phrase goes, in peculiarly beautiful red-banded peaked caps, heavy with gold braid. Crowns and stars, ribbons, epaulettes, belts and bands of the utmost significance, adorned their persons. War was the most important function in life for them and they dressed for it. They sat down, like men who had given some thought to sitting down in the best possible manner. They produced their voices; they did not merely emit audible turbid thoughts as we did. If you had listened only to the sounds they made, you would have felt they were simple clear-headed men, speaking with a sane determination, and yet the things they said were by my standards almost inconceivably silly. Over against them sat my civilian colleagues, and only David Low could convey to you how comparatively ignoble we looked in our untidy every-day costumes, our bowler hats, our wilted collars, our carelessly chosen and carelessly tied war-time cravats. Judged by the way we carried ourselves we might almost as well have had no chests at all. And though our vocabulary was much more extensive there was no click about it. The noises we made came in shambling loose formation—from Scotland and Lancashire and Cockney London.

That contrast stuck in my mind and haunted me. It exercised me profoundly. It set me thinking of the implacable determination of so many types of life—and perhaps of all types of life—not to over- adapt, to make concessions indeed up to a certain extent, but not to make too fundamental concessions,—to perish rather. It made me waver towards the dogma of the class war. Here were these fine, handsome, well-groomed neighing gentlemen, the outcome of some century or so of army tradition, conscientiously good to look at but in no way showy or flashy, and they had clear definite ideas of what war was, what was permissible in war, what was undesirable about war, what was seemly, what was honourable, how far you might go and where you had to leave off, the complete etiquette of it. We and our like with our bits of stick and iron-pipe and wire, our test tubes and our tanks and our incalculable possibilities, came to these fine but entirely inconclusive warriors humbly demanding permission to give them victory—but victory at the price of all that they were used to, of all they held dear. It must have been obvious to them for instance, that we hated saluting; we were the sort that might talk shop at mess; we had no essential rigidities, no style; our loyalties were incomprehensible; our effect on "the men" if men had to be instructed, might be deplorable. We had therefore in plain English to be outwitted, cheated, discredited and frustrated; and we were.

It was not a plot against us; it was an instinct. Not one of those soldiers would have admitted, even in his secret heart, that that was what he meant to do. But it was what he did. Damn these contrivances! It was far easier to understand a fellow officer from Berlin or Vienna than these Inventors. It was fundamentally more important for those finished products of our militant sovereign state system to beat us than to beat the Germans; they felt that, even if they did not recognize it clearly. We were trying to get hold of their war and carry it God knows where—it would be the story of those beastly tanks over again. It was a fresh encroachment. At any cost it must not become our war; it must remain theirs. Or it might really turn out to be "the war to end war"—and end all sorts of associated things.

In the behaviour of the War Office and Foreign Office and in the strenuous and intelligent resolve of the Crown to keep itself authoritatively in the limelight, the struggle to keep things in their places and resist novelties became more and more manifest as the war continued. The history of the Great War, regarded as an intensifying clash between old forms and new forces, still remains to be written. And yet that is perhaps the most interesting aspect of all. The war between the Allied Powers and the Central Powers was a war between similars; it was the established proper vertical aspect of the war; it was like any old war except that it was bigger. War had been declared; one side had taken the offensive and the other the defensive according to rule. But within the fighting body of each combatant state, there speedily began this more novel struggle, a horizontal struggle, between class tradition and the insistent need for decisive original inventions and new methods. The soldiers could not invent; it had been drilled out of them. And this struggle again was complicated by the progressive disillusionment of the common man who had neither social nor technical standing. He displayed a deepening dislike to being killed either in the old style or the new. At first he had been fiercely patriotic everywhere and then, as the wilting discipline of 1917 and 1918, the mutinies and refusals showed, more and more desperately recalcitrant. These three elements interacted in different proportions and with varying results in every combatant country, and to trace their interplay would carry me far beyond the region of autobiography into an essay in recent history.

In Britain, as in France, the old order contrived to keep in the saddle and its obstinate loyalty to itself prolonged the struggle through two years of intensified and totally unnecessary waste and slaughter. Radical critics obsessed by Marxist suggestions are apt to ascribe this prolongation of the war simply to the wickedness of armament and financial interests. That is only partially true. It is so much easier to denounce "capitalism" than to denounce real categories and specific governmental institutions capable of reprisal. War industry and financial influences, though unquestionably they were evil influences, could not have worked except through the legal forms of the old order. The steel framework of the obstruction was, everywhere, the self-protective obstinacy of the formal government in control, which would not accept even compromise, much less admit defeat. The profiteers no doubt flattered and used the formal government for their own ends but they were never the masters of it. Much more were they its by-products. They sheltered and did their mischief behind its implacable resistance to efficiency.

To the very end of the war not one of all the generals who prance across the page of history developed the ability to handle the vast armies and mechanisms under his nominal control. Nor was any flexible and effective method of collaboration ever brought into being. The Great War was an All Fools' War. But there was no admission of this fact. The system just went on with the witless slaughter until discipline dissolved, first in Russia and then—luckily for us and the immobilized French—in Germany. And instantly upon the German collapse our populace forgot its gathering doubts. The monarchy, lest there should be any question about the way in which the War to End War had ended, went in state through the beflagged streets of London, unashamed amidst a blaze of uniforms and a great blare of military music, to thank our dear old Anglican Trinity, Who had been, it seems, in control throughout, in St. Paul's Cathedral.

Girls, children, women, schoolboys, undergraduates, unfit, middle-aged and elderly men, indispensables and soldiers from the home front, thronged the streets rejoicing; glad that the national martyrdom was over and quite uncritical already of either Army, Navy or Crown. There were a million of us dead of course, and half of those deaths, even from the military point of view had been sheer waste, but after all *we* had won. And the dead were dead. A Grand Inquest on those dead would have been a more reasonable function, but how disagreeable that would have been!

I remember starting out with Jane during one of these pompous, swarming occasions to get from our flat in Whitehall Court to Liverpool Street Station and so escape to the comparative disloyalty of our home at Easton Glebe. Our cab was held up and we had to abandon it and struggle with our bags through the press as well as we could. We squeezed through at last and caught a later train than we intended. It was one of those occasions when my love for my fellow man deserts me. The happy complacency of survivorship shone on every face in that vast crowd. What personal regrets appeared were richly sentimental and easily tearful. "Poor dear Tommy! How he would have *loved* all this!"

We were going to hang the Kaiser and make the Germans pay. The country was now to be made a country "fit for heroes." God save the King!

"And this," thought I, "is the reality of democracy; this is the proletariat of dear old Marx in being. This is the real people. This seething multitude of vague kindly uncritical brains is the stuff that old dogmatist counted upon for his dictatorship of the proletariat, to direct the novel and complex organization of a better world!"

The thought suddenly made me laugh aloud, and after that it was easier to push along and help steer Jane through the crowd about the Royal Exchange....

But I am digressing and telling things out of their proper order.

Aldershot, I presently realized, was resolved not to have anything to do with this telpherage of ours—at least as we had devised it. It was bad enough for soldiers and gentlemen to be bothered with tanks, but this affair of sticks and string was even worse. After mechanical toys—cat's cradle. It was the sort of contraption any one might make mistakes about—and then where were you? However, in its earnest desire to keep the business in professional hands, Aldershot produced alternative systems. They were much heavier and clumsier than ours and one, much in favour, required men to walk along the track, so— as we had to explain to these professional soldiers—exposing the system to air photography and air-directed fire. A bugbear we could never banish from these inflexible minds was the dread that our lines—which could be lowered in an instant and cleared away in an hour—would interfere with "lateral movements."

This in no-man's land with its shell holes and old trenches and jungle thickets of cut wire! The thought of a "line," any line, hypnotized these warriors, just as a chalk line will hypnotize a hen.

I was baffled and worried beyond measure by these perverse

difficulties. I felt my practical incompetence acutely. I did not know whom to get at and how to put the thing through. I had only a dim apprehension of the forces and instincts that were holding back not merely our little contrivance, but a multitude of other innovations that might have changed the face of the war. Meanwhile on every wet night so many poor lads fell and choked in the mud, and the little inadequate offensives squittered forward beyond their supports and succumbed to the counter-attack. I could not sleep for it. I was so worried and my nerves were so fatigued that I was presently afflicted with *allopecia areata*, well known in the flying corps of those days as an anxiety disease, in which the hair comes out in patches. Ridiculous patches of localized shiny baldness appeared and did not vanish for a year or so, when first they sprouted a down of grey hair and then became normally hairy again. It was not much in the way of a war wound, but in all modesty I put it on record.

I returned from the western front in 1916 with, among other things, a very clear conviction that cavalry was a useless nuisance there. I wrote some disagreeable things about the fodder waggons that choked the roads, about spurs and about our military efficiency generally, in a series of articles which became a book, *War and the Future* (1917). But there was a war Censorship in existence, and an excellent gentleman, Colonel Swettenham—or General I forget which—who had for some obscure reason been put in authority over the mind of England, presently summoned me to his presence and remonstrated with me over the galley proofs of my book. I went home with these proofs considerably emasculated, blue-pencilled and amended in the Colonel's handwriting. I meditated over his alterations. They seemed to me to be intended to save rather the prestige of the military authorities than the country, for if people like I were not to chide the military authorities and tell the public about them, who would? These soldiers would go on with their bloody muddle. Muddle until disaster was assured.

I took another set of proofs, made no material changes in what I had said, sent them to my publisher with my explicit assurance that the Censor had seen a set, and then, though it hurt me greatly to destroy many of the painstaking improvements he had made, I burnt the Colonel's set. The book appeared and he must have read it with a certain astonishment. After some consideration of the situation he wrote me a very nice letter asking me to return the set of proofs that he had corrected. I wrote him an even nicer letter, explaining that that set was not now to be found, and assuring him of my utmost esteem. With quite exemplary civility our correspondence ceased at that point and the censorship troubled me no more.

The chief point of permanent value in that book was my insistence on the fact that the progressive mechanization of war was making war impossible for any countries that did not possess a highly developed industrial organization and adequate natural resources. Five or six countries at most had it in their power to make modern war, and it needed only an intelligent agreement among these powers to end war, if they so wished it, for ever. This is a reality I have never ceased to press upon the attention of people in general. From 1916 to 1933 I have been sprinkling the world with repetitions of this important truth. I was stressing it in the *Daily Herald* in March 1930, in a series of articles "The A.B.C. of World Peace," reprinted in *After Democracy* (1933). The consent of all the sovereign powers of the world to world pacification is quite unnecessary. Indeed, as I point out in the latter series of articles, three or four powers alone could impose an enduring World Pax. This idea will be found very frankly expressed in the Crewe House memorandum I shall presently quote.

War and the Future, however, is a very mixed bag. There is a gusto in some of its war descriptions that suggests that that mighty statesman- strategist, that embryo Hitler-Cromwell (aged 13) who won the various Battles of Martin's Hill, Bromley, was by no means dead in me, even in 1916.

§ 6. WORLD STATE AND LEAGUE OF NATIONS

To return to my education by the Great War; 1917 is marked in my records by a letter published in the *Daily Chronicle*for June 4th, entitled "Wanted a Statement of Imperial Policy," by a paper in the *Daily News* August 14th, "A Reasonable Man's Peace" and by a third article, in the *Daily Mail*, which I was invited to write by the editor, "Are we sticking to the Point? A Discussion of War Aims."

These writings show a very considerable consolidation of my ideas and in that respect they followed the movement that was going on in the general mind. They are collected together in a book called *In the Fourth Year* (May 1918) which is an immense advance upon *What Is Coming?*, uncompromising, bolder and more forcible. And in these the idea of a League of *Free* Nations, a plain anticipation of a federal world-state, is stated with the greatest explicitness. One of these papers, "A Reasonable Man's Peace" was twice reprinted as a pamphlet and had an issue, in that form, of about a quarter of a million.

The idea of some supernational Union of States for the preservation of peace is a very old one indeed and its history quite beyond my present range, but the way in which it came into my purview has to be told. The origin of the term "League of Nations" is obscure. Theodore Marburg's *Development of the League of Nations Idea* (1932), is concerned rather with the voluminous participation of that gentleman in the world's affairs than with history—and so the precise facts are difficult to disentangle. His book is essentially an autobiography in the form of letters, and as a general history it over-emphasizes the importance of Theodore Marburg in developing what one may call the Wilsonian notion of a League. A "League to enforce

Peace" was certainly begotten in the Century Club in New York in January 1915 and it seems to have owed something to the private propaganda of Sir George Paish. But the term "League of Nations" is of English origin and it seems to have been first used by a small group of people meeting in the house of Mr. Walter Rea and including Sir Willoughby (now Lord) Dickinson, G. Lowes Dickinson, Raymond Unwin, J. A. Hobson, Mrs. Claremont and Aneurin Williams. (E. M. Forster in his life of Lowes Dickinson (1934) gives reasons for ascribing the term to that writer, who may have used it for the two possible "leagues" he sketched in the first fortnight of the war.) These people founded a League of Nations Society, with Lord Shaw as president, early in 1915. L. S. Woolf also was associated with this group but not, I think, at the beginning.

The world was ripe for the lead embodied in such a phrase and it caught on very rapidly. I was late in recognizing its value. I do not seem to have used the term before the end of 1916, but then I seem to have taken it up abruptly and noisily; it is all over my war writings in 1917, with a very characteristic emendation for which I think I was wholly responsible, the insertion of the word "Free." I put in that word Free because I hoped then for republics in Russia and Germany and possibly in Great Britain. I did not believe in world peace without revolution and my efforts to keep the revolutionary impulse in touch with the peace-making movement were very persistent. Early writings to which I make acknowledgment in *In the Fourth Year* are Marburg's *League of Nations* (1917-18), André Mater's *Société des Nations* (an excellent French comment first published, I think, about 1917 and translated in its entirety in Sir George Paish's excellent collection of early projects, *The Nations and the League*, 1920), and H. N. Brailsford's *A League of Nations* (1917). Several organizations using the term, "League of Nations" in their titles, were active in 1917 on both sides of the Atlantic. I joined the London society in 1917 and was later associated with a League of Free Nations Association formed in 1918. My mind fixed upon this word League, as being just the needed formula that might give a World State its first concrete form. It helped pull my outlook together and point it. *In the Fourth Year* is a crystallization of all the incoherent aspirations of *What Is Coming?* and of my past generally. It contained a few outspoken phrases about such matters as "The Future of Monarchy," which were at that time considered extremely indelicate. English people have still to brace themselves up to the obvious fact that there can be no world pax without a practical retirement of monarchy, graceful or graceless as royalty may choose.

During these war years my always friendly relations with Lord Northcliffe became closer. I have told already in Chapter the Sixth § 4 how we first came to know each other and explained how much this remarkable intruder into the British peerage and British public life, had to improvise to meet the colossal opportunities that were thrust upon him. Whenever I met him I talked plainly to him and he respected even when he did not agree with my ideas. He was never at his ease in the old system; his peerage had not bought him; he knew the old social order accepted him, and his newly titled brothers, by duress and with furtive protest and he felt the continual danger of treacheries and obstructions. There were times when he reminded me of a big bumble bee puzzled by a pane of glass. The court, the army people, the Foreign Office treated him with elaborate civility but regarded him with hard, defensive eyes. When the first Russian revolution (March 1917) occurred, I created a small scandal by inducing him to print a letter in *The Times* in favour of a more explicit appeal to the Republican sentiment in the world. This gave great offence in the highest quarters. "There goes my earldom," said Northcliffe to me, with a gleam from the ineradicable schoolboy in his make-up. One had a sense of fuss behind the scenes, and the young subalterns of the Third Army, who had been in the habit of playing hockey and taking baths and teas and supper at my house at Easton every Sunday, were suddenly forbidden my now leprous neighbourhood by their superior officers. "King and country" had got them surely enough; it was "*his* war"—it was the war of the "tin hats." The war for world civilization had vanished. But one or two of these young men wrote me pleasant notes of apology for this uncivil loyalty imposed upon them.

The government had created two new ministries for the sake of keeping the inquisitive noses of Northcliffe, and his younger competitor Lord Beaverbrook, out of the ancient mysteries of the Foreign Office. This could be done most unobtrusively by busying them elsewhere. The Ministry of Information was devised to prevent Lord Beaverbrook from becoming too well-informed and the Ministry of Propaganda served a similar purpose in occupying and disordering the always rather febrile mind of Lord Northcliffe. Northcliffe asked me to visit him in Crewe House, where the new Ministry of Propaganda was installed, and discussed the general idea of his activities with me.

We sat together in the drawing-room of Crewe House, hastily adapted to the new requirements of ministerial headquarters. "You want a social revolution," he said. "Isn't our sitting here social revolution enough for you?"

I might have replied that that depended on the use we made of our time while we were there.

The upshot of our conversation was that in May 1918 in collaboration with that excellent scholar, Dr. J. W. Headlam, (who afterwards became by knighthood and a change of name Sir J. W. Headlam Morley), I became responsible for the preparation of propaganda literature against Germany. This was almost simultaneous with the publication of *In the Fourth Year* and its exposition of such still admirable common-sense as this that follows:

"The League of Free Nations must, in fact, if it is to be a working reality, have power to define and limit the military and naval and aerial equipment of every country in the world. This means something more than a restriction of state forces. It must have power and freedom to investigate the military and naval and aerial establishments of all its constituent powers. It must also have effective control over every armament industry. And armament industries are not always easy to define. Are aeroplanes, for example, armament? Its powers, I suggest must extend even to a restraint upon the belligerent propaganda which is the natural advertisement campaign of every armament industry. It must have the right, for example, to raise the question of the proprietorship of newspapers by armament interests. Disarmament is, in fact, a necessary factor of any League of Free Nations, and you cannot have disarmament unless you are prepared to see the powers of the council of the League extend thus far. The very existence of the League presupposes that it and it alone is to have and to exercise military force. Any other belligerency or preparation or incitement to belligerency becomes rebellion, and any other arming a threat of rebellion, in a world League of Free Nations.

"But here, again, has the general mind yet thought out all that is involved in this proposition? In all the great belligerent countries the armament industries are now huge interests with enormous powers. Krupp's business alone is as powerful a thing in Germany as the Crown. In every country a heavily subsidized 'patriotic' press will fight desperately against giving powers so extensive and thorough as those here suggested to an international body. So long, of course, as the League of Free Nations remains a project in the air, without body or parts, such a press will sneer at it gently as 'Utopian,' and even patronize it kindly. But so soon as the League takes on the shape its general proposition makes logically necessary, the armament interest will take fright. Then it is we shall hear the drum patriotic loud in defence of the human blood trade. Are we to hand over these most intimate affairs of ours to 'a lot of foreigners?' Among these 'foreigners' who will be appealed to to terrify the patriotic souls of the British will be the 'Americans.' Are we men of English blood and tradition to see our affairs controlled by such 'foreigners' as Wilson, Lincoln, Webster and Washington? Perish the thought! When they might be controlled by Disraelis, Wettins, Mountbattens and what not! And so on and so on. Krupp's agents and the agents of the kindred firms in Great Britain and France will also be very busy with the national pride of France. In Germany they have already created a colossal suspicion of England.

"Here is a giant in the path....

"But let us remember that it is only necessary to defeat the
propaganda of this vile and dangerous industry in four great
countries....

"I am suggesting here that the League of Free Nations shall practically control the army, navy, air forces, and armament industry of every nation in the world. What is the alternative to that? To do as we please? No, the alternative is that any malignant country will be free to force upon all the rest just the maximum amount of

644

armament it chooses to adopt. Since 1871 France, we say, has been free in military matters. What has been the value of that freedom? The truth is, she has been the bond-slave of Germany, bound to watch Germany as a slave watches a master, bound to launch submarine for submarine and cast gun for gun, to sweep all her youth into her army, to subdue her trade, her literature, her education, her whole life to the necessity of preparations imposed upon her by her drill-master over the Rhine. And Michael, too, has been a slave to his imperial master for the self-same reason, for the reason that Germany and France were both so proudly sovereign and independent. Both countries have been slaves to Kruppism and Zabernism—*because they were sovereign and free!* So it will always be. So long as patriotic cant can keep the common man jealous of international controls over his belligerent possibilities, so long will he be the helpless slave of the foreign threat, and 'Peace' remain a mere name for the resting-phase between wars....

"The plain truth is that the League of Free Nations, if it is to be a reality, if it is to effect a real pacification of the world, must do no less than supersede Empire; it must end not only this new German imperialism, which is struggling so savagely and powerfully to possess the earth, but it must also wind up British imperialism and French imperialism, which do now so largely and inaggressively possess it. And, moreover, this idea queries the adjective of Belgian, Portuguese, French, and British Central Africa alike, just as emphatically as it queries 'German.' Still more effectually does the League forbid those creations of the futurist imagination, the imperialism of Italy and Greece, which make such threatening gestures at the world of our children. Are these incompatibilities understood? Until people have faced the clear antagonism which exists between imperialism and internationalism, they have not begun to suspect the real significance of this project of the League of Free Nations. They have not begun to realize that peace also has its price."

With this much on record I went to Crewe House. I think that Northcliffe knew something of what I had in mind. Or to be more accurate I think that at times—in exceptional gleams of lucidity—he knew something of what I had in mind and sympathized with it and wanted to forward it. But his undoubtedly big and undoubtedly unco-ordinated brain was like a weather-chart in stormy times, phases of high and low pressure and moral gradients and depressions chased themselves across his mental map. His skull held together, in a delusive unity, a score of flying fragments of purpose. He was living most of his time in the Isle of Thanet and rushing to and fro between that house of refuge and the excitements of London. I put it to him that we had no clear idea of the work his Ministry of Propaganda had to do, as a whole, and that to make our exertions effective it was necessary that our objectives should be defined.

Before the creation of the ministry, such propaganda as existed had been a business of leaflet distribution by secret agents and by the air, the forging of pseudo-German newspapers with depressing suggestions and the like, and this was already being expanded very energetically when I took up my duties. Descriptions and details are to be found in the *Secrets of Crewe House*. I did what I could to forward all that and to make such modifications as occurred to me, but these activities did not seem to me to exhaust the possibilities of our organization. Telling lies—and occasionally revealing the concealed truth of the situation—to the German rank and file and the Germans behind the front, "attacking morale" as it was termed, was perhaps a necessary operation in this new sort of warfare we were waging, but it was really much more important now to get to something in the nature of a common understanding between the combatant populations if a genuine peace were to be achieved. The best counter-check to the very vigorous war propaganda sustained by the enemy governments, was honest peace propaganda, and I did my utmost to make Crewe House an organization not merely for bringing the war to a victorious end, but also for defining that end with an explicitness equally binding upon us, our Allies and the enemy.

I had no illusions left about the fundamental wisdom of the British and French Foreign Offices. They were, I realized, in the hands of men of limited outlooks and small motives, whose chief control was their servitude to tradition. They had far less grasp of the world situation than an average intelligent man, and the duty of everyone who had a chance, was to help force their hands towards such a "Reasonable Man's Peace" as was now everywhere defining itself in the liberal mind.

One great desideratum was that there should be a plain statement of "War Aims" to the whole world. Then the combatants would realize the conditions of cessation. I persuaded Crewe House that our work necessitated such a statement of what we were fighting for, properly endorsed by the Foreign Office and in conjunction with Headlam Morley a memorandum was prepared, submitted to an Advisory Committee and fully discussed. This Committee, by the bye, consisted of the Earl of Denbigh, Mr. Robert Donald (then Editor of the *Daily Chronicle*), Sir Roderick Jones, Sir Sidney Low, Sir Charles Nicholson, Mr. James O'Grady, Mr. H. Wickham Steed (foreign Editor and later Editor-in-Chief of *The Times*), Dr. Headlam Morley, Mr. H. K. Hudson (Secretary) and myself, and the memorandum to which we agreed said among other things:

"It has become manifest that, for the purposes of an efficient pro-Ally propaganda in neutral and enemy countries, a clear and full statement of the war aims of the Allies is vitally necessary. What is wanted is something in the nature of an authoritative text to which propagandists may refer with confidence and which can be made the standard of their activities. It is not sufficient to recount the sins of Germany and to assert that the defeat of Germany is the Allied war aim. What all the world desires to know is what is to happen *after* the war. The real war aim of a belligerent, it is more and more understood, is not merely victory, but a peace of a certain character which that belligerent desires shall arise out of that victory. What, therefore, is the peace sought by the Allies?

"It would be superfluous even to summarize here the primary case of the Allies, that the war is on their part a war to resist the military aggression of Germany, assisted by the landowning Magyars of Hungary, the Turks, and the King of Bulgaria, upon the rest of mankind. It is a war against belligerence, against aggressive war and the preparation for aggressive war. Such it was in the beginning, and such it remains. But it would be idle to pretend that the ideas of the Governments and peoples allied against Germany have not developed very greatly during the years of the war.... There has arisen in the great world outside the inner lives of the Central Powers a will that grows to gigantic proportions, that altogether overshadows the boasted *will to power* of the German junker and exploiter, *the will to a world peace*. It is like the will of an experienced man set against the will of an obstinate and selfish youth. The war aims of the anti-German Allies take more and more definitely the form of a world of States leagued together to maintain a common law, to submit their mutual differences to a conclusive tribunal, to protect weak communities, to restrain and suppress war threats and war preparations throughout the earth.... The thought of the world crystallizes now about a phrase, the phrase 'The League of Free Nations.' The war aims of the Allies become more and more explicitly associated with the spirit and implications of that.

"Like all such phrases, 'The League of Free Nations' is subject to a great variety of detailed interpretation, but its broad intentions can now be stated without much risk of dissent. The ideal would, of course, include all the nations of the earth, including a Germany purged of her military aggressiveness; it involves some sort of International Congress that can revise, codify, amend and extend international law, a supreme Court of Law in which States may sue and be sued, and whose decision the League will be pledged to enforce, and the supervision, limitation, and use of armaments under the direction of the international congress. ...The constitution of this congress remains indefinite; it is the crucial matter upon which the best thought of the world is working at the present time. But given the prospect of a suitable congress there can be little dispute that the Imperial Powers among the Allies are now prepared for great and generous limitations of their sovereignty in the matter of armaments, of tropical possessions and of subject peoples, in the common interest of mankind.... Among the Allies, the two chief Imperial Powers, measured by the extent of territory they control, are Britain and France, and each of these is more completely prepared to-day than ever it has been before to consider its imperial possessions as a trust for their inhabitants and for mankind, and its position in the more fertile and less settled regions of the world as that of a mandatory and trustee....

"But in using the phrase 'The League of Nations,' it may be well to dispel certain misconceptions that have arisen through the experimental preparation, by more or less irresponsible persons and societies, of elaborate schemes and constitutions of such a league. Proposals have been printed and published, for example, of a Court of World Conciliation, in which each sovereign State will be represented by one member—Montenegro, for example, by one, and the British Empire by one—and other proposals have been mooted of a Congress of the League of Nations, in which such States as Hayti, Abyssinia, and the like will be represented by one or two representatives, and France and Great Britain by five or six. All such projects should be put out of mind when the phrase 'League of Free Nations' is used by responsible speakers for the Allied Powers. Certain most obvious considerations have evidently been overlooked by the framers of such proposals. It will, for example, be a manifest disadvantage to the smaller Powers to be at all over-represented upon the Congress of any such League; it may even be desirable that certain of them should not have a *voting* representative at all, for this reason, that a great Power still cherishing an aggressive spirit would certainly attempt, as the beginning of its aggression, to compel adjacent small Powers to send representatives practically chosen by itself. The coarse fact of the case in regard to an immediate world peace is this, that only five or six great Powers possess sufficient economic resources to make war under modern conditions at the present time, namely, the United States of America, Great Britain, France, Germany, Japan, and doubtfully, Austria- Hungary. Italy suffers under the disadvantage that she has no coal supply. These five or six Powers we may say, therefore, permit war and can prevent it. They are, at present, necessarily the custodians of the peace of the world, and it is mere pedantry not to admit that this gives them a practical claim to preponderance in the opening Congress of the World League...."

This memorandum was sent, with a covering letter from Lord Northcliffe, to Lord Balfour for the endorsement of the Foreign Office. We had all been kept in the dark as to the cramping secret engagements which had been made by our diplomatists, and we had no suspicion that our broad and reasonable proposals were already impossible. We were not enlightened. Dr. Headlam Morley and I were invited for a conversation with Lord Tyrrell who was then Sir William Tyrrell. Possibly he intended to give us a hint about the secret treaties but, if so, he never did as he intended or the hint was too feeble to register upon our minds. Tyrrell was a compact self-assured little man, who tacitly put our memorandum on one side, rested his elbow on it, so to speak, and delivered a discourse on our relations to France and Germany and on the "characters" of these countries, that would have done credit to a bright but patriotic school-boy of eight, and so having told us exactly where we were, he dismissed biologist and historian together unheard. I suppose he had learnt that stuff for gospel from his governess at his knickerbocker stage, and had never had the wit to doubt it. Most upper-class mentality is founded on governesses. According to such lights as he had acquired in his tender years, he was perfectly honest and patriotic—if a little "pro-French."

It is terrifying to think that these vast powers, the Foreign Offices of the world, are being run to a very large extent by little undeveloped brains such as Tyrrell's, that they are immensely protected from criticism and under no real control from educated opinion. And what they do affects and endangers hundreds of millions of lives.

That conversation was the utmost Crewe House got out of the Foreign Office. We assumed rather rashly that our memorandum had been tacitly accepted and pursued our propaganda activities on those lines. That, from the diplomatic point of view was admirable, because in our quasi-official rôle we gave assurances to doubtful Germans, that could afterwards be repudiated. We were in fact decoys. Just as T. E. Lawrence of the "Seven Pillars" was used all unawares as a decoy for the Arabs. And all for nothing! Plainly I had not learnt the A.B.C. of diplomacy.

There were at that time several small organizations promoting the League of Nations idea. I took part in a successful attempt to consolidate these into one League of Nations Union, which would not merely spread but develop the idea. I put the stress upon the development. It was conspicuously evident that, so far, the idea was lacking in detail and definition; it was like a bag into which anything might still be put and there were a number of things that I felt were very undesirable as occupants of that bag and others that were vitally important. I was already alive, as that Crewe House memorandum shows, to the danger of a pseudo-parliamentary organization, with an enfeebling constitution, and I felt we had to get ahead of that by working out some clearer statement of the possibilities of the occasion. We evolved therefore a "Research Committee" which could press on with this necessary preliminary work. It consisted of the following members, most of whom, I must admit, did no work whatever upon it; Mr. Ernest Barker, Mr. Lionel Curtis, Mr. G. Lowes Dickinson, Viscount Grey of Fallodon, Mr. John Hilton, Professor Gilbert Murray, Mr. H. Wickham Steed, Mr. J. A. Spender, Mr. L. S. Woolf, Mr. A. E. Zimmern, and myself, with Mr. William Archer as secretary. It produced only two pamphlets "The Idea of a League of Nations" and "The Way to the League of Nations" before events superseded it.

The former of these pamphlets ends with this passage:

> "Negative peace is not our aim. It is something, of course, to have a rest from suffering and the infliction of suffering; but it is a greater thing to be set free, and peace sets people free. It sets them free to live, to think, to work at the work that is best worth doing, to build instead of destroying, to devote themselves to the pursuit or the creation of the things that seem highest, instead of having to spend all their time in trying to avoid being killed. Peace is an empty cup that we can fill as we please; it is an opportunity which we can seize or neglect. To recognize this is to sweep out of one's mind all dreams of a world peace contrived by a few jurists and influential people in some odd corner of the world's administrative bureaux. As well might the three tailors of Tooley Street declare the millennium in being. Permanent world peace must necessarily be a great process and state of affairs, greater indeed than any war process, because it must anticipate, comprehend, and prevent any war process, and demand the conscious, the understanding, the willing participation of the great majority of human beings. We, who look to it as a possible thing, are bound not to blind ourselves to, or conceal from others, the gigantic and laborious system of labours, the immense tangle of co-operations, which its establishment involves. If political institutions or social methods stand in the way of this great good for mankind, it is fatuous to dream of compromises with them. A world peace-organization cannot evade universal relationships.

"It is clear that if a world league is to be living and enduring, the idea of it and the need and righteousness of its service must be taught by every educational system in the world. It must either be served by or be in conflict with every religious organization; it must come into the life of every one, not to release men and women from loyalty, but to demand loyalty for itself. The answer to the criticism that world peace will release men from service is, that world peace is itself a service. It calls, not as war does for the deaths, but for that greater gift, for the lives, of men. The League of Nations cannot be a little thing: it is either to be a great thing in the world, an overriding idea of a greater state, or nothing. Every state aims ultimately at the production of a sort of man, and it is an idle and a wasteful diplomacy, a pandering to timidities and shams, to pretend that the World League of Nations is not ultimately a State aiming at that ennobled individual whose city is the world."

We got as far as that. And then President Wilson essentially ill- informed, narrowly limited to an old-fashioned American conception of history, self-confident and profoundly self-righteous, came to Europe and passed us by on the other side. Men of my way of thinking were left helpless, voiceless and altogether baffled outside the fiasco of Versailles. What had seemed to be the portal of a World Control standing wide open to us, was shut and slammed in our faces.

My friend Philip Guedalla, discussing this period of memorandum-writing with me the other day, recalled a letter which he declared I had sent to President Wilson, at the President's request, through the hands of Mr. Bainbridge Colby in November 1917. He alleged that through this letter I had contributed materially to the President's "Fourteen Points." I think very poorly of the Fourteen Points and at the time I was unable to recall any communication justifying this accusation. A search was made, however, and finally a copy of the following letter was disinterred. The original was conveyed, with Mr. Guedalla's assistance, past any risks of war-time censorship to Mr. Colby who had gone on to Paris.

I doubt whether this letter was ever actually read by President Wilson though we have Colby's word for it that it reached his hands. I never heard from President Wilson in the matter. Colonel House came to Easton Glebe while the President was in England, but he and Mrs. House were so anxious to hurry on to "see over" Hatfield, the historical mansion of the Cecils, that there was no possibility of any political talk. A chance to see Hatfield might not recur. My letter therefore has no grain of historical importance, but in the light of the concluding passage of the preceding section it has considerable autobiographical significance.

It runs:—

Dear Mr. Bainbridge Colby,

You asked me, after our conversation at the Reform Club on the evening of November the fourteenth, to set down on paper my views upon the part America might and should play in this war. It was not the military side of the matter that engaged us, though I feel very strongly that by a bold use of scientific inventions the American intelligence, accustomed to a large handling of economic problems and the free scrapping of obsolescent material and methods, may yet be of enormous service and stimulus to the Allied effort; it was rather the political rôle of America about which we talked. I warned you that I was perhaps not to be taken as a representative Englishman, that I was scientifically trained, a republican, and "pro-American." I repeat that warning now. Here are my views for what they are worth.

They are based on one fundamental conviction. There is no way out of this war process—there may be a peace of sorts but it will only lead to a recrudescence of war—except by the establishment of a new order in human affairs. This new order is adumbrated in the phrase, *A League of Nations*. It lies behind that vaguer, more dangerous because less definite, phrase, "a Just Peace." We have, I am convinced, to set our faces towards that order, towards that just peace,*irrespective of the amount of victory that falls to us.* We may achieve it by negotiations at any point when the German mind becomes open to the abandonment of militant imperialism. If by a sudden change and storm of fortune we found Germany deserted by her allies, prostrate at our feet, our troops in Berlin and her leaders captive, we could do no more, we should do ourselves and the whole future of mankind a wrong if we did more, than make this same "Just Peace" or set up this League of Nations. There is, I hold, a definable *Right Thing* for most practical purposes in international relations; there are principles according to which boundaries can be drawn and rights of way and privileges of trade settled and apportioned (under the protection of the general League) as dispassionately as a cartographer makes a contour line.

This I believe is the conviction to which a scientific training leads a man. It is the conviction, *more or less* clearly developed, of rational-minded people everywhere. It is manifestly the idea of President Wilson. It is the conviction that has to be made to dominate the world.

And this conviction of a possible dispassionate settlement is one for which the world is now ready. I am convinced that in no country is there even one per cent of the population anxious to prolong the war. The ninety and nine are seeking helplessly for a way out such as only a dispassionate settlement can give. But they are kept in the war by fear. And by mental habit. Few men have the courage to reach their own convictions. They must be led to them or helped to them. They fear the greed of their antagonists, fresh wars, fresh outrages, and an unending series of evil consequences, if they seem to accept anything short of triumph. No one can read the newspapers of any belligerent country without realizing the overwhelming share of fear in now prolonging the struggle. Germany as much as any country fights on and is helpless in the hands of her military caste, *because there is no confidence in Germany in the possibility of a Just Peace.* There is an equal want of confidence in London and Paris and New York. To create a feeling of confidence in that possibility of a Just Peace everywhere is as necessary a part of our struggle for a right order in the world as to hold the German out of Calais or Paris.

It is easy to underrate the pacific impulse in men and to overrate their malignity. All men are mixed in their nature and none without a certain greed, baseness, vindictiveness. After the strain and losses of such a struggle as this it is "only in human nature" to prepare to clutch and punish whenever the scales of victory seem sagging in our favour. Too much importance must not be attached to the aggressive patriotism of the Press in the belligerent countries. Let us keep a little humour in our interpretation of enemy motives and remember that though a man has still much of the ape in his composition, that does not make him an irredeemable devil. The same German who will read with exultation of the submarining of a British passenger ship, or pore over a map of Europe to plan a giant Germany reaching from Antwerp to Constantinople, founded on blood and dreadfulness and ruling the earth, will, in his saner moments, be only too ready to accept and submit himself to a scheme of general good will, provided only that it ensures for him and his a tolerable measure of prosperity and happiness. The belligerent element is present in every man, but in most it is curable. The incurably belligerent minority in any country is extremely small. There is a rational pacifist in nearly every man's brain, and the right end of the war can come only by evoking that.

It is here that the peculiar opportunity of America and of President Wilson comes in. America is three thousand miles from the war; she has no lost provinces to regain, no enemy colonies to capture; she is, in comparison with any of our Allies except China, a dispassionate combatant. (If China can be called a combatant.) No other combatant except America can talk of peace without relinquishing a claim or accepting an outrage. America alone can stand fearlessly and unembarrassed for that rational settlement all men desire. It is from America alone that the lead can come which will take mankind out of this war. It is to America under President Wilson that I look as the one and only medium by which we can get out of this jangling monstrosity of conflict.

What is wanted now is a statement of the Just Peace, a statement without reservations. We want something

more than a phrase to bind the nations together.
America has said "League of Nations" and everywhere
there has been an echo to that. But now we want America
to take the next step and to propose the establishment of
that League, to define in general terms the nature of the
League, to press the logical necessity of a consultative,
legislative, and executive conference, and to call together
so much of that conference as exists on the Allied side.
*There will never be such a conference until America
demands it.* There will never be a common policy for
the Allies or a firm proposal of peace conditions, unless
America insists. This war may drag on for another year
of needless bloodshed and end in mutual recriminations
through the sheer incapacity of any Ally but America to
say plainly what is in fact acceptable to all.

In addition to the moral advantage of its aloofness,
America has a second advantage in having a real head,
representative and expressive. Possessing that head,
America can talk. Alone in our system America is
capable of articulate speech. Russia is now headless, a
confusion; Italy is divided against herself; in France and
Britain politicians and party leaders make speeches that
are welcomed here and abused there. No predominant
utterance is possible. It will be no secret to an observant
American such as you are, that Britain and France
are divided in a quarrel between reactionary and
progressive, between aggressive nationalism and modern
liberalism. All the European allies are hampered by
secret bargains and pacts of greediness. They have soiled
their minds with schemes of annexation and exploitation
in Syria, in Albania, in Mesopotamia and Asia Minor.
Russia was to have had Constantinople, and so forth and
so forth. This ugly legacy of the old diplomacy entangles

our public men hopelessly to-day. Even where they are willing to repudiate these plans to-day for themselves they are tied by loyalty to the bright projects of their allies, and silenced. Their military operations have had no real unity because their policy, their war aims, have been diverse. The great alliance against the Central Powers has been a bargain system and not a unification. The allied statesmen, challenged as to their war aims, repeat time after time the same valiant resolution to "end militarism," free small nations, and the like, standing all the time quite resolutely with their backs to the real issues which are the control of the Tropics, the future of the Ottoman Empire, and international trade conditions. So it seems likely to go on. Any voice that is raised to demand a lucid statement of the Allied aims in these matters is drowned in a clamour of alarmed interests. In Britain and France "hush" in the interests of diplomacy is being organized with increasing violence. Only America can help us out of the tangle by asserting its own interpretation of the common war purpose, and demanding a clear unanimity on the part of the Allies. The war was begun to defeat German imperialist aggression. It is with extreme reluctance that the European powers will accept the one way to salvation, which is the abandonment of all imperialist aggression and the acceptance of a common international method. The League of Nations is a mere phrase until it is realized by a body whose authority is supreme, overriding every national flag in the following spheres, in Africa between the Sahara and the Zambesi, as a trustee in Armenia, Syria and all the regions of the earth whose political status has been destroyed by the war, and permanently upon the high seas and vital channels (such as the Dardanelles) of the world.

America in the last three years has made great strides from its traditional isolation towards a responsible share in framing the common destinies of mankind. But America has to travel further on the same road. The future of America is now manifestly bound up with the peace of Europe, for that peace cannot be secured unless these sources of contention in the supply of tropical raw material and in the transport and trading facilities of the world are so controlled as to be no longer sources of contention. It is easy to argue that America has "no business" in Central Africa or Western Asia, that these are matters for the "powers concerned" to decide. But it is just because America has no "business" in Central Africa and Western Asia that it is necessary that America should have a definite will about Africa and Western Asia. Her aloofness gives her her authority. The "powers concerned" will never of their own initiative decide. They are too deeply concerned, and they will haggle. It is, I fear, altogether too much to expect a generous scheme for the joint settlement of regions by powers who have for a century cultivated a scheming habit of appropriation. But none of these powers can afford to haggle against the clear will for order of America at the present time.

What is suggested here is not a surrender of sovereignty nor a direct "international control" of tropical Africa, but the setting up of an over-ruling board composed of delegates from the powers concerned: Frenchman, Englishman, Africander, Portuguese, Belgian, Italian and (ultimately) German, to which certain functions can be delegated, as powers are delegated to the government of the United States of America by those states. Among these functions would be transport control, trade control, the arms and drink trades, the revision of legislation affecting the native and his land, the maintenance of a supreme court for Central Africa, the establishment of higher education for the native, and the systematic disarmament of all the African possessions. A similar board, a protectorate board, could take charge of the transport, waterways, customs, and disarmament of the former Ottoman empire. Only by the establishment of such boards can we hope to save those regions from becoming at the end of this war, fields of the bitterest international rivalry, seed-beds of still direr conflicts. It is in the creation and support of such special boards, and of other boards for disarmament, international health, produce control and financial control, that the reality of a League of Nations can come into being. But Europe is tied up into a complexity of warring and jostling interests; without an initiative from America it is doubtful whether the world now possesses sufficient creative mental energy to achieve any such synthesis, obvious though its need is and greatly as men would welcome it. In all the world there is no outstanding figure to which the world will listen, there is no man audible in all the world, in Japan as well as Germany and Rome as well as Boston—except the President of the United States. Anyone else can be shouted down and will be shouted down by minor interests. From him, and from him alone, can come the demand for that unity without which the world perishes, and those clear indications of the just method of the League of Nations for which it waits.

There is another area, an area beyond the scope of international controls, which remains an area of incalculable chances because no clear *dominant idea* has been imposed upon the world. This is Eastern Europe from Poland to the Adriatic. The Allies have no common idea, and they never have had a common idea and do not seem to be capable of developing a common idea about this region. They do not even know whether they wish to destroy or enlarge the Austro-Hungarian system. Vague vapourings about the rights of nationality conceal a formless confusion of purposes. Yet if the Allies have no intention of rending the Austro-Hungarian empire into fragments, if they do not propose to cripple or dismember Bulgaria, it is of the extremest importance that they should say so now. There is no occasion to make the Austrian and Bulgarian fight, as if he fought for his national existence, when he is really only fighting for Germany. All liberal thought is agreed upon the desirability of a practically independent Poland, of a Hungary intact and self-respecting, of a liberated Bohemia, of a Yugo-Slav autonomous state. None of these four countries are so large and powerful as to stand alone, and there are many reasons for proposing to see them linked into a league of mutual protection, mutual restraint and mutual guarantees. Add only to this system the present German states of the Austrian empire, and such a league would be practically a continuation of that empire. But the European Allies lack the collective mental force, lack the mouthpiece, lack the detachment and directness of purpose necessary for the declaration of their intentions in this matter, and they will probably go into the peace conference unprepared with a decision, a divided and so an enfeebled crowd, unless America for her own good and theirs, before the end of the war, gives the lead that will necessitate a definite statement of war aims. Only President Wilson and America can get that statement. To us in Europe our statesmen have become no better than penny-in-the-slot gramophones, who at every challenge for their war aims, say "Evacuate Belgium, restore Alsace-Lorraine to France and Italia Irredenta to Italy, abandon militarism and—*Gurrrr!*" The voice stops just when it is beginning to be interesting. And because it stops the war goes on. The war goes on because nothing can be extracted from the Allies that would induce any self-respecting Bulgarian, Austrian or democratic-minded German to regard peace as a practicable proposition. They have their backs up against the wall, therefore, side by side with the German militarist—who is the real enemy—because we will not let them have any alternative to a fight to the death.

There, my dear Mr. Bainbridge Colby, are the views you ask for. You have brought them on yourself. You see the rôle I believe America could play under President Wilson's guidance, the rôle of the elucidator, the rôle of advocate of the new order. Clear speech and clear speech alone can save the world. Nothing else can. And President Wilson alone of all mankind can speak and compel the redeeming word.

§ 7. WORLD EDUCATION

My awakening to the realities of the pseudo-settlement of 1919 was fairly rapid. At first I found it difficult to express my indignant astonishment at the simulacrum of a Peace League that was being thrust upon Europe. I was embarrassed and rather puzzled to find that men I had reckoned upon surely as associates, Gilbert Murray for instance, Zimmern, Ernest Barker and J. A. Spender and that dignified figurehead Grey, were all, it seemed, content with this powerless pedantic bit of stage scenery. In spite of the fact that they had committed their names to the most explicit denunciation of a sham world parliament, of an uncontrolled armament trade and of a weaponless league from which the former enemy states were to be indefinitely excluded, they not only accepted this incredibly defective organization, but became eager apologists for it. I clung to the original demands and promises of Crewe House and the League of Nations Union. This I insisted was not the thing that had to be.

What looked like everyday commonsense but was, in effect, sheer imaginative destitution was all against me. I was rather in the position into which a man would have been put by Dr. Johnson if he had talked to him of the possibility of electric lights and air liners. The fact that in the violent passage that would no doubt have ensued, he would have been right and the great Doctor altogether wrong, would not have prevented him from looking and feeling like an egregious fool. I was invited most urgently to feel that my ideas were preposterous and unacceptable. My futile voice mingled feebly with the feeble protests of a few other intelligent men behind the wainscot while the conference rooms reverberated to the feet of the "statesmen" and the pompous expressions of their "policies." I think the first intelligent man to emerge from behind the wainscot and make himself really audible was J. M. Keynes in his *Economic Consequences of the Peace* (1919).

I will not here enter into any discussion of Woodrow Wilson, I never met him, and the quintessence of what I have to say about him is to be found in Book V § 6 of that most discursive novel, *The World of William Clissold*, in which I contrast his triumphant reception in Rome in January 1919 with the funeral of David Lubin, forced to travel obscurely and circuitously to the cemetery through side streets because of the Wilson parade. Nor will I expatiate again upon the strange phase of docility and expectation in the world at the end of 1918, which mocked the limitations of Wilson and Lloyd George and Clemenceau. That I have conveyed (chiefly by quotations from Dr. Dillon and J. M. Keynes) in the *Outline of History* (Chapter XXXIX §§ 3 and 4 in the 1932 Edition). Slowly I realized the full significance of that passage cited from *The Idea of the League of Nations* about the "gigantic and laborious system of labours, the immense tangle of co-operations" demanded of us, and set about seeking how among the new conditions, the still non-existent foundations of a real and enduring World State might yet be planned and laid.

During the various discussions, committee meetings and conferences that occurred in the course of the consolidation of the earlier League of Nations organizations into the League of Nations Union, I had been very much impressed by the perpetually recurring mental divergences due to the fact that everyone seemed to have read a different piece of history or no history at all, and that consequently our ideas of the methods and possibilities of human association varied in the wildest manner. The curious fact dawned upon me that because I was not a "scholar" and had never been put under a pedant to study a "period" intensely and prematurely, and because I had a student's knowledge of biology and of the archæological record, I had a much broader grasp of historical reality than most of my associates in this mixture of minds which, as the League of Nations Union, was trying to fuse itself into a directive and controlling public opinion. I began to talk more and more decisively of the need for "general history" and to express opinions such as I embodied finally in a pamphlet "*History Is One*" (1919). I proposed that our Research Committee should organize the writing and publication of a history of mankind which should show plainly to the general intelligence, how inevitable, if civilization was to continue, was the growth of political, social and economic organizations into a world federation.

My idea was at first an outline of history beginning with an account of the Roman and Chinese empires at the Christian era, and coming up to contemporary conditions. It was to be a composite Gibbon, with Eastern Asia included and brought up to date. But it became very speedily plain to me that no such broad but compact historical synthesis by authoritative historians was possible. They lived in an atmosphere of mutual restraint. They would not dare to do anything so large, for fear of incidental slips and errors. They were unused to any effective co-operation and their disposition would be all towards binding together a lot of little histories by different hands, and calling the binding a synthesis; and even if they could be persuaded to do anything of the sort it would certainly be years before it became available. I was already making a note-book for my own private edification and for use in the controversies that I felt were gathering ahead, and the idea of writing up this note-book of how the present human situation had come about and publishing it—if only to demonstrate that there was some other method possible in history than that of sheer indiscriminate aggregation—became more and more attractive.

It did not occur to me that this Note-Book or Outline of History would be a particularly saleable production. I wanted to sketch out how the job might be done rather than to do it. Before I began it I had a very serious talk with my wife about our financial position. The little parcel of securities we had accumulated before 1914 had been badly damaged by the war. Its value had fallen from about £20,000 to less than half that amount. But the success of Mr. Britling had more than repaired that damage and my position as a journalist had improved. We decided that I could afford a year's hard work on this *précis* of history, although it might bring in very little and even though I risked dropping for a time below the habitual novel reader's horizon. As a matter of fact I dropped below that horizon for good. I lost touch with the reviewers and the libraries, I never regained it, and if I wrote a novel now it would be dealt with by itself by some special critic, as a singular book, and not go into the "fiction" class. I set to work, undeterred by my burning boats, with the *Encyclopaedia Britannica* at my elbow, to get the general shape of history sketched out. It planned itself naturally enough as a story of communications and increasing interdependence. It became an essay on the growth of association since the dawn of animal communities. Its beginning was carried right back before the appearance of viviparous types of life, to those reptiles which shelter their eggs and protect their offspring, and it came on in one story of expanding relationship to the aeroplane-radio-linked human world of to-day. The essay grew beyond expectation, but that stress upon continually more effective communications, upon the gathering co-ordination of lives, is still, as even the reader of the *Outline's* List of Contents can see, the gist of it all.

I will not here detail how with the *Outline*, as with *Anticipations*, my sense of the importance of my subject grew as I worked upon it. I saw more and more plainly that this was the form, the only right form, in which history should be presented to the ordinary citizen of the modern state, this, and not "King and Country" stuff, was the history needed for general education, and I realized too that even my arrangement of notes, if it was properly "vetted" by one or two more specialized and authoritative helpers, might be made to serve, provisionally at least, for just that general review of reality of which we stood in such manifest need if any permanent political unity was to be sustained in the world. I persuaded Sir Ray Lankester, Sir Harry Johnston, Gilbert Murray, Mr. Ernest Barker, Sir Denison Ross, Philip Guedalla and various other men of knowledge among my friends, to go over my typescript for me, I got J. F. Horrabin, who makes charts that talk, to help me with some exceptionally eloquent maps, and I suggested to Newnes and Co. the possibility of a publication in parts prior to the publication of the *Outline* in book form by Cassells. In America, Mr. G. P. Brett of The Macmillan Co., was very doubtful about the prospects of the book, but finally he brought it out at the rather odd price of 10 dollars and 10 cents.

The public response was unexpectedly vigorous, both in Britain and America. Edition after edition was sold on both sides of the Atlantic. It made a new and wider reputation for me and earned me a considerable sum of money. Over two million copies of the *Outline* in English have been sold since 1919, it has been translated into most literary languages except Italian—it is proscribed in Italy because it detracts, they say, from the supreme grandeur of Mussolini's Rome—and it continues to sell widely. *A Short History of the World* (1922) has also had an extensive sale. The ordinary man had been stimulated by the war to a real curiosity about the human past; he wanted to be told the story of the planet and of the race, plainly and credibly, and since the "historians" would not or could not do it, he turned to my book. It was quite open to those worthy teachers to do the job over again and do it beyond measure better, but until they could manage to do that, people had either to remain in ignorance of this exciting subject, as one whole, or else go on reading me, or Van Loon, or some other such outsider who had not been sterilized by an excess of scholastic pretension.

Unhappily, though the professional teachers of history could not bar the reading public from access to the new history of all mankind that was now unfolding itself, they were much more successful in keeping it out of the schools. To this day, in school and syllabus, King and Country and Period still prevail and it is still just a matter of luck whether or no an intelligent boy or girl ever comes to the newer rendering of historical fact. Yet beginning history point-blank with mediæval England is as logical and sensible as it would be to begin chemistry with the study of cookery recipes or patent medicines.

The immense popularity of the *Outline of History* was a very exciting success for me. My self-conceit has always had great recuperative power; it revived bravely now; and I saw a still wider possibility behind the *Outline*, the possibility of giving Mr. Everyman an account not merely of past events, but of the main facts about the processes of life in general and the social, economic and political state of the world. I gave this possibility a preliminary airing in some lectures I wrote but never delivered— they were intended for America—and which I reprinted in a book *The Salvaging of Civilization.*

Therein I developed a scheme which I called the "Book of Necessary Knowledge" or the "Bible of Civilization." That idea was first broached by Comenius, and, some time before me, Dr. Beattie Crozier was insisting that every culture needed its "Bible." I owe the phrase to him. My League of Nations Union experience had enforced my conviction that for a new order in the world there must be a new education and that for a real world civilization there must be a common basis of general ideas, that is to say a world-wide common-school education presenting the same vision of reality. Someone had to begin upon that restatement of educational ideas. I was in no way qualified for such a beginning, yet no one else was stirring, and presently I found myself casting about for colleagues and collaborators in order to complete that first sketch of a world citizen's ideology of which my *Outline of History* was a part. Instead of arguing endlessly about what had to be done, it seemed simpler and more effective to demonstrate, however roughly, what had to be done.

I should have liked to call these books that were taking shape in my mind an *Outline of Biology* and an *Outline of Social and Economic Science*. But following the success of the *Outline of History* a number of so-called "Outlines" of Art—of Literature— of Science—of this and that, had been put upon the market and widely advertised and distributed. They were not really outlines at all; they were miscellanies of articles by various hands with hardly any common thread of interest, but they exhausted the meaning of the word so completely that when at last after much toil and tribulation I got the books I wanted done, I called them

The Science of Life and *The Work, Wealth and Happiness of Mankind*respectively.

In organizing the writing of the *Science of Life* I was greatly helped by my early association with biological work and by the facts that my eldest son was a biological teacher and that the able grandson of my teacher Huxley, Julian Huxley, was my friend. He has an extraordinary full and detailed knowledge of the whole biological field. We three got together in 1927 and we made a scheme that covered every division of our immense subject. We worked very harmoniously throughout and, after a part publication, produced the book in 1930.

I had already been casting about for suitable helpers to collaborate in the same fashion upon a summary of social, political and economic science, but in this I was less successful. I entangled my scheme with an inconvenient associate and it had to be disentangled. I need not go into the particulars of my troubles here. The plan I had in mind for this work was bold and more novel than that of either of its predecessors; it was nothing less than an attempt to fuse and recast all this group of "subjects" into one intelligible review of Man upon his planet. It was to begin with a description of his material life and its evolution and it was then to describe the social, legal, political and educational organizations that had grown up as necessary concomitants of developments. Just as the *Outline of History* was an experiment in analytical history, so this was to be an experiment in synthetic, descriptive economics and politics. The exactest name for such a synthesis would be the Outline of Human Ecology. But I did not call it that because the word Ecology was not yet widely understood.

Hendrik Van Loon, I may note, has done three books which, in an entirely different manner, approach much the same popular conspectus as my own. They are called *The Story of Mankind*, *The Liberation of Mankind* and *The Home of Mankind*; and if presently he does *The Work of Mankind*, he will have covered practically all my territory, outside the *Science of Life*, and with a very useful and desirable extension into the field of topographical geography. I do my work in my own style and so does he, and for many readers his type of survey may prove to be more attractive and stimulating than mine. *The Work, Wealth and Happiness of Mankind*, I have felt for some time, might very well be supplemented by a broad geographical survey.

My trouble with my hastily selected assistant wasted most of my working time for half a year. Two privately printed pamphlets distributed to the members of the committee of the Authors' Society embalmed that tiresome dispute. In the end I brought in a number of fresh advisers and helpers and did the *Work, Wealth and Happiness of Mankind* as I had done the *Outline of History* by "mugging up" the material and writing or rewriting practically all of it myself, and then getting the various parts vetted and revised and, in one part, rewritten by specialists. It appeared in 1931 and it has sold very well, but not at all on the scale of the *Outline of History*. It is only now appearing in a popular edition. On the whole considering the greater novelty of the design, I am quite as well satisfied with it as I am with its two companions.

These three works taken together do, I believe, still give a clearer, fuller and compacter summary of what the normal citizen of the modern state should know, than any other group of books in existence. They shape out something that will presently be better done. Clearly there must be some factor, in the relative unsuccessfulness of the latter two thirds of the trilogy, which escapes me. They must need further simplification and consolidation. I have not, I think any extravagant delusions about their quality, but I have perhaps too high an estimate of the value of their general conception.

I am convinced that the informative framework of a proper education should be presented as the three sides of the triangle I have drawn in them; Biology, History and Human Ecology. A child should begin with Natural History, a History of Inventions, Social

Beginnings and Descriptive Geography, that should constitute its first world picture, and the treatment of these subjects should broaden and intensify before specialization. I believe that minds resting on that triple foundation will be equipped for the rôle of world citizens, and I do not believe that a world community can be held together in a common understanding except upon such a foundation. This is not to say that my books are anything more than first exploratory experiments in this foundation work. But they do constitute a very serious first experiment and they foreshadow a new education as it was not foreshadowed until I wrote them.

* * * * *

In this account rendered of the purpose and substance of my life-work I must here insert in a sort of parenthesis one or two other subsidiary books which will otherwise find no place in this story. In 1920 I made a brief visit to Russia, talked to a number of Communist leaders, including Lenin, and published my impressions in a book, *Russia in the Shadows*, and in 1921 I went to Washington to report upon the Disarmament Conference of that year, in a series of newspaper articles which became *Washington and the Hope of Peace*. Since these books were incidents in my development they must be mentioned here, but I need not expatiate upon them.

Here too I must mention, though I need not enter at length into the particulars of it, the Decks Case which came to an end, after five years of legal proceedings, in 1933. Miss Deeks was a Canadian spinster who conceived the strange idea that she held the copyright in human history. She was permitted and encouraged to sue me, as the author of the*Outline of History*, for infringement of copyright and to produce a manuscript, which she alleged had existed in the form in which she produced it before the publication of my Outline, in support of her claim for

£100,000 and the suppression of my book. No evidence of the prior existence of her manuscript, as produced, was ever exacted from her, and she was allowed to carry this silly case from court to court—each court dismissing it contemptuously with costs against her—up to the Privy Council. When finally that court disposed of her conclusively, with costs, she declared her inability to pay a penny of the £5,000-worth of fees and charges that these tedious and vexatious proceedings had entailed upon me. And there the matter ended. Life is too short and there is too much to do in it for me to spend time and attention in hunting out whatever poor little assets Miss Deeks may have preserved from her own lawyers and expert advisers. She has to go on living somehow and her mischief is done. I hope she is comfortable and that she is still persuaded she is a sort of intellectual heroine. I saw her once in court, when I had to give sworn evidence in my own defence, and I found her rather a sympathetic figure. She impressed me as quite honest but vain and foolish, with an imagination too inflamed with the idea of being a great litigant for her to realize what an unrighteous nuisance she was making of herself; there was something faintly pathetic, something reminiscent of Dickens' Miss Flyte, in the way in which she fussed about with her lawyers, with much whispering and rustling of papers, giving her profound and subtle instructions for the undoing of our dire conspiracy; and it is not against her, but against those who encouraged and egged her on, that I am disposed to be resentful.

Since 1914 I had been on very friendly terms with F. W. Sanderson, the headmaster of Oundle, to whom I sent my boys at the outbreak of the war. Sanderson was an original and vigorous teacher, who was feeling his way in a manner all his own, towards a modernized education. He was at the practical end of the business in immediate contact with boys, parents and school governors and I was at the other end in contact with public affairs and the League of Nations, and we converged very interestingly in our talks. My boys, as children at home, had acquired very good French and German and I, just back from my first visit to Russia in 1914 (see *Joan and Peter*), persuaded him to add a Russian teacher to his staff for their benefit, the first Russian teacher, I believe, in any English public school.

Sanderson was a ruddy plethoric man, with his voice in his throat, and always very keen to talk. His mind found its best expression in his very characteristic school sermons; the actual practice of his school and the ideas of his staff lagged far behind his ambitions. He was greatly occupied with the development of a special building at Oundle when he died, The House of Vision, in which boys were to go and think out life. It was to be a sort of museum displaying universal history and the world as a whole; it was to give very much what my three outline books were designed to give, a unified conception of the world drama in which they had to play their parts.

Sanderson was growing mentally and his reach and boldness were increasing to the very day of his death. That came very suddenly and shockingly to me, for I was in the chair at a lecture at University College in the summer of 1922 when—at the end of a rather wandering discourse, his overtaxed and neglected heart stopped beating and he fell dead on the platform beside me.

This lecture was to have opened new ground and he had made great preparations for it. He had added the toil of a sort of mission to Rotarians and people of that sort, to his already heavy work as a headmaster, and this lecture was to have been a key utterance. Apart from my keen sense of the loss of his intimacy and co-operation I was greatly distressed at this abrupt truncation of his work; he was only sixty-five and he seemed full of a panting vitality that might have gone on for years.

I did all I could to put him on record before his prestige faded. I got together an official *Life* (1923) and, finding myself hampered by the reserves and suppressions customary in such compilations, I also wrote my own impression of him in*The Story *of a Great Schoolmaster* (1924). It is so personal and affectionate an impression and it is so expressive of my own educational conceptions as well as his, that if I could I would incorporate it, just as I would like to incorporate my introduction to *The Book of Catherine Wells*, in this already greatly distended autobiography. His successor had none of his distinctive spirit and understanding, and the light of that House of Vision was never lit. In *The Story of a Great Schoolmaster*, I have described how I visited it and found that lantern for the imagination, empty and abandoned six months after his death. Oundle lacked and still lacks the understanding or the piety to carry out his scheme.

I will merely mention here such other incidental books of mine as *A Year of Prophesying*, 1924, and *The Way the World Is Going*, 1929. They are collections of newspaper articles in which I hammer away at my leading ideas, not always very tactfully, and the rare, curious reader who may wander into these volumes will find variations perhaps in the method of approach but nothing of essential novelty.

With this I round off my account of another main mass of my work, my own personal attempt to shape out the informative content of a modern education. Necessarily it is a lopsided account, almost Marburgesque in the way in which the parallel work and thought of other people fall into the background. I have for instance got through this section with no mention of such a book as James Harvey Robinson's *Mind in the Making* or the New History movement in America. But I am not writing a history of modern ideas in the world. I am writing the story of modern ideas in the mind of one sample person, H. G. Wells.

And as I look at the table in my study piled up with my own books and with correspondence and controversial books and pamphlets—quite a little heap for example, including Hilaire Belloc's *Companion to the Outline of History* and *Some Errors of H. G. Wells* by Dr. Downey the Roman Catholic Bishop of Liverpool, I have, except for a passing allusion to Catholic controversialists in Chapter the Eighth, § 3, passed over altogether—I am quite unable to make up my mind how far these millions of printed words are already dead litter and how much is still touching and moving minds. Is all this, and the kindred stuff of similar writers, producing any sensible and permanent effect upon education throughout the world? Much of it has certainly failed, because it was written hastily or just badly, because it was directed at the wrong brains, because it was alloyed with baser metal, prejudices or brief angers that let in corruption. But is it mostly going to be missed? Never in this world will it be possible to make a just estimate of what it has done.

There is a queer little twist in my private vanity, a streak of snobbish imitativeness, which disposes me at times to parallel my lot with Roger Bacon's. I dress up my *persona* in his fashion. This disposition is in evidence in the opening chapter of *The Work, Wealth and Happiness of Mankind*. When I am most oppressed by the apparent lack of direct consequence to all my voluminous efforts, when I doubt whether the modernization of the content of education upon the lines I have drawn in my triple outlines can possibly be done in time to save our present social order, then is it most comforting to me to compare myself with Bacon in his cell scribbling away at those long dissertations of his about a new method of knowledge, which never even reached, much less influenced, the one sole reader, his friend the Pope, in whom he had hope for the realization of his dream. Which nevertheless in the course of a few centuries came to the fullest fruition. I play at being such a man as he was, a man altogether lonely and immediately futile, a man lit by a vision of a world still some centuries ahead, convinced of its reality and urgency, and yet powerless to bring it nearer.

But this is just an imaginative indulgence, a private vice I nurse, and directly I set it down here in plain black and white its absurd unreasonableness is plain. It is only my present preoccupation with my own work that gives me that single-handed feeling. Inflammation of the ego, I began to realize, is inevitable to any autobiographer in action, and that intensifies this disposition. In truth I am neither solitary nor suppressed. I merely happen to be the one I know best among a number of people who are all thinking very closely upon the same lines. Instead of writing manuscripts that will rest unread or be merely glanced at for centuries, we are printing and scattering our ideas by the million copies.

As I write here there must be between two and three million copies of my own books scattered about the world, and many more millions of other books and newspaper articles, lectures and discourses by other hands, all driving in the same direction. Every day several thousands of fresh minds respond to some part of the suggestions we are making; a teacher here alters his teaching a little; a reader thinks over a point and argues with his friend; a journalist gets a new idea of things and echoes it in an article; an orthodox parson suddenly feels insecure. It was not to be expected that all at once all the schools would experience a change of heart, have a great burning of textbooks and start off at a tangent towards the new learning; nor is it reasonable to complain that even among those who advocate a fresh education for citizenship the apprehension of what we are driving at is usually very inadequate. If the Eric Yarrow Memorial, that House of Vision, stands, misused and abortive, at Oundle, it is only like some gun that has been hit by a shell on the road to victory.

There is no proof that the seed we have already sown has died. On the contrary, the signs of vitality increase. Now it is a series of lessons in some elementary school; now it is a string of broadcast talks like those of Commander King-Hall; now it is a book for children or the newspaper report of a provincial lecture, that comes reassuringly, another fresh green blade forcing its way to the light. The new ideology creeps upon the world *now*. There is nothing in our circumstances to-day to justify this comparison with the spiritual and imaginative isolation of that untimely man who first proclaimed the strange possibilities of experimental science. Our period is far more like the seventeenth than the thirteenth century in its realization of mutation and progressive possibility.

The thoughts of Roger Bacon were like a dream that comes before dawn and is almost forgotten again. The sleeper turns over and sleeps on. All that Roger Bacon wrote was like humanity talking in its sleep. What is happening now is by comparison an awakening. In a dream we can in a flash of time see things complete because what is happening is happening without resistance in a single brain—and then they pass; but the realization of a new day comes to thousands before it comes to millions; at first the illumination is almost imperceptible, everything is touched by it while nothing stands out; there is a slow leisureliness in its manner of approach that belies its steady and assured incessancy.

§ 8. WORLD REVOLUTION

Concurrently with those laborious and troubled efforts to anticipate the necessary informative content of a modern education, my brain was also returning to the problem I had first raised as that New Republic of *Anticipations* which fructified in my *Modern Utopia*, the problem of organizing the coming world-order, in the body and out of the existing substance of the order of things as they are.

The temptation for active men eager for results to shirk this problem, or to stave it off with some immediately workable but essentially evasive formula, has always been very great. The first French Revolution was conducted upon an assumption of "natural" virtue and the American Revolution was essentially a political change and an economic release from an alleged and grossly caricatured "tyranny," a change and release which brought with it scarcely any modification in the liberated system. But Marx did not shirk this fundamental problem. My habitual polemical disposition to disparage Marx does not blind me to the fact of his pioneer awareness of this forest of difficulties in the theory of revolution. He did realize that a movement to reconstruct a society is unlikely to receive the immediate enthusiastic support of the majority of those who fit into and profit by its existing arrangements.

Such people may of course produce profound changes without intending it, as the curiosity of the gentlemen of the Royal Society or the excitement of the South Sea speculators evoked inventions, discoveries and developments of the most world-shaking sort, but they did these things quite unaware of the dangerous dragons they were releasing. It is necessary to find discontent before conscious revolutionary effort is possible; and, in insisting upon that point, Marx was leading his generation. But it has been the refrain of my lifetime that Marx antagonized property and the expropriated too crudely, and that he confused mere limitation and unhappiness with the rarer and more precious motive of creative discontent. He was himself too energetic and self-centred to realize how meekly human beings can be put upon if they are caught young, how susceptible they are to mass as well as to individual self-flattery and how unwilling to admit and struggle against disadvantages. Most men are ready to sympathize with the under-dog but few will allow they are themselves under-dogs. Nor did Marx realize how acutely people who have wealth and position can be bored and distressed by the existing state of affairs. He looked therefore to the Indignant Proletarian evolved by his own imagination as the sole driving force of his revolution and he stamped the theory of the Class War upon human affairs with immense and fatal determination.

I have pointed out already that the dead impracticability of the Socialism of the opening twentieth century was due to the want of any realizable conception of a Competent Receiver for collectivized property and enterprises. The untutored masses of expropriated people are obviously unable to discharge the functions of an administrative receiver. Something had to be done about it. The "Dictatorship of the Proletariat" of the Communists, is a jerry-built Competent Receiver run up in a hurry to meet this objection. It is not good enough for its job. It is a controversial answer and not a practical solution. But Lenin's reconstructed Communist Party was a much more effective step towards an organized receivership.

To abandon the Class War theory of revolution is to give up the use of a very sustaining opiate and to face an intricate riddle. For many rough immediate purposes, drugged fighters may do better than clear-headed ones, but not in the long run.

One is forced to admit that in periods of tolerable general prosperity (as in America up to 1927) or stabilized repression (as in Hanoverian England), there is little hope for direct revolutionary effort. The illusion of stability must have been undermined in some way before the human intelligence will brace itself up to the stresses and vexations of constructive work. In the past the driving discontent has often appeared as a conflict between oppressed and oppressors, either as a class or as a race conflict, and it is still insufficiently realized that the peculiar discontents and instabilities of the present time do not follow that time-honoured formula. The issues are polygonal, they are not two-sided. And it is to mental and not to social classes that we have to appeal.

The other day at the Film Society show (March 11th, 1934) I saw Eisenstein's stirring film *October*, in which noble and enthusiastic proletarians chase corrupt and over-fed imperialists and capitalists and their parasites out of the Winter Palace. The peculiar rôle of a third party in the fight, the Russian Navy, is understressed throughout. Never have I encountered a statement more obstinately misleading. Navies have played a large part in revolutionary history, in Turkey and Germany, notably, as well as in Russia. Every armed technical force is a living weapon with a solidarity of its own, that may turn upon a mentally feeble government which does not use it effectively. The real unorganized proletarians were in fact, if not in film, merely the chorus in the October revolution. That will be their lot in any revolution still to come.

A constructive revolution under modern conditions must begin fragmentarily, it must begin here and there, and it will have associated with it a considerable riff-raff of merely eccentric, extravagant, disgruntled and discredited individuals. These have to be handled with care and discrimination. Revolution begins with the misfits. Every revolutionary process arises out of developing dislocations and disproportions. And the interesting thing about our present situation is the fact that there is no social stratum, no organization, state, nation, school, army, navy, air force, bank, law, industry where the realization among the personnel that things are out of adjustment is not becoming acute. It is a ridiculous travesty of the situation to deal with our western world as a self-complacent "Capitalist System," squatting ruthlessly on masses of enslaved victims who have merely to revolt and evoke a millennium. Russia, after overthrowing the Capitalist System as it manifested itself under the Tzar, has floundered back through several experimental stages to state capitalism, and except that she has rid herself of some very encumbering traditions and types and broached some important experiments, she is still confronted by essentially the same riddles as the western world.

Now, if this is sound, then, I submit, it follows that *everywhere* in the social complex we shall find certain main types of mental reaction dependent upon innate or very intimate personal characteristics. We shall find an originally preponderating number of people carrying on from the phase of apparent stability, hanging on to the current usages to which they are accustomed and trying to the very last to believe that things will go on according to precedent, we shall find an increasing proportion, the resentfully defensive type, disposed to resist, by violence, any change in their habits and we shall also have a number of the open-minded innovating types who will be ready to recognize that something has to be done in the way of adaptation and rearrangement, even if this involves a sacrifice of old customs and privileges and preconceived ideas. As the sense of instability grows, the numbers of both these latter sorts of people, the revolutionaries and the violent reactionaries, will increase at the expense of the first, the contented sort which wants to escape bothers, and the intelligence and will-for-change of the third kind, in particular, will be quickened. In certain social groups dependent largely upon the general liveliness of mind prevailing in them, the tendency to become either viciously defensive or alertly innovating may vary. Such an artificial occupation as that of a stockbroker or a professional betting man naturally attracts people of a narrow-minded smart type and is not likely to turn the mind to any social rearrangements that may threaten the technique of the stock-exchange or the turf, and fewer retired rentiers are likely to give their minds to revolutionary reconstruction than public health officials or hydraulic engineers. But in most spheres of interest, in law, public administration, medicine, engineering, industry, education and even the compulsive services, intensifying dislocation is likely to call an increasing proportion of questioning and planning brains into constructive activity. These are the only brains to which we can look for creative drive. For the purposes of revolutionary theory the rest of humanity matters only as the texture of mud matters when we design a steam dredger to keep a channel clear.

These questioning, planning and executive brains which will be stimulated by the realization of social impermanence and insecurity, will start, every one of them, from some fixed system of ideas. Their immediate reactions and activities will be determined at first by the established routines out of which they awaken, and so the early stages of their activities, at any rate, are likely to be not only extremely diverse and chaotic but conflicting. On the other hand the violent reactionaries will have a natural solidarity about the Thing that Is. The primary problem in revolutionary theory is to discover the general formulae, which will reduce the waste through diversity and imperfect apprehension to a minimum, and evoke the most rapid and efficient co-ordination of creative effort.

I have told already of my conception of a New Republic (in 1900) and of my elaboration of this idea in *A Modern Utopia* (1906) and how I tried to make the Fabian Society into an order of the Samurai—to the great excitement of Pease, Shaw, Bland and Sidney Webb, and, to my own effectual discomfiture. I tried to put an acceptable face on my retreat from the Fabian conflict, but that was by no means easy. I had to swallow the dose that I had attempted to do something and failed completely. I had to realize that I had no organizing ability and no gift for leading or directing people. To make up for that, I told myself I would write all the better. But *The New Machiavelli* (1911) with its pose of the deflated publicist in noble retirement is obviously a compensatory production. *The Research Magnificent* (1914) betrays a mind still looking for some method of effective public action. Before it was half written, the livid glares and deepening shadows of the Great War fell across its pages and a new grade in my education began.

I have traced already how the war process stormed across my mind and how my attention was shifted from social structure to international affairs and so to the relation between popular education and international feeling. The idea of doing all I could for the reconstruction of the content of education became so dominant with me that it ruled my intellectual life and shaped my activities for some years. For a time I was so busied with the production of those three books embodying a modern general ideology, that I gave little attention, far too little attention, to the question whether my general idea was being put over to any large number of people. Then I began to feel that I was going on "in the air," that at the best I was producing fairly saleable but, it might be, essentially ineffective books. I might be shooting beside the mark altogether. I became impatient for palpable results.

In some manner the new education had to be got into the education office and the syllabuses and the schools, and since no one else seemed to be doing it, I felt under an obligation to try, however ineffectively, to do something about it myself. I turned my reluctant face towards meetings and committee-rooms again. I had had nothing to do with such things since my Fabian withdrawal. I heard with dislike and a sinking heart my straining voice once more beginning speeches. I dislike my voice in a meeting so much that it gives me an exasperated manner and I lose my thread listening to it. I still thought the Labour Party might be the party most responsive to constructive ideas in education, and in order to secure a footing in its councils I stood as Labour candidate for the London University at the 1922 and 1923 elections. I had no prospect of being returned, but I thought that by writing and publishing election addresses and such leaflets as *The Labour Ideal of Education* (1923) I might impose a modernization of the schools curriculum, upon the party policy and so get general history at least into its proper place as elementary school history.

In a speech at the University of London Club, in March 1923, reprinted as *Socialism and the Scientific Motive*, I find I was trying to persuade myself and my liberal-minded hearers of the essential identity of these two things. But I was not really persuaded. I was declaring what ought to be was fact. I was poking about in this political stuff not because I believed it to be the way to my ends, but because I did not certainly know any way to my ends, and this seemed to hold out possibilities. But the older men in control of the Labour Party at that time were quite impervious to the idea of changing education. They did not know that there could be different kinds and colours of education. A school, any school, was a school to them and a college a college. They thought there was something very genteel and desirable about education, just as there was about a municipal art gallery, and they wanted the working classes to have the best of everything. But they did not consider education as a matter of primary importance. They had themselves managed very well with very little.

A phase of great restlessness and discontent came upon me in 1923-24. I was doing what I felt to be good work in making a digest of modern knowledge and ideas available for the general reader, but this did not fully engage my imagination. I could not subdue myself to the idea that this was the limit of my effectiveness. I made speeches and when I read the reports of them I could not believe I had said so little. I gave interviews and was overwhelmed by a sense of fatuity when they came home to roost. I wrote articles and they seemed to me more and more like the opening observations to something that was never really said. I was oppressed by a sense of encumbrance in my surroundings and of misapplied energy and time running to waste.

In the introduction to this autobiography I have already remarked upon the fugitive element in most intellectual lives, but it is only now as I bring facts and dates together that I realize the importance of fugitive impulses throughout my own story. At phase after phase I find myself saying in effect: "I must get out of this. I must get clear. I must get away from all this and think and then begin again. These daily routines are wrapping about me, embedding me in a mass of trite and habitual responses. I must have the refreshment of new sights, sounds, colours or I shall die away."

My revolt against the draper's shop was the first appearance of this mood. It was a flight—to a dream of happy learning and teaching in poverty. To a minor extent and with minor dislocation this fugitive mood no doubt recurred but it did not come back again in full force until my divorce. Then it is quite clear that it clothed itself in the form of a dream of a life of cheerfully adventurous writing. The concealed element was that my work with Briggs was boring me. That divorce was not simply the replacement of one wife by another; it was also the replacement of one way of living by another. It was a break away to a new type of work.

I detect all the symptoms of the same flight impulse again about 1909, but then there was not the same complete material rupture with my established life. But *The New Machiavelli* (published in 1911) is quite plainly once more the release of the fugitive urgency, a release completed in imagination if not in fact. I realize now (and the queer thing is that I do realize only now) that the idea of going off somewhere—to Italy in the story—out of the tangle of Fabian disputes, tiresomely half-relevant politics and the routines of literary life, very nearly overwhelmed me in my own proper person, and the story of Remington and Margaret and Isabel is essentially a dramatized wish. I relieved my tension vicariously as Remington. He got out of my world on my behalf—and wrote in lofty tranquillity of politics in the abstract, à la *Machiavelli*, as I desired to do.

We shifted house from Sandgate to London (1909) and from London to Easton Glebe (1910) and there I settled down again. All that is quite sufficiently told in *The Book of Catherine Wells*. The huge issues of the War and the Peace held my mind steady and kept it busy for some years. But in 1924 the same mood returned, so recognizably the same, that I am surprised to realize how little I apprehended the connection at the time. If I did not get to writing in Italy in the pose of *The New Machiavelli*, I got to the south of France. It was much the same thing. It was the partial realization of my own fantasy after twelve years. What I did I did with the connivance and help of my wife, who perceived that I was in grave mental distress and understood how things were with me. I did not immediately head for France. I went by air first to the Assembly of the League of Nations at Geneva with the idea of going on thence to wander round the world. It was at Geneva that I changed my plans and turned southward to Grasse. I found it was quite possible to get out of things, for some months at least, much as Remington did, establish myself in a quiet corner among the hills, stay there cut off from the daily urgencies of England, sift my thoughts and purposes in peace and presently write.

I began a life in duplicate. The main current of my ostensible life still flowed through my home at Little Easton in Essex; there the mass of my correspondence was dealt with and all my business done, but at the *mas* known as Lou Bastidon near Grasse, I dramatized myself as William Clissold, an industrialist in retreat,—the prophet Hosea could not have been more thorough in 'his dramatization—and I set this Mr. William Clissold to survey and think out how the world looked to him. For three winters I lived intermittently in that pleasant sunlit corner, living very plainly and simply, sitting about in the sun, strolling on the flowery olive terraces about me, going for long walks among the hills behind, seeing hardly anything of the fashionable life of the Riviera that went on so near to me. And the main thread of my thought and writing for all that time was how to realize the New Republic and bring it into active existence.

I wish that seasonal retirement to Lou Bastidon could have gone on to the end, but obscure difficulties and complications; a craving for an efficient bathroom, electric light and a small car, it may be, presently undid me. I attempted to reproduce Lou Bastidon on a firmer foundation and behold! the foundation became a pitfall. I began to play with house-building and garden-planning. There is a vividness, an immediate gratification of the creative instinct in this amusement, which can distract the mind very readily from reality. Men and women take to building and gardening as they take to drink, in order to distract their minds from the whole round world and its claim upon them, and all the Riviera is littered with villas that testify to the frequency of this impulse. I acquired some land with a pretty rock, vines, jasmin and a stream close by, and I planned and built a house which I called *Lou Pidou*, and after that rash act the cares of house-holding and car-owning and gardening began to grow up about me. The Riviera also got wind of me and reached up sociable tentacles towards my retreat. Lou Pidou was an amateurish, pretty house with a peculiar charm of its own but it insisted upon growing and complicating itself; it became less and less of a refuge and more and more of an irksome entanglement with its own baffling bothers and exactions. I worked there with dwindling zest and energy and stayed less and less willingly and for briefer periods, as those good long sunlit hours in which I could think became rare and ragged and the necessity for management and attention more clamorous, until presently a time came, in May 1933, when I realized I could work there effectively no more.

It was early in 1933 that the opening section of this autobiography was written and the mood of this phase is fully described in that section.

I cast Lou Pidou at last as a snake casts its skin. It needed an effort, but once more the liberating impulse was the stronger. I resolved that I would sell it, or if necessary give it away, and have done with it. I took a farewell stroll in my olive orchard up the hill, said good-bye to my new and promising orange-trees and rose-beds, gave my parental benediction to the weeping-willows and the banks of iris I had planted by my stream, sat for awhile on my terrace with a grave black cat beside me, to which I was much attached, and then went down the familiar road to Cannes station for the last time.

I returned to London by way first of a stormy but entertaining International P.E.N. Congress at Ragusa, over which I presided, and then a holiday in what was altogether new country for me, the fresh green loveliness of Austria in early summer. My flat in London is now my only home. The two small boys who figure at the end of Chapter the Eighth are parents to-day with pleasant households and sons and daughters of their own, and Easton

Glebe which is described in *The Book of Catherine Wells* was sold after her death in 1927. It had become too large for me and too empty altogether. I have indeed seen family life right round now from beginning to end. That stage is over. A flat above the rumble of Baker Street and Marylebone Road is as good a place as any to work in and easy to maintain; I can go away when I please and where I please for as long as I please; and London, for all my outrageous radicalism, is a very friendly and pleasant city to me. If I have no garden of my own, Regents Park just outside my door grows prettier every year; there are no gardens like Kew Gardens and no more agreeable people in the world than the people in the London streets.

The World of William Clissold, the book I wrote in Lou Bastidon, has a rambling manner but it seems to ramble more than it actually does from my main preoccupation. Its gist, to which, after four Books mostly of preparatory novel writing to get the Clissold brothers alive, I came in Book Five, is the possibility of bringing the diffused creative forces of the world into efficient co-operation as an "Open Conspiracy." I am supposing myself to be in the position of an intelligent industrialist with a sound scientific training and this is how I make him see it:

> "It is absurd to think of creative revolution unless it has power in its hands, and manifestly the chief seats of creative power in the world are on the one hand modern industry associated with science and on the other world finance. The people who have control in these affairs can change the conditions of human life constructively and to the extent of their control. No other people can so change them.

> "All other sorts of power in our world are either contributory or restrictive or positively obstructive or positively destructive. The power of established and

passive property, for example, is simply the power to hold up for a price. The power of the masses is the strike, it embodies itself in the machine-breaking, expert-hunting mob.... It is only through a conscious, frank and world-wide co-operation of the man of science, the scientific worker, the man accustomed to the direction of productive industry, the man able to control the arterial supply of credit, the man who can control newspapers and politicians, that the great system of changes they have almost inadvertently got going can be brought to any hopeful order of development.

"Such men, whether they mean to be or not, are the actual revolutionaries in our world.... I believe that we industrials and the financiers are beginning to educate ourselves and broaden our outlook as our enterprises grow and interweave. I believe that if we can sufficiently develop the consciousness of contemporary business and associate with it the critical co-operation and the co-operative criticism of scientific and every other sort of able man, we can weave a world system of monetary and economic activities, while the politicians, the diplomatists, and the soldiers are still too busy with their ancient and habitual antics to realize what we are doing.... We can build up the monetary and economic world republic in full daylight under the noses of those who represent the old system. For the most part I believe that to understand us will be to be with us, and that we shall sacrifice no advantage and incur no risk of failure in talking out and carrying out our projects and methods quite plainly.

"That is what I mean by an Open Conspiracy.... Many things that now seem incurably conflicting, communism and international finance for example, may so develop in the next half-century as to come to drive side by side, upon a parallel advance. At present big distributing businesses are firmly antagonistic to co-operative consumers' associations; yet one or two of the big distributors have already made important deals with these large-scale economic organizations from the collectivist side. Both work at present upon very crude assumptions about social psychology and social justice. Both tend to internationalize under the same material stresses.

"I find it hard to doubt the inevitability of a very great improvement in the quality and intellectual solidarity of those who will be conducting the big business of the world in the next century, an extension and an increased lucidity of vision, a broadened and deepened morale. Possibly my temperament inclines me to think that what should be must be. But it is patently absurd to me to assume that the sort of men who control so much of our banking to-day, limited, traditional, careless or doctrinaire, are the ultimate types of banker. It seems as irrational to suppose that such half-educated, unprepared adventurers as Dickon and myself and our partners and contemporaries are anything but makeshift industrial leaders, and that better men will not follow us. Dickon and I are, after all, at best early patterns, 1865 and 1867 models...."

All this was written before anyone was thinking of such an American President as Franklin Roosevelt and his astonishing effort so to regulate a loose capitalist system as to thrust it rapidly towards State Socialism. Where the Clissold version of the Open Conspiracy is least defensible is in its easy disregard of the fact that though privately created productive, industrial and distributive organization is to a large extent capable of direct socialization, *private finance is something absolutely and incurably different in its spirit and conduct from any conceivable sort of public finance.* It is an attempt to extract profit out of what should be a public service, the exchange machinery. It is as anti-social as it would be to attempt to get profits by falsifying the standard yard. That, we have since found out. The industrious reader will find it in course of being found out in the *Work, Wealth and Happiness of Mankind.* The public control of credit and a scientific reorganization of the world's monetary system is the necessary preliminary stage in carrying out a planned world economy. Like myself and our English labour leaders and indeed practically everybody in 1926, William Clissold was still in need of some hard thinking about the relations of money and credit to private ownership.

Furthermore—in an exaggeration of my own aversion from the class-war doctrine—too wide a gap was set by Clissold in his world between the industrial organizer and the technological assistant and skilled artisan. The workers were dismissed as being just workers and the political possibilities and capacity of their better equipped stratum was ignored. I was identifying myself with my imaginary business man almost too thoroughly. I was evidently still sore about the Labour Party as I had found it. In my reaction against the mass democracy that had produced Macdonald, Snowden, Thomas, Clynes and the like as its representative heads, I underrated the steadily increasing intelligence of the more specialized workers and of the ambitious younger working-men. To them at any rate William Clissold is an impersonation to apologize for.

The World of William Clissold was published in 1926. It was published as an important book and it received a very considerable amount of useful destructive criticism. So that I reconsidered this Open Conspiracy almost as soon as it was launched. It was a sound instinct which made me do that book not in my own first person but in the form of a trial personality. I was soon struggling to disentangle myself from various rash commitments of Clissold's and get on to a revised view. I had had this first exercise in general political statement handed back to me with ample corrections—mostly in red ink,—and I wanted to profit by them.

In the spring of 1927, I was asked to lecture in the Sorbonne and I chose as my subject *Democracy under Revision,* in which I insisted on the necessity for some such organization as my Samurai to replace the crude electoral methods of contemporary politics. This was, so to speak, Open Conspiracy propaganda adapted to the peculiarly narrow French outlook. My wife, I may note here, was with me in that Paris journey, we were fêted and entertained and very happy together, and neither of us realized that death was already at work in her and that in six months we should be parted for ever. The title page of that printed lecture is the last of all the title pages on which I ever drew a "picshua" for her. I reproduce it here as a reminder of the life-long companionship and the persistent, unassertive help that underlies all this tale of work. Our last half year together I have described in *The Book of Catherine Wells.*

After her death I sat down to alter and explain my conception of the Open Conspiracy more exactly—to myself first and then to others. I wrote a little book The *Open Conspiracy: Blue Prints for a World Revolution* (1929) and I was so convinced of its unavoidably tentative quality that I arranged its publication so as to be able to withdraw it, revise it completely and republish it again after a lapse of two years. I did this under the new title of *What Are We to Do with Our Lives?* (1931). In this, the third version of the Open Conspiracy plan, I began to feel I was really settling down to definitive detail. *The Work, Wealth and Happiness of Mankind,* which was launched after many difficulties in 1932, also contained in its political and educational chapters, and based on a description of current conditions, an even more explicit statement of the Open Conspiracy plan. The definition was still clearer; and the touch surer.

In all this work I was really only cleaning up, working out, and sharpening the edges, dotting the i's and crossing the t's of the problem of the New Republic. The Open Conspiracy was my New Republic plus a third of a century of experience. It was a working plan in the place of Anticipations. I was moving with my generation from a speculative dreamland towards a specific project.

Picshua: Title page of "Democracy Under Revision."

In *After Democracy* (1932) I collected together a number of diverse papers, a lecture given in the Reichstag building in Berlin (1928), a lecture given to the Residencia des Estudiantes in Madrid (1932), a memorandum on the world situation prepared at the request of one or two influential people in America in 1932, and at first privately circulated, a lecture to the Liberal Summer School at Oxford (1932) and arising out of the latter, a paper, *A Liberal World Organisation*, in which I gave still further definition from this point of view and that of the same conception. I also tried out my general idea, with very little response, in the *Daily Herald* (December 1932) under the title *There Should Be a Common Creed for Left Parties Throughout the World*. This has been reprinted as an Introduction to the *Manifesto* of the new Fellowship of Progressive Societies— which is a sort of Fellowship of the New Life fifty years later. The exploratory note in these papers diminished to a minimum as my ideas grew more precise. Each successive change was smaller than the one that went before.

The Shape of Things to Come (1933) is the last important book I have written. It is as deliberate and laborious a piece of work as anything I have ever done and I took great pains to make it as exciting and readable as I could without any sacrifice of matter. There are one or two episodes of quite lively story-telling. I was becoming sufficiently sure of my ground to let my imagination play upon it. The device of a partially deciphered transcription of a fragmentary manuscript got over a multitude of the technical difficulties that arise in an anticipatory history. I think I have contrived to set out in it my matured theory of revolution and world government very plainly.

The World of William Clissold was written during a "boom" phase in the world's affairs, the profound rottenness of the monetary-credit system was still unrealized, and so Clissold turned to social boredom and the irritation of seeing industrial and mechanical invention misused, in order to evoke the discontent necessary for a revolutionary project. But by the time *The Work, Wealth and Happiness of Mankind*, which was, so to speak, the workshop in which was built *The Shape of Things to Come*, was in hand, the artificiality and unsoundness of those boom conditions had become glaringly obvious. The realization was spreading through all the modern categories of workers, the men of science, the men of invention, the big-scale industrial organizers, the engineers, the aviators, the teachers and writers, the social workers, the mass producers, every sort of skilled artisan, every honest and creative-minded man, indeed, everywhere, that if the new mechanical civilization by which they lived was to carry on, they had to be up and stirring. The Open Conspiracy of William Clissold was essentially speculative, optional and amateurish; the Open Conspiracy of De Windt which took possession of a derelict world, was presented as the logical outcome of inexorable necessity. Only through personal disaster or the manifest threat of personal disaster can normal human beings be sufficiently stirred to attempt a revolutionary change of their conditions.

Step by step through that logic in events, the new pattern of revolution has been brought from Utopia and from the vague generalizations of the New Republic, towards contact with contemporary movements and political actuality. I have moved with my class and type, to more and more precise intentions. Small groups and societies to explain and realize the Competent Receiver are springing up; periodicals are being started in relation to it; its phraseology is appearing in actual political discussion. Independent beginnings of a kindred spirit are coming into relations with one another. They are giving and taking. These people are not merely propagandists of an idea. Every one of them according to his or her abilities or opportunities is in training for the Civil Service, and the industrial teaching and compulsive services of the new order of things. It is from the skilled artisans, the technically educated middle-class, the fraternity of enlightened minds, rather than from the proletarian masses that its energy will come. But it cannot be pretended that constructive revolutionary organization is anything like as advanced as yet even as educational modernization and the spread of cosmopolitan ideas. It is still in the phase of germination. For the reorientation of revolution, just as for the modernization of education, one must accept what the Webbs have called so aptly "the inevitability of gradualness."

Remembering always that "gradual" need not mean slow.

Of the reality of our progress towards constructive world revolution I have no doubt. All revolutionary organizations are snowball organizations. The Open Conspiracy whether under that name or under some other name, or as a protean spirit, will in the long run win schools and colleges to its ends; it will get the worth-while young men, the skilled men and women, the simple and straightforward, the steadfast and resolute. That is to say that ultimately it will get mankind. It supplies the form and spirit of that "competent receiver," the lack of which made the frustration of the earlier socialism inevitable. It is law and order modernized and ennobled. It will find a job for everybody; the sacrifices it demands are temporary and conditional. When it is fully and fairly displayed it is a handsome and hopeful loyalty; the better it is known the finer it appears, the nature of man necessitates loyalty of some sort and there is no other loyalty now that can stand comparison with it.

And there, for a time at any rate, the description of the main arch of my work must end. My brain has been the centre of the story throughout, but just as with the new education, so here also in this conception of the idea of world revolution as the ruling and directive interest in life, similar things have happened and are happening to myriads of brains. I tell how I in particular travelled upon a road along which more and more people are travelling, but my egoism is far more apparent than real. There used to be a popular recitation in my young days telling how

Bill Adams won the Battle of Waterloo. Except for a transitory appearance of the "Dook," the victory seemed all the work of Bill. Nevertheless the Battle of Waterloo *was* won by Bill Adams multiplied by some score thousands, and it is small discredit to Bill Adams that he was too busy on his personal front to take much note of what the other fellows were doing.

What is plain to me is that the modern world-state which was a mere dream in 1900 is to-day a practicable objective; it is indeed the only sane political objective for a reasonable man; it towers high over the times, challenging indeed but rationally accessible; the way is indicated and the urgency to take that way gathers force. Life is now only conflict or "meanwhiling" until it is attained. Thirty-four years ago the world-state loomed mistily across a gulf in dreamland. My arch of work has bridged the gulf for me and my swinging bridge of ropes and planks and all the other ropes and wires that are being flung across, are plainly only the precursors of a viaduct and a common highway. The socialist world-state has now become a to-morrow as real as to-day. Thither we go.

§ 9. CEREBRATION AT LARGE AND BRAINS IN KEY POSITIONS

The particular brain whose ups and downs and beatings about in the world you have been following in this autobiography, has arrived at the establishment of the socialist world-state as its directive purpose and has made that its religion and end. This, it has been abundantly apparent, has involved for it very definite and distinctive standards of judgment upon both individual conduct and the conduct of public affairs. It had been perpetually meeting and jostling against other brains, brains in crowds and brains apart, summing them up, learning from them what to attempt and what to avoid; and so it seems worth while to conclude this elaborate description of my own mental growths and reactions, with a few comments upon other mentalities I have encountered at work upon these same intricate challenges and problems that have taken possession of and unified my own.

Social life has presented itself to me at last as a vast politico-educational problem. It is, as it were, a sea of active brains. My individual life is a participating unit in this multitudinous brain-life, the mind of the species. Its general problem is vastly simple, though its individual variations are infinite. It is required to orient all this diverse multitude of brains, about two thousand millions of them at present, in one particular direction so as to bring about a new morale and government of life. It is under penalty to do that. In a measurable time mankind has to constitute itself into one state and one brotherhood, or it will certainly be swept down cataracts of disaster to an ultimate destruction.

It is no novelty that life should present itself in this form of a problem of unification. Men have been seeing it more and more plainly so for at least five-and-twenty centuries. Every one of the universal religions, Buddhism, Christianity, Islam, every one in its valiant beginnings, set out to do as much for mankind. All, it is true, failed to attain that universality. They rose like floods and after a time they rose no further. The whole world over never became Buddhist, Christian or Moslem. At first in every case, the onset of the new faith was like the magnetising of an iron bar in an electric coil and many millions of the little individual particles, originally pointing higgledy-piggledy in the general mass, were swung round towards a common objective. Hitherto there has always been a limit set to this process of conversion; the bar was too big for the induction, much of it stretched beyond the influence of the coil, or the inducing current diminished and died out too soon. But that is no reason for declaring that it is impossible to achieve a general peace and a common faith and law for mankind. On the contrary, the success of these pioneer faiths, in spite of philosophical inadequacy and the handicap of local theological associations and unjustifiable miraculous pretensions, started as they were under conditions of tremendous disadvantage by weak individuals and a feeble initial group of disciples, is an extraordinary manifestation of the power of a unifying appeal and of the receptivity of common men to such an appeal. The human animal is more disposed than not for a universal social life, for peace and co-operation, and what has been done during the relatively brief space of twenty-five centuries and a few score generations of men, is merely a first demonstration of what will yet be achieved.

What we have seen in the course of my one brief lifetime has been a great development of our biological and psychological knowledge, and this last science in particular carries still with it almost untouched possibilities of self-restraint, self-direction, mutual sympathy and group and mass co- operation. The art of conduct is in its infancy. Concurrently the advance of physical technique has carried our facilities of mental exchange to undreamt-of levels. We can tell each other and show each other with unprecedented ease. When we consider the beginnings of the great world faiths; the weak voice of the Founder talking in some small dusty market-place to casually assembled crowds, the going to and fro of the undistinguished disciples, the faint and feeble records, the faulty gospels, the obscure epistles, the mis-hearings, the misunderstandings, the distortions of rumour, the heretical blunderings, the difficulties of correction and verification, and compare the ease and clarity with which to-day statements can be made, consistency sustained and co-operation ensured, then the wide prevalence and partial success of these former disseminations become the surest augury for the rapid and conclusive establishment of the new way of living to which not one Founder but myriads of quickening intelligences are awakening to-day. They are not now the disciples of this man or that. This time they are the disciples and apostles of the logic of human necessity. It is not that one man alone has received

701

a revelation and realized the substance of a new and necessary education and planned reconstruction of economic and political relations. The revelation has been prepared by the scientific work and invention of a century, and the call has been broadcast by events.

I have already described some intimate encounters which very importantly affected the final shaping of my *persona* and ideas. Here in a concluding section I think I will set down what I have seen at close quarters and what I have thought of one or two brains which seemed to be exceptionally placed in the world, so that they had apparently unusual directive opportunities. Their conduct was just as much a resultant of innate impulse and suggestion and circumstance as the lives of Gissing or Crane or Bennett or myself, but because relatively they happened to occupy key positions, their reaction on great multitudes of other brains was much more powerful and immediate. Leadership was their rôle. All of them belong to my own generation, the generation of disillusionment, perplexity and mental reconstruction, and all of them are far less lucid, assured and decisive than the men of to-morrow are likely to be.

An outstanding figure in my middle years was Theodore Roosevelt. He had a tremendous effort in his time of masterful direction. He was the Big Noise of America. He was a great release. Political life in America seemed to have become a wholly base technique, and the American outlook upon world affairs, narrowly patriotic, sentimental and selfish, when he broke through and became, by sheer accident, President. He made the liveliest use of his opportunities. His personality became more visible and his voice more audible about the planet than those of any of his predecessors since Lincoln. It was natural for me in my Spade House days, when I seemed only to be talking unheeded beside the flow of events, and quite unable to affect them, to exaggerate the Power he could exercise and to want to meet him. I had still to realise what an obscure and elusive thing political Power is. I had still to doubt whether there are really any powerful individuals now at all.

I went to America to write a series of articles for the London *Tribune* in 1906 and I lunched with the President and walked about the grounds of the White House with him while he talked. He talked easily and frankly, as Mr. Arthur Balfour used to talk. He "stuck through" the formulated politicians of his time. He betrayed none of the uneasiness of the normal politician that any phrase of his might be quoted unfairly against him, and he interested me enormously. I asked him, though in less direct phrases, what he imagined he was "up to" and I think he did his best to tell me.

In those days mental adaptation to the idea of a change of scale in human affairs was still in its opening phases. Nobody had got the thing in its full immensity but everywhere its disturbance was in evidence. His talk was tremendously provisional and speculative. In my book I called him "a complex of will and critical perplexity."

At that time hardly anyone had dared to face up to the conception of a planned world-state. Roosevelt was round about where Cecil Rhodes had been when he died; he probably owed a great deal to the Milner-Kipling-Rhodes school of thought, he was thinking vaguely of a loose combine, an understanding rather than an alliance, of the liberal northern powers to control the next phase of human affairs. He was sceptical of continental Europe, contemptuous of Asia, and oblivious, as we all were then, of the revolutionary possibilities of Russia. And neither of us as we talked that day had the remotest suspicion of the earthquakes that were latent in the monetary system of our world.

Though he had heard of socialism he evidently could not imagine it as an organised reality, as anything more practical than a legal modification of the baronial freedoms of big business by government control. You must remember that in those days there was no such striking evidence as we now possess of the self-terminating nature of the private capitalist system. That possibility was indeed cardinal in Marxist theory but only a very few people knew about it and still fewer understood and believed it. The current system was generally supposed to get along in a looping sort of way by trade cycles of depression and recovery, it had the air of a going concern that might jar perhaps at times but could not fail to go; and it was only after 1928 that any considerable number of people could be made to realize that these alleged trade cycles were not necessarily cycles at all and that there was no reason to suppose that a depression might not go on indefinitely with no effectual recovery at any point. That was outside his imaginative scheme. Such being the limitation of his ideas, it was natural that he should be a hearty individualist, convinced that no man who sought work could fail to find it, that there was room for an unlimited multitude of healthy workers everywhere (so that he passionately opposed "race suicide") and that all that was needed to keep the world going was strenuous "go." The utmost danger he would admit as threatening the glorious torrent of individualistic life as he saw it about him, was the restraint and choking of competition by the growth of monopolistic combinations, and this could be checked first by very vigorous anti-trust legislation and secondly by a greater wariness in granting public utility and other franchise for the exploitation of natural resources to private lessees. He was in particular the champion of an imaginary citizen farmer, the legendary pioneer western farmer,—and his power of overriding doubts in a sort of mystical exaltation was very great. I tried to insinuate my still not very completely formulated criticism of the current order. I tried to convey my persuasion that all competitive systems must be self-terminating systems....

But here let me quote my very own book:

"It is a curious thing that as I talked with President Roosevelt in the garden of the White House there came back to me quite forcibly that undertone of doubt that has haunted me throughout this journey. After all, does this magnificent appearance of beginnings, which is America, convey any clear and certain promise of permanence and fulfilment whatever?... Is America a giant childhood or a gigantic futility, a mere latest phase of that long succession of experiments which has been and may be for interminable years—may be, indeed, altogether until the end—man's social history? I can't now recall how our discursive talk settled towards this, but it is clear to me that I struck upon a familiar vein of thought in the President's mind. He hadn't, he said, an effectual disproof of a pessimistic interpretation of the future. If one chose to say America must presently lose the impetus of her ascent, that she and all mankind must culminate and pass, he could not conclusively deny that possibility. Only he chose to live as if this were not so.

"That remained in his mind. Presently he reverted to it. He made a sort of apology for his life, against the doubts and scepticisms that, I fear, must be in the background of the thoughts of every modern man who is intellectually alive. He mentioned my *Time Machine* ...He became gesticulatory, and his straining voice a note higher in denying the pessimism of that book as a credible interpretation of destiny. With one of those sudden movements of his he knelt forward in a garden-chair— we were standing, before our parting, beneath the colonnade— and addressed me very earnestly over the back, clutching it and then thrusting out his familiar gesture, a hand first partly open and then closed.

"'Suppose, after all,' he said slowly, 'that should prove to be right, and it all ends in your butterflies and morlocks. *That doesn't matter now.* The effort's real. It's worth going on with. It's worth it. It's worth it—even so.' ...

"I can see him now and hear his unmusical voice saying, 'The effort—the effort's worth it,' and see the gesture of his clenched hand and the—how can I describe it?—the friendly peering snarl of his face, like a man with the sun in his eyes. He sticks in my mind at that, as a very symbol of the creative will in man, in its limitations, its doubtful adequacy, its valiant persistence, amidst perplexities and confusions. He kneels out, assertive against his setting—and his setting is the White House with a background of all America.

"I could almost write, with a background of all the world; for I know of no other a tithe so representative of the creative purpose, the *goodwill* in men as he. In his undisciplined hastiness, his limitations, his prejudices, his unfairness, his frequent errors, just as much as in his force, his sustained courage, his integrity, his open intelligence, he stands for his people and his kind."

I might have written that to-day. "Teddy" was an interesting brain to come up against and it gives a measure of just how much of a constructive plan for the world's affairs there was in the current intelligence of the world twenty-eight years ago. By our modern standards it was scarcely a plan at all. It was a jumble of "progressive" organization and "little man" democracy. Afforestation, "conservation of national resources," legislation against any "combination in restraint of trade" were the chief planks of the platform and beyond that "woosh!" the emotional use of the "big stick," a declaration of the satisfying splendour of strenuous effort—which, when one comes to think it over, was, on the intellectual side, not so very strenuous after all.

That I suppose was the most vigorous brain in a conspicuously responsible position in all the world in 1906—when I was turning forty. Radical speculative thought was ahead of this, but that was as far as any ruling figure in the world had gone.

A man I never met, who must have been a very curious mixture of large conceptions and strange ignorances, was Cecil Rhodes. Of ignorances—Sir Sidney Low told me once that he never learnt properly to pronounce the name of his protagonist "Old Krooger." I would have liked to have known more about the operations of his cerebral hemispheres, as they rolled about South Africa. Much the same ideas that were running through my brain round about 1900, of a great English-speaking English-thinking synthesis, leading mankind by sheer force of numbers, wealth, equipment and scope, to a progressive unity, must have been running through his brain also. He was certainly no narrow worshipper of the Union Jack, no abject devotee of the dear Queen Empress. The institution of the Rhodes scholarships which transcended any existing political boundaries and aimed plainly at a sort of common understanding and co-operation between all the western peoples and more particularly between all the "Nordic" peoples—he was at just about the level of ethnological understanding to believe in Nordic superiority—indicates a real greatness of intention, though warped by prejudices and uncritical assumptions.

I wish I knew much more about that brain and still more would I like to know about the brain history of Mr. Rudyard Kipling, whom also I have never met. He is to me the most incomprehensible of my contemporaries, with phases of real largeness and splendour and lapses to the quality of those mucky little sadists, Stalky and Co. I do not understand his relation to Rhodes nor Rhodes's attitude to him. He has an immense vogue in the British middle-class and upper-class home; he is the patron saint of cadet corps masters, an in-exhaustive fount of sham manly sentiment, and one of the most potent forces in the shrivelling of the British political imagination during the past third of a century.

The only representative of that Boer War Imperialist group I ever met was Lord Milner. He seemed to me a bold-thinking man, hampered by politic reservations. In 1918 he wrote a preface for a little pamphlet I published, *The Elements of Reconstruction.* I came against him in a curious little talking and dining club, the "Coefficients," which met monthly throughout the session between 1902 and 1908 to discuss the future of this perplexing, promising and frustrating Empire of ours. These talks played an important part in my education. They brought me closer than

I had ever come hitherto to many processes in contemporary English politics and they gave me juster ideas of the mental atmosphere in which such affairs are managed.

In certain respects our club represented something that seems now, I think, to have faded out from contemporary English life. It had the gestures if not the spirit of free interrogation. It had an air of asking "What are we doing with the world? What are we going to do?" Or perhaps I might put it better by saying: "What is being done to our world? And what are we going to do about it?"

The club included the queerest diversity of brains. Its foundation was, I believe, suggested by Mrs. Sidney Webb. It was inaugurated by a meeting in the flat of Sir Edward Grey and Mr. Haldane (neither as yet peers) in Whitehall Court and the first assembly included such incongruous elements as Bertrand Russell (now Earl Russell), Sidney Webb (who is now Lord Passfield), Leo Maxse, (already in 1902 denouncing the German Peril and demanding the Great War), Clinton Dawkins, who linked us to finance, Carlyon Bellairs, a Big Navy man, Pember Reeves, a New Zealand progressive settled in England, W. A. S. Hewins, L. S. Amery and H. J. Mackinder, all three on the verge of revolt under Joseph Chamberlain against Free Trade. Later on we were joined by Lord Robert Cecil, Michael Sadler, Henry Newbolt (of "Drake's Drums"), J. Birchenough, to strengthen the financial side, Garvin who helped remove the last traces of Encyclopaedism from the *Encyclopædia Britannica*, Josiah Wedgwood the Single Taxer, Lord Milner, John Hugh Smith, Colonel Repington, F. S. Oliver, C. F. G. Masterman and others. We found our talks interesting and we kept up a quite high average of attendances. For some years we met in the St. Ermin's Hotel, Westminster, and later in a restaurant which has now given way to a theatre in Whitehall.

Most of these men were already committed to definite political rôles, and Russell and I were by far the most untied and irresponsible members. I had much more to learn than anyone from those conversations and less tradition and political entanglement to hamper my learning. The earlier discussions were the most general and, from my point of view, the best. Could the British Empire be made a self-sustaining system, within a Zollverein? That was at first an open question for most of us. I argued against that idea. The British Empire, I said, had to be the precursor of a world-state or nothing. I appealed to geography. It was possible for the Germans and Austrians to hold together in their Zollverein because they were placed like a clenched fist in the centre of Europe. But the British Empire was like an open hand all over the world. It had no natural economic unity and it could maintain no artificial economic unity. Its essential unity must be a unity of great ideas embodied in the English speech and literature.

I was very pleased with that metaphor of the fist and the open hand—but I did not find it a very contagious suggestion.

As I look back now across a gap of two and thirty years upon that talk among the coffee cups and the liqueur glasses, I see England at a parting of the ways. I was still clinging to the dear belief that the English-speaking community might play the part of leader and mediator towards a world commonweal It was to be a free-trading, free-speaking, liberating flux for mankind. Russell, Pember Reeves and Webb and possibly Haldane and Grey had, I think, a less clearly expressed disposition in the same direction. But the shadow of Joseph Chamberlain lay dark across our dinner-table, the Chamberlain who, upon the "illimitable veldt" of South Africa, had had either a sunstroke or a Pauline conversion to Protection and had returned to clamour influentially for what he called Tariff Reform, but what was in effect national commercial egotism. He was impatient with what he felt to be the impracticable world-liberalism of Balfour, the Cecils and the Liberals. Foreign powers, he thought, were taking an immediate advantage of our longer views. He had no long views. He began a struggle to impose the crude commonsense and hard methods of a monopolistic Birmingham hardware-manufacturer upon international relations. More and more did his shadow divide us into two parties. Year by year at the Coefficient gatherings, I saw the idea of the British commonweal being decivilized and "Imperialized." I was in at the very beginning of the English recoil from our pretensions—and with many they were more than pretensions—to exceptional national generosity, courage and world leadership.

The undeniable contraction of the British outlook in the opening decade of the new century is one that has exercised my mind very greatly, and I fear it would produce an immense bulge in this present already bulging bale of a book if I were to attempt a complete analysis. Gradually the belief in the possible world leadership of England had been deflated, by the economic development of America and the militant boldness of Germany. The long reign of Queen Victoria, so prosperous, progressive and effortless, had produced habits of political indolence and cheap assurance. As a people we had got out of training, and when the challenge of these new rivals became open, it took our breath away at once. We did not know how to meet it. We had educated our general population reluctantly; our universities had not kept pace with the needs of the new time; our ruling class, protected in its advantages by a universal snobbery, was broad-minded, easy-going and profoundly lazy. The Edwardian monarchy, court and society were amiable and slack. "Efficiency"—the word of Earl Roseberry and the Webbs was felt to be rather priggish and vulgar. Our liberalism was no longer a larger enterprise, it had become a generous indolence. But minds were waking up to this. Over our table at St. Ermin's Hotel wrangled Maxse, Bellairs, Hewins, Amery and Mackinder, all stung by the small but humiliating tale of disasters in the South Africa war, all sensitive to the threat of business recession and all profoundly alarmed by the naval and military aggressiveness of Germany, arguing chiefly against the liberalism of Reeves and Russell and myself, and pulling us down, whether we liked it or not, from large generalities to concrete problems.

These Young Imperialists, as they were then, found it impossible to distinguish between national energy and patriotic narrowness. Narrowing the outlook is a cheap immediate way of enhancing the effect of energy without really increasing it. They were all for training and armament and defensive alliances, and they were all careless or contemptuous of that breadth and vigour of education in which the true greatness of a people lies. I tried to be more fundamental, to trace the secret springs of our inertness. I talked—it was considered a barely pardonable eccentricity—of the crippling effect of the monarchy, of the cultivated suspicion of real capacity in high quarters, and of the monopolization of educational direction by Oxford and Cambridge. I was of opinion that if Great Britain had become a Republic early in the nineteenth century and set up an adequate modern university organization centering in London and extended throughout the Empire, in the place of those privileged mediaeval foundations and the intensely domestic personal loyalties it has cherished, it would have drawn the United States back into a closer accord and faced the world with an altogether greater spirit than it was now displaying. Our mentality, I reasoned, was still in the great-estate, gentlemen's servants tradition of the eighteenth century because we had missed our revolution. These are all if's and and's, but that was the disposition of my mind.

Presently Bertrand Russell flung out of the club. There was an argument at which unfortunately I was not present. Hewins, Amery and Mackinder declared themselves fanatical devotees of the Empire. "My Empire, right or wrong," they said. Russell said that there were a multitude of things he valued before the Empire. He would rather wreck the Empire than sacrifice freedom. So if this devotion was what the club meant——! And out he went—like the ego-centred Whig he is—without consulting me. Later the discussion was summarized to me. I said I was quite of his mind. The Empire was a convenience and not a God. Hewins in protest was almost lyrical. He loved the Empire. He could no more say why he loved the Empire than a man could say why he loved his wife. I ought to resign. I said I had no taste for exile; I never have had a taste for exile; and so I would not follow Russell unless they threw me out. The more this Imperialist nonsense was talked in the club, the more was it necessary that one voice at least should be present to contradict it. And so nailing my colours to the mast and myself to the dinner table, I remained— and we all continued to get on very well together.

Milner, oddly enough, I found the most satisfactory intelligence among us. He knew we had to make a new world, but he had nothing of my irresponsible constructive boldness. So that he fell into Imperialist Monarchist forms—which a partly German education may have made easier for him. But upon many minor issues we were apt to agree.

Haldane on the contrary I found intellectually unsympathetic, although his general political attitude was nearer to mine. He was a self-indulgent man, with a large white face and an urbane voice that carried his words as it were on a salver, so that they seemed good even when they were not so. The "Souls," the Balfour set, in a moment of vulgarity had nicknamed him "Tubby." He was a copious worker in a lawyer-like way and an abundant—and to my mind entirely empty—philosopher after the German pattern. He had a cluster of academic distinctions which similar philosophers had awarded him. I used to watch him at our gatherings and wonder what sustained him. I think he floated on strange compensatory clouds of his own exhalation. He rejoiced visibly in the large smooth movements of his mind. Mostly he was very busy on his immediate activities; his case, his exposition, his reply, his lecture, and it was probably rare for him to drop down to self-scrutiny. When other men lie awake in the small hours and experience self-knowledge, remorse and the harsher aspects of life, crying out aloud and leaping up to pace their rooms, Haldane I am sure communed quite serenely with that bladder of nothingness, the Absolute, until he fell asleep again.

When Einstein came to England and was lionized after the war, he was entertained by Haldane. Einstein I know and can converse with very interestingly, in a sort of Ollendorffian French, about politics, philosophy and what not, and it is one of the lost good things in my life, that I was never able to participate in the mutual exploration of these two stupendously incongruous minds. Einstein must have been like a gentle bright kitten trying to make friends with a child's balloon, very large and unaccountably unpuncturable.

Haldane found time to produce various books on philosophy. They are still spoken of with profound respect and a careful avoidance of particulars in academic circles, but they mark no turning point in the history of the human mind. They move far away from any vulgar reality in a special universe of discourse. *The Pathway to Reality* was not actually written; it was poured out from notes as the Gifford Lectures in that mellifluous voice, taken down in shorthand and corrected for publication. It is like a very large soap bubble that for some inexplicable reason fails to be iridescent. He also produced a translation of Schopenhauer, omitting an indelicate but vitally important discussion of perversion.

His abundant methodical mind was at its best in formal organization. It is generally admitted that it was his reform of the army in 1905 which made possible the prompt dispatch of the British Expeditionary Force to France in August 1914. His intelligence was certainly better trained and more abundant than that of any of the British professional military authorities, and he might have done great service during the actual struggle. But in a moment of enthusiasm for Teutonic metaphysics he had declared that Germany was his "spiritual home" and Northcliffe, in an access of spy mania, hunted him from office at the outbreak of the war. It was a great disappointment for him, for he was acutely conscious of strategic capacity. But measured against such brains as those of Kitchener and French, almost anyone might be forgiven an acute consciousness of strategic capacity.

I will not speculate about what might have happened if we had had Haldane as war-director instead of the fuddled dullness of Kitchener, the small-army cleverness of French, Haig's mediocrity and the stolid professionalism of the army people throughout. It would lead me far away from this wandering lane of autobiography into a wilderness of entertaining but futile hypothesis, and I have already made some heartfelt observations about the army caste in an earlier section. Moreover after a section on "If Haldane had been at the War Office in 1914," it would be impossible not to go on to what might have happened if we had had Winston Churchill for our war lord—brilliant, I feel sure he would have been, if unsound—and so on to even stranger possibilities. My concern here is simply with Lord Haldane as a man with a voice in human destiny. How was this undeniably big brain concerned with change and the incessant general problem of mankind? I have told how Theodore Roosevelt was touched by that problem. Was Lord Haldane really touched by it at all?

I do not think that between contemporary practicality and the Absolute there was any intermediate level at which the mind of Haldane halted to ask himself what he was doing with the world. His mind was unquickened by any serious knowledge of biology or cosmology, his idea of science was of a useful technical cleverness and not of a clearer vision, and I think it improbable that he brought the conception of unlimited fundamental change into his picture of the universe at all. A legal training directs the mind to equity and settlement rather than progress. And the Absolute is very constipating to the mind. I imagine he just thought that "history goes on—much as ever" and left it at that.

Another of our Coefficients who certainly found a belief in the steady continuity of conventional history a full and sufficient frame for his political thoughts was Sir Edward Grey (who became Viscount Grey of Fallodon). Here again was a brain that I found almost incredibly fixed and unaware of the violent mutability of things. His air of grave and responsible leadership was an immense delusion, for who can lead unless he be in motion? Never had a human being less stimulus for getting on to anywhere or anything. He was a man born to wealth and prominence; he inherited his baronetcy and estates at the age of twenty and he entered parliament with the approval of everyone, the nicest of nice young men, at the age of twenty-three. He was tall and of a fine immobile handsomeness; he played tennis very well and he was one of the most distinguished of British fly-fishers. At the age of thirty-seven in the full tide of his gifts, he wrote an excellent book on the latter art. He was never very deeply interested in internal politics for naturally enough he could see very little to complain of in the condition of the country, but as a matter of public and party duty he was made under-secretary for foreign affairs when he was thirty, and an opinion grew about him and within him that he understood them. He understood them about as much as Lord Tyrrell, upon whose outlook I have already animadverted in my account of my Crewe House experiences.

I have already said that Tyrrell's mind was governess-made. I would almost extend that to the whole Foreign Office personnel. People of this class are caught young before any power of defensive criticism has developed in them and told stories of a series of mythical beings, France, Germany, England, Spain, with such assurance that they become more real than daddy and mummy. They are led to believe that "Spain" is cruel, "Holland" little and brave, "Germany" industrious and protestant and "Ireland" tragic, priest-led and unforgetting. They think that there are wicked countries and good countries. Once a modernized education has cleared up the human mind in this matter, such widespread delusions will be inconceivable. Readers in those days to come will not believe what I am writing here. But the minds of these people are set in that shape, as the bandaged skulls of the Mangbetu of the Belgian Congo are set in the shape of a sugar loaf, and few so formed ever come round to a sane scepticism about these foolish simplifications. In my *Outline of History* I have done my best to show plainly how the belief in these plausible inventions, as unreal as Baal or Juggernaut, has warped all human life and slaughtered countless millions in the past two centuries. Slowly a clearer vision of the human complex is spreading, but Grey in his grave solemn way talked, just as Tyrrell chattered, of "What France feels in the matter" or "If Germany does so and so, the time will come for us to act."

He would not even disperse these personifications to the extent of saying "They."

I thought Grey a mentally slow, well-mannered, not unpleasantly dignified person until after August 1914. Then I realized what a danger such blinkered firmness of mind as his could be to mankind.

I think he wanted the war and I think he wanted it to come when it did. Sooner or later, on the international chequerboard which he saw in place of reality, Germany would attack. It was better she should attack while her navy was still quantitatively inferior to ours and while the web of precautionary alliances we had woven against her held firm. He would never have taken part in an attack on Germany, a preventive war as they call it in France nowadays, because that was not in accordance with the rules of the game, not at all the sort of thing a gentlemanly country does, but if Germany saw fit to attack first, then, well and good, the Lord had delivered her into our hands.

It is charged against him that he did not definitely warn Germany that we should certainly come into the war, that he was sufficiently ambiguous to let her take a risk and attack, and that he did this deliberately. I think that charge is sound.

His faith in the reality of national personifications outlived the war. When I was working for the creation of a League of Nations Union, it was with a sort of despair that I found that everyone in the movement was insisting on the necessity of having Grey for our figurehead. For him a League of Nations was necessarily a League of Foreign Offices. His intelligence was as incapable of thinking multitudinously of the human beings under the shadow of "France" or "Russia" as a Zoo bear is of thinking of the atoms in a bun.

Another of these governess-moulded minds I encountered was Lord Curzon who was at the Foreign Office in 1920, when I returned from a visit to Soviet Russia. I went to him to suggest a working understanding with the new régime. I tried to explain first that it was now the only possible régime in Russia and that if it was overthrown Russia would come as near to Chaos as a human population can; secondly that it was a weak régime in sore need of manufactured material, scientific apparatus and technical help of every sort and thirdly, that however strong our objection to Marxist theory might be and however intransigeant their Marxism, a certain generosity and understanding now, a certain manifest readiness to help must inevitably force reciprocal concessions. The new Soviet Russia was the best moral and political investment that had ever been offered to Britain. And our Foreign Office turned it down—like a virtuous spinster of a certain age refusing a proposal to elope and bear ten children. Most of this is said quite plainly in my*Russia in the Shadows*.

Lord Curzon listened to me as a man listens to a language he does not understand, but which he is unwilling to admit is strange to him. For him Russia was something as unified and personally responsible as Aunt Sally or the defendant in the dock. When it came to his turn to speak, he began, incorrigibly and with a slight emphasis on his master words, in this fashion; "But so long as *Russia* continues to sustain a *propaganda* against us in *Persia*, I do not see how we can possibly do anything of the sort you suggest...."

I declare that the greatest present dangers to the human race are these governess-trained brains which apparently monopolize the Foreign Offices of the World, which cannot see human affairs in any other light than as a play between the vast childish abstractions we call nations. There are people who say the causes of war, nowadays at least, are economic. They are nothing so rational. They are hallucinatory. Men like Grey, Curzon and Tyrrell present a fine big appearance to the world, but the bare truth is that they are, by education and by force of uncritical acceptance, infantile defectives, who ought to be either referred back to a study of the elements of human ecology or certified and secluded as damaged minds incapable of managing public affairs.

Another outstanding man, of that period before the Great War, with whom I had some mental exchanges was Mr. Balfour—"Mr. Arthur." I used to meet him at Stanway and Taplow Court and in various London houses. He at any rate was high above the governess-made level. There was always an odour of intelligence about him that made his average Conservative associates uncomfortable. He had a curious active mind, he had been attracted by my earlier books and, through him and through Cust, I came to know something of the group of people who centred round him and Lady Mary Elcho, the "Souls." That too was a vague Open Conspiracy, an attempt to get away from the self-complacent dullness and furtive small town viciousness of *fin-de-siècle* England, and to see life freshly. He had grown up in an atmosphere of scientific thought; Francis Balfour, his younger brother, was a brilliant biologist and his *Text Book of Embryology* had been my first introduction to the Balfour family. Arthur Balfour had none of the forceful energy of Theodore Roosevelt; he was a long-limbed, simple-living but self-indulgent, bachelor man. He was a greater British private gentleman even than Sir Edward Grey. He was so comfortably wealthy, so well connected and so secure that a certain aloofness from the dusty sweaty conflict of life, was in his habit of living.

It is hard to say where, in aloofness, is set the boundary between divinity and cowardice. He could show such courage as he did when as Irish Secretary he was continually under a threat of assassination, because he could not believe that anything of that sort could really happen to him; but when his essential liberalism came face to face with this new baseness of commercialized imperialism, with all its push and energy, he made a very poor fight for it. He allowed himself to be hustled into the background of affairs by men with narrower views and nearer objectives.

He argued sceptically on behalf of religion. His way of defending the Godhead was by asking, What can your science know for certain? and escaping back to orthodoxy under a dust-cloud of philosophical doubts. He anticipated my own remark that the human mind is as much a product of the struggle for survival as the snout of a pig and perhaps as little equipped for the unearthing of fundamental truth. But while that enabled him to accord a graceful support to the Church of England—which might be just as right or wrong about ultimates as anything else—I used my release from rigid conviction for a systematic common-sense interpretation of my world.

In the smooth-water years before 1914 and the subsequent cataracts, I had a great admiration for Balfour. In that queer confused novel, *The New Machiavelli*, one of my worst and one of my most revealing, I have a sort of caricature-portrait of him as Evesham in which I magnify him unduly. (There is also, by the bye, in the same book a remote sketch of the Coefficients as the "Pentagram Club.") I put various discourses into Evesham's mouth, of which the matter is clearly my own. Here is a vignette, which shows also my own phase of development about 1912.

"Have I not seen him in the House, persistent, persuasive, indefatigable, and by all my standards wickedly perverse, leaning over the table with those insistent movements of his hand upon it, or swaying forward with a grip upon his coat lapel, fighting with a diabolical skill to preserve what are in effect religious tests, tests he must have known would outrage and humiliate and injure the consciences of a quarter—and that perhaps the best quarter—of the young teachers who come to the work of elementary education?

"In playing for points in the game of party advantage Evesham displayed at times a quite wicked unscrupulousness in the use of his subtle mind. I would sit on the Liberal benches and watch him, and listen to his urbane voice, fascinated by him. Did he really care? Did anything matter to him? And if it really mattered nothing, why did he trouble to serve the narrowness and passion of his side? Or did he see far beyond my scope, so that this petty iniquity was justified by greater, remoter ends of which I had no intimation?

"They accused him of nepotism. His friends and family were certainly well cared for. In private life he was full of an affectionate intimacy; he pleased by being charmed and pleased. One might think at times there was no more of him than a clever man happily circumstanced, and finding an interest and occupation in politics. And then came a glimpse of thought, of imagination, like the sight of a soaring eagle through a staircase skylight. Oh, beyond question he was great! No other contemporary politician had his quality.... Except that he had it seemed no hot passions, but only interests and fine affections and indolences, he paralleled the conflict of my life. He saw and thought widely and deeply; but at times it seemed to me his greatness stood over and behind the reality of his life, like some splendid servant, thinking his own thoughts, who waits behind a lesser master's chair."

There is something very youthful in that passage. I have hardened and grown wiser since then. It is easier to be taken that way when one is thirty- eight than in the cooler longer perspective of sixty-eight. Later on I realized that Balfour was letting one thing after another be wrested from his hands by lesser men. He allowed *The Times* when it was sold, go to the highest bidder; it fell to Northcliffe and it might have fallen into far worse hands; Balfour would have done nothing disturbing to himself to prevent it. None of our richer aristocrats seem to have risked any money at that time to keep this public organ in public-spirited hands. Yet the control of that paper was quite essential to their predominance. They trusted to the snobbishness of some *nouveau riche*. So they got Northcliffe who was anything but a snob—and in due course a new mercantile conservatism arose which adopted B.M.G. (Balfour Must Go) as its animating slogan. He could not control these new people but he hampered them and so they turned upon him.

Balfour might perhaps have been a very great man indeed if his passions had been hotter and his affections more vivid. The lassitudes of these fine types, their fastidiousness in the presence of strong appeals, leave them at last a prey to the weak gratifications of vanity and a gentle impulse to pose. He posed. He was aware of himself and he posed—as Mr. Humbert Wolfe has recently told in the *English Review* (June 1934). As the war went on his poses became more and more self-protective.

Amidst the clamour and riot of the war he faded away from power to eminence. I had one queer glimpse of some struggle going on in him and about him. We were at the house of Lady Wemyss in Cadogan Square, talking about the early reactions of the various classes to the war. He had an impulse to tell me something. "The worst behaviour," he began, "has been on the part of our business men." Emphasis. "The *very* worst."

He thought better of it and I was not clever enough or resolute enough to make him say more.

After the war, power left him altogether. He was merely a very eminent person, at last indeed almost the most eminent person in Britain. His last flare of charm and activity was at the Washington Conference of 1924. He helped make it the most amiable conference imaginable and the fund of sympathy between Washington and Westminster was greatly enhanced. There I saw and talked with him but nothing he said has remained in my memory. No doubt he and Grey were very fine gentlemen, but they were expensive to produce and they did not give back to human society anything like an adequate return in mental toil and directive resolution, for its expenditure upon them, for their great parks and houses and the deference that was shown them.

One day—in 1920 or 1921 I think, I went with Jane to the Institute of International Affairs and saw Balfour speaking on the platform. The light fell on his skull and I had a queer impression that quite recently I had seen an almost exactly similar cranium, similarly lit. My mind flashed back to Moscow. I whispered to Jane: "He's got a brain box that is the very pair to Lenin's.... It's incredible."

Perhaps it was only a matter of lighting and I will not embark upon any systematic search for correlated resemblances. Lenin by all his circumstances was as insecure, active and aggressive as Balfour was assured and indolent, but both had curious brains with a live edge of scepticism that put them on a far higher level than the blinkered stupidity of Grey and Curzon or the elaborate unreality of Haldane. Neither I think were orthodox minded and Lenin believed in the dogmas of Marx about as much as Balfour believed in the Holy Trinity and both were capable of the most destructive conformity. But while Lenin was using Marxism to make things happen because he was under the urgency of change, Balfour was using Christianity and Christian organization, to resist changes that, whatever else they did, were bound to disturb the spacious pleasantness of his life. I went to Russia as I have recounted in *Russia in the Shadows*, and I had a long talk with Lenin and a number of talks about him.

Now here was a fresh kind of brain for me to encounter and it was in such a key-position as no one had dreamt of as possible for anyone before the war. He appeared to be the complete master of all that was left of the resources of Russia. He was not by any means the master he seemed to be; he had a difficult team of supporters to handle and such an instrument as the Ogpu, which could twist round in his grip and wound him—as it did when it executed the Grand Dukes after his reprieve. And above all he was tied very closely to the sacred text of Marx. A real or assumed reverence for that was what held his following together, and his modification of the sacred Word to meet the great emergencies before him had to be subtle and propitiatory to an extreme degree. He had all these checks and entanglements to hinder him. But the authoritative effect of him was very great indeed.

He had a personal prestige based on his sound advice and lucid vision during the revolutionary crisis. He became then the man to whom everyone ran in fear or doubt. He had the strength of simplicity of purpose combined with subtlety of thought. By imperceptible changes, to an extent that only began to be measured and recognized after his death, he changed Marxism into Leninism. He changed the teachings of a fatalistic doctrinaire into a flexible creative leadership. So long as it was the substance of Lenin, he did not care in the least if it bore the label of Marx. But this year I have seen that his portrait and image in Russia everywhere are quietly elbowing his bearded precursor out of the way. His was by far the more vigorous and finer brain.

Like everybody else he belonged to his own time and his own phase. We met and talked each with his own preconceptions. We talked chiefly of the necessity of substituting large scale cultivation for peasant cultivation—that was eight years before the first Five Year Plan—and of the electrification of Russia, which was then still only a dream in his mind. I was sceptical about that because I was ignorant of the available water power of Russia. "Come back and see us in ten years' time," he said to my doubts.

When I talked to Lenin I was much more interested in our subject than in ourselves. I forgot whether we were big or little or old or young. At that time I was chiefly impressed by the fact that he was physically a little man, and by his intense animation and simplicity of purpose. But now as I look over my fourteen year old book and revive my memories and size him up against the other personalities I have known, in key positions I begin to realize what an outstanding and important figure he is in history. I grudge subscribing to the "great man" conception of human affairs, but if we are going to talk at all of greatness among our species, then I must admit that Lenin at least was a very great man.

If in 1912 I could call Balfour "beyond question great," it seems almost my duty here to put that flash of enthusiasm in its proper proportion to what I think of the Russian. So let me say with all deliberation that when I weigh the two against each other it is not even a question of swaying scale-pans; Balfour flies up and kicks the beam. The untidy little man in the Kremlin out-thought him—outdid him. Lenin was alive to the last, whereas Balfour ended in an attitude. Lenin was already ailing when I saw him, he had to take frequent holidays, early in 1922 the doctors stopped his daily work altogether and he became partly paralysed that summer and died early in 1924. His days of full influence therefore, extended over less than five crowded years. Nevertheless in that time, he imposed upon the Russian affair, a steadfastness of constructive effort against all difficulties, that has endured to this day. But for him and his invention of the organized Communist party, the Russian revolution would certainly have staggered into a barbaric military autocracy and ultimate social collapse. But his Communist party provided, crudely no doubt but sufficiently for the survival of the experiment, that disciplined personnel for an improvised but loyal Civil Service without which a revolution in a modern state is doomed to complete futility. His mind never became rigid and he turned from revolutionary activities to social reconstruction with an astonishing agility. In 1920, when I saw him, he was learning with the vigour of a youth about the possible "electrification of Russia." The conception of the Five Year Plan—but as he saw it, a series of successive provincial Plans—a Russian grid system, the achievements of Dnepropetrovsk, were all taking shape in his brain. He went on working, as a ferment, long after his working days had ended. He is still working perhaps as powerfully as ever.

During my last visit to Moscow, in July 1934, I visited his Mausoleum and saw the little man again. He seemed smaller than ever; his face very waxy and pale and his restless hands still. His beard was redder than I remembered it. His expression was very dignified and simple and a little pathetic, there was childishness and courage there, the supreme human qualities, and he sleeps— too soon for Russia. The decoration about him was plain and noble. The atmosphere of the place was saturated with religious feeling and I can well believe that women pray there. Outside down the Square there still stands the inscription: "Religion"— which in Russia it must be remembered always means Orthodox Christianity—"is the opium of the people." Deprived of that opium Russia is resorting to new forms of dope. In Moscow I was shown one evening Dziga Vertov's new film: *Three Songs for Lenin*. This is a very fine and moving apotheosis of Lenin. It is Passion Music for Lenin and he has become a Messiah. One must see and hear it to realize how the queer Russian mind has emotionalized Socialism and subordinated it to the personal worship of its prophets, and how necessary it is that the west wind should blow through the land afresh.

* * * * *

In the spring of 1934 I took it into my head to see and compare President Franklin Roosevelt and Mr. Stalin. I wanted to form an opinion of just how much these two brains were working in the direction of this socialist world-state that I believe to be the only hopeful destiny for mankind.

In what has gone before I have done my best to set out before the persevering reader as precisely and plainly as possible the foundations and nature of this picture of the world problem that has been painted bit by bit on my own brain tissues since I played in the back-yard of Atlas House, and I have tried to show the successive phases through which my belief has grown definite, until at last it has become altogether clear to me (as to many others) that the organization of this that I call the Open Conspiracy, the evocation of a greater sounder fellow to the first Communist essay, an adequately implemented Liberal Socialism, which will ultimately supply teaching, coercive and directive public services to the whole world, is the immediate task before all rational people. I believe this idea of the planned world-state is one to which all our thought and knowledge is tending. It is an idea that is quietly pervading human mentality because facts and events conspire in its favour. It is appearing partially and experimentally at a thousand points. It does not dismay me in the least that no specific political organization to realize this idea, has yet appeared. By its very nature the formal conflicts of politics will be almost the last thing in the world to be affected by it. When accident finally precipitates it, its coming is likely to happen very quickly. We shall find ourselves almost abruptly engaged in a new system of political issues in, which the socialist world-state will be plainly and consciously lined up against the scattered vestigial sovereignties of the past.

I am quite unable to form an opinion how long it will be before this happens and the socialist world-state enters the field of political actuality. Sometimes I feel that it may be imminent. Sometimes I feel that generations of propaganda and education may have to precede it. The war danger and economic stress are both forcing men's minds towards it as the one way out for them. These grim instructors may do much to make up for the negligence and backwardness of the schoolmaster. Plans for political synthesis and economic readjustment seem to grow bolder and more extensive. It was natural therefore, if a little impulsive and premature, that I should go to America and Russia with the question, Is this it already? What is the relation of the New Plan in America to the New Plan in Russia and how are both related to the ultimate World-State?

Some readers will object that this is political discussion and not autobiography. It is political discussion but also it is autobiography. The more completely life is lived the more political a man becomes. My democratic reading of the rights of man is not so much a matter of voting—usually for candidates put up for me by other people—as asking questions, getting answers and passing judgments on my own behalf. I ask my questions. These two visits are essential events in my life and telling about them is as intimate and personal a rounding off of my story as I can imagine. Modern life is expansion and then effacement. We do not round off, we open out. We do not end with valedictions; we open doors and then stand aside.

Just before I sailed for America I went to a queer exhibition of futility in the Albert Hall. It was a gathering of Mosley's blackshirts and it would be hard to imagine anything sillier— from the slow pompous entry of this queer crazy creature, dressed up like a fencing instructor with a waist fondly exaggerated by a cummerbund and chest and buttocks thrust out, stalking gravely and alone down the central gangway, to the last concerted outburst confined entirely, I remarked, to his disciplined following, of boyish shouting and hand-lifting: "We *want* Mosley."

I have met Mosley intermittently for years, as a promising young conservative, a promising young liberal, a promising new convert to the Labour party, with Communist leanings, and finally as the thing he is. He has always seemed to me dull and heavy, imitative in his politics and platitudinous in his speeches, and so I was not greatly interested in what he had to say to this meeting. As his banalities boomed about the hall, without a single flicker of wit or wisdom, their dullness vastly exaggerated by loud speakers, we noted how the habit of mouthing his words was growing upon him—he has for some obscure reason invented a sort of dialect of his own—and then we discussed particulars of his Sandhurst days and his war-record which were new to me. What chiefly held my attention were his supporters and the audience generally. The audience was miscellaneous, curious and little moved, and it did not fully fill the hall. Quite a quantity of pleasant boys and nice young men, and quite a number of others who were not so nice, dressed up in black shirts and grey trousers, were acting as ushers, selling idiotic songs about their glorious Leader, supplying the applause, pervading the meeting, and generally keeping the affair from becoming a complete slump. They seemed drawn chiefly from the middle and upper class. There was something shy about many of them, something either desperately grave and assertive, or faintly apologetic. They were not throwing themselves into their parts as the hairy young Italians they were aping would have done. There was no romantic conviction about them. The thing that really intrigued me was why they did this. What sort of feeble imaginations, I asked, could be flicking about in their nice young cerebral cortices to bring them to this pass?

That question went with me across the Atlantic. Is there really anything we can call education in England at the present time? Or is what passes for education only a sort of systematic softening of the brain? What history had been put before these young men, what vision of life had been given them, that they should start out upon their political life "wanting"—of all conceivable desiderata!—Mosley?

Only after a huge cultural struggle can we hope to see the world-state coming into being. The Open Conspiracy has to achieve itself in many ways, but the main battle before it is an educational battle, a battle to make the knowledge that already exists accessible and assimilable and effective. The world has moved from the horse-cart and the windmill to the aeroplane and dynamo but education has made no equivalent advance. The new brains that are pouring into the world are being caught by incompetent and unenlightened teachers, they are being waylaid by the marshalled misconceptions of the past, and imprisoned in rigid narrow historical and political falsifications. We cannot do with such a world population. We cannot build a new civilization out of two thousand million pot-bound minds. It is all poor, damaged material we have to deal with. Such cramped and crippled stuff might serve well enough for the comparatively unshattered social and political routines of the nineteenth century but it will not serve to-day. It is as dangerous, as catastrophically inert, as loose sand piled high, and always rising higher, over the excavation for a highway.

I prowled round the promenade deck at night thinking how little we were doing for education and how little I had done. I wished I had some virus with which one might bite people and make them mad for education. I was going from one dismally miseducated country to another, and when all was said and done these two were the most enlightened countries as yet in all the world. And I was hoping against my better knowledge to find the seeds of a new way of life already germinating and sending out green shoots.

It is not spring of the world's great year yet.

> *The world's great age begins anew,*
> *The golden years return,*
> *The earth doth like a snake renew*
> *Her winter weeds outworn.*

That was written a hundred years ago and it is still prophetic.

Coming into New York harbour there was fog, a quite appropriate and disturbing fog, with fog-horns about us so like political leaders that you could not in the least ascertain their direction, and the *Washington* in which I was a passenger was as nearly as possible run down by the *Balin* in the Ambrose Channel. The German liner jumped out of the fog abruptly, and passed within ten yards of us on the wrong side. I heard a babble of voices close at hand and looked out of my port-hole into the astonished faces of a group of passengers on the *Balin's* deck within spitting distance of me. She swept by and vanished in the fog and I went up on deck to hear what other people thought of the occurrence. Opinions differed as to how near we had been to a smash; the estimates varied from six feet to twenty yards. The two boats had sucked in towards each other as they passed. Some of us tried to imagine just what a touch would have meant. Nobody was very much upset about it; it seemed to be just a part of the general large dangerousness of human affairs at the present time.

When I arrived in New York I began to hear opinions of the "New Deal" from every point of view. I wanted to sample the atmosphere in which the President was working before I went to see him. Various good friends had gathered talk parties of the most diverse composition, and I had written to one or two men I knew would give me first-hand information. Everyone talked freely and it is not for me to document what was said by this individual or that. I found myself sitting next to an unassuming young man whose name I had not quite caught and he began to unfold a view of the world to me which seemed to contain all I had ever learnt and thought, but better arranged and closer to reality. This I discovered was A. A. Berle of the so-called Brains Trust. "And how many more of *you* are there?" I wanted to ask him—and didn't.

And then, by way of contrast, I heard across the table the distinguished head of a big corporation, a fine grey-headed, rotund-voiced gentleman, denouncing every new thing in America from the President down to the last man in the queue of unemployed, and demanding to be put back forthwith to the happy days of 1924. Or was it 1926? He had observed nothing material since then. "And how many," thought I, "are there of *you*?" His faith in economic anarchism and the eternal succession of trade-cycles was unshaken. Since the present depression was particularly intense and prolonged he argued, the recovery would be all the brighter. He was like a strong infusion of Herbert Spencer and Harriet Martineau in the tradition of that valiant optimist, Ambassador Choate—whom I described as Mr. Z, "Pippa's rich uncle" in *The Future in America*.

Between these extremes of understanding and resistance to reality, was an extraordinary variety of types. I had a brush with a delightful couple of New York "Reds," pure Communists, as pure and intolerant as their Puritan forebears. They were of quite wealthy origin, and they recited their belief in Karl Marx, his philosophy, his psychology, his final divine wisdom, as though Lenin had lived in vain, and they were in just as complete and effective an opposition to the New Deal as my grey-haired corporation president. Roosevelt they said was just "bolstering up capitalism." He was trying to sneak past a social catastrophe and cut out their dear dictatorship of the proletariat altogether—contrariwise to Holy Writ. The better he did the worse it would be, for there could be no real blessing on it, said these real bright Reds.

In the New Willard, in Washington, I found myself in contact with those fine flowers of American insurrectionism, my old friends Clarence Darrow and Charles Russell. They had been summoned to the capital to report on the working of various codes and they were reporting as unhelpfully and destructively as they knew how. They were "agin the government" all the time and the wildfire of freedom shone in Darrow's eyes.

I have a great affection and sympathy for Clarence Darrow. It is deep in my nature also to be restive under government and hostile to dogma. But he is, by ten years or more, of an older generation, and the American radicalism in which he grew up was very different from the early formative influences I have described in my own case. I believe in the free common intelligence, in freely criticized commonsense, but Darrow believes superstitiously in the individual unorganized free common man. That is to say he is a sentimental anarchist. He is for an imaginary "little man"— against monopoly, against rule, against law—any law.

It is remarkable how widespread among American brains is this fantasy of the sturdy little independent "healthy" competitive man, essentially righteous: the Western farmer, the small shop-keeper, the struggling, saving, hard-working entrepreneur. To this first onset of publicly directed large-scale economic organization in Washington, that New York corporation president I have described and Clarence Darrow, the extreme radical, responded in almost identical terms. "Leave us alone," they said—with passion. The same ideal, of perpetuating a fundamental individualism of small folk, was manifest in the anti-trust legislation of Theodore Roosevelt. It is a dream. The problem of personal freedom is not to be solved by economic fragmentation; that Western farmer lost his independence long since and became the grower of a single special crop, the small shop-keeper either a chain-store minder or a dealer in branded goods, and the small entrepreneur a gambler with his savings, and a certain bankrupt in the end; nevertheless the dream survives. To borrow a phrase from Russia: it is a kulak ideal. I found it still living even among the directors of the A.A.A. in Washington.

In their report upon the codes, Darrow and Russell went so far as to impute motive. That heroic small man of their imaginations was, they said, being deliberately sacrificed to big business—*sold* to big business. But it is not the New Deal and the N.R.A. which are sacrificing the small man to large-scale operations. The stars in their courses are doing that. Nevertheless in this fashion these two anarchistic Old Radicals were able to line up with our wealthy young Communists, who thought Roosevelt was "bolstering up capitalism" and that angry public utility exploiter who declared the New Deal was smashing it. There are manifestly common subconscious elements underlying this amazing unanimity.

What struck me most about the New York atmosphere, and the impression was intensified in Washington, was the mixture of praise and detraction with which the President was mentioned. It had become almost a ritual. There would be a prelude upon his courage, his integrity, his personal charm and then "but——". The varied contexts to that "but," taken altogether, made me realize that Franklin Roosevelt is one of the greatest shocks that has ever happened to the prevalent mental assumptions of the United States. A man's formulated and expressed opinions may be one thing, we have to remember, and his tacit or subconscious assumptions quite another. Premonitions of a new social and economic order which have hitherto seemed the harmless talk of an ineffectual intelligentsia have been broadcast abruptly over vast surfaces of conventional business and political expression. The time-honoured crust of pompous insincerity characteristic of the old order has been broken and has revealed the underlying capacity of the American mind for stark reality. With an air of just giving the old deck of cards a new deal for the century-old game of political poker, the President seems to have taken up a new deck altogether, with strange new suits and altered values, and to be playing quietly and resolutely a different game. What game is he playing? Does he know himself? Does he realize he is a revolution? Imaginative answers to these perplexing questions, often highly imaginative and experimental answers, furnished the material for all those "buts."

Were they trying to pull him down or trying to make him out? I listened undecided. Principally, I think, they were puzzled about him and, being puzzled, they were alarmed. They did not want to have him—with all due acknowledgments—and they did not know what else they could have. The world of American wealth and enterprise has been so sure of its freedoms, so convinced of its boundless areas and possibilities and so uncritically assured of its own essential goodness and necessity, that it has received the onset of even a certain scrutiny of its operations with a kind of exaggerated claustrophobia. It is disposed to fight and embarrass any form of regulation. It had got itself into the most hideous economic and industrial mess; only a year ago it was scared white and helpless with the terror of immediate catastrophe, but already it is recovering its ancient confidence and declaring, now that the immediate danger is past, that there was never any danger at all. It means to be carping and obstructive—and to the best of its power and ability it will be. In 1906 in my *Future in America* I emerged with the obvious reflection that Americans rich and radical alike had no "sense of the state." Now they are getting a sense of the state put over them rather rapidly, and they are taking it very ungraciously.

This disposition to detract from the President's effort to reconstruct the American front and to hamper him in every possible way, is unaccompanied by any real alternative policy. It is an irresponsible instinctive opposition, a mulish pulling back. There is no going back now for America. If Roosevelt and his New Deal fail altogether, there will be further financial and business collapse, grave sectional social disorder, political gangsterism and an extensive decivilization of wide regions. And these still wealthy and influential people who are carping and making trouble will be the first to suffer.

The absence of any sense of the state in America, the irresponsible habit of mind fostered by beginning the teaching of history with a rebellion and carrying it on to a glorification of individual push and the mystical democracy of the "Peepul" is the essential difficulty ahead of this eleventh-hour attempt to salvage the immense material accumulations of the past century before they topple over, and to set up an ordered and disciplined direction for the new powers of mankind before it is too late. Order and collective direction means an efficient and devoted Civil Service. The doubt whether America will succeed in making the great adjustments it is facing in time to escape catastrophe, turns largely upon the manifest inadequacy of its present Civil Service to the immense tasks that will necessarily be thrust upon it. Can this Civil Service be supplemented rapidly and effectively? The most momentous question before the United States community is the possibility of improvising ministers, officials and functionaries sufficiently honest and public-spirited, sufficiently clear-headed, courageous and competent to carry through the inevitable reconstruction.

Now outside the limits of the undermanned and underpaid Federal Civil Service there has long been considerable speculative activity in intellectual circles, among the university professoriate, among writers, scientific and technical workers and mentally active men of leisure, about the constructive defects that were becoming more and more patent in the American community. An intelligentsia has developed—much more considerable altogether than the corresponding strata on the British side. It thinks as a whole more *roughly* than its British equivalents, but more boldly and less deferentially. American business has hitherto ticked these people off as "long-haired Radicals" or "parlour socialists" or "cranks" and turned its back on their extending influence. Then, when the crisis was at its blackest, it discovered that these "cranks" might perhaps prove to be "experts." With very mixed feelings it realized that the new President, instead of entrusting himself to the grave and dignified advice of tried "Experience" to heal—or at any rate to go through the motions of healing—at eight per cent let us say, until the ultimate smash—the disaster its routines had made inevitable, was calling these new brains into consultation. Some journalist, not quite sure whether the suggestion of intellectual activity was a curse or a blessing invented the phrase the "Brains Trust," and the report of it went about the world.

It was inevitable after all my broodings upon a possible world-wide Open Conspiracy of clear-headed people, that this report should stir my interest profoundly. I wanted to know just what integrating forces this talk about the Brains Trust might imply, and how they could be brought into relationship with the steady growth of creative revolutionary thought upon the European side.

I have seen enough of this Brains movement to realize that it is no sort of conspiracy; that it is not a body of men formally associated by a concerted statement of ideas. It represents nothing so much in agreement as the radicals who made the republic in Madrid, nothing nearly so close-knit as the pre-revolutionary Bolshevik party. It has indeed scarcely anything to hold it in any sort of unity except that in this miscellany of widely scattered men there is a common determination to bring scientific analysis to bear upon financial and industrial processes, and to make a practical application of the results in the common interest. Its members are miscellaneous both in tradition and in character. It is the President who has drawn them together and it is necessarily from their ranks and associates, rather than from the rascal heelers of the party politicians, grafters by profession, that the supplementing and extension of the Civil Service must be drawn if there is to be any hope for the salvaging of America.

Raymond Moley has interested himself in the history of this Brains Trust movement, and he spread it out very intelligibly to me in a long talk we had in the Hangar Club in New York. He distinguished three main groups of mental influences, the monetary realists, such as Professor Irving Fisher and Professor Rogers, who constitute the rudiments of a scientific monetary control, the economic organizers such as Johnson, Tugwell and Berle, who stand chiefly for an extension of employment and exploitation by the State, and the lawyers—of whom only Felix Frankfurter is known to me personally—who are concerned with the development of legal restraints upon socially destructive speculative enterprise, and upon the use of large scale organization for private aggrandizement. Many of these people have never met each other. The link between them all was first the Executive Mansion at Albany, when Franklin Roosevelt was Governor of New York State and is now the White House. It is the President's notes of interrogation that have drawn them all together into a loose constructive co-operation.

That is the outstanding difference—so far as form goes—between the constructive effort in Washington and Moscow. The one is a receptive and co-ordinating brain-centre; the other is a concentrated and personal direction. The end sought, a progressively more organized big-scale community, is precisely the same.

I have been four times to the White House, and twice to the Kremlin, to see the man in occupation. But I have never been, and I am never likely to go, inside the gates of Buckingham Palace. Very early impressions may have something to do with that; I have told of my resistance to my mother's obsession about the dear Queen and my jealousy of the royal offspring; but the main reason for my obstinately republican life, as I see it in my own mind, is my conviction that here in England something has been held on to too long, and that nothing is doing here. A constitutional monarchy substitutes a figure-head for a head and distributes leadership elusively throughout the community. This gives the British system the resisting power of an acephalous invertebrate, and renders it equally incapable of concentrated forward action. In war-time the Crown resumes, or attempts to resume, a centralized authority—with such results as I have already glanced at in my account of my war experiences. Quite in accord with the tenacity of an acephalous invertebrate, the empire can be cut to pieces legally, have its South Ireland amputated, see half its shipping laid up and its heavy industries ruined, reconcile itself to the chronic unemployment and demoralization of half its young people, and still, on the strength of a faked budget and a burst of sunny summer weather, believe itself to be essentially successful and invulnerable. So it came about that, almost without thinking it over, as the various League of Nations documents I have quoted bear witness, I had become accustomed to looking westward for the definitive leadership of the English speaking community—and anywhere but in London for the leadership of mankind.

I have told already of my visit to Theodore Roosevelt. It was like visiting any large comfortable, leisurely, free-talking country house. Seeing President Harding had been like attending a politicians' reception in an official building, all loud geniality and hand-shaking and the protean White House, had taken on the decoration and furniture of a popular club. My call upon President Hoover was a sort of intrusion upon a sickly overworked and overwhelmed man, a month behind in all his engagements and hopeless of ever overtaking them, and the White House, in sympathy, had made itself into a queer ramshackle place like a nest of waiting-rooms with hat-stands everywhere, and unexpected doors, never perceptible before or since, through which hurrying distraught officials appeared and vanished. President Hoover did not talk with me at all; he delivered a discourse upon the possible economic self-sufficiency of America that was, I imagine, intended for M. Laval from Paris, who had left Washington a week or so before. I did not find it interesting. After the Harding days there had been a foolish development of etiquette in Washington and instead of going to the President as man to man, the foreign visitor during the Coolidge and Hoover régimes was led—after due enquiries—down to the White House by his ambassador. Henceforth America and the English, it had been decided, were to talk only through a diplomatic pipette. Sir Ronald Lindsay took me down, apologetically, and sat beside me during the encounter, rather like a gentleman who takes a strange dog out to a tea-party, and is not quite sure how it will behave. But I respected the trappings of government and nothing diplomatically serious occurred.

I just listened and contained myself. Diplomatic usage, will I suppose, prevent Sir Ronald from ever producing his memories of Men I have Chaperoned to the White House.

All this had been swept away again in 1934, I had had some slight correspondence with the President already, I went to him on my own credentials, and found that this magic White House had changed back again to a large leisurely comfortable private home. All the Hoover untidiness had vanished. Everything was large, cool, orderly and unhurried. Besides Mr. and Mrs. Roosevelt, his daughter Mrs. Dall, Miss Le Hand his personal secretary, and another lady, dined with us and afterwards I sat and talked to him and Mrs. Roosevelt and Miss Le Hand until nearly midnight, easily and pleasantly—as though the world crisis focused anywhere rather than upon the White House.

As everyone knows, the President is a crippled man. He reminded me of William Ernest Henley. He has the same big torso linked to almost useless legs, and he lacked even Henley's practised nimbleness with stick and crutch. But when we sat at dinner and when he was in his study chair, his physical disablement vanished from the picture. Mrs. Roosevelt I found a very pleasant, well-read lady; I had been warned she was a terrible "school marm," but the only trait of the schoolmistress about her was a certain care for precision of statement. There was no pose about either of them. They were not concerned about being what was expected of them, or with the sort of impression they were making; they were just interested in a curious keen detached way about the state of the world. They talked about that, in the manner of independent people who had really not so very much to do with it. We were all in it and we had to play our parts, but there was no reason because one was in a responsible position that one should be mystical or pompous or darkly omniscient about it.

Even if my memory would serve for the task, I would not report the drift and shifting substance of our talk. Only one thing need be recorded, the President's manifest perplexity at some recent turns of British diplomacy, and the wonder that peeped out—a wonder we all share—over the question as to what Sir John Simon imagines he is up to, whether he represents any obscure realities of British thought and, if not, why on earth, in the far east and elsewhere, the two big English-speaking communities seem perpetually discordant and unexpected to each other. My own fixed idea about world peace came naturally enough to the fore. If it were not, I said, for questions of mere political mechanism, stale traditions, the mental childishness of our British Foreign Office and what not, it would be perfectly possible even now for the English speaking masses and the Russian mass, with France as our temperamental associate, to be made to say effectively that Peace shall prevail throughout the earth. And it would prevail. Whatever dreams of conquest and dominion might be in a few militant and patriotic brains outside such a combination, would burn but weakly in the cold discouragement of so great a unison. And what was it—prevented that unison?

But that was only one of the topics we touched upon. What concerns me here is not what was said, but the manner in which it was thought about and advanced. I am not thinking primarily of policies and governmental actions here, but of an encounter with a new type of mind. My own ideas about the coming socialist world-state are fixed and explicit. But they are, I am persuaded, implicit in every mind that has been opened to the possibility of unrestricted change. I do not say that the President has these revolutionary ideas in so elaborated and comprehensive a form as they have come to me; I do not think he has. I do not think he is consciously what I have called an Open Conspirator and it is quite clear his formula are necessarily limited by the limitations of the popular understanding with which he has to come to terms. But these ideas are sitting all round him now, and unless I misjudge him, they will presently possess him altogether. Events are reinforcing them and carrying him on to action. My impression of both him and of Mrs. Roosevelt is that they are *unlimited* people, entirely modern in the openness of their minds and the logic of their actions. I have been using the word "blinkered" rather freely in this section. Here in the White House, the unblinkered mind was in possession.

The Roosevelts are something more than open-minded. Arthur Balfour was greatly open-minded, but he lacked the slightest determination to realize the novel ideas he entertained so freely. He was set in the habitual acceptance of the thing that is, church, court, society, empire, and he did not really believe in the new thoughts that played about in his mind. President Roosevelt does. He has a brain that is certainly as receptive and understanding as Balfour's but, with that, he has an uncanny disposition for action and realization that Balfour lacked altogether. This man who can sit and talk so frankly and freely is also an astute politician and a subtle manager of masses and men. As the President thinks and conceives, so forthwith, he acts. Both he and his wife have the simplicity that says, "But if it is right we ought to do it." They set about what they suppose has to be done without exaltation, without apology or any sense of the strangeness of such conduct. Such unification of unconventional thought and practical will is something new in history, and I will not speculate here about the peculiar personal and the peculiar American conditions that may account for it. But as the vast problems about them expose and play themselves into their minds, the goal of the Open Conspiracy becomes plainer ahead. Franklin Roosevelt does not embody and represent that goal, but he represents the way thither. He is being the most effective transmitting instrument possible for the coming of the new world order. He is eminently "reasonable" and fundamentally implacable. He demonstrates that comprehensive new ideas can be taken up, tried out and made operative in general affairs without rigidity or dogma. He is continuously revolutionary in the new way without ever provoking a stark revolutionary crisis.

Before I visited Washington, I was inclined to the belief that the forces against such a replanning of the American social and political system as will arrest the present slant towards disaster, the individualistic tradition, the individual lawlessness, the intricate brutal disingenuousness of political and legal methods, were so great that President Franklin Roosevelt was doomed to an inevitable defeat. I wrote an article *The Place of Franklin Roosevelt in History* (Liberty Magazine, October, 1933) in which I made my bet for his over-throw. But I thought then he was a man with a definite set of ideas, fixed and final, in his head, just as I am a man with a system of conclusions fixed and definite in my head. But I perceive he is something much more flexible and powerful than that. He is bold and unlimited in his objectives because his mental arms are long and his courage great, but his peculiar equipment as an amateur of the first rank in politics, keeps him in constant touch with political realities and possibilities. He never lets go of them and they never subdue him. He never seems to go so far beyond the crowd as to risk his working leadership, and he never loses sight of pioneer thought. He can understand and weigh contemporary speculative economics, financial specialism and international political psychology, and he can talk on the radio—over the heads of the party managers and newspaper proprietors and so forth—quite plainly and very convincingly to the ordinary voting man.

He is, as it were, a ganglion for reception, expression, transmission, combination and realization, which I take it, is exactly what a modern government ought to be. And if perhaps after all he is, humanly, not quite all that I am saying of him here, he is at any rate enough of what I am saying of him here, for me to make him a chief collateral exhibit in this psycho-political autobiography.

* * * * *

On July the 21st I started from London for Moscow in the company of my eldest son, who wished to meet some Russian biologists with whose work he was acquainted, and to see their laboratories. We left Croydon in the afternoon, spent the night in Berlin and flew on by way of Danzig, Kovno and Welilikje Luki, reaching Moscow before dark on the evening of the 22nd. We flew in clear weather as far as Amsterdam, then through a couple of thunderstorms to Berlin. We were late in reaching the glitter of illuminated Berlin; the raining darkness was flickering with lightning flashes and our plane came down to make its landing with flares burning under its wings along a lane of windy yellow flame against the still red and white lights of the aerodrome. The flight next day from Welilikje Luki to Moscow, flying low and eastward in afternoon sunshine, was particularly golden and lovely.

In 1900, when I wrote *Anticipations*, this would have been as incredible a journey as a trip on Aladdin's carpet; in 1934 it was arranged in the most matter of fact way through a travel agency, it was a little excursion that anyone might make; and the fare was less than the railway fare would have been a third of a century before. In a little time such a visit will seem as small a matter as a taxi-cab call does now. It is our antiquated political organization and our retrograde imaginations that still hold back such a final abolition of distance.

Moscow I found greatly changed—even from the air this was visible; not set and picturesque, a black-and-gold barbaric walled city-camp about a great fortress, as I had seen it first in 1914; nor definitely shabby, shattered and apprehensive as it had been in the time of Lenin, but untidily and hopefully renascent. There was new building going on in every direction, workers' dwellings, big groups of factories and, amidst the woods, new *datchas* and country clubs. No particular plan was apparent from the air; it looked like a vigorous, natural expansion such as one might see in the most individualistic of cities. We came down over a patchwork of aerodromes and saw many hundreds of planes parked outside the hangars. Russian aviation may be concentrated about Moscow, but this display of air force was certainly impressive. Twenty-two years ago, in my *War in the Air*, I had imagined such wide fields of air fleet, but never then in my boldest cerebrations did I think I should live to see them.

I confess that I approached Stalin with a certain amount of suspicion and prejudice. A picture had been built up in my mind of a very reserved and self-centred fanatic, a despot without vices, a jealous monopolizer of power. I had been inclined to take the part of Trotsky against him. I had formed a very high opinion perhaps an excessive opinion, of Trotsky's military and administrative abilities, and it seemed to me that Russia, which is in such urgent need of directive capacity at every turn, could not afford to send them into exile. Trotsky's Autobiography, and more particularly the second volume, had modified this judgment but I still expected to meet a ruthless, hard—possibly doctrinaire—and self-sufficient man at Moscow; a Georgian highlander whose spirit had never completely emerged from its native mountain glen.

Yet I had had to recognize that under him Russia was not being merely tyrannized over and held down; it was being governed and it was getting on. Everything I had heard in favour of the First Five Year Plan I had put through a severely sceptical sieve, and yet there remained a growing effect of successful enterprise. I had listened more and more greedily to any first-hand gossip I could hear about both these contrasted men. I had already put a query against my grim anticipation of a sort of Bluebeard at the centre of Russian affairs. Indeed if I had not been in reaction against these first preconceptions and wanting to get nearer the truth of the matter, I should never have gone again to Moscow.

This lonely overbearing man, I thought, may be damned disagreeable, but anyhow he must have an intelligence far beyond dogmatism. And if I am not all wrong about the world, and if he is as able as I am beginning to think him, then he must be seeing many things much as I am seeing them.

I wanted to tell him that I had talked to Franklin Roosevelt of the new prospect of world co-operation that was opening before mankind. I wanted to stress the fact upon which I had dwelt in the White House, that in the English-speaking and Russian-speaking populations, and in the populations geographically associated with them round the temperate zone, there is a major mass of human beings ripe for a common understanding and common co-operation in the preparation of an organised world-state. Quite parallel with that double basis for a world plan, I wanted to say, there is a third great system of possible co-operation in the Spanish-speaking community. These masses, together with the Chinese, constitute an overwhelming majority of mankind, anxious—in spite of their so-called governments—for peace, industry and an organized well-being. Such things as Japanese imperialism, the national egotism of the Quai d'Orsay and of Mussolini, the childish disingenuousness of the British foreign office, and German political delirium, would become quite minor obstacles to human unity, if these common dispositions could be marshalled into a common understanding and a common method of expression. The militancy of Japan was not so much a threat to mankind as a useful reminder for us to sink formal differences and spread one explicit will for peace throughout the world. Japan, with a possible but very improbable German alliance, was the only efficient reactionary menace left for civilization to deal with. France was inaggressive in spirit; Great Britain incurably indeterminate. I wanted to find out how far Stalin saw international matters in this shape and, if he proved to be in general agreement, to try and see how far he would go with me in my idea that the present relative impotence of the wider masses of mankind to restrain the smaller fiercer threats of aggressive patriotism, is really due not to anything fundamental in human nature but to old inharmonious traditions, bad education and bad explanations; to our failure, thus far, to get our populations clearly told the true common history of our race and the common objective now before mankind. That objective was the highly organized world community in which service was to take the place of profit. The political dialects and phrases which were directed towards that end were needlessly and wastefully different. Creative impulses were being hampered to the pitch of ineffectiveness by pedantries and misunderstandings.

Was it impossible to bring general political statements up to date, so that the real creative purpose in the Russian will should no longer be made alien and repulsive to the quickened intelligence of the Western World, by an obstinate insistence upon the antiquated political jargon, the class-war cant, of fifty years ago? All things serve their purpose and die, and it was time that even the passing of Karl Marx, intellectually as well as physically, was recognised. It was as absurd now to cling to those old expressions as it would be to try to electrify Russia with the frictional electric machines or the zinc and copper batteries of 1864. Marxist class-war insurrectionism had become a real obstacle to the onward planning of a new world order. This was particularly evident in our English-speaking community.

This ancient doctrine that the proletariat or the politician temporarily representing him, can do no wrong, estranged the competent technologist, who was vitally essential to the new task, and inculcated a spirit of mystical mass enthusiasm opposed to all disciplined co-operation. I wanted to bring it plainly into our talk that Russia was now paying only lip service to human unity and solidarity; that she was in actual fact drifting along a way of her own to a socialism of her own, which was getting out of touch with world socialism, and training her teeming multitudes to misinterpret and antagonize the greater informal forces in the West making for world socialization and consolidation. Was it not possible, before opportunity slipped away from us, to form a general line of creative propaganda throughout the earth?...

It was typical of the way in which mental interchanges lag behind the swift achievements of material progress, that Stalin and I had to talk through an interpreter. He speaks a Georgian language and Russian and he does not even smatter any Western idiom. So we had to carry on our conversation in the presence of a foreign-office representative, Mr. Umansky. Mr. Umansky produced a book in which he made a rapid note in Russian of what each of us said, read out my speeches in Russian to Stalin and his, almost as readily, to me in English, and then sat alert-eyed over his glasses ready for the response. Necessarily a certain amount of my phraseology was lost in the process and a certain amount of Mr. Umansky's replaced it. And our talk went all the slowlier because I was doing my best to check back, by what Stalin said, that he was getting the substance at least, if not the full implications, of what I was saying.

All lingering anticipations of a dour sinister Highlander vanished at the sight of him. He is one of those people who in a photograph or painting become someone entirely different. He is not easy to describe, and many descriptions exaggerate his darkness and stillness. His limited sociability and a simplicity that makes him inexplicable to the more consciously disingenuous, has subjected him to the strangest inventions of whispering scandal. His harmless, orderly, private life is kept rather more private than his immense public importance warrants, and when, a year or so ago, his wife died suddenly of some brain lesion, the imaginative spun a legend of suicide which a more deliberate publicity would have made impossible. All such shadowy undertow, all suspicion of hidden emotional tensions, ceased for ever, after I had talked to him for a few minutes.

My first impression was of a rather commonplace-looking man dressed in an embroidered white shirt, dark trousers and boots, staring out of the window of a large, generally empty, room. He turned rather shyly and shook hands in a friendly manner. His face also was commonplace, friendly and commonplace, not very well modelled, not in any way "fine". He looked past me rather than at me but not evasively; it was simply that he had none of the abundant curiosity which had kept Lenin watching me closely from behind the hand he held over his defective eye, all the time he talked to me.

I began by saying that Lenin at the end of our conversation had said "Come back and see us in ten years". I had let it run to fourteen, but now that I had seen Franklin Roosevelt in Washington I wanted to meet the ruling brain of the Kremlin while my Washington impressions were still fresh, because I thought that the two of them between them indicated the human future as no other two men could do. He said with a quite ordinary false modesty that he was only doing little things—just little things.

The conversation hung on a phase of shyness. We both felt friendly, and we wanted to be at our ease with each other, and we were not at our ease. He had evidently a dread of self-importance in the encounter; he posed not at all, but he knew we were going to talk of very great matters. He sat down at a table and Mr. Umansky sat down beside us, produced his note book and patted it open in a competent, expectant manner.

I felt there was heavy going before me but Stalin was so ready and willing to explain his position that in a little while the pause for interpretation was almost forgotten in the preparation of new phrases for the argument. I had supposed there was about forty minutes before me, but when at that period I made a reluctant suggestion of breaking off, he declared his firm intention of going on for three hours. And we did. We were both keenly interested in each other's point of view. What I said was the gist of what I had intended to say and that I have told already; the only matter of interest here is how Stalin reacted to these ideas.

I do not know whether it illuminated Stalin or myself most penetratingly, but what impressed me most in that discussion was his refusal to see any sort of parallelism with the processes and methods and aims of Washington and Moscow. When I talked of the planned world to him, I talked in a language he did not understand. He looked at the proposition before him and made nothing of it. He has little of the quick uptake of President Roosevelt and none of the subtlety and tenacity of Lenin. Lenin was indeed saturated with Marxist phraseology, but he had a complete control of this phraseology. He could pour it into new meanings and use it for his own purposes. But Stalin was almost as much a trained mind, trained in the doctrines of Lenin and Marx, as those governess-trained minds of the British Foreign Office and diplomatic service, of which I have already written so unkindly. He was as little adaptable. The furnishing of his mind had stopped at the point reached by Lenin when he reconditioned Marxism. His was not a free impulsive brain nor a scientifically organized brain; it was a trained Leninist-Marxist brain. Sometimes I seemed to get him moving as I wanted him to move, but directly he felt he was having his feet shifted, he would clutch at some time-honoured phrase and struggle back to orthodoxy.

I have never met a man more candid, fair and honest, and to these qualities it is, and to nothing occult and sinister, that he owes his tremendous undisputed ascendency in Russia. I had thought before I saw him that he might be where he was because men were afraid of him, but I realize that he owes his position to the fact that no one is afraid of him and everybody trusts him. The Russians are a people at once childish and subtle, and they have a justifiable fear of subtlety in themselves and others. Stalin is an exceptionally unsubtle Georgian. His unaffected orthodoxy is an assurance to his associates that whatever he does would be done without fundamental complications and in the best possible spirit. They had been fascinated by Lenin, and they feared new departures from his talismanic directions. And Stalin's trained obduracy to the facts of to-day in our talk simply reflected, without the slightest originality, the trained and self-protective obduracy of his associates.

I not only attacked him with the assertion that large scale planning by the community, and a considerable socialization of transport and staple industries, was dictated by the mechanical developments of our time, and was going on quite as extensively outside the boundaries of Sovietdom as within them, but also I made a long criticism of the old-fashioned class-war propaganda, in which a macédoine of types and callings is jumbled up under the term bourgeoisie. That is one of the most fatal of the false simplifications in this collective human brain-storm which is the Russian revolution. I said that great sections in that mixture, the technicians, scientific workers, medical men, skilled foremen, skilled producers, aviators, operating engineers, for instance, would and should supply the best material for constructive revolution in the West, but that the current communist propaganda, with its insistence upon a mystical mass directorate, estranged and antagonised just these most valuable elements. Skilled workers and directors know that Jack is not as good as his master. Stalin saw my reasoning, but he was held back by his habitual reference to the proletarian mass— which is really nothing more than the "sovereign Peepul" of old fashioned democracy, renamed. That is to say it is nothing but a politician's figment. It was amusing to shoot at him, with a lively knowledge of the facts of the October revolution, an assertion equally obvious and unorthodox, that "All Revolutions are made by minorities." His honesty compelled him to admit that "at first" this might be so. I tried to get back to my idea of the possible convergence of West and East upon the socialist world state objective, by quoting Lenin as saying, after the Revolution, "Communism has now to learn Business," and adding that in the West that had to be put the other way round. Business had now to learn the socialization of capital—which indeed is all that this Russian Communism now amounts to. It is a state-capitalism with a certain tradition of cosmopolitanism. West and East starting from entirely different levels of material achievement, had each now what the other lacked, and I was all for a planetary rounding off of the revolutionary process. But Stalin, now quite at his ease and interested, sucked thoughtfully at the pipe he had most politely asked my permission to smoke, shook his head and said "Nyet" reflectively. He was evidently very suspicious of this suggestion of complemental co-operation. It might be the thin end of a widening wedge. He lifted his hand rather like a schoolboy who is prepared to recite, and dictated a reply in party formulae. The movement of socialization in America was not a genuine proletarian revolution; the "capitalist" was just saving himself, pretending to divest himself of power and hiding round the corner to come back. That settled that. The one true faith was in Russia; there could be no other. America must have her October Revolution and follow her Russian leaders.

Later on we discussed liberty of expression. He admitted the necessity and excellence of criticism, but preferred that it should be home-made by the party within the party organization. There, he declared, criticism was extraordinarily painstaking and free. Outside criticism might be biased....

I wound up according to my original intention by insisting upon the outstanding positions of himself and Roosevelt, and their ability to talk to the world in unison. But that came lamely because my hope for some recognition, however qualified, on the part of the man in control of Russia, of the present convergence towards a collective capitalism in the East and West alike, was badly damaged. He had said his piece to all my initiatives and he stayed put. I wished I could have talked good Russian or had an interpreter after my own heart. I could have got nearer to him then. Normal interpreters gravitate inevitably towards stereotyped phrases. Nothing suffers so much in translation as the freshness of an unfamiliar idea.

As I saw one personality after another in Moscow, I found myself more and more disposed to a psycho-analysis of this resistance which is offered to any real creative forces coming in from the West. It is very marked indeed. In a few years, if it is sustained, we may hear Moscow saying if not "Russia for the Russians," then at least "Sovietdom for the followers of Marx and Lenin and down with everyone who will not bow to the Prophets," which, so far as the peace and unity of the world is concerned, will amount to the same thing. There is a strong incorrigible patriotism beneath this Russian situation, all the more effective because it is disguised, just as there was an incorrigible French patriotism beneath the world-fraternisation of the first French revolution.

A day or so later I discussed birth control and liberty of expression at considerable length with Maxim Gorky and some of the younger Russian writers, in the beautiful and beautifully furnished house the government places at his disposal. Physically Gorky has changed very little since 1906 when I visited him, an amazed distressful refugee, upon Staten Island. I have described that earlier meeting in *The Future in America*. I stayed with him again in 1920 (*Russia in the Shadows*). Then he was a close friend of Lenin's but disposed nevertheless to be critical of the new régime. Now he has become an unqualified Stalinite. Between us also, unhappily, an interpreter had to intervene, for Gorky, in spite of his long sojourn in Italy, has lapsed back to complete mono-lingualism.

Some years ago John Galsworthy helped to create an international net of literary societies called P.E.N. Clubs. At first they served only for amiable exchanges between the writers of the same and different countries, but the violent persecution of Jewish and leftish writers in Germany, and an attempt to seize and use the Berlin Pen Club for Nazi propaganda, raised new and grave issues for the organization. Just at that time Galsworthy died and I succeeded him as International President. I was drawn in as President and chairman to two stormy debates in Ragusa and Edinburgh respectively. The task of championing freedom of expression in art and literature was practically forced upon this weak but widespread organization. It had many defects, but it had access to considerable publicity, and in these questions publicity is of primary importance. Local battles to maintain the freedom and dignity of letters were fought in the Berlin, Vienna and Rome P.E.N. Clubs, and I now brought to these new Russian writers the question whether the time had not come to decontrol literary activities in Russia, and form a free and independent P.E.N. Club in Moscow. I unfolded my ideas about the necessity of free writing and speech and drawing in every highly organized state; the greater the political and social rigidity, I argued, the more the need for thought and comment to play about it. These were quite extraordinary ideas to all my hearers, though Gorky must have held them once. If so, he has forgotten them or put them behind him.

We wrangled for an hour or so at a long tea table, which had been set in a high sunny white portico, with fluttering swallows feeding their young above the capitals of the columns. About half a dozen of the younger Russian writers were present and the Litvinoffs came in from their equally beautiful villa on the far side of Moscow to join in the discussion. To me the most notable things by far about this talk were the set idea of everyone that literature should be under political control and restraint, and the extraordinary readiness to suspect a "capitalist" intrigue, to which all their brains, including Gorky's, had been *trained*. I did not like to find Gorky against liberty. It wounded me.

I must confess indeed to a profound discontent with this last phase of his. Something human and distressful in him, which had warmed my sympathies in his fugitive days, has evaporated altogether. He has changed into a class- conscious proletarian Great Man. His prestige within the Soviet boundaries is colossal—and artificial. His literary work, respectable though it is, does not justify this immense fame. He has been inflated to a greatness beyond that of Robert Burns in Scotland or

Shakespeare in England. He has become a sort of informal member of the government, and whenever the authorities have a difficulty about naming a new aeroplane or a new avenue or a new town or a new organization, they solve the difficulty by calling it Maxim Gorky. He seems quietly aware of the embalming, and the mausoleum and apotheosis awaiting him, when he too will become a sleeping Soviet divinity. Meanwhile he criticizes the younger writers and gathers them about him. And he sat beside me, my old friend, the erstwhile pelted outcast dismally in tears whom I tried to support and comfort upon Staten Island, half deified now and all dismay forgotten, looking sidelong at me with that Tartar face of his, and devising shrewd questions to reveal the spidery "capitalist" entanglement he suspected me of spinning. One sails westward and comes at last to the east, and here in Russia after the revolution, just as in Russia before the revolution, all round the world to the left, we have come to the worst vice of the right again, and literary expression is restricted to acceptable opinions.

It does not matter to Gorky, it seems, that our poor little P.E.N. organization has fought for a hearing for left extremists like Toller, and that all its battles so far have been to liberate the left. In this new-born world of dogmatic communism, he insisted, there was to be no recognition for White or Catholic or any sort of right writer, write he ever so beautifully. So Maxim Gorky, in 1934, to my amazement made out a case for the Americans who had hounded him out of New York in 1906.

I argued in vain that men had still the right to dispute the final perfection of Leninism. Through the media of art and literature, it was vital that they should render all that was in their minds, accepted or unorthodox, good or bad. For political action and social behaviour there must be conventions and laws, but there could be no laws and conventions in the world of expression. You could not lock up imaginations. You could not say, "thus far you may imagine and no further." Socialism existed for the dignity and freedom of the soul of man, and not the soul of man for socialism. There were sceptical smiles as the translator did his best to render this queer assertion. Perhaps I made things too difficult for him by speaking of the soul of man.

Gorky, the reformed outcast, wagged his head slowly from side to side and produced excuses for this control of new thought and suggestion by officials. The liberty I was demanding as an essential in any Russian P.E.N. that might be founded, might be all very well in the stabler Anglo-Saxon world; we could afford to play with error and heresy; but Russia was like a country at war. It could not tolerate opposition. I had heard this stuff before. At Ragusa, Schmidt-Pauli, speaking for the Nazis, and at Edinburgh, Marinetti, the Fascist, had made precisely the same apologies for suppression.

I was inspired to produce an argument in the Hegelian form. I asserted that nothing could exist without the recognition of its opposite and that if you destroyed the opposite of a thing altogether the thing itself went dead. Life was reaction, and mental processes could achieve clear definition only by a full apprehension of contraries. From that I argued that if they suppressed men who sang or painted or wrote about the glories of individual freedom, the picturesqueness of merchandising, the mysteries of the religious imagination, pure artistry, caprice, kingship, sin or destruction and the delights of misbehaviour, then their Leninism also would lose its vitality and die. This was I think translated correctly to these exponents of the orthodox Russian temperament but they contrived no sort of reply.

Litvinoff cut across their indecision with a question whether I wanted to have the exiled White writers come to Moscow. I said that was for him to decide, it might do them and Russia a lot of good to have them back and listen to what they had to say, but anyhow the principle of the P.E.N. club was that no genuine artist or writer, whatever his social or political beliefs and implications might be, should be excluded from its membership.

I had brought them my proposal and I promised I would leave a written version of it to put before the approaching Congress of Soviet Writers. If they chose to enter into the liberal brotherhood of the P.E.N. Clubs, well and good. If they did not, I should do my best to make their refusal known to the world. In the long run it would be the Russian intellectual movement that would suffer most by this insistence upon making its cultural relations with the outside world a one-way channel, an outgoing of all that Russia thought fit to tell the world and the refusal of any critical return. Mankind might even grow bored at last by a consciously heroic and unconsciously mystical Soviet Russia with wax in its ears.

Later on I found a rather different atmosphere in the household of Alexis Tolstoy at Detskoe Selo (which is Tsarskoe Selo rechristened). There too I met a number of writers and propounded this idea of a thin web of societies about the world associated to assert the freedom and dignity of art and literature. There has always been very marked mental, temperamental and political contrast between Leningrad and Moscow. The bearing of the two populations is very different and the former place has a large cold seventeenth century dignity and a northern quality which compares very vividly with the disorderly crowded street bustle, the bazaar animation of Moscow. Even the religiosity of the new faith has a different quality. There is nothing in the northern city with the emotional value of Lenin's tomb, and the anti-God museum in the great church of St. Isaac opposite the Astoria Hotel is a mere argumentative brawl within the vast cold magnificence of that always most unspiritual fane. Christianity never was alive in Leningrad as it was at the shrine of the Black Virgin in Moscow and neither is the new Red religion as alive.

Perhaps I put my case to the Leningrad writers with better skill after my experience in Gorky's villa, but I encountered none of the suspicion and rigid preconceptions of that first meeting. They were quite ready to accept the universalism of the P.E.N.

proposal, and to assert the superiority of free scientific and artistic expression to considerations of political expediency. They promised to support my memorandum to the approaching Congress of Soviet Writers, proposing the constitution of a Russian P.E.N. centre, open to every shade of opinion, and I shall await the report of their clash with the definite intolerance of the Moscow brains with a very keen interest. But at the time of writing this Congress has still to meet.

I argued with Gorky also about birth control, because he, with many others of these Russian leaders, in a confusion between subconscious patriotism and creative optimism, is all for a Russia of four hundred or five hundred millions, regardless of how the rest of mankind may be faring. Russia may want soldiers to defend its Russianism, which is exactly on the level of Mussolini's reasons for damning the thought of birth control in Italy. In the old days Gorky was a dire pessimist with a taste for gloomy colours, but now his optimism has become boundless. Under the red ensign the earth can support an increasing population, he seemed to argue, until standing room is exhausted. To the Proletariat under the new régime, as to God under the old, nothing is impossible. Where it gives mouths it will give food. The Soviet men of science, he imagines, can always be instructed and, if necessary, disciplined to that effect.

In Gorky's study was a great book of plans which he thrust upon me. They were the plans of an almost incredibly splendid palace of biological science. It outdid the boldest buildings of the Czardom. Five hundred (or was it a thousand?) research students from abroad were always to be working there. Among other activities. Where *is* this? I asked. He produced a plan of Moscow and indicated the exact spot. I said I would like to go and see it. But, he smiled, it was not yet completed for me to see. I had a flash of understanding. I would like to go and see the foundations. But they have not yet begun the foundation! You shall see it, said Gorky, when you come again. It is only one of a group of vast research and educational establishments we are making. You need have no anxiety about the quality of scientific work in Soviet Russia or of its capacity to meet whatever calls are made upon it. In view of these plans.

From Gorky evoking biology in a land of controlled literature by waving an architect's drawing at it, it was an immense relief to go and see some of the most significant biological work in the world actually in progress, in Pavlov's new Institute of Psychological Genetics outside Leningrad. This is already in working order and still being rapidly enlarged under its founder's direction. It is the least grandiose and most practicable group of research buildings in the world. Pavlov's reputation is an immense asset to Soviet prestige and he is now given practically everything he asks for in the way of material. That much is to the credit of this government. I found the old man in vigorous health, and he took me and my biological son from one group of buildings to another at a smart trot, expounding his new work upon animal intelligence with the greatest animation as he did so. My son who has always followed his work closely, plied him with lively questions. Afterwards we sat in the house over glasses of tea and he talked on for a couple of hours. He is ruddy and white-haired; if Bernard Shaw were to trim and brush his hair and beard they would be almost indistinguishable. He is eighty-five and he wants to live to a hundred-and-five just to see how the work he has in hand will turn out.

My son and I had visited him in 1920 (in *Russia in the Shadows*), when Gip was still a Cambridge undergraduate, and so it was natural that a comparison of Russia in 1920 and Russia in 1934, should get into the stream of the discourse. He talked down his two Communist assistants who were at the table with us. He talked indeed as no other man in Russia would be permitted to talk. So far, he said, the new régime had produced no results worth considering. It was still a large clumsy experiment without proper controls. It might be a success in time, it was certainly a considerable nuisance to decent people with old-fashioned tastes, but at present there was neither time nor freedom in which to judge it. He seemed to see very little advantage in replacing the worship of the crucified by the worship of the embalmed. For his own part he still went to church. It was a good habit, he thought. He delivered a discourse quite after my heart on the need for absolute intellectual freedom, if scientific progress, if any sort of human progress, was to continue. And when I asked him what he felt about dialectical materialism, he exchanged derisive gestures with me, and left it at that. He will not be bothered by minor observances; he sticks to dating by the old weekday names, and his always very simple way of living has carried over, just as his magnificent researches have carried over, with scarcely a modification, from the days before the great change. There was by the bye a nursery with a real governess for his two grandchildren! I doubt if there is another governess in Soviet territory. As we came away my son said to me; "Odd to have passed a whole afternoon outside of Soviet Russia."

That I thought was a good remark. But if we had been outside Soviet Russia, where had we been? That was not so easy. It wasn't the Past. It was a little island of intellectual freedom? It was a scrap of the world republic of science? It was a glimpse of the future? But in the end we decided that it was just Pavlov.

If I had to talk to Stalin and Gorky and Alexis Tolstoy and Pavlov through a sort of verbal grille, there were other people about who could talk English, and who wilfully or inadvertently exposed some acutely interesting minor aspects of the new Russia. It seems beyond disputing that while the political controls incline to be excessive and oppressive, the lay-out of the material scheme, as one sees it in Moscow at least,—for I saw nothing whatever of the planning of Leningrad—is hasty, amateurish and often shockingly incompetent. Disproportion is visible everywhere and all sorts of ineffectivenesses forced themselves on my attention during my ten-day stay quite without my looking for them; there is for instance still a shortage of paper to print even the books in greatest demand, and the paper used is often like thin packing paper; vitally important educational work is held up in consequence; the street traffic again in Moscow, although it has nothing like the volume of the traffic in London or Paris, is disorganised and dangerous, and if one does not belong to the automobile-using class—there are still classes of that sort—getting about is toilsome and tediously slow; the distribution of goods through a variety of shops with different prices and using different sorts of money is preposterously inconvenient. Moscow is growing very rapidly and the re-planning and rebuilding seemed to me poorly conceived. Since other great cities have their tube system, Moscow also is making an imitative tube system, although its alluvial water-bearing soil is highly unsuitable for the tubes they are making at the inadequate depth of thirty feet or so. It will be the least stable "Metropolitan" in the world, and it is plain the problem should have been approached from some other and more original direction. I was told by various apologists that what is being done in Moscow is not representative of the real Russian effort; that at different points, usually they are remote points, marvellous things are being achieved. But I suppose there are the same sort of people there as here in Moscow, and in Moscow, as planners and constructors, they are anything but marvellous.

The outstanding achievement of the new régime, when all is said and done, is the great change in the bearing of the new generation, which has cast off altogether the traditions of serfdom and looks the world bravely in the eye. Coupled with this, an integral part of it indeed, is the "liquidation of illiteracy." But are either of these advances unprecedented? The common folk of the United States of America were as free, equal and confident in the days of simplicity a hundred years ago. And they had their common schools. It is really nothing so very miraculous to be almost the last country in Europe to respond to the need for a common citizen who can read. These people do not know anything of the rest of the world. But wait and see what *these* young people will *do*, interpolates my Bolshevik guide. A hundred years ago America was just such a land of promise.

Still more similar to this Russian change in manners, was the swift establishment of equalitarian phrases and attitudes after the first French Revolution. Neither American nor French democracy prevented a subsequent development of inequalities of power and fortune. Plutocracy succeeded Aristocracy. "This time," say the Bolsheviks, "we have guarded against any similar relapse." But though they may have abolished profiteering and speculation they have not abolished other sorts of advantage. Their defensive obscurantism makes just the shadows in which fresh infringements of human dignity can occur. As the initial revolutionary enthusiasm dies away, officialdom, protected from independent criticism, is bound to find its way to self-indulgence and privilege. All over Moscow and Petersburg you can bribe with foreign currency because of the absurd Torgsin system, and the population everywhere is learning to hop quickly and deferentially out of the way of an aggressively driven Lincoln car. The Communist propaganda is altogether too self-satisfied about the intensity and uniqueness of its revolution.

The perpetual reference of those who showed me about to something away over there or coming to-morrow, recalled the Spanish *mañana*. "Come and see us again in ten years' time," they say, at every revelation of insufficiency. If you say that a new building is ramshackle or flimsy they assure you that it is merely a temporary structure. "We don't mind tearing things down again," they explain. The impulse to shift things and pull them about seems to be stronger than the impulse to make. They are transferring the Academy of Sciences from Leningrad to Moscow for no reason that I can understand. Possibly it is to render the control of general scientific thought more effective. One Pavlov is enough for them; they do not want any revival of that old world radical mentality with its unrestrained criticism, its scepticism and its ridicule. They want their men of science to be industrious bees without stings and live in Gorky's hive.

When Bubnov, the Commissar of Public Education, parted from me outside a charming exhibition of original paintings by little children, very like the original paintings by little children exhibited in every other country in the world, he broke out into happy anticipations of the lives this new generation would lead in a reconstructed Russia. "All this," he said, pointing to a disorderly heap of builders' muck which had submerged a little garden before us, "is temporary." The constructors of the new Metropolitan had, it seems, just made this dump and then gone away for a bit. "This used to be a pretty park," said Bubnov. But it would be all right ten years hence.

Bubnov and Stalin are now among the last survivors of the leaders who did the actual fighting of the revolution, and he said they both meant to live to be a hundred just to see the harvest of Russian prosperity coming in at last. But besides the children in the model schools there are plenty of unaccountable little ragamuffins flitting about the streets. If Stalin and Bubnov live to be two hundred, I feel, Russia will still remain the land of half fulfilled promises and erratic wanderings off to new beginnings.

I came out of Russia acutely frustrated and disappointed in my dream of doing anything worth while to define an understanding between the essentially revolutionary drives towards an organized socialism in America and Russia respectively. They will certainly go on apart and divergent with a maximum of mutual misunderstanding, at least until there is a new type of intelligence dominating the intellectual life of Communism. If I could have talked Russian, or if I had been clever enough to pervert the Marxist phraseology in Lenin's fashion, I might perhaps have come near to my intention. I might have got into real contact with a mind here or there, if not the leading mind. I was fairly beaten in an enterprise too big for me.

As I thought it over in the homeward aeroplane, I felt that Russia had let me down, whereas I suppose the truth of what has happened is that I had allowed my sanguine and impatient temperament to anticipate understandings and lucidities that cannot arrive for many years. I shall never be able to imagine that what is plain to me is not plain to everyone. I had started out to find a short cut to the Open Conspiracy and discovered that, by such abilities as I possess, there is no short cut to be found to the Open Conspiracy.

I had expected to find a new Russia stirring in its sleep and ready to awaken to Cosmopolis, and I found it sinking deeper into the dope-dream of Sovietic self-sufficiency. I found Stalin's imagination invincibly framed and set, and that ci-devant radical Gorky, magnificently installed as a sort of master of Russian thought. There are no real short-cuts perhaps, in the affairs of men, everyone lives in his own world and between his blinkers, whether they be wide or narrow, and I must console myself, I suppose, as well as I can, for my failure to get any response out of Russia, with such small occasional signs of spreading contemporary understanding as may appear in our own western life. There has always been a certain imaginative magic for me in Russia, and I lament the drift of this great land towards a new system of falsity as a lover might lament estrangement from his mistress.

The truth remains that to-day nothing stands in the way to the attainment of universal freedom and abundance but mental tangles, egocentric preoccupations, obsessions, misconceived phrases, bad habits of thought, subconscious fears and dreads and plain dishonesty in people's minds—and especially in the minds of those in key positions. That universal freedom and abundance dangles within reach of us and is not achieved, and we who are Citizens of the Future wander about this present scene like passengers on a ship overdue, in plain sight of a port which only some disorder in the chart room, prevents us from entering. Though most of the people in the world in key positions are more or less accessible to me, I lack the solvent power to bring them into unison. I can talk to them and even unsettle them but I cannot compel their brains to see.

§ 10. ENVOY

I went by the train called the "Red Arrow," the Soviet echo of the *Flèche d'Or*, from Moscow to Leningrad and thence I flew to Tallin. I am finishing this autobiography in a friendly and restful house beside a little lake in Esthonia....

I have done my best now to draw the outline and development of a contemporary mind reacting freely to the disintegrating and the synthetic forces of its time. Copious as this book has become I have still omitted a great bulk of comment and detail that did not seem to me to be of primary importance in this story of the awakening of world citizenship in a fairly normal human intelligence. It has not always been easy to disentangle irrelevant matter without desiccating the main argument. But in a life of eight-and-sixty years there accumulates so great a miscellany of memories and material that, but for some such check upon discursiveness as my design has given me, my flow of reminiscence might have gone on for ever. I confess to an uneasy realization now as I draw to my conclusion that I have not done any sort of justice to the keen interest of countless subsidiary happenings, to the fun of life and the loveliness of life and to much of the oddity of life, beyond the scope of its main essentials. I feel I have been so intent on my thesis, particularly in this very long concluding chapter, that I may have failed to convey my thankfulness to existence for being all else that it so incessantly and generously is. My generalizing impulses have perhaps ruled too much and made my picture of life bony and bare. In my effort to combine the truthful self-portrait of a very definite individual with an adequate reflection of the mental influences of type and period and to keep my outlines firm and clear, I have deliberately put many vivid memories and lively interludes aside, ignored a swarm of interesting personalities I have encountered, cut out great secondary systems of sympathy and said nothing whatever about all sorts of bright, beautiful and pleasant things that have whirled about me entertainingly for a time and then flown off at a tangent. I could write gaily of travels, mountain tramps, landfalls, cities, music, plays, gardens that have pleased me....

What remains is the story of one of the most pampered and irresponsible of "Advanced Thinkers," an uninvited adventurer who has felt himself free to criticize established things without restraint, who has spent his life planning how to wind up most of them and get rid of them, and who has been tolerated almost incredibly during this subversive career. Exasperation there has been, bans and boycotts from Boots to Boston; public schoolmasters and prison chaplains have intervened to protect their charges from my influence, Nazis have burnt my works, the Catholic Church and Italian Fascism have set their authority against me, and dear old voluble indignant Henry Arthur Jones in *My Dear Wells!* and many better equipped writers—Hilaire Belloc and Archbishop Downey for example—have been moved to write vehement controversial books. But refusals to listen and cries of disagreement are not suppression, and it would ill become an advanced thinker to complain of them. They are recognition. If they are not recognition of the advanced thinker himself, they are recognition of his supports and following, and of the greater forces of which he is the expression. I take it, therefore as a fair inference from the real immunity I have enjoyed, that such revolutionary proposals as mine are anything but unique and outstanding offences. What I have written openly and plainly is evidently in the thoughts of many people. In spite of much sporadic repressive activity, this new ferment of world-state ideas is spreading steadily throughout the world.

Repression, even violent and murderous repression, there is, no doubt, in Germany, in Italy and elsewhere but, where it occurs, it has a curiously forced and hysterical quality; it is no longer whole-hearted repression by assured authority, it is indeed not so much the result of intolerant counter-conviction as resistance to conviction. It is on the defensive against itself. Its violence, in more cases than not, is the convulsive tightening of a slipping grip. The supporters of the thing that is, seem everywhere touched by doubt. Even more plainly is that the case with reactionaries. We advanced thinkers owe our present immunity, such as it is, very largely to the fact that even those of our generation who are formally quite against us, have nevertheless been moving, if less rapidly and explicitly, in the same direction as ourselves. In their hearts they do not believe we are essentially wrong; but they think we go too far,—dangerously and presumptuously too far. Yet all we exist for,—our sort,—is to go too far for the pedestrian contingent....

I began this autobiography primarily to reassure myself during a phase of fatigue, restlessness and vexation, and it has achieved its purpose of reassurance. I wrote myself out of that mood of discontent and forgot myself and a mosquito swarm of bothers in writing about my sustaining ideas. My ruffled *persona* has been restored and the statement of the idea of the modern world-state has reduced my personal and passing irritations and distractions to their proper insignificance. So long as one lives as an individual, vanities, lassitudes, lapses and inconsistencies will hover about and creep back into the picture, but I find nevertheless that this faith and service of constructive world revolution does hold together my mind and will in a prevailing unity, that it makes life continually worth living, transcends and minimizes all momentary and incidental frustrations and takes the sting out of the thought of death. The stream of life out of which we rise and to which we return has been restored to dominance in my consciousness, and though the part I play is,

I believe, essential, it is significant only through the whole. The Open Conspirator can parallel—or, if you prefer to put it so, he can modernize—the self-identification of the religious mystic: he can say, "personally when I examine myself I am nothing"; and at the same time he can assert, "The Divinity and I are One"; or blending divinity with democratic kingship, "The World-State, c'est Moi."

There is a necessary parallelism in the matured convictions of all intelligent people, because brains are made to much the same pattern and inevitably follow similar lines of development. Words, colourings and symbols can change very widely but not the essential forms of the psychological process. Since first man began to think he has been under a necessity to think in a limited number of definable shapes. He has to travel by the roads his ancestry made for him and their fences are well nigh insurmountable. So mystical Christianity, Islamic mysticism, Buddhist teaching, in their most refined and intense efforts towards distinctive penetration, have produced almost identical and quite easily interchangeable formulae for their mysteries. The process of generalization by which the mind seeks an escape from individual vexations and frustrations, from the petty overwhelming pains, anxieties and recriminations of the too acutely ego-centred life, is identical, whatever labels it is given and whatever attempts are made to establish exclusive rights in it. All these religions and every system of sublimation, has had to follow the same route to escape, because there is no other possible route. The idea of creative service to the World-State towards which the modern mind is gravitating, differs widely in its explicitness, its ordered content and its practical urgency, from the All of Being, the Inner Life, the Ultimate Truth, the Personal Divinity, the Friend who sticketh closer than a brother, who is nearer than breathing and closer than hands and feet, and all those other resorts of the older religions, but its releasing and enveloping relation to the individual *persona* is, in spite of all that difference in substance, almost precisely the same.

The difference between our modern consolation systems on the one hand and their homologues in the religions and conduct-philosophies of the past on the other, lies almost entirely in the increasingly monistic quality of the former. They imply an abandonment, more or less tacit or explicit, of that rash assumption of matter-spirit dualism, which has haunted human thought for thousands of generations. The change from egoism to a larger life is consequently now entirely a change of perspective; it can no longer be a facile rejection of primary conditions and a jump into "another world" altogether. It is still an escape from first-hand egoism and immediacy, but it is no longer an escape from fact. And the modern escape to impersonality is all the more effective and enduring because of this tougher, unambiguous adhesion to exterior factual reality. The easy circuitous return through shadowy realms of abstract unreality to egoism on a higher plane is barred; the Life of Contemplation and receptive expressionism, are no longer possible refuges. The educated modern mind, constrained to face forward is systematized but not abstracted. For all his devotion to larger issues, for all his subordination of lesser matters, the Open Conspirator like the Communist or the positivist man of science, remains as consistently *actual* as blood or hunger, right down to the ultimates of his being.

So ends this record of the growth and general adventure of my brain which, first squinted and bubbled at the universe and reached out its feeble little hands to grasp it, eight and sixty years ago, in a shabby bedroom over the china shop that was called Atlas House in High Street, Bromley, Kent.

A List of H. G Wells Books in this Series

FICTION COLLECTIONS

The Short Stories of H. G. Wells

Tales of Space and Time

The Country of the Blind, and Others

The Door in the Wall, and Others

The Plattner Story and Others

The Stolen Bacillus and Others

The Time Machine and Others

Twelve Stories and a Dream

NON-FICTION

A Year of Prophesying

Anticipations

Certain Personal Matters

Crux Ansata

Experiment in Autobiography

First and Last Things: A Confession of Faith and Rule of Life

God, the Invisible King

Mankind in the Making

Marxism vs. Liberalism - An Interview

Mr. Belloc Objects to "The Outline of History"

New Worlds For Old: A Plain Account of Modern Socialism

Scientific War

Select Conversations with an Uncle (Now Extinct) and Two Other Reminiscences

Socialism and the Family

Text Book of Biology, Part 1: Vertebrata

The Anatomy of Frustration

The Common Sense of War and Peace

The Discovery of the Future

The Elements of Reconstruction

The Future in America

The Idea of a League of Nations

The Salvaging of Civilization

The Story of a Great Schoolmaster

The War That Will End War

This Misery of Boots (1907)

War and the Future:

What is Coming? A Forecast of Things after the War

World Brain

Printed in Great Britain
by Amazon